Movies and Meaning

An Introduction to Film

Sixth Edition

Stephen Prince

Virginia Polytechnic Institute and State University

PEARSON

Boston   Columbus   Indianapolis   New York   San Francisco   Upper Saddle River
Amsterdam   Cape Town   Dubai   London   Madrid   Milan   Munich   Paris   Montréal   Toronto
Delhi   Mexico City   São Paulo   Sydney   Hong Kong   Seoul   Singapore   Taipei   Tokyo

Editor-in-Chief, Communication: Karon Bowers
Editor: Ziki Dekel
Marketing Manager: Blair Zoe Tuckman
Editorial Assistant: Megan Hermida
Associate Development Editor: Corey Kahn
Senior Digital Editor: Paul DeLuca
Digital Editor: Lisa Dotson
Associate Managing Editor: Bayani Mendoza de Leon
Production/Project Manager: Raegan Keida Heerema
Project Coordination, Text Design, and Electronic Page Makeup: Integra
Senior Cover Design Manager: Nancy Danahy
Cover Designer: Nancy Sacks
Cover Image: ©Fox Searchlight Pictures/courtesy Everett Collection
Senior Manufacturing Buyer: Mary Ann Gloriande
Printer/Binder: RR Donnelley
Cover Printer: RR Donnelley

Library of Congress Cataloging-in-Publication Data

Prince, Stephen.
   Movies and meaning: an introduction to film/Stephen Prince.—6th ed.
      p. cm.
   Includes bibliographical references and index.
   ISBN 978-0-205-21102-9
   1. Motion pictures.   I. Title.
   PN1994.P676 2012
   791.43—dc23

                                        2011051040

29 2021

www.pearsonhighered.com

ISBN 13: 978-0-205-21102-9
ISBN 10:   0-205-21102-X

CONTENTS

PREFACE

Movies and Meaning focuses on narrative filmmaking, and on fictional narratives in particular, because this is the most popular and pervasive form of filmmaking, seen by the largest audiences, and what most people mean when they talk about "the movies." Throughout the text, boxes extend the major topics of discussion into more specialized areas and supplement film examples with brief profiles of major directors. The reader will gain a more comprehensive understanding of cinema by exploring these boxed discussions. Each chapter ends with a few suggested readings to direct the interested reader's attention to more intensive treatments of basic issues. Boldface terms throughout the text designate items defined in the glossary.

New to This Edition

With each new edition, I've aimed to improve the coverage of existing topics, add coverage of new topics, and update the film examples and chapter information. The sixth edition includes the following changes:

- I have incorporated new examples and pictures to illustrate fundamental concepts and terminology as well as film syles and filmmakers and have broadened the inclusion of international films and older, classic films.
- Spotlight discussions of directors Dorothy Arzner, Yasujiro Ozu, and Sergei Eisenstein, sound designer Ben Burtt, and the traditions of French New Wave and Italian neo-realist filmmaking.
- New spotlight discussions also examine 9/11 in the context of documentary filmmaking and in terms of its influence upon Hollywood film.
- New case studies examine production design in *Schindler's List* and the use of fantasy in *Pan's Labyrinth*.
- A new chapter examines visual effects and their use throughout cinema history.
- I have abbreviated the discussion of film criticism and have enlarged the coverage of film theory, particularly psychoanalytic and feminist approaches.
- As in earlier editions, I've updated the coverage of digital tools used in filmmaking.

HOW THIS BOOK IS ORGANIZED

Movies and Meaning provides a comprehensive introduction to the motion picture medium. The text is organized around three basic questions: How do movies express meanings? How do viewers understand those meanings? How does cinema function globally as an art and a business?

Most introductory film textbooks concentrate on the first question and tend to minimize or disregard the other two questions. A special feature of this book is the attention that it gives to the ways that viewers understand and interpret the elements of film structure and the attention that it gives to cinema as a global business as well as an art. To fully understand the medium of cinema, the reader needs to know what filmmakers do with the tools of their craft, how viewers respond to the designs those tools create, and how the art and business of film are interrelated. Film is an art form, but it is also a business enterprise. These two domains are not separate; they map onto each other, and knowing one requires knowledge of the other.

These three core questions frame the essential attributes of cinema. The first question—How do movies express meaning?—asks what filmmakers do and how they do it. The basic tools of filmmaking include cinematography, production design, the actors' performance, editing, sound design, and narrative structure. Each of these areas contributes to the organizing design of a film, and, by manipulating these tools, filmmakers are able to express a range of meanings.

To look only at what filmmakers do to create meaning, though, is to leave out a crucial part of the picture. One also needs to know what viewers do with the movies they watch because, without viewers, there are no meanings in film. The medium of cinema depends on a contract between filmmaker and viewer. Together, they co-create the film experience.

Thus, the second core question—How do viewers understand film?—asks what viewers do when watching movies. How do viewers interpret the audiovisual designs that filmmakers have created? How do filmmakers anticipate in their work the likely ways that viewers will react to certain kinds of stories and audiovisual designs? What makes movies understandable to viewers in the first place? How can filmmakers facilitate the viewer's ability to understand and interpret the images and sounds on screen?

Viewers respond to film, and understand it, by applying significant aspects of their real-life visual, personal, and social experience as well as their knowledge of motion picture conventions and style. The upcoming chapters emphasize both aspects of this response: the mapping of real experience onto the screen and the knowledge of medium-specific codes and style. This dual response is a function of the medium's own duality, its ability to *document* visual reality and to *transform* it. These functions receive special emphasis throughout the chapters because they are fundamental to much of what the cinema does and how.

The third question—How does cinema operate as an art and business on a global scale?—asks about the medium's capacity as a business enterprise and a vehicle of creative expression. An account that emphasized the cinema only as an art form would be inadequate and incomplete, and it would fail to grasp some of the medium's essential features, namely, the remarkable interrelation between art and commerce that has defined cinema since its inception. Filmmakers today work in a medium that faces grave economic problems, and these problems are affecting the kinds of films that get made. Furthermore, commercial filmmaking operates as part of a global communications industry, which exerts considerable influence on film content and style. At the same time, the global context carries with it considerable diversity, with filmmakers representing a range of countries, cultures, and styles. Although these issues of art and commerce, of cultural diversity and homogenization, are complex, no comprehensive examination of the medium should ignore them.

About the Photographs

The photographs that appear in this textbook are frame enlargements. This ensures that the images from films under study correspond exactly to the images on screen that viewers see when watching a film. The use of frame enlargements is intended to provide a major teaching advantage over other textbooks that use mainly publicity stills. Regarding publicity stills, these are taken by an on-set photographer during the course of a film's production, and they only *approximate* the actual shots and compositions in a film. To exactly reproduce these, frame enlargements must be used, and I have spent many hours producing these in optimal condition. The frame enlargements used in this text are identified as such in the captions.

SUPPLEMENTS

Instructor's Manual

The accompanying Instructor's Manual, written by Stephen Prince, includes an outline of the main emphases in each chapter, suggested teaching approaches for the content, exercises, and sample test questions for every chapter. It is available for download in our Instructor's Resource Center, www.pearsonhighered.com/irc (access code required).

PowerPoint Presentation Package

Available for download in our Instructor's Resource Center, www.pearsonhighered .com/irc (access code required), this text-specific package provides PowerPoint slides for each chapter of the book.

ACKNOWLEDGMENTS

For their valuable help on this and previous editions, I owe great thanks to Kevin Davis, Linda Montgomery, Donald Larsson, Richard Terrill, Blake Wood, Paul Helford, Joe Opiela, Karon Bowers, Terry Geeskin, Edd Sewell, Gerry Scheeler, Carl Plantinga, Richard Dillard, Eric Poe Miller, Grant Corley, Bob Denton, Teresa Darvalics, Marjorie Payne, Myrna Breskin, Marty Tenney, and Molly Taylor. Also thanks to Susan Mattingly, Executive Director of the Lyric Theater, who kindly allowed me to photograph the historic site. Philip Cho designed the visual effects drawings and diagrams that appear in Chapter Eight.

The author gratefully acknowledges the following reviewers of the new edition:

Nancy Andreasen, Inver Hills Community College
Daniel Linton, University of Memphis
Robert Matorin, Middlesex Community College
Helen Robbins, Lyons University

Film Structure

OBJECTIVES

After reading this chapter, you should be able to:

- explain the nature of film structure and its relation to the ways movies express meaning

- describe the production process and its relation to film structure

- describe the relation between film structure and the cinema's properties of time and space

- distinguish the three basic camera positions and their expressive functions

- describe how camera position can clarify the meaning of an actor's facial expression and gestures

- distinguish the three basic camera angles and describe the ways they influence viewer response

- differentiate telephoto, wide-angle, and zoom lenses and explain their optical effects

- explain the basic categories of camera movement and their expressive functions

- explain how a film's structural design is shaped by a filmmaker's choices about how to use the tools of style

1

■ describe the relation between the camera's view of things and human perception

■ explain how the camera creates images that both correspond with and transform the viewer's visual experience

The shark in *Jaws* (1975) and the digital characters in *The Lord of the Rings: The Return of the King* (2004) thrilled and amused moviegoers throughout the world. Audiences have embraced films as diverse as *Toy Story 3* (2010), *True Grit* (2010), *The Social Network* (2010), and *The Dark Knight* (2008). Each of these pictures provided its viewers with a strong cinematic experience, crafted by filmmakers using the elements of film structure: camerawork, lighting, sound, editing. To understand how movies express meanings and elicit emotions, one must begin by understanding their structural design. This chapter explains the concept of film structure, the camera's role as an element of structure, and the relation between the camera's method of seeing and a viewer's understanding of cinema.

ELEMENTS OF FILM STRUCTURE

Structure refers to the audiovisual design of a film and the particular tools and techniques used to create that design. (Scholars sometimes refer to this by the term **film form**. Thus, one might speak of formal design or of structural design. The terminology is interchangeable.) A convenient way to illustrate this concept is to make a distinction between structure and content. Consider the average newspaper movie review. It provides a description of a film's story and a paragraph or two about the characters and the actors who play them. In addition, the reviewer might mention the theme or themes of the film. These descriptions of story, character, and theme address the content of the movie.

Now, instead of thinking about content, one could ask about those things that help to create the story, give shape to the characters, and illustrate and visualize the themes. These are questions about the elements of cinema—the camera, lights and color, production design, performance, editing, sound—and their organization in a given film.

The Production Process

A helpful way of understanding film structure—and the material presented in upcoming chapters—is to map its components according to their place in the production process. When does production design occur? Cinematography? Editing? Filmmaking involves three basic steps or stages. **Preproduction** designates the planning and preparation stage. It typically involves the writing of a script; hiring of cast and crew; production design of sets, costumes, and locales; and planning the style of cinematography. Set design and camera style are both previsualized using software programs that enable filmmakers to "see" in advance how camera setups and lenses will look on the sets that are planned. Preproduction also sometimes includes a brief period of rehearsal for the actors. **Production** designates the work of filming the script (cinematography) and sound recording of the action. The director may request a temp track, a temporary musical score that is similar to the one that will be created for the film. **Postproduction** involves the editing of sound and image, composition and recording of the music score, additional sound recording for effects (Foley) and dialogue replacement (ADR), creation of digital visual effects (these also may occur during production), and color timing to achieve proper color balance in the images. This may be

PREPRODUCTION	PRODUCTION	POSTPRODUCTION
Script	Shooting & Sound	Editing of Sound & Image
optioning	Recording of Scenes	Music Scoring
writing		Foley
revisions		ADR
Hiring of Cast and Crew		Digital Effects
Design of Sets and Costumes		Color Timing (Digital/Lab)
Plan Style of Cinematography		Release Prints
Rehearsals		

FIGURE 1.1
The production process.

done digitally (known as digital grading) or using traditional lab methods. Copies of the film are then made for exhibition, either as prints (on film) or as digital video.

Because filmmakers apply the elements of structure at different points in the production process, these elements can be used to modify or influence one another. A director might realize that a scene as filmed lacks emotional force and may turn to the composer for music to supply the missing emotion or to the editor to sharpen its dramatic focus. A cinematographer in postproduction may alter the image captured on film by using digital grading to adjust color, contrast, and other elements.

TITANIC (PARAMOUNT/20TH CENTURY FOX, 1997)
Titanic's production design evokes a now-vanished early-twentieth-century world. Meticulously detailed costumes and sets are an essential part of the film's structural design. Frame enlargement.

The Role of the Director

A wide range of creative personnel design picture and sound on any given production. While filmmaking is a collaborative enterprise, one individual has chief artistic authority, and this is usually the **director**. The director coordinates and organizes the artistic inputs of other members of the production team, who generally subordinate their artistic tastes or preferences to a director's stated wishes or vision. The director, in turn, answers to the **producer,** who generally has administrative control over a production (e.g., making sure the production stays on schedule and within budget). In practice, though, many producers hold more than administrative authority and are actively engaged with the director's creative decisions, especially if the producer is a powerful figure in the industry.

Great variety exists in the working methods of directors. Some directors, such as Robert Altman (*Gosford Park*, 2001; *The Player*, 1992), welcome input from other production team members in a spirit of shared collective artistry. Other directors, such as Alfred Hitchcock or Charles Chaplin, tend to be more autocratic and commanding in their creative approaches. Some directors, such as Woody Allen (*Match Point*, 2005; *Deconstructing Harry*, 1997), Steven Spielberg (*The War of the Worlds*, 2005; *Saving Private Ryan*, 1998), and Stanley Kubrick (*Full Metal Jacket*, 1987; *Eyes Wide Shut*, 1999), take an active role in the editing of their pictures. Most directors place special emphasis on the quality of the script, believing a polished script to be essential to making a good film. Clint Eastwood's best films as director, *Million Dollar Baby* (2004), *Mystic River* (2003), and *Unforgiven* (1993), feature exquisitely written scripts.

Most directors maintain enduring relationships with key production personnel. As these relationships deepen over the course of several productions, the creative, collaborative work that results becomes richer. Steven Spielberg, for example, has used cinematographer Janusz Kaminski for *War Horse* (2011), *Munich* (2005), *The War of the Worlds* (2005), *The Terminal* (2004), *Saving Private Ryan* (1998), and others. Clint Eastwood relied on production designer Henry Bumstead for eleven films, including *Million Dollar Baby* (2004), *Mystic River* (2003), and *Unforgiven* (1993). Woody Allen invariably relies on editor Susan E. Morse, as does Martin Scorsese with editor Thelma

THE IMMIGRANT (MUTUAL FILM CORP., 1917)

Charles Chaplin was the complete filmmaker. He wrote, directed, performed in, edited, and composed the music for his films. Many said that, were it possible, he'd have played all the characters as well. He rarely worked from a completed script. He preferred to build a set, dress it with props, and then explore its comic possibilities, making up gags as he went along. Performance, not camerawork, was the centerpiece of his films. Here, Charlie and his companion (Edna Purviance) have no cash to pay for the meal they've just eaten. The hulking waiter (Eric Campbell) suspects the worst. Frame enlargement.

Schoonmaker. George Lucas relied on Ben Burtt as the sound designer for all six of the *Star Wars* films. The continuities established by these professional relationships are vitally important to a director's ability to get what he or she wants on the screen.

Time and Space in Cinema

The elements of cinematic structure, organized by directors and their production teams, help to shape the distinctive properties of time and space in a film. A convenient way of thinking about the arts is to consider the properties of time and/or space that they possess. Music, for example, is primarily an art of time. Its effects arise through the arrangement of tones in a musical composition that has some duration or length. Movies, by contrast, are an art of time as well as space.

The time component of movies has several aspects. **Running time** designates the duration of the film, the amount of time it takes a viewer to watch the film from beginning to end. Most commercially released films are called **feature films**, which means that they typically run from 90 to 120 minutes. Some films, however, are much longer. *The Lord of the Rings: The Return of the King* (2004), in its theatrical release, was 201 minutes long, and the director's extended version on DVD runs even longer, 251 minutes.

Story time designates the amount of time covered by the narrative, and this can vary considerably from film to film. In Fred Zinnemann's Western, *High Noon* (1952), the story spans 1.5 hours, roughly equivalent to the running time of the film itself. Story time, on the other hand, can span many epochs and centuries, as in Stanley Kubrick's *2001: A Space Odyssey* (1968), which goes from the dawn of the apes well into the age of space travel. Filmmakers also may organize story time through the use of flashbacks so that it becomes fragmented, doubling back on itself, as in Orson Welles's *Citizen Kane* (1941), in which the story of Charles Foster Kane is told largely through the recollections of friends and associates who knew him.

Internal structural time, a third distinct aspect of cinematic time, arises from the structural manipulations of film form or technique. If a filmmaker edits a sequence so that the lengths of shots decrease progressively, or become shorter, the tempo of the sequence will accelerate. A rapid camera movement will accelerate the internal structural time of a shot. Regardless of the shot's actual duration on screen, it will seem to move faster. (The term **shot** designates the basic building block of a film. During production, a director creates a film shot by shot. In this context, a shot corresponds to the amount of film footage exposed by the camera from the time it is turned on until it is turned off. Films are composed of many shots that are joined together in the process of editing. In a completed film, a shot is the interval on screen between edit points.)

In *Open Range* (2003) and *Dances with Wolves* (1990), the editing imposes a slow pace on the story by letting many shots linger on screen for a long time. Director Kevin Costner felt that a slow pace suited those stately epics about an era when horse and wagon were major modes of transportation. By contrast, contemporary action films like the *Mission Impossible* series (1996, 2000, 2006) race at breakneck speed, rarely pausing long enough for an audience to catch its breath.

A film's internal structural time never unfolds at a constant rate. It is a dynamic property, not a fixed one. Filmmakers modulate internal structural time to maintain viewer interest by changing camera positions, the lengths of shots, color and lighting design, and the volume and density of the soundtrack.

Viewers experience internal structural time as a series of story events held in dynamic relations of tension and release. Viewers often describe films as being fast or

Stanley Kubrick

During his 46-year career, Stanley Kubrick made only 12 feature films. Despite the relatively small body of work that he left, however, he had an extraordinary impact on the medium and is recognized as one of its major filmmakers. A director of legendary stature, he was renowned for spending years planning a film and years more shooting it and working on postproduction. Famous for doing many takes of each shot and for the precision of his visual designs, Kubrick honed a style that is unique and unmistakable, and his films offer bleak but compelling visions of human beings trapped and crushed by the systems—social, military, technological—they have created.

Kubrick's reputation was that of an intellectual director, keenly interested in a range of subjects and whose films explored issues and ideas, yet he never finished high school. At age 17 he dropped out and began work as a photographer, working at *Look* magazine for several years before completing two documentary shorts for the March of Time newsreel company (*Day of the Fight* [1951] and *Flying Padre* [1951]). Borrowing money from family and friends, he then completed his first two features as director, *Fear and Desire* (1953) and *Killer's Kiss* (1955). In a move that announced his conviction that cinema was a medium of personal artistry and that he would control his own work, Kubrick produced, wrote, directed, photographed, and edited these films.

After another crime film, *The Killing* (1956), Kubrick made *Paths of Glory* (1958), a powerful drama of World War I and the first of his films to pursue what would be his great theme, the domination of people by the systems they have created (envisioned in this film as the machinery of war and the pitiless chain of command). Influenced by the moving camera of director Max Ophuls, Kubrick's sustained tracking shots became a signature element of his style.

Kubrick's next film, *Spartacus* (1960), was a production on which he, uncharacteristically, did not have complete authority (the picture belonged to its star–producer Kirk Douglas), and as a result, Kubrick was careful to work as his own producer on

THE SHINING (WARNER BROS., 1980); A CLOCKWORK ORANGE (WARNER BROS., 1971)

Kubrick made some of the most imaginative and precisely designed films in cinema history. His passion for design led him to shoot 30 and 40 takes of a shot until he had what he wanted. The results were mysterious, haunting, and poetic and included Jack Nicholson's spectacular madness in *The Shining* and visions of a violent, authoritarian future in *A Clockwork Orange*. Frame enlargements.

all subsequent films. He next went to England to film *Lolita* (1962), from the controversial Vladimir Nabokov novel, and he then settled there, using English production facilities for most of his ensuing films. He was becoming a filmmaker whose work transcended national boundary.

Dr. Strangelove (1963) is a modern classic, a shrewd and superb satire of the Cold War and the policy of nuclear deterrence aptly named MAD (Mutual Assured Destruction). Kubrick's startling marriage of baroque imagery and popular music (detonating atom bombs accompanied by the sentimental ballad "We'll Meet Again") became one of his trademarks, used famously in *2001: A Space Odyssey* (spaceships pirouette to the Blue Danube waltz) and *A Clockwork Orange* (lurid violence set to Beethoven's "Ode to Joy").

With *Strangelove*, these two films solidified Kubrick's reputation as a social and cinematic visionary. *2001* (1968) is a visual feast whose startling effects are married to a mystical and mind-bending narrative that takes humankind on a cosmic journey from the dawn of the apes to the era of space travel. Controversial for its violence, *A Clockwork Orange* (1971) depicted a brutal vision of future society where the state learns to control the violent impulses of its citizens. Kubrick said, "The central idea of the film has to do with the question of free will. Do we lose our humanity if we are deprived of the choice between good and evil?" By making the main character a thug and a menace to society, Kubrick aimed to give the question resonance.

With dazzling Steadicam shots of a labyrinthine hotel, Kubrick explored the effects of space on the mind in *The Shining* (1980), which depicts the hotel's sinister influence on a mentally unstable caretaker and his family and ends with one of the director's bleakest images of futility and alienation.

Kubrick extended his pessimistic visions of human failure to eighteenth-century Ireland in *Barry Lyndon* (1975) and the battlefields of Vietnam in *Full Metal Jacket* (1985). His untimely death followed completion of *Eyes Wide Shut* (1999), a haunting and mysterious evocation of erotic fantasy and its emotional consequences.

Kubrick never made the same kind of film twice. Each picture is uniquely different and uniquely resonant and must be seen more than once before it begins to yield up its treasures. Kubrick dedicated his life to making films, and he believed that cinema was an art. Few filmmakers gain the authority to pursue this conviction without compromise. Kubrick's achievements in this regard place him in very select cinematic company. By showing filmmakers what the medium can achieve, Kubrick's work remains a continuing inspiration. ■

slow moving, but in fact, the pacing of any given film typically varies as filmmakers use structure to create narrative rhythms that alternately accelerate and decelerate. While internal structural time results from a filmmaker's manipulations of cinema structure, viewers experience this type of time subjectively, and their responses often vary greatly. One viewer may love the dramatic intensity and emotional lyricism of *The Bridges of Madison County* (1995) or *Monster's Ball* (2001), whereas another may find the overall pacing of these films to be too slow.

Cinema is an art of time *and* space. The spatial properties of cinema have several components. One involves the arrangement of objects within the **frame** (the dimensions of the projected area on screen; the term also refers to the individual still image on a strip of film). This is the art of framing, or **composition,** which is discussed in the next chapter because it is a part of the cinematographer's job.

The spatial properties of the cinema, though, go beyond the art of framing. Cinema simulates an illusion of three-dimensional space on a flat screen. To do so, it corresponds in key ways with the viewer's experience of physical space in daily life, and filmmakers create these correspondences in the design of their films. Cinematographers control the distribution of light on the set to accentuate the shape, texture, and positioning of objects and people. Film editors join shots to establish spatial constancies on screen that hold regardless of changes in the camera's position and angle of view. Sound designers use the audio track to convey information about physical space. The spatial properties of cinema are multi-dimensional and can be expressed through many elements of structure. This chapter and succeeding chapters explain these spatial properties and how filmmakers manipulate them.

OPEN RANGE (TOUCHSTONE, 2003) AND MISSION: IMPOSSIBLE 2 (PARAMOUNT, 2000)

This Western, directed by Kevin Costner, has a slow pace because he wants to concentrate on the characters and their situation rather than rushing over these for action or special effects. Costner also believes that a slow pace works well in Westerns where characters travel by horse or wagon. Snappy editing and a fast pace would be as ill-suited to this material as a leisurely pace would be for contemporary action films, such as the *Mission: Impossible* series. Frame enlargements.

STRUCTURE AND THE CAMERA

Let us begin our understanding of film structure by discussing the fundamentals of camera usage. The basic issues of camera position and lenses as discussed in this chapter are actually part of cinematography. But it will be helpful to cover them here separately as an introduction to the camera. These must be grasped before more complex issues of cinematography can be examined in the next chapter. The camera's position, angle, lens, and the camera's movement have a major impact on the visual structure of every film. The reader seeking to understand cinema should begin with a clear sense of the relationship among these characteristics and the differences between them.

Camera Position

The most basic way of classifying camera usage is in terms of **camera position**. This refers to the distance between the camera and the subject it is photographing. Obviously, the camera-to-subject distance is a continuum with an infinite series of points from very close to very far. In practice, however, the basic positions usually are classified as variations of three essential camera setups: the **long shot,** the **medium shot,** and the **close-up.** Each of these positions has its own distinct expressive functions in the cinema.

Filmmakers typically use the long shot to stress environment or setting and to show a character's position in relationship to a given environment. In *Titanic* (1997), the majesty of the ship's enormous size is conveyed with a series of long shots that contrast the huge ship with the tiny passengers that crowd its decks. When they are used to open a film or begin a scene, long shots may be referred to as **establishing shots**. Many detective films, for example, begin with a long shot of the urban environment, often taken from a helicopter.

In contrast to the long shot, the medium shot brings viewers closer to the characters while still showing some of their environment. In *The Phantom of the Opera* (2004), a medium-shot framing shows the Phantom (Gerard Butler) embracing Christine (Emmy Rossum) while revealing details of the Phantom's candlelit lair underneath the opera house. Sometimes medium shots are labeled according to the number of characters who are present within the frame. Accordingly, this shot from *The Phantom of the Opera* would be termed a *two-shot*. A *three-shot* and a *four-shot* would designate medium shots with larger numbers of people.

By contrast with long and medium shots, the close-up stresses characters or objects over the surrounding environment, usually for expressive or dramatic purposes, and it can be an extremely powerful means for guiding and directing a viewer's attention to important features of a scene's action or meaning.

Once the filmmaker chooses a camera position, the camera is typically locked down on a tripod or other type of platform in order to produce a steady image without jitter. Alternatively, rather than locking the camera down, the filmmaker

AN AMERICAN IN PARIS (MGM, 1951)

Longer, full-figure framings in the dance sequences of classic Hollywood musicals showcase the beauty of the dance. The longer framing allows the viewer to see the performer's entire body in motion. By contrast, contemporary filmmakers "cheat" when they film dance, using fast editing and close-ups to create the impression of a dance performance without showing the real thing. Here, Gene Kelly dances in an elaborate production number designed around the styles of Impressionist painting. Frame enlargement.

THERE WILL BE BLOOD (PARAMOUNT, 2007)

Medium-shot compositions can stress the relationship among characters while integrating them into their environment. This medium shot, in widescreen, preserves the intimacy of this moment between Daniel Plainview (Daniel Day-Lewis) and an orphaned child that he has adopted. The widescreen frame enables the viewer to see a great deal of the train compartment in which they are riding. Frame enlargement.

might work with a **hand-held camera**. In this case, the camera operator physically holds the camera, either on his or her shoulder or on a harness strapped to his or her body. Long shots, medium shots, and close-ups can be filmed in this fashion. Going hand-held enables a filmmaker to cover the action of a scene in a more flexible and spontaneous way, but the challenge is to produce a smooth and steady image. (The Steadicam can help to achieve this—it is discussed in the section on camera movement.) All the shots in *Jaws* (1975), when the characters are at sea, are done with a

THE LORD OF THE RINGS: THE FELLOWSHIP OF THE RING (NEW LINE, 2001)

Galadriel (Cate Blanchett) is a strong, spiritual presence as ruler of the domain of Lothlorien, where the film's heroes journey seeking refuge. Note how the close-up framing concentrates attention on her face. The framing is tight, and the focal plane of the shot does not extend beyond her face. This gives the close-up additional punch. The halo of light and Galadriel's glowing, luminescent appearance were created digitally in post-production. Frame enlargement.

JAWS (UNIVERSAL, 1975)

All the shots in the second half of *Jaws*, once the characters are at sea, are done with a hand-held camera. They look remarkably steady, however, because the camera operator used his body to absorb the rocking of the boat. The camera had to be hand-held because locking it to a tripod or other fixed platform would have induced seasickness in the viewer. The camera operator was Michael Chapman, who went on to become cinematographer of *Raging Bull* and *Taxi Driver*. Frame enlargement.

hand-held camera. It was impossible to do otherwise—locking the camera down on a rocking boat would have made the film's viewers seasick!

The fact that filmmakers can choose among different camera positions illustrates a basic difference between cinema and theater. In theater, the spectator views a play from a single fixed vantage point, a position in the auditorium, usually from a distance. By contrast, in film, viewers watch a shifting series of perspectives on the action, and their ability to understand the story requires synthesizing the shifting points of view as the filmmaker moves from one camera position to another, from shot to shot. How viewers make sense of changing views of a scene supplied by different camera positions is a major issue to be examined in the chapter on editing.

CAMERA POSITION, GESTURE, AND EXPRESSION   By varying the camera-to-subject distance, the filmmaker can manipulate the viewer's emotional involvement with the material in complex ways. What the camera sees is what the spectator sees. As the camera moves closer to a character, viewers are brought into the character's personal space in ways that can be very expressive and emotional.

People express emotion and intention in ways that go beyond the words they speak. Posture, gesture, facial expression, eye contact, and vocal inflection express feelings and help to define relationships. These signals vary by culture, but all members of a society learn how to read the expressions and gestures of other people as a way of inferring what they are thinking or feeling. By varying camera placement, filmmakers can call attention to significant expressions and gestures and thereby help viewers understand the meaning of the relationships and situations depicted on screen.

When a filmmaker cuts to a close-up, the director can emphasize and clarify a character's reaction, as well as bring viewers into the action and the personal emotional space of the character. Depending on how the viewer feels about that character, this can give rise to either positive emotions (e.g., compassion, empathy) or negative ones (e.g., fear, anxiety).

In George Cukor's *A Star Is Born* (1954), James Mason plays a tragic Hollywood actor, Norman Maine. With his acting career destroyed, the alcoholic Maine collapses into despair and considers suicide. He begins to cry. The camera draws in to a medium close-up, and director Cukor keeps the shot on screen for a surprisingly long time. Cukor said, "To see that man break down was very moving. All the credit for that goes to James [Mason]. He did it all himself. What I did was to let him do it and let it go on and on, let the camera stay on him for an eternity." The shot is designed to elicit the viewer's empathy by revealing an intimate glimpse of a man's private hell.

Facial expressions do not have to be realistic to express emotion or intention. Close-ups of Gollum (Andy Serkis) in *The Lord of the Rings: The Return of the King* (2004) emphasize his semi-human character, rendered with visual effects. These effects *transform* normal human reality but also *correspond* with real facial cues. The bulging eyes and open mouth accurately convey the character's anger, but they do so with exaggeration.

A STAR IS BORN (WARNER BROS., 1954)

Changing facial expressions in a single, extended shot from *A Star Is Born* convey the despair of Norman Maine (actor James Mason). As a photographic medium, the cinema is especially powerful in its ability to capture and emphasize the smallest details of human facial expression as signs of emotion. The face is one of cinema's most profound channels for emotional expression. Frame enlargements.

THE LORD OF THE RINGS: THE RETURN OF THE KING (NEW LINE, 2004)
Unreal faces in fantasy films still can have a special expressive power. Gollum's bulging eyes and snarling mouth accurately convey his greed for the ring and his anger at those who stand in his way, but the emotions are conveyed with some exaggeration. Frame enlargement.

The application of digital tools in filmmaking has made great progress in little over a decade, with digital artists learning to represent a great variety of images and lighting conditions. Breakthroughs in the representation of water, for example, made possible the convincing digital oceans in *Finding Nemo* (2003) and *The Perfect Storm* (2000). (Compare the tidal wave in that film with the one in *The Abyss* (1989), a decade earlier.) But the emotional richness and complexity of facial expression have not yet been among these breakthroughs. The facial reactions of digital characters in *Madagascar* (2005), *Shrek 2* (2004), or *The Incredibles* (2004) are conveyed very effectively as caricature rather than in a photorealist style.

THE POLAR EXPRESS (WARNER BROS., 2004)
To date, most digitally created faces have involved cartoon or nonhuman characters because their expressions can be rendered in broader terms. For this film, motion capture techniques converted the performances of live actors (such as Tom Hanks, pictured here) into cartoon figures. The results were disappointing. The faces look stiff and do not show the range of expression of a real person. Frame enlargement.

Few filmmakers understood the emotional implications of camera position better than Charles Chaplin. Chaplin used a formula to guide his camera placements: long shot for comedy, close-up for tragedy. He understood that the long shot was best suited for comedy because it allowed viewers to see the relationship between Charlie the tramp and his environment, particularly when he was causing chaos and confusion, as he might when tackling a waiter carrying a tray of food or stepping on a board with a brick on one end, causing it to catapult onto the head of a policeman. Laughter depended on seeing these relationships and having sufficient emotional distance from the character. The long shot helped provide viewers with that emotional distance. By contrast, Chaplin knew that the close-up, by emphasizing a character's emotional reaction, could invite tears rather than laughter. Aiming for the heartstrings of his audience, he used his close-ups sparingly so that they would have exceptional dramatic intensity.

The ending of *City Lights* (1931) illustrates this quite well. Charlie has been courting a blind flower girl who believes that he is a millionaire. Charlie happily plays along. At the end of the film, the flower girl regains her eyesight, chances upon Charlie, the disreputable tramp, and realizes with disappointment who he is. At this moment, Chaplin shows Charlie's extraordinary expression in close-up, a mixture of hope, love, fear, embarrassment, and humiliation. This is one of the most perfect close-ups in film history. It emphasizes the complex feelings between the characters, magnifies the emotions on screen, and intensifies them for the film's viewers.

This scene elicits positive emotions from viewers. Obviously, though, many films and genres, like horror, appeal to viewers by eliciting such negative emotions as fear, disgust, and anxiety. Within the safe confines of a fictional film world, these negative emotions can be pleasurable to experience. In this context, a strategically placed close-up can be disturbing and frightening if it brings the viewer into a relationship of proximity

CITY LIGHTS (UNITED ARTISTS, 1931)

Chaplin's sublime expression in the final image of *City Lights*. Chaplin intuitively understood the emotional implications of camera position, and he reserved the close-up for special moments of pathos and sentiment. His extraordinary face, the tentative gesture of his hand, the rose it clutches—these emphasize his romantic yearning and his pained embarrassment at being revealed as a tramp and not a millionaire. Frame enlargement.

and spatial intimacy with a terrifying or dangerous character, as in *The Exorcist* (1973).

The effects of camera position, then, are context-dependent, a matter of how a given position is related to the dramatic or emotional content of a shot or scene. By using camera position, filmmakers can enhance or inhibit the viewer's emotional involvement with a character or situation and can elicit both positive and negative emotions. Good filmmakers are intelligent in their choice of camera position, understanding when to cut in to close-up and when to pull back to long shot. Each position gives the viewer a unique perspective on the action, and filmmakers understand that the effects of these positions can be enhanced by a careful choice of camera angle. ■

Camera Angle

The camera's angle of view typically varies from shot to shot. Camera angles are classified as variations of three essential positions: low, medium (or eye-level), and high. Low- and high-angle positions are usually defined relative to what the camera is filming. A low-angle shot in *Spider-Man 2* (2004) shows Peter Parker (Tobey Maguire) throwing away his Spider-Man costume, having decided to stop being a superhero. The low-angle framing emphasizes the seriousness and drama of this moment.

Filmmakers use camera angles for a variety of expressive purposes. These include conveying information about a character's view of the world and accompanying emotions. In *Citizen Kane*, director Orson Welles uses camera angle to evoke young Charlie Kane's boyhood feelings of bewilderment and powerlessness in his new foster home. Charlie's imposing guardian gives him a sled for a Christmas present. To magnify Charlie's feelings of helplessness, Welles shoots the man towering above him, from the boy's point of view, using an extremely low camera angle that forces viewers to look up to this figure, much as Charlie has to do.

THE EXORCIST (WARNER BROS., 1973)
Facial close-ups can be a very powerful way of eliciting negative emotion from viewers. When the possessed Regan (Linda Blair) stares into the camera, as here, it is difficult to avoid flinching. The camera's proximity to a dangerous or frightening character can generate in viewers a sense of being threatened. Frame enlargement.

Camera angle also can complicate emotional responses by playing against the visual relationships viewers want to have with characters, as Hitchcock does in his use of high angles during moments of extreme emotional crisis. In *Psycho* (1960), he used one of these extremely high angles as a way of solving a dramatic and narrative problem and of working at cross-purposes with the viewer's desired response. A first-time viewer believes that the psychopathic killer in the film is the deranged mother of motel owner Norman Bates. In the film's climax, Norman is revealed as the killer. The mother has been dead for many years, and Norman has kept her alive in his mind, keeping her body in the house, even dressing up like her and speaking in her voice. Hitchcock's narrative problem was to keep the audience from realizing midway through the film—when Norman moves her body from the upstairs bedroom to the basement—that the mother was dead.

DR. STRANGELOVE (COLUMBIA PICTURES, 1964)

The psychotic General Jack Ripper (Sterling Hayden) launches a nuclear war because he feels his "precious bodily fluids" are being drained by communist spies. The low camera angle emphasizes Ripper's looming presence and his madness. The oversized cigar points to his sexual anxieties. Frame enlargement.

PSYCHO (PARAMOUNT PICTURES, 1960)

Hitchcock solves a narrative problem in *Psycho* by using this high camera angle. The bizarre, distorting perspective conceals the fact that Norman's mother is dead as he carries her down to the fruit cellar. Frame enlargement.

Hitchcock attached his camera to the ceiling and filmed from directly overhead as Norman carries the corpse down to the cellar. The extremely high angle, coupled with the jostling movement as Norman goes down the stairs, prevents the audience from realizing he is carrying a corpse. The viewer is even fooled into thinking that the mother is kicking in protest.

ETERNAL SUNSHINE OF THE SPOTLESS MIND (FOCUS FEATURES, 2004)

Camera angle can visualize point of view, even one that cannot literally exist. When Clementine (Kate Winslet) and Joel (Jim Carrey) lie on a frozen pond and look at the stars, the camera looks down on the characters as if from the heavens. The stars cannot be gazing at the characters, but the camera angle creates an effect that suggests something like this idea. The angle adds a moment of visual poetry. Frame enlargement.

Hitchcock's use of the high angle in this scene is an ingenious solution to his narrative problem. It introduces a bizarre, distorting perspective into the scene that plays against the viewer's desired visual relationship with the characters. Because of the questions that the narrative has raised about this mysterious figure, viewers want to see Norman's mother clearly and up close, not from the odd angle Hitchcock provides. But, by delaying the desired response, Hitchcock builds

FILMMAKER SPOTLIGHT

Alfred Hitchcock

Alfred Hitchcock was a consummate showman and entertainer and a serious artist who used film to explore dark currents of human thought and behavior. He thrived in the classical Hollywood studio system because his films were popular with audiences and enjoyed considerable critical respect. As a result, Hitchcock became one of the most powerful Hollywood directors and one of the few known to the public by name.

Born into a Catholic family in the East End of London in 1899, Hitchcock grew into a solitary boy possessed of an active imagination and fascinated by crime. Uncommonly anxious, he believed his many fears motivated his preference for making films about innocent characters suddenly caught up in an unpredictable whirlpool of danger, madness, and intrigue. "I was terrified of the police, of the Jesuit Fathers, of physical punishment, of a lot of things. This is the root of my work."

In 1920, Hitchcock entered the British film industry as a scriptwriter and set and costume designer. In 1924–1925, he worked as an assistant director, and then director, in Germany on several British–German co-productions. He studied and absorbed the style of German Expressionism, and in all his subsequent films he relied on expressionistically distorted images to suggest an unstable world.

Hitchcock rose to the peak of the British industry with a cycle of elegant spy thrillers—*The Man Who Knew Too Much* (1934), *The 39 Steps* (1935), *The Lady Vanishes* (1938). Seeking greater creative freedom and technical resources, Hitchcock left Britain for Hollywood and completed his first U.S. film, *Rebecca*, in 1940. An auspicious debut, it won an Academy Award for Best Picture. In the years that followed,

VERTIGO (PARAMOUNT PICTURES, 1958)
James Stewart portrays a detective terrified of heights in *Vertigo*, Hitchcock's most passionate and poetic film. Stewart's pose here is a classic Hitchcock image of the individual haunted by the darkness in his mind and beset by chaos in the outer world. Hitchcock's darkest films offer no places of safety. Frame enlargement.

Hitchcock rapidly consolidated his reputation as a leading director and defined his unique screen world.

Using suspense as his method for drawing the audience into the fictional screen world, Hitchcock concentrated on stories of crime, madness, and espionage in which ostensibly innocent characters confront their guilt and complicity in unsavory or villainous activities. In *Shadow of a Doubt* (1943) a psychopathic serial killer (Joseph Cotton) visits his sister in a small California town, and his idealistic young niece discovers his secret and the many ties that bind her to him. In *Notorious* (1946), two U.S. spies (Cary Grant and Ingrid Bergman) fall in love

(continued)

while manipulating and emotionally betraying one another. In *Strangers on a Train* (1951), a charming psychopath (Robert Walker) proposes an exchange of murders to a celebrity tennis player. "You do mine, I do yours," he tells the shocked but intrigued athlete.

Hitchcock reached the height of his powers, and the zenith of his career, in the 1950s with a series of now-classic films. In *Rear Window* (1954), about a wheelchair-bound photographer intent on proving one of his neighbors is a murderer, Hitchcock explored the theme of voyeurism, applying it both to characters in the narrative and to audiences watching the film.

To Catch a Thief (1955) was a classy, witty Technicolor romp on the Riviera, and *The Man Who Knew Too Much* (1956) was a glossy, big-budget remake of his 1934 British hit. *Vertigo* (1958), a complex tale of detection, murder, and madness, was Hitchcock's most intensely personal, romantic, and poetic creation. Widely regarded as his masterpiece, it is hypnotic, dreamlike, with a remarkable depth of feeling and an uncompromisingly bleak ending. Disappointed with *Vertigo*'s commercial performance, Hitchcock made *North by Northwest* (1959), a fast, witty, hugely entertaining summation of the espionage and chase thrillers he had perfected in his 1930s British career.

Hitchcock's next film, *Psycho* (1960), proved to be his most influential. This story of murder, madness, and perversion at a seedy roadside motel was a calculated exercise in audience manipulation in which Hitchcock wanted only to make his viewers scream. He succeeded brilliantly. In its coldness, its savage brutality and violence, and its merciless attitude toward the audience, *Psycho* anticipated, and introduced, the essential characteristics of modern horror.

Hitchcock had one more hit in the 1960s—*The Birds* (1963)—and then began a period of decline. *Marnie* (1964), *Torn Curtain* (1966), and *Topaz* (1969) were critical and commercial disappointments. The industry and the modern audience were changing, and Hitchcock could not adapt. The old studio system was dead, and many of the stars (Grace Kelly, Cary Grant, James Stewart) who were essential to Hitchcock's films had retired or were now too old for the parts he needed to fill. The brutality and cynicism of modern film, which Hitchcock had helped inaugurate with *Psycho*, swept by him. Hitchcock had relied for his best effects on suggestion and implication and felt unable to relate to a world in which, and to a public for whom, extraordinary acts of violence were becoming increasingly commonplace.

Hitchcock achieved a brief popular comeback with *Frenzy* (1972), a hit about a British serial killer. Movie censorship had fallen, and Hitchcock included horrific and distasteful scenes of explicit violence, inadvertently demonstrating how creatively beneficial Hollywood censorship had been for him. His last film, *Family Plot* (1976), was an entertaining but unremarkable thriller. Hitchcock's declining health prevented completion of additional films, and he died on April 29, 1980.

Hitchcock's genius for self-promotion (realized through his cameo appearances in films and his witty introductions on his television show, which ran from 1955–1965), and his brilliance at frightening viewers made him one of the most popular and famous directors in screen history. But he was also a serious and sophisticated artist who made brilliant use of cinema as a vehicle for expressing the forces of darkness and chaos in human life. ■

considerable suspense, and when the payoff finally comes at the end of the film—a close-up of the mother's skeletal face—it is heart-stopping.

Other Angles   The **canted angle,** involving a tilted camera leaning to one side or the other, can be an effective way of making the world look off-kilter, often to express a character's anxieties or disoriented, disorganized frame of mind. In *Thirteen* (2003), director Catharine Hardwicke uses a tilted camera to visualize the distress of a mother (Holly Hunter) who learns that her 13-year-old daughter is into drugs. In a similar fashion, the off-kilter angles visualize the disturbed world of *Natural Born Killers*

NATURAL BORN KILLERS
(WARNER BROS., 1994)

Unstable, tilted camera angles help to establish the nightmarish, off-kilter world of serial killers in Oliver Stone's *Natural Born Killers*. Stone purposely created a wildly chaotic visual design to give the film a psychotic tone. Frame enlargement.

(1994). Tilted camera angles are an excellent means of visualizing emotional or psychological instability.

Angle in Context   While camera angles are capable of eliciting some of the kinds of emotional responses from viewers described here, it is important to remember that all these responses are context-dependent. The information they convey depends on the emotional content and action of a given scene. They must be carefully matched by filmmakers to the material of the scene. In other contexts, other scenes, low, high, and canted angles may have other effects than those mentioned here.

Japanese director Yasujiro Ozu, for example, used low camera positions and angles extensively, but they are not correlated with any of the effects discussed here. To a large extent, they are motivated by the action of the films, which feature characters sitting on tatami mats while conversing (as is the custom in traditional Japanese homes). The camera gets closer to the ground to film them. One critic has suggested that these low positions and angles work to include the viewer in the world of the film, like a guest sitting on a tatami mat. To assess the function of camera position and angle, then, one must bear in mind their potential for structuring emotional response and also consider the expressive requirements of the scene. What are its dramatic, comedic, emotional, or cultural requirements, and how is their expression facilitated by camera position and angle?

Camera Lens

Besides position and angle, a third factor defines the relationship between the camera and what it photographs. This is the type of lens used in each shot. The lens is the device that gathers light and brings it into the camera to a focused point on the film, thereby creating an image that is recorded on the light-sensitive surface of the film, called the **emulsion**. A filmmaker's choice of lens can drastically affect the look of the image in terms of (1) the apparent size of objects on screen and (2) the apparent relationships of depth and distance between near and far objects. Camera positions generally are defined by the amount of distance between the camera and what it is photographing, but without knowing something about the lenses employed, a viewer is liable to misjudge the camera's position. Certain lenses, for example, can make the camera seem much closer to what it is photographing than it really is.

INGLOURIOUS BASTERDS (UNIVERSAL PICTURES, 2009)

Lt. Aldo Raine (Brad Pitt) admires his handiwork, having just carved a swastika on the forehead of a Nazi colonel. The low camera angle shows Raine from the colonel's pont of view, lying on the ground. Although the camera itself is not tilted, the extreme wide angle lens creates parallax distortion, making the characters seem tilted and the tree behind them to lurch at an angle. The tilted composition is achieved with the lens rather than the camera's position. Frame enlargement.

FILMMAKER SPOTLIGHT

Yasujiro Ozu

Most movies resemble one another because filmmakers use standard methods of setting their cameras, lighting a scene, and editing the shots. Interesting variations on the standard pattern are possible, but it is rare for a filmmaker to define a unique, singular visual style, essentially inventing a novel method of scenic construction.

Yasujiro Ozu did just this in a career that lasted from 1927–1963. He made most of his films for Shochiku Studio, and almost all of his films are family dramas that focus on transitional events—children drift away from their parents or marry and start new lives, aging relatives pass away. Ozu was so committed to these portraits of family life that he rarely strayed from the topic, and the titles of his films demonstrate the regularity of the pattern—*Early Spring* (1956), *Late Spring* (1949), *Early Summer* (1951), *The End of Summer* (1961), *Late Autumn* (1960), *An Autumn Afternoon* (1962), *I Graduated, But...* (1929), *I Flunked, But...* (1930), *I Was Born, But...* (1932).

Ozu's films are often very funny, but they are also serene and at times quite melancholy, as he calmly views the transient nature of life and the disappointments that living inevitably brings. He frequently collaborated with screenwriter Kogo Noda and relied on a stock company of actors that included Chishu Ryu, Setsuko Hara, and Haruko Sugimura.

He disliked melodrama and avoided the heated emotions that movies often portray. He gave his actors meticulous directions about how to hold a pair of chopsticks, how to lift a glass of sake, the angle at which to look right, then left and then down. And he often wanted them to do this without projecting strong emotions. The paradox, though, is that watching an Ozu film can be a very emotional experience. His emphasis on minimalism pays great dividends. Less is more.

Most famously, Ozu's visual style was rigorous and almost unvarying. He set his camera about three feet off the ground, which for many scenes corresponded with the seated position on tatami matting in a traditional Japanese home. But even in outdoor scenes where characters are standing or walking, Ozu's camera often stayed close to the ground.

EARLY SUMMER (SHOCHIKU, 1951); LATE SPRING (SHOCHIKU, 1949)
Ozu placed his camera a few feet off the ground, which corresponded with the traditional seating in a Japanese home, but he maintained this practice even with outdoor scenes in which characters are not seated on tatami matting. Frame enlargements.

LATE SPRING (SHOCHIKU, 1949); EQUINOX FLOWER (SHOCHIKU, 1958)
Ozu did not use over-the-shoulder framings in dialogue scenes. He preferred the frontal compositions seen here in which characters look almost into the camera lens. The set-ups draw the viewer into the scenes in a singular fashion. Frame enlargements.

He didn't use fades or dissolves but preferred the straight cut to join shots. He rarely moved the camera, and he often cut away from a scene's action to shots of inanimate objects—an umbrella leaning against a doorway, a glowing lantern outside a restaurant, a lotus flower in bloom. The still-life imagery provided moments of transition within the narrative and also a space in which the viewer might contemplate character behavior and conflict and reach a calm understanding of these.

(continued)

Ozu's camera set-ups did not follow the standard over-the-shoulder style of framing that became so universally accepted among filmmakers. He often filmed his characters in a head-on, frontal fashion, and had them look back at the camera in a way that was just slightly off-angle of its lens. This compositional style draws the viewer inside the scene by making it seem as if the characters are addressing themselves to the camera and the viewer. And he often cut between shots in ways that shifted the line-of-sight by 180 degrees, as each shot offered a reverse-field view of the scene's playing area.

These stylistic traits emerged early in Ozu's career and he sustained the pattern across the body of his work. They give Ozu's films an unmistakable profile. Ozu's films look like nobody else's movies. But the style was not gratuitous or a meaningless exercise to establish authorship. Ozu was a great artist, and his visual style is precisely calculated. It defines a cinema of great poetry and delicacy and uncommon emotional sensitivity. ∎

FOCAL LENGTH AND DEPTH OF FIELD   When the lens is focused on a distant object, the distance between the film inside the camera and the optical center of the lens is known as the **focal length**. The properties of different lenses are understood in relation to their respective focal lengths. A focal length of 50 mm conventionally designates a **normal lens** for 35-mm film, which is the film format used in commercial theaters. Lenses with focal lengths greater than the normal range are **telephoto lenses,** or long-focal-length lenses. Those with focal lengths less than normal are **wide-angle lenses,** or short-focal-length lenses.

FINDING NEVERLAND (MIRAMAX, 2004)

Changing the lens's focal plane within a shot (a technique called **rack focusing**) can make a dynamic contribution to the composition. It creates a kind of editing within the frame as the filmmaker racks focus instead of cutting to a new shot. In a long, uninterrupted shot, Sylvia Davies (Kate Winslet) and James Barrie (Johnny Depp) talk about her children, and the changes in focal plane bring first one and then the other character into focus. Frame enlargements.

The focal length of a lens is directly related to how much it sees, termed the **angle of view**. At a shorter focal length, the angle of view increases, allowing filmmakers to film a wider area. At longer focal lengths, the angle of view decreases, limiting filmmakers to photographing a more narrow area.

Also varying with the focal length of the lens is the **depth of field**, the amount of area from near to far that will remain in focus. A wide-angle lens can capture much greater depth of field than a telephoto lens. With a wide-angle lens, the distance between near objects in focus and distant objects in focus can be very great. By contrast, a telephoto lens will tend to give filmmakers a shallow depth of field, an inability to hold near and far points in focus.

These issues of depth of field are connected to important aesthetic traditions in cinema. Using **deep focus**, filmmakers like Orson Welles (*Citizen Kane*) and Jacques Tati (*Playtime*, 1967) created complex compositions featuring a rich interplay of foreground and background detail. By shooting in deep focus and extending the duration of their shots, these filmmakers work with an aesthetic that respects the wholeness of time and space; that is, the playing area of each shot is extended in time (the shot's long duration) and space (depth of field). This is a distinct stylistic alternative to the use of editing to carve up space into many brief shots. The deep focus tradition is covered in more detail in the section on Realism in Chapter 11.

Yet another characteristic differentiating wide-angle from telephoto lenses is the ability of telephoto lenses to make distant objects appear much closer than they really are. In this respect, the effects of the telephoto lens can overwhelm the impression of

THE UNTOUCHABLES (PARAMOUNT, 1987)

The wide-angle lens gives filmmakers an expansive depth of field. It also can exaggerate depth perspective. Sean Connery and Kevin Costner's hands appear very large, relative to the apparent size of their heads—this is a distortion of depth perspective created by the wide angle lens. In the closer framing, note how close Costner is to the camera, while Connery in the middle distance remains in focus. Wide angle depth of field enables filmmakers to put things right into the face of the camera while retaining the ability to focus on the midground or background. Frame enlargements.

Two portraits of the same subject, one taken a few yards away with a normal (55-mm) lens and the other at a much greater distance using a telephoto (205-mm) lens. Which composition is a function of camera position, and which is a function of lens focal length?

true camera position. What might appear to be a close-up can, in fact, be shot using a telephoto lens with the camera in a long-shot position. In the two portraits of the wooden bridge, the bridge is the same size in each photo, but in one case the size is due to a close camera position, whereas in the other it is due to the magnifying effects of a telephoto lens. Viewers will have developed a sophisticated eye for cinema if they can tell when object size on screen is due more to camera position or to the choice of lens.

In sum, wide-angle lenses have a greater angle of view and depth of field than telephoto lenses. Unlike wide-angle lenses, telephoto lenses will magnify distant objects and make them seem closer than they are.

Zoom Lenses   In addition to normal, wide-angle, and telephoto lenses, a fourth category of lens is important in the cinema. This is the **zoom lens**. The zoom is a lens with a variable focal length. It can shift from wide-angle to telephoto settings within a single shot. This can create the appearance of camera movement, making it seem as if the camera is moving closer to or farther from its subject. In fact, however, the camera in a zoom shot remains stationary. Viewers with a sophisticated cinematic eye can discriminate zoom shots from true moving-camera shots. In a moving-camera shot, perspective changes; that is, the spatial relationship of the camera to the objects around it shifts because the camera is moving through three-dimensional space.

In a zoom shot, by contrast, perspective does not change because the camera does not move. Zooming in will magnify all objects on screen evenly. Zooming out will shrink all objects evenly. This is what produces the impression of camera movement. As objects in the shot enlarge, the viewer has the impression of moving closer to them. Whereas the zoom shot provides simple magnification, the moving camera provides a series of changing spatial relationships produced by movement and known as **motion parallax** or **motion perspective**. The absence of motion perspective in a shot where the camera seems to be moving is a clear sign that the shot is a zoom and not a true moving camera shot.

Filmmakers sometimes use zoom lenses as alternatives to camera movement, especially if they are filming on a low budget and a quick schedule. Zoom lenses, though, can be used for sophisticated effects. In *McCabe and Mrs. Miller* (1971), director Robert Altman and cinematographer Vilmos Zsigmond employ a zoom to create a moment of dramatic emphasis when the hero realizes a gang of gunmen has come to kill him. Altman and Zsigmond rapidly zoom in on the gang, conveying the hero's sense of anxiety and the rush of excitement he feels. The optical effect suggests these emotional reactions.

USING LENSES   Filmmakers often employ the telephoto lens when they are filming a scene on city streets in which the characters are engaged in conversation and surrounded by real pedestrians. A realistic impression depends on the pedestrians being unaware of the camera and the actors. Filmmakers can hide the camera by placing it at some distance from the action and then use the telephoto lens to bring the characters into the medium shot or close-up framing suitable for the dramatic content of the scene. Telephoto lenses also can facilitate the staging of stunts. When Tom Cruise runs across a busy city street in *The Firm* (1993), viewers jump when a car nearly crashes into him. The car's apparent proximity, though, is an illusion created by a telephoto lens.

Viewers acquire greater cinematic sophistication when they become sensitive to the effects produced by different lenses used in the shots of a given scene. Just as filmmakers change camera positions and angles throughout a scene, they change lenses as well, fitting these to the unfolding dynamics of the dramatic action. In a shot with extreme depth of field, where near and distant objects are in focus, the lens is likely to be a wide angle. If, on the other hand, depth of field looks very shallow, with a compression of distance so that an object that definitely is very far off looks close, the lens is likely to be a telephoto.

Some filmmakers are closely identified with certain types of lenses. Orson Welles, Martin Scorsese, and Tim Burton tend to favor wide-angle lenses, whereas Akira Kurosawa, Robert Altman, and Sam Peckinpah favor the telephoto. In *Touch of Evil*, his last U.S. picture, made for Universal Studios in 1958, Orson Welles filmed his gargantuan detective hero, Hank Quinlan, with extremely short lenses to exaggerate and enhance his huge and grotesque dimensions. Evaluating a filmmaker's choice of lenses requires that one be sensitive both to structure—in this case, the visual properties of lenses—and the requirements of the scene or shot. Consider the lead-in to the gunfight at the OK Corral in *Tombstone* (1993), when Wyatt Earp, his brothers, and Doc Holiday make their fateful walk down the town's streets toward the corral. A building blazes behind them for dramatic effect. The camera shoots them head-on as they stride toward it. The long lens isolates the heroes in a shallow plane of focus, giving them an unequivocal visual dominance in the frame. By excluding the fire from the plane of focus, the filmmakers ensured that it would not distract unduly from the foreground drama of the heroes' determination. As an out-of-focus object, the fire is

TOMBSTONE (BUENA VISTA, 1993)

Telephoto lens perspective used to isolate, emphasize, and intensify a point of dramatic climax. Frame enlargement.

TOUCH OF EVIL (UNIVERSAL, 1958)

Orson Welles was the master of wide-angle filmmaking, as practiced in *Citizen Kane* and subsequent films like this one about a corrupt sheriff in a Mexican border town. Filming on a small set during this police interrogation scene, Welles fills the camera's wide angle of view with numerous characters and gives them a dynamic staging in deep focus. Note the strategic positioning of characters at four planes of distance from the camera. Frame enlargement.

BEOWULF (PARAMOUNT, 2007)

Digital effects often simulate many features of camera perspective, including camera movement and depth of field. The exaggerated depth perspective seen here mimics what an extreme wide-angle lens might capture. Building virtual camera perspectives into effects shots enables filmmakers to make the effects seem consistent with the way in which a camera might view the world. Frame enlargement.

a subordinate element in the frame, but its presence is nevertheless dramatic, serving to prefigure the violence to come. Assessed in these terms, the telephoto framing is an effective one. By contrast, a wide-angle lens would have increased depth of field and thereby eliminated the concentrated visual focus on the heroes.

RED BEARD (TOHO, 1965)

Japanese director Akira Kurosawa preferred the telephoto lens. He also liked to film scenes with multiple cameras, creating occasional problems of perspective when he cut between shots. In this case he cuts between two cameras whose lines of sight form a 90-degree angle. The first camera setup uses a telephoto lens and makes the characters seem very close together, whereas the second setup reveals their true positioning. The perspective change between the two shots is very striking. Frame enlargements.

Camera Movement

The camera's perspective not only changes from shot to shot, but it also can shift and move within the shot. The camera can move in virtually any fashion through space. To simplify things, this discussion will focus on four basic categories of camera movement: (1) **pan and tilt**, (2) **dolly or tracking**, (3) **boom or crane**, and (4) **Steadicam**. All these types of camera movements shift the boundaries and coordinates of the frame. Moving the camera creates a fluid perspective, unlike a static shot with its fixed framing.

PAN AND TILT   A pan shot produces lateral movement on screen. The camera head rotates in a horizontal fashion from side to side on top of the tripod, which remains stationary. By contrast, in a tilt, the camera pivots vertically, up or down. If a filmmaker were shooting a skyscraper, she or he could start with a camera focused on the bottom of the building and then tilt slowly up to the top to reveal, perhaps, King Kong swatting at airplanes. The accompanying diagrams illustrate the action of panning and tilting.

Pans and tilts tend to establish linking movements, which filmmakers often use to connect objects or establish relationships between them or to call attention to new areas of the scene. Pans also may be used to readjust the frame to accommodate character movement. If a character crosses the room to open a door, the camera operator might pan to follow the movement. An early example of this use of the pan occurs in

Edwin S. Porter's *The Great Train Robbery* (1903). When the robbers make their daring escape from the train after holding it up, they go down an embankment and across a stream to get to their horses. As they do this, the camera operator pans left and tilts down to follow them. It is done a bit sloppily, however, because the robbers get almost out of frame at one point before the camera operator picks them back up again.

In most instances, pans are brief, with the camera only pivoting a small degree. However, its physical design permits the camera to rotate an entire 360 degrees on the mounting attached to its tripod. Nothing, therefore, except for conventional usage, prevents filmmakers from executing a fully circular, 360-degree panning shot. These tend to be rare, but they do occur. In *Easy Rider* (1969), when the heroes Wyatt (Peter Fonda) and Billy (Dennis Hopper) visit a hippie commune and its members gather in a circle to pray for their harvest, cameraman Haskell Wexler uses a 360-degree pan across the faces of all the characters, who are grouped in a circle. The camera's movement brings each character's face into frame, creating a symbolic image of unity and completeness.

DOLLY, TRACK, AND BOOM   Unlike the pan and tilt, in dolly, tracking, and boom or crane shots, the camera, along with its tripod or base, physically travels through space. As a result, these shots produce motion perspective, unlike pans and tilts. A **dolly** is simply a wheeled platform used for mounting the camera in a tracking shot. Sometimes these are called *dolly shots* because of their platform mount. In tracking, or dolly, shots, the camera may move briefly toward or away from an object, such as a character's face, or it may describe more extended and elaborate movements. In the latter case, a tracking shot may follow a character who is moving. As Rocky sprints along the streets of south Philadelphia to train for his big fight, the camera tracks with him. The rapid track helps to visualize Rocky's power and adds energy to the shot.

Tracking, or dolly, shots generally move in a direction parallel to the ground. By contrast, boom, or crane, shots execute elaborate movements up or down through

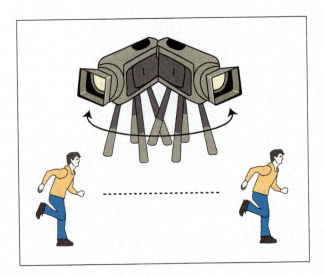

FIGURE 1.2
Pan.

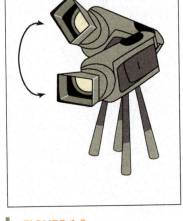

FIGURE 1.3
Tilt.

THE GREAT TRAIN ROBBERY (EDISON, 1903)

After holding up the train, the robbers run for their horses to escape. In the next moment, as they turn left and run down a hill, the camera operator will pan and tilt to follow the action. Frame enlargement.

space. They take their name from the apparatus—boom or crane—on which the camera is mounted. A famous boom shot occurs in *Gone With the Wind* (1939), during the scene where Scarlet O'Hara visits wounded confederate soldiers at the railroad station. The shot begins with a full-figure framing of Scarlet. The camera then pulls back and booms up to a high angle that shows Scarlet surrounded by a huge field of the dead and dying. This change of perspective creates a powerful dramatic effect by revealing the scale of the carnage surrounding Scarlet, a scale that the initial framing of the shot had concealed.

STEADICAM   The Steadicam has revolutionized camera movement in contemporary film. It is a mechanical system that produces a very steady, jitter-free image from hand-held camerawork. It consists of a vest worn by the camera operator, a stabilizing support arm connecting the camera to the operator's vest, and a monitor through which the operator views what the camera is seeing. (The Steadicam operator does not look through the camera itself.)

Using Steadicam, the operator can move the camera through space in a completely smooth and fluid way as an extension of his or her own body. The operator extends his or her arm and produces a "dolly" shot. The operator walks or runs along a street and produces a "tracking" shot.

Steadicam was introduced in *Bound for Glory* (1976) and *Rocky* (1976) and was used extensively in Stanley Kubrick's *The Shining* (1980). Today it is used in countless productions and is the means for achieving the restless, continuously moving camera work that is such a feature of contemporary film. A common shooting practice today is to have one or two Steadicam operators following the actors through a scene and providing a full 360 degrees of coverage. *Cinderella Man* (2005) and *Alexander* (2004) exemplify this approach. *Atonement* (2007) features a 5-minute-20-second Steadicam shot that reveals an epic landscape of war, the British retreat at Dunkirk in World War II. It is a single, unbroken shot; no digital effects are used to "glue" several shots together. *Children of Men* (2006) is shot entirely with a hand-held camera, but not a Steadicam. The filmmakers wanted to avoid the

FIGURE 1.4
Tracking shot.

mechanical look that Steadicam sometimes creates. As in *Atonement*, many sequences seem to be composed of a single, lengthy moving camera shot, except that in this case digital effects were used to invisibly join several shots into one.

FUNCTIONS OF MOVING-CAMERA SHOTS   This is a common and powerful function of camera movement: to reveal dramatic information by enlarging the viewer's field of view. A complementary function is to narrow and focus attention on significant objects or characters. As a director, John Ford rarely moved his camera, but when he did, it had tremendous effect, as in *The Searchers* (1956), where a dolly in to John Wayne's face emphasizes the character's intense and pathological hatred of Indians. Note the difference of emphasis between the opening and closing frames of the dolly as pictured in the frame enlargements as pictured on page 33.

In addition to revealing action or concentrating the viewer's attention, moving-camera shots can serve other purposes. One extremely common function is to express a dynamic sense of movement that makes a shot or scene more sensuous and dramatically exciting. When the Joker hijacks a police car and speeds through Gotham City in *The Dark Knight* (2008), the traveling camera plunges the viewer into the scene's frenzied action. Japanese director Akira Kurosawa is a master of sensuous camera movements that add extraordinary dramatic and visual impact to his scenes. In films such as *Seven Samurai* (1954) and *Throne of Blood* (1957), where characters on foot or horse race through a dense forest, Kurosawa tracks the camera rapidly with them, darting in and out of trees, over streams and under branches, plunging the viewer into dense foliage and expressing in the most visually convincing manner the sensation and experience of flight.

U.S. directors Martin Scorsese (*Shutter Island*, 2009; *Taxi Driver*, 1976) and Brian De Palma (*The Untouchables*, 1987) are masters at using sweeping, sensuous camera movements. In *Goodfellas* (1990), Scorsese uses a hand-held camera in a single shot to follow the main character, a New York gangster, as he gets out of his car, crosses the street, enters the side door of a nightclub, winds through narrow hallways and a crowded kitchen, and walks into a ballroom filled with hundreds of people and a stand-up comic in midroutine. In *Snake Eyes* (1998), De Palma used a hand-held camera to simulate a 20-minute moving-camera shot that follows Nicolas Cage as he walks through a sports arena filled with a capacity crowd. This was a deceptive sequence, however, because it was composed of several shots. These were joined at hard-to-see edit points when a wall or a person passed closely in front of the camera. Another bravura moving-camera shot—9 minutes long—opened Robert Altman's *The Player* (1992) as a way of letting the audience know that this would be a very self-conscious film. In the shot, characters discuss their love for the elaborate opening tracking shot of Orson Welles's *Touch of Evil*, as Altman essentially repeats the famous Welles shot.

Filmmakers also use moving-camera shots to visualize important thematic ideas. In such cases, the camera's movement is metaphoric and symbolic, its motion correlating, as a visual design, with important issues in a film's narrative. In *Seven Samurai* (1954), for example, to suggest the developing friendship and unity between samurai and peasants, Kurosawa groups them in a circle and tracks the camera around its periphery. In *We Were Soldiers* (2002), to suggest

**THE EARRINGS OF MADAME DE...
(GAUMONT, 1953)**

Camera movement in contemporary film often has an unstructured and sometimes sloppy look because the proliferation of lightweight equipment makes cameras very portable and hand-held shots relatively easy to execute. In contrast with this contemporary trend, director Max Ophüls was the master of elaborately choreographed, precisely designed tracking shots. *The Earrings of Madame de...* is composed with the camera in continuous motion. Its movements reveal décor, simulate character perspective, visualize social connections among groups of people, and create a series of fluid framings that are exacting in their focus and design. The film is composed as an elaborate series of dances by the camera. Ophüls' brilliance at choreographing tracking shots and using them as vehicles for narrative and theme has never been equaled. Frame enlargement.

the Vietnamese enemy closing in on an army lieutenant colonel (Mel Gibson) and his men, the cinematographer did an inwardly spiraling tracking shot that loops around and in on Gibson. In *The Sea Inside* (2004), a digitally enhanced helicopter shot expresses a paralyzed man's fantasy of flying.

Some of the most unique and carefully conceived moving-camera shots occur in the films of French director Jean-Luc Godard. Godard's structural designs are extremely self-conscious; that is, they call attention to the technique at work. *Weekend* (1967) is Godard's dark, savagely funny satire of the barely repressed violence of an absurd Americanized consumer society. In the film, an amoral couple, Corrine and Roland, travel by car to Oinville, where they plan to murder Corrine's mother so that they might claim the family inheritance. On the way to Oinville, they are caught in a traffic jam. On a narrow country road, a long line of vehicles impedes their progress. Anxious to get past the stalled line, Roland impatiently edges his car along the shoulder of the road, past the other vehicles.

Godard films the sequence in a single, unbroken tracking shot that lasts over 7 minutes. The camera tracks along the road and the line of stalled vehicles, keeping

ATONEMENT (UNIVERSAL, 2007)

Camera movement can work to reveal details and vistas by enlarging perspective. Trying to rejoin British forces at Dunkirk in World War II, Robbie Turner (James McAvoy) finds a group of schoolgirls who have been killed by German soldiers. The camera move reveals the horror gradually. At first, Robbie is framed alone (a). Then the camera pulls away a short distance to reveal a few bodies (b), and then it continues moving to reveal the full scale of the outrage (c). Frame enlargements.

THE SEARCHERS (WARNER BROS., 1956)

Camera movement can work to concentrate the viewer's attention on dramatically important objects or details. John Wayne's character in this John Ford Western has an intense racial hatred for the Commanche, and Ford uses a dolly shot to emphasize the depth of this animosity. Pictured here are the beginning and ending frames of the shot. Notice how the dolly brings Wayne's face forward, emphasizing his extraordinary expression. Frame enlargements.

pace with Roland as he inches his way forward. The camera frames the scene slightly to the rear, preventing viewers from seeing what lies ahead. The effect of this maddening and funny sequence depends on the length of the shot—lasting an extremely long time—as well as on the slow, methodical progress of the camera along what seems an endless line of stalled vehicles. The tracking shot becomes a metaphor for the experience of being stalled in traffic and enables the filmmakers to subject the audience to that oppressive experience.

These examples of camera movement point toward an important conclusion. Whether a filmmaker uses it to reveal detail, to convey the sensory experience of motion, or to symbolically express thematic and narrative ideas, camera movement provides filmmakers with an essential means of shaping and organizing the visual space of a scene. Camera movement gives structure and meaning to the composition of a shot.

TECHNOLOGICAL COMPONENTS OF FILM ART   Technological developments in recent years have made camera movement especially easy to achieve. The elaborate camera moves in *Snake Eyes* and *Goodfellas* were achieved with the Steadicam, as were the sweeping camera moves during the climactic battle in Terrence Malick's *The Thin Red Line* (1998).

Malick's film also benefited from the use of an Akela crane for scenes showing U.S. soldiers hunting their Japanese foes through waist-high grass. These grassy

THE DARK KNIGHT (WARNER BROS., 2008)

Rapid movement by objects or by the camera produces motion blur. Even digital effects sequences simulate motion blur because it is so characteristic of the camera's way of seeing. The Joker (Heath Ledger) takes a maniacal ride through Gotham City, and the fast-moving camera makes the background appeared blurred. Frame enlargement.

WEEKEND (NEW YORKER FILMS, 1967)

Godard's tracking camera slowly travels the length of a line of stalled cars. The framing prevents a view of what lies ahead, deliberately frustrating the viewer. Finally, after several minutes, the camera reveals the cause of the accident. Frame enlargements.

fields on the Australian location (subbing for Guadalcanal in the Solomon Islands, where the story was set) were dense, with rocks and holes underneath, an impossible terrain for a camera operator to move about. But the Akela could be positioned securely on solid ground and the camera extended on its 72-foot arm into the grassy areas that were vital to the story. On the crane, the camera could execute sweeping moves through the fields. In *Ali*, a film biography of boxer Muhammad Ali, Michael Mann used a "lipstick" camera—as tiny as its name implies—that he could hold in his hand as he moved between the boxers in order to film the fight scenes from unconventional angles.

Camera moves also can be simulated digitally today. Computer-effects shots in *Panic Room* (2002) create effortless camera moves through floors in a house, through air vents, and other impossible objects. This is animated footage that imitates the appearance of a camera move. And filming digitally enables a filmmaker to create an endless camera move, or at least one that doesn't, of necessity, end when the camera runs out of film. Shot on digital video, *Russian Ark* (2002) is composed of a single moving-camera shot that runs the entire length of the film's 96 minutes.

Obviously, filmmakers in earlier decades did not have the luxury of such devices. When viewing older films, therefore, one must be aware of the physical resources available in earlier periods. Sometimes filmmakers had to struggle with clumsy or cumbersome equipment, and it is often their ingenuity at devising solutions to these technical problems that is a mark of their talent.

During production of *The Last Laugh* (1924), for example, F. W. Murnau experimented with many different ways of producing camera movement. The camera was attached to a ladder, to scaffolding, to a rubber-wheeled trolley, and to the stomach of cameraman Carl Freund while he rode a bicycle. So impressed was Hollywood with the work of Murnau and Freund in *The Last Laugh* that it sent a telegram to Ufa, the German studio that produced the film, inquiring about the special camera that had been used to take the shots, adding that in the United States there was apparently no such device. Robert Herlth, the set designer for *The Last Laugh* and several other Murnau films, remarked that what the Americans didn't know was that Murnau and the crew had not used sophisticated equipment but only the most primitive and basic methods to achieve outstanding results.

Technical sophistication, by itself, provides a misleading yardstick for measuring the quality of films. Film equipment is so advanced today that filmmakers of only moderate talent (a category that does *not* include Malick, Mann, Scorsese, or De Palma) can produce images with a sophistication that the early masters—Renoir, Murnau, D. W. Griffith—could only dream of. Technology without intelligence, however, is just mechanics. It must be balanced by artistic vision and ingenuity.

STRUCTURAL DESIGN AND CREATIVE CHOICE

A film's structural design results from the creative choices made by filmmakers, who confront a range of options as a project moves into production. There is no single, right way to film a scene. Where to position the camera, from what angle, which lens to use, whether to employ camera movement, how to light the set, how to choreograph the actors on screen, how to record the sound and balance dialogue, music, and sound effects, a filmmaker wrestles with all these decisions. How they are resolved defines the style or structure of a given film.

Case Study SAVING PRIVATE RYAN *AND* FLAGS OF OUR FATHERS

Two prominent World War II films—Steven Spielberg's *Saving Private Ryan* (1998) and Clint Eastwood's *Flags of Our Fathers* (2006)—include vivid scenes of combat that are accentuated by an intentionally harsh visual design. But the filmmakers on each production used different tools and took different creative approaches in achieving their designs.

Saving Private Ryan (1998) begins with a startlingly graphic depiction of the D-Day invasion of the Normandy beaches, a battle that helped turn the tide of World War II in June 1944. In a harrowing 25-minute sequence, Spielberg and cinematographer Janusz Kaminski depict the carnage on Omaha beach, where the Allied forces suffered their greatest casualties

(continued)

under withering fire from German troops barricaded on high ground overlooking the beach.

Spielberg wanted the violence in *Saving Private Ryan* to have a chaotic quality that would correspond to the subjective experience of the men on the beach, knowing that death could come at any time, regardless of how one tried to avoid it.

He and Kaminski used the documentary footage shot by combat cameramen on the Normandy beaches as a model. They aimed to emulate the striking features of this footage, much of which was shot in color and had a flat look, with reduced contrast. Accordingly, they decided to film in color, in contrast to their previous World War II collaboration, *Schindler's List* (1993), shot in black-and-white in order to correspond with much of the historical footage of Nazi atrocities.

They used two photochemical (non-digital) techniques—flashing and ENR—to render the colors more monochromatic and to reduce contrast. When film is flashed, the negative is exposed to a small amount of light prior to filming. This has the effect of de-saturating color and reducing the density of shadows, allowing more detail to come through in shadow areas. ENR (named after the technician, Ernesto N. Rico, who helped develop the process) is a somewhat complementary process and has been used widely in recent films (*Evita*, 1996; *Amistad*, 1998; *Bulworth*, 1998). ENR retains a portion of the silver in film emulsion, which is normally removed during developing. This has the effect of making shadows blacker, de-saturating color, and highlighting the texture and edges of surfaces. As a result of ENR, the patterns on the uniforms in *Saving Private Ryan* grew more vivid, as did the edges of helmets and guns and the reflective surface of the

water, heightening the physical effect Spielberg was after. To darken the blood so it would stand out amid the de-saturated colors, the effects crew added dyes to make it more blue.

Because the lenses used by combat cameramen were inferior to what a modern filmmaker would use, Kaminski and Spielberg ordered that the protective coating be stripped from some of their lenses. This gave the photographed images a sharp but cloudy appearance, with reduced contrast. To heighten the sense of chaos, they shot scenes with cameras using mismatched lenses, with and without the coating, to give the resulting footage a disjointed and disconnected feel.

To accentuate this off-kilter feeling, they manipulated the camera's shutter (a device that regulates how light reaches the unexposed film) to create strange, memorable effects in some shots. They threw the shutter out of synch to create a streaking, teary effect from top to bottom of the image and set the shutter at unusual angles to give the action a stroboscopic appearance. (*Pearl Harbor* (2001) copied this effect.) To create a disturbed, visually unsettled perspective, they used handheld cameras and employed a Clairmont Camera Image Shaker to vibrate camera perspective both horizontally and vertically.

Through all these choices about technique, Spielberg and Kaminski aimed to capture the jarring experience of being inside combat. As Spielberg said, the film's style is hard and rough. He stated that he and his crew were trying to capture fear and chaos. Technical imperfections actually worked to achieve this end. If blood or sand hit the lens, no attempt was made to clean it off. Spielberg wanted the footage

SAVING PRIVATE RYAN (DREAMWORKS, 1998)

The ferocious intensity of this film's battlefield sequences resulted from highly stylized manipulations of cinema technique. In cinema, there is no one "right" way to shoot a scene. Structural design results from the creative choices made by filmmakers. Frame enlargement.

to look as if it had been filmed by a combat camera-man. The film's design has its visual point of origin in combat photography, even though many of the techniques they used had no basis in such photography. Their design choices—rendering a monochromatic look, emulating the visual qualities of the documentary footage of the invasion, creating a subjective view of the battle—led them to elaborate technological manipulations to achieve these ends.

Flags of Our Fathers depicts the brutal fighting on the Pacific island of Iwo Jima between American troops and Japanese soldiers who were determined to hold the island. Eastwood wanted the battle scenes to have a monochromatic look, but, unlike Spielberg, he achieved this look using digital methods.

Cinematographer Tom Stern and Eastwood had planned to use ENR in order to de-saturate the color, but they ran tests comparing ENR with comparable results that could be achieved digitally. They decided to use digital methods because these allowed results that could not be achieved through traditional photochemical means. Because ENR is applied during the creation of a positive release print, the smallest increment in which it can be used is one lab reel (about 10 minutes of film), and it cannot be varied within that unit. By contrast, working digitally Stern could not only replicate the de-saturated ENR look but he could vary it dynamically within a shot, adjusting individual colors and areas of the frame. Accordingly, the film footage was scanned to digital video where the extensive color manipulations could be carried out. Once these were finished, the results were scanned back to film for distribution to theatres. (This process of scanning to digital video for color correction is known as the digital

intermediate (DI) and is explained in more detail in Chapter 2.)

Eastwood likes rich, deep blacks (shadows and dark areas in the image), and digital color correction enabled him to "crush" the blacks—making them so dark that little or no detail is visible—to a degree that went beyond what he had achieved using photochemical means on films such as *Million Dollar Baby*.

The film has a severely monochromatic look that verges on black-and-white, but individual colors were intensified in portions of the image—blood erupting from soldiers hit by gunfire, the reds on the American flag raised on Mt. Suribachi, skintones on faces and hands. The film was shot in Iceland, and the sandy beaches were digitally darkened to depict the volcanic soil of Iwo Jima.

The de-saturated design of the battle scenes contrasts with other sequences in the film that take place in the United States and that have more vivid colors. The de-saturation was meant to evoke the hellish and brutal conditions faced by the soldiers doing battle on the island.

Flags of Our Fathers marked the first time that Eastwood had used digital methods of color correction, and he continued to do so on each of his subsequent films.

Structural design results from a filmmaker's inevitable need to choose one or more sets of techniques and tools, based on an organizing design concept. On *Saving Private Ryan*, Spielberg emphasized traditional photochemical methods of achieving his goals, while Eastwood on *Flags of Our Fathers* used a digital approach to achieve his goals. While the imagery of both films is severe looking, de-saturated in color, and heavy in contrast, Spielberg and Eastwood took different

FLAGS OF OUR FATHERS (PARAMOUNT PICTURES, 2006)

Clint Eastwood used digital methods of color correction for the first time on this production. The film's severely monochromatic design verges on black-and-white. The film footage was shot and processed normally but then was converted to digital video for manipulation to achieve the extremely de-saturated look that Eastwood wanted. Frame enlargement.

(continued)

routes to achieve these goals. The many potential ways to design a film are narrowed to a single approach as filmmakers decide how to organize the tools of film-making. Decisions about where to place the camera, whether to move it, and what type of lenses to use must be integrated with other decisions about lights, color, sets, costumes, editing, and sound—as well as the relationship between traditional analog methods of production and digital tools—in order to arrive at a coherent and expressive audiovisual design. ◾

THE CAMERA AND HUMAN PERCEPTION: CINEMA'S DUAL CAPABILITY

The camera records screen action through a changing series of positions, angles, lenses, and movements, and as they make their creative decisions, filmmakers need to anticipate how viewers will see and make sense of their images. To what extent does the camera's way of "seeing" approximate the viewer's customary habits of viewing the world? Is there a relationship between the appearance of images on the movie or television screen and the appearance of real-world objects and things in the viewer's mind's eye? These issues are relevant for comprehending how film structure operates and how viewers understand films.

Transforming Visual Reality

Obviously, both camera and human eye can see color, texture, movement, and the location of people and things in three-dimensional space. Motion pictures seem very lifelike, and even impossible objects, like Godzilla, can be rendered with apparent photographic realism. The camera, though, can see selectively in ways the human eye cannot. In other words, it has the property of **perceptual transformation,** the ability to show things in ways that differ from ordinary visual experience. Telephoto and wide-angle lens perspectives have no counterpart in human vision. The eye cannot magnify the size of distant objects, as a telephoto lens can, or increase the apparent distance between near and far objects, as a wide-angle lens can. A cinematographer who cranes up to a high-angle long shot employs a unique cinematic technique that

DO THE RIGHT THING (40 ACRES AND A MULE FILMWORKS, 1989)

A wide-angle lens alters normal visual reality by stretching and exaggerating perspective in this shot of Radio Raheem (Bill Nunn). His hands and rings seem unnaturally large compared to the rest of his body, and the lines of perspective in the image are bent. Note the way the roofline on the buildings seems to curve. The optics of the lens have transformed the ordinary appearance of things. Frame enlargement.

the viewer's eye cannot duplicate, as does an editor who cuts among shots taken from different camera positions and angles, and with different lenses, to provide a shifting series of perspectives on the action. Viewers quickly learn that motion picture images and stories can define their own rules of representation. Stylized films like *The Crow* (1994) or *The Matrix* (1999) take viewers on imaginary journeys to screen worlds that differ remarkably from the one they inhabit in daily life. Viewers accept the unusual images, characters, and stories established in these films as a representational reality that is true on its own stylized terms.

Corresponding with Visual Reality

But the camera and other elements of film structure do not simply alter and transform the viewer's experience of people, places, and physical environments. Cinema also has the capability of **perceptual correspondence,** the ability to show things in ways that reference and correspond with the viewer's visual and social experience. Close-ups, for example, emphasize facial expressions. Social experience has taught viewers how to interpret these as signs of a person's thoughts, feelings, and intentions.

CLOSE-UP

How Movies Create the Impression of Motion on Screen

Viewers see only *apparent* motion on screen. As a strip of film runs through the projector, each frame is projected individually. Inside the projector is a device called the **shutter,** which blocks the light for a fraction of a second while the next frame is pulled down into place. The projector thus emits light in a pulsating beam that turns on and off. In the theater, viewers see a series of still frames projected on the screen and sit in alternating periods of light and dark.

The illusions of cinema—the viewer's impressions of movement and of a continuously illuminated screen—are due to several factors of perception. The retina of the eye retains an image for a fraction of a second after the source is gone (a phenomenon called **persistence of vision**). If a light source is switched on and off rapidly enough, a threshold is reached where **flicker fusion** occurs, a blending together of the individual pulses of light. 24 frames per second, the projection speed of sound film, is adequate to sustain retinal after-images and produce flicker fusion. At 24 frames per second, viewers cannot see the pulsing light that the projector

is emitting. (A popular nickname for the movies is *flicks*. This term dates from the silent era when slower projection speeds were used, enabling spectators to see a flicker effect, produced by the pulsing light from the projector. Hence the term *flicks*.)

Retinal after-images and flicker fusion explain why viewers fail to perceive the projector's pulsating light. They do not, however, explain why viewers see moving objects on screen. Motion perception is a complex phenomenon, and under the right conditions spectators will see apparent motion when no real movement has occurred. If a series of closely spaced light bulbs are illuminated in rapid sequence in a darkened room, a spectator will see a single light source moving across the room rather than a series of lights illuminated one after another. This phenomenon has been called **beta movement.** If the intervals between a series of illuminated lights, or the positions of a galloping horse captured in a series of film frames, are small enough, the eye's motion detectors encode this information as movement. The viewer sees a single travelling light or a galloping horse on screen.

(continued)

Many viewers today watch movies on electronic display devices such as computer screens or widescreen monitors and image resolution varies considerably depending on the video source and the display device. Electronic images are scanned as lines of pixels (a pixel is the smallest unit of picture information in an electronic display). A standard DVD outputs 720 x 480 pixels (width by height) to create an interlaced image that is composed of two fields (odd-numbered scan lines are one field, even-numbered lines are the other). A DVD video frame is composed of the two fields, presented in an alternating fashion. Resolution suffers in an interlaced image because it is prone to distortion and noise. HD (high definition) video, as found on Blu-ray offers a resolution of 1920 x 1080 pixels that are progressively scanned, that is, the lines of pixels composing each frame are created in sequence, producing superior resolution and a much cleaner image. In each case, the output of scan lines is above the critical fusion threshold, ensuring that a viewer sees a continuously illuminated image rather than scan lines or individual pixels. In these ways, the most fundamental features of cinema—the appearance of continuous light and motion—are built on shared characteristics of perception common to all viewers. These features are automatic. Viewers

FIGURE 1.5
Intermittent motion at 24 frames per second.

FIGURE 1.6
Successive events perceived as apparent motion.

do not have to make any effort to bring them into play. The cinema activates universal perceptual abilities held by all members of its audiences. This fact underlies the medium's great appeal and accessibility. ■

The Na'vi of planet Pandora in *Avatar* (2009) are tall, blue, cat-people created as digital characters, but their behavior is modeled on the performances by live actors. The animators preserved the actors' distinctive facial features in their Na'vi counterparts so that the characters played by Zoe Saldana, Wes Studi, Sam Worthington, Sigourney Weaver, and others would seem recognizably human. They did this even when it resulted in a 'wrong' face. Sigourney Weaver, for example, has a thin, aquiline nose that is one of her most distinctive features. Na'vi, though, have broad, flat noses consistent with their cat-like appearance. Even so, Weaver's Na'vi character was animated to have the actresses' distinctively thin nose so as to visually connect the digital character with the famous face of the actress playing that character. Throughout the film viewers study the faces of the Na'vi for clues about their feelings, thoughts and motivations. These blue, cat-like faces were built to correspond with a viewer's understanding of human behavior and feeling.

Among the most powerful correspondences that cinema can establish with the viewer's experience are perceptual ones. On the movie screen, the viewer sees depth, distance, and motion in ways that seem remarkably lifelike. A fully three-dimensional world comes to life on the flat two-dimensional screen. When the Na'vi ride atop the giant flying banshees, a viewer experiences the sensation of gliding through space

AVATAR (TWENTIETH CENTURY FOX, 2009)
Even in highly stylized films, facial expression corresponds with the viewer's understanding of behavior and personality. Zoe Saldana's performance as Neytiri was captured using an innovative camera that focused exclusively upon her face. The facial information captured by this camera, in turn, was used to digitally animate the character. Frame enlargement.

because of the highly detailed and emphatic motion perspective that has been built inside the computer-generated flying shots. But movement and depth on screen are both visual illusions. Neither really exists.

The camera captures the same information about light, shadow, color, texture, motion, and location in space that viewers use in perceiving and responding to the real three-dimensional world. Movies build this information into shots in ways that emphasize the three-dimensionality of the image appearing on the flat screen. This opens the door to tricks of all kinds in cinema. In *The Matrix*, some of the most memorable visual effects are the high-speed moving camera shots that envelop the characters in scenes of fast action. But during production these shots did not involve *any* camera movement. Keanu Reeves and the other performers were photographed by a series of still cameras arranged into the circuit that the nonexistent moving camera would travel. Computer software interpolated the missing pictures to fill out the orbit of a continuous camera move. Moreover, Reeves and the others were photographed against a blank background (a "greenscreen") and were then digitally inserted into computer-animated environments. The filmmakers jokingly referred to their work as "virtual cinematography." Neither the interactions of character and location nor the moving camera that the viewer "sees" in *The Matrix* in fact existed. But because the perceptual cues in the shots about movement and space seemed true, the illusions were credible and compelling.

Cinema, then, has a dual capability: It corresponds with, and also transforms, the viewer's visual and social experience. These functions—correspondence and transformation—establish a very complex relationship between movies and viewers. To understand how filmmakers design their work, one needs to grasp how those structures build on and connect with the viewer's perceptual skills and how they can go beyond these as well. The first condition furnishes the grounds that make film intelligible, while the second underlies much of the delight that the medium provides. We will have more to say about these issues in upcoming chapters.

Hitchcock's *Vertigo* (1958) has a main character who is afraid of heights. To visualize the character's dizziness, Hitchcock films a city street from an extremely high angle and combines a zoom and track in opposite directions to suggest the feeling of falling through space. The resulting image deforms normal visual reality, but viewers readily accept this in the interest of style and for the delight that it provides.

THE MATRIX (WARNER BROS., 1999)

The illusion of high-speed moving camera shots in *The Matrix* was created without any actual camera movement. Sophisticated digital software supplied the motion perspective that created the effect. Because the 3-D motion cues in the images were realistic, viewers found the effect credible. Frame enlargement.

SUMMARY

Film structure or style results from the ways a filmmaker chooses to manipulate the camera, editing, light, sound, and color. This chapter has explained the fundamentals of the camera, specifically the factors of position, angle, lens, and movement, and how these factors affect the way a viewer perceives the content of a shot or scene. By understanding the range of creative choices filmmakers confront, and by appreciating their options in resolving those choices, one begins to understand a film's structural design.

Camera positions are variations of three basic set-ups: the long shot, the medium shot, and the close-up. While long shots typically stress landscape or environment over character, close-ups usually privilege character over environment. By varying the camera-to-subject distance, the filmmaker manipulates the viewer's emotional involvement with the scene or character in complex ways. Camera position can emphasize facial expressions as signs of a character's inner emotional life or can even work at cross-purposes to a viewer's desired relationship with a scene or character.

Camera angles are variations of low, medium (or eye-level), or high angles. Like camera position, camera angle can be used to manipulate the viewer's reactions. Camera angles can represent a character's point of view and emphasize a character's strength or, conversely, his or her insignificance. Angles can be consistent with, or play against, a viewer's desired relationship with a scene or character. As with camera position, the effects of camera angle are always dependent on the emotional context and action of a given scene.

Camera lenses supply distinctive optical characteristics to shots. Telephoto lenses reduce depth of field and angle of view, while wide-angle lenses enlarge these. Zoom lenses can substitute for camera movement, although they will not produce motion perspective as does a moving camera.

Camera movement includes pan and tilt shots, dolly or tracking shots, and boom or crane shots. Pans and tilts create linking movements, connecting objects or establishing relationships between them. Tracking and crane shots can add a dynamic sense of movement to a shot or express thematic ideas.

The camera and the structural designs it helps create both record and transform the outward appearance of things, the way they look. The cinema has a fundamental connection with the viewer's perceptual skills and experience. The viewer's impressions in film of continuous light, apparent motion, and spatial depth all derive from this fundamental connection. What makes the cinema such a rich imaginative experience is the way it builds on and creatively enhances this connection. Style, then, can be understood as a kind of creative response by filmmakers to the tendency of the motion picture camera to reproduce the surface appearance of the objects it photographs. By intervening stylistically—by choosing to use a wide-angle lens or a high camera angle—a filmmaker can creatively shape the material of the shot and the world of the film to the dimensions of the imagination.

KEY TERMS AND CONCEPTS

angle of view   23
beta movement   39
boom or crane   27
camera position   8
canted angle   18
close-up   9
composition   7
deep focus   23
depth of field   23
director   4
dolly or tracking   27
emulsion   19
establishing shots   9
feature films   5
film form   2

flicker fusion   39
focal length   22
frame   7
hand-held camera   10
internal structural time   5
long shot   8
medium shot   9
motion parallax   24
motion perspective   24
normal lens   22
pan and tilt   27
perceptual
   correspondence   39
perceptual
   transformation   38

persistence of vision   39
postproduction   2
preproduction   2
producer   4
production   2
rack focusing   22
running time   5
shot   5
shutter   39
Steadicam   27
story time   5
structure   2
telephoto lens   22
wide-angle lens   22
zoom lens   24

SUGGESTED READINGS

Geoff Andrew, *The Director's Vision: A Concise Guide to the Art of 250 Great Filmmakers* (Brooklyn, NY: Lawrence Hill, 1999).

David Breskin, ed., *Inner Views: Filmmakers in Conversation* (Winchester, MA: Faber and Faber, 1997).

John P. Frisby, *Seeing: Illusion, Brain, and Mind* (New York: Oxford University Press, 1980).

E. H. Gombrich, *Art and Illusion* (Princeton, NJ: Princeton University Press, 1984).

Eve Light Honthaner, *The Complete Film Production Handbook* (Boston: Focal Press, 1996).

Steven D. Katz, *Film Directing Shot by Shot: Visualizing from Concept to Screen* (Boston: Focal Press, 1991).

Sidney Lumet, *Making Movies* (New York: Alfred A. Knopf, 1995).

Ken Russell, *Directing Films: The Director's Art from Script to Cutting Room* (London: B. T. Batsford, 2000).

Cinematography

OBJECTIVES

After reading this chapter, you should be able to:

- describe the work of previsualization

- describe what the cinematographer contributes to a film's visual design

- explain how cinematographers work with film stock, lenses, and aspect ratios

- differentiate between realist and pictorial lighting designs

- describe the creative challenges of light source simulation

- explain why pictorial lighting designs work especially well for creating visual symbolism

- differentiate between hard and soft light and explain their expressive functions

- explain the differences between high- and low-key lighting setups

- explain the principles of lighting continuity

- explain the differences between lighting for color and lighting for black-and-white

■ describe how color design establishes symbolic meaning, narrative organization, and psychological mood and tone

■ explain the relationship between cinematography and digital effects

■ explain how visual conventions help establish representational reality and how filmmakers may "quote" from other films

During production, a film's visual design results from the way that filmmakers arrange elements before the camera—sets, costumes, actors, props, light, and color. *Titanic* (1997), for example, featured extremely detailed sets and costume design, and the film's meticulous re-creation of that vanished historical world held extraordinary fascination for audiences. Viewers responded to the romance at the center of the film's narrative but also to the luxuriance of its imagery. The term **mise-en-scène** is sometimes used to designate a film's overall visual design and to refer to all the elements placed before the camera to be photographed.

Filmmakers also control the visual design of their work through editing, but this occurs during postproduction, after they have implemented the designs achieved through light, color, production design, and performance. Accordingly, we will examine editing after considering these other elements of production proper.

Cinematography, examined in this chapter, pertains to the use of light and color. **Production design** involves the creation of sets, locations, costuming, and all visual environments that are depicted on screen. **Performance style** deals with the actor's contribution to the film and how filmmakers incorporate actors as visual elements within the frame. A filmmaker's use of actors can be quite realistic or extremely stylized and pictorial. Chapter 3 examines production design, and Chapter 4 looks at performance.

COLLABORATION AND PRE-VISUALIZATION

The director, cinematographer, and production designer work together in close collaboration to create an effective visual design. Production designers and cinematographers translate the director's vision into the terms of their respective crafts, and in practice, they subordinate their own artistic inclinations to the director's wishes. Production designer Mel Bourne, whose credits include Woody Allen's *Annie Hall* (1977) and *Manhattan* (1979) and Adrian Lyne's *Indecent Proposal* (1993), characterizes the creative partnership necessary to plan the visual design of a film by stressing that the production designer and cinematographer should be working on the same wavelength, which, in turn, comes from the director.

During preproduction, the cinematographer and production designer consult with the director to discuss and define the film's design. This work is called **pre-visualization** because it is an initial attempt to formulate the basic features of how the film will look. As aids to pre-visualization, the director, cinematographer, and production designer often will look for references in such visual fields as architecture, painting, and photography. On *The Passion of the Christ* (2004), cinematographer Caleb Deschanel and director Mel Gibson based the look of the film on Renaissance painting, especially the work of Caravaggio. The Romantic paintings of J. M. Turner helped establish the look of Ridley Scott's *Kingdom of*

AMERICAN BEAUTY (DREAMWORKS, 1999)

The relationship between the director and cinematographer is a crucial one on any production, and it can vary considerably depending on their talents and personality. Many
first-time directors lack the aptitude for strong visual design and depend on their cinematographer's choices about lighting and camera placement. By contrast, Conrad Hall,
the cinematographer for *American Beauty*, found first-time director Sam Mendes to be
a strong visual stylist with very precise ideas about framing, lighting, and camera placement. Stimulated by Mendes's ideas and cinematic talents, Hall produced work that won
the 1999 Academy Award for Best Cinematography. Frame enlargement.

Heaven (2005). To visualize J. R. R. Tolkien's Middle Earth, the filmmakers of
The Lord of the Rings studied the book covers and the watercolor paintings used
to illustrate the novels and hired two of the illustrators to serve as conceptual artists on the films. To design *L.A. Confidential* (1997), director Curtis Hanson and
cinematographer Dante Spinotti used photographer Robert Frank's 1958 book,
The Americans. This collection of Frank's work showcased the visual elements they
wanted in their film—high-intensity light that "burns out" in the photos, high contrast, and the incorporation of light sources within the photos—as well as a 1950s
time period that coincided with the film's narrative. Even comic books might supply inspiration, as Japanese *manga* did for the directors and cinematographer of
The Matrix (1999).

Other motion pictures are a common source for pre-visualization. To plan the lighting for *Insomnia* (2002), cinematographer Wally Pfister studied modern film classics
distinguished by their moody lighting, *The Godfather, Part III* (1990), *Apocalypse Now*
(1979), *Seven* (1995). The film noir classic *The Third Man* (1949) influenced the lighting style of *Sky Captain and the World of Tomorrow* (2004). To pre-visualize the Mel
Gibson Vietnam war film, *We Were Soldiers*, cinematographer Dean Semler studied the
classic war films *All Quiet on the Western Front* (1930) and *Pork Chop Hill* (1959).
Cinematographer Robert Elswit and director Paul Thomas Anderson used *The Treasure
of the Sierra Madre* (1948) as a visual model for *There Will Be Blood* (2007), and to
achieve the look of an old film they also used old-fashioned, outdated lenses on the
camera. Several crime films of the 1970s, including *The French Connection* (1971) and
Serpico (1973) furnished the influence for Ridley Scott's *American Gangster* (2007), a film
set in that period.

THE ESSENTIALS OF CINEMATOGRAPHY

The cinematographer creates the images that viewers see on screen, manipulating their elements to establish a unified and memorable design. Memorable compositions, as pictured on pages 48–49, result from the careful control of image elements and their balancing within the frame. Such compositions can vividly express a film or scene's underlying emotional dynamics or themes.

How does a cinematographer organize visual elements to produce such images? Working with the director, the cinematographer determines the film stock on which the picture will be shot, the aspect ratio, the lenses and camera positions used in filming scenes, and the lighting and color design of the scenes.

Film Stocks, Lenses, and Aspect Ratios

Cinematographers work with a variety of **film stocks,** which are identified by their manufacturer and stock number (e.g., Kodak 5298). Selecting one or more stocks for a production enables the cinematographer to control a large number of image characteristics. Film stocks vary in terms of their sensitivity to light, color reproduction, tolerance for diverse lighting conditions, amount of grain (grain is visible as tiny specks or dots within the image), contrast levels, sharpness, and resolving power (the ability to discriminate fine detail). A cinematographer will select a given stock depending on how it handles these characteristics and its suitability for the design of a given production.

Cinematographer Darius Khondji, for example, shot all the nighttime scenes for *Seven* (1995), a dark thriller about a serial killer, on Kodak 5287 because this stock gave him exceptionally dark blacks, suitable for the film's mood and theme. To accentuate this effect even more, Khondji used ENR to restore silver to the negative, increasing the density of its blacks. To create the off-kilter visual style of *Natural Born Killers* (1994), Oliver Stone and cinematographer Robert Richardson intermixed five 35-mm stocks, four 16-mm stocks, and three 8-mm stocks to create vivid changes in color, contrast, grain, and resolution. In *U Turn* (1998), during an argument and fight between two principal characters, Stone and Richardson switched film stocks in mid-scene to create glaring changes of color and grain. These were intended to visualize the scene's volatile emotional swings. On *Alexander* (2004), Stone used color infrared stock to portray Alexander the Great's mystical visions.

Filmmakers often emulate the inspiring innovations of other directors and cinematographers. On Spike Lee's *Clockers* (1995), cinematographer Malik Sayeed employed a stock never before used in a motion picture, Kodak 5239, which was manufactured for use by NASA and the Air Force. The grain structure of the stock made its images look extremely raw—suitable for this grim film about urban drugs and violence—and it vividly rendered primary colors, making reds and blues glow on screen and leap out of the frame. The unusual look of *Clockers* impressed Oliver Stone and Robert Richardson, who used the stock in *U Turn* to create selectively lurid color effects. Spike Lee again employed 5239 on *Summer of Sam* (1999). Since then, the "cross-processing" of a raw, grainy stock has come into general use. Recent examples include the dream sequences in *From Hell* (2001), the Hughes brothers' film about Jack the Ripper, and the 1950s flashback scenes in *Blow* (2001), which starred Johnny Depp as a drug dealer.

Cinematographers select their lenses to give images the visual properties that will express a film's underlying themes or the dramatic requirements of given scenes. *Pleasantville* (1998) is a fantasy about a 1950s-style sitcom whose characters become progressively more

ATONEMENT (UNIVERSAL, 2007)

Controlling a shot's depth of field—the area in focus—can be a powerful way of achieving an effective composition. The shallow plane of focus makes all of the foreground objects a blur and thereby concentrates the viewer's attention on one character (Keira Knightley), as her face is reflected in a mirror. Frame enlargement.

LAWRENCE OF ARABIA (COLUMBIA PICTURES, 1962)

Great depth of field can also help create powerful compositions. In this famous shot—held by editor Ann V. Coates and director David Lean for a long time—Lawrence (Peter O'Toole, left) and his guide watch a mysterious figure ride toward them from the horizon. Positioning the foreground characters on each side of the widescreen frame and having them gaze at the approaching rider create a fulcrum that draws the viewer's eye irresistibly toward the rider. The extreme depth of field and the way the shot is held on screen without cutting create remarkable tension about what in the story is going to happen next. Frame enlargement.

THE MATRIX (WARNER BROS., 1999)

When Neo (Keanu Reeves) learns the truth about the Matrix from Morpheus (Laurence Fishburne), he appears as a reflection on Morpheus' eye-glasses. By making Morpheus the dominant visual element in the shot, it stresses his power and wisdom compared with Neo's lack of knowledge about the world he has entered. Frame enlargement.

THERE WILL BE BLOOD (PARAMOUNT, 2007)

Composition can visualize a scene's emotional content through a careful arrangement of objects in the frame. Henry (Kevin J. O'Connor, left) claims to be the long-lost brother of Daniel Plainview (Daniel Day-Lewis, left). Plainview is skeptical, and the composition depicts the emotional gulf between the men by placing them on opposite sides of the widescreen frame. The visual distance between them corresponds to their emotional state. Frame enlargement.

A NIGHTMARE ON ELM STREET (NEW LINE CINEMA, 1984)

Horror films regularly make use of disturbing compositional styles. His knife-like claws make the killer, Freddy Kreuger (Robert Englund), look monstrous, but so does the composition. Kreuger is back-lit, making him a silhouette. His face is lit from below, reversing the normal way that shadows are distributed on a human face. The camera angle is low, making him into a looming figure. And he looks directly, and threateningly, at the camera and therefore at us, the viewers. Frame enlargement.

modern in their outlook. To suggest this change at a visual level, the cinematographer began shooting with shorter lenses that corresponded with those used in 1950s films and then, as the story progressed, began moving to the longer focal lengths characteristic of contemporary filmmaking. In a subliminal fashion, this gave the images an evolving historical look and context. To suggest a world in which everything was for sale, the cinematographer of *The Truman Show* (1998) used the extreme wide-angle perspectives often seen in television advertising. To capture a 1970s look for scenes in *The Velvet Goldmine* (1998) occurring in that time period, the cinematographer used zoom lenses rather than camera movement. Zooms were featured prominently in films of that era, and the cinematographer liked the way the zoom emphasized surfaces (because it merely magnifies an image) rather than depth and perspective, as true camera movement does.

When choosing an **aspect ratio** (the dimensions of the screen image), cinematographers must balance several considerations. Which of the available ratios is best

CLOSE-UP

What Are Light and Color?

Light and color are the tools of the cinematographer's art. In addition to planning camera setups and movements, the cinematographer organizes the lighting design of scenes and the placement of color gels to augment or enhance certain colors on screen.

Light is a form of radiant energy, a part of the total electromagnetic spectrum. Light is visible only at its source or as it is reflected off another object. Colors are visible when white light is broken down into its component **wavelengths**. Colored objects reflect or transmit their color values depending on whether they are solid objects or translucent. A rose appears red because it absorbs all visible wavelengths with the exception of red light, which it reflects. A bottle of green dishwashing liquid looks green because the liquid transmits only green light and acts as a filter to block out all other colors.

In the cinema, colors can be created on the set by using these processes of reflectance and transmission. Lighting a blue object on the set will increase its ability to reflect blue to the camera. Using a red gel or filter over a white light source will cause that source to transmit only red light.

Properties of Color

Three properties of color are important. **Hue** refers to the color itself. Red, blue, green, and yellow are hues. These four hues are unique. They do not resemble one another. By contrast, pink, a derivative of red, is not a unique hue. **Saturation** refers to the strength of a color. Red is more highly saturated than pink.

Intensity, or brightness, refers to how much light a given colored object reflects. In respect of this property, the viewer makes certain assumptions that influence the way colors are perceived. For example, a viewer will judge a red cloth seen at high noon and again at dusk as the same color, but its intensity will vary. Seen at high noon, it will appear much brighter than at dusk. In this regard, perceptions of hue and intensity do not always correspond. Viewers assume color constancy while correcting for perceived variations in brightness.

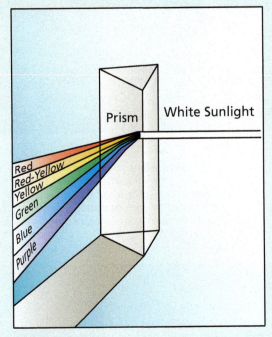

FIGURE 2.1
Prism.

The Gray Scale

Until the 1960s, black-and-white was a common film format. Since the 1960s, by contrast, black-and-white has been used rarely but with powerful artistic effect. Steven Spielberg shot his film about the Holocaust, *Schindler's List* (1993), in black-and-white because it would give his film a harsher, stark look appropriate to its grim subject matter.

Black-and-white film and television cameras see only degrees of brightness, ranging from white to black through intermediate shades of gray. This spectrum is known as the **gray scale**, and it determines which colors are used or avoided in costumes and sets during filming. Different colors have the same degree of brightness. In black-and-white cinematography, this creates a problem. Objects of different colors but the same intensity, or gray-scale value, will blend together on screen. Black-and-white film will not distinguish them.

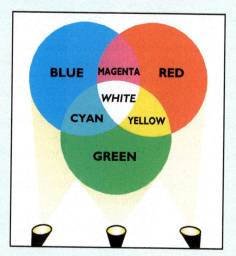

FIGURE 2.2
Additive mixing.

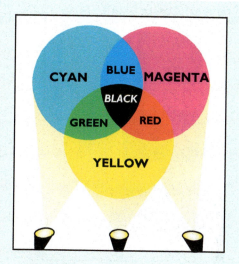

FIGURE 2.3
Subtractive mixing.

In color film, hues will naturally separate objects. Shooting in black-and-white, cinematographers must separate objects by their degrees of brightness. Cinematographer Laszlo Kovacs (*Easy Rider*, 1969; *Ghostbusters*, 1984) points out that in color a brown head will separate naturally from a beige wall, but in black-and-white the two may run together. The cinematographer has to keep in mind not only how the human eye will see the colors in a scene but also how the black-and-white camera will read the brightness values of those colors.

Additive and Subtractive Color Mixing

The earliest color systems in film history were **additive**. By adding varying proportions of red, green, and blue light (achieved through the use of filters to convert the white projector light into these hues), they produced a diverse range of colors on screen. Adding green and red, for example, will produce yellow. Additive systems in film, though, were soon replaced by **subtractive** color mixing, which removes various wavelengths from white light. To accomplish this, subtractive color filters are used. These colors are magenta, yellow, and cyan. They are contained as layers of dye in the strip of raw, unexposed film, and as white light enters the camera, they filter and transmit only those few wavelengths needed for subtractive mixing. ■

suited for the themes or action of the film? *Memento* (2000) was shot in **anamorphic** widescreen (2.35:1) because the shallow-focus lenses typically used in that format could be used to isolate the main character (who is confused and suffering from memory loss) from his surroundings. *The Phantom of the Opera* (2004) also was shot in anamorphic widescreen, but for a different reason. The filmmakers liked the way the anamorphic lenses handled candlelight, which featured prominently in many scenes.

A second critical consideration involves the consequences of converting a film exhibited theatrically in widescreen to home video and conventional television monitors. During the classic Hollywood period of the 1930s and 1940s, frame size remained fairly standard, with an aspect ratio (width to height) of 1.37:1. (The frame enlargements from

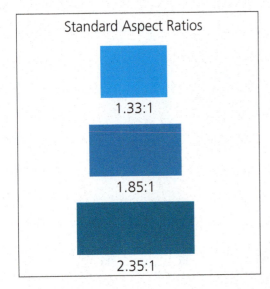

Standard Aspect Ratios

1.33:1

1.85:1

2.35:1

FIGURE 2.4

Standard aspect ratios.

Brute Force, Strangers on a Train, and *Singin' in the Rain* appearing in Chapter 7 illustrate this ratio.) This was a nearly square ratio and one that approximated the dimensions of conventional television screens.

Since the 1950s, however, **widescreen ratios** have been standard. Today, viewers see films projected in ratios of 1.85:1 or 2.35:1. These ratios are wider and more rectangular than the classic Hollywood ratio. Accordingly, cinematographers must be careful to compose their shots in ways that make best use of the chosen aspect ratio. A 2.35:1 ratio, for example, facilitates compositions using the horizontal axis of the frame more effectively than the vertical axis, as the frame enlargement from *Yojimbo* (1961) demonstrates. Filmmakers working in this ratio can spread things out across the frame, but the ratio is not good for depicting tall objects. Because of this, Janusz Kaminski shot *The Lost World* in a 1.85:1 ratio to give the dinosaurs more headroom than a 2.35:1 ratio would supply. The latter ratio, however, is well suited for epics, Westerns, and historical dramas and has been used extensively in such pictures.

Anamorphic widescreen produces its image through a process of squeezing and stretching. Cinemascope, brought to market in the 1950s, was an early and widely-used example of the process, and anamorphic films sometimes are referred to generically today as 'scope' films. During filming an anamorphic lens squeezes the widescreen field of view onto the square frame of film. During projection, a corrective lens on the projector unsqueezes the image, correcting the distortion and reproducing the widescreen image dimensions. Christopher Nolan shot *Inception* (2010) in anamorphic widescreen, and the frame enlargements on page 54 demonstrate the squeezed and unsqueezed versions of the image.

YOJIMBO (TOHO, 1961)

The widescreen 2.35:1 ratio accentuates horizontal space across the screen surface, and skilful filmmakers fully utilize this compositional area. Director Akira Kurosawa loved to arrange his characters in a lateral fashion across the screen, making maximum use of the frame. Frame enlargement.

AMARCORD (F.C. PRODUZIONI, 1973)

The 1.85:1 ratio allows filmmakers plenty of width for compositions as well as a comfortable amount of headroom for vertical elements in the frame. The great Italian filmmaker Federico Fellini used the ratio for strikingly pictorial images in this autobiographical film about his youth. For theatrical release, films in this ratio will be **soft-matted**: An aperture matte in the projector will mask the top and bottom of the image captured on the square frame of film, producing the 1.85:1 ratio on the theater screen. Frame enlargement.

HOW THE WEST WAS WON (MGM, 1962)

Cinema adopted widecreen ratios in the 1950s as a way of competing with television, which, at the time, offered a small, square 4 x 3 image. Numerous widescreen processes proliferated. Cinerama was the grandest, offering a huge, curved screen onto which three projectors cast an image. The screen's curvature stimulated the viewer's peripheral vision and immersed spectators deeply within the image. The 'smilebox' presentation pictured here is available on Blu-ray and DVD and attempts to reproduce in miniature the visual experience of the huge Cinerama screen. Frame enlargement.

To reproduce proper aspect ratio for home video viewing, a 2.35:1 film typically is **letterboxed**. The image is **hard-matted** for video; that is, frame bars will mask the top and bottom of the image displayed on the monitor, producing a wider-ratio picture in the center of the screen (and without eliminating anything from the top and bottom of the image). Viewers of a letterboxed video get to see proper, or nearly proper, screen ratio.

(a)

(b)

(c)

INCEPTION (WARNER BROS., 2010)

Director Christopher Nolan often films in anamorpic widescreen. The first two pictures (A and B) illustrate the frame image unsqueezed for viewing and the squeezed image capturing during filming. Many cable television channels today show cropped versions of 2.35:1 films, reproducing only a part of the frame, as illustrated in image C. Frame enlargements.

Digital formats like DVD, electronic delivery systems such as cable television and the Internet, and digital imaging routinely used in post-production have led the industry toward wide use of an alternative method of producing a 2.35:1 image—a scope extraction. A tremendous number of films today are shot digitally or in **Super 35,** which uses the full aperture of the 35mm negative frame, including the area normally masked for a soundtrack. The film images can then be scanned digitally (electronically captured images will already be digital) and can then be formatted for release in a variety of aspect ratios and for distribution to electronic delivery systems like disk or Internet. A scope extraction, for example, may be performed to produce a 2.35:1 image for theatrical release in anamorphic widescreen, and since the footage has already been digitized, it's ready for release into electronic non-theatrical markets. *Gladiator* (2000), *The Lord of the Rings, The*

Aviator (2004), and *Cinderella Man* (2005) were all shot in Super 35 and given a scope extraction for theatrical release.

When a filmmaker shoots in anamorphic widescreen during production, the images are usually well-composed because it is an unambiguous format. Super 35 scope extractions can be more ambiguous because shots are composed simultaneously for two ratios, the square, full-frame and the widescreen area selected for extraction. The frame enlargements from *Harry Potter and the Scorserer's Stone*, pictured below, illustrate this problem well. The shot of Hermione (Emma Watson) and Harry (Daniel Radcliffe) is arguably more pleasing in its full-frame version than in the scope extraction, which feels cramped by comparison.

In recent years, filmmakers have mixed aspect ratios and film gauges. *The Dark Knight* (2008), the sequel to *Batman Begins,* and *Inception* were shot in two very different aspect ratios and film gauges. (A film's gauge designates the width of the film; the wider the film, the higher the resolution because the frames are larger.) Director Christopher Nolan and cinematographer Wally Pfister shot most of these films in anamorphic widescreen on 35mm gauge film, which is the conventional gauge used in ordinary theaters. They also shot selected scenes on 65mm Imax. On *The Dark Knight*, these included the opening and closing sequences and all of the aerial sequences. Imax is a super high-resolution gauge that is typically reserved for special attractions that are presented in Imax theaters.

Shooting this way enabled the film to be shown in both ordinary and Imax theaters. The aspect ratio of an Imax film frame is 1.33:1, so for conventional theaters a 2.35:1 image was extracted from the 1.33:1 frame for the footage that had been shot in Imax. The benefits of having shot in Imax were still apparent, even after extracting part of the frame and printing it in 35mm. It had a superior resolution to the rest of the 35mm footage, which had originated on that gauge. For presentation in Imax theaters, 35mm widescreen footage was digitally scanned to Imax 65mm and

HARRY POTTER AND THE SORCERER'S STONE (WARNER BROS., 2001)

Super 35 is widely used today in movies shot on film (as distinct from digital capture) because it enables easy scope extractions. The *Harry Potter* series was shot on Super 35 and was screened in theaters as scope extractions. The left frame shows the full image as captured during production; the right image shows the scope extraction. Frame enlargements.

electronically cleaned and sharpened. These scenes were combined with the material originally shot in Imax. A viewer watching the films in an Imax theater would see a widescreen movie, but when the scenes shot in Imax appeared, the aspect ratio suddenly changed and the huge Imax screen was filled with imagery. *The Dark Knight* was the first feature film to combine footage shot in two such different gauges.

The aspect ratio selected often will influence the lenses employed during production. Many cinematographers dislike shooting wide-angle in anamorphic 2.35:1 because of the curvature the lens introduces into the composition during moving camera shots. If they are committed to working at the shorter focal lengths, they will often shoot 1.85:1 or on Super 35. However, director Christopher Nolan and cinematographer Wally Pfister shot many of the action scenes in *Batman Begins* wide angle because they felt it provided greater realism.

Having decided on the film stock, lenses, and aspect ratio, the cinematographer determines with the director the camera's placement for each shot in a given scene and how the shot will be lit. Camera placement and lighting are interconnected issues: The lighting of each shot is a function of where the camera is positioned.

Lighting Design

Depending on the style and subject matter of a given film and the dramatic requirements of the scene, the cinematographer may employ a realistic or a pictorial lighting design or some combination of each approach.

REALISTIC LIGHTING   A lighting design that distributes light to simulate an explicit source on screen, whether it be the sun or a table lamp indoors, is a **realistic lighting design**. It suggests that the light on screen is cast by one or more specific sources. If it is an exterior scene, the light source is usually, by implication, the sun. If it is an interior scene, then the table lamps, overhead ceiling lights, or street lights visible through windows become the implied source lights. These are "effect" lights because the cinematographer uses them to convey the effect that they are casting the visible light in the scene. This may or may not actually be true. If the table lamp in the set is rigged to be a real source of lighting for the camera, then it is called a **practical** because it is a visible light source on the set that actually works for exposure of the film. In other cases the actual lights for exposure may be off screen. Lights for effect, then, may be distinct from the lights for exposure. In the case of those lights termed *practicals*, the light source that creates the effect and the exposure is the same.

Burnout effects sometimes may be an important part of a realistic design. The term refers to an overexposed portion of an image in which details are lost. Much of the action of *The English Patient* (1996) takes place in the Sahara Desert. To convey the heat of that landscape, cinematographer John Seale photographed the film's characters by exposing on their shadowed faces and letting the sunlit areas of the desert burn out with overexposure. This made the desert look hotter.

Cinematographer Michael Ballhaus devised a very creative approach to simulating light sources in Francis Ford Coppola's *Bram Stoker's Dracula* (1992). There were no electric lights in Dracula's time, all light being supplied by candles, lanterns, oil lamps, or torches. The light these instruments cast was flickering and unsteady. To simulate this, Ballhaus placed his electric lights on flicker boxes, which created wavering, flickering illumination. Coppola's film is a gaudy and stylized fantasy. *Realism* is not the sort of term that one would apply to such a film. Nevertheless, the filmmakers sometimes observed realistic principles of light-source simulation.

CLOSE-UP

Cinematographers

Moviegoers often think about cinema as being mainly a director's medium. Many movie critics discuss films as being the exclusive creation of their directors. In fact, the cinematographer is a key influence on the visual design of a film, and a convenient way of thinking about films—and classifying them—is in terms of the cinematographer.

Gregg Toland is well known for collaborating with Orson Welles on *Citizen Kane* (1941) and that film's deep focus compositions. But Toland had already used deep focus to striking effect on *The Long Voyage Home* (1940) for director John Ford, and he would continue to use deep focus in other films, such as *The Best Years of Our Lives* (1946), directed by William Wyler. Deep focus cinematography is one of Toland's signatures as an artist, and directors interested in this technique found him to be a natural collaborator.

The most radical cinematographer in the classical Hollywood period was probably John Alton, who shot a series of film noirs, often with director Anthony Mann (*T-Men*, 1947; *Raw Deal*, 1948), that featured single-source lighting, extremely dark blacks, huge areas of the frame in shadow, and an extremely wide-angle look. The most extreme instance of Alton's style can be seen in the film noir *The Big Combo* (1955). Alton also shot part of the concluding ballet sequence in the musical *An American in Paris* (1952) and broke the rules by shooting directly into the light sources.

The striking visual look and design for which many films and directors become famous actually must be achieved by the cinematographer. Ingmar Bergman *(Persona, 1966)* relied on Sven Nykvist, Sergio Leone (*The Good, the Bad and the Ugly,* 1966) on Tonino Delli Colli, and Akira Kurosawa *(Ran, 1985)* on Takao Saito. Kurosawa, in fact, did not begin shooting in color until he partnered with Saito as his cinematographer. Steven Spielberg frequently has relied on Janusz Kaminski, and the Coen brothers often work with Roger Deakins.

Other outstanding cinematographers include James Wong Howe (*Body and Soul,* 1947), Haskell Wexler (*Matewan,* 1987), Nestor Almendros (*Days of Heaven,* 1978), and Gordon Willis (*The Godfather,* 1972). Studying the careers of cinematographers can be an excellent way of learning about film. Seeking out films shot by Sven Nykvist, Tonino Delli Colli, or Gordon Willis enables one to understand the key contribution made by cinematographers. ∎

THE SEVENTH SEAL (SVENSK FILMINDUSTRI, 1957)

Sven Nykvist shot many of acclaimed Swedish director Ingmar Bergman's films, and Nykvist's sensitive and bold use of light made Bergman's films into paintings-in-motion. Nyvkist's deep shadows and chiaroscuro lighting enhanced the brooding nature of this film, a medieval parable about death and salvation. Frame enlargement.

(continued)

THE GODFATHER (PARAMOUNT, 1972)

Cinematographer Gordon Willis created a unique look for the *Godfather* series by using an amber color palette to unify the story across all of the films. He also broke several rules of traditional cinematography, such as the one stipulating that an actor's eyes must be lit. Instead, Willis often placed faces deep in shadow. His work on these films is a classic example of how a cinematographer helps establish a look, mood, and tone on a production. Frame enlargement.

THE LAST EMPEROR (COLUMBIA PICTURES, 1987)

Vittorio Storaro is a legendary cinematographer acclaimed by his peers as one of the great masters of cinema. Storaro brings an elaborate theory of color to his work, believing that color is a universal form of communication and that it can be orchestrated to evoke specific emotional tones and responses in viewers. Like all great cinematographers, he is a master of lighting. Much in demand, he has worked most famously and regularly with Italian director Bernardo Bertolucci. Their films together include *The Last Emperor* as well as *The Conformist* (1970), *Last Tango in Paris* (1972), *1900* (1976), and *The Sheltering Sky* (1990). Frame enlargement.

THE MALTESE FALCON (WARNER BROS., 1941)

Light-source simulation in a realistic design, whose effect is that the table lamp is casting the visible illumination. The actual lights illuminating the set are off-camera, and they have been set up to light the character in ways that seem consistent with what the table lamp would do. Although realistically motivated, the overall design is stylish and moody, fitting the character, Brigid O'Shaughnessy (Mary Astor), a wicked and dangerous murderer. Cinematographer Arthur Edeson was an expert at handling shadows and moody tones, as illustrated by his work on such key films as *Frankenstein* (1931), *The Old Dark House* (1932), and *Casablanca* (1942). Frame enlargement.

Sometimes the way to achieve a realistic design is to avoid lighting set-ups that look calculated or complicated. Using practicals as exposure lights, and underlighting the actors or set, can work very well, as cinematographer Emmanuel Lubezki demonstrated on *Children of Men* (2006). That film's director, Alfonso Cuaron, wanted the movie to have a documentary feel even though it was fiction, and Lubezki lit numerous locations using only practical sources. This helped give the film a rawness and immediacy that a glossy lighting design could achieve.

PICTORIAL LIGHTING   **Pictorial lighting design** stresses purely pictorial or visual values that may be unrelated to strict concerns about source simulation. Realistic and pictorial approaches are not rigid categories, and many films may use both

CHILDREN OF MEN (UNIVERSAL, 2006)

Cinematographer Emmanuel Lubezki wanted to avoid the pretty, glossy look that conventional film lighting often creates. He used as few lights as possible in order to make the action seem harsh and real. This climactic birth scene was filmed with a single, practical light simulating a lantern. Frame enlargement.

BARRY LYNDON (WARNER BROS., 1975)

Candlelit scenes are almost always filmed using electric lights to simulate the glow of candles. Stanley Kubrick and cinematographer John Alcott (who had worked together previously on *2001* and *A Clockwork Orange*) wanted to break with tradition and, in the interest of realism, shoot by candlelight alone. The film, about the rise in society of an 18th century Irish rogue, was shot entirely on location in England using period houses and castles. There were no studio sets, and Kubrick wanted to capture the special quality of light that people living in these old buildings had experienced after sunset when candles provided the only illumination. Kubrick and Alcott used a super-light-sensitive lens, specially constructed for their purpose. Because the light levels were so low, there was virtually no depth of field in which to stage the action. But the results were extraordinary, unlike anything moviegoers had seen before, and became one of the film's most talked-about features. Frame enlargement.

approaches. *Bram Stoker's Dracula* includes many scenes in which the lighting design is governed by extravagantly pictorial considerations. When Dracula (Gary Oldman) meets with real estate representative Jonathan Harker (Keanu Reeves), who has journeyed by train and coach to the vampire's remote Transylvanian castle, Coppola and Ballhaus achieve one of their most striking pictorial effects.

Harker shows Dracula the portrait of Mina, the woman he is engaged to marry. Dracula realizes that she is the reincarnation of his own true love lost many centuries ago. Wanting to possess Mina as his own beloved, Dracula feels murderous rage toward Harker. As the two converse, Dracula's shadow, which had been cast on the back wall, disengages itself from the vampire. The shadow advances on Harker and begins to strangle him.

The effect is not only visually striking but surprising and uncanny. Coppola and Ballhaus creatively violate the logic of shadow phenomena. Shadows are either attached to or cast by the object to which they belong, but in neither case do they behave independently of that object. Coppola violates the perceptual regularities governing cast-shadow behavior, shocking viewers and guiding their interpretations toward ideas of supernatural power. It is a purely pictorial (and physically impossible) moment in the scene.

The effect was created by shooting part of the scene live and part of the scene with **rear projection**. Dracula's cast shadow on the wall is not a true shadow at all but was created by a dancer working in sync with actor Gary Oldman's movements. The dancer was placed behind the "wall," which was actually a screen onto which the dancer's shadow

BRAM STOKER'S DRACULA (COLUMBIA PICTURES, 1992)

Pictorial lighting designs suggest purely visual effects unconnected to issues of realism. Dracula's shadow disengages itself from the vampire count, advances on Jonathan Harker (Keanu Reeves), and begins to strangle him. The effect is pictorial and poetic. Frame enlargement.

was projected. When the "shadow" disengages itself from Dracula, the effect is created by the dancer breaking sync with Gary Oldman and pantomiming the act of strangulation.

PICTORIAL LIGHTING FOR THEMATIC SYMBOLISM   Filmmakers often employ pictorial designs to visually symbolize the thematic content of a scene or film. Pictorial designs do this more successfully and explicitly than realistic designs because filmmakers can manipulate light and color in ways that are unfettered by concerns about realism and

THE SILENCE OF THE LAMBS (ORION, 1990)

After a long scene with subtle, restrained lighting, the filmmakers suddenly switch to this extravagant design for a shot showing one of serial killer Hannibal Lecter's victims. The lighting is completely unmotivated in that it has no connection to any sources established within the dramatic action of the scene. With no attempt to hide them, the cross lights and backlights are visible in the frame. The effect is purely pictorial, a visual flourish designed to give impact to this moment of horror. Frame enlargement.

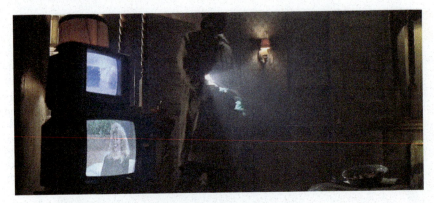

SEVEN (NEW LINE, 1995)

Filmmakers often create pictorial effects by showing and filming a light source within the scene. Investigating a murder scene, police inspector Morgan Freeman cradles his flash-light on his forearm. The dust suspended in the hazy air reflects in the flashlight beam to make it visible. Director David Fincher's film portrays a world of absolute moral and spiri-tual darkness for which the flashlight's inability to illuminate the room becomes a potent metaphor. Frame enlargement.

ALL THAT HEAVEN ALLOWS (UNIVERSAL INTERNATIONAL PICTURES, 1955)

Flagging a light source means blocking a selective portion of it, and cinematographers use flags—square wire frames wrapped in non-reflective cloth—to control where light will fall within the frame. Flags enable cinematographers to create highly expressive lighting designs. Director Douglas Sirk and cinematographer Russell Metty collaborated on sev-eral films that showcased elaborate color and lighting effects. In this scene, Ned (William Reynolds) harshly criticizes his widowed mother, Cary (Jane Wyman), for dating a much younger man. The flagged light gives his face a sinister cast and adds a volatile and dan-gerous emotional tone to their confrontation. Frame enlargement.

that can directly relate to the underlying social, psychological, or emotional themes of a scene. Pictorialism enables filmmakers to use light and color to visually embody the underlying significance of a given scene or film.

TYPES OF LIGHT: HARD AND SOFT LIGHT   Once the cinematographer and director de-cide on the overall balance of realistic and pictorial elements, they further specify their lighting design in terms of the proportions of **hard** and **soft light**.

Case Study APOCALYPSE NOW

Cinematographer Vittorio Storaro's pictorial designs for Francis Ford Coppola's *Apocalypse Now* (1979) create a precise visual statement of the existential moral issues at the heart of the film. The Vietnam War drives a renegade U.S. soldier named Kurtz (Marlon Brando) insane, and the military brass sends an assassin named Willard (Martin Sheen) upriver to Kurtz's compound to murder the colonel. Most of the narrative takes place during Willard's trip upriver and raises the question about what Willard will do when he finally meets Kurtz. Will he kill him as he has been instructed, or, because both men are equally murderous and bestial, will he join Kurtz instead?

To suggest the psychological and spiritual bond between the two characters, Storaro employed a strikingly similar lighting design for each man. Kurtz is filmed with his face half in and half out of shadow to convey the character's cruelty and moral darkness and the inner struggle between good and evil that has driven him insane. After Willard kills Kurtz, the same lighting design is used to make him look Kurtz-like. Willard's face

is partially eclipsed, half in the light, half in the shadow. The lighting tells the viewer that Willard has become Kurtz. Postproduction editing of the film, however, weakened the visual and thematic force of this pictorial statement. After early test screenings indicated that the original ending did not work for audiences, Coppola added a different conclusion in which Willard rejects Kurtz's kingdom and leaves.

Coppola's original ending was more ambiguous. In both the original and revised endings, Willard kills Kurtz, but in Coppola's original version, Willard remains behind on the steps of Kurtz's compound facing Kurtz's army, his face lit to look like Kurtz. Coppola's preferred version ended here. He wanted the film to conclude with the question of whether Willard has become Kurtz, and Storaro's lighting clearly implied that he has. The way this ending was changed—by showing Willard leaving Kurtz's compound—undermined the meaning established by Storaro's lighting design, and this made the film thematically less coherent. ▪

APOCALYPSE NOW (UNITED ARTISTS, 1979)

Pictorial lighting for thematic symbolism: the faces of Kurtz (Marlon Brando) and Willard (Martin Sheen). Cinematographer Vittorio Storaro's lighting design stresses the moral conflict between good and evil within each character and suggests an essential equivalence between both men. Frame enlargements.

**OUT OF THE PAST
(RKO, 1947)**

Low-key lighting in a sophisti-cated, complex design typical of 1940s film noir. Small portions of the frame are selectively exposed using hard light, leaving other areas to fall quickly into shadow. The effect is moody and omi-nous. Frame enlargement.

Hard and soft lighting differ in terms of **fall-off** and **contrast.** Hard lighting typically creates high contrast and fast fall-off. The boundaries between the illuminated areas and the areas in darkness or shadow are sharply defined. The rate of fall-off, or change be-tween light and dark, is rapid. This creates a high contrast between light and dark areas as they are distributed throughout the frame. Another way of understanding contrast is in terms of shadow definition. High-contrast lighting produces very strong shadow definition, as in the shot from *Out of the Past* (1947), a **film noir** made during a period when high-contrast black-and-white cinematography was very popular.

By manipulating fall-off and contrast, cinematographers enhance the three-dimensional appearance of film images. Notice how vividly the shadow information renders the folds of Robert Mitchum's trenchcoat in the shot from *Out of the Past.* Light organizes and defines space. The distribution of light and shadow conveys physical properties of depth, distance, and surface texture, expressed by the ways light falls across objects in a room or scene. Motion picture images easily copy this source

FILMMAKER SPOTLIGHT

Francis Ford Coppola

Along with Martin Scorsese, George Lucas, and Brian De Palma, Coppola belonged to a young generation of university-trained film students-turned-directors who established careers in the early 1970s. His earliest films (*Dementia 13*, 1963; *Finian's Rainbow*, 1968) are undistinguished and do not hint at the talent that suddenly burst forth in *The Godfather* (1972), the most successful example of epic narrative filmmaking produced by a major

studio since *Gone With the Wind* (1939). Starring Marlon Brando and Al Pacino, *The Godfather* offers a richly romanticized and harshly brutal portrait of the rise to power of the Corleone crime family. Feeling he had oversentimentalized the Corleones in the first film, Coppola set out to destroy them in the harsher, bleaker sequel, *The Godfather, Part II* (1974), which many critics consider superior to its predecessor.

Between these two epics, Coppola made *The Conversation* (1974), an edgy, sophisticated portrait of the psychological disintegration of an electronics wizard and domestic spy (played by Gene Hackman). An extraordinarily stylized and ambiguous work, *The Conversation* avoids the formulaic features of the bigger-budgeted *Godfather* films.

These three films remain Coppola's greatest achievements as director. His subsequent career is checkered with grandly conceived but incompletely realized ambitions. Seduced by a huge budget and ballooning ambitions, Coppola released *Apocalypse Now* (1979), a visually spectacular but conceptually muddled account of the Vietnam War. For much of its length it is undeniably hypnotic, but after the precision and clarity of his previous three films, its diffuseness is disappointing.

His next films, *One from the Heart* (1982), *The Outsiders* (1983), *Rumble Fish* (1983), *The Cotton Club* (1984), *Peggy Sue Got Married* (1986), *Gardens of Stone* (1987), and *Tucker* (1988), generally failed to connect with critics or the public and often seemed more conventional than visionary. Part of Coppola's problem was a faltering economic base. He attempted to establish his own studio by creating Zoetrope Studios in 1980, but *Apocalypse Now* saddled him with huge debts, and the disastrous box-office performance of *One from the Heart* compounded his problems. The more conventional films that followed are partly a result of Coppola's efforts to extricate himself from a mountain of debt by crafting less audacious and more commercial products.

Coppola returned to epic form with *The Godfather, Part III* (1991), a compelling but uneven conclusion to the saga of Michael Corleone, and *Bram Stoker's Dracula* (1992), a controversial but genuinely visionary and audacious adaptation of the Stoker novel. The latter film is one of Coppola's most ambitious and artistically successful works.

Coppola's up-and-down career has been marked by an unresolved tension between grandiose artistic ambitions and the budgetary limitations and need for box-office success inherent in studio-financed productions. Unlike Woody Allen, who works successfully and well on limited resources, Coppola often required huge budgets for his visions and had difficulty accommodating the inevitable compromises such budgets entail. Presently, he has semi-retired from filmmaking in order to concentrate on his vineyard and wine-making business. ∎

THE GODFATHER: PART 2 (PARAMOUNT PICTURES, 1974)
Coppola brilliantly integrated masterful storytelling with an ambitious visual design in *The Godfather*, an enduring modern classic. And then he surpassed that film with its sequel focusing on Michael Corleone (Al Pacino) and the disintegration of his empire. Gordon Willis' cinematography used light and color to create a consistent through-line that helped to unify the two films. Frame enlargement.

of everyday perceptual information, and filmmakers use this information in light to create a convincing impression of three-dimensional space on a flat screen.

In contrast with hard light, soft light is highly diffused or scattered. It is produced by using a filter in front of the light source or by bouncing light off a reflective surface (cinematographers use "bounce cards" to accomplish the latter goal). Once light is scattered in this fashion, it will move in all directions to wrap around and envelop the actors and set. For this reason, soft light is much less directional than hard light, which can be precisely controlled to spotlight small details or areas of a set or an actor's face. During the Last Supper scene in *The Passion of the Christ* (2004), Caleb Deschanel's cinematography creates a strong, single-source effect, with the light seeming to come from the candles on the table. The soft light creates a gradual transition between light and shadow, and the design is realistic. It looks as if the candle is casting all the visible light within the frame. By contrast, the lighting in *Sky Captain and the World of Tomorrow* (2004) simulates a hard-light look by using soft light. The soft light is precisely controlled to create sharp fall-off. The light does not wrap around the actor.

Hard and soft lighting can establish time of day very effectively in a scene by mimicking the way sunlight changes during the course of a day. At noon, sunlight tends to be very hard, and shadows tend to be short. During the morning and dusk, sunlight is more highly diffused and produces longer shadows. Bright exterior lights visible through windows of an indoor set and diffused light on the interior of the set will establish daytime, whereas night is indicated by using dark or dim exteriors and hard, contrasting illumination on the interior. In Peter Weir's *Fearless* (1993), cinematographer

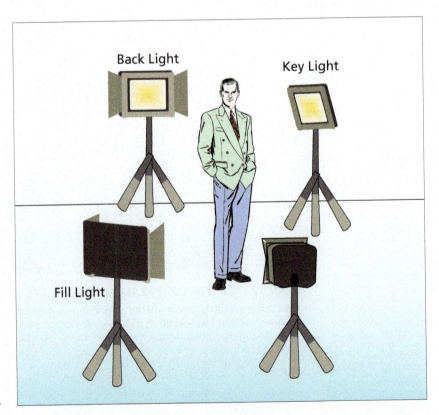

FIGURE 2.5
Three-point lighting.

Allen Daviau used hard light to establish the late-morning hour during which a critical airline flight occurs. He positioned lights at a high angle to cast short shadows through the windows of the airplane set. The lighting arrangement realistically replicated qualities of light at this time of day.

Hard and soft light also can convey emotional qualities. In *Batman Begins*, the filmmakers used soft light to film the flashback scenes to Bruce Wayne's childhood, before the trauma of losing his parents and being attacked by bats. The soft light helped to establish this as a happier time—thereafter, he is depicted with harder light.

HIGH- AND LOW-KEY SETUPS   Hard and soft lighting designs can be achieved by using **high-key** and **low-key** lighting setups. The **key light,** in the traditional three-point lighting employed in Hollywood films, is the main source of illumination usually directed on the face of the performer. The other two light sources are the **fill light** and the **back light.** The back light illuminates the rear portion of the set and/or the performer to establish a degree of separation between the actor and the rear of the set. The fill light fills in undesirable areas of shadow that are created by the positioning of the key light and the back light.

Low-key lighting features a relatively bright key light in comparison with a small use of fill light. This produces abundant shadows. In low-key lighting, most of the frame is underlit, whereas other, usually small, portions are adequately exposed. Typically, low-key lighting employs hard light in a high-contrast, fast fall-off image. This style was very popular in crime films throughout the 1940s and early 1950s. Many of these were called *film noir*, meaning "black film," a term designating the low-key lighting setups they employed as well as the moral darkness of their stories and characters. The shot from *Out of the Past* (page 64) is low-key.

High-key lighting is the opposite of low-key. High-key employs similar, bright intensities of key and fill, producing an even level of illumination throughout the scene with low contrast and few shadow areas. While low-key setups are suited to the gloomy, sinister films noir, high-key styles brightened the tone of Hollywood's popular musicals. High-key styles assertively displayed the cheerful sets, colors, costumes, and dancing in such films as *Singin' in the Rain, An American in Paris*, and *The Band Wagon*. The MGM studio in particular favored high-key styles to showcase the sumptuous sets and costumes in their productions, musical and nonmusical alike.

AN AMERICAN IN PARIS
(MGM, 1951)

High-key lighting balances key, fill, and backlights to create an even level of illumination throughout the frame. Notice how minimal is the shadow information in this shot of Gene Kelly. The brightness of high-key lighting was suited to the optimism of the Hollywood musicals. Frame enlargement.

LIGHTING CONTINUITY

Continuity of Lighting across Shots   Viewers watching a narrative motion picture generally want to believe in the plausibility and integrity of the world represented on screen. In other words, it should behave much as the viewer's own world does and obey the same kinds of physical laws of time and space, unless, as in adventure, fantasy, or science fiction, there is a clearly established reason for not doing so. Filmmakers manipulate cinematic style to represent *and* transform the viewer's sense of reality. Viewers, in turn, expect films to reference, and correspond in key ways with, their experience of the world while granting filmmakers a great deal of freedom in the ways they do this. Stylistic manipulations operate within limits. These are partly dictated by the logical demands of the style itself. Sylvester Stallone's character Rambo can have superhuman abilities, but if these are too excessive, his adventures will lose all sense of danger and peril, and the films will lack suspense.

Stylistic manipulations are also limited by the viewer's demands for reference and correspondence in the represented screen world. In this respect, continuity principles impose fundamental limitations on style in the interest of achieving reference and correspondence. In the areas of image editing and sound editing, principles of continuity are fundamental to narrative filmmaking. The same is true for lighting, irrespective of whether a filmmaker employs a realistic or pictorial design.

Cinematographers follow principles of continuity in their lighting designs. They are not free to drastically change light values from shot to shot. Changes of camera perspective from shot to shot should not produce major changes in the light values that have been established for the scene. A cinematographer, therefore, must take adequate measurements of the amount of light available within a scene and understand how to make small adjustments in that light depending on the camera's position. Close-ups, for example, are generally lit a bit brighter than long or medium shots, but viewers do not notice these small variations.

Filming on location can introduce complications into the way cinematographers plan for lighting continuity. When shooting out-of-doors, filmmakers often must supplement naturally available sunlight with artificial lights. The position of the sun in the sky overhead changes during the course of the day, and so does the apparent hardness of the light. Light is hardest at noon. While filming *The Last of the Mohicans* (1993), cinematographer Dante Spinotti found that artificial electrical lights offered several advantages during location shooting in the forest where much of the film's action is set.

In designing a visual look for the film, Spinotti wanted to be faithful to the story's eighteenth-century period. At that time, there were no electric lights, so illumination in the forests would have been produced by sunlight during the day and by moonlight and firelight at night. To simulate the effect of powerful shafts of sunlight pouring into the forest, Spinotti used a few very large, very powerful electric lights. These cast narrow beams of light to effectively simulate rays of sunshine penetrating the dark forest.

This use of artificial light accomplished two things. It established lighting continuity across shots regardless of the different times of day or dusk when filming occurred. Using electrical lights that could be positioned at appropriate angles enabled filmmakers to compensate for changes in the sun's position. Using these lights also extended principal hours of cinematography beyond the noon hour when light was at its hardest and least diffused. Supplementing sunlight with the electrical lights permitted shooting to occur well past the noon hour, even at dusk.

Continuity of Lighting within Shots   A cinematographer must plan for lighting continuity within shots as well as across shots. Many shots involve camera movement, and most involve actors who change positions in the frame. Lights that provide adequate exposure and atmosphere for a camera in one position will not do so if the camera moves to another portion of the set. The cinematographer must plan for a lighting design that can accommodate the entire range of the camera's movement. This may require adjusting the light level and the exposure level in the camera during the shot itself. Cinematographer Vittorio Storaro (*Bulworth*, 1998) regularly uses an elaborate dimmer board that enables him to raise and lower light levels during filming and while the camera and actors are in motion.

Filming Robert Altman's *Short Cuts* (1993), cinematographer Walt Lloyd confronted a scene in which a chauffeur drives a limousine in bright, hard sunlight, parks it by a trailer, and goes into the trailer's dim interior. In one shot, the camera follows the chauffeur as he gets out of the car in the hard sunlight and walks over to the trailer, opens the screen door, and goes inside. To accommodate this drastic change in light levels from exterior to interior within the moving camera shot, Lloyd executed a wide range of "stop pulls," changes in the lens aperture setting that determines how much light the lens is letting into the camera. The stop pulls helped maintain light continuity as the action of the shot moved from the bright exterior to the dim interior.

These examples indicate one of the key requirements of a cinematographer's job: the ability to quickly and creatively solve artistic and practical challenges. Cinematographers must strategically fit the demands of a location shoot or a director's preferred visual design with available camera resources and the imperative for lighting continuity. This may entail supplementing natural light with artificial light, executing elaborate on-set lighting adjustments during the course of a shot, or readjusting exposure levels in the camera to compensate for changes in light level.

LIGHTING FOR COLOR   Black-and-white film registers only brightness levels, not colors. Brightness values range from white through gray to black. When shooting black-and-white, the cinematographer must be careful to avoid using colors in a scene, such as red and green, that have the same degree of brightness and will be indistinguishable on film.

By contrast, the cinematographer who works in color can use it to add to the tone and atmosphere of the scene. By appropriately choosing film stocks with an understanding of their sensitivity to color, by employing color gelatins over the lights to intensify a dominant color motif within a scene, and by working closely with the production designer to establish the range of colors to be employed in sets and costumes, the cinematographer helps organize the color design of a given film.

Functions of Color Cinematography   Color design performs three basic functions in film. It establishes symbolic meaning, narrative organization, and psychological mood and tone.

Conveying Symbolic Meaning Filmmakers often use color to establish a symbolic association or idea in the mind of the viewer. In *Thirteen* (2003), to express the downward arc of a young girl's life as she gets involved with drugs, the filmmakers slowly, gradually drained most of the color out of the film. In *Pleasantville*, a teenage brother and sister find themselves trapped within a 1950s-era television sitcom whose characters lead humdrum and predictable lives. The siblings disrupt the scripted equilibrium of the show, causing some of its characters to reflect on and examine their personalities and identity. Color emblemizes this dawning self-awareness. The sitcom world is initially a black-and-white world, corresponding to the simplified morality of the show. But as the characters awaken into complex selves, color begins to appear, at first in selective parts of the black-and-white image and eventually into the entire image. The shift from black-and-white to color suggests the transition by the sitcom characters to a fuller, more emotionally rounded life.

Cinematographer Vittorio Storaro (*Apocalypse Now*, *Bulworth*) believes that colors have an inherent symbolism, based in their wavelength, to which viewers respond physiologically. Of all contemporary cinematographers, Storaro has the most elaborate theory of color expression in cinema, and he typically uses colors for highly specific purposes. In *Bulworth*, he used an elaborate color palette to suggest the spiritual crisis and regeneration of the title character, played by Warren Beatty. To suggest Bulworth's initial despair, the film opens in darkness, with no color, and then its scenes move through the hues of red, orange, yellow-cyan-magenta, blue, indigo, and white. Storaro's color design bookends the film with the absence of color (black) and, at the end, the unity of all colors (white). For Storaro, the aesthetic structure of *Bulworth* is determined by this color plot and the symbolic ideas associated with its progression of hues.

Establishing Narrative Organization Many contemporary films use color design in an overt way to establish narrative organization, and this function often overlaps with providing symbolic meaning. *Ray* (2004), about the life of singer Ray Charles, marks the flashbacks to his youth with bright, vibrant color. Scenes showing his adult life—after he had lost his eyesight—have a more limited range of desaturated color. The complex narrative of Steven Soderbergh's *Traffic* takes place in three locations, two of which are color-coded. The Washington, DC, sequences were shot unfiltered to achieve a cold, blue look. Scenes in Mexico were overexposed and shot with a tobacco filter to give them a hot, brown look. As the story switches between the locations, the color change is quite striking. In *Blow*, the story spans the 1950s–1990s, and each decade gets a distinctive color

characterization. Steven Spielberg's *Schindler's List* and *Saving Private Ryan* bracket their narratives with a prologue and epilogue and use color to differentiate these sections from the narrative body of the films. In both films, the prologue and epilogue are shot in naturalistic color, whereas the narrative body of *Schindler's List* is filmed in black-and-white and that of *Saving Private Ryan* is filmed in desaturated color. These color differences create a counterpoint within the structure of each film that invites the viewer to reflect on what each section of the films is expressing.

The narrative of Spike Lee's *Malcolm X* (1993), about the life of the charismatic black leader, is divided into three sections. The first section of the film, dealing with Malcolm's life as a young man, is the most colorful, the most visually romantic, and the section that features the warmest colors. The sections dealing with Malcolm's time in prison contrast with the warmth of the earlier episodes by using a color scheme that stresses grays, blacks, and bluish grays. The lighting scheme is very cool and hard, eliminating all diffusion.

The third section of the narrative, dealing with Malcolm's career as a civil rights leader and relationship with the Nation of Islam, features browns, greens, and very natural tones. Dickerson wanted each of these schemes to work on the viewer subliminally and to provide a way of visually characterizing the content of Malcolm's life during these periods.

Conveying Mood and Tone The most common use of color design in film is probably to augment and intensify the emotional mood and tone of a scene. The filmmakers constructed a color plot for *The Lord of the Rings* films, using color to convey emotional tones for the diverse locations. Bags End, the Hobbits' village, has a cozy, comfortable feel, with a warm, yellow-orange fire in the fireplace. In the sinister village of Bree, in contrast, the fireplace has a dirty greenish-yellow glow. Autumnal colors help give Rivendell, the decaying empire of the Elves, a melancholy quality. Green light, draining color from the actors' faces, gives the Moria Mines a tomblike atmosphere. In *L.A. Confidential* (1997), Kim Basinger plays Lynn Bracken, a Hollywood hooker who lives in a palatial Los Angeles

MALCOLM X (40 ACRES & A MULE FILMWORKS, 1992)

Cinematographers often use a color arc to organize a film, orchestrating color changes across the running time of the film in ways that correspond with changes in the characters and their situations. In collaboration with director Spike Lee, cinematographer Ernest Dickerson used changes in color to define the film's three narrative sections. Pictured here are the first, in which bold, saturated colors characterize an era of excitement, energy and recklessness in Malcolm's youth. In the film's third section, a more restrained and balanced palette emphasizing earth tones typified the mature and settled phase of his adult life. Frame enlargements.

house where she has two bedrooms, one the working bedroom, the other her own. Cinematographer Dante Spinotti used color to contrast the emotional tone of these two rooms. He shot the working room with cool blue light to give it a slightly harsh and emotionally distant aura. By contrast, when Lynn takes a man she loves to her real bedroom, Spinotti used a romantic amber lighting to create a sense of warmth and emotional security.

In James Cameron's *The Terminator* (1984), a science fiction fantasy set in Los Angeles during two time periods, 1984 and 2029 A.D., cinematographer Adam Greenberg used hard, strong, blue light to photograph the terminator (played by Arnold Schwarzenegger). Greenberg found that hitting Schwarzenegger with this light from a high angle made the character seem less human and more savage. When he lit Schwarzenegger with strong light, the actor looked like a piece of sculpture. The high angle of the light increased the shadows on Schwarzenegger's physique and created a harder look, and the blue cast of the light accentuated his coldness.

Much has been written about the psychological and emotional effects of color schemes, and many cinematographers have very intense preferences for and against certain colors and a belief that specific colors can have precise effects on the emotional responses of viewers. In general, however, the emotional effects of color are

THE TERMINATOR (ORION, 1984)
Cinematographer Adam Greenberg used hard, blue lighting to bring out the violence and savagery of the title character. Color and lighting design intensify the dramatic and emotional impact of the film's narrative. Frame enlargement.

strongly context-dependent. Color can augment, intensify, and sometimes contrast and cut against the dominant emotional tone and mood of a scene, but an individual color in itself rarely can supply emotional and psychological content that is otherwise missing in a scene. In the case of the contrasting color schemes of the two bedrooms in *L.A. Confidential,* the action of the scenes in those locations works with the lighting to help set a unified emotional tone in each locale. Rather than imposing extraneous meaning on a scene or film, color design extends, sharpens, heightens, or, conversely, minimizes, mitigates, or contrasts with the existing narrative, dramatic, or psychological material of a given scene.

CINEMATOGRAPHY AND THE DIGITAL DOMAIN

Digital imaging is now a standard part of contemporary film, and the cinematographer's job intersects with the work of computer-effects artists. Light, color, camera perspective, and movement can be created either digitally or through traditional cinematography. Digital tools enable filmmakers to pre-visualize (or "previz") their shots before any footage is actually exposed. Software tools such as Frame Forge 3D allow filmmakers to build a virtual set in the computer, to plan their camera positions, and to specify the type of lenses and focal lengths that will be on the cameras. The software package will then show how the set and characters will look when filmed with, say, a Primo E-Series line of lenses. Filmmakers can simulate lens changes and camera moves, can move furniture around inside the virtual set, and can see when a shot is so wide that the ceiling or other unwanted information is visible. This kind of preparation can save valuable time once production actually begins.

DIGITAL CAPTURE   For much of its history, cinema meant *film,* strips of celluloid that run through cameras and projectors. Cinema is no longer exclusively a film medium, and it is moving swiftly to replace film with **digital video.** Many films originate as digitally captured images. High-end digital cameras, like the Red (used to film David Fincher's *The Social Network*) or the Thomson Viper (used to shoot Michael Mann's *Collateral and Miami Vice*) capture images that have remarkable resolution and tonal values approaching that of film. These cameras operate like computers, crunching huge amounts of data, require a process of rebooting after they are shut down, and get regular software and hardware updates.

The luminous, sumptuous imagery in Steven Soderbergh's *Che* (2008) and Fincher's *Zodiac* (2007) and *The Social Network* (2010) show what can be accomplished with the new generation of data cameras, making these among the most beautifully rendered digital films yet produced. These filmmakers—Fincher, Soderbergh, Mann, along with James Cameron on *Avatar* (2009)—have been leading the industry toward a digital future, and they have embraced digital capture for aesthetic reasons as well as convenience. (The convenience factor is the elimination of dailies. A cinematographer shooting in digital video sees the results immediately; shooting on film requires waiting for the footage to be developed and printed by a lab, a process that came to be known as waiting on "dailies.")

Film still offers superior resolution and tonal values, but not by much. Viewers watching *Che, The Social Network,* or *Zodiac* see images that look remarkably film-like. That is because these are **high-definition video** images or are ultra-high. HD (high-definition) cameras, like the Viper or Sony's CineAlta used by George Lucas to film his second batch of *Star Wars* movies, produce 1920 x 1080 pixels. The Red, by contrast, can shoot at 4K, producing 4096 x 3072 pixels (ultra-high-definition). Many filmmakers and cinematographers believe that a 4K image is indistinguishable from an image projected from 35mm celluloid film. At this high end of digital capture, the gap with what film provides is increasingly narrow. The main giveaway to the films' digital origins is the difficulty that digital video has in handling highlights. Bright areas tend to clip and burn out, looking harsh as compared with film. But careful filmmakers can handle this issue to minimize the limitation, as Soderbergh

THE SOCIAL NETWORK (COLUMBIA PICTURES, 2010)
Cinematographer Jeff Cronenweth shot David Fincher's film using the Red camera operating at 4K resolution. He found that the Red enabled him to work fast, shoot in low light levels, and get rich, luxurious-looking images. And digital capture facilitated color and image correction in the DI (digital intermediate). In the film, Jesse Eisenberg (pictured) plays Mark Zuckerberg, the inventor of Facebook. Frame enlargement.

showed with *Che* and Fincher did with *The Social Network*. Moreover, digital video compensates for this limitation by seeing more information in shadow areas than does film, and Michael Mann shot his crime films—*Collateral, Miami Vice, Public Enemies* (2009)—in HD for this very reason.

The Digital Intermediate

Whether productions are shot on video or film, *digital timing* (or **digital grading**) is used increasingly to adjust and balance color and tweak other image elements. Traditional laboratory methods, using photochemical processes, in earlier periods (a process known as *lab timing*) enabled cinematographers to make color adjustments in the entire image overall, whereas today they can selectively remove or alter individual colors or sections of the image, as cinematographer Andrew Lesnie did on *The Lord of the Rings* films. Whereas traditional lab timing only makes gross adjustments in the three primary colors of red, blue, and green, digital timing enabled Lesnie to work directly with delicate blends, such as lavenders and salmons, and in small, precisely defined areas of the image (skin tones, for example). *O Brother, Where Art Thou?* was the first feature film to be entirely digitized and color corrected using this method. Because of the image control that digital timing affords, cinematographers are becoming increasingly involved in this area of postproduction, whereas in previous decades their work was largely finished with the completion of principal photography.

An entire film may be digitally graded or select scenes only. In either case, the first step involves making a **digital intermediate (DI)**—the film images are converted to digital video (if the movie was digitally captured in production, this step is skipped), where they undergo the grading process. The corrected digital footage (the digital intermediate) is then scanned back out to film for exhibition in theaters. If the movie is to be shown in a 2.35:1 ratio, then the scope extraction typically is performed during the DI.

Many light and color effects that were once accomplished during filming are now achieved with a digital intermediate. The intensely saturated colors of *House of Flying Daggers* (2004), as well as the monochromatic, desaturated color palette of *Flags of Our Fathers* (2006), were achieved with a digital intermediate. Lighting problems also can be fixed. While filming the appearance of the samurai in a twilit, smoky forest in *The Last Samurai* (2003) and the many day exterior scenes in *Alexander* (2004), the cinematographers accepted problems of lighting continuity, knowing these would be fixed with digital grading.

The great advantage offered by a DI is the precision with which alterations in the image can be made. Filmmakers can select a small area, for example, and alter it. A selecting and masking function, called power windows, enables artists to work on one part of an image and leave the rest unchanged.

When cinematographer John Alton wrote *Painting with Light*, this description of the cinematographers' art was mainly a metaphor. The DI takes it closer to reality by virtue of the expanded aesthetic powers it gives to a cinematographer. At the same time, while many cinematographers welcome the new levels of control that digital grading gives them, others prefer the traditional photochemical methods of color correction. On *There Will Be Blood* (2007), *Batman Begins* (2005), and *Inception* (2010), the filmmakers used traditional tools of light and color because they did not want a digitally graded look.

KING KONG (UNIVERSAL, 2005)
Naomi Watts commands the viewer's attention in this shot because the focal plane is shallow and also because the highlights in her eyes add the spark of life to her face. Director Peter Jackson used power windows in the DI to make many subtle alterations in the film, which included emphasizing the highlights in Watts' eyes. Frame enlargement.

Case Study   RATATOUILLE

Filmmakers today can accomplish many tasks of cinematography—color, lighting, camera movement—using digital tools. Pixar's animated film *Ratatouille* (2007) features exquisitely rendered lighting effects. Indeed, lighting was essential to the story, which is about a clever rat working as a gourmet chef in one of the world's great restaurants. Making the animated food on screen look real enough to eat was accomplished by careful digital lighting. The **digital light designer** works with key, fill, and back lights but these are not real in the physical manner of traditional cinematography. They are virtual lights, created in a computer. *Ratatouille* presented numerous lighting challenges because so many of its scenes presented a kitchen full of food, and the food needed to look real. The digital designers created virtual lighting effects that emphasized texture and surface detail, and made the food look fresh. To do so, they studied the photography that appears in food magazines and cookbooks. As they wrote about this kind of photography, "Light falls across cuts of meat to reveal their perfectly cooked texture, a soft backlight hints that fruits and vegetables are plump and juicy, and highlights glisten on sauces."

In particular, the digital lighting of the animated food conveyed the properties of softness (to avoid a hard and plastic look), reflection (to convey an appealingly moist texture), and color saturation (to indicate freshness). They also used the technique of **subsurface scattering**, which had been developed on *The Lord of the Rings* for simulating Gollem's skin. This technique mimics the way that light penetrates an object, scatters below the surface, and then exits at a different place from where it entered. They also used a complementary technique they called "Gummi," which emulated light transmission through an object, such as a glass of wine. To get both techniques to work required running a series of computations to determine how light would behave in contact with different surfaces, densities, and degrees of translucence. Consultants on the film who were gourmet cooks instructed the CG artists in how food looks, how sauces behave when stirred, and how food reacts when chopped with a knife.

The result in the film is food that looks good enough to eat, an illusion created by the careful way that digital light is used to model the surface properties of texture, color, and translucence. While the film is an animated fantasy, the lighting is quite realistic—the digital lighting behaves according to the known properties of real light. The illusion created on screen is a convincing one. ■

RATATOUILLE (PIXAR, 2007)
Remy, the film's hero and a gourmet rat, surveys some tempting bread. All of the food in the film had to look real and edible, an illusion accomplished by digital lighting and careful rendering of surface textures and colors. Frame enlargement.

VISUAL STYLE AND DESIGN QUOTATIONS

The discussion thus far has tended to emphasize how cinematography functions within individual films, with a stylistic design suited to expressing the needs of a given production. But one also can understand cinematography in terms of visual styles across groups of films. The cinema is now more than a century old, and cinematography has established some important visual traditions. Certain lighting and color designs, used extensively across many films, have emerged as enduring features of style. Filmmakers can quote from these in their own work, and what is "real" for an audience is sometimes a function of how films in the past have represented the world.

During the decade of the 1940s, hard, low-key lighting was an established visual convention pervasive in Hollywood cinema. (A **convention** is an agreement shared by filmmaker and audience about what will be valid and acceptable in a film.) Dark, moody, shadowy compositions were firmly established in crime and detective films, especially film noir. The low-key shot from *Out of the Past* is such an example.

Contemporary cinematographers photographing crime films whose narratives are set during the 1940s consciously try to evoke this lighting style. In *Bugsy* (1991), dealing with real-life gangster Ben Siegel's experiences in Hollywood in the 1940s, cinematographer Allen Daviau used abundant hard lighting because this was one of the staples of 1940s crime film cinematography. Barry Levinson, the director of *Bugsy*, wanted the dark areas of the compositions to be extremely dark, and to comply, Daviau worked small pieces of highly directional hard light.

What is striking about this aesthetic choice, from the standpoint of visual conventions, is that to evoke a period style and setting for *Bugsy*, the filmmakers chose to imitate the lighting style of 1940s Hollywood pictures. In this regard, the lighting style has established its own reality and its own validity. To visually represent the world of 1940s crime on film means to evoke the lighting style that Hollywood employed in its films during those years. Roger Deakins's black-and-white, low-key cinematography for *The Man Who Wasn't There* (2001) reproduces the look of Hollywood film during this period, appropriately because the story is set in the 1940s.

Hollywood is a very small community whose artists know each other and study one another's work. This accentuates the speed at which influences can operate. The striking visual designs created by one cinematographer can shape the work of other artists and their films. In *JFK* (1991), cinematographer Robert Richardson created a distinctive

JFK (WARNER BROS., 1991); INGLOURIOUS BASTERDS (UNIVERSAL, 2009)

In Oliver Stone's *JFK*, cinematographer Robert Richardson's lighting created a glowing, halo effect, a design that he repeated in films for other directors, such as Quentin Tarantino, and which other cinematographers have employed in homage to Richardson. Frame enlargements.

halo-style lighting that made the characters glow under hot lights. Richardson has used this lighting style on other productions, and it has come to be known as the Richardson style. Shooting Spike Lee's *Clockers*, cinematographer Malik Sayeed emulated this look during a police interrogation scene. Using floor and ceiling lights and a reflective table surface, Sayeed replicated "the Richardson aura."

Among their many visual innovations in *Saving Private Ryan*, Steven Spielberg and Janusz Kaminski used an oddly configured shutter inside the camera, which created a streaking effect on the image because shutter and film frame were out of synchronisation. In reviewing the footage shot by combat cameramen in World War II, they noticed these streaking effects (which occurred when the cameras lost their loops), and they wanted to reproduce that look.

It became one of the memorable visual effects in *Saving Private Ryan*, and it has impressed other filmmakers, who have incorporated it into their own work. Michael Bay used it in *Pearl Harbor* (2000) during the bombing attack. In *The Limey* (2000), Steven Soderbergh removed it from the combat context of these films and used it for a flashback scene in which a character accidentally kills his girlfriend. The streaking effect helps to stylize the flashback and to visually suggest the tension and stress of the moment.

In *Vertigo* (1958), Alfred Hitchcock and cinematographer Robert Burks created a highly influential shot—the combination zoom and track in opposite directions—used to simulate the main character's fear of heights. In the years since,

SAVING PRIVATE RYAN (PARAMOUNT/DREAMWORKS, 1998); THE BOURNE ULTIMATUM (UNIVERSAL PICTURES, 2007)

Filming with the shutter inside the camera out of synch produces these streaks of light in the image. Steven Spielberg and cinematographer Janusz Kaminski were emulating the look of World War II combat footage, which frequently had this flaw. The look they achieved was so striking that other filmmakers have incorporated it into their own work, often with greater exaggeration. It has evolved into a stylistic device for expressing emotional or physical distress, as in this scene from *The Bourne Ultimatum* where Jason Bourne (Matt Damon) learns the truth about his origins as a trained killer. Frame enlargements.

the combination zoom-track has been used by a great number of filmmakers to express unease, disturbance, or anxiety. Steven Spielberg used it in *Jaws* (1975) to capture the fears of police chief Brody (Roy Scheider) as he nervously watches bathers frolicking offshore. Martin Scorsese used it in *Goodfellas* (1990) to capture the disorientation of a gangster who realizes a trusted friend might be planning his execution. Spike Lee employed it in *Clockers* to show a mother's reaction to the spectacle of her son's being beaten by a policeman. In *The Ghost and the Darkness* (1996), the zoom-track visualizes the rush of fear in a hunter facing a killer lion when his gun misfires. Hitchcock and Burks did more than create an effective visual metaphor for their main character's psychological affliction. They fashioned an enduring visual symbol for emotional disorientation, a template for other filmmakers interested in evoking this quality of mind, a convention that has passed into the general vocabulary of contemporary filmmaking.

The repetition of visual conventions establishes compelling artistic realities not only for audiences but also for the artists who make films and who borrow from and are influenced by the designs of their peers. Memorable cinematographic designs establish powerful artistic traditions and influences on the work of subsequent filmmakers.

SUMMARY

The cinematographer helps the director to achieve a desired visual design by using the camera to capture images that reflect the director's visual goals for the film. To do this, the cinematographer chooses a film stock and aspect ratio, and controls and designs the use of light and color in film and the planning and placement of camera setups. Cinematographers employ realistic and pictorial lighting designs. In the first they simulate the effects of a real light source on screen, whereas in the second approach they aim for more purely pictorial effects.

Either approach to lighting design will employ varying proportions of hard (high-contrast) and soft (low-contrast) light. Specific lighting setups tend to create a hard or soft look. Low-key lighting is hard. High-key lighting is often soft. Like image and sound editing, lighting designs follow continuity principles. Light levels and angles must match across shots and even within shots when the moving camera is employed.

With respect to color design, a cinematographer lights objects on the set or uses colored gels over white lights to manipulate color hue, saturation, and intensity. Color can be used to separate and define objects in a composition, but when shooting black-and-white, a cinematographer has to use gray-scale values when organizing a composition. Color cinematography establishes symbolic meanings, narrative organization, and psychological moods and emotional tones. In each of these functions, color is integrated into the overall dramatic context and design concept of a scene or film.

The cinematographer's tools are shared by digital effects artists, and the scope of cinematography, as traditionally defined, has expanded to include the collaboration necessary for creating convincing digital effects.

Light and color designs, once established, can become enduring features of style, repeated across many films. When this happens, those designs take on a high level of representational reality. Filmmakers are sensitive to this, and if they need to express a particular social milieu, such as urban crime, or a time period, such as the 1940s, they may deliberately imitate famous lighting designs from older movies picturing those settings or periods. Filmmakers also may replicate the striking visual designs of fellow filmmakers, deliberately borrowing design elements in a way that "quotes" from other films.

KEY TERMS AND CONCEPTS

additive 51
anamorphic 51
aspect ratio 49
back light 67
burnout 56
cinematography 45
contrast 64
convention 77
digital grading 75
digital intermediate (DI) 75
digital light designer 76
digital video 73
fall-off 64
fill light 67

film noir 64
film stocks 47
gray scale 50
hard light 62
hard-matted 53
high-definition video 74
high-key lighting 67
hue 50
intensity 50
key light 67
letterboxed 53
low-key lighting 67
mise-en-scène 45
performance style 45

pictorial lighting design 59
practical (light) 56
pre-visualization 45
production design 45
realistic lighting design 56
rear projection 60
saturation 50
soft-matted 53
soft light 62
subsurface scattering 76
subtractive 51
Super 35 54
wavelengths 50
widescreen ratio 52

SUGGESTED READINGS

Dan Ablan, *Digital Cinematography and Directing* (Indianapolis, IN: New Riders, 2002).

John Alton, *Painting with Light* (Berkeley: University of California Press, 1995).

American Cinematographer, monthly journal of film and electronic production techniques published by ASC Holding Corp., Hollywood, CA.

Kris Malkiewicz, *Cinematography: A Guide for Film Makers and Film Teachers* (New York: Simon and Schuster, 1992).

Kris Malkiewicz, *Film Lighting: Talks with Hollywood's Cinematographers and Gaffers* (New York: Simon and Schuster 1992).

Pauline B. Rogers, *The Art of Visual Effects: Interviews on the Tools of the Trade* (Boston: Focal Press, 1999).

Pauline B. Rogers, *Contemporary Cinematographers on Their Art* (Boston: Focal Press, 1998).

Dennis Schaeffer and Larry Salvato, *Masters of Light: Conversations with Contemporary Cinematographers* (Berkeley and Los Angeles: University of California Press, 1986).

3

Production Design

OBJECTIVES

After reading this chapter, you should be able to:

- explain the work of production design

- describe costumes, sets, mattes, and miniatures, the basic tools of production design

- explain how production creatively transforms existing locations

- explain how production design can fabricate locales that are made to seem real

- describe how a design concept organizes a film's production design

- explain changing production designs in contemporary science fiction films

- describe how production design in fantasy films utilizes realistic perceptual information

In addition to cinematography, filmmakers use sets, props, costumes, and actors to achieve a film's total visual "look." This chapter examines the contributions of **production design**, and the next chapter looks at film acting.

WHAT THE PRODUCTION DESIGNER DOES

The production designer is the individual who supervises the design of a film's visual environments. The production designer oversees the work of set decorators and designers, costume designers, and the prop crew. This array of artists and technicians creates costumes and sets using colors and concepts supplied by the production designer, who arrives at an overall visual organization through close consultation and collaboration with the director and cinematographer. As a result of these conferences, the production designer prepares a series of sketches that illustrate the basic **design concept** and organization of the film. Set and costume designers then work to produce settings and costumes that embody the concepts outlined in the production designer's sketches. During preproduction, the sketches are turned into storyboards and into miniature models that are used to plan camera and lighting positions.

Stages of Work

The first step in the production designer's work is reading the script and visualizing the look of the film that might be made from it. Production designer Wynn Thomas (*Do the Right Thing*, 1989) explains this in terms of "How do you want the movie to feel?" Films that have a powerful and enduring "feel"—*The Wizard of Oz, Alien, The Lord of the Rings*—establish this through their production design.

The production designer will next break the script down in terms of budgeting issues. What kind of sets will be needed? How much of the film should be shot in a studio, and how much on location? What will all this cost? One of the production designer's most important jobs is to find ways to trim these costs. In other words, the production

THE DUCHESS (PARAMOUNT VANTAGE, 2008)

Skillful production design vividly recreates historical eras, as in this film about Georgiana Cavendish (Keira Knightly), the 18th-century Duchess of Devonshire. Filming occurred at more than a dozen historic homes across England, such as Holkham Hall, an 18th-century country house on the coast of Norfolk. As selected by production designer Michael Carlin, these locations enhanced the realism of the film's settings and costumes. Frame enlargement.

designer will explain to the producer how the film can be made for its allotted budget. As Stuart Craig (*The English Patient*, 1996) explains, "The designer addresses the script and the amount of money available and offers the producer a viable way of making the film."

It's often cheaper today to build sets or to film locations overseas. All the exteriors in *The Last Samurai* (2003) were shot in New Zealand, not Japan, where the story takes place. *Cold Mountain* (2004), about the Civil War, was shot in Europe.

As the production designer breaks down the script in terms of budget issues, he or she also breaks it down into visual concepts, which are expressed in sketches. These sketches of proposed sets that the production designer prepares from the script provide a first indication of how the film will look and feel. Many designers prefer to do these in pencil first—because lines and shadows stand out with more clarity—and only then move on to colored drawings.

Production Design as Character and Story Design

Creating the sketches and then the sets requires the designer to think about very specific issues of character and story. To design a set is also to design the characters that will live in it. A set makes a statement about the characters, and, therefore, to visualize a set often means thinking about the personality and the life history of the characters who will use it. John Beard, whose work as a designer includes *The Last Temptation of Christ* (1988), points out that to do good work, "you should know what art a character would have on their walls, what books they would read, and even what music they would listen to." Wynn Thomas, who has collaborated frequently with director Spike Lee, speaks of this process as "character design," and he encourages the actors to come on set a few days before shooting to explore it and become familiar with it. "I encourage

THE ROAD (DIMENSION FILMS, 2009)

Choosing locations is one of the chief responsibilities of a production designer. But the locations where a film is shot do not always correspond to the locations of the story, and real locations may be altered, enhanced or changed to serve story and drama. Based on a respected novel by Cormac McCarthy, *The Road* shows a post-apocalyptic landscape, an unspecified locale devastated by a mysterious, unnamed catastrophe. The film was shot in Pennsylvania and Louisiana. The neighborhood pictured here was a row of houses abandoned in New Orleans after Hurricane Katrina. In the actual location, an open freeway occupied the left of the frame, and the row of houses that appears there now in the shot is a digital element added to the image. The car in the foreground is a real prop, but the brooding sky is a digital matte painting standing in for the clear and more tranquil sky that existed on the day of filming. Frame enlargement.

them to explore the space, open the drawers and look inside; I always provide the sort of stuff their characters might have to be dealing with, paperwork in a desk, for example."

While these items may have a subliminal presence for viewers, they provide motivation for drama, setting and character. In a good design, their presence helps actors to give better performances. The Hollywood star Burt Lancaster travelled to Italy to appear in *The Leopard* (1963), directed by the great Luchino Visconti. At Visconti's insistence, production designer Mario Garbuglia's recreation of the film's 19th-century aristocratic world was so detailed and lavish that Lancaster was stunned to open the drawers of a dresser and find them fully stocked with clothing. Hollywood's norm was only to design and build what the camera will see. Visconti had gone far beyond this, and Lancaster felt humbled, and he resolved to work extra hard on his performance in order to be worthy of this kind of attention.

A good example of the way that production design can motivate the drama is found in Spike Lee's *Do the Right Thing*. One of the main sets is Sal's Pizzeria, run by Sal (Danny Aiello), a white Italian, and his two sons, but located in a black neighborhood. While Sal is proud that he has served food to the neighborhood for years, tensions with some of the black patrons flare up periodically. Framed photos that Sal has hung on the walls of the pizzeria provide one source of conflict. These show prominent Italian-American entertainers, like Al Pacino, Robert De Niro, and Frank Sinatra, but the portraits do not contain any famous African-Americans. Buggin' Out (Giancarlo Esposito), who eats a lot of pizza there, gazes at the "Wall of Fame" and challenges Sal about the absence of prominent black celebrities. Sal tells him if he gets his own pizzeria, he can put up any pictures he wants, but here only Italian Americans go on the wall.

Sal's remark provokes a confrontation with Buggin' Out, and the conflict flows naturalistically from the setting and the performances. Thomas points out that the actors spent time on the set prior to filming so that it would seem as if the characters had worked there or eaten pizza there for years, and this illusion comes across vividly in the scene. "I think it's important that there's a point where a set ceases to be a world I have designed and begins to become the world the actors live in."

The celebrities on Sal's "Wall of Fame" were pre-selected by director Spike Lee and Thomas in order to motivate this action. In turn, the action enabled Lee to make a thematic point. He agreed with Sal's view, that the owner of the business gets to say what goes. One of the film's sub-themes is the need for black-owned businesses, that black entrepreneurs would provide a vital link between economic development in the city and an expanding social authority. The pictures on Sal's wall help to make this larger theme concrete.

Where the production designer puts a window in a set or places interior lights will determine how the set is lit by the cinematographer, so the two must consult early on. The production designer will show the cinematographer his or her sketches and models and get feedback about potential camera positions. These, in turn, will affect how a set is dressed with props. The film stock chosen by a cinematographer will affect how skin tones look, and this, in turn, will influence a production designer's choice of colors on the set.

As in other areas of contemporary filmmaking, digital tools have become important aids to production design. Digital pre-visualization enables filmmakers to build three-dimensional computer models of sets and locations. By rotating and reformatting these models, filmmakers can simulate views of the set from different camera positions and with lenses of differing focal lengths. The process enables filmmakers to see in advance how the set will look under a variety of filming conditions. Based on this information, filmmakers can plan camera setups or, if necessary, revise the design of a set.

DO THE RIGHT THING (40 ACRES & A MULE, 1989)

Buggin' Out (Giancarlo Esposito) demands to know why there are no African-American portraits on the Wall of Fame. Brilliant production design motivates characters, drama, setting and theme and stimulates actors to do their best work. Sal's "Wall of Fame" illuminates one of the film's core themes, the role that African-American entrepreneurs can play in transforming the city. Frame enlargement.

During all of this, the production designer also will make trips to scout locations. These trips are called **recces** (pronounced "wreckies"), and the objective is to find places that will be economical to use and also will fit with the evolving look and feel of the film.

As the sketches become models and full-scale sets, the production designer supervises a crew that he or she often has hired. These people include the **art director** (a kind of second-in-command who oversees the translation of sketches into sets), the **set decorator** (who dresses a set with curtains, lamps, furniture), the **prop master** (who supervises the design and construction of props, such as a cigar lighter or walking stick), the **scenic artist** (who supervises matte paintings and other backdrop portions of a set), and the **costume designer** (who designs what the characters will wear).

Creating a Unified Design

The production designer thinks about the visual statements made by the layout of sets, architectural styles and building materials, coloring and texture of buildings and costumes, and the interplay of all design elements in the frame. The goal is to use these elements to make a unified and coherent design statement or series of such statements. *Chinatown* (1974) was one of the best-designed films of the 1970s, and it is instructive to hear how its production designer, Richard Sylbert, conceptualized the different details that went into that film's highly distinctive mise-en-scène. The film takes place in 1937 in a drought-stricken Los Angeles and follows Jake Gittes (Jack Nicholson), a private eye investigating the death of Hollis Mulwray. Sylbert insisted there be no clouds visible in the sky because clouds suggest rain; that buildings be colored white because white denotes heat; that glass windows on office doors be cloudy and opaque to make it hard to see through them and enhance a sense of mystery; and that the color green, because it denotes lushness and moisture, be used only in significant scenes where the viewer feels something important is about to happen.

As Sylbert's design suggests, each element in a well-designed film has a reason for being there, some contribution that it is making to the story, theme, or style of the production. Throughout cinema history, films have been designed in this fashion, even though the title "production designer" is of relatively recent vintage. While the title is commonly employed in contemporary productions, during the studio era of the Hollywood period the title barely existed. During the 1930s and 1940s, each studio had an art department that employed illustrators, model builders, set decorators, prop men and prop women, and costume

CHINATOWN (PARAMOUNT, 1974)

Detective J. J. Gittes (Jack Nicholson) and the mysterious Evelyn Mulwray (Faye Dunaway, pictured) grapple with murder and deceit in 1930s Los Angeles. The film's unified production design evokes the period setting with exceptional concentration and metaphoric suggestiveness. Frame enlargement.

designers, all of whom worked under a given production's **unit art director**. (The Motion Picture Academy of Arts and Sciences, which awards the Oscars, still employs this older terminology, giving the award for "Best Art Direction.") The head of the art department who oversaw all the films in production was the **supervising art director**. At MGM, this individual was Cedric Gibbons. At 20th Century Fox, the equivalent figure was Lyle Wheeler.

Producer David O. Selznick first employed the term *production designer* on *Gone With the Wind* (1939) as a tribute to the importance of William Cameron Menzies's design sketches. These sketches and storyboards provided the unifying visual structure that helped give *Gone With the Wind* its stylistic coherence. This contribution was especially important in light of the fact that several different directors worked on *Gone With the Wind*. The man who gets screen credit as director is Victor Fleming, but during production Selznick changed directors several times, and it was Menzies's design concept that furnished a unifying visual structure. Menzies was a brilliant visual artist whose work has inspired generations of production designers. For this reason, he is sometimes referred to as the "father of production design," although, as we shall see, imaginative set design extends well back into silent cinema. As a director, he made one of the classic early science fiction films, *Things to Come* (1933), notable for its flamboyant and imaginative futuristic sets.

FILMMAKER SPOTLIGHT

Henry Bumstead

Henry Bumstead was one of Hollywood's most successful production designers. He worked at Paramount Studios from 1937 to 1960, during the great era of studio filmmaking, then at Universal Pictures, and then as an independent. He formed lasting partnerships with directors Alfred Hitchcock, Robert Mulligan, George Roy Hill, and Clint Eastwood, leaving an enduring visual imprint on their films through the sets and locations that he created.

Bumstead described Paramount as being like a miniature city, bustling with creative people under long-term contract. He worked in many genres—Westerns (*Run for Cover*, 1955), war films (*The Bridges at Toko-Ri*, 1954), comedy (*My Friend Irma*, 1949)—and moved quickly from one architectural style to another. "One day you might have to do something Gothic, next day, art nouveau," he recalled. He learned how to break down a script into locations and set designs that would include key character details and a color scheme suited to character and situation.

He met Hitchcock while at Paramount through Hitchcock's cinematographer, Robert Burks, who was shooting a picture—*The Vagabond King* (1956)—for which Bumstead was doing the art direction. On Burks' recommendation, Hitchcock asked to meet Bumstead, and they then collaborated on four films,

(continued)

The Man Who Knew Too Much (1956), *Vertigo* (1958), *Topaz* (1969), and *Family Plot* (1976). Bumstead's memorable designs for *Vertigo*—which included the church bell tower where the climax occurs—helped provide the film with its singular visual power.

At Universal Studios, Bumstead designed five films for Robert Mulligan, of which the most important was *To Kill a Mockingbird* (1962), based on the Harper Lee novel of a small Alabama town in the 1930s. Bumstead created a believable town built not in Alabama but on the Universal back lot. Even the trees on the set were built. So real did the sets seem that numerous art directors asked him where in Alabama he had found this town! It was Bumstead's attention to detail—dressing the sets with period décor, including porch swings and a house with brick pillars elevating its foundation above the flood plain and creating a little crawl space underneath—that made the sets seem so real.

Bumstead designed eight films for George Roy Hill, which included *Slaughterhouse-Five* (1972), *Slap Shot* (1977), *The World According to Garp* (1982), and their Oscar-winning film, *The Sting* (1973). For this Depression-era story set in Chicago, Hill wanted to shoot on location, but Bumstead persuaded him to build the sets in the studio, and Hill later said that the best-looking stuff in the film was that shot on Bumstead's studio sets. In designing the sets, Bumstead used the period photographs of Walker Evans as inspiration, and he created a dominant palette of red and brown to set mood and tone.

Bumstead's longest relationship was with Clint Eastwood, for whom he designed twelve films beginning with *High Plains Drifter* (1973) and ending with *Flags of Our Fathers* (2006) and *Letters from Iwo Jima* (2006). Eastwood is noted for working very fast and efficiently, and Bumstead's training during the studio period enabled him to adapt to the fast schedule of an Eastwood shoot. In *Unforgiven* (1991), for example, Bumstead created the Western town of Big Whiskey on a location in Calgary, Canada, in 43 days. It was one of many Western towns that he had created for the movies, and he always ran the main street on an east-west axis so that cinematographers would have backlight available for dramatic framing. Toward the end of his life, Bumstead planned to retire, but Eastwood kept coming by with new scripts, and "Bummy," as he was affectionately known, found each new collaboration with Eastwood to be irresistible. When Bumstead won the Lifetime Achievement Award from the Society of Motion Picture and Television Art Directors, Eastwood paid him a high compliment, saying "Dear Bummy, you take the BS out of filmmaking." ■

TO KILL A MOCKINGBIRD (Universal, 1962)
Bumstead built the sets for a Depression-era Alabama town on the back lot at Universal Studios, and the sets looked so authentic that many people believed the film had been shot on an actual Alabama location. Frame enlargement.

GONE WITH THE WIND (MGM, 1939)

William Cameron Menzies's design sketches helped provide a unifying visual structure for a production that frequently changed directors. Menzies's architectural visions brought the novel's settings memorably to life. Ashley Wilkes's Twelve Oaks plantation is the stage for several critical scenes in the film's first act. The sumptuous sets and costumes provide a vivid backdrop for the drama, and the filmmakers take care to display them in a luxuriant fashion. Frame enlargement.

BASIC TOOLS OF PRODUCTION DESIGN

Filmmakers design the visual environments of a film by using a set of tools that have remained essentially the same over many decades of filmmaking, although today they are augmented by digital effects. These tools are costumes, sets, matte paintings, and miniatures. **Costumes,** of course, are worn by performers on the set in front of the camera. Period films use historical costuming whose style and fashions designate a particular time period. The sumptuousness of James Cameron's *Titanic* (1997) is evident in the lavishly detailed costumes (and sets) that evoke the early modern world of 1912.

Sets are the physical locations on which the action occurs. These locations can be outdoors or indoors in the studio. At times, an indoor location may masquerade as an outdoor location. In Steven Spielberg's *Amistad* (1998), scenes that were supposed to be taking place outdoors in the courtyard of a New England prison holding African slaves actually were filmed on an indoor set. The filmmakers hung a giant silk shroud from the ceiling of the stage and lit it brightly from behind so that it would "burn out" on film. To the camera—and the viewer—it looked like a bright, cloudy sky.

Matte paintings are printed into the shot in the laboratory or, more often today, are digitally composited as a part of the background of a setting. Mattes very effectively extend the scale and depth of the represented scene. Matte work can be exceptionally sophisticated and subtle and, when done well, is virtually impossible for the casual viewer to spot. Digital mattes, created on the computer, are employed in many contemporary films.

Miniatures are small models that stand in for a portion of the set. Filmmakers often need miniatures when a very large set, such as a castle or, in the case of the *Batman* films, the entire city of Gotham, is required for a scene but cannot be built on its true scale. In the opening, pre-credit sequence of *Goldeneye* (1995), James Bond blows up a poison gas factory. While the effect is spectacular, it was executed using a small-scale model surrounded by a replica of the Swiss Alps. Let us now examine each of these tools in more detail.

Costumes

Costume design performs several functions. It furnishes details of period or setting appropriate to the story. Second, it provides opportunities for color and spectacle. Third, it provides a commentary on the characters, suggesting or revealing essential aspects of their personality or function in the story. Let's consider some examples of these functions.

Costume designers typically research the clothing styles associated with a film's period or locale because these styles can vividly evoke time and place. On the Civil War film *Glory* (1989), the filmmakers wanted to be as authentic as possible and used Matthew Brady's documentary photographs as guides and relied on a large community of Civil War re-enactors, buffs who had designed their own uniforms with exacting historical precision, down to the salt stains on their jackets and the scuffs on their boots.

In contrast to the historical realism of *Glory*, the costume designs Cecil Beaton furnished for the classic musical *My Fair Lady* (1964) are considerably more flamboyant. They demonstrate the way that costuming creates opportunities for spectacle. Audrey Hepburn plays an uneducated, working-class woman who, by learning to speak proper English, is transformed into a beautiful and poised epitome of high fashion. Note the extraordinary hat that Beaton has furnished her with, as pictured on page 91. As an article of clothing, it is impractical and dysfunctional. But as a visual design, it is sumptuous and magnificent, commanding the viewer's attention and suggesting the gorgeous butterfly into which the drab character has changed.

The costuming in *Planet of the Apes* (2001) provides one of the film's main attractions, and makeup designer Rick Baker improved on the ape designs used in the 1968 version of the film. In the earlier film, the actors in ape makeup could not move their lips and teeth independently because the teeth were glued onto the prosthetic lips. Moreover, their masks were relatively inflexible, so they couldn't show much facial expression. Baker designed masks that were much more flexible and made the teeth and lips as separate rigs. This enabled the actors to move their lips over their teeth and to convincingly simulate ape speech.

Costuming also provides a way of revealing character, creating subliminal messages about the person wearing the costume. In *The Graduate* (1967), an older woman, Mrs. Robinson (Ann Bancroft), makes a habit of seducing young men, and when she sets her sights on the film's hero (Dustin Hoffman), a recent college graduate, she wears a predatory costume, a leopard-print coat. The costumes worn by Satine (Nicole Kidman) in *Moulin Rouge* (2001)—red dress, black top hat, garters, and stockings—link her to the famous movie temptresses, and the actresses who played them, on whom she is modeled. In *Titus* (1999), director Julie Taymor shows the growing weakness and vulnerability of Rome's General Titus (Anthony Hopkins) using costume changes, taking him from dark colors, armor, and hard fabrics early in the film to light colors and soft, revealing fabrics later on. In *Bram Stoker's Dracula* (1992), costume designer Eiko Ishioka reserved the color red for Dracula. He is the only character in the film to wear this color, except when the plot foreshadows his next victim, who then also appears in red.

MY FAIR LADY (WARNER BROS., 1964)

When Eliza Doolittle (Audrey Hepburn) makes her high-society debut, her effect is electric, due in no small part to the eye-catching attire costume designer Cecil Beaton provided. Her hat is beyond words. Frame enlargement.

Sets, Matte Paintings, and Miniatures

Using sets, **matte paintings,** and miniatures, production designers have an opportunity to create extraordinary visual statements that become an essential part of a film's mise-en-scène. Viewers remember not only what happened in a movie but how a given film *looked*. Memorable screen environments, achieved through set design, can be an indelible part of the film experience.

SATURDAY NIGHT FEVER (RSO, 1977)

John Travolta's famous white suit became an enduring emblem for this movie. Production designer Patrizia von Brandenstein had something very specific in mind: "We wanted to make a world where people came alive on Saturday night, lived for Saturday night, expressed their true selves on Saturday night (the rest of the week was putting in time)." The flamboyant suit expressed the dreams and desires of Tony Manero (Travolta), a working-class kid who lived to dance. Frame enlargement.

**THE
GRAPUATE
(EMBASSY
PICTURES,
1967)**

When Mrs.
Robinson (Ann
Bancroft) se-
duces Benjamin
(Dustin
Hoffman), she
wears a leopard-
print coat, pro-
viding a visual
commentary on
her predatory
behavior. Frame
enlargement.

Inspired by William Cameron Menzies's work, Ken Adam has been one of cinema's most imaginative production designers, designing two films for Stanley Kubrick
(*Dr. Strangelove* and *Barry Lyndon*) and seven of the James Bond films, an enormously popular and influential series. Adam's work on the first Bond production,
Dr. No (1962), established an essential feature of the series: the villain's huge, futuristic headquarters, the designs for which blended serious and comic elements and which
have influenced many films in the action–thriller genre. Built to colossal proportions,
these sets often were constructed on the huge soundstage at Pinewood Studios in
England. So essential has Adam's design become for the series that even productions

**STAR WARS
EPISODE I: THE PHANTOM
MENACE (20TH CENTURY
FOX, 1999)**

Queen Amidala's (Natalie
Portman) costumes create an
exaggerated futuristic spectacle. They blend a variety of
ethnic and regional elements
into a series of outlandish designs. From scene to scene, the
viewer never knows in what
flamboyant manner she will
appear. Frame enlargements.

such as *Goldeneye*, on which he did not work, use Ken Adam–like sets for the villain's lair. Trained like many production designers as an architect, Adam was skilled at using space to create a visual statement. His brilliant set for the war room in *Dr. Strangelove*—where the president and military generals gather to plan for nuclear war—used a giant round table suspended beneath a hanging circular light panel. The design was eye-catching and explicitly metaphoric, a giant poker table around which the president and military had gathered to gamble on the fate of the world.

The tradition of building huge sets to serve as film locations has very deep roots in cinema, going well back to the silent period. One of the most famous examples in early cinema is the mammoth set D. W. Griffith erected to serve as a Babylonian palace in *Intolerance* (1916). The set was so huge that it could accommodate scores of extras, and its most famous feature was six fabulous white elephants, statuary atop glistening marble pillars. Griffith introduced the set to viewers with a dramatic crane shot, with the camera slowly descending through the vast open space of the set. For many years after the film's production, the set remained standing, a reminder of this opulent chapter in the history of production design.

In the 1920s, the German expressionist filmmakers preferred to work on sets because they could design them to perfectly embody a film's style and theme. Fritz Lang's *Metropolis* (1926) used imaginatively designed large-scale sets to evoke a city of the future and, together with Menzies's *Things to Come*, established the tradition in cinema of using set design to visualize ultramodern cityscapes, a tradition that includes the *Batman* movies, *Dick Tracy* (1990), *Blade Runner* (1982), *Robocop* (1987), *Dark City* (1988), *The Fifth Element* (1997), and other films.

Large-scale set design in contemporary film includes the climax of *Saving Private Ryan*, a fierce battle between the Allies and the Germans in the fictitious French town of Ramelle. The Ramelle set, built from scratch, was three blocks long, with multistory buildings and a bridge over a canal, with massive buildings constructed in various states of rubble to simulate the effects of years of war. Because the set enabled the lighting crew to bury its electrical cables beneath the rubble and to hang fixtures inside its buildings, it facilitated many elaborate and complex lighting setups.

BRAM STOKER'S DRACULA (COLUMBIA PICTURES, 1992)

The imaginative design of Dracula's suit of armor evokes a body flayed of its skin. The helmet is batlike, with horned ears and menacing slits for eyes. It is both angel and devil and is rust-colored, a variation of red. Frame enlargement.

Case Study   SCHINDLER'S LIST

Stylized films like *Moulin Rouge* or *The Lord of the Rings* clearly depend on production design for achieving the visual look appropriate for their imaginary screen worlds. But filmmakers who shoot on real locations depend as deeply on the production designer to find locales and to create sets that will further a film's themes and visual tone. Shooting on location is not a substitute for production design. Patrizia von Brandenstein (*Saturday Night Fever, The Untouchables, Working Girl*) has said that her trademark as an artist is building on location.

Steven Spielberg shot on location in Poland for *Schindler's List* (1993), a factually based film about a German factory owner, Oskar Schindler, who used his business connections with the Third Reich to shield Jews from extermination and also to help them escape from the Nazis. Spielberg relied on Polish production designer Allan Starski to find sets and locations for his film, and Starski's work won an Oscar for Best Production Design.

Starski grew up in Lodz, one of the principal locales for the film, and he had worked on numerous films with the great Polish director, Andrzej Wajda, which included a movie that challenged and changed the Communist system in Poland, *Man of Marble* (1976). Prior to *Schindler's List,* Starksi had visualized the Nazi era in a black-and-white film for Wajda (*Korczak*, 1990) and a color film for Agnieszka Holland (*Europa, Europa,* 1991). His experience designing filmic portraits of the World War II era and his intimate knowledge of Lodz locations made him the right choice for the project. Starski felt that strong production design could push a film deeply into the viewer's consciousness. He wanted his sets to work as strong images conveying story, theme, setting, period, and character.

Spielberg gave him great freedom to find locations and design sets and wanted to be surprised by the results, so that he could adapt quickly to them like a documentary filmmaker coming into an uncontrolled situation and having to respond. Spielberg wanted mainly hand-held cameras on the shoot, in order to avoid the glossy look

that equipment like booms and cranes will produce, and Starski designed sets that facilitated a free approach to camerawork. Starski said that for the story to feel real, the camera should be able to move as in a documentary, and his set designs aimed to facilitate this.

Spielberg noted that Holocaust photos had been in black-and-white. Accordingly, working in black-and-white became essential to achieving the film's realist, documentary-like style. This required Starski to design a tonal palette for the film, finding colors and textures that would separate naturally in black-and-white and would be consistent with the kind of naturalism that Speilberg wanted.

Production design requires careful research into period and style, and Starski's designs were based on detailed historical research. He collected numerous books, drawings, and photographs from the period. He studied the Nazi SS architectural plan for the Plaszow forced labor camp (presided over by Kommandant Amon Goeth, played in the film by Ralph Fiennes), and he simplified the design for the film while retaining its essential features, such as the triple-tiered bunks inside the prison houses and the circular, outdoor assembly area (A).

But research is in service to drama, and some of the sets departed from known facts in the interests of theme, idea and style. The windows in the film's depiction of Schindler's factory, for example, were unnaturally big (B) because this enabled Spielberg to convey a visual idea that he thought was essential. Spielberg asked for large windows so that the office overlooking the plant would seem like a paradise to the workers below, and Starski complied even though he knew authentic windows would have been smaller.

Starski's sets and locations were a major factor in the film's ability to sustain a sense of historical realism. About his objectives, Starski emphasized that his design goal was to make viewers believe that what they are watching is real. His success is demonstrated in frame enlargement C, which looks compellingly like a newsreel image and not like something from a Hollywood feature film.

(a)

(b)

(c)

Global nuclear war as a high-stakes poker game. Ken Adam visualized the Pentagon war room in these memorably metaphoric terms for director Stanley Kubrick. Illuminated maps against the back wall track the flights of bomb-laden planes. The hanging circular light panel supplied the source lighting in the scene. Frame enlargement.

USING REAL LOCATIONS   Filmmakers frequently "dress up" real locations to make them part of a film's unified style. Spike Lee's *Do the Right Thing* explores racial tensions that explode into violence on a hot summer's day in a New York City neighborhood. Translating the ideas of heat and tension into a visual design for the film, production designer Wynn Thomas transformed a real location in ways suitable for the film's themes and visual concepts.

While scouting locations, Thomas wanted to find a block with few trees to suggest the absence of shade and the inescapability of the summer heat. When he found the location, the filmmakers had to refurbish the buildings because the brownstone exteriors were decayed. Their fronts were cleaned and repainted in warm browns to evoke the summer climate. Because the action was largely confined to this block, however, Thomas wanted to add additional colors to the setting, and he began to see his own function on the film in terms of finding opportunities to add color to existing scenes. A recurring set of characters are the three men who sit on the street corner under an umbrella and gossip about their neighborhood. The action in these scenes was static; the men sit in their chairs in front of a concrete wall. To add energy to the scene, Thomas wanted to paint the wall red. When he suggested this to director Spike Lee, Lee visualized it as fire-engine red, and that is how it exists in the film. The wall's fiery coloring intensifies the film's mise-en-scène and its underlying concepts of heat, fire, and explosion. By skillfully applying color to the setting, the production designer made the locale an embodiment of the film's themes.

In many films, locations that may seem real and authentic are actually the work of clever production design. The conclusion of *Terminator 2* (1991) is set in a steelworks factory where the evil Terminator hunts his victims and eventually perishes in a vat of molten steel. The location was a real steel mill, but it had been shut down since the mid-1980s and was about to be dismantled. It was totally inoperative, but in the film it had to appear active, with fiery, sparking furnaces. To create the illusion—to make the factory spit fire and glow with molten heat—the filmmakers used lights and colored gels.

To create the vats of molten steel in which the Terminator perishes, the filmmakers placed powerful lights inside the vats and used orange gels over the lights to give a fiery glow. They then covered these with sheets of plastic, on which they placed a mixture of water, mineral oil, and white powder. This created the impression of molten steel

DO THE RIGHT THING (40 ACRES & A MULE, 1989)

Production designer Wynn Thomas came to movies with a background in theatre, which trained him to think conceptually and not to feel confined by a need to be realistic. Color is Thomas' emotional response to the world of the script, and he envisioned this wall as red because it enlivened the scenes at this location and corresponded well with the themes of heat and anger that the film dramatizes. Frame enlargement.

moving in the vat. To simulate flame, they manipulated the lights to create a flickering effect, which they augmented with the use of heaters near the camera to create ripples in the atmosphere, heat waves from the molten steel. In the background, artificially produced sparks added atmosphere and a sense of realism to the scene. With these techniques, the dead factory came alive. The molten steel on screen had a terrifying reality, but the illusion rested on some very basic manipulations of light and color.

On many films, real locations in one region or country may double for those in another, primarily to save money. It's often cheaper to shoot somewhere other than where the story dictates. *From Hell* (2001), about Jack the Ripper, was shot in Prague, Hungary, with East European castles and museums doubling for 19th-century London, the period and locale of the story. In Oliver Stone's *Born on the Fourth of July* (1989), scenes set in Vietnam and Mexico were filmed in the Philippines, and those set in Massapequa, Long Island, were filmed in Texas.

MATTE PAINTINGS   To extend the size and scope of their sets, filmmakers use matte paintings, which are usually placed behind a set or miniature model and may show a distant horizon or landscape. When these are used effectively, viewers do not notice the shift from a three-dimensional set or model to a two-dimensional matte painting.

Matte painting is based on the techniques of **tromp l'oeil**, first practiced by Renaissance painters, which are designed to fool the eye into seeing three dimensions on a

TERMINATOR 2 (TRI-STAR PICTURES, 1991)

Through some basic manipulations of light and color, an abandoned steel mill comes to fiery life in *Terminator 2*. Frame enlargement.

flat surface. The illusion has to be a good one because matte shots are often held on screen longer than other optical effects. Matte paintings are used to establish locations, and in order for the viewer to feel the reality of the locale, it needs to be on screen for some time.

The matte painter has to convey size and scale—sometimes many miles in height or depth—on the flat painted surface. Unlike a cinematographer who uses real light, the painter must draw and color the light effects into the picture—how will the atmosphere look, how will the tonal quality of light change, how will color relate to distance? To fool the eye, all this must be convincing. And the painting technique needs to produce a picture that will resemble a photograph when viewed from six or more feet away.

Some of the greatest matte paintings ever created appear in *Black Narcissus* (1947). The story takes place in the Himalayan Mountains of Nepal, but the film was made indoors on studio sets in suburban London. Nothing was shot on location. And yet the matte paintings of the Himalayas, when conjoined in effects shots with sets and live actors, powerfully establish the remote locale of the story. The tromp l'oeil illusion is very powerful.

A more recent example is provided by *Raiders of the Lost Ark* (1981). The warehouse in the film's last scene is, in fact, a matte painting.

Today, filmmakers often create digital matte paintings in the computer. Light and color effects on a simulated landscape are achieved easily by coloring **pixels** in the computer image. Once the digital matte has been painted by computer, it is composited with the live-action components of a shot. The opening scene in *The Passion of the Christ* (2004), in the Garden of Gethsemane, is a studio set with a digital matte painting representing the sky. The spectacular long shot in *True Lies* (1994) of a Swiss chateau nestled by a lake and the Alps was a digitally composited image employing a computer matte painting of the Alps. In working with digital mattes, filmmakers sometimes face an interesting problem. Light and color in a digital painting can be optimized for style and beauty, whereas live-action imagery cannot. In Martin Scorsese's *Kundun* (1997), for a scene where the Dalai Lama leaves the Tibetan capital in a small boat, digital artists added mountains and a star-filled sky to the background of the shot. The soft, beautiful

BLACK NARCISSUS (RANK ORGANIZATION/ THE ARCHERS, 1947)

The majestic Himalaya Mountains provide the story setting, but the film was shot on indoor sets in suburban London. A series of matte paintings visualized the mountains and valleys surrounding a convent, where the action takes place. Here, one of the nuns rings the morning bell. Everything except the floor of the set on which the actress stands and the bell tower is a matte painting created by Walter Percy Day. Frame enlargement.

moonlight in the matte, however, was better looking than what the cinematographer could achieve with the live-action elements. The digital artists had to redo their lighting, making the light harder and more directional so that it would match the cinematography.

Similar to a matte painting, a **translite** is another common way of creating a distant background for a scene or set. A translite is a photograph, blown up to huge proportions, mounted on a translucent screen, and then lit from behind. A translite provides the dramatic skyline in the background of the set at the climax of *Fight Club* (1999). The translite was composed of several 8 × 10 inch photographs, combined and blown up to a size measuring 130 feet wide by 36 feet tall. This is a very common method for creating landscapes or city views glimpsed outside the windows of indoor sets. The views of the city outside the windows of the Nakatomi Plaza building in *Die Hard* (1988) are translites, as are the views of rural countryside surrounding the home in the first section of *A.I.: Artificial Intelligence* (2001).

Throughout most of cinema history, matte paintings—whether painted traditionally or digitally—have been flat, unmoving components of a scene, typically placed in the background, behind actors, props, and sets. Actors and the camera could not interact with them. Today, by contrast, **3D digital mattes** can be manipulated to simulate the perspective of a moving camera, as in the David Fincher film, *Zodiac* (2007).

NORTH BY NORTHWEST (MGM, 1959)

Roger Thornhill (Cary Grant) carefully approaches the luxurious mansion of arch-villain Philip Vandamm in Alfred Hitchcock's popular thriller. Hitchcock never hesitated to wink at the audience. The house is a matte painting. Frame enlargement.

FIGHT CLUB (20TH CENTURY FOX, 1999)

The dramatic skyline in this scene at the climax is a translite, an enormous photographic image mounted on a translucent screen. A thin netting hung in front of the translite, and as it moved in the air currents on the set, the distant lights of the city seemed to twinkle. Frame enlargement.

Case Study   ZODIAC

Digital tools enable filmmakers to place actors inside virtual sets that look photographically real. *Zodiac* featured extensive digital effects work, but most of this was quite subliminal and subtle. Most viewers do not experience this movie as a showcase for effects. The film is a historical portrait of the Zodiac killer's rampage in the San Francisco area beginning in 1969 and of police efforts to apprehend him. Because the film chronicles true events, Fincher wanted to be as faithful as possible in visually portraying the San Francisco Bay area as it existed in that period.

But the city has changed a great deal, and many of the crime scenes no longer look as they did in the late sixties. So when a location could not be photographed so as to represent this earlier period, the filmmakers used digital methods of creating their locations. A prominent establishing shot of the harbor, showing the ferry terminal, which has the camera flying in over the water as if on a helicopter, was entirely computer generated. Photographs of the area taken from a U-2 spy plane in the early 1970s provided information about buildings in the area that no longer existed, and using methods of **photogrammetry** the filmmakers were able to construct a three-dimensional environment from these photographs. Photogrammetry is a process of tracing lines of sight from the cameras in several photographs and then mathematically plotting their intersections to yield the 3D landscape.

ZODIAC (WARNER BROS., 2007)

A spectacular establishing shot of the San Francisco harbor was entirely computer generated, with the 3D models built from archival photographs to achieve historical accuracy. Frame enlargement.

ZODIAC (WARNER BROS, 2007)

The crime scene at Washington and Cherry Streets was recreated on a studio set, with actors and a few props against a bluescreen. The distant buildings are a 3D digital matte, capable of being rotated to simulate the view of a moving camera. The near police car is a real prop, while the distant one is a CGI element. Frame enlargement.

Such information can assist in **camera mapping** a virtual 3D environment. A good example of this occurs later in the film when the police investigate one of Zodiac's killings at the intersection of Washington and Cherry Streets. The area looks wealthier today than it did in 1969, and so parts of the scene were shot in a studio with actors and a few props against a bluescreen. The surrounding buildings were added through camera mapping as a 3D digital matte. Camera mapping involves projecting a matte painting or photograph onto a 3D wireframe geometry built in the computer that corresponds with the objects in the matte. Period photographs of buildings in the area were projected onto a geometrical rendition of the area. Because the wireframe geometry of the virtual set can be rotated and moved in the computer, once the photographic information has been projected onto this geometry, the digital matte can then be moved and rotated to simulate such things as camera movement. When the camera follows Inspector David Toschi (Mark Ruffalo) as he walks down the street at the intersection (Ruffalo is actually on the bluescreen set), the digital matte background moves according to the camera's changing line of sight. This creates a convincing 3D illusion and enables the actors to credibly interact with a virtual set that is dynamic.

3D digital mattes are used extensively in films today. In earlier periods of filmmaking matte paintings were static and flat. They were two-dimensional areas added to the background of a set. By contrast, the dynamic properties of 3D mattes enable the camera and the actors to credibly interact with them and can make virtual sets seem photographically real and authentic. ■

THE DESIGN CONCEPT

Production designers typically work from a detailed visual concept that organizes the way that sets and costumes are built, dressed, and photographed. Let's examine two examples of this.

Case Study THE LORD OF THE RINGS: THE RETURN OF THE KING

Director Peter Jackson and his team of filmmakers used set and costume design with great care and intelligence to convey the illusion that the fanciful locations in the story were real and authentic. To accomplish this, although the film involved a considerable amount of digital effects, the filmmakers relied on traditional tools of production design—hand-built sets, miniatures, props, and costumes. They believed that these hand-built sets and costumes would establish the reality of the film's fictional worlds and help to anchor the digital effects. As a result, the film achieves a careful and successful balance of digital and traditional design methods. This helps to avoid the cartoonish quality that sometimes results when a film goes overboard on digital effects.

As visual-effects cinematographer Alex Funke noted, "At some subconscious level, viewers can tell when they're seeing real photography."

The size of the film (actually, it was three films because the entire trilogy was shot at once—principal photography lasted over 15 months, and total production time was 4 years!) was unusually large. Three hundred and fifty sets were constructed, plus 68 miniatures, and each of the Middle Earth civilizations visited by the characters required an average of 150 costumes. Forty-two tailors, cobblers, jewelers, and embroiderers worked on these.

The most complicated sets and miniatures were those for the seven-tiered city of Minas Tirith. A lot of the film's action takes place in that city, including a long siege and battle. The art department's conceptual designer, Alan Lee, first visualized the city's design in a series of pencil sketches, in which he pictured the city's culture and its architecture. These were meant to be reminiscent of medieval Europe. The pencil sketches furnished the basis for set and model construction.

The entire city could be constructed only as a miniature model, which would be used in long shots such as the one where Gandalf approaches it on horseback. Before building it, the miniatures unit consulted with cinematographer Andrew Lesnie to work out lighting

(continued)

THE LORD OF THE RINGS: THE RETURN OF THE KING (NEW LINE, 2004)

The city of Minas Tirith is a principal setting of the third film in the trilogy. It appears as a miniature model, as in the scene where Gandalf approaches it on horseback. It also appears as a series of full-scale sets inhabited by live actors, accentuating the authenticity of the setting. Frame enlargements.

design, color, and texture so that shots of the miniature (not photographed by Lesnie) would match with his footage of other scenes.

Miniatures of the city and its selected parts were then built at 1/72 scale, with exacting detail. More than 1000 houses populated the city, with fine detailing in the architecture, yards, and even the interiors. This was necessary because director Peter Jackson wanted elaborate camera moves, swooping across the rooftops, between the buildings, and down through the streets, especially in the battle scene.

These moves were accomplished with a **snorkel lens**. Attached to a camera at the end of a long flexible tube, or snorkel, the lens can be maneuvered through the very small and tight spaces of a miniature model, and it has a pitch-and-roll mechanism that enables it to move in an acrobatic fashion, as if the camera were mounted in an airplane. This produces a convincing illusion of elaborate and extended camera moves. In

many of the shots, the lens passed so close to the miniature that it almost scraped the paint on its surfaces.

Other sequences in the film—Faramir and his men riding out of the city to their deaths, Gandalf and Pippin galloping through the streets—required that live actors interact with their surroundings. Therefore, portions of Minas Tirith also were built as full-scale sets. These were constructed at the huge Dry Creek Quarry (also used for the Helms Deep Castle sets in *The Two Towers*). Building these sets required six months because Jackson wanted the size and scale of a true city and wanted it captured in real photography rather than as a digital effect.

Director Peter Jackson said that he wanted viewers to feel like the film had been shot on actual locations in Middle Earth. He wanted everything on screen to seem real. He knew that digital effects alone could not achieve this. Thus traditional methods of production design became key ingredients in this strategy of visiting Middle Earth "for real." ■

Case Study   THE EVOLUTION OF DESIGN IN CONTEMPORARY SCIENCE FICTION FILMS

Stanley Kubrick's *2001: A Space Odyssey* (1968) had special effects far more sophisticated than any film of its time, and even today they remain impressive. Kubrick's model spaceships were remarkably detailed and three-dimensional, and he used mattes to insert moving images of people into their interiors, glimpsed behind windows. Inside the spacecraft, the production design emphasized blank, white, controlled, and regulated environments that suggested an antiseptic future, in which human behavior was rational and orderly rather than unpredictable and impulsive. The designs spoke to control and authority rather than decay and chaos. Doing so, they embodied the central irony of the film, namely, the way in which people had ceded control over their lives to the mechanical systems and synthetic environments they created. The pessimism inherent in this view would inspire the next generation of science fiction film and give rise to an alternative way of visualizing the future. *Alien* (1979) initiated this alternative visual design.

Ridley Scott, director of *Alien* and *Blade Runner*, has acknowledged the importance and influence of Kubrick's film. *Alien* replicated the antiseptic Kubrick design in selected sets of the spaceship, Nostromo, but in other ways it established a new design template for the next decade and a half of science fiction filmmaking. The Nostromo has two faces. The control rooms and science bays upstairs are gleaming and antiseptic. By contrast, sets in the bowels of the ship—its engine rooms and storage areas—were grimy, dark, and dank. These established a mise-en-scène that became the norm not just for the *Alien* series but for subsequent science fiction films in general,

including such pictures as *Blade Runner* (1982), *Escape from New York* (1981), *Robocop* (1987), and *Dark City* (1998). Locales are dirty and dimly illuminated, with rain- and smoke-filled air. This mise-en-scène might be termed future noir because of its similarity to the gloomy and oppressive look of classic film noir. It has another root in Fritz Lang's *Metropolis* (1927), specifically that film's underground city where the workers reside and labor, a place of enormous machinery, darkness, and congestion.

Alien's future noir transitioned film away from the antiseptic *2001* look, and *Blade Runner's* landmark production design reinforced this shift with its dark vision of a future city. Production designer Lawrence G. Paull based his design concept on the social realities evoked in the film's script and the novel from which it derived. The film is set in a futuristic society where the middle class has relocated to pleasurable off-world colonies, leaving the cities to choke in urban decay, architectural collapse, and overpopulation. The visual design of the film creates a world of clutter, a ghettoized alley environment in which transient, jobless, urban poor jostle together in a mix of nationalities and languages, whereas, far overhead, video monitors and electronic billboards carry corporate advertisements and media messages. High-rise buildings of high-tech opulence coexist with the crumbling alley environment, creating a striking mix of contrasting architectural and social styles and realities. Paull's production design is a stunning translation of the social realities of the story into extremely powerful visual environments.

2001: A SPACE ODYSSEY (MGM, 1968)

Human figures against a sterile, white environment. The production design evokes an antiseptic, sterile future in which human beings have ceded authority to the technological systems they have created. Frame enlargement.

(continued)

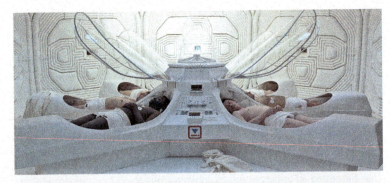

ALIEN, ALIENS (20TH CENTURY FOX, 1979, 1986)

Production design of the spacecraft Nostromo evoked two sharply contrasting environments. The sterile, antiseptic science bays and computer rooms showed the influence of Kubrick's *2001*. But it was the dark, grimy interior of the Nostromo, and its low-key lighting, that helped establish "future noir" in science fiction films for years to come. Frame enlargements.

BLADE RUNNER (THE LADD COMPANY, 1982)

Blade Runner's influential design concept followed the social realities depicted in script and novel. The visual clutter evokes a ghettoized urban future marked by social breakdown. The film's production design brilliantly embodies the novel's themes of entropy and decay.

The noirish, pessimistic mise-en-scène established by *Alien* and *Blade Runner* predominated in science fiction films for the next 15 years. Even fantasies such as the *Batman* series visualize a noir environment. So prevalent had it become that when director Luc Besson and designer Dan Weil were planning *The Fifth Element* (1997), they felt it imperative to break with this style and define an alternative. Accordingly, *The Fifth Element*'s city is seen mostly by day, and has a recognizable Manhattan skyline, and in place of the tangled and shadowy architectural styles in sci-fi noir, it was built on a grid pattern, like Manhattan, with vanishing single-point perspective. This design connects this futuristic cityscape with the recognizable metropolis of today. Innovative and startling in its time, the future noir look had become conventional, a mise-en-scène to avoid for *The Fifth Element*'s filmmakers, interested in creating new imagery. Like cinematographers, production designers study and borrow from the work of their peers, and really successful design concepts in time can become obstacles to fresh creation. ■

PRODUCTION DESIGN AND VISUAL EFFECTS

As with cinematography, production design in contemporary filmmaking overlaps with the creation of digital effects. Many special effects sequences in film blend miniature models with digital mattes or digital animation. In *The Truman Show* (1998), the tall buildings on the main street set of Seahaven, Truman's home town, were only partially constructed as ground-level facades. The upper floors were digital creations, giving the sets greater mass and height than they actually possessed. The same strategy was used to create the huge Coliseum in *Gladiator* (1999). Audiences delight in these manipulations of place and setting and embrace the movie magic that makes them possible.

In some cases, sets, locations, and props may be entirely digital, with live actors inhabiting computer-designed environments. In this case, production design occurs within a digital realm, and films like *Sin City* (2005) and *300* (2006) illustrate this approach. Chapter 8 offers a detailed look at this aspect of digital environment creation within the larger context of cinematic visual effects.

SUMMARY

The term *mise-en-scène* refers to the design and manipulation of all the objects placed in the frame in front of the camera. These typically include sets, costumes, light and color, and the actor's performance. The three chief members of the filmmaking team who are responsible for mise-en-scène are the director, cinematographer, and the production designer. They form a close three-way partnership to arrive at the visual concepts that will underlie and guide the visual design of the film.

Both cinematographer and production designer have the responsibility of helping the director to realize his or her vision for the film. The cinematographer does this by planning lighting and camera setups and assisting in the coordination of color as it will appear in the scene, often by placing colored gelatins in front of the lights. The production designer assists the director, organizing a visual design for the environments of the film. Components of these environments include sets, costumes, mattes, and miniatures. The production designer, in conference with the cinematographer, helps organize the film's color design through the choices that are made about sets and costumes.

The importance of an organizing visual design for a film, agreed on by the director, cinematographer, and production designer, is to facilitate a unified mise-en-scène in which all of the elements—costumes, sets, lights, color, and performance—work together to advance the narrative and to represent mood and atmosphere on screen and to evoke appropriate interpretive and emotional responses by the viewer.

KEY TERMS AND CONCEPTS

art director 86	photogrammetry 100	set decorator 86
camera mapping 101	pixels 98	snorkel lens 102
costumes 89	production design 83	supervising art director 87
costume designer 86	prop master 86	3D digital mattes 99
design concept 83	recces 86	translite 99
matte paintings 91	scenic artist 86	tromp l'oeil 97
miniatures 90	sets 89	unit art director 87

SUGGESTED READINGS

Sybil DelGaudio, *Dressing the Part: Sternberg, Dietrich, and Costume* (Madison, NJ: Fairleigh Dickinson University Press, 1992).

Peter Ettedgui, *Production Design and Art Direction* (Woburn, MA: Focal Press, 1999).

Jane M. Gaines and Charlotte Herzog, eds., *Fabrications: Costume and the Female Body* (New York: Routledge, 1990).

Beverly Heisner, *Hollywood Art: Art Direction in the Days of the Great Studios* (Jefferson, NC: McFarland, 1990).

Andrew Horton, *Henry Bumstead and the World of Hollywood Art Direction* (Austin: University of Texas Press, 2003).

Vincent LoBrutto, *By Design: Interviews with Film Production Designers* (Westport, CT: Praeger, 1992).

4

Acting

OBJECTIVES

After reading this chapter, you should be able to:

- list the basic types of film performers

- differentiate between method and technical approaches to performing

- describe four ways in which performance becomes an element of visual design

- explain how performance elicits interpretive and emotional responses from viewers

The actor is the human element in film. Many components of cinema involve machinery—lights, camera, computers for editing and visual effects—but performance puts the reality of human emotion directly onto screen. Carl Dreyer, one of cinema's greatest directors, felt that the human face was the most important element of cinema, and many filmmakers agree with him. Dreyer's most emotionally intense film, *The Passion of Joan of Arc* (1928), is composed almost entirely of close-ups of faces.

Nearly all film acting derives from the tradition of naturalism established by Constantin **Stanislavsky** (1863–1938), a Russian teacher, actor, and director who emphasized that performance should be anchored in the emotional reality of the script and story, the characters, and their situation. Good film actors aim to find these moments of emotional truth in a scene and to play these as honestly as they can using the tools of their craft—their face, voice, and body. Many of cinema's greatest actors—Barbara Stanwyck, Jean Arthur, Bette Davis, James Stewart, Spencer Tracy, Tom Hanks—are so honest that they don't seem to be acting at all. Their performances become transparent, revealing the characters with exceptional clarity.

Actors have different methods of preparation, but the good ones all try to find the emotional arc in the story and to play that. They search for correspondences between their inner emotional life and the situation of the characters they are playing. A good actor is always "in the moment," speaking and moving in ways that honestly embody the drama at each moment in a scene.

Good film acting has an element of unpredictability, and that is why some directors are uncomfortable with actors. Directors have to turn actors loose in front of a camera, and to get good results, they can't control actors with the mechanical precision that they can exercise over lighting or editing.

But this lack of control is where the artistry of acting resides, where the actor's interpretation of the material arises. During a tender scene between actors Marlon Brando and Eva Marie Saint in *On the Waterfront* (he plays a tough dockworker and ex-boxer; she's a proper young lady), Saint accidentally dropped her white glove on the ground. Brando picked it up, but instead of handing it back to her, he put it on and wore it for the remainder of the scene. Watching the scene, you can see that Saint expects him to give her back the glove. She reaches for it, but Brando holds onto it, plays with it as they talk, and then wears it. It was a spontaneous, unscripted moment that is wonderful because it's true to the scene. It conveys the tenderness in Brando's tough character and the unspoken attraction he feels for her.

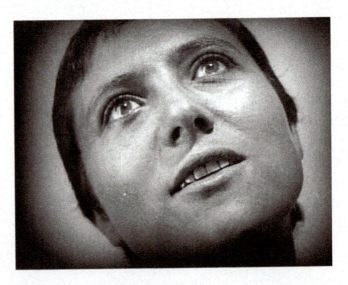

THE PASSION OF JOAN OF ARC (1928)

Director Carl Dreyer felt that the human face was the most cinematic element of all, and he composed this film, about the trial and execution of Joan of Arc, almost entirely as a series of facial close-ups. Most films are not as stylistically radical as this, but Dreyer was right about the special emotional truth that the actor's presence before the camera uniquely conveys. Frame enlargement.

ON THE WATERFRONT (COLUMBIA PICTURES, 1954)
Good acting conveys the emotion of a scene with truth and honesty. Good actors can be so "in the moment" that they create new, un-scripted material in their performance that adds to and improves the scene. Brando's brilliant gesture with the glove reframes all the scene's dialogue with this spon-taneous expression of his character's attraction to Edy (Eva Marie Saint). In this frame enlargement, Saint clearly expects Brando to give back her glove.

ACTING IN FILM AND THEATER

What are the basic characteristics of acting in the cinema, and how does performance style become an element of a film's visual design? Acting in the cinema is a uniquely difficult challenge. While screen acting would seem to bear some similarity with performance in the theater, the differences between acting in the two mediums are significant. Only in live theatre can actors be said to own their performances. Film actors do not own their performances. In cinema, an actor's performance is recon-figured by editing, sound design, music, and other elements of structure. Filmmakers use these elements to redesign performance. While this makes the actor's contribution to the medium of cinema somewhat more ambiguous than it is in theatre, it remains true that narrative cinema is heavily reliant upon good acting. Five characteristics of the motion picture medium make the actor's task different from what it is in theatre: lack of rehearsal; out-of-continuity shooting; the amplification of gesture and expres-sion by the camera and sound recording equipment; the effects of lighting, lenses, and greenscreening; and the absence of an audience.

Lack of Rehearsal

In theater, rehearsal is an essential part of the production process. Actors do not go before a live audience until the play and their performance in it have been thoroughly rehearsed. This enables actors to achieve the right nuances and timing in their performance and to work on, and hopefully resolve, problem areas in the production.

By contrast, in cinema, rehearsal is a relative rarity. For a film production to accord its actors a two-week rehearsal period is a luxury. With thousands of dollars consumed by each day of a shoot, the great expense of film production works against a lengthy rehearsal period. Moreover, the sad fact is that many film directors dislike working with actors and mistrust the actor's contribution to a scene or shot and feel relatively insecure about collaborating with performers to secure the right nuance in a scene. Other directors who are skilled at working with actors, such as Sydney Pollack (*Out of Africa*, 1985), prefer to avoid rehearsing because the time that is available is simply too short. Because of these factors, actors in film lack the elaborate prep time to develop a role and a performance that is standard in theater. Film actors have to hit the ground running, learn their lines, arrive on the set, and play their character for the camera. This is an extraordinary demand, but it is compensated by the fact that, in most cases, the performer is one element among many in the frame, and the filmmaker can use lighting, camerawork, editing, and sound to modulate and strengthen the actor's performance.

Shooting Out of Continuity

Motion pictures are filmed out of continuity. The order in which scenes are filmed is very different from the order in which they appear in the finished film. The sequencing of scenes as they appear in the final finished film is achieved during the process of editing and does not occur during shooting. Economies of time and cost determine the order in which scenes are filmed, the goal being to do it in the most cost-efficient way possible. To save time and money, all scenes occurring in a given location or on a particular set may be filmed at one time, regardless of how they are distributed throughout the narrative. When the filming of all scenes occurring in a given location or set has been completed, the production company moves on to the next set or location to film the scenes that occur there.

The filming of each scene also fails to observe proper continuity. Typically, the **master shot** is filmed first, and the performers run through the entire action of the scene from the master shot camera position. This is generally a framing of the action in medium long shot that shows an overall view of the set and the actors in it. Then the actors recreate bits of the action for inserts and close-ups. These supply what is known as **coverage**, which the editor will intercut with the master shot to create the edited scene. When filming coverage, an actor typically will deliver all his or her dialogue that is recorded from a given camera position, regardless of when it may appear in the scene.

All of this can complicate the actor's job. One of cinema's great actors, Michael Caine, wrote a highly respected book, *Acting in Film*, in which he discussed how strange this way of working might seem to an actor. "If the last scene in a picture takes place outside, you can count on the fact that it will get shot first and then you will move to the studio to shoot all the scenes leading up to it. You might shoot the master in the morning, then rush out in the afternoon to shoot another scene because suddenly the sun came out. Then you have to come back some other time and continue with the morning scene, then perhaps do the medium shot and close-up a week later." One of the most famous acting scenes in U.S. films, the so-called Brother Charlie scene from *On the Waterfront* (1954), dramatically illustrates these challenges. Terry Malloy (Marlon Brando) and his brother Charlie (Rod Steiger) are part of the mob that controls the longshoremen's union on the New York dockyards. Sickened by its corruption, Terry wants to leave the mob, but his brother tries to persuade him to stay because he knows if Terry leaves and turns informant, as the state prosecutor wishes him to do, a mob contract will be issued on his life.

ON THE WATERFRONT (COLUMBIA PICTURES, 1954)

Rod Steiger and Marlon Brando in two camera setups from *On the Waterfront*. In the two-shot, both actors are present, and each can build a performance by playing off the other. In the close-up, however, Rod Steiger (pictured) had to deliver his lines while Brando was absent from the set. The angle of Steiger's eyes makes it seem as if he is looking at Brando, but he had to create his character in the scene under highly artificial conditions. Frame enlargements.

In the scene, a master shot of the two actors alternates with close-ups of each. In the close-ups, actor Rod Steiger had to deliver all his dialogue in the scene that was to be recorded from this camera position, regardless of when the dialogue occurred. Complicating this task, Steiger later reported, was the fact that Brando left the set on the days Steiger had to deliver these lines. Steiger played his scene and projected his emotions to an actor who was not there.

These conditions of filming require that actors be able to recreate their character at any moment in the drama as required by the shooting schedule. By contrast, the performer in the theater has it a bit easier. He or she creates a character sequentially and chronologically in real time, from act one to the last act of the play.

Amplification of Gesture and Expression

On stage, the actor plays to an audience that is sitting some distance away in the auditorium. The actor's gestures and vocal inflections must be large and loud enough to reach the most distant point in the auditorium. By contrast, the film camera and sound equipment act as magnifying instruments, amplifying even the tiniest of gestures and the smallest of vocal inflections. The film actor has to understand when a little is too much and has to know how to precisely calibrate the smallest degree of facial and vocal reaction with the knowledge of how that will play when magnified on the giant motion picture screen.

The acting styles of many famous motion picture stars would be totally inappropriate and ineffective on stage. The quavering, tremulous undertone in Judy Garland's voice is a subtlety of performance that precisely and powerfully conveys the vulnerability of her characters in movies like *The Wizard of Oz* (1939) and *A Star Is Born* (1954). It is a characteristic captured by the motion picture medium in its ability to amplify voice and gesture. Humphrey Bogart's nervous facial tics and James Cagney's trademark shrug of the shoulders, repeated from film to film, helped establish the star presence of these performers. These tiny gestures would be lost if played in a theater auditorium.

Lighting, Lenses, and Effects Work

The film actor has to know not just the emotional arc of the character in the story and how to play this arc but also how to play for the camera's view of the scene. In other words, the actor has to know how the camera is viewing the area within its frame. What is the depth of field? Where is the focal plane of the shot—the area in focus—and where are its borders? Where does the light fall off into shadow *as the camera reads it*, not as it appears to the eye? These considerations complicate how an actor must move on screen.

Performing with these considerations in mind is called *hitting the mark*. Actors hit their mark when they move in precise accord with the constraints imposed by lighting and depth of field. In a complex and highly specific lighting setup, if an actor misses his or her mark by taking one extra step crossing the set, he or she may deliver his or her line from an unexposed or out-of-focus area of the frame. Hitting the mark without letting the audience see this dimension of performance requires tremendous skill from a performer.

How the camera frames a shot will influence the way an actor plays the scene. In a master shot, where the camera is some distance away, actors often will put more energy into their scene and then recalibrate their energy level for closer shots. Some directors, like Japan's Akira Kurosawa, like shooting with multiple cameras running simultaneously so that actors won't feel the need to play to a specific camera and will therefore give a more natural performance.

Director Paul Greengrass used multiple cameras when he made *United 93* (2006), about the aircraft hijacked on 9/11 which crashed in Pennsylvania after a

THE GENERAL (BUSTER KEATON PRODUCTIONS, 1926)

Minimalist acting styles can be highly effective in cinema because the camera is so sensitive it sees everything a performer does, no matter how tiny. Buster Keaton was, with Chaplin, one of the great masters of silent comedy. Unlike Chaplin, though, Keaton avoided expressing emotion. He was called the "Great Stoneface." In situations of chaos and danger, his characters are calm and stoic, their faces unresponsive to crises. This contrast is part of what makes his films so funny. Keaton's extraordinary ability to underplay his characters offers the purest example of the general rule in art that "less is more." Frame enlargement.

THE HOURS (MIRAMAX, 2002)

Makeup effects can be an essential tool of the actor's craft. Many actors, for example, have worn false noses. Orson Welles often did so, and Kevin Spacey in *Beyond the Sea* wore one to better resemble his character, singer Bobby Darin. Playing writer Virginia Woolf, Nicole Kidman wore a prosthetic nose to enhance her resemblance to Woolf. Changing one's appearance in this manner can help the actor to get "in character." Frame enlargement.

struggle onboard between the hijackers and the passengers. By shooting scenes with several cameras and starting each camera at a different time, Greengrass could film an entire, lengthy scene without interruption. He did this for the benefit of the actors, enabling them to stay in character for a much longer time than is the norm in movies shot with only one camera and therefore to give more naturalistic, extended performances.

Visual effects scenes in film impose an additional set of demands on performers. Actors play these scenes in nonexistent sets and often to nonexistent characters, if those characters are effects creations like Godzilla or the bugs in *Starship Troopers*. The actor performs in front of a greenscreen, a blank-colored wall that will be digitally subtracted from the shot, leaving the performer as an element that can be composited with other digital elements in a special effects shot. Much of Keanu Reeves's performance in *The Matrix* (1999) and Liam Neeson's in *The Phantom Menace* (1999) were greenscreened. Acting in a visual effects context will be covered in Chapter 8.

Lack of a Live Audience

On stage, performers play to a live audience, and they typically modify their performance based on the immediate feedback they get from the audience. The film performer does not have this luxury. To shape a performance, the actor has to depend on the guidance of the director, and those who have the reputation of handling actors well—Robert Altman, Woody Allen, Sydney Pollack, Oliver Stone—have consistently attracted the industry's finest performers to their films.

Some film actors periodically do stage work precisely because they value the immediate feedback of a live audience and consider this to be essential to developing their skills as an actor. By contrast, other performers have found film acting more congenial precisely because the audience is absent. Perhaps the most famous example of this is Charlie Chaplin, who had a fear of playing to live audiences and felt more comfortable perfecting his performances in the relative seclusion of the motion picture studio.

Case Study   THE PASSION OF THE CHRIST

Jim Caviezel gives a very intense performance as Jesus, one that helps to create the film's emotional power and appeal. Caviezel's enactment of Christ's agonies during his torture and crucifixion struck many viewers as emotionally true and deeply moving. It is a very physical performance, as Caviezel graphically depicts the anguish of a man whose body is being systematically broken.

But the most powerful moments in the film were digital effects, requiring that Caviezel pretend that some action was occurring when, in fact, it was not. The scourging scene, for example, shows a Roman guard whipping Jesus with a flagrum, a torture device with sheep bones and iron balls attached to the ends of leather thongs. The flagrum tears out large chunks of Jesus' flesh, which the viewer sees on camera as Caviezel pretends to react in pain.

While the action may seem convincing, in fact, it was assembled from many different elements combined digitally, which included the actors' performances. The flagrum was a digital effect. The actor playing the Roman guard did not hold any such device. Instead, he merely pantomimed the action of whipping. The wounds that seem to open on Jesus' back when the flagrum hits also were effects. Caviezel wore a body

prosthesis that contained the wounds, but these were covered digitally in postproduction with fake skin. To simulate the whip strikes, the digital skin was removed, revealing a prosthetic wound.

The climax shows the flagrum tearing out a large chunk of flesh from Jesus' side. Caviezel was not involved in this action. Another actor wore a chest prosthesis with a flagrum attached to it, and the camera filmed the action of it being torn loose. This imagery was then digitally pasted onto Caviezel's body. Caviezel pretended to react to something that was not there.

This provides one measure of the quality of his acting—he convinces us that what we are seeing is actually occurring. Viewed in a naive way, the scene seems to put the actor's performance at the center of the action. In fact, however, the detailed performance provided by Caviezel occurred in very artificial conditions—without a key prop (the flagrum), with the scene's action conveyed in pantomime, and with no on-camera depiction of the climax (the tearing of Jesus' side).

This is the kind of artificiality that is commonly encountered by actors today. They must share the screen with missing elements that are added in postproduction, long after the actor has gone home. ▪

THE PASSION OF THE CHRIST (DIMENSION FILMS, 2004)

Jim Caviezel's performance helps lend credibility to this special-effects scene in which none of the pictured action happened on camera. The whip and the wounding were digital effects added in postproduction. Film actors today increasingly must do their work in relation to nonexistent (digital) props, sets, and even other characters. Frame enlargement.

CATEGORIES OF FILM PERFORMERS

Motion picture actors tend to fall into three categories. There are **stars, supporting players,** and **extras.** The star is an indelible feature of motion pictures. Audiences go to the movies in large part because of the stars who appear in them, and this has been the case for decades. This is true not just for the U.S. film industry but for virtually every film industry in the world.

Stars are distinct from supporting players in that the star commands the largest salary, usually gets top billing, and is foremost in the minds of viewers. Supporting players, as their name implies, have secondary and supporting, rather than starring, roles in a production. By contrast, extras occupy the smallest amount of screen time. Extras are performers who appear incidentally and briefly—pedestrians crossing a street, the crowd watching a baseball game.

Although stars typically get the most attention from viewers, many supporting players have established careers with considerable distinction and have created recognizable screen personalities. Supporting players such as Walter Brennan, for example, developed very distinct screen personalities in such films as *Mr. Deeds Goes to Town* (1936), *Red River* (1948), and *Rio Bravo* (1959). Brennan frequently portrayed cantankerous old coots who came close to stealing the film from the established stars. Other supporting players, such as Danny Aiello and Robert Duvall in more recent years, have approximated star status. Duvall began his career with memorable supporting work in pictures such as *To Kill a Mockingbird* (1962) and *The Godfather* (1972) and, by virtue of his star turn in *Lonesome Dove* (1989), graduated to leading-player status. *The Apostle* (1997), which he wrote, directed, and starred in, showcases his charismatic personality and subtle, nuanced playing style. It is very much an actor-centered film, emphasizing the human emotional drama for which performance, not effects, is essential.

The Star Persona

The **star persona** is the collective screen personality that emerges over the course of a star's career from the motion pictures in which he or she appears. The star persona or on-screen personality is a collective creation generated by many films and is greater than any single performance in an individual film. One of the easiest ways of gauging whether a performer has become a star is to evaluate whether a star persona exists. Names such as John Wayne, Charlie Chaplin, Bette Davis, and Katharine Hepburn instantly call to mind a very fixed, distinct screen personality that exists beyond their individual film appearances and that unifies these.

Stars with long careers evidence interesting changes in their star personas. If one looks at the screen appearances of a performer before they became a star, one often sees a different persona, resulting from atypical roles that the performer, once a star, thereafter avoided. Before he became a star, Humphrey Bogart spent many years as a supporting player in Warner Bros. crime films. In such pictures as *Angels with Dirty Faces* (1938) and *The Roaring Twenties* (1939), Bogart portrayed a series of unsympathetic, if interesting, villains. These roles did not showcase the essential feature of his star persona, namely, Bogart's world-weary romanticism, his cynicism with a heart.

It was not until *High Sierra* in 1941 that Bogart, still playing a gangster in a Warner Bros. picture, became a star in a role that allowed him to embody the kind of bruised romantic idealism that he would go on to perfect in such enduring pictures as

CASABLANCA (WARNER BROS., 1942); THE AFRICAN QUEEN (UNITED ARTISTS, 1951)

Evolution of a star performer. Two phases of Humphrey Bogart's career: the romantic leading man (with Ingrid Bergman) in *Casablanca* and the player of grizzled, quirky, neurotic characters, as with Katharine Hepburn in *The African Queen*. Frame enlargements.

The Maltese Falcon (1941), *Casablanca* (1942), *To Have and Have Not* (1944), and *Key Largo* (1948). In Bogart's later career, his star persona underwent another change. In the late 1940s and early 1950s, he stopped playing romantic leading men and turned toward interesting character types in such pictures as *The Treasure of the Sierra Madre* (1948), *The African Queen* (1951), and *The Caine Mutiny* (1954). Gone from these pictures were his romantic star qualities. In their place was a series of neurotic, quirky, and eccentric characterizations.

The greatest stars give their pictures an electricity and charisma that ordinary performers can't provide. Consider Julia Roberts and the excitement of her star-making performance in *Pretty Woman* (1990). When she is on screen, she dominates the scene.

ERIN BROCKOVICH (COLUMBIA TRISTAR, 2000)

As a star vehicle, this film provides a showcase for Julia Roberts' screen personality and charisma. She commands the camera's attention with her beauty and force of personality. Frame enlargement.

THE SEARCHERS (WARNER BROS., 1956)

After years of struggling in low-budget B Westerns, John Wayne achieved stardom in *Stagecoach* (1939) and during the next four decades projected a powerful masculine image characterized by physical strength, moral dignity, fair play, and stubborn independence. Directors John Ford and Howard Hawks appreciated Wayne's physical power on screen and considered it essential to the making of a good Western. Wayne's physical presence easily dominates the frame. Frame enlargement.

Her star performance carries *Erin Brockovich* (2000), a picture for which she won an acting Oscar. In *Ocean's Eleven* (2001), her character doesn't appear until halfway through the film, and director Steven Soderbergh was counting on her to make a strong impression on the viewer very quickly, and she did. There is an indefinable quality of charisma that stars provide, and each of these pictures is a vehicle for the star.

Some stars have a greater acting range than others. John Wayne tended to play the same type of characters from film to film. His acting range is quite small compared with Robert De Niro's, but this is not to say that he was a poor actor. His performances in *Red River* (1948), *The Quiet Man* (1952), *The Searchers* (1956), *The Cowboys* (1972), and many other films are carefully crafted, and his power and charisma are essential components of those films.

TRAINING DAY (WARNER BROS., 2002)

Playing against type can be very effective but also risky. Sometimes audiences don't want to see their stars in a different kind of role. Denzel Washington has tended to play very courageous and moral characters. Here, though, he plays an evil, corrupt cop and gives the role a savage intensity. Washington's daring switch of character, and the brilliance of his performance, had a sensational effect on the film's critical and box-office performance. For the role, he earned an Oscar for Best Actor. Frame enlargement.

Other stars, such as Meryl Streep, have an extraordinary range. She has played an actress and country-western singer in *Postcards from the Edge* (1990), a distraught Australian mother accused of murdering her baby in *A Cry in the Dark* (1988), a Polish woman who has survived internment in the Nazi concentration camps in *Sophie's Choice* (1982), a Danish author who establishes a life in Nairobi in *Out of Africa* (1985), a whitewater adventurer in *The River Wild* (1994), and an Italian-American housewife living in the midwestern farm belt in *The Bridges of Madison County* (1995).

Even stars who can play a range of characters often project a relatively consistent personality from role to role. Robert De Niro, for example, is known for his psychopaths in such films as *Taxi Driver* and *GoodFellas*, whereas Dustin Hoffman tends to play more introverted, withdrawn characters who have trouble expressing themselves, in films such as *The Graduate* (1967), *Midnight Cowboy* (1969), *Hero* (1992), and *Rain Man* (1988).

What finally counts in cinema is not acting range, but the magnetism of the actor's personality before the camera. John Wayne is a great film actor, as are Streep, De Niro, and Hoffman, despite the differences in their range.

CLOSE-UP

Meryl Streep

Born in 1949, Meryl Streep found rapid success and acclaim as a film actress and currently holds the record for the most Academy Award nominations. She has also won numerous Golden Globe Awards, Emmy Awards, and Screen Actors Guild Awards. As these honors suggest, many professionals in the film and television industries view her as one of the finest—perhaps the finest—actors currently working in motion pictures. The film industry today does not produce many films with a female lead at their center, and yet Streep has sustained a long and distinguished career in the face of this obstacle. She has worked regularly and often, and has supplemented her film roles with performances on television and the stage.

Her first film roles in the 1970s, as supporting characters, were in very prominent films by major directors. These included Fred Zinnemann's *Julia* (1977), Michael Cimino's *The Deer Hunter* (1979), Woody Allen's *Manhattan* (1979), and Robert Benton's *Kramer vs. Kramer* (1979). She had an Oscar nomination as Best Supporting Actress for *The Deer Hunter* and won in that category for *Kramer vs. Kramer*.

In the next decade, she became a major star, playing lead roles in a variety of highly prestigious films, many of which were historical dramas that showcased her exceptional command of language,

dialect, and diction. These included *The French Lieutenant's Woman* (1981), *Sophie's Choice* (1982), *Out of Africa* (1985), *Ironweed* (1987), and *A Cry in the Dark* (1988). She won an Oscar for Best Actress for her role in *Sophie's Choice* as a Polish mother forced by a Nazi officer to choose which of her children will be executed.

Most of her roles in the 1980s were in serious and very literate dramas, and beginning in the 1990s she expanded her range of characters by playing flamboyant villains and comic characters in movies that had a more popular orientation. Her comic villains in *She-Devil* (1989) and *Death Becomes Her* (1992) were startling changes of pace, as was her rugged, white-water-rapids-shooting character in the action film, *The River Wild* (1994). But she kept returning to serious drama for her best work, as in Clint Eastwood's *The Bridges of Madison County* (1995), as an Iowa housewife vaguely unhappy in her marriage who falls in love with a visiting photographer. In *The Hours* (2002), she costarred with two other outstanding contemporary actors—Nicole Kidman and Julianne Moore—in a finely directed and performed story of three generations of women coping with despair.

Streep formed a very productive relationship with director Mike Nichols on the films *Silkwood* (1983), *Heartburn* (1986), *Postcards from the Edge* (1990),

THE DEVIL WEARS PRADA (20TH CENTURY FOX, 2007)

Streep's performance as fashion magazine editor Miranda Priestly added another powerful character to her portfolio. While Miranda is not a villain, she is an unsympathetic character, one of many that Streep has bravely played. Many stars are reluctant to play characters they know the audience will not like. Other films in which she does not try to elicit the audience's favor include *Rendition* (2007) and *The Manchurian Candidate* (2004). Frame enlargement.

and *Angels in America* (2003), a television mini-series in which she played four different characters and won an Emmy Award. Nichols also directed her on the stage in a production of Chekhov's *The Seagull*. She has lent her voice to cartoon characters in the television series *The Simpsons* and *King of the Hill* and in film, *The Ant Bully* (2007). She also has a splendid singing voice, which can be heard in *Postcards from the Edge* and *A Prairie Home Companion* (2006).

Off-screen Streep has lent her name and prestige to various environmental, health, family, and arts charities and benefits, remaining extremely active in social and community causes.

At a time when major roles for women in Hollywood film are in short supply, Streep has not only endured; she has prospered and has accumulated a significant body of work, enduring films that define her as one of the screen's great performers. ■

ANGELS IN AMERICA (HBO, 2003)

As a performer, Meryl Streep has few limits. She is equally adept at comedy and drama, and there seems to be no role she cannot play. She plays four roles in this film, including the elderly rabbi pictured here. Frame enlargement.

METHOD AND TECHNICAL APPROACHES TO PERFORMING

In creating a character, film actors today tend to use a blend of **method** and **technical** approaches. For the sake of clarity, these approaches will be discussed in distinction to one another, although in practice most actors use some elements of both. Method acting grew out of acting teacher Lee Strasberg's workshops and exerted a powerful influence over a generation of actors in U.S. motion pictures beginning in the 1950s. This generation included Marlon Brando (*A Streetcar Named Desire*, 1951; *On the Waterfront*, 1954); James Dean (*Rebel without a Cause*, 1955); Paul Newman (*The Left-Handed Gun*, 1958; *Cat on a Hot Tin Roof*, 1958), and others. They brought to their roles a more reflective psychological dimension than had existed in preceding decades of screen acting. In a performance by Brando or Newman, one senses a reservoir of thought and feeling within the character, a rich inner life, that is only partly disclosed through dialogue and gesture. Their playing style was emotionally rich and projected volatile and at times contradictory psychological dynamics.

The method involved using emotional recall to play a role. Called on to portray fear, anxiety, sadness, or other emotions, the method actor searches his or her personal experience for moments when these emotions were experienced and tries to reimagine the situations that led to those feelings and internally recreate them. Re-experiencing the emotion, or one similar, becomes the basis for its performance. The method actor searches for the relevant personal experiences that will enable him or her to feel the character.

Marlon Brando is one of the supreme exemplars of this approach. One of his greatest performances is in Bernardo Bertolucci's *Last Tango in Paris* (1972). During a lengthy scene in the middle of the film, shot largely in a single take to accentuate the continuity of Brando's performance, his character reminisces about his youth and his parents. Brando improvised the scene on camera and largely drew on his own life to flesh out the memories of the character he was playing, as he did in other scenes of the picture. The result is a performance of authentic emotion that shocks and disturbs the viewer with its candor.

An alternative to the method is a more technical approach. Here, instead of basing a character on personal emotional memories, the actor plays the script and creates the character by performing the behavior and dialogue called for in the scene. The classic Hollywood actors of the 1930s and 1940s represent this approach, perhaps none better than James Cagney. Cagney was one of the industry's finest actors and possessed an impressive range, excelling in gangster movies (*The Public Enemy*, 1931; *The Roaring Twenties*, 1939), light comedy (*The Strawberry Blonde*, 1941), and the musical (*Yankee Doodle Dandy*, 1942).

In his autobiography, he discussed one of his most famous scenes in *White Heat* (1948), where, as gangster Cody Jarrett, he goes berserk in a prison cafeteria on learning of his mother's death. Cagney wrote his autobiography after the method performers had arrived in the 1950s, and his discussion contains an implied criticism of that approach. He recalled being asked by reporters whether he prepared himself in some special way for the extraordinary emotional and physical outburst he displays in the scene. He said that he didn't psych himself up in any special way and (here was the implied criticism) that he didn't understand actors who felt the need to emotionally pump themselves up in order to do a scene. Cagney said that he remembered seeing some lunatics in an asylum when he was a boy and tried in the scene to imitate the way they looked and sounded. While Cagney admitted drawing on personal experi-

In this single, lengthy shot, Marlon Brando used details from his own childhood to create his character in *Last Tango in Paris*. The raw emotional candor of this performance remains unsurpassed in his career. Frame enlargement.

ence to play the scene, it is significant that he did not phrase it in emotional terms. He did not try to recall the emotions he felt as a boy viewing people in the asylum or to imagine what those so confined must have felt. He merely tried to imitate some of the inmates' gestures and behavior patterns. He created the role from the outside in rather than from the inside out. Cagney took pride in maintaining that the pro knows how to do a scene without extensive "psyching up" and just goes and does it.

Prior to the arrival of the method performers, most Hollywood acting tended to be of this sort, extremely accomplished but without excessive psychologizing about a character's motivations and personality. It was in this context that the more introspective approach of Brando, Newman, and their generation of actors seemed so revolutionary. While today it may seem less so, that is because the playing styles of so many contemporary actors—Johnny Depp, Brad Pitt, Sean Penn—owe much to the 1950s method actors.

WHITE HEAT (WARNER BROS., 1948)

Exemplifying a technical approach to acting, James Cagney, as gangster Cody Jarrett, goes beserk on learning of his mother's death. The scene is a classic in the history of American screen performance. Frame enlargement.

THE PERFORMER AS AN ELEMENT OF VISUAL DESIGN

Now that the fundamentals of motion picture acting are clear, it is time to examine how performance style becomes an element of mise-en-scène. Filmmakers can treat actors as design elements in several ways: by emphasizing a performer's unique body language, by choreographing performance and regulating its intensity, by transforming the performer into a visual "type," and finally, by relating the performer to additional structural elements of design.

Unique Body Language

Many stars have distinctive, highly identifiable ways of moving. Denzel Washington, for example, has a centered, rolling gait that projects calmness and power. Filmmakers often capitalize on the body language of an established star so that it becomes part of the visual design of a film. John Wayne had a peculiar manner of walking that, in time, became famous. A large and very graceful man, his feet were quite small in relation to his bulk, and he developed an easy, fluid gait that riveted attention—such a large man moving so easily on small feet. Actress Katharine Hepburn (with whom he worked in *Rooster Cogburn*, 1975) was very impressed by his light movements. Wayne's graceful, catlike movements became a justly famous part of his screen persona, evident in scores of films over many decades. In *Red River*, Wayne walks through a herd of cattle, and they scatter to get out of his way. It's an impressive thing to see.

In 1976, at the end of his career, Wayne appeared in *The Shootist*, a film with strong biographical elements in which he played an aging gunfighter dying of cancer, much as Wayne, the actor, would soon do. At the climax of the film, Wayne's character, J. B. Books, agrees to meet three gunfighters for a shoot-out in the town saloon. Wayne enters the saloon, and the film's director, Don Siegel, privileges his walk by letting Wayne traverse the length of the saloon from the front door in the background to the bar in the foreground. Siegel lets the moment play without cutting, enabling the viewer to observe and enjoy the walk one final time in what was to be his last film.

By emphasizing the unique body language of its star, the visual design of *The Shootist* tailors its mise-en-scène to blend Wayne's screen persona and the character of J. B. Books into a seamless whole. It does so most explicitly during the opening credit sequence, when Books is introduced through clips from earlier John Wayne Westerns. In each clip, Wayne gracefully performs some physical action—galloping a horse across a river, diving off a wagon under gunfire, snatching a thrown rifle from midair. The clips span 20 years of filmmaking, their images encoding a history of John Wayne's physical performances, a history that in *The Shootist* becomes the identity of the character he plays.

Charlie Chaplin is another performer whose films center on his unique and expressive body language. Chaplin's famous exit at the conclusion of his pictures showed him walking away from the camera with his back to it, waddling in his famous splay-footed fashion and twirling his cane. Chaplin's camerawork was extremely simple and functional. He avoided extravagant camera movements and fancy angles, preferring, instead, to use the camera as a passive observer of his pantomime performance, believing, correctly, that what he did in front of the camera was more important than how the camera itself might move to comment on the action of a scene. The mise-en-scène of his films centers on his body language and costume.

FUNNY FACE (PARAMOUNT, 1957)

Born in Belgium and trained as a ballet dancer, Audrey Hepburn became one of Hollywood's biggest stars in the 1950s. With her lean, dancer's body and natural beauty, she commanded the screen with exceptional whimsy and charm. She was very adept at physical comedy, and her movements were light, airy, and graceful, even when a scene called on her to play clumsy. Hepburn was a unique personality on screen in the period, and even when playfully costumed as she is here, her star appeal shines through. Frame enlargement.

Choreographing Expression

Filmmakers regulate acting style in keeping with their design objectives for a film. This often entails a deliberate placement of the performers in relation to the camera. Alfred Hitchcock, for example, precisely choreographed his performers, and they had very limited freedom to bring material of their own devising that affected the content and design of Hitchcock's shots. During a love scene in *Notorious* (1946), in one extended shot Cary Grant and Ingrid Bergman walk from a balcony to the interior of a hotel room, and Grant picks up a telephone and converses with his boss. Hitchcock insisted that Grant and Bergman maintain an embrace, kiss, and nuzzle during the length of the shot as they walked across the set, and they were filmed by a moving camera. The maneuver was extremely difficult to execute. It required that the actors maintain a very unnatural posture, but Hitchcock wanted the visual effect of the sustained embrace and the camera's intimate involvement with the lovers.

A filmmaker also can regulate performance by controlling its degree of emotional expression. At one extreme, severe restraint can work to orient the viewer to surface rather than depth. *Citizen Kane* (1941) revolves around the mystery of how Charles Foster Kane came to be the man he was. In a crucial scene from childhood, where he is taken from his parents to be raised by a rich guardian, director Orson Welles has actress Agnes Moorehead play Kane's mother in an opaque and impenetrable way. Her facial expressions and voice are flat and unmodulated, even when the character appears in close-up framings. As a result, the viewer can only attend to the surfaces of this character—her face, her posture—as Moorehead's performance establishes these. It is very difficult to "read" beyond them, to see into the character, to infer her motives and feelings in abandoning her child and to understand the nature of Kane's relationship with his parents. This difficulty helps state the film's overall theme and design, which stress that Charles Foster Kane is, in fundamental ways, unknowable. The impenetrability of the mother deepens the mystery of Kane. The acting style expresses the theme that is evoked elsewhere in the film by low-key lighting, camera movement, and editing.

French director Robert Bresson was a master filmmaker who worked from a set of unique ideas about the proper role of actors in cinema. He generally preferred that his performers be empty vessels. He regarded his performers not as actors but as models who should pose in an emotionally flat manner for the camera. He avoided using actors whose facial expressions and gestural styles projected specific emotions. He wanted his actors to be recessive, passive, and neutral in their playing style, and he directed them to speak in a monotone. By reducing all stylistic ornamentation, he wanted to illuminate the interior, spiritual lives of the characters. Conventional acting, he felt, turned cinema into theatre and did not get at the interior realities he wanted to explore.

Bresson explained his creative philosophy in a series of memos published in book form as *Notes on Cinematography*. His preference for relatively emotionless acting is very different from the norms of U.S. filmmaking, which tend to emphasize acting that communicates a great deal of emotional information. Bresson's style, however, has influenced U.S. filmmakers. The end of Bresson's *Pickpocket* (1959) shows the titular thief, now in jail, finally acknowledging the grace a woman's love has brought into his life. By acknowledging this, he achieves a kind of spiritual redemption. Director Paul Schrader was so impressed with this ending and its emotional restraint that he recreated it as an **homage** in two of his own films, *American Gigolo* (1980) and *Light Sleeper* (1992). (An *homage* is a reference in a film to another film or filmmaker.)

Compare Bresson's approach with the expression on Chaplin's face in the concluding close-up of *City Lights* in Chapter 1. Chaplin conveys a great deal of

CITIZEN KANE (RKO, 1941)

Mrs. Kane (Agnes Moorhead) gazes at the young son she is sending away and whom she will never see again. As directed by Orson Welles, Moorhead's expression is un-readable. Is the character sad? Relieved? What is she feeling? By making the expression un-readable, Welles plays against the viewer's desire to under-stand the character. Doing so, he treats the relationship of Mrs. Kane and her son as a mystery. Frame enlargement.

A MAN ESCAPED (GAUMONT, 1956)

Bresson said that he liked keeping actors in the dark about the nature of the film they were making. The less actors knew, he felt, the better. He was a radical filmmaker. His working methods and goals were quite unusual. By stripping the ornamentations of theatre from an actor's performance, by directing them *not* to project emotion, Bresson aimed to illuminate the poetry of a person's interior life. The film portrays the efforts of Fontaine (Francois Leterrier), a French Resistance fighter in World War II, to escape from his Nazi captors. Characteristic of Bresson's lack of interest in melodrama, the film's title—in past tense—removes the elements of surprise and suspense from the narrative. Frame enlargement.

emotional information about his character, and consequently, his expression is richer. In each case, though, the playing style results from specific decisions made by the filmmakers. These differences are tied to the respective mise-en-scènes of the films and the creative approach of their directors. In each case, the actor's level of expression becomes a crucial element in the design of the film.

Many films feature more extroverted playing styles. Much comic acting depends on exaggerating a character's responses and emotions. Jim Carrey (*The Mask*, 1994) or Mike Myers (*Austin Powers*, 1997) are funny because their reactions are disproportional to the situation in which the character finds himself. But outside of comedy there are important examples of this playing style. Akira Kurosawa's *Rashomon* (1950) is set in twelfth-century Japan and deals with a rape and murder, the circumstances of which are told differently by all the witnesses who recall it. As they recall the crime, they assume extremely exaggerated and flamboyant acting styles. Actors in the film gesture wildly, laugh hysterically, and contort their faces into extreme emotional expressions.

Many viewers are struck by what seems to be a flamboyantly melodramatic and excessive acting style. In part, this was precisely Kurosawa's intention. In *Rashomon* he wanted to recover some of the visual aesthetics and performance styles of the silent cinema. Acting in early silent films was coded in uniquely different terms than those that would become established during the sound period.

One scholar has termed early silent performance style *histrionic* because it was based on a series of precise and exaggerated gestures. The histrionic gesture for fear was to extend the arm palm out and clutch the throat with the other hand, whereas shame was indicated by covering the face with one's hands or arms. The histrionic style of silent film melodrama was replaced in sound films by a more naturalistic style, incorporating a more subtle and wider range of gestures based on concepts of realism and naturalism. But Kurosawa had his performers overplay their roles as if they were in a silent film.

Filmmakers regulate expression to integrate the actor into the design structure of a shot. Acceptable modulations range from the extremely minimal, as in the films of

RASHOMON (1950)
Exaggerated performance styles may deliberately break with traditions of naturalism and realism. Toshiro Mifune's mannered acting enables director Kurosawa to recover the visual aesthetics of silent cinema. Frame enlargement.

Bresson or the acting of Clint Eastwood, to the histrionically exaggerated, as in the films of Kurosawa, early silent cinema, or popular comic performers.

Typage

A third way in which performance style becomes an element of mise-en-scène is through the employment of **typage**. Here, actors and their performances are visually stylized, often in extreme terms, to suggest that the character embodies a particular social or psychological type or category. This visual encoding of social or psychological information often predominates in a film's mise-en-scène.

SOCIAL TYPAGE   Social typage was a major feature of classic Soviet filmmaking in the 1920s. Directors such as Sergei Eisenstein cast performers whose physical appearance could be made to suggest the more abstract characteristics of social class. In Eisenstein's *Battleship Potemkin* (1925), the sailors on board the battleship who mutiny against their oppressive officers are embodiments of working-class virtue. The actors portraying these sailors are beefy, muscular, and handsome. The actors portraying the ship's officers have unappealing physiques, alternately thin and wizened or obese. A master of visual caricature, Eisenstein correlated the appearance of actors, their faces and bodies, with more general ideas about social identity.

A recent instance of this kind of visual caricature is evident in *Starship Troopers* (1997), in which the military officers wear Nazi-like uniforms and insignias and are filmed in stark, geometric patterns to express the film's underlying theme that war makes fascists of everyone. Like many of the combat veterans in the film, Rasczak (Michael Ironside) is an amputee with a mechanical appendage, making the character an emblem of the state's war machine.

In Sergio Leone's epic Western *Once upon a Time in the West* (1969), the spread of corrupt business practices into the undeveloped American West is symbolized in the bone cancer that has twisted and crippled the body of the wealthy railroad baron, J. P. Morton (Gabriel Ferzetti). Morton's twisted body is given significant visual attention in the scenes

BATTLESHIP POTEMKIN (1925); ALEXANDER NEVSKY (1936)

Social typage in the films of Eisenstein. In *Battleship Potemkin*, a snarling naval officer personifies the evil of the old regime. He commands a firing squad about to execute the film's noble heroes. In *Alexander Nevsky*, helmets give the evil Teutonic Knights a sinister and dehumanized appearance. Frame enlargements.

where he appears. In Sylvester Stallone's *Rocky IV* (1985), a political belief that Soviet communist society dehumanizes its citizens is expressed through the social typage of Rocky's Soviet opponent, Drago (Dolph Lundgren), who has a robot-like appearance and behaves as a merciless fighting machine.

PSYCHOLOGICAL TYPAGE   Psychological typage can be seen in the **expressionist** style of filmmaking that has its origin in 1920s German cinema. Expressionist films such as *The Cabinet of Dr. Caligari* (1919) and *Nosferatu* (1922) present grotesque characters, pathological emotional states, and fantastic settings in which the visual distortions were indicators of twisted minds or spirits. The expressionist style entered U.S. cinema in the 1930s in the cycle of horror films made at Universal Pictures. The physical deformities in characters such as Frankenstein's monster externalize their warped inner humanity.

The *Night of the Hunter* (1955), a psychological thriller about good and evil focusing on a maniacal preacher's pursuit of two young children who know the whereabouts of a fortune, used expressionist pictorial and performance styles. Actor Robert Mitchum's contorted face intentionally recalls the expressionism of early German cinema. Conceived in homage to this tradition is the villain Max Schreck (Christopher Walken) in *Batman Returns* (1992). The character is named for the German actor who played the vampire in *Nosferatu*, and he sports a hairpiece that makes him look like Rotwang, the mad inventor in *Metropolis* (1926).

Performance style, then, can be manipulated to evoke ideas of social category or psychological condition. Soviet political typage evoked the idea of the virtue of the proletariat, whereas the visual typage operative in expressionist styles elicits the anxieties associated with the supernatural, madness, or psychological disturbance. Warren Beatty's production *Dick Tracy* (1990) illustrates a combination of psychological and social typage. The visual style of the film is borrowed from comic strips, and the grotesquely

NOSFERATU (1922); FRANKENSTEIN (UNIVERSAL STUDIOS, 1931)

Contorted bodies, twisted psyches in the German expressionist style. In Germany, the vampire killer in F. W. Murnau's version of Dracula. In Hollywood, the expressionist style used in the horror classic *Frankenstein*. Frame enlargements.

exaggerated features of the gangsters, in comparison with Dick Tracy's clean-cut good looks and the virtuous appearance of his lover, Tess Trueheart, are a powerful shorthand way of visually expressing the social Darwinian view that criminals are mentally deformed and sick and that the law-abiding are virtuous and emotionally sound.

Visual Design of Performance

Filmmakers use elements of visual design in ways that affect how a viewer understands a character at given moments in the story. In such ways, the performer is integrated as one component in the visual design of shots and scenes. It is for this reason that an actor in cinema is not the author of their performance as in theatre. In cinema, too many

THE DARK KNIGHT (WARNER BROS., 2008)

The Joker's disfigured face points to his disfigured mind. Heath Ledger's performance internalizes the visual typage suggested by the makeup in ways that enable him to portray the Joker as a grotesque psychological monster. Frame enlargement.

THE SILENCE OF THE LAMBS (ORION PICTURES, 1991)

The lighting of Hannibal Lecter (Anthony Hopkins) reverses the normative distribution of shadows on the human face to give him an eerie and unnatural appearance. Hopkins's performance accentuates Lecter's disturbing qualities, but the lighting and composition (he looks directly into the camera) enhance and intensify the performance, integrating the actor into the shot's visual design. Frame enlargement.

other variables come into play to structure, rework, or revise the performance. In the expressionist style of early German films, low-key lighting enclosed grotesque characters in a surrounding sea of darkness. The lighting adds to the performance styles used in those films, accentuating the creepiness of the characters and situations. In a somewhat different fashion, the lighting in *The Silence of the Lambs* (1991) makes serial killer Hannibal Lecter look especially creepy. Placing a light below his face reverses the normative distribution of shadows. Actors are virtually always lit from an elevated angle, and reversing this practice gives the character an unnatural appearance.

A love scene in *L.A. Confidential* (1997) between Lynn Bracken (Kim Basinger) and Bud White (Russell Crowe) was filmed with warm amber light. A subsequent argument between the characters was shot in harder, bluish light. The color design visualizes a tone that extends the emotions of the characters as conveyed by the actors. The two are not separable. The viewer's emotional impression of the scenes is a product of both the performances and the color design. By being compatible with the psychological mood of the scenes, the color design externalizes the emotional quality of the performances and the shift from passion to psychological distance in the characters.

Consider another example. In *Citizen Kane* (1941), the title character, newspaper owner Charles Foster Kane, announces to his employees that his newspaper will be guided by a series of principles. Among these are truthfulness in reporting and a commitment to look out for the interests of the poor. Kane announces these by leaning over his desk. As he does so, his face goes into the shadows. (The scene occurs at night and is lit using low-key setups.)

Because of the lighting, the viewer has an ambivalent response to Kane's declaration of principles. The viewer suspects that he doesn't really mean them. On the one hand, this conviction is based on the understanding of Kane that has been developing

CITIZEN KANE (RKO, 1941)

Lighting and composition add information to an actor's performance to make it part of a film's visual design. Charles Foster Kane reads his declaration of principles but steps into the shadows as he does so, enhancing the viewer's suspicion that he is insincere. Frame enlargement.

through the narrative and from the performance of Orson Welles, who masterfully suggests Kane's mercurial, opportunistic, and ever-changing personality. On the other hand, however, the viewer's ambivalence arises from the lighting design. The shadowing of Kane's face as he reads the principles extends and comments on his opportunism and lack of sincerity. Performance style and visual design become part of a unifying whole called *mise-en-scène*.

PERFORMANCE, EMOTION, AND THE VIEWER'S RESPONSE

As with other areas of film structure, the performance component includes stylistic transformations of human behavior and feeling but also establishes clear references and correspondences with that behavior. Viewers evaluate performances and characters by drawing comparisons with their knowledge of human behavior and what seems to be a plausible, likely, or consistent response by a character in a scene's dramatic or comedic situation. These judgments are based on standards derived from real-life experience, as well as expectations based on genre or other storytelling conventions.

Experimental evidence indicates that people are extremely skilled at evaluating and identifying the emotions that can be conveyed through gesture and facial expression. Many of these emotions are context-dependent. Certain expressions have particular meanings in given cultures. Other kinds of expressions, though, seem to cross cultures and function as universal signs of human emotion (in particular, expressions associated with the emotions of fear, anger, happiness, sadness, surprise, and disgust). A viewer can watch a movie from another country or culture and easily identify from the actors' expressions many of the emotions being conveyed in the scene. This universal aspect of facial expression, and the camera's ability to emphasize it, are major reasons for the cinema's appeal throughout the world and across cultures.

Interpretive and Emotional Responses by Viewers

Because the facial and gestural components of performance invite comparisons with real-life emotions, situations, and circumstances, they elicit both interpretive and emotional responses from viewers. Interpreting the performance, a viewer asks whether the character's response is plausible, likely, convincing, and/or proportional to the situation. These are cognitive judgments that influence emotional responses. In many older movies, characters behave quite differently than in contemporary cinema. In Hitchcock's *Shadow of a Doubt* (1943), for example, a young woman and a police detective, who have just met only a few days ago, declare their love for one another and talk of marriage. Despite the evident sincerity of the actors' performances, many contemporary viewers find this turn of events implausible. It doesn't square with their understanding of how people under those circumstances would behave. This judgment, in turn, underlies such viewers' decision not to invest their emotions in the scene.

On the other hand, if viewers decide that a character's behavior and an actor's performance are appropriate and convincing, given the narrative circumstances, they may go on to share in the character's emotions by way of empathy. Empathy is a willingness to understand a character's feelings and even, under the right circumstances,

THE SILENCE OF THE LAMBS (ORION PICTURES, 1991)

Watching *The Silence of the Lambs,* viewers react to Clarice Starling (Jodie Foster) and serial killer Hannibal Lecter (Anthony Hopkins) by forming complex cognitive, emotional, and moral judgments about the characters. The elements of structural design guide viewers in forming these judgments. Frame enlargements.

to feel similar emotions. It is based on complex allegiances with characters, as viewers evaluate the moral and emotional acceptability of a character's screen behavior. This, in turn, influences their readiness to empathize with the characters and situations.

In *The Silence of the Lambs* (1991), most viewers are probably scared of the insane serial killer Hannibal Lecter, although they may find him a compelling and fascinating figure. By contrast, the film's heroine, Clarice Starling, behaves in a way that most viewers probably deem exceptionally heroic, displaying extreme honesty and courage in her dealings with both Lecter and her male superiors at the FBI. As a result of the cognitive, emotional, and moral judgments they make about these characters, viewers have differing emotional responses toward them. They are frightened *of* Hannibal Lecter but are frightened *for* Clarice Starling when she is in a situation of danger. Of the two serial killers in the film—Lecter and Buffalo Bill—viewers respond with loathing and disgust toward Bill because he has no redeeming qualities. Lecter, by contrast, is funny, witty, and cultivated and shows real tenderness toward Clarice, qualities that Anthony Hopkins emphasizes in his performance. Thus, while viewers morally condemn both killers, their response to Lecter is far more ambivalent.

A viewer's reaction to a character and the actor's performance is a complex process. It involves an intricate series of inferences and evaluations, judgments, and appraisals at cognitive and emotional levels. In films displaying high levels of craft and artistry, performance style becomes part of a unified mise-en-scène in evoking these reactions. Camera placement, color, composition, and other aspects of mise-en-scène work to emphasize the emotional displays by performers. A director can cut to a closer camera position—the better to highlight a character's response and the actor's facial display at a crucial moment in the narrative—or a cinematographer and production designer can employ a palette of colors expressly designed to heighten the psychological mood or atmosphere of the scene. The design of a coherent mise-en-scène gives the filmmaker a uniquely powerful way of guiding the viewer toward a desired set of intellectual and emotional responses.

SUMMARY

Acting links cinema with theater as a medium of performance, but the film actor is not always the center of the show. A filmmaker typically combines an actor's performance with other elements of design furnished by the camera, sets, lights, and props, and in the final combination of elements, the actor may or may not be central.

Compared with theater, film acting is more challenging because its conditions are more artificial. The film actor must make do with little rehearsal, must know how much the camera will magnify what he or she does, must play to a nonexistent audience, must know how a camera reads a scene, and must share the scene with nonexistent props, characters, or effects that will be added in postproduction.

Film acting has emphasized a naturalistic playing style, and historically, actors have been divided into stars and supporting players. Among stars, the personality star has been the most common type. Since the beginning of cinema, viewers have been attracted to personality stars, and their appeal continues undiminished.

Film actors today may combine method and technical approaches, although the method approach did not itself appear in cinema until the 1950s.

KEY TERMS AND CONCEPTS

coverage 110	master shot 110	stars 115
expressionist 127	method acting 120	supporting players 115
extras 115	Stanislavsky 108	technical acting 120
homage 124	star persona 115	typage 126

SUGGESTED READINGS

Charles and Mirella Jona Affron, *Sets in Motion: Art Direction and Film Narrative* (Piscataway, NJ: Rutgers University Press, 1995).

Michael Caine, *Acting in Film: An Actor's Take on Movie Making* (New York: Applause, 1997).

Steve Carlson, *Hitting Your Mark: What Every Actor Really Needs to Know on a Hollywood Set* (Studio City, CA: Michael Wiese Production, 1999).

James Naremore, *Acting in the Cinema* (Berkeley and Los Angeles: University of California Press, 1990).

Roberta Pearson, *Eloquent Gestures: The Transformation of Performance Style in the Griffith Biograph Films* (Berkeley and Los Angeles: University of California Press, 1992).

Carole Zucker, *Figures of Light: Actors and Directors Illuminate the Art of Film Acting* (New York: Plenum, 1995).

Editing: Making the Cut

OBJECTIVES

After reading this chapter, you should be able to:

- define the role of editing in the production process

- describe the difference between linear and nonlinear editing systems

- explain the basic methods of joining shots

- explain how editing helps create continuity, dramatic focus, tempo, and narration and point of view

- explain how editing establishes parallel action

- describe the basic rules of continuity editing and the ways in which they establish continuity of action from shot to shot

- explain how continuity editing establishes a coherent and orderly physical world on screen

- explain how editing approaches that emphasize jump cuts, spatial fragmentation, and thematic montage work as alternatives to continuity editing

- describe how editing cues viewers to draw connections and interpretations across shots
- explain how editing establishes perceptual constancies across shot and scene transitions

Many filmmakers regard editing as the single most important creative step in determining the look and shape of the finished film. A good editor can save a film that has been directed in a mediocre fashion, and poor editing can damage the work of even the finest director. This chapter looks closely at the role of editing in the production process, continuity editing codes (these are the rules of editing that are found in most commercial feature films), and alternatives to continuity editing.

WHAT IS EDITING?

Editing is the work of joining shots to assemble the finished film. The **editor** selects the best shots from the large amount of footage the director and cinematographer have provided, assembles these in order, and connects them using a variety of optical transitions. In theory, the process of editing begins with the completion of filming or cinematography. In practice, however, the editor may begin consultations with the producer and director and may even begin cutting the film while principal filming is being completed. Most editors, however, will not watch the process of filming or view the locations where the film is shot. This allows them to view the footage unhampered by knowledge about the actual conditions that existed in front of the camera and to visualize with greater freedom various ways of combining the shots.

The amount of authority that the editor has may vary from production to production and, consequently, so may the editor's relationship with the director and producer. These factors determine when the editor may begin work and in what capacity on any given production.

Despite these variations, the basics of editing have remained relatively constant. The first task is to assemble a **rough cut,** which is done by eliminating all the unusable footage containing technical or performance errors. These may include out-of-focus shots or shots containing unstable camera movement, flubbed lines by an actor, inaudible sound recording, or lighting problems. Once all this footage has been removed, the editor then assembles the remaining footage in scene and sequence order. This rough assembly will be pruned, refined, and polished to yield the **final cut.** The final cut is the completed product of an editor's work. It includes the complete assembly and timings of all shots in the film's finished form. It is in going from the rough cut to the final cut that the real art and magic in editing lies.

LINEAR AND NONLINEAR SYSTEMS

Editors today use a **nonlinear editing system** to accomplish their work. A nonlinear system, such as the Avid, is computer-based and works with digital video (footage shot on film must be converted to digital video), giving an editor instantaneous access to any frame, shot, or edited sequence distributed anywhere in the existing footage. The editor decides which footage to work on by using notes that describe the characteristics, strengths, and flaws of particular shots. Prior to the 1990s, when the film industry adopted digital editing systems, editors worked directly on celluloid film and had to search manually through all the footage to find a desired shot or segment. This older approach was a **linear system** because the editor could only search for one shot at a time and had to do so by viewing footage sequentially, from beginning to end.

Digital systems have made editing a much faster process, and the complex and instantaneous control they give an editor over the digitized footage helps to explain why so many films—*Mission Impossible 2* (2000), *An Enemy of the State* (1999), *Armageddon* (1998)—have such fast and aggressive editing.

Films today have many, many more cuts and shot transitions than in earlier decades. Many shots are only a few frames long, less than a second of screen time. *The Bourne Ultimatum* (2007) features a dizzying array of speedy shot changes that often disorient the viewer because the camera perspective is shaky and unsteady. Nonlinear systems facilitate this more intensive editing style. To create the hyperfast shot transitions of *Moulin Rouge* (2001), editor Jill Bilcock worked with a massive amount of digitized footage. Scenes in the film were covered with a huge number of camera angles and set-ups. She then created files of shots labeled "men in top hats and tails" or "glamour shots of Nicole [Kidman]" and had instant electronic access to this material to use in building the film's montage sequences. (A **montage** is a scene composed of a rapid series of shots.) Nonlinear systems enable editors to organize and manipulate such vast amounts of footage. A film such as *Moulin Rouge* could not exist without computerized editing.

While digital systems have given editors greater control over their footage and increased their abilities to manipulate it in ever more elaborate ways, these systems have disadvantages. Unlike linear systems, the editor does not view a film image but rather an electronic image on a small monitor, which is degraded in quality, with poor resolution. This can bias editors toward close-ups because they will look better on the monitor than long shots. Furthermore, because the monitor's image is a poor guide to the visual qualities of the actual film images, it forces an editor to rely more heavily on his or her notes about the footage. It is arguable that editors using linear systems get to know their footage

MAN ON FIRE (PARAMOUNT, 2004)

Like many films today, *Man on Fire* has an especially fast cutting rate, with shot transitions occurring at a rate of more than one per second. This quick shot of Denzel Washington in a gun battle is only a few frames long, a fraction of a second in duration. The viewer barely sees it as a single shot. Nonlinear editing systems have accelerated the editing rate of contemporary films, giving editors new levels of control over huge amounts of footage and enabling them to create the complex montages that have become typical of modern film. Frame enlargement.

THE BOURNE ULTIMATUM (UNIVERSAL, 2007)

Director Paul Greengrass has developed a style that many have called "shaky-cam." It marries jerky, unstable camerawork to super-fast editing, creating an explosive style for action filmmaking. Shot lengths are extremely brief, and the film as a whole becomes an aggressive montage. Frame enlargement.

better because they must search manually through all of it to find what they need. The editor working on a digital system will not access footage that the notes have excluded.

Types of Visual Transitions

In joining the shots together into a rough and then a final cut, the film editor typically employs three basic types of visual transition. The most commonly used transition is the straight **cut**, which is visible on screen as a complete and instantaneous change of one image or shot to another. The cut is typically used to join shots where there is no change of narrative time or place involved. A cut from a shot of Julia Roberts looking off-frame right to a shot of Denzel Washington looking off-frame left tells the viewer that Roberts and Washington are looking at each other and that no changes in time or place have occurred in the story between the shots.

When changes of time or place do need to be specified, the editor has several techniques available. One is the **dissolve**. One shot begins to fade out to black, but before it is gone completely, the next shot begins to appear on top of it so that there is a moment of superimposition in which the two shots are visible together. If an editor dissolved from a shot of Julia Roberts to a shot of Denzel Washington, the viewer would know that some change in time or place in the story had occurred. The shot after the dissolve might be taking place several hours after the shot preceding the dissolve, or it may be occurring in a new location.

A substantial change of time or place is often indicated by the use of a **fade**. In this case, the first shot fades completely to black. The darkness lasts on screen for a few moments, and then the next shot begins to fade in. In a fade, there is no moment of superimposition. If the editor faded from a shot of Roberts to Washington, the shot after the fade could be taking place several days or even weeks after the first.

By using these basic transitions, editors can establish important relations of time and place in the story. These visual codes developed early in the history of film to enable filmmakers to organize their story material and construct complex narratives by, for example, using a fade to establish that one set of events is occurring at a later time than a

A VERY LONG ENGAGEMENT (WARNER BROS., 2004)

Because the dissolve overlaps images, editors often use this transition for poetic effects. Matilde (Audrey Tautou) is searching for her fiancé, who was lost on the battle-field during World War I. She telephones a woman who has information and is told about a group of soldiers who found a body hidden in an underground bunker— perhaps this was her fiancé. As the call ends, she reflects on this information. The scene plays in a single frame containing a series of shots that dissolve in and out as split-screen effects. This design presents the story infor- mation in a very fluid and poetic manner. Frame enlargements.

LAWRENCE OF ARABIA (COLUMBIA PICTURES, 1962)

Editors pay very close attention to the visual properties of the shots they join together. They carefully choose the edit points, where they place cuts and other optical transitions. This famous cut in *Lawrence of Arabia*—from a close-up of Lawrence (Peter O'Toole) blowing out a match to a long shot of the Arabian desert with the sun just below the horizon—startles the viewer with its radical change of scale and with the poetic association that motivates the cut, one that links the burning match with the fiery desert. Frame enlargements.

previous scene. But filmmakers also use these optical transitions for their poetic and expressive visual effects. Editors examine the footage closely, and when they join shots together, they often do so because of the suggestive effects and ideas these combinations can create. An editor may use a cut to join shots with similar graphic properties. The instantaneous change of images produced by the cut calls attention to the graphic similarities or differences, as the frame enlargements from *Lawrence of Arabia* (1962) demonstrate. In *Apollo 13* (1995), the cut was used poetically to show astronaut Jim Lovell (Tom Hanks), stranded in a crippled spacecraft thousands of miles from Earth, and his anxious wife "looking" at one another (across the cut and the thousands of miles that separate them).

Because it overlaps images, a dissolve can create many poetic effects. For a scene in *Blow* (2001), when drug kingpin George Jung (Johnny Depp), in prison for the remainder of his life, writes a tender letter to his father (Ray Liotta), whom he will never see again, the editor joined shots of the characters, seen in separate locations, with dissolves. One series of shots shows George taping a letter in prison, and the other shows his father listening to the letter at a later date. The edited scene goes back and forth between shots in each series. Each pair of shots is linked with a dissolve, which connects the images of each character and suggests that the emotional bond between them persists despite their physical separation.

In *The English Patient* (1996), editor Walter Murch used a dissolve as the transition out of a flashback to show the youthful Count Almashy (Ralph Fiennes) touching the face of his older self (by overlapping these images at the midpoint of the dissolve) as he lay dying at a point many years later in the story.

APOLLO 13 (UNIVERSAL, 1995)

Separated by thousands of miles, Jim Lovell (Tom Hanks) and his wife (Kathleen Quinlan) "see" each other across the cut. Their matching eyelines and the camera angles imply that they are looking at one another, despite the literal impossibility at this point in the story for them to do so. The film's editor has created a moment of visual poetry. Frame enlargements.

OTHER OPTICAL TRANSITIONS   Editors can use other optical transitions to sequence story information and create visual effects. In this regard, however, contemporary film is relatively impoverished. A viewer who looks at films from the silent period, for example, may notice devices such as the **iris**. Irises were used much like fades to signal the end of an important chapter in the story or to conclude a scene or film. In an iris-out, a circular

THE CIRCUS (UNITED ARTISTS, 1928)

Contemporary films seldom use the iris, which is a shame because it offers filmmakers a uniquely expressive visual effect. It directs the viewer's attention to a selected portion of the frame, providing visual emphasis. When used to conclude a scene or film, it does so with great finality. At the end of *The Circus*, Chaplin's melancholy tramp walks away from the camera as an iris slowly closes down around his figure. Visually poetic, it makes for a splendid exit and conclusion to the film. Frame enlargement.

SEVEN SAMURAI (TOHO, 1954)

Japanese director Akira Kurosawa frequently used the wipe. He liked the aggressive, decisive way that it replaced one shot with the next. In *Seven Samurai*, a wipe traveling from screen right to screen left erases the shot of an old farmer and reveals a crowded town square. The wipe is visible as the hard bar or line bisecting the frame and dividing the two shots. Frame enlargement.

pattern appeared on screen and gradually closed over the image. To open a scene, an iris-in might be employed, in which case the image appeared inside a small circular opening that gradually expanded on the screen.

In the 1930s and 1940s, Hollywood's editors used **wipes** quite frequently. The wipe is visible as a solid line traveling across the screen, sometimes vertically, sometimes horizontally. As it moves, it pushes one shot off the screen to reveal another. Unlike fades and dissolves, which tend to be more gradual and more subtle transitional devices, the wipe is a very aggressive, highly visible, and noticeable device. Perhaps for this reason, Hollywood eventually stopped using it.

However, when contemporary filmmakers want to evoke early film style, they may choose to use these archaic editing devices. Joel and Ethan Coen use irises in *O Brother Where Art Thou!* (2000), a film whose story is set during the Great Depression, and George Lucas uses wipes throughout his *Star Wars* films, emulating the early movie serials that were an inspiration for the series.

CLOSE-UP

Film Editors in the Hollywood Era

Historically, women have been shut of out many key film production positions. Until the modern period, very few women could be found working as directors, cinematographers, producers, or sound designers. Even in the modern period, by comparison with men in the Hollywood industry they are underrepresented in these positions. But this was never true for editing.

During the Hollywood studio era, many of the industry's most prominent film editors were women.

Margaret Booth, for example, began work with the great silent film director D. W. Griffith and then, in the early 1930s, became one of the chief editors at MGM, the most prestigious of Hollywood's studios. She edited such prominent MGM films as

(continued)

Mutiny on the Bounty (1935) and *Camille* (1936). In 1939, the studio promoted her to be the head of all of its film editing operations. This was a tremendously influential position, enabling her to shape the emergence of Hollywood's classical continuity editing in its mature form.

She ran the studio's editing operations until the late 1960s, when MGM fell on hard times. She then worked as a freelance editor, extending classical continuity editing into the modern period on such films as *The Way We Were* (1973), *The Sunshine Boys* (1975), *The Goodbye Girl* (1977), and others.

In some ways, Barbara McLean was her counterpart at 20th Century Fox. She began work as an editor in 1929, joined Fox in 1935 and was promoted to chief editor in 1949. She edited many of Fox's now-classic films, including *12 O'Clock High* (1949), *All About Eve* (1950), *The Gunfighter* (1950), *The Snows of Kilamanjaro* (1952), and *The Robe* (1953). The editing of *The Gunfighter* is especially brilliant, maintaining a tight running time of less than 90 minutes while sustaining a tense, exciting tone.

At MGM, Adrienne Fazan cut many of the great musicals, including *Anchors Aweigh* (1945), *An American in Paris* (1951), *Singin' in the Rain* (1952), and *Gigi* (1958). At Paramount, Anne Bauchens edited all of director Cecil De Mille's movies from 1918 to 1956, and these included the two versions that De Mille made of *The Ten Commandments* (1923, 1956). Partnerships between an editor and a director have been very common throughout cinema history.

Dede Allen, for example, exerted a major influence on modern cinema style through her work with key 1960s-era filmmakers. She literally changed the look and rhythms of modern film with the jumpy, discontinuous editing of *Bonnie and Clyde* (1967), and she continued working with that film's director, Arthur Penn, on *Alice's Restaurant* (1970), *Little Big Man* (1970), *Night Moves* (1975), and *The Missouri Breaks* (1976). She also worked extensively with director Sidney Lumet on such key classics as *Serpico* (1973) and *Dog Day Afternoon* (1975), and her innovative editing helped to give those films a nervous, jumpy tension and rhythm. She won an Oscar for best editing for her work on the historical epic *Reds* (1981), about the American journalist John Reed, who witnesses the Russian Revolution of 1917.

Verna Fields edited numerous television Westerns during the 1950s and feature films in the 1960s before emerging in the 1970s as a major collaborator with key figures in the new generation of Hollywood filmmakers. After editing Haskell Wexler's classic *Medium Cool* (1969), she edited three films for Peter Bogdanovich (*What's Up Doc*, 1972; *Paper Moon*, 1973; *Daisy Miller*, 1974) and did the sound editing on his *Targets* (1968). Bogdanovich was an important new directorial talent in the period, as were George Lucas and Steven Spielberg. Fields edited the breakthrough film for both Lucas (*American Graffiti*, 1973) and Spielberg (*Jaws*, 1975). Her extraordinary gifts for telling a story through editing helped to make *Jaws* into a blockbuster.

Anne V. Coates' career has had extraordinary breadth. She began work as an editor in 1952 with *The Pickwick Papers* and cut numerous films in Britain, which included the classic comedy *The Horse's Mouth* (1958). She emerged as one of cinema's greatest editors with her peerless work on the magnificent *Lawrence of Arabia* (1962). She continued in this vein of historical period films with *Beckett* (1964), *Murder on the Orient Express* (1974), and *Chaplin* (1992). But her work also includes pictures in nearly every genre, including comedy (*What About Bob?*, 1991; *Catch and Release*, 2006), drama (*Erin Brockovich*, 2000) action films for Clint Eastwood (*In the Line of Fire*, 1992) and Arnold Schwarzenegger (*Raw Deal*, 1986), and fantasy (*The Golden Compass*, 2007).

Thelma Schoonmaker has worked as Martin Scorsese's editor of choice since *Raging Bull* (1980). Their collaboration is one of the most significant director–editor partnerships in cinema history. Schoonmaker's aggressive shot combinations, freely mixing jump cuts, long takes, freeze frames, montage, slow motion, and propulsive music video-style cutting, have provided Scorsese's films with one of their dominant stylistic signatures. Their work together includes *Goodfellas* (1990), *The Age of Innocence* (1993), *Gangs of New York* (2002), and *The Departed* (2006). ◼

THE TEN COMMANDMENTS (PARAMOUNT, 1956)

This spectacular epic from producer-director Cecil B. DeMille was the last picture from the editor–director team of Anne Bauchens and DeMille. The two had worked together regularly since the silent era, making Bauchens one of the key authors on these films. Frame enlargement.

FUNCTIONS OF EDITING

In close consultation with a film's director, an editor combines shots to create narrative and expressive effects. Let us now examine the editor's work in more specific terms. In turning a rough cut into a fine cut, the editor works to create (1) continuity, (2) dramatic focus, (3) tempo, rhythm, mood, and (4) narration and point of view.

Continuity

Continuity is a fundamental principle of narrative filmmaking. The story, and the images used to tell it, must move along in an orderly and organized fashion. Editors join shots in ways that emphasize relationships of continuity—of orderliness—between them. If, during the course of a story, a character grows a beard, then shots must be carefully selected to establish the proper continuity of growth. In an early scene, the beard should not be longer or fuller than it appears in a later one.

Proper continuity also may apply to movement. During a chase scene, if camera positions establish that the escaping prisoner is running from screen right to left, followed by a posse hot on his trail, it will not do to change direction by editing subsequent shots with the escaping prisoner running from left to right while the posse moves from right to left. If this were to happen, it would seem as if both the prisoner and the posse were running toward each other. These principles of continuity are a little complicated, but they are extremely important, and we will cover them fully later in the chapter.

The continuity that editing creates often exists only on screen and not in the material *as it was filmed*. A dialogue scene in Julie Taymor's *Titus* (1999), for example, is composed of reverse-angle shots of two groups of characters. In the film's story, they are conversing in one location. In reality, as the scene was filmed, each reverse-angle setup was filmed in a different location, miles away from one another, and was shot a month apart. The editing joined the locations together and made them seem connected as one. Many films are made this way.

This conversation scene
composed of reverse-angle
shots was photographed
in two different loca-
tions and a month apart.
One setup (A), showing
Tamora (Jessica Lange)
and Saturninus (Alan
Cumming) on the stairs,
was shot at Mussolini's
government building in
Rome. The other setup
(B), showing them with
Titus (Anthony Hopkins,
center background), was
shot a month later at the
Villa Adriana, a historical
site outside Rome. The
editing joins the locations
as if they were one. The
continuity that editing
creates may be very dif-
ferent from the reality of
what the camera actually
has photographed. Frame
enlargements.

(a)

(b)

Dramatic Focus

The editor cuts the footage to find or emphasize the dramatic focus of a scene. In this respect, the editor actually can improve an actor's performance by deleting footage in which
the actor may give an improper line reading or by tightening up the reaction time between
shots to make the actor appear to have swifter psychological reflexes. In extreme cases,
the editor may entirely reshape the film so that a secondary character becomes a major
character. This happened in Woody Allen's Academy Award-winning *Annie Hall* (1977).

In Allen's initial conception and all through shooting, the character of Annie Hall
was a subsidiary one. The focus was on Alvy Singer, the character played by Woody
Allen, and rather than telling a story about a relationship, the film was conceived as a
loosely connected series of skits emphasizing Alvy's personality and psychological hang-
ups. But the editing changed the nature and structure of the film, making Annie a major
character and the movie a story of the affair between Alvy and Annie. During editing,
it became apparent that the original conception for the film was not working. With
Allen's approval, editor Ralph Rosenblum began to cut to emphasize the Alvy–Annie relationship. The resulting film won Academy Awards for Best Picture and Best Direction.

In finding the dramatic focus of the scene, the editor may, on occasion, create
scenes that did not exist in the script or the filming but result purely from editing.
Annie Hall furnishes another example. At the end of the film, after Alvy and Annie
have broken up, the story concludes with Alvy in a reflective mood thinking back

ANNIE HALL (UNITED ARTISTS, 1977)

Intensive collaboration between director Woody Allen and editor Ralph Rosenblum drastically rearranged the design of *Annie Hall*. Most significantly, Annie (Diane Keaton, pictured) became a major character, and a stronger narrative emerged. Frame enlargement.

on their relationship. Editor Rosenblum put together a memory sequence in which Alvy speaks in **voice-over** about his attitudes toward relationships while the images show a series of highlights from previous episodes in Alvy and Annie's affair. The sequence was cut to music, a reprise of Annie singing "Seems Like Old Times" from an earlier scene. This concluding montage enabled the film to end in a visually creative way and one that was emotionally complex and evocative. But the montage had not been scripted; it resulted purely from the editing process.

A similar experience occurred during the editing of Francis Ford Coppola's *The Godfather* (1972). At the end of production, Coppola had to go to Sicily to film some sequences there, the last he needed to complete even though they dealt with material much earlier in the story. The script called for the film to conclude with the baptism of Michael Corleone's son followed by the assassination of Michael's enemies. While Coppola was in Sicily, editor Peter Zinner, believing the original conception to be somewhat flat, decided to create a montage in which the baptism was intercut with the assassination scenes. This sequence, conjoining the baptism with the bloody executions, is one of the most memorable and powerful montages in modern cinema, concluding the film on an exceptionally strong note.

Tempo and Mood

By varying the lengths of shots, the editor establishes rhythm, tempo, and pacing. Brief shots will produce a faster pace, whereas shots of longer duration typically produce a fuller, more measured pacing. The length of the shots never remains constant throughout a film. By varying their length, the editor modulates the pacing of a film. Action films today are cut at an extremely fast pace, whereas a historical epic such as *Dances with Wolves* (1990) establishes a measured tempo with shots of longer duration.

The editor also may cut to establish appropriate moods. In a horror film, for example, the cutting can help to create suspense and shock. If a character goes into a dark room where viewers know a monster is lurking, the editing might emphasize tight close-ups of the character's face. Typically, the director and cinematographer would have filmed these with the express purpose of facilitating this approach to the scene's editing. The tight close-ups prevent viewers from seeing the room and what may be lurking there. If the monster suddenly lurches into the frame, or if the editor abruptly cuts to a longer shot showing the monster just behind the character, viewers will jump with fright.

In *The Bridges of Madison County* (1995), director Clint Eastwood and editor Joel Cox purposely created a slow pace, letting shots linger on screen, in order to give the screen romance room to develop in a convincing manner and to let the lovers have ample time with one another and the viewer with these characters. The lush, full-bodied romantic tone of the film is very much a function of its editing.

Narration and Point of View

Editing permits filmmakers to control the flow of story information and point of view as it is established through changing camera positions. Editing determines the way in which a scene's story information is conveyed.

A sequence from Alfred Hitchcock's *Rear Window* (1954), edited by George Tomasini, demonstrates this relationship between editing, storytelling, and the control of point of view. Hitchcock designed *Rear Window* as an experiment. He wanted to restrict the physical scene and setting of the action while maintaining dramatic interest. Most of the camera's positions are restricted to what the main character—a professional photographer with a broken leg who is confined to a wheelchair—can see from his apartment window. The photographer, Jeffries (James Stewart), begins to eavesdrop on his neighbors; from his window, he can see into the windows of their apartments across the courtyard. Jeffries comes to believe that a murder has been committed by one of his neighbors, a salesman named Thorwald (Raymond Burr). Jeffries hears a mysterious scream during the night and then sees Thorwald going in and out of his apartment carrying a large suitcase. Because this is a Hitchcock film, viewers are not surprised to learn that the contents of the suitcase turn out to be quite ghoulish. They are the dismembered pieces of Thorwald's wife.

Throughout this sequence, the editing implies associations between the shots. This is an important principle of narrative filmmaking. Each shot means what it

(a)

(b)

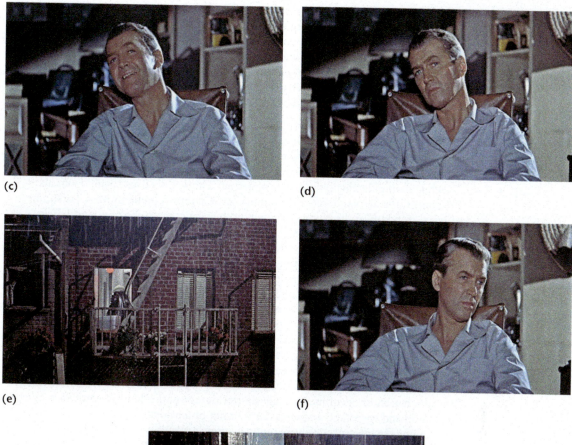

(c)

(d)

(e)

(f)

(g)

REAR WINDOW (PARAMOUNT PICTURES, 1954)

In cross cutting shots of Jeffries (James Stewart) looking off frame with shots presenting views of the apartment courtyard, the editing gives the shot series a point-of-view structure. Viewers infer that the courtyard views are what Jeffries sees. The shots A-B-C show a comic series—Jeffries sees a couple struggling to get out of the rain and is amused. Shots D-E-F-G show Jeffries watching the killer Thorwald leaving his apartment in the middle of the night. Note that the more extreme angle of Jeffries' glance in shot F points to a new location, the street beyond the apartment complex. The angles at which Jeffries looks off-frame tell us where things are located. In reality, actor James Stewart is not seeing anything pictured here. Hitchcock simply told him "look off-camera right" and "look up and off-camera left" and then created the associations and story meanings in the editing. Frame enlargements.

does by virtue of its surrounding context. Hitchcock and Tomasini cut back and forth between Jeffries's face and shots of what he is meant to be seeing across the courtyard. These latter are his point-of-view shots; they simulate what he can see out his window. Hitchcock and Tomasini want viewers to interpret Jeffries's facial expressions and reactions as responses to what has occurred in the point-of-view shots. Notice, however, that Jeffries and what he sees and reacts to are never shown within the same shot. It is the editing that creates the association.

PARALLEL ACTION   To tell sophisticated stories, filmmakers need a way of suggesting (simultaneous) parallel action, that is, that two or more things are happening at the same time. This enables them to weave together several lines of action in the telling of their story. **Parallel action** is achieved through editing. The editing in *Rear Window* manipulates multiple lines of action: Thorwald's trips to and from his apartment, the arrival home of the composer, the return home of Miss Torso, the comical response of the couple sleeping on their balcony in the rain, and Jeffries's surveillance of all this and his reactions to it. The editing references each of these lines of action to the others by establishing relationships of time and location. Without the use of parallel editing, that is, editing that interrelates multiple lines of action, filmmakers could not create complex narratives involving the actions of numerous characters, story lines, and subplots.

One especially important form of parallel action is **cross-cutting**. In cross-cutting, the editor goes back and forth, typically with increasing speed, between two or more lines of action. *The Fugitive* (1993) opens with a spectacular train wreck during which the fugitive (Harrison Ford) escapes from his jailers. The cross-cutting goes back and forth with increasing speed between shots of the oncoming train and the frenzied, panicked reactions of prisoners trapped inside a bus that has fallen across the tracks. By cross-cutting shots of increasingly shorter duration, the editor creates an accelerating tempo and speed and an increasing amount of tension.

Among the inferences viewers routinely draw across cuts are inferences of simultaneous action. The cross-cut shots of the train and the frantic prisoners prompt the viewer to make an unambiguous interpretation: The train is about to smash the bus. Filmmakers guide viewers in drawing these inferences by composing and editing shots to create a strong flow of action across the cuts. How is this accomplished?

THE PRINCIPLES OF CONTINUITY EDITING

As its name implies, **continuity editing** is a style of cutting that emphasizes smooth and continuously flowing action from shot to shot. Instead of noticing the abruptness of a cut in a popular movie, the viewer pays attention to story information and character relationships. Shots are joined so that the action flows smoothly over the cut. The remarkable achievements of the continuity editing system are sometimes disparaged in discussions that describe the style as "transparent" or "invisible." In reality, continuity editing is a highly constructed and accomplished style that creates an impression of realism and naturalism from carefully applied editing rules.

A Continuous Flow of Action

The goal of continuity editing is to emphasize the apparent realism and naturalness of the story and to minimize the viewer's awareness of film technique and the presence of the camera. The remarkable achievement of continuity cutting lies in successfully meeting this goal. When viewers see a popular commercial film in the theater, they rarely notice details of camera position and movement. Instead, they are swept up by the story and the characters. There is a major paradox here. As viewers watch a movie, they see a rapid succession of individual shots on screen accompanied by an ever-changing series of camera positions and angles. What they *see*, therefore, is fragmentary and discontinuous. A film is assembled from hundreds of individual shots. Its structure is inherently fragmentary. What viewers *experience*, however, is the impression of a smoothly flowing, unbroken stream of imagery in which the story and the characters come convincingly to life. How is this apparent contradiction between the reality of what viewers see and the impression of what they experience explained?

The answer is that filmmakers have discovered methods of connecting their shots that minimize the disruption of shot changes. In other words, continuity editing makes possible the impression of narrative wholeness and completeness. Continuity editing also has helped make cinema very popular because it can be so easily understood. Films edited according to these principles do not pose difficult perceptual or interpretive challenges. Films can be edited so that they will be easy to understand and will therefore appeal to wide segments of the market.

Here lie the true achievements of the continuity system. The system emphasizes visual coherence and ease of comprehension. These are things that must be created in film. Because of the camera's ever-changing angle of view, the potential in film for incoherence and discontinuity is always much greater, and filmmakers accordingly have to strive very hard to achieve the opposite.

Case Study CASABLANCA

The Hollywood classic *Casablanca* (1942) provides some representative sequences that display continuity editing codes in action. Among the most important codes of the continuity system are the following: the use of a master shot to organize the subsequent cutting within a scene, matching shots to the master, the shot-reverse-shot series with the eyeline match, and the 180-degree rule.

Casablanca is a wartime adventure film about heroic resistance against the Nazis, and it is also a lush romantic melodrama. Rick (Humphrey Bogart), a nightclub owner, has come to Casablanca to get over a disastrous love affair with Ilsa Lund (Ingrid Bergman). Ilsa turns up unexpectedly one night in Rick's cafe and sets in motion the romantic fireworks that move the plot along to its exciting conclusion.

Matching to the Master Shot

In the first scene illustrated here, one of the attendants in Rick's nightclub awaits Rick's approval before admitting some customers into the room where roulette and gambling occur. Rick is filmed from behind, in the foreground, and the door to his casino is visible in the background of the shot (**a**). This shot functions as the master shot position for this scene. The **master shot** shows the spatial layout of a scene, all the characters' positions in relation to each other and to the set. The master shot is typically filmed first, with all the action in a scene from beginning to end photographed from this position. Then directors typically go back to film inserts, close-ups, and medium shots that will be cut with the master shot to create the final edited scene and whose compositional elements will match with the master.

Rick sees the doorman pausing in the entrance with several guests, awaiting his approval to enter the casino. Shot 2 (**b**) is an example of a **matched cut**. The two compositions—the master shot and the medium close-up of the doorman and guests—match. The camera's angle of view is similar in each shot. The only difference is that the camera is closer to the

(continued)

characters in shot 2 (**b**). A second matching element is the positioning of the doorman and guests. They are oriented toward screen left, a similar position in both shots. The match here is so strong that a casual viewer does not notice the cut.

The Eyeline Match

The doorman glances off-frame left (**c**) (implying that he is looking at Rick, who is off-screen), and the film cuts to Rick in shot 4 (**d**) looking off-frame right. Each looks in an opposing direction, one to the right, the other to the left, creating the impression that they are looking at each other. This match is known as the **eyeline match**, and it is an important code used to link the spaces in separate shots. The eyeline match establishes that two characters are indeed looking at each other and that the spaces they inhabit, though seen in different shots, are connected. Often in a scene, characters are interacting with each other but are presented in separate shots. The eyeline match helps to create continuity between the separate images.

In organizing the cut to shot 4, the master shot remains important. What else, besides the eyeline match, establishes that these characters are looking at each other? It is the information viewers remember from the master shot about the spatial layout of the room. From the master shot, viewers know there is a direct line of sight from Rick's table to the door and that Rick and the doorman have an unobstructed view of each other. The angles of their glances in shots

(a)

(b)

(c)

(d)

(e)

(f)

(g)

(h)

(i)

(*continued*)

3 and 4 (**c, d**) match the information viewers were given in the master shot.

The Master Shot and Viewer Perception

As viewers watch a movie, they are responding to more than the information that is on-screen at any one moment. Viewers interpret shots by relating them to the larger context of an edited scene. In this regard, the master shot furnishes viewers with a map or visual schema of the set or locale (a room in this scene from Casablanca). Using this schema, viewers integrate fragmentary details, like the composition of the shot (**b**), with their recollected sense of the layout of the room. Using master shots facilitates a viewer's understanding of the action of a scene.

The Shot-Reverse-Shot Series

In shot 5, a Nazi supporter tries to enter Rick's casino (**e**). In shot 6 (**f**), the doorman and the German talk outside the room, where Rick shortly joins them in shot 7 (**g**). The cutting now goes into a brief **shot-reverse-shot series** (**g–i**) as Rick and the German exchange words. The camera is positioned over the shoulder of one character and then, in the reverse shot position, over the shoulder of the other character. This series of alternating compositions is a standard method for filming dialogue scenes. It creates something of a ping-pong effect as the composition continually shifts into reverse shot positions. The cutting is typically coordinated with the flow of dialogue so that, as speakers change, so does the camera position. Should the camera shift into an extreme close-up isolating each character in a single shot, the eyeline match would be employed. In shot-reverse-shot cutting, editing follows the flow of dialogue, and the shifting camera positions mark the changes of speakers in the conversation. This emphasizes the dialogue and facilitates the viewer's pickup of story information.

The 180-Degree Rule

The **180-degree rule** is one of the most important codes of the continuity system. This rule is the foundation for establishing continuity of screen direction. The right–left coordinates of screen action remain consistent as long as all camera positions stay on the same side of the line of action. Crossing the line entails a change of screen direction.

Because filmmakers change camera positions and angles from shot to shot, screen direction is something that must be established and maintained carefully. Right and left must remain constant across shot changes, but the potential for creating inconsistent right and left orientations from shot to shot is very great. The 180-degree rule specifies how this may be prevented.

Within any given scene, a line of interest or action can be drawn between the major characters. The 180-degree rule counsels filmmakers to keep their cameras on one side of this line from shot to shot within a scene. If a filmmaker were to cross the line by cutting to a camera position taken on the other side of the line, the right–left coordinates on screen would be reversed. Characters who were on screen right in one shot would appear on screen left in the next.

The 180-degree rule operates in the next scene in the film (**j–m**) on page 154. Ugarte (Peter Lorre) comes into the casino to tell Rick that he has some "letters of transit" that guarantee their bearer safe passage from Casablanca, and he asks Rick to keep them for him. As Ugarte talks to Rick, they are seated at the table. The line of interest extends between them. Notice that the camera stays on the same side of the line in all the subsequent shots (**k–m**). When both characters are in the shot, Ugarte is always on screen right and Rick is always on screen left despite the changing camera positions. When a close-up isolates Rick, he is facing screen right, consistent with his position in the two-shot.

Notice also that the line of interest is consistent with the line of interest established in the previous scene with the doorman and guests. Rick sits at his table in both scenes, and the camera positioning has kept Rick on screen left. In this sense, visual continuity has been maintained from scene to scene because a consistent line of interest is used as the basis of the 180-degree rule.

Scenes are dynamic, however, and filmmakers frequently need to define new lines of action to follow changes of character positioning as the drama unfolds. How does a filmmaker define a new line of action by crossing the existing one? There are several possible ways. A filmmaker may cut first to a series of camera positions on or near the line before crossing it. A filmmaker may use a moving camera to cross the line within a shot. Whatever strategy is employed, the

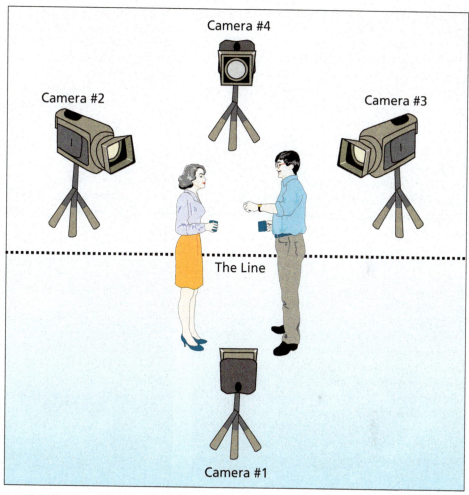

FIGURE 5.1
The 180-degree rule.

problems associated with maintaining or crossing the line raise issues about the relationship between visual change and perceptual constancy in the represented action on screen.

Camera Position and Perceptual Constancies

Filmmakers typically provide viewers with continuously changing visual perspectives on the action. They build a scene by cutting among different camera setups. The problem is how to create this variety without confus-

ing and disorienting the viewer, particularly when it is important to establish a coherent sense of a fixed visual landscape. The viewer must understand that although the camera's angle of view may change, the layout of the physical world on-screen remains constant. In other words, if a character is shown standing at the bottom of a hill, the character must seem to remain there, unless shown moving elsewhere, regardless of whether a high-angle or a low-angle shot is employed, regardless of whether the camera photographs that character from the left or right

(continued)

(j)

(k)

(l)

(m)

side. The camera's relative positions, which change as the action unfolds on screen, are distinct from the perceptual constancies (e.g., up, down, left, right) that must prevail, that must not change, in the represented action. The sheriff pursuing the prisoner always must be understood to be chasing his quarry regardless of the directions in which pursuer and pursued are shown moving on screen.

This relationship between the editing codes pertaining to screen direction and the constancies of the physical world that is represented on screen can be demonstrated with an example from *Out of Africa* (1985). Karen Blixen (Meryl Streep) arrives in Kenya and rides by coach from the train station to meet her new husband. During the shots that show her riding

in the coach, screen direction is reversed. The reversal, though, occurs in a way that is consistent with principles of continuity.

The first shot (**a**) showing Blixen traveling by coach is a telephoto long shot in which she appears, through crowds of pedestrians, riding toward screen left. The filmmakers then cut to a new camera position framing her as she rides directly toward the camera. Consequently, this new framing (**b**), which is on the line of action (motion) established in the previous shot, erases the right–left coordinates. In this shot, movement occurs toward the camera, not to the right or left.

The next shot (**c**) shows Blixen riding toward screen right and represents a reversal of screen direction relative to the first shot (**a**). The editing, however, softens the abruptness of the reversal by using the intervening shot in which she rides directly toward the camera. By establishing a dominant line of action and then cutting to a camera position on the line, filmmakers can cross it subsequently it and define a new line.

This method preserves screen continuity perfectly. Directional change occurs gradually, and the viewer understands that the layout of the physical world on-screen has remained constant, despite changes in the camera's angle of view and the direction of motion on-screen. ◼

(a)

(b)

OUT OF AFRICA (UNIVERSAL, 1985)

In *Out of Africa*, continuity of movement is maintained despite a change in its right–left orientation. The shot (b) of Karen Blixen (Meryl Streep) riding toward the camera erases the right–left coordinates established in (a) and provides the transition necessary for maintaining continuity across the change (a and c) in screen direction. Note also the motion blur produced by the panning camera in the first and last shots of the series. Because the camera is panning with the coach's movement, stationary pedestrians and buildings are subject to motion blur. Frame enlargements.

(c)

Errors of Continuity

Filmmakers never achieve perfect continuity, and viewers with sharp eyes often can spot errors. **Errors of continuity** are mismatched details in a series of shots. The vanishing water jug in the shots from *The Waterboy* (1998) is an especially flagrant example.

Continuity errors arise because moviemaking proceeds on a shot-by-shot basis, with everything, from character positions and costumes to lights and props, recreated for each new shot. The possibilities of flubbing these recreations, of mismatching their details, are enormous. The conditions of film production make it difficult for filmmakers to avoid such errors. Take, for example, Kevin Costner's *Robin Hood: Prince of Thieves* (1991). When Robin (Costner) and Azeem (Morgan Freeman) land on the shores of England, Azeem helps Robin up from the beach. In medium close-up, Robin holds out his right arm for assistance, and in the following shot viewers see Azeem helping Robin up by grasping his left arm.

THE WATERBOY (TOUCHSTONE, 1998)

The disappearing water jug—now you see it, now you don't. A brief cutaway to the face of another character separates these two shots of Adam Sandler. In the second shot, the water jug is conspicuously missing. This is a relatively glaring continuity error. Frame enlargements.

The error arose because the action had to be created separately for each shot and was done so without the proper matching continuity. In such cases, the editor's best hope is that the viewer will not notice the discrepancy, and indeed, if the gaff is not glaring, viewers often fail to notice because they are busy following the story.

Continuity errors can develop when portions of a scene are shot at widely spaced intervals. For example, in *Cocktail* (1988), Tom Cruise passes a New York theater whose marquee advertises the film *Barfly* and then, a few minutes later, when he passes that theater again, the marquee advertises *Casablanca*. As many readers know, some films have abundant continuity problems. In *Pretty Woman* (1990), continuity errors ranged from scenes in which Richard Gere's tie appears and disappears from shot to shot to other scenes in which his shoes and socks do the same thing, and still others in which Julia Roberts takes a bite at breakfast from what is alternately a pancake and a croissant.

Facilitating the Viewer's Response

The editing codes just reviewed—cutting to match the master shot and use of the 180-degree rule, the shot-reverse-shot series, and the eyeline match—are cornerstones of the continuity system. The system emphasizes naturalism and realism to the extent that it minimizes the amount of perceptual work that the viewer needs to do. This work is minimized because the positioning of characters, the direction of their movement, and the camera's angles of view are related across shots in an orderly way. This enables the perspective of each shot to link up with the perspectives in other shots, establishing for the viewer the sense of a unified landscape stretching across all the shots, of which each offers only a partial view.

Think of film viewing as an activity like a picture puzzle in which the overall picture—Rick's casino or Jeffries' apartment complex—emerges when all the little pieces have been fit together. Each piece is a shot, and if they fit properly, the viewer sees the overall picture and not the pieces, just as with a puzzle. In this way, continuity editing helps to make the visual perspectives of each shot easy to interpret and movies themselves very easy to understand.

Continuity editing codes are so successful at simplifying the viewer's perceptual task that they actually can facilitate comprehension of story information. Ample experimental evidence indicates that viewers understand story information more easily when continuity editing is used than when it is not. Rather than interfering with normal perception, continuity editing facilitates it. As a result, it makes films more accessible and attractive for diverse audiences whose educational and cultural backgrounds vary. To the extent that continuity editing poses few interpretational problems for viewers, it has helped establish the enormous popular acceptance and emotional appeal of motion pictures.

Case Study   SUBVERTING CONTINUITY EDITING: THE SILENCE OF THE LAMBS

Because audiences are so familiar with continuity editing, clever filmmakers can fool viewers by applying its rules in a misleading way. An especially brilliant example of this occurs in *The Silence of the Lambs* (1991). FBI agents encircle a house in Calumet City, believing it to be the lair of serial killer Buffalo Bill. This action is intercut with shots of Bill in his basement tormenting one of his victims. Outside, an agent is sent to ring the doorbell. Other agents crouch nearby, hidden in the bushes. When Bill opens his door, however, viewers are startled and frightened to find not an FBI SWAT team but lone agent Clarice Starling (Jodie Foster), unaware that she is face-to-face with Buffalo Bill. Meanwhile, the SWAT team breaks into an empty house. It turns out that the viewer is seeing two different locations. How did the filmmakers trick viewers and spring this surprise on them?

The sequence opens with an establishing shot of the Calumet City house (**a**). FBI agents swarm the property and hide. Extensive intercutting joins this action with shots of Bill in his basement. Outside, one agent, disguised as a man delivering flowers, approaches the front door and rings the bell (**b**). The next shot shows a bell ringing in Bill's basement (**c**) and Buffalo Bill listening with annoyance (**d**). When the bell stops ringing, the next shot (**e**) shows the FBI agent taking his finger off the doorbell outside. The shot series implies continuity of action and place, and the viewer concludes that the Calumet City house is, indeed, Bill's lair.

The agent rings the bell again, followed by shots of Bill listening. Bill goes upstairs to answer his door, and the action cuts to an exterior view of the Calumet City house as the agents decide they will have to break in. In the next moment, Bill opens his door to reveal Clarice (**f**), alone and unsuspecting. In shock, viewers realize that they have been misled, that the Calumet City house is not occupied by Bill. The sequence ends with an establishing shot of the real house where Bill lives.

The cross-cutting of the FBI's maneuvers with Bill's activities in his basement prompts the viewer to make a correct assumption of *temporal continuity* (the sequence of events is properly chronological, with no distortions of time) but a false assumption of *spatial*

(continued)

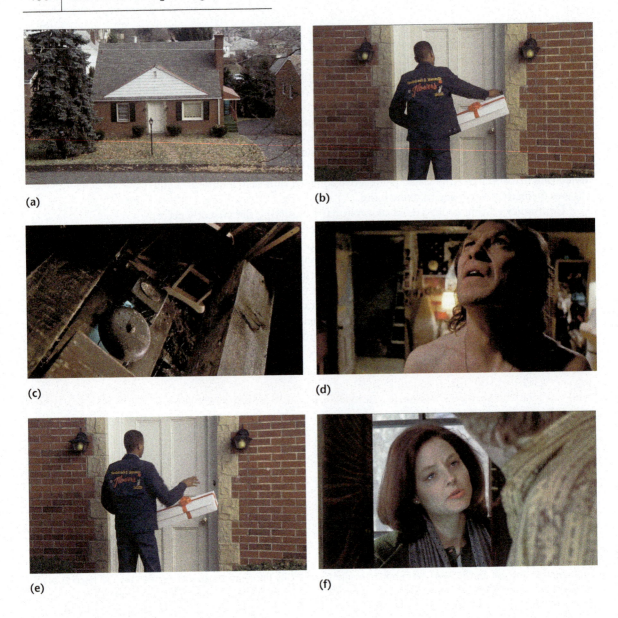

(a)

(b)

(c)

(d)

(e)

(f)

contiguity (that the locales shown in the cross-cut shots are connected). The deception depends on the viewer's familiarity with parallel editing, conventionally used to establish linkages of time and/or place among several lines of action. It depends also on using matching sound and visual elements to make the viewer infer continuity of action. The agent rings the bell; the viewer sees it ring and Bill react. The viewer cannot know from the editing that these are two separate bells and different locations.

When Bill opens his door to reveal Clarice, viewers realize with shock that their schema of time–space relations, constructed by the editing, is wrong. Clarice's situation gives the shock its emotional power. A character for whom the viewer cares deeply, she is now in mortal danger. ◼

ALTERNATIVES TO CONTINUITY EDITING

Although it predominates in popular cinema, continuity editing is not the only method of editing used by filmmakers. Several alternatives exist, some of which disrupt continuities of time and space to varying degrees. Filmmakers often seek to create vivid stylistic effects by breaking from the naturalistic rendering of time and space that continuity editing provides. To do this, they commonly employ jump-cutting and/or montage.

Jump Cuts

This type of editing produces abrupt breaks in the continuity of action by omitting portions of an ongoing action. Imagine that an editor is examining a strip of film that contains one shot showing a woman walking across a room and opening a door. If the editor removes several frames from the middle of that shot, it will produce a break in the action, which will seem to jump over the interval of missing frames. The editor has created a **jump cut**.

Inspired by the use of jump-cutting in such French films as *Breathless* (1959), U.S. filmmakers in the late 1960s and early 1970s experimented with the technique in *Easy Rider* (1969) and *Bonnie and Clyde* (1967), the latter edited by Dede Allen. She has reported that the film's director, Arthur Penn, kept telling her to make the story go faster, and to do this, she used jump-cutting to omit portions of the action and speed things along. The first scene of the film shows Bonnie (Faye Dunaway) in her bedroom. She paces restlessly about the room and lies down on the bed. Allen cuts from a shot of Bonnie walking over to her bed with her back to the camera to a shot in which Bonnie faces the camera and is already reclining on the bed. The cut between these two shots produces a jump, or discontinuity, in both her orientation relative to the camera and her position on the bed. This tiny break in the action creates a small acceleration in time, propelling the story forward a bit faster than standard continuity editing could accomplish.

The editors of *Easy Rider* used jump-cutting extensively to give many scenes a rough and jagged rhythm. In addition to jump-cutting, they employed a very unusual method of scene transition. Instead of using a dissolve, a fade, or a cut,

BONNIE AND CLYDE (WARNER BROS., 1967)

This jump cut shows Bonnie standing and looking down at her bed, then reclining on the bed. The intervening action is omitted. The result for the viewer is a brief moment of perceptual disorientation. Frame enlargements.

they employed a unique technique that can best be described as flash cross-cutting. Cross-cutting is typically used within a scene to reference and compare two or more lines of action. As used in *Easy Rider*, flash cross-cutting is a method of scene transition in which the last shot of the first scene and the first shot of the next scene are intercut very rapidly. The viewer oscillates rapidly, back and forth, between the end of one scene and the beginning of the next.

Flash cross-cutting is a unique method of scene transition that, like the jump cut, produces a very noticeable break in continuity. These techniques disrupt the smooth flow of action and call attention to themselves as visual devices. While flash cross-cutting is a rarely employed device, jump-cutting is a standardly employed method of producing discontinuity. It tends to be used, however, within scenes that have been constructed according to overall continuity principles. The contrast with these makes the jump cut vivid and effective.

Montage

Montage editing builds a scene out of many brief shots, each of which typically presents a fragmentary view of action and locale. The shots are often edited to a very rapid pace, subjecting the viewer to a barrage of visual information. With each shot offering an incomplete view, the total picture of the event emerges from the montage as a whole. Montage editing is typically used (1) to fragment time and space and (2) to visually embody thematic or intellectual ideas.

THE SOVIET MONTAGE TRADITION   Soviet filmmakers in the 1920s first practiced this method of editing, and the most famous of these filmmakers is Sergei Eisenstein. Eisenstein was very familiar with the continuity editing of U.S. pictures, particularly the work of D. W. Griffith (*The Birth of a Nation*, 1915; *Intolerance*, 1916), who used it with great sophistication. *Intolerance*, for example, in telling four stories simultaneously, represents the pinnacle of parallel editing and cross-cutting. Eisenstein resolved to break with continuity principles, and he developed a montage style based on the creation of visual conflict between and among shots. His motivation was a sociopolitical one. As a Marxist, he believed that conflict was the essence of history, society, and art. In *Battleship Potemkin* (1925), *October* (1928), and other films,

---

FILMMAKER SPOTLIGHT

Arthur Penn

Along with Sam Peckinpah, Arthur Penn is one of the great poets of screen violence. Unlike Peckinpah, though, who treated violence as an essential and instinctual component of human behavior, Penn places violent behavior within a clear social context and uses it to illuminate the political atmosphere of an era. *The Chase* (1966) presciently treats the United States as a gun culture and studies its festering climate of violence. In its horrific climax, the town sheriff (Marlon Brando) is savagely beaten and cannot prevent the public

assassination of a small-time criminal under police custody. Here, as elsewhere in Penn's films, the killing of John F. Kennedy provides the model and resonant reference point for explorations of U.S. social violence.

Penn trained as a television director and debuted as a feature filmmaker with an unusually psychological Western, *The Left-Handed Gun* (1958). *Mickey One* (1965) was a European-style, existential art film whose unconventional visual style and ambitious story were too far ahead of

U.S. film culture when it was released. Penn applied the style of the French New Wave, primarily jump cuts and other unconventional edits and optical effects, to a mainstream U.S. film with *Bonnie and Clyde* (1967), an important work of modern cinema. Using slow motion and multicamera filming for its scenes of violence, audaciously mixing high comedy and brutal violence, Penn's film captured the rebellious spirit of the times with its unconventional style and countercultural portrayal of Bonnie and Clyde as youthful heroes taking on the establishment. *Alice's Restaurant* (1969) and *Little Big Man* (1970) quickly followed, essential documents of late 1960s film and society.

Penn faltered in the 1970s. With the eclipse of the social idealism and political excitement of the 1960s, and with Watergate the dominant metaphor of social corruption in the next decade, Penn was disillusioned and cut off from the social ferment that nourished his films. However, he managed a stunning artistic expression of a bleak cultural period. *Night Moves* (1975), a detective film, brilliantly captures the national darkness, despair, and confusion experienced in the wake of the assassinations of John and Bobby Kennedy and Martin Luther King, Jr., and the collapse of the 1960s' social movements. It is, perhaps, Penn's best film.

Following *The Missouri Breaks* (1976), a big-budget Western teaming Brando with Jack Nicholson and widely regarded as a failure, Penn worked infrequently and without commercial impact. *Four Friends* (1981) was barely released, *Target* (1985) was an efficient demonstration of Penn's ability to make a plot-driven thriller, and *Dead of Winter* (1987) was an effective, if cold-blooded, psychological chiller that Penn directed as a favor to friends who would have otherwise been unable to get their script produced.

Penn's checkered film career demonstrates the essential interconnection of film and society. Penn thrived during a period of social turbulence when the film industry welcomed innovative, cutting-edge work and when he could connect his artistic visions to the political dramas unfolding around him. Disillusioned with the 1970s and disappointed with the special-effects-driven blockbuster fantasies that dominated U.S. film from the latter half of that decade, Penn simply stopped working in films, except on an irregular basis, and turned his energies to a deepening involvement with the New York-based Actor's Studio. Returning to his roots, he had been directing for television when he died in 2010. ∎

BONNIE AND CLYDE (WARNER BROS, 1967)

The slow-motion, bloody deaths of Bonnie and Clyde changed American cinema forever. Penn's gut-wrenching images established a new threshold of brutality on film, yet they seem almost tame by today's standards. Unlike later filmmakers interested in gore for its own sake, Penn used violence as a way of exploring the cultural climate of violence in American society. Frame enlargement.

Eisenstein's elaborate montages created conflicts of movement, rhythm, tone, lighting, and graphical properties among the shots. In many scenes, the editing has a harsh and jagged quality, as Eisenstein pushes these conflicting visual elements to the limit.

The huge and extended massacre of civilians by Czarist troops in *Battleship Potemkin* is the most famous and influential example of Eisensteinian montage. Eisenstein's editing fragments space and time by fracturing it into a multitude of brief shots that violate continuity principles. Actions are repeated, omitted, viewed simultaneously from multiple angles, slowed down, and speeded up and have their screen direction abruptly reversed. The editing is as violent as the drama that it visualizes. In this sequence and elsewhere, Eisenstein showed other filmmakers the power of montage as a tool for fragmenting time and space, and in this regard, it has been profoundly influential.

Eisenstein also practiced what he called "intellectual montage," using the editing to suggest ideas and guide the viewer's thought process. The massacre sequence in *Battleship Potemkin* concludes with a vivid example of intellectual montage. To defend the massacre victims, a battleship fires its guns at the headquarters of Czarist troops. As their palace explodes, Eisenstein cuts together three quick shots of different statues of lions. The first stone lion sleeps, the second sits upright, the third roars. The montage, however, makes it look like a single, sleeping lion has awakened with fury. The symbolic idea is that the wrath of the people against the Czar is now aroused; the lion of revolution stalks the land.

(a)

(b)

(c)

BATTLESHIP POTEMKIN (1925)

Eisenstein's thematic montage creates a symbol for the people's revolution. Three separate statues of lions, skillfully edited, become a single lion, roused from its slumbers and roaring its defiance. Because the shots are so brief, the editing imparts a sense of movement to the statuary. Frame enlargements.

SPATIAL FRAGMENTATION   Montage editing used to create spatial fragmentation tends to forgo the use of a clear master shot, the matching of action to that master shot, and the systematic repetition of familiar camera setups. *Moulin Rouge*, for example, breaks almost all the rules of continuity in its editing. Eyelines, camera angles, and object positioning fail to match from shot to shot. The cutting is so quick, though, that the viewer has little time to concentrate on these continuity problems.

FILMMAKER SPOTLIGHT

Sergei Eisenstein

Sergei Eisenstein was one of the greatest Soviet filmmakers working in the silent and early sound period, and his ideas about film editing have exerted tremendous influence over filmmakers throughout the world. While most directors recognize editing as a key element of filmmaking, for Eisenstein it was decisive. He felt that cinema, more than anything else, was an art of montage.

We know exactly what Eisenstein thought because, unlike most filmmakers who do not think and write analytically, he wrote numerous essays about cinema and about the art of editing. The most important of these are collected in volumes entitled *Film Form* and *The Film Sense*. Eisenstein wrote that meaning in film depends far more on editing—on how shots are arranged in a sequence—than on their content, on what is photographed. Montage determines meaning, according to Eisenstein.

Eisenstein practiced what he called "dialectical montage," ordering his shots according to principles of conflict. This might involve conflict of movement from shot to shot, of lines, of volumes (for example, masses of people in the frame), or of tempo. As a Marxist, he believed conflict—or the dialectic, as it is termed in Marxist philosophy—was the fundamental truth of life and of history. And as a good dramatist, he knew that conflict was essential to his stories.

Strike (1923) portrays a rebellion by factory workers and the violent repression it elicits from fat-cat businessmen and politicians. *Battleship Potemkin* (1925) portrays a mutiny by sailors aboard a battleship in pre-Revolutionary Russia, and *October* (1926) dramatizes key events in the October Revolution. Eisenstein builds the stories according to a Marxist analysis of history, in which groups of people matter far more than individual heroes, and he uses montage to show class conflict as a motor of social change.

Unlike the continuity editing that prevailed in American cinema, Eisenstein used editing analytically, to clarify the class basis of the conflicts in his stories. *Strike* (1923), his first film, climaxes with an attack by soldiers on the striking factory workers. As the soldiers slaughter the workers, Eisenstein abruptly intercuts shots of a bull being killed by a butcher, and the idea motivating this shocking montage is that the soldiers treat the workers as so many animals.

Eisenstein avoided using establishing shots or matches of direction and motion because he wanted viewers to supply the missing information and build a comprehensive sense of the screen world in their minds, based on the fragmentary views that he gave them. This gives the montages in many of Eisenstein's films a nervous, jumpy, aggressive quality that he believed was an accurate mirror of dynamic energies at work in the world.

In the 1930s, Eisenstein fell out of favor with Soviet authorities who felt his work was too radical and cutting-edge. They wanted a more realistic, naturalistic style in cinema, and Eisenstein's films were anything but. In the sound era, therefore, he did not work as frequently, and he worried that the addition of spoken dialogue in cinema would diminish the medium's poetic force by making filmmakers more literal and less imaginative in how they edited scenes.

Eisenstein was right to worry. Sound did take cinema in a more naturalistic direction, and the wildly imaginative montages of the silent era grew less common. Eisenstein made three sound films— *Alexander Nevsky* (1936), *Ivan the Terrible Part I* (1944), and *Ivan the Terrible Part II* (1946)—in which

(continued)

he attempted to create poetic combinations of image and sound. But dialectical montage was now frowned upon by the authorities, and the editing in these films is far less aggressive than what he had practiced during the silent era.

The rapid, poetic, often brutal editing of Eisenstein has exerted a strong influence over contemporary film. Hitchcock staged the shower murder in *Psycho* (1960) using Eisensteinian montage, and the rapid montages that violate continuity principles in such films as *The Bourne Ultimatum* would not exist were it not for Eisenstein. These films, though, borrow Eisenstein's technique but not his worldview and Marxist rationale. In his work—and the theories of editing he developed in his essays—Eisenstein presented cinema as a construction rather than a mirror on the world, as a medium constructed according to the laws of montage, in which meaning was not something to be recorded by a camera but was created and arranged by a filmmaker using the art of editing. ■

BATTLESHIP POTEMKIN (1925)

This kind of shot is rare in Eisenstein's work. It provides an expansive and clear view of a key moment in the drama—during the Odessa Steps massacre, a mother carrying her wounded child (foreground) confronts the murderous soldiers (background) who have fired on the citizenry. More typically, he built a scene by showing fragments of its action. Frame enlargement.

Viewers probably notice them subliminally, however, because the editing does feel wild and jagged, not smooth and flowing.

During the dance scenes in the Moulin Rouge, the editing fragments the club's spatial layout by showering the viewer with visual information at a fast rate and by showing many, many close-ups and few master shots. The club is a dizzying montage offering glimpses of people, lights, signs, and faces. Editor Jill Bilcock said that her experience constructing the scenes out of so many close-ups was "like being given thousands of different kinds of colored beads and asked to make a necklace."

The editing builds the scene by accumulating details, bits and pieces of space and action. The editing aims to create a collage of discrete visual impressions rather than a spatially ordered, coherent, and stable environment. The scene is organized by a cumulative principle—the piling up of detail.

While the montage cutting of contemporary films descends from the Soviet model of editing, there are other clear historical precedents. In Alfred Hitchcock's *Psycho* (1960), the film's main character, Marion Crane (Janet Leigh), is murdered in her shower one-third of the way into the film. The murder itself lasts for 40 seconds and is composed of 34 shots. These tend to fall into three categories: (1) shots of Marion struggling with her attacker, holding the killer's knife arm with her hand, (2) shots of Marion's face

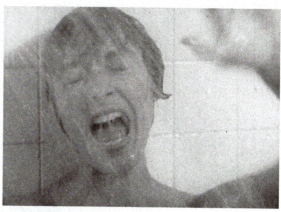

PSYCHO (PARAMOUNT, 1960)

Rapid montage editing creates the sensation of a violent murder in *Psycho* by assembling flash cuts of murderer and victim. The violent pace of the editing intensifies the brutal nature of the scene. Frame enlargements.

and hands as she writhes in the shower, and (3) shots of the killer stabbing toward the camera. By rapidly intercutting these categories of shots, Hitchcock and editor George Tomasini create a scene of extraordinary violence, but one in which most of the actual violence is suggested because viewers almost never see the knife actually touching flesh. The impression of the murder is built up in the mind's eye by virtue of the rapid editing.

As Eisenstein showed, montage can fragment space *and* time, and contemporary filmmakers have used editing in vivid ways to fracture space and distort time. In Sam Peckinpah's *The Wild Bunch* (1969), montage editing slowed action down, interrupted it with cutaways to parallel lines of action, and intercut normal speed and slow-motion footage to create stylish distortions of time and space. During the elaborate gun battle that opens the film, two snipers are shot from their rooftop perch. One man falls from the roof to the ground in slow motion; the other falls forward and into the rooftop ledge at normal speed. The editing intercuts these different time frames to establish an impossible parallel. The man who falls off the roof—traveling a much greater distance and in slow motion—strikes the ground at the same instant that the other victim hits the ledge. The viewer accepts these manipulations as permissible stylistic organizations of the action despite their evident unreality.

THEMATIC MONTAGE Like Eisenstein, filmmakers may use montage to create ideas in the mind of the viewer. The arrangement of shots cues intellectual, and sometimes emotional, associations by the viewer.

Familiar with Eisenstein's work, Charles Chaplin in *Modern Times* (1936) used a similar bit of associational editing (though it is not a montage because it consists of only two shots). At the beginning of the film, he cuts from a shot of sheep being herded into a pen to a shot of workers leaving a subway and crossing the street to enter their factory. The viewer is asked to draw the appropriate conclusions based on the comparison of the two categories of images.

In *Pat Garrett and Billy the Kid* (1973), director Sam Peckinpah used **thematic montage** to emphasize the irony in the fate of sheriff Pat Garrett, killed by the same politicians who hired him years earlier to kill the outlaw Billy the Kid. Peckinpah intercuts two time frames, one set in 1908 showing Garrett's assassination, the other set in

Two rooftop victims, two different film speeds, and the simultaneous resolution of these lines of action. The editing reconfigures space and time. Frame enlargements.

1880 showing Billy and his gang shooting the heads off of some chickens. The intercutting shows Billy firing from the 1880 time frame and seeming to hit Garrett in the 1908 frame. The historical irony is clear. By killing the Kid, Garrett unintentionally brought about a chain of events that ultimately led to his own death many years later.

Sequence Shots

In closing this chapter on editing, it is important to note the existence in cinema history of a stylistic tradition in opposition to montage and to the general contribution of editing in structuring a scene. This is the use of the **long take**, sometimes also known as the **sequence shot**. The term refers to a shot of very long duration which, in some cases, may last for the entire length of a scene. If a filmmaker chooses to construct a scene using the long take, this decision will substitute for the normative practice of building a scene by cutting among different camera set-ups. In other words, the long take becomes the foundation of the scene, not editing. In *Easy Rider* (1969), as noted in an earlier chapter, the harvest prayer scene is composed of an extended 360-degree panning shot across the faces of the commune members. Because the scene is composed of one shot, there is no editing.

Long takes do not always have to be sequence shots. Sometimes a scene can be composed of several very lengthy takes. In Orson Welles's *Citizen Kane* (1941), Kane's parents strike a deal with a banker, Mr. Thatcher, in which the bank will act as Kane's guardian and assume control over his estate until he comes of age. The scene is largely presented in two long takes that, together, run for almost four minutes of screen time. Instead of relying on editing to maintain visual interest, Welles sustains it by choreographing elaborate moves by the characters and the camera. In the work

MODERN TIMES (UNITED ARTISTS, 1936)

Associational editing invites viewers to draw intellectual connections among images. Chaplin compares factory workers and sheep at the beginning of *Modern Times*. Frame enlargements.

Case Study   THE GRADUATE

One of the most creative and imaginative sequences in *The Graduate* (1967) uses associational montage to show the hero, Benjamin (Dustin Hoffman), spending his days floating in his parents' backyard swimming pool and his nights making love with the family friend Mrs. Robinson (Ann Bancroft) in a hotel room. The montage blurs time and place. The viewer knows that a great deal of time is passing, days, probably weeks, but can't say exactly how much. Most remarkably of all, different places and locations blend into one another in a dreamlike way.

In the first shot of the montage (**a**), Ben gets out of the pool, puts on a white shirt, and walks into his parents' house, pushing open the patio door. In shot 2 (**b-1**), Ben enters through a door wearing the white shirt but has entered the hotel room where Mrs. Robinson awaits. The match in action—Ben exiting screen left in shot 1 and entering screen right in shot 2—implies, falsely, that these spaces are connected as part of a single location.

Ben sits with his head against the black headboard of a bed as Mrs. Robinson unbuttons his shirt (**b-2**). Shot 3 (**c-1**) is a close-up of Benjamin's head against a black background. The viewer assumes it to be the bed on which he was lying in the previous

shot, especially because his facial expression matches in both shots. Ben then gets up, crosses the room, and closes a door, beyond which his parents are sitting at a dining room table (**c-2**). They glance at him as he closes the door. Ben then recrosses the room and sits in a black chair before a television set (**c-3**). Obviously, this cannot be the hotel room; he is at home with his parents.

Shot 4 (**d-1**) shows Ben's face against a black background, this time assumed to be the chair in front of the television. The camera then zooms out to reveal the hotel room with Mrs. Robinson dressing (**d-2**). She leaves. Again the viewer has been misled. The room in shot 4 is different than the one in shot 3. Shot 5 (**e-1**) is another close-up of Ben's face against a black background. The viewer thinks it to be the bed on which he was lying in the previous shot, but the camera zooms out to reveal that he is in his bedroom at his parents' house (**e-2**). He glances out his window, puts on his swim trunks, and goes down the stairs. In shot 6 (not illustrated), his mother watches him dive into the pool. Shot 7 (**f**) is a close-up of Ben swimming underwater. In shot 8 (**g**), he leaps up onto the pool's inflatable raft,

(continued)

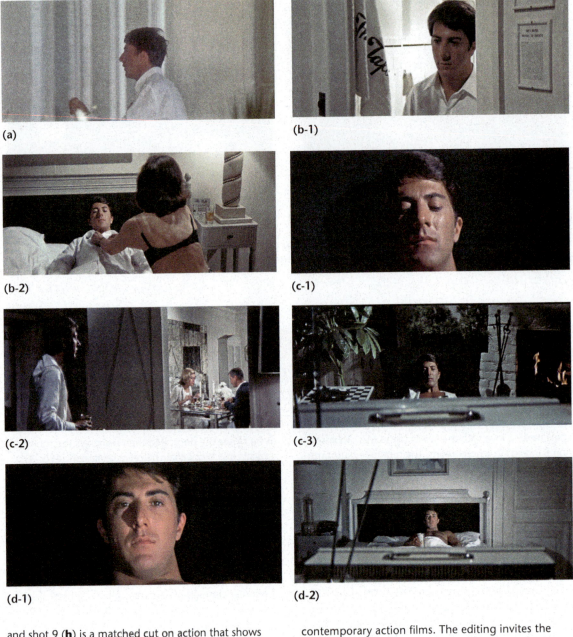

(a)

(b-1)

(b-2)

(c-1)

(c-2)

(c-3)

(d-1)

(d-2)

and shot 9 (**h**) is a matched cut on action that shows Benjamin moving on top of Mrs. Robinson in bed.

The filmmakers use continuity principles, such as matching action, to create the disorienting, dream-like effect in which times and places are indistinct and melt into one another. This is a slower, more seductive presentation of the breakdown of time–space than in the violent, hard-edged montages of

contemporary action films. The editing invites the viewer to draw associations across the cuts. In this case, the associations are psychological, having to do with Ben's alienated frame of mind. He is in a daze, disconnected from all of his environments, lonely and unhappy, sleepwalking through his life, barely conscious of his connection either to his parents or to Mrs. Robinson.

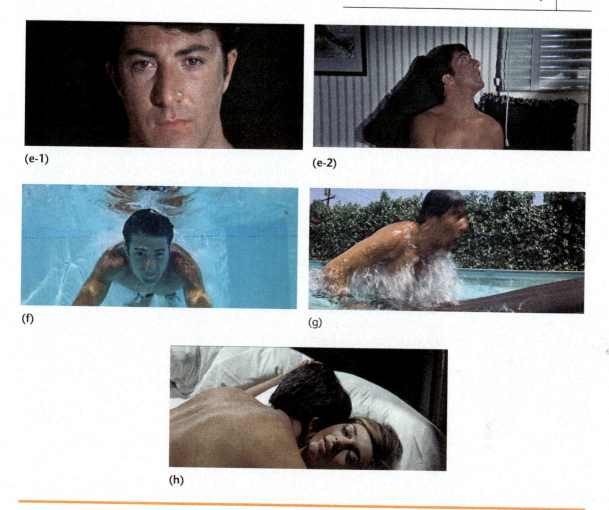

(e-1)

(e-2)

(f)

(g)

(h)

of Welles, and such other directors as Woody Allen, William Wyler (*The Best Years of Our Lives*, 1946), and Miklós Jancsó (*Red Psalm*, 1972), the long take is a recurrent and essential feature of style that provides an alternative to film editing.

Here, too, however digital tools are changing the manner in which a long take can be created. Separate shots can now be joined seamlessly to create the impression of a long take. Joining shots digitally in this manner, the cinematographer of *Children of Men* (2004) created several lengthy moving camera sequences that looked like long takes. The edits were invisible and subliminal.

SUMMARY

Almost universally, filmmakers regard editing as the decisive phase of production, giving a film its distinct shape, organization, and emotional power. There is, however, no single way to cut a scene or a film.

Continuity editing is the predominant approach used in narrative cinema. It establishes a coherent and orderly physical world on screen, despite variations in the camera's placement and angle. The rules that deal with screen direction and matched visual elements are an essential means of creating this coherence and order. Continuity errors occur when mismatched visual elements violate the perceptual constancies that a viewer looks for in the world represented on screen. If Julia Roberts is eating a croissant for breakfast, it should not suddenly turn into a pancake.

Realism is an elastic concept, however, and the physical and perceptual laws that continuity editing seeks to honor can be subjected to distortion and manipulation. Viewers accept many such manipulations, regarding them as permissible expressions of style or artistry. Montage editing enables filmmakers to create striking distortions of time and space, some of which are inconsistent with strict continuity principles. The craft of editing is infinitely powerful in its ability to reorganize time and space, and many things are permissible under the rubric of style.

Whatever approach a given filmmaker might use, if he or she is making a feature film and telling a story, the option of completely avoiding editing does not exist. Even where a filmmaker like Woody Allen may shoot each of his scenes in a single master shot, he and his editor must still join these shots together and make decisions about the points at which to do so. Hitchcock, a director for whom editing was of great importance, once tried to do without it. In *Rope* (1948), he cut only when the camera physically ran out of film (approximately every 10 minutes) and tried through elaborate means to hide the cuts when they did occur. The result is an interesting experiment but a sluggish film that lacks the dramatic rhythms and intensity that only editing can create. To be a filmmaker is to select, manipulate, sequence, and cut!

KEY TERMS AND CONCEPTS

continuity editing 148	final cut 135	180-degree rule 152
cross-cutting 148	iris 140	parallel action 148
cut 137	jump cut 159	rough cut 135
dissolve 137	linear system 136	sequence shot 166
editing 135	long take 166	shot-reverse-shot
editor 135	master shot 149	series 152
errors of continuity 155	matched cut 149	thematic montage 165
eyeline match 150	montage 136	voice-over 145
fade 137	nonlinear editing system 135	wipes 141

SUGGESTED READINGS

Ken Dancyger, *The Technique of Film and Video Editing* (Stoneham, MA: Focal Press, 1996).
Sergei Eisenstein, *Film Form* and *The Film Sense* (New York: Harcourt, Brace and World, 1949).
Vincent LoBrutto, *Selected Takes: Film Editors on Film Editing* (New York: Praeger, 1991).
Walter Murch, *In the Blink of an Eye: A Perspective on Film Editing* (Los Angeles: Silman-James Press, 1995).
Gabriella Oldham, *First Cut: Conversations with Film Editors* (Berkeley and Los Angeles: University of California Press, 1995).
Karel Reisz and Gavin Millar, *The Technique of Film Editing*, 2nd ed. (Boston: Focal Press, 1995).
Ralph Rosenblum, *When the Shooting Stops...the Cutting Begins: A Film Editor's Story* (New York: Da Caps, 1988).
Michael Rubin, *Nonlinear: A Guide to Digital Film and Video Editing* (Gainesville, FL: Triad Pub. Co., 1995).

6

Principles of Sound Design

OBJECTIVES

After reading this chapter, you should be able to:

- describe the development of contemporary multichannel sound

- describe the three basic types of sound in cinema

- explain the uses and functions of dialogue in film

- explain the functions of ADR

- describe sound effects design and Foley techniques

- describe five steps for creating movie music

- explain five basic functions music performs in film

- explain the nature of sound design, its expressive uses, and how it builds on the viewer's real-life acoustical skills and experience

- distinguish between realistic and synthetic sounds

- explain the fundamental differences between sound and image

- explain five codes of sound design and their expressive uses

- differentiate direct sound, reflected sound, and ambient sound

- explain how sound establishes continuity in film as well as intellectual and emotional effects

- explain why switching between on-screen and off-screen sound helps makes camera positions more flexible

Image editing employs standard rules and techniques that (1) provide editors with methods for organizing shots, (2) establish constancies of time and space between the story world on screen and viewers' experiences of their physical environment, and (3) are based on correspondence with the viewer's perceptual experience and have become familiar to viewers through constant repetition over many films. Like image editing, film sound has its own rules (or codes) of structural design. One can speak of sound fades, sound cuts, sound dissolves, and sound perspective. This chapter examines the three categories of sound in film: dialogue, effects, and music. It explains the concept of sound design and examines its rules and techniques.

SOUND IN CONTEMPORARY FILM

Today, film sound is digitally recorded and edited, and it is often created digitally. Indeed, sound went digital long before images did. As a result, sound is much more complex and expressive than in the films of decades past. As recently as the 1980s, for example, it was common for a film's soundtrack to be put together from 20 tracks of sound elements. Today, a soundtrack of 200 or more tracks is the norm.

THE SOCIAL NETWORK (COLUMBIA PICTURES, 2010)

Director David Fincher thought of this film as a docudrama and wanted the audio backgrounds to enhance a sense of place and authenticity. The story locations included Boston and Palo Alto in the San Francisco Bay Area, and environmental sounds recorded in these areas were included as ambient information in the sound mix, in order to accurately characterize place using sound. The film dramatizes the creation of Facebook, and to create an audio environment for the Facebook offices in the film, located in Palo Alto, ambient sound was recorded in numerous Silicon Valley and Bay Area offices. The ambient audio environments created in this way are subliminal, enhancing the film's docudrama style in ways an audience feels without consciously noticing. Pictured, Jesse Eisenberg as Facebook founder Mark Zuckerberg, with Justin Timberlake (right) as Sean Parker, co-creator of Napster. Frame enlargement.

Consider what sound accomplishes in contemporary film. Many sound effects are layered; that is, they are composed of numerous sounds blended together. Doc Ock's tentacles in *Spider Man 2* (2004) were created from a blend of the sounds of a motorcycle chain, piano wire, and a pump-action shotgun. The blend was manipulated in a software program, Pro Tools, to create hundreds of variations, producing whooshes, screeches, ratchety noises, servo-motor sounds, and even vocalizations to give the tentacles personality.

There were so many tentacle variations that they occupied 100 tracks, separated by right tentacle, left tentacle, and upper and lower tentacles. This variety, and the fact that the tentacles are always moving on screen, was perfect for surround sound. A viewer watching the film experiences the tentacle sounds whooshing across all the speakers, front and back. The film's sound designer said that the character was ideal for surround sound because the tentacles were moving in all directions, which multichannel sound could capture perfectly. Bass or low-frequency sounds are a key part of the contemporary soundtrack, adding power and presence to voices or effects.

TOY STORY 3 (PIXAR, 2010)

This was the first film released theatrically in Dolby Surround 7.1, an eight-channel sound system that spreads four channels across the rear to create enhanced directionality within a 360-degree sound field. When Barbie and Ken first meet in the film, Gary Wright's song "Dreamweaver," about the appeal of dreams and fantasy, starts out as a mono (single-channel) recording and then it swells and spreads in audio space, filling all eight channels. The audio change playfully points to the flush of love seizing Barbie and Ken. Frame enlargement.

SPIDER MAN 2 (COLUMBIA, 2004)

Multitrack sound mixing in contemporary film produces richly layered sound effects composed of numerous sound sources blended together. Doc Ock's tentacles take on a personality of their own owing to the many different sounds that they make and the distribution of this sound information in multiple-channel playback. Frame enlargement.

THE PASSION OF THE CHRIST (NEWMARKET, 2004)

Sound is a subliminal element of cinema. Often, a viewer feels its contribution without being explicitly conscious of it. The sound mix of *The Passion* did not use the bass channel very often, reserving it for scenes where Christ carried the cross. When the cross thuds against the ground, the bass channel anchored that sound effect and gave it considerable force. Viewers experienced the force of the effect without being aware it was there. Frame enlargement.

The sound design of *The Passion of the Christ* (2004) reserved the subwoofer for the thudding of the cross on the ground, giving this action added power and emotional presence as a metaphor for the sins of the world.

In earlier decades, scenes that had a lot of repetitive sounds—guns firing, for example—often sounded a bit flat because the sound was not varied. The same gunshot, or ricochet effect, might be used throughout the scene or even from film to film. Today, these effects, like Doc Ock's tentacles, are given tremendous variation. Sounds were individually recorded for each of the iron balls and sheep bones of the flagrum used to whip Jesus in *The Passion of the Christ*, and these were then mixed in expressive combinations.

A huge variety of punching sounds was created for the boxing film *Cinderella Man* (2005) to give each of the film's fights a different tone and personality. Two professional boxers sparred with one another over several days, punching in a variety of styles while the sound crew recorded them. These were the sounds heard in the film. Sound also can be used to change an actor's performance. In one scene of *Cinderella Man*, Mae (Renee Zellweger) argues with her husband (Russell Crowe) about his going back in the boxing ring. Afraid he will be killed, she becomes nearly hysterical. During postproduction, the sound crew lowered the pitch of her voice to make it sound less shrill, fearing that otherwise the audience would lose sympathy with her.

Sound also can be subliminal and subjective. At the beginning of *Collateral* (2004), when a hired killer played by Tom Cruise appears in an airport, the sound is nonspecific and diffused, unfocused, until he bumps into his contact man, at which point the sounds of the airport become very clear and defined.

Later in the film, when a cab driver (Jamie Foxx) realizes that Cruise is a hit man, the soundtrack expresses Fox's alarm. The background city noises all convey anxiety—one hears people yelling, the siren of an alarm, car speakers booming rap music. The sound mix weaves a tapestry of urban noises that convey and symbolize the current of emotions that run through the film.

EVOLUTION OF FILM SOUND

Of all the components of film structure, sound has shown the greatest improvements in recent decades. Contemporary film uses multiple channels of sound information to envelop viewers in a dynamic, three-dimensional **sound field** (the acoustical area covered by speaker placement in a surround setup and activated by multichannel sound coming from the speakers). In the 1930s and 1940s, in contrast, film sound was essentially a monaural, single-channel experience, with each speaker in a theater auditorium receiving the same signal. Sound was encoded as an optical track on the strip of film, and directors and sound mixers were invariably disappointed at the loss of volume, limited frequency range, and distortion in the upper register that occurred when they encoded their sound onto the optical track. Low-volume sound effects vanished into the hiss of the track. High volumes produced a different problem. On optical tracks, the louder the sound, the larger its visual encoding (i.e., the more space it occupies on the track). Because the track space available between frame line and sprocket holes is fixed, volume levels that exhaust this space edge into harsh noise, a frequent problem with soundtracks from these years.

To compete with television in the 1950s, Hollywood moved to widescreen film formats, some of which carried multichannel stereo sound, using magnetic stripes to encode the sound signal. To play such soundtracks, projectors had to be outfitted with special playback heads, much like a tape recorder. Widescreen formats such as Cinemascope (35 mm) and Todd-AO (70 mm) carried from four to six channels of sound. (In this regard, film stereo was distinct from home stereo, a two-channel system used for playing music.) Mag-stripe stereo on widescreen film, however, was reserved for special appeal films, and until the mid-1970s, the industry norm remained a single-channel optical track.

Debuting in 1976, Dolby Stereo carried two optical tracks that were encoded with four channels of sound information. These were configured for playback as left, center, right, and rear (surround) channels. With Dolby Stereo, multichannel sound gained widespread acceptance in the film industry. For the consumer market of home video, Dolby Surround debuted in 1982, enabling home viewers to play Dolby Stereo movies as stereo videocassettes. Initially, though, Dolby Surround only decoded the left, right, and surround channels, but Dolby Prologic decoders, marketed in 1987, enabled center channel decoding as well.

Cinema sound became even richer when Dolby moved to a digital six-channel system in 1992. Known as Dolby Digital, the system carried three channels across the front—left, center, right—plus two fully independent rear channels (left and right surrounds) and a dedicated channel for low-frequency (bass) signals. The digital soundtrack data were placed between the sprocket holes on the film, which also carried an analog stereo soundtrack.

Dolby added yet another channel in 1999. Dolby Digital Surround EX is a seven-channel system, adding a third surround channel positioned behind the viewer, in addition to the rear left and rear right split surrounds of the 5.1 system. This extra channel can be used to create flyover effects, useful in films such as *Star Wars Episode III: The Revenge of the Sith*. An eighth channel is now commonly used to increase directionality. *Toy Story 3* (2010) was the first film released theatrically in Dolby Surround 7.1.

Today, the industry uses several competing digital sound formats: Dolby Digital, Digital Theater Systems (DTS, using a CD for the soundtrack synched with time code

High Definition Audio

Blu-ray DVD (BD) offers tremendous improvement in the audio performance of movies viewed in the home. It offers high definition audio in conjunction with high definition video. It can do this because BD can store a greater amount of audio-visual information than standard DVD. A dual-layer BD can hold 50 gigabytes of information as compared with 8.5 gigabytes on a standard DVD. As a result Blu-ray discs have introduced new audio formats that require more disc space than standard DVDs can accommodate and are far more expressive and enveloping.

Dolby Digital 5.1 and DTS Digital Surround (also 5.1) are the audio tracks offered on standard DVD, and they can be found on many Blu-ray discs as well. But BD also may carry the eight-channel extensions—Dolby Digital Plus (DD+) and DTS-HD—of these formats which expand the number of audio channels in playback. Eight-channel formats are configured as 7.1 systems. Relative to 5.1 systems, they have two additional rear channels.

More exciting, however, are the lossless formats that BD can carry. On standard DVD, Dolby Digital and DTS 5.1 compress the audio information by discarding sections of the soundtrack that are inaudible to human hearing or that tend to be covered by other audio information. By contrast, Dolby TrueHD and DTS HD-MA offer lossless compression and are new formats introduced for high definition DVD. Because there is no loss of audio information, in theory, listening to a Dolby TrueHD or a DTS HD-MA soundtrack is like listening to the original studio master that filmmakers created.

In addition to these lossless compression formats, many Blu-ray discs also carry an LPCM (linear pulse code modulation) soundtrack. LPCM soundtracks are uncompressed and therefore take up even more disc space than Dolby True HD or DTS HD-MA. But, like them, an LPCM track is lossless and is akin to hearing a studio master. Films viewed conventionally, in a standard movie theater, are not capable of delivering this kind of sound quality. Thus, the audio capabilities offered by Blu-ray are superior to what celluloid film can deliver.

Much, though, depends on the technical setup of the home viewing environment. While many BD

THE SAND PEBBLES (20TH CENTURY FOX, 1966)

This epic adventure starring Steve McQueen was originally released in the era of analog audio. However, because the film was exhibited in 70mm, it carried six channels of sound. These were digitally restored and re-mastered for the Blu-ray release, which features a DTS HD-MA soundtrack, with lossless multichannel audio, as well as a four-channel Dolby Digital soundtrack. Neither format existed at the time of the film's release. The film sounds better on Blu-ray today than it did in conventional theaters in 1966. Many older films released on high definition DVD feature this kind of sound upgrade. Frame enlargement.

players may be capable of decoding the lossless formats, the best results are obtained by letting a high-end receiver do the decoding while the player merely passes the lossless Dolby, DTS or PCM signal to the receiver. And because the bandwidth of the lossless signal is much higher than is standard Dolby or DTS, HDMI (High Definition Multimedia Interface) cables are needed to connect player and receiver. Viewers watching movies on Blu-ray, then, have more audio options than standard DVD has offered. The

BD of *300* (2007), for example, offers 5.1 channels of sound in uncompressed LPCM, in Dolby TrueHD, and in Dolby Digital. *Pan's Labyrinth* (2007) and *Rush Hour 3* (2007) offer 7.1 channels in DTS-HD MA. *Blade Runner* (1982) carries a Dolby Digital 5.1 track as well as a Dolby TrueHD track, an audio format that did not exist when the film was originally produced and released. Viewed on Blu-ray, *Blade Runner* sounds better than it did upon its initial release nearly 30 years ago. ■

printed on the film), and Sony Dynamic Digital Sound (SDDS). Each film print, however, still carries an optical soundtrack, as a backup in case a problem arises with the digital information and because many theaters are only equipped for optical playback.

Digital playback revolutionized the art of film sound. Filmmakers no longer had to contend with the restrictions imposed by an optical track. Spread across three channels in the front, the **soundstage** (the acoustical space established by the front speakers) is broad and expansive and is anchored with an impressive bottom register supplied by the dedicated bass channel. The thunderous explosions in contemporary action films illustrate the potential this channel has given cinema. The rear surround channels make the sound field dynamic and three-dimensional, enveloping the viewer in multidirectional sound. Until the 1990s, the surround channels were used infrequently for the occasional sound effect, but they are now used very aggressively, along with all the other channels, to spatialize the sound field (i.e., to render it in highly directional terms) and provide the viewer with an immersive sound experience. The Oscar-winning (for sound-effects editing) *The Ghost and the Darkness* (1996) boasts an exceptionally complex and aggressive six-channel mix.

Cinema is now oddly unbalanced. In sound, it is fully three-dimensional, but its picture remains two-dimensional. Viewers are surrounded by sound but must watch a picture on a flat screen positioned in front of them. It seems likely that the ideal toward which cinema is evolving is a totally 3-D experience, in picture *and* sound. At some future point, cinema viewers will have an immersive visual experience, but so far the medium has achieved this ideal only with sound.

ARMAGEDDON (TOUCHSTONE, 1998)

Multi-channel playback of digital film sound routes bass signals to a separate, dedicated channel. This gives the modern film sound stage an impressive acoustic floor and adds tremendous power to special effects imagery. Frame enlargement.

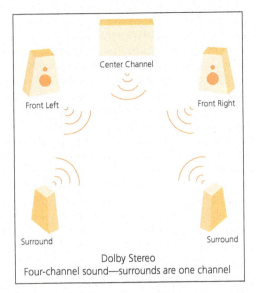

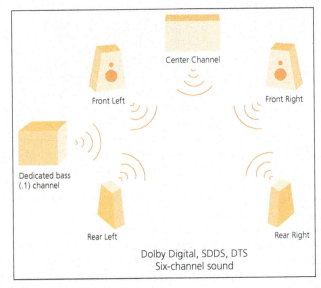

FIGURE 6.1   **FIGURE 6.2**

Dolby Digital brought six-channel sound to the home video environment on laser disc in 1995 and on DVD (digital video disc) in 1997. Indeed, the successful launch of DVD has encouraged studios and filmmakers to undertake multi-channel remixes of older film soundtracks for release in this format. Warner Brothers' DVD of *Dirty Harry* (1972) carried an impressive Dolby Digital remix, and director Wolfgang Peterson supervised an outstanding six-channel remix of the track for *Das Boot* (1981) on DVD. The Blu-ray release in 2010 carried an eight-channel digital mix. The film portrays submarine warfare in World War II, and its new soundtrack creates a total sonic environment that places viewers inside a narrow, cramped German submarine deep in the Mediterranean. Other older films given multiple-channel remixes include titles that were restored for theatrical release and subsequent DVD and

DAS BOOT (COLUMBIA TRISTAR, 1981)

Digital, multichannel soundtracks create a spatial, three-dimensional sound field by surrounding the viewer with discrete, directional sound. Wolfgang Peterson's film about submarine warfare in World War II is one of the outstanding sonic experiences in contemporary cinema; sound is both the subject and structure of this film. The U-boat captain and his officer listen anxiously for sonar signals warning of the approach of Allied warships. Frame enlargement.

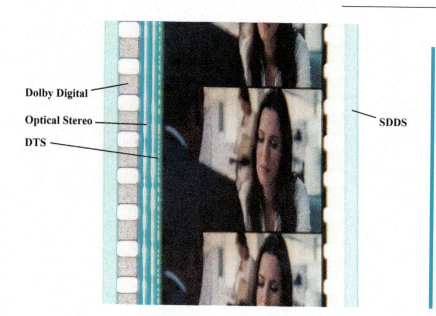

Dolby Digital

Optical Stereo

DTS

SDDS

Celluloid film carries multiple soundtracks positioned in different places around the frames (the picture area on the film strip). The Dolby Digital track is located between the sprocket holes. The optical track is between the sprocket holes and the frames. The DTS track appears as time code between the optical track and the frames. The SDDS track appears outside the sprocket holes along the edge of the film strip. (This is an anamorphic scope film so the frames exhibit the characteristic anamorphic squeeze.) Frame enlargement.

Blu-ray distribution. These include *Gone with the Wind* (1939), *The Wizard of Oz* (1939), Hitchcock's *Vertigo* (1958) and the classic musicals *My Fair Lady* (1964) and *West Side Story* (1961).

Sound in cinema has never been better than in the contemporary period. One cannot make similar claims for cinematography, editing, or many other elements of cinema structure. In this regard, sound is making a uniquely improved aesthetic contribution to cinema. Viewers today are privileged to enjoy a total sonic experience that was not available to moviegoers in earlier periods.

TYPES OF SOUND

Three basic types of sound figure in cinema. These are **dialogue, effects,** and **music.**

Dialogue

Since the late 1920s when synchronous sound became a permanent feature of the movies, two primary kinds of dialogue have been employed in the cinema. **Speech** is delivered by characters on screen usually in conversation with one another. **Voice-over narration** accompanies images and scenes but is not delivered by a particular character from within the scene. Voice-over narration typically is provided by an all-seeing, all-knowing, detached narrator or by a character in the story, usually from some time later than the events portrayed on screen.

SPEECH   Motion pictures use a wide range of dialects and speech types. Shakespearean adaptations faithfully transpose the Bard's language to the screen and frequently employ classically trained actors such as Laurence Olivier, Ralph Richardson, or John Gielgud. Kenneth Branagh's trilogy—*Henry V* (1989), *Much Ado about Nothing* (1993), and *Hamlet* (1996)—are among the most cinematic of

MUCH ADO ABOUT NOTHING (SAMUEL GOLDWYN, 1993)

Kenneth Branagh and Emma Thompson play bickering lovers in this delightful version of Shakespeare's comedy. Branagh's Shakespeare films respect the Bard's language while giving it a completely cinematic showcase. Frame enlargement.

these adaptations. By contrast, other films adopt a more playful attitude toward Shakespeare. Oliver Parker's *Othello* (1995) successfully casts an actor lacking classical training—Laurence Fishburne—in the title role, and Baz Luhrmann's MTV-style *Romeo and Juliet* (1996) grafted the play's language onto a thoroughly modernist visual style. More recently, *Shakespeare in Love* (1998) used naturalistic, nonpoetic language to portray a fictional episode from the playwright's life.

At the other extreme from the poetry of Shakespeare lies the colloquialism of modern life. The dynamic impact of sound in the late 1920s and early 1930s was due largely to the electrifying presence of a new generation of screen actors. James Cagney, for example, brought his scrappy, high-voltage personality to a series of gritty, tough, urban dramas that allowed him to draw on his boyhood experiences growing up in the slums of New York's Upper East Side. The way Cagney moved and spoke electrified audiences because it was so different from the mannerisms and speech of stage-trained actors. In the Cagney classic *Angels with Dirty Faces* (1938), he plays a good-hearted crook named Rocky who greets his friends with the salutation, "Whadda ya hear? Whadda ya say?" rattled off in rapid-fire delivery. Cagney got this greeting from a pimp he had known when he was a youth.

The screen appeal of many stars, like Cagney, resides partly in their distinctive manner of speaking. Will Smith's lilting voice, often barbed with a wisecrack, and Eddie Murphy's trademark laugh have endeared them to audiences. In *Face/Off* (1997), actors John Travolta and Nicolas Cage swap each other's mannered speaking style in an impressive display of the connection between speech and star charisma.

By speaking to audiences in a colloquial, familiar manner, movies forge a strong rapport and powerful emotional bonds with viewers. In the 1950s, when Marlon Brando, playing an outlaw motorcyclist in *The Wild One* (1953), was asked what he is rebelling against, he replied, "Whadda ya' got?" and a young generation instantly understood his insolence and contempt for established society. In Spike Lee's *Clockers* (1995), the thick street dialects of Brooklyn gangs vividly establish their authority and authenticity.

VOICE-OVER NARRATION   While rarely used today, voice-over narration in earlier periods was an essential part of certain genres. In the 1940s and 1950s, many films noir—*Out of the Past* (1947), *Criss Cross* (1949), *The Killers* (1946)—told their stories through intricate flashbacks accompanied by voice-over narration. In voice-over, the

tough private eye or the world-weary criminal delivered hard-boiled lines of dialogue. At the beginning of *Double Indemnity* (1944), with a bullet wound slowly leaking blood from his shoulder, a cynical insurance agent confesses his crime: he killed a man for money and a woman and, as fate would have it, didn't get either.

Voice-over narration can be used for ironic or playful effects. In one of the most famous films noir, *Sunset Boulevard* (1950), the narrator turns out to be a dead man. The film opens with shots of a man's body floating in a swimming pool. The police arrive and remove the body as the narrator, a screenwriter named Joe Gillis, tells how the murder occurred. It is not until the end of the movie that viewers realize the dead man *is* Joe Gillis. He talks wistfully about how it feels when the police fish him out of the pool and lay him out "like a harpooned baby whale."

DOUBLE INDEMNITY (PARAMOUNT, 1944)

Hard-boiled, tough-guy dialogue, spoken as voice-over narration, coupled with dark, low-key lighting to establish the hardedged, cynical atmosphere of classic film noir. Fred MacMurray, as the doomed Walter Neff, provides the gripping narration about a murder scheme gone awry. Frame enlargement.

Of course, in the case of *Sunset Boulevard*, the narration is unreliable and misleading. Dead men don't talk. Director Billy Wilder plays against an established convention of voice-over narration, which is that the character doing the narration must survive the events of the story. In this case, he doesn't, and it enabled Wilder to pull off one of his darkest jokes. In a similar manner, the narrator of *American History X* (1998) is murdered but continues his narration, commenting on the things that his death has taught him. *American Beauty* (1999) is another film that uses this device.

While voice-over narration is closely identified with U.S. films noir, it also has been used in documentary filmmaking, especially that subcategory of documentaries known as the newsreel. Newsreels routinely accompanied feature films, cartoons, and serials in the nation's movie theaters in earlier decades, and they typically employed the so-called "voice of God" narrator. Such a narrator was male and spoke with a deep, booming, authoritative tone.

In *Citizen Kane* (1941), director Orson Welles satirized the "voice of God" newsreel narrator. The film tells the life story of Charles Foster Kane, a rich newspaper man who rose from humble beginnings. The film opens with Kane's death; a newsreel follows, viewed by newspaper reporters for background on their stories about Kane's death. The newsreel features a "voice of God" narrator as director Welles expertly mimics the conventions of this kind of documentary.

Beyond the fake newsreel, however, *Citizen Kane* offers a host of other voice-over narrators. *Citizen Kane* is a classic and superlative example of voice-over narration used for complex effect and as an essential ingredient of film structure. The plot of the film is constructed as a series of flashbacks, each one narrated by a different

SUNSET BLVD. (PARAMOUNT, 1950); DAUGHTERS OF THE DUST (AMERICAN PLAYHOUSE, 1991)

Voice-over narration can be quite playful. Joe Gillis (William Holden) narrates *Sunset Blvd.*, despite the fact that he's a murder victim. As the film begins, the police find Joe floating face down in a swimming pool, and he proceeds to tell us how he ended up there. Billy Wilder's film plays with the movie convention that narrators will survive the stories they tell. An unborn child narrates Julie Dash's *Daughters of the Dust* and makes fleeting appearances in the film as a kind of phantom. She tells the film's story about the Gullah people of the Sea Islands and their migration to the U.S. mainland, events that are not yet a part of her own life-to-come. Frame enlargements.

CITIZEN KANE (RKO, 1941)

Jed Leland (Joseph Cotton), one of the principal narrators in *Citizen Kane*, explains why Kane's first marriage failed. As he begins his speech, the image dissolves to the past to show the first Mrs. Kane at breakfast. The narrative voices are not easily reconciled. Leland describes events he couldn't possibly have witnessed. Frame enlargement.

character, which makes the emerging portrait of Charles Foster Kane into a kaleidoscope. Characters recollecting Kane include the millionaire banker, Walter P. Thatcher, who was given custody of Kane as a little boy; Susan Alexander, Kane's second wife; Jed Leland, the drama critic who worked briefly on Kane's newspapers; Mr. Bernstein, Kane's chief editor and close friend; and Raymond, Kane's personal valet.

Each of these characters narrates a section of the film, recalling events in ways that clash with the memories of the other narrators. For example, Jed Leland recalls the Charles Foster Kane who betrayed his ideals and principles, whereas Mr. Bernstein emphasizes those principles, remembering how Kane used his newspaper to fight crime and expose official graft and corruption.

The voice-over narration frames the various flashbacks and colors them with a variety of psychological perspectives. *Citizen Kane*, in part, is a mystery film. The mystery is Kane's personality, which ultimately remains unknowable. It is difficult to reconcile the various Kanes disclosed in the narrators' memories because each is so different from the others. In this way, the respective voice-over narrations deepen the emotional and psychological mystery of film, the nature of Kane's personality. Few films in cinema history have used voice-over narration so skillfully and with such profound structural and emotional effects.

ADR AND DIALOGUE MIXING   Most of the dialogue heard in the average feature originates from the **production track** (the soundtrack recorded at the point of filming), but 30 percent or more of a film's dialogue is the result of **ADR** (automated dialogue replacement). Following shooting, actors recreate portions of a scene's dialogue in a sound studio, and this postproduction sound is mixed in with dialogue from the production track. The mixer must smooth out the audible differences of tone and timbre and make sure that no audio cuts are apparent to the listener. Digital software facilitates the ADR process, alleviating the need for an actor to speak in perfect synch with the picture; the software can match the ADR speech with the lip movements on screen.

(a)   (b)

PRETTY WOMAN (TOUCHSTONE, 1990)

The blocking of a scene can create opportunities to add new dialogue using ADR. These two frames from a single shot show how changing character positions facilitated the addition in postproduction of the salesman's line of dialogue about helping her use the credit card. The salesman is visible at the rear (a) between Julia Roberts and Richard Gere, but when Roberts walks out of the store, she blocks the salesman from the camera's view (b), at which point the new line of dialogue was inserted. Frame enlargement.

ADR is typically used when portions of the production track are unusable or unsatisfactory, and some films, such as Sergio Leone's *Once upon a Time in America* (1984), have extraordinarily high amounts of ADR. All the dialogue in that picture was done as ADR; none originated from the production track.

Camera placement can facilitate opportunities for using ADR. One of the highlights of *Pretty Woman* (1990) occurs when Julia Roberts goes on a Beverly Hills shopping spree. The ensuing montage is scored to the titular Roy Orbison song, and a dialogue exchange between Richard Gere and the shop clerk (Larry Miller) kicks off the start of the montage. Gere tells the clerk that she has the credit card, and the clerk incautiously replies he'll help her use it. The clerk's dialogue was dropped in as late-in-the-game ADR, an opportunity facilitated by the blocking of the scene, as the accompanying frame enlargements demonstrate.

Sound Effects

Sound effects are the physical (i.e., nonspeech) sounds heard as part of the action and the physical environments seen on screen. They include **ambient sound,** which is the naturally occurring, generally low-level sound produced by an environment (wind in the trees, traffic in the city). They also include the sounds produced by specific actions in a scene, such as the rumble of the spaceship Nostromo in *Alien* (1979) as it passes nearby, or the crash of broken glass as Mookie throws a trashcan through the window of Sal's Pizzeria in *Do the Right Thing* (1989). Digital methods of sound recording and mixing enable sound engineers to achieve an impressive aural separation of individual sound elements. This gives the effects in contemporary film a richer texture than in decades past and enables selective emphasis of individual effects without a corresponding loss of the overall sonic context.

Virtually all the sound effects that one hears in contemporary film are the result of postproduction manipulation. Sound effects recorded as part of the production track may be electronically cleaned and optimized, but most are recorded separately and in places other than the filming environment. Many effects are created using **Foley technique.** Foley technique refers to the live performance and recording of sound effects in synchronization with the picture. As the film is projected in a sound recording studio, a Foley artist watches the action and performs the necessary effects. A Foley artist might walk across a bare floor using hard shoes in synchronization with a character on-screen to produce the needed effects of footsteps. The Foley artist may open or close a door or drop a tray of glasses on the floor to create these effects as needed in a given scene.

Foley techniques require considerable physical dexterity, often verging on the acrobatic, from the artists creating these live effects. Foley is often needed because many of today's films involve the use of radio microphones that are attached to individual actors in a scene. Unlike mikes on a boom overhead, radio mikes fail to pick up natural sounds in the environment, and these often have to be dubbed using Foley techniques.

Because of the nonspecific nature of sound—taken out of context, many sounds are difficult to identify—Foley often uses objects that are not part of the scene. To create sound effects in *Star Wars Episode 2: Attack of the Clones* for the skin surfaces of alien creatures, when other aliens or objects touch them, the Foley artists used pineapples, coconuts, and cantaloupes. The rough texture of their surfaces proved to be ideally suited to evoking the imaginary sound of alien skin.

Whether or not Foley is employed to create a given effect, digital tools enable sound engineers to electronically enhance effects and introduce changes in the soundwave characteristics of a given source. The effects track of a film is the highly processed outcome of these electronic methods of sound manipulation. Leading the industry's transition to digital audio in 1984, Lucasfilm had a proprietary digital sound workstation (ASP, Audio Signal Processor) that stored and mixed sound in digital format. For *Indiana Jones and the Temple of Doom* (1984), when Jones is surrounded by a bevy of arrows flying toward him, ASP electronically extended the arrows' whizzing sounds and added Doppler effects (Doppler is a means of spatializing sound by altering its pitch).

The simple, raw recording of a given effect usually lacks emotional impact, so audio engineers typically manipulate the effect, by layering in other components, to make it suitably expressive. In *Apocalypse Now* (1979), during the scene where panicky Americans machine-gun a group of Vietnamese in their boat, sound designer Walter Murch wanted to affect the viewer's psychological and emotional response to the machine-gun sound. He wanted the viewer to feel that the sound was realistic even though it was not a live recording of a single source but a synthetic blend of multiple, separate recordings.

Murch backed the microphone away from the gun to get a clean recording and then, later, added supplementary elements such as the clank of discharging metallic cartridges and the hiss of hot metal. By layering these additional features over the softer sound of the gun firing, Murch artificially created a convincing realism in ways that were compatible with his recording technology. Doing this involved "disassembling" the sound rather than capturing it live and direct on tape.

In *Terminator 2* (1991), for the gun battle in an underground parking garage, sound designer Gary Rydstrom recorded guns firing in this reverberant space. But to make the sound interesting, he also recorded the sound of two-by-fours slapping together in the garage and layered this echoing sound into the effect to "fatten" it up. In *Backdraft* (1991), Rydstrom gave blazing fires an audio presence and personality by layering in animal growls and monkey screams. Given the film's context—about deadly urban fires—he knew the audience would not hear these sounds as animal noises but as attributes of the fire. For the backdrafts, produced when a huge fire sucks in oxygen before exploding, he used coyote howls, which gave the backdrafts

BACKDRAFT (UNIVERSAL, 1991)
Taken out of context, the meaning of an isolated sound can be very fluid and difficult to identify. This enables sound designers to attach sounds to unrelated images to great effect. The fires in *Backdraft* were mixed with animal sounds, although viewers did not identify these sounds as such. This audio design suggested that fire was a kind of living organism, with intelligence and personality. Frame enlargement.

a subliminal personality and intelligence. Expressive sound effects are complex, artificial creations that transcend their live sound components.

Music

Music has always accompanied the presentation of films for audiences. During the silent period, film music was often drawn from public-domain, noncopyrighted classical selections or from the popular tunes of the era. Numerous catalogues offered filmmakers or musical directors a guide for selecting appropriate music depending on the tempo of the scene and its general emotional content. In addition, some original symphonic scores were composed for silent films.

The original score composed especially for motion pictures became standard practice in the sound period. While many different musical styles can be employed in film scoring—jazz (*Mo' Better Blues*, 1990), rock (*Bill and Ted's Excellent Adventure*, 1989), ragtime (*Ragtime*, 1981), symphonic orchestral (*Star Wars*, 1977)—music is typically used to follow action on-screen and to illustrate a character's emotions.

CREATING MOVIE MUSIC   The production of movie music involves five distinct steps: spotting, preparation of a cue sheet, composing, performance and recording, and mixing. The first stage is **spotting**, during which the composer consults with the film's director and producer and views the final cut in order to determine where and when music might be needed. Spotting determines the locations in the film that require musical cues, where and how the music will enter, and its general tempo and emotional color.

Much of this is left up to the composer, although detailed discussions with a film's director are not uncommon, especially when the director has strong preferences as to the style of scoring. Sometimes the director will impose a **temp track**—a temporary musical track derived from a score the director likes—onto the soundtrack of an edited scene, or even the entire film, and ask that the composer create something like the temp track. Not surprisingly, many composers find this stifling.

After the film has been spotted, the music editor then prepares a **cue sheet.** The cue sheet contains a detailed description of each scene's action requiring music plus the exact timings to the second of that action. This enables the composer to work knowing the exact timing in minutes, seconds, and frames of each action requiring music. As a result, musical cues can catch the action and enter and end at precisely determined points.

Once the cue sheet has been prepared, the third step is actual composition of the score. This is done by the composer using a video copy of the film. The video contains a digital time code that displays minutes, seconds, and frames for all the action. Using the cue sheet and video, the composer creates the score, carefully fitting the timing of music and action.

Digital programs known as *sequencers* enable the composer to lock the score onto the video's digital time code. Once this is done, any scene can be played back, and the computer can call up the score, enabling the composer to check timings. Tempo adjustments—speeding up or slowing down the music—also can be made by computer to precisely match music with action. The sequencer also can generate a series of clicks that many composers use to establish a desired tempo for a given scene and that is then used as a guide for composition.

Digital technology also has altered the phase of composition in which the composer demonstrates the score for the director. Digital samplers enable composers to electronically simulate all needed instrumentation in their scores and play the results for the director, who can hear a close approximation of the film's score-in-progress. Before the age of samplers, composers demonstrated their scores on the piano, which required that directors be able to understand how the piano performance would translate into a full-bodied instrumentation. The disadvantage of digital sampling is that demonstrations now give directors more input into scoring—an area most are not qualified to handle—because, using a sampler's keyboard, anyone can easily manipulate the musical characteristics of a composition. Some directors, to their composer's dislike, find this an irresistible temptation.

Once the music has been composed, the next step is performance and recording of the score on a sound stage while a copy of the film is projected on a large screen or video monitor. Timing of music to film action is facilitated by the use of clicks to

PLATOON (ORION PICTURES, 1986)

The score for *Platoon* deliberately avoids using conventional war-film music. Instead, composer Georges Delerue employed an already-existing classical composition—Samuel Barber's melancholy "Adagio for Strings"—and used it to emphasize the film's haunted, tragic tone. Frame enlargement.

establish tempo, *streamers*—lines imprinted on the film or video—that travel across the screen and mark the beginning and end of each cue, and a large analog clock with a sweep second hand. The performance of the score is often attended by the director and producer of the film.

The final stage in the creation of movie music is the process of mixing, which is the blending of the various sound tracks, effects, music, and dialogue. The fact that movie music is mixed along with dialogue and effects has influenced the attitude of composers to the kind of music they create. Because dialogue is regarded as the most important sound in a movie, music typically is mixed at a lower volume when it accompanies dialogue. Composers know this and work accordingly.

Hollywood composer Miklos Rosza pointed out that when music accompanies dialogue, it should be simple, without a lot of ornamentation, because this will be lost in the mix when the music is buried beneath the dialogue. He also recommended that music in dialogue passages be scored with strings rather than brass instruments because he felt that strings blend better with the human voice. While there is much variation among composers in their approach to scoring, these remarks indicate something most would agree on—the film score is not autonomous. It should be written with the action in mind and be capable of blending with all other sound sources in the movie.

So much for the technical steps involved in producing movie music. What of its dramatic functions? Why is it used, and what does it accomplish in movies?

FUNCTIONS OF MOVIE MUSIC   The great U.S. concert hall composer Aaron Copland occasionally ventured into the world of filmmaking to compose scores for such pictures as *Of Mice and Men* (1940), *Our Town* (1940), *The Red Pony* (1949), and *The Heiress* (1949). Copland discussed the functions of movie music as he saw them, emphasizing five basic functions.

Setting the Scene   Film music creates a convincing atmosphere of time and place. Movie music characterizes the locations, settings, and cultures where the story occurs. Often, this may involve the use of special instrumentation that reflects regional or ethnic musical characteristics. Jerry Goldsmith, who was one of the industry's most prolific and respected composers, employed pan flutes in his score for *Under Fire* (1983), a film dealing with the

UNDER FIRE (ORION PICTURES, 1983)
Movie music helps establish place and locale, often by employing regional or ethnic musical instruments and traditions. Jerry Goldsmith's score for *Under Fire* used pan flutes, associated with peasant cultures of Central America, to musically characterize the film's Nicaraguan setting and the popular basis of that country's revolution. Frame enlargement.

revolution in Nicaragua in 1979. By using an instrument that was not specifically tied to Nicaragua but was found in many peasant cultures in Central America, Goldsmith was able to create a musical score that tied the Nicaraguan revolution, musically, to its peasant origins, but in a way that included echoes of the peasant cultures of other Central American countries, much as the revolution itself did in the 1980s.

Sometimes the time and place that a composer wishes to create do not exist in reality. For his celebrated score for the science fiction film *Planet of the Apes* (1968), Goldsmith relied on the use of unusual instruments, such as ram's horns and brass slide whistles, and unusual musical techniques, such as clicking the keys of woodwind instruments directly on the microphone. The result was a score that many people thought was electronic, though Goldsmith has pointed out that he did not use any electronic techniques. He used existing instruments in an unusual fashion to enlarge the sound possibilities of the orchestra. These new and unusual sounds perfectly suited the film's futuristic fantasy set in an alien and frightening world.

Unfortunately, the scene-setting function of movie music sometimes draws on and fosters cultural stereotypes. Dimitri Tiomkin, who composed the score for Howard Hawks's Western *Red River* (1948), needed music for a scene in which Indians attack a wagon train. He wrote music with a stereotypical tympani beat in order to telegraph the idea that the Indians were about to attack. Tiomkin knew that this Indian music was quite artificial and without any real historical basis, but he believed that authentic tribal music would have been less effective because it was unconventional. Tiomkin elected to use the musical stereotype because the audience was familiar with it.

Adding Emotional Meaning All motion picture composers stress the importance of this function. Composer Hugo Friedhofer pointed out that music has the special ability of hinting at the unseen, whereas images can only show what is visible. Music extends an image's range of meaning by adding psychological or emotional qualities not in the picture.

The tonal range of Western music, particularly the highly coloristic rendering used in the Romantic period of the late nineteenth century, has become the model for orchestral movie music because the emotional content of this musical style is extremely familiar to audiences. Think of all the romantic melodramas in which the teary lovers are about to be parted and the violins are sawing away on the soundtrack

BLACK HAWK DOWN (COLUMBIA PICTURES, 2001)

The sound design eliminates realistic sound from portions of the helicopter attack sequence and uses music to quietly imitate the whooshing helicopter blades. The design creates a subjective perspective that portrays the mental concentration of the American soldiers in the helicopters, about to go into combat. Frame enlargement.

or the way the strings in John Williams's soaring score for *E.T.* capture the pathos of Eliot's goodbye to E.T. at the conclusion of that film.

Movie music emphasizes emotional effects most often by direct symbolization: The music embodies and symbolizes an emotion appropriate to the screen action. An alternative approach is to employ a contrast of image and music. Though less common than direct musical symbolization, it can be quite effective.

An especially impressive example occurs during the helicopter attack sequence in Ridley Scott's *Black Hawk Down* (2001). The Black Hawk helicopters in reality are very loud, but the film's sound editor minimized the realistic sound of the engines, sometimes eliminating it entirely. Hans Zimmer's music score substituted for the engine sounds and musically portrayed the whooshing of the helicopter blades. The result was subjective and psychological. The musical evocation of an absent sound effect worked to convey the stress and concentration of American soldiers about to land in a battle zone. Their minds on the upcoming battle, they were not "hearing" the helicopters. The film viewer does, but only indirectly, by way of the music.

Director Stanley Kubrick famously combined picture and music in counterintuitive ways. In *Dr. Strangelove* (1963), the world ends in a nuclear holocaust, which is scored with the lilting 1940s melody "We'll Meet Again." More cruelly, in *A Clockwork Orange* (1971), Kubrick used the exuberant title song from MGM's beloved musical *Singin' in the Rain* (1952) as the accompaniment to a rape scene.

Japanese director Akira Kurosawa loved to contrast music and image. In *Drunken Angel* (1948), the central character of the film, a small-time gangster, loses control of the local neighborhood he dominated. Furthermore, he is dying of tuberculosis. He wanders the streets shunned by shopkeepers, coughing his life out. To emphasize the character's despair, Kurosawa instructed his composer, Fumio Hayasaka, to accompany the action with a silly and mindless cuckoo waltz. Kurosawa knew that the mindless optimism of the waltz, in its extreme contrast with the character's situation, would underline and emphasize the gangster's despair and sadness.

Serving as Background Filler   This use of movie music was more typical in older films than it is in contemporary filmmaking. During the Hollywood period in the 1930s and 1940s, films were distinguished by so-called wall-to-wall music. Music accompanied almost every scene, and it often assumed a kind of background filler function, just as Copland noted. Contemporary films tend to use music more

A CLOCKWORK ORANGE (WARNER BROS., 1971)

The thug Alex (Malcolm McDowell, center) dances and sings "Singin' in the Rain" while his gang assaults a husband and wife in their home. Director Stanley Kubrick's appropriation of this cheerful song, best remembered from the classic MGM musical that starred Gene Kelly, was an act of cruel subversion, placing the music in a new, horribly violent context. Frame enlargement.

LEAVING LAS VEGAS (MGM, 1995)

For this grim story about an alcoholic (Nicolas Cage) and a hooker (Elizabeth Shue) who have a brief affair while he drinks himself to death, the filmmakers used music to counterpoint the bleakness of the story. The main musical theme is the song "My One and Only Love," a tender and sentimental ballad given a lush, sweet orchestration for the film. The song creates a sharp counterpoint to the drama. Frame enlargement.

sparingly, and composers such as Jerry Goldsmith have believed that less music is better because, when used, it becomes more significant.

Creating Continuity As with dialogue and effects, music can bridge shots in ways that link and unify them. In montage scenes, for example, where many shots are edited together, music often supplies a unifying structure for the montage. When Julia Roberts goes on her shopping spree in *Pretty Woman*, the Roy Orbison song, from which the film derives its title, accompanies and unifies the montage.

A classic example of music unifying a montage occurs in Bernard Herrmann's score for *Citizen Kane* (1941). A famous sequence in the film shows Charles Foster Kane and his first wife Emily in a series of brief encounters across the breakfast table. The montage telescopes many years of marriage into these breakfasts. Each encounter registers further decay and disintegration in their marriage. Herrmann wrote a little waltz for the montage,

CITIZEN KANE (RKO, 1941)
Composer Bernard Herrmann provided a waltz and variations to link musically the different shots of *Citizen Kane*'s famous breakfast montage. Frame enlargement.

established it in the first scene, and then used a series of variations for each succeeding scene in the montage, with the music growing colder and more forbidding as the montage progresses in order to capture the deepening alienation between Charles and Emily.

One of the most important ways that film music creates continuity is by using a **leitmotif** structure. Indeed, this is one of the most common ways of scoring a motion picture. A leitmotif is a kind of musical label that is assigned to a character, a place, an idea, or an emotion. Once assigned, a leitmotif can be repeated each time the character or idea or emotion reappears. This helps to make the music recognizable to an audience, especially after stretches of film where no music has been heard, and it also helps to characterize the character, place, idea, or emotion. The leitmotif can be presented with great invention and variation, restated in differing rhythms and colors. Leitmotif is derived from the operas of Richard Wagner, who used it as a way of helping his audience recognize and understand the characters and their emotional situations.

The Italian composer Ennio Morricone's score for Sergio Leone's *Once upon a Time in the West* (1969) employs a very explicit leitmotif structure. Each of the four major characters in the film has his or her own theme, and the themes reappear as the characters do throughout the film so that one can easily follow the story and its conflicts simply by listening to the music. Almost every motion picture score is structured as a set of themes and variations, and this repetition of familiar musical material is a powerful means of creating continuity.

Music also can establish continuity by creating pacing and tempo within scenes. As soon as music is added to a scene, the images take on a rhythm and pace they did not otherwise possess because relationships are established musically across the shots. Elmer Bernstein, composer of the score for the popular Western *The Magnificent Seven* (1960), has pointed out that his music for this film is actually faster than the action on screen. He wanted the music to help speed along an otherwise slow film. Bernstein's now-classic score adds immeasurably to the pacing of the movie, providing excitement in scenes that would otherwise lack it.

Emphasizing Climaxes   Movie music emphasizes climaxes and concludes scenes or the end of a film with finality. Music in movies tends to begin and end on specific

Each character in this epic Sergio Leone Western has his or her own highly distinctive musical theme. The leitmotif structure of the score is especially explicit. Frame enlargement.

actions: doors opening and closing, cars pulling away, monsters jumping out of the dark. In these ways, musical cues alert the audience to the climaxes and the emotional high points of scenes. Danny Elfman's score for *Batman* (1989) is exceptionally accomplished in catching action and emphasizing climaxes.

Music need not always be used to heighten action. Sometimes, its absence can be very effective. In *The Silence of the Lambs* (1991), the climactic confrontation in a dark basement between Clarice Starling (Jodie Foster) and serial killer Buffalo Bill features spooky ambient sounds and source music coming from Bill's boom box, but no film score. One had been composed for the scene, but the filmmakers elected to go instead with the ambient sound. In the police thriller *Bullitt* (1968), during the famous car chase, the music ceases early on. As detective Steve McQueen starts his pursuit of a pair of suspected killers, the music begins in a tense and ominous fashion, but then it stops so that sound effects—screaming engines, squealing tires—take over to carry the sequence. Most movies use music to make car chases more exciting, but the chase in *Bullitt* is historically important for avoiding this obvious stratagem.

CONTEMPORARY TRENDS IN FILM SCORING   Although movie music today performs the basic functions noted by Copland, the styles employed and the importance of music for the industry have changed since his era. The use of romantic orchestral

THE SILENCE OF THE LAMBS (ORION, 1991)

Sometimes no music at all is more effective than a score. One mark of intelligent scoring is knowing when not to score. Composer Howard Shore wrote music for the climactic scene where an FBI agent (Jodie Foster) confronts a serial killer in a dark basement. On seeing the edited sequence, however, he felt it worked better, with more suspense, without the music. Frame enlargement.

music to score films in the Hollywood period gave way in the 1950s to more modern approaches. Elmer Bernstein composed a jazz-oriented score for *The Man with the Golden Arm* (1955), and Leonard Rosenman composed an atonal, 12-tone serial score for *The Cobweb* (1955). Folk and rock scores in the late 1960s distinguished *The Graduate* (1967) and *Easy Rider* (1969). At this time, the symphonic orchestral score fell out of style, but it made a triumphant comeback in the mid-1970s in the work of John Williams. His scores for the *Star Wars* films and Steven Spielberg's pictures re-established the symphony orchestra as an essential scoring resource.

Today, film music is a key part of the movie business. Studios often market films using contemporary music supplied by popular bands and singers and rely on sales of recorded film music as a supplementary source of income. (The parent corporations that own studios also own music publishing and recording businesses.) Because of this, studios are often interested in scores that can be marketed in the format of popular songs. This trend goes back at least to David Raksin's score for *Laura* (1944) and could be found in the 1950s with films such as *High Noon* (1952) and in the 1960s in *The Magnificent Seven, Breakfast at Tiffany's* (1961), and *Dr. Zhivago* (1965). Today, it is firmly established and is extremely common. The soundtrack of *Forrest Gump* (1994) was essentially a collection of popular tunes from the 1960s, whereas *Natural Born Killers* (1994) featured the work of popular 1990s performing groups.

The crafting of movie music as a series of pop hits has become a permanent fixture of the industry and has had a detrimental effect on the art of film scoring. The artistry of film scoring aims to create a fusion of music and image rather than detachable songs that can be marketed on their own and have only a marginal relationship with the images on screen. It was this development that effectively ended the long-time partnership between director Alfred Hitchcock and composer Bernard Herrmann. Herrmann had composed extraordinary music for the Hitchcock films *The Trouble with Harry* (1955), *The Man Who Knew Too Much* (1956), *The Wrong Man* (1956), *Vertigo* (1958), *North by Northwest* (1959), *Psycho* (1960), and *Marnie* (1964) and had served as a musical consultant on *The Birds* (1963). Herrmann composed a score for Hitchcock's next film, *Torn Curtain* (1966), which was grim and foreboding, but the producers at Universal wanted a pop song that could be hummed and played on the radio. Responding to their pressure, Hitchcock threw out Herrmann's score and substituted a more conventional composition in its place. Miffed at this treatment, Herrmann never worked with Hitchcock again.

Like Herrmann, most serious film composers think that the pop song approach compromises the integrity of their scores. Sometimes the application of pop songs

PSYCHO (PARAMOUNT PICTURES, 1960)
Bernard Herrmann contributed brilliant scores for Alfred Hitchcock's pictures. The score for *Psycho*, for example, used only string instruments. The shrieking strings heightened the impact of the film's brutal violence. Frame enlargement.

is done in an almost schizophrenic fashion. *Robin Hood, Prince of Thieves* (1991), starring Kevin Costner, employed a score that used many period instruments, but at the end of the film, over the final credits, a pop rock love ballad provided the exit music, roughly jolting moviegoers out of the medieval period of the movie.

The cross-marketing of movies and pop songs is now a firmly established feature of the industry. To some extent, film scoring suffers from this emphasis. Many films feature scores that, musically, have little to do with the action or emotions on screen. Despite this, however, the art of film scoring remains very much alive. Exciting, ambitious original scores by Hans Zimmer (*Black Hawk Down*, 2001; *The Thin Red Line*, 1998), James Horner (*A Beautiful Mind*, 2001; *Field of Dreams*, 1989; *Glory*, 1989), John Barry (*Out of Africa*, 1985; *Dances with Wolves*, 1990), Danny Elfman (*Planet of the Apes*, 2001; *Men in Black*, 1997; *Edward Scissorhands*, 1990), and others continue to make a distinguished contribution to modern movies.

Case Study   NO COUNTRY FOR OLD MEN

Sound design on *No Country for Old Men* (2007), directed by Joel and Ethan Coen, breaks with the tradition in suspense thrillers of using a lot of music and relying on it to create tension and excitement. The Coens' film has very little music, and when it does appear it's in a subliminal fashion, barely heard underneath ambient sounds like prairie wind and the rumble of an automobile engine. Unless really listening for it, a viewer will not hear it consciously. Composer Carter Burwell avoided traditional instrumentation and used, instead, singing bowls, used in Buddhist meditation rituals, that produce a continuous tone. He manipulated the sonic properties of this tone in creative ways. When the hired killer, Chigurh (Javier Bardem), menaces a gas station owner, Burwell

set the frequency of the bowls' tone to be the same as the noise of a refrigerator.

The goal throughout the film was to let silence and ambient noises create the tension that in more traditional films music is expected to produce. As a result, the film's sound effects are precisely crafted and edited. Rather than taking a huge number of effects, laying them on top of one another into a dense mix, and then adding a lot of music, the Coens, Burwell, and sound designer Craig Berkey went in the opposite direction, toward a design that was lean and spare and highly calibrated.

Many scenes in the film are sustained entirely by image and by sonic design and feature no dialogue at all. The best of these occurs in a dark hotel room, as

(continued)

Llewelyn Moss (Josh Brolin), who has stolen a suitcase full of drug money, awaits the approach of Chigurh, who has been hunting him. Moss sits on the edge of the bed, straining to hear noises that shouldn't be there. As in a similar scene in Hitchcock's *Rear Window*, the killer's stealthy approach is betrayed by a few key, muffled sounds—the scrape of a chair in the lobby downstairs, the distant ringing of the desk clerk's phone that goes unanswered, the soft pad of feet on the floorboards in the hallway outside the door, the squeaking of the light-bulb in the hallway as it is unscrewed from its socket, the explosive thump of the door's lock as the unseen Chigurh shoots it out of the door frame. The scene is a pure example of storytelling through sound design.

The sound design that Berkey created for Chigurh's shotgun equipped with a silencer did not include any recording of gun noises. It was a synthetic blend of numerous high-pitched sounds, including screaming, blended with an acoustical thump.

Overall, the creative sound work on *No Country for Old Men* was intended to get the viewer to behave as Moss does in his hotel room, sitting forward a little, listening intently to a sonic landscape that offers clues to the action and that in many contemporary films is buried under too much audio information that is too loud and unrelenting. The film is about letting silences and discrete noises create the tension. ■

NO COUNTRY FOR OLD MEN (MIRAMAX, 2007)
This film's sound design is lean and spare but highly controlled. Ambient sounds rather than music predominate in most scenes. The filmmakers elected not to use music to carry the action and comment on it. When it does appear, the music score is muted and subliminal. Frame enlargement.

SOUND DESIGN

The complexity of modern film sound, and its importance for the artistic design of a film, has brought forth a new creative member of the production team: the **sound designer**. Walter Murch's brilliant work on *Apocalypse Now* (1979) elicited the credit "sound design" because of Murch's key contributions to the film's total artistic design. On *Apocalypse Now*, Murch and his crew manipulated 160 tracks of recorded sounds. These were mixed together to create the finished soundtrack. Since then, the term has come into general usage.

Sound design goes far beyond the routine technical challenges of getting audible sound and mixing effects and music with dialogue. Sound designers create a total sound environment for the film's images, an environment that not only supports the images but also extends their meaning in dynamic ways. The sound design of a film builds a mix of **realistic** and **synthetic sounds.** Realistic sound matches the properties of a real source. Unlike realistic sounds, synthetic sounds are invented and have no counterpart in actual life, but they bond with the images on screen and extend their meaning. The voice of Steven Spielberg's character E.T. resulted from a mix of human speech and animal sounds, incorporating up to 18 different sound elements. In *Return of the Jedi* (1983), the sounds of the laser guns and the air motorcycles were created by electronically modifying and rerecording a mixture of sound sources.

The modern film audience is privileged to experience film soundtracks of unprecedented complexity and subtlety. Sound designers create highly sophisticated manipulations of sound information. These manipulations are rule-governed and exploit unique properties of sound that differentiate it from a film's image track.

Differences between Sound and Image

Sound and images uniquely differ from one another. Two kinds of differences exist: (1) what viewers notice about pictures and sound and (2) how pictures and sound structure time.

PERCEPTION OF IMAGE AND SOUND Obviously, images are visible and can be seen, and sound cannot. Image edits, whether cuts, fades, or dissolves, can be seen on screen. Sound edits are inaudible. Images can be touched. Sound cannot. As a result, viewers notice images but tend to be less aware of sound design. Viewers tend to think of cinema as an essentially visual medium, with sound as the backup element, there to support the images.

Because of this, viewers think that they interpret sound in reference to images. In most instances, however, sound shapes the image as much as the image shapes the sound. Walter Murch created a memorable image-sound juxtaposition in *Apocalypse Now* (1979) by adding a helicopter sound to a shot of a spinning ceiling fan. Viewers hear a helicopter engine and rotor blades but see the spinning blades of the fan. In this striking contrast, sound and image are equally assertive, equally important. Viewers may think of images as being more important, but in this instance the helicopter sound contextualizes the image as much as it contextualizes the sound.

Sound design is an extremely powerful but nearly subliminal element of film structure. Furthermore, sound has a fluid nature that images do not. Taken out of context, many sounds can be difficult to identify, which enables sound designers to

APOCALYPSE NOW (UNITED ARTISTS, 1979)

To this shot of a spinning ceiling fan, sound designer Walter Murch added the sound of a helicopter propeller. This audiovisual combination places equal stress on image and sound; each conditions the other. Frame enlargement.

THE CONVERSATION (PARAMOUNT, 1974)

Featuring brilliant sound design by Walter Murch, Francis Ford Coppola's *The Conversation* is that rare film that deeply probes the psychological components of sound. Harry Caul (Gene Hackman) is a pathologically withdrawn man who works as a professional wiretapper. As he labors to discover the meaning behind a mysterious conversation he has taped, Murch and Coppola show the subjective nature of sound. Harry psychologically projects a meaning onto the audio information that proves to be tragically incorrect. In this scene, he crouches in a hotel bathroom to tape a conversation in the next room. Frame enlargement.

use them with great freedom, attaching them, for example, to a variety of images, as in the sound effects used in *Terminator 2* and *Backdraft*. Sound can stimulate the imagination in ways images do not. In *The Conversation* (1974), Gene Hackman plays a surveillance expert, Harry Caul. He overhears a murder committed in an adjoining hotel room. The violence of the killing is conveyed in the noises that come through the wall into Harry's room. Sound designer Walter Murch knew that what the audience (and Harry) would imagine based on the sounds would be far worse than what a picture might show.

STRUCTURING TIME   Unless they contain explicit movement, many images are ambiguous with respect to time. They can be run forward or backward with little noticeable difference. A long shot of a forest or the exterior of a house is ambiguous in this way, but not a shot of traffic or joggers. Viewers can tell if the latter two images were run backwards, but not necessarily the first two.

Sound adds directional time to images. With sound, viewers perceive images as moving forward unambiguously. George Stevens's Western *Shane* (1953) provides an interesting illustration of this principle. Stevens realized that a man dismounting a horse looks more graceful than when climbing into the saddle. Accordingly, when the film's villain climbs into the saddle, the editor used a shot of the character *dismounting* but played it in reverse. The sound in the scene—a gurgling stream, wind, off-screen dialogue from other characters—gives the shot a clear forward momentum. Viewers who are aware of the trick can see that the shot is played backwards, but for most viewers, unaware of the editing magic at work, the sleight-of-hand passes unnoticed because of the way the shot is paired with sound that is clearly directional in time.

Sound gives images forward momentum or adds to the momentum that the shots already possess. Sound temporalizes images. This is the principle that underlies the codes of sound continuity. But creating continuity is only one of the achievements of sophisticated sound design, which, like image editing, is a rule-governed practice. What are the basic rules and procedures for manipulating sounds and for establishing relationships with images?

The Codes of Sound Design

To construct the finished soundtrack viewers hear when watching a movie, designers employ five essential codes: (1) the sound hierarchy, (2) sound perspective, (3) sound bridges, (4) off-screen sound space, and (5) sound montage.

THE SOUND HIERARCHY   Because of the variety of sounds in the audio environment and the need to organize them to facilitate the viewer's understanding of story information, sound designers customarily treat them in terms of a hierarchy of importance. When filmmakers manipulate dialogue, sound effects, and music within a scene, the hierarchy of relationships typically emphasizes dialogue. A sound mixer understands that inaudible or unclear dialogue can take a viewer out of the movie and break its spell. If a viewer has to ask someone sitting next to them what a character just said, the viewer is no longer "in" the film. Thus dialogue tends to be the determining element in a sound mix. It is generally the first element to be mixed, and the volume of effects and music is usually kept at a softer level to run underneath the dialogue.

Everyone has seen movies in which an important character dies during a noisy battle. Often, the character makes a little speech before dying. When this occurs, the volume of the battle sounds invariably drops below the dialogue. Once the character has died, the battle sounds rise again to their previous level. Prevailing assumptions stipulate that dialogue always should be clear, crisp, and understandable to the viewer.

Filmmakers do not always construct a standard sound hierarchy; some have deliberately sought to avoid it. In the early 1970s, one major U.S. filmmaker revolutionized sound recording techniques in ways that challenged the dominant place of the actor's voice in the hierarchy of sound. Beginning with *California Split* (1974) and *Nashville* (1975), director Robert Altman pioneered the use of multichannel, multitrack sound recording. Rather than using a boom mike—a microphone hung on a long pole suspended over a scene to record the voices of the actors—Altman employed radio mikes. Each actor was separately miked, their voices transmitted to a recording receiver.

In the sound mix, Altman aimed to produce a profusion of voices, much as one hears in a crowded room. In the crowd scenes in *California Split*, for example, many actors speak at once, and the dialogue is multilayered, full of overlapping speech. In addition, the radio mikes picked up ambient noises, like the rustle of clothing, that are usually not captured by more standard recording techniques. The resulting audio mix was extremely rich and multidimensional, and a single character's voice did not always predominate over other voices in a scene. The mix gave Altman an audio equivalent to what his images were showing, namely, many things happening at once.

Altman's approach frustrated critics because they were used to a more normative sound hierarchy in which all voices were clearly modulated and balanced to give a single speaker primacy of position in the audio mix. His films of the early 1970s were somewhat controversial, but multitrack recording methods are today an industry standard, even though most films do not aim for the audio density of Altman's pictures.

ON THE WATERFRONT (COLUMBIA PICTURES, 1954)

Breaking the sound hierarchy can create startling effects. When Terry Malloy (Marlon Brando) tells Edie (Eva Marie Saint) that he was involved in her brother's murder, the sound mix eliminates nearly all of their dialogue, replacing it with loud, harsh sounds from the environment, the New York harbor. These piercing sounds portray the characters' anguish and stand in for the missing dialogue. These sounds are the most important and prominent ones in the scene and carry its emotion, a function more typically performed by dialogue or music. Frame enlargements.

The Sound Hierarchy in Early Cinema   While contemporary sound design typically features a highly articulated mix of dialogue, effects, and music, films from the early sound period blended fewer elements to create the soundtrack. Rather than working with many tracks each of dialogue, effects, and music, early sound films mixed a couple of dialogue tracks, a mono music track, a few sound effects, and an ambient track. In contrast to the profusion of sound detail in contemporary film, the audio design of early sound films included less information. Occasionally, one finds an incomplete sound hierarchy in these films, a mix of dialogue, effects, and music that runs counter to the practices that would soon become normative in the industry.

In Sergei Eisenstein's first sound film, *Alexander Nevsky* (1938, about a Russian folk hero who repulsed a German invasion in the thirteenth century, music and dialogue tend to predominate in the sound structure of the film, with background ambient sound and sound effects used less extensively. Some scenes or shots completely lack the ambient sound and effects that are clearly denoted by the images and action.

At the beginning of the movie, for example, a group of Mongol warriors visits Alexander Nevsky's fishing village. Viewers hear the sounds of their horses and armor as they arrive, but leaving, they make no sound at all. Their exit is completely silent.

 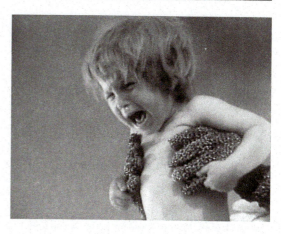

ALEXANDER NEVSKY (1936)

The soundtrack of many films in the early sound period have a minimal range of effects and ambient noise, even when images, such as these shots showing a screaming child, suggest highly specific sounds. Frame enlargements.

Later in the film, during the visually impressive sequence that details the burning of the city of Pskov and the slaughter of its inhabitants by the invading German army, viewers hear only music and dialogue without any sound effects. Close-ups of screaming, crying children lack these sound effects.

During the climax of the film, the epic battle on a frozen lake between Nevsky's armies and the invading Germans, music and sound effects alternate one at a time. The music plays for a while and then stops, and viewers hear sound effects (swords clashing, men shouting). Then the sound effects stop, and the music begins again. These manipulations of sound may strike a modern moviegoer's ears as rather crude and unrealistic because of the peculiar manner in which effects and music have been edited so that they are never present together and because of the lack of detail in the film's audio space when compared to its often striking images.

While most films establish a clear hierarchy of sound relationships that gives the voice a privileged pride of place and surrounds the voice with music and important sound effects, Altman's work and Eisenstein's *Alexander Nevsky* are significant alternatives to this practice. Their deviant structure demonstrates, by its omission, the prevalence of the conventional hierarchy in which voice, effects, and music are present together but in carefully regulated volumes.

SOUND PERSPECTIVE   **Sound perspective** designates the ways that sound conveys properties of the physical spaces seen on screen. Sound perspective in film is based on correspondences with the viewer's acoustic perception of space in everyday life. The sound of an approaching or receding object, for example, changes its pitch in a predictable way depending on its direction of movement, a phenomenon known as the *Doppler effect*. Sound designers routinely use Doppler effects to acoustically convey the movement of a sound-producing object through three-dimensional space. Recall that the sound engineers at Lucasfilm added Doppler effects to the arrows whizzing at Indiana Jones to give them a convincing three-dimensional presence in the scene. In the *Star Wars* films and other science fiction pictures, Doppler spatializes the approach of CGI or miniature-model spacecraft and helps sell these special-effect images to viewers.

Ben Burtt

Ben Burtt has created some of the most famous sounds in modern movies—the mechanical breathing of Darth Vader, the crack of Indiana Jones' whip, the voices of E.T. and R2D2, the resonant hum of Luke Skywalker's lightsaber. His long association with George Lucas and Steven Speilberg helped to change modern movie sound by emphasizing the invention of original sounds for a production.

Before the 1970s, film studios compiled stock libraries of audio effects that they used and re-used in their films. Warner Bros.' movies sounded different than Paramount's films because each studio drew from its in-house audio archive. Many of the gunshots heard in years of Warner Bros. gangster movies were created originally for *G-Men* (1935), and the studio recorded numerous bullet ricochets for *The Charge of the Light Brigade* (1936). Audiences continued to hear these ricochets in movies for decades. They even were altered to become the cartoon sound of the Road Runner dashing away. Burtt points out that one ricochet was played backwards to supply the sound of Superman landing on the 1960s-era television show. These practices meant that sound effects often were repetitive, familiar, and unsurprising.

The "Wilhelm scream" is a famous example of recycled audio. The scream—recorded for a scene in *Distant Drums* (1951) where a man is bitten by an alligator—was archived at Warners and used in many of the studio's films, including *The Charge at Feather River* (1953) where it was used when a character named Wilhelm is shot with an arrow. Researching sound at studio libraries, Burtt noticed this recurring scream and named it "Wilhelm," after the *Feather River* character. The scream is very distinctive, and Burtt affectionately used it in several *Star Wars* movies. It's now a kind of legendary audio effect and can be heard in *Inglourious Basterds* (2008), *Monsters vs. Aliens* (2009), and *Iron Man 2* (2010)

When George Lucas hired Burtt to design the sounds of *Star Wars* (1977), he wanted the film to have an original audio profile, not recycled sound effects. He broke with existing studio practices. As a result, *Star Wars* sounded unlike earlier science fiction films. The Federation's beat-up space ships, for example, sounded like Model T automobiles rather than having the electronic hum so common in 1950s-era sci-fi. Sound was uniquely assertive in defining the experience, emotions, characters, and settings of *Star Wars*. Burtt's creative sound design on that film helped to usher in a new era of audio invention in motion pictures in which sound was conceived as an active part of the moviegoer's experience.

Because many of the characters and situations for which Burtt had to invent sound were novel and imaginary, he tried to map them onto sound experiences familiar to viewers, ones they would associate with particular emotions. To create the sounds of large spaceships in the *Star Wars* movies, Burtt blended audio of thunder, animal growls, and jet airplanes. Animal sounds are also part of the mix for the engines on military vehicles appearing in *Raiders of the Lost Ark* (1981).

Because sounds taken in isolation are often hard to identify, sound design is an art of elegant substitution, and a designer needs to be able to

THE EMPIRE STRIKES BACK (20TH CENTURY FOX, 1980)

Darth Vader's lack of humanity was unforgettably characterized by the mechanical sound of his breathing, a sound designed by Ben Burtt to embody the essence of the character. Frame enlargement.

think analytically about sound in order to get the right combinations of elements. Burtt created Darth Vader's heavy breathing by putting a microphone inside a scuba tank regulator. Light-sabers were the combined sounds of Simplex movie projectors, the electric hum of television sets, and a moving microphone re-recording the combined sounds to convey a sense of object movement. Raccoon noises helped supply the voice of E.T. and the skittery sounds of the cockroach that appears in *WALL-E* (2008).

Because *WALL-E* is a computer-animated film, no audio was recorded as part of a production track. All of the images were created without sound, requiring Burtt to invent the mechanical sounds of the robots WALL-E and EVE, their planet and spacecraft. He created more than 2000 individual sounds for the film. The noise of wind, for example, was produced by running audio of Niagra Falls through an echo chamber, and when the wind is heard from inside WALL-E's trailer, the sound is produced by dragging a canvas bag across the floor. Why not simply record wind? Because literal, realistic sound sources often are insufficiently dramatic. Other sources can be blended and manipulated to evoke the necessary emotional tone or personality. The sound of EVE's laser gun in the film is produced by stretching a slinky out to full length, placing a microphone at one end and tapping the other end. Because of the slinky's length, high-frequency tones reach the microphone first, then the midtones, and then the low. The resulting sound is metallic and resembles an explosive discharge, making a good fit with the images of EVE shooting her laser gun.

Burtt's work on the *Star Wars* and *Indiana Jones* films, and Walter Murch's inventive work for Francis Coppola on *Apocalypse Now* (1979), helped to make the 1970s the first great era of sound design in motion pictures. The inventive, singular, and unique audio profiles of these films established the essential role that original sound, expressly designed for a film, would play in the art of cinema. ∎

WALL-E (Pixar, 2008)
Robots in love—WALL-E and EVE are personified through highly articulated and individuated sounds. A low-tech robot, his sounds are very mechanical, while hers are more electronic and airy. Sound design plays a major role in bringing this sci-fi world to life. Frame enlargement.

Sound perspective also can be created by using reverberance and changes in volume. **Direct sound** is sound that comes immediately from the source. It is spoken or recorded directly into the microphone, and because of this, it typically carries minimal or no reverberance and conveys little environmental information. By contrast, **reflected sound** carries reverberance. It reflects off of surrounding surfaces in the environment to produce reverberation. Differing surfaces reflect sounds in differing ways, and these differences convey important information about the kind of physical environment in which the sound is occurring. Hard surfaces such as glass or metal tend to bounce sound very quickly and very efficiently, whereas softer surfaces such as carpeting or cushioned furniture are less reflective. They tend to absorb sound and, in extreme cases, may deaden sound. In *The Conversation* (1974), the noises of the murder that Harry Caul hears through an adjoining hotel room wall are muffled and deadened.

Sound environments, then, can be characterized in terms of their sound-reflective or sound-deadening properties. Sound designers pay close attention to these features so that the audio environments they create for a film match the physical conditions of the scene or shot. Sound needs to reverberate in Edward Scissorhands's huge, vacant castle but not on the western plains in *Dances with Wolves*.

Another, very important characteristic of sound in the audio environment is ambient sound. As explained earlier, this term refers to generalized noises in the recording environment. If shooting takes place out-of-doors, ambient sounds may include the airplane traveling overhead, the cries of children playing in the distance, or the sound of wind in the trees. Ambient sound is found in all recording environments, even in an empty room. When a scene occurs in an empty room, the soundtrack will not be dead or silent. It will carry **room tone**, the acoustical properties of the room itself, the imperceptible sounds that it makes. Room tone is a very low level of ambient noise, and it indicates that the audio environment created by contemporary sound design is never silent or dead but always conveys some audio information.

Sound perspective often correlates with visual perspective. If the action is presented in long shot, viewers also hear the sound as if in long shot. As the sound source gets more distant from the camera in a reverberant environment, the properties of reflected sound increase. As the sound source comes closer to the camera, the amount of reflected sound decreases. By varying the amount of reflected sound, filmmakers establish the location of a sound source within the visual space on screen.

If the action is presented to the viewer in close-up, direct sound should predominate over reflected sound. The actors' voices should be intimate and sound as if they are spoken closely to the microphone. Sound designer Walter Murch has stated that he records not just sounds in the environment but also the spaces between the listener

THE OTHERS (MIRAMAX, 2001)

Digital, multichannel sound can create tremendously vivid sound perspective. When Grace (Nicole Kidman) is terrorized by what she believes are ghosts, disembodied voices fly around the room, jumping from channel to channel, speaker to speaker, across the front soundstage and into the rear surrounds. As the unseen spirits flutter about the character, the sound reproduces this action in three-dimensional audio space. The effect becomes subjective, immersing the film viewer into the character's experience. Frame enlargement.

and those sounds. In actual practice, however, microphone placement does not exactly parallel camera placement. While the difference in camera placement between a close-up and a long shot may be very great, the difference in actual microphone placement may only be a matter of several feet. Moreover, many contemporary films invert visual and sound perspectives by filming actors in long shot and miking them for direct sound. Peter Weir's *Dead Poets' Society* (1989) deals with the relationship between an unconventional English teacher (Robin Williams) and his students in an elite prep school in 1959. One of the boys discusses with his friend his excitement over getting the lead role in the school play. The two boys stand on a pier next to the water and are filmed in extreme long shot. Their voices, however, are miked in intimate terms. The audio space is very close. The visual space is very distant.

Sound Perspective in Early Cinema   As with other attributes of film structure, filmmakers did not grasp the complexities of sound design all at once. Sound technology came to the movies in the late 1920s, and filmmakers gradually discovered the creative possibilities of sound and how to use it in a rich and naturalistic fashion. As a result, and because early sound technology was quite limiting, the soundtracks in many early films tend to be less detailed and less reflective of the realities of sound space.

French director René Clair's *Under the Roofs of Paris* (1930), for example, is a mixture of pantomime, music, and dialogue. Much of the film was shot silent, with a few talking sequences added later. At the beginning of the film, the camera booms down from the rooftops to the streets of Paris where a song salesman is performing a new tune for a group of onlookers. Viewers hear the song throughout the camera movement, and as the camera draws closer, the song's volume increases. There is, however, no apparent change in reverberation.

At the end of the scene, the camera booms back up to the rooftops. This time the volume of the song does not decrease as much as it should given the amount of physical space the camera crosses. Again, there is no change in reverberation. The perspectives established by visual space and audio space do not correlate very well.

UNDER THE ROOFS OF PARIS (TOBIS, 1930)
Correct sound perspective is not a feature of every film. The relationship of audio space and camera perspective often proves to be quite flexible. In *Under the Roofs of Paris*, as the camera travels from the rooftops to the street below, the appropriate changes in audio space do not occur. Frame enlargement.

Case Study   JACQUES TATI

As with all rules and conventions of film structure, sound perspective can be satirized and played with by smart filmmakers. French director Jacques Tati was one of the masters of sound cinema. Tati was a pantomime comedian whose films bear some relationships to silent comedies. Dialogue in his films is minimal, and the sound space is dominated by a multitude of carefully organized environmental sounds. Tati **postdubbed** his soundtracks to achieve a maximum of control over their sound design.

In Tati's masterpiece, *Playtime* (1967), he playfully distorts standard sound perspective. Early in the film, the main character, Mr. Hulot (played by Tati himself), is trying to keep an appointment with an official named Mr. Giffard. When Hulot tries to meet the official, he is instructed by the building's doorman to wait beside a bank of elevators while Mr. Giffard is paged. Hulot waits patiently, framed at screen left, while, onscreen right, a vast, receding hallway extends into the distance. Hulot is seated around the edge of the wall, however, so he cannot look down this hallway. But the viewer can.

As Hulot waits, loud footsteps occur off-screen. Because of their loud volume, the viewer assumes the person these feet belong to must be very near. In the next moment, however, a tiny figure appears in the distance at the end of the hallway. This is joke number one, reversing the expectation viewers developed based on the probable sound space–image space relation. The glass, metal, and tile hallway conveys the reverberant footsteps very effectively; they remain loud and only grow slightly in volume as the man approaches. This is joke number two. The third joke in the scene occurs as Tati, hearing the man but unable to see him, keeps trying to get up, assuming that he must be close given the loudness of his steps. The doorman, however, who can look down the hallway, keeps gesturing for Hulot to stay seated.

This scene is composed of a single shot, and the three distinct jokes that occur in it are based on Tati's playful manipulation of the sound space–image space relation. In this case, sound perspective is an unreliable indicator of visual space and of the physical relations in the scene. It illustrates the cinema's transformational property, its ability to alter and play with perceptual realities in ways that viewers readily accept. The cinema records *and* transforms audiovisual information, and filmmakers are constantly negotiating the creative possibilities of these functions. ◼

PLAYTIME (1967)

Director Jacques Tati satirizes sound perspective by making it an unreliable indicator of visual space. The sound of Mr. Giffard's footsteps remains extremely loud and distinct despite his changing location in a long hallway. Frame enlargement.

Pointing out this feature of *Under the Roofs of Paris* does not imply that René Clair is an inferior filmmaker. Clair, in fact, was one of the most important early practitioners of sound and a filmmaker whose career straddled the silent and sound periods. He devised many inventive gags in his films where the humor depends on a particular manipulation of sound. Moreover, his work was a decided influence on the U.S. master Charlie Chaplin. Clair's film, *À Nous la Liberté* (1931), was the inspiration for Chaplin's *Modern Times* (1936). The point here is to emphasize that these codes of sound design are learned applications of style that filmmakers gradually discovered as a way of creating credible audiovisual relationships on screen. The design differences between an early film like *Under the Roofs of Paris* and more contemporary films shows the development and maturation of sound aesthetics.

SOUND BRIDGES   Sound may be connected to a source on screen or disconnected from an on-screen source. In the latter instance, the sound-producing source is off-camera. It is source-disconnected sound because, though viewers hear the sound, they cannot see its source. In any given scene, sound designers employ both categories. Source-connected sound occurs if viewers see Daniel Day-Lewis as Hawkeye in *The Last of the Mohicans* (1993) tell a British officer that he will not serve in the English army. If, by contrast, the camera stays on the British officer while Hawkeye speaks off-screen, the sound is source-disconnected.

Switching between on-screen and off-screen sound gives filmmakers enormous flexibility in the editing of their films. Not everything that is heard needs to be shown. This frees the camera from being a slave to dialogue or other sounds and enables it to reveal aspects of the scene independently of what viewers hear on the soundtrack. All a filmmaker need do is return periodically to source-connected sound in order to sustain the viewer's sense of the important audiovisual relationships. Filmmakers often "cheat" in the editing of dialogue scenes by using reaction shots of a character's face taken from other points in the scene or film. The editing encourages viewers to read the expression as a reaction to the immediate dialogue, which is heard off-camera.

Filmmakers use sound to establish continuity across shots by alternating between on-screen and off-screen sound. Because sound gives images a clear direction and orientation in time—with sound, film images clearly move forward—sound can establish continuity of time across the shot changes in a scene. This often occurs through the use of a **sound bridge** in which dialogue or effects carry over, or bridge, two or more shots, unifying them in time and/or space. Sound bridges are one of the most powerful and important ways of creating continuity in film. In *Glory* (1989), Col. Robert Shaw (Matthew Broderick) must tell his African-American regiment that the War Department has ordered that black soldiers in the Union army will receive less pay than their white counterparts. As Shaw speaks, the editor cuts to reaction shots of the black soldiers, showing their dismay at this insulting decree. Shaw continues to speak off-screen during these shots, establishing the sound bridge and creating continuity among the shots. The sound information tells viewers that all the shots, which show completely different groups of characters, are part of a common space and within a single moment of time.

In the early German sound film *The Blue Angel* (1930), as the schoolmaster (played by Emil Jannings) removes his handkerchief to blow his nose, the action cuts to a reaction shot of the schoolboys. While looking at them, viewers hear the sound of Jannings blowing his nose. The editing switches from source-connected to source-disconnected sound. Sound flows over the cut, establishing a continuity that links up the different images. In dialogue scenes using the shot-reverse-shot technique, passages of spoken dialogue will flow over the cuts to establish continuity across the shot changes.

In contemporary films, filmmakers often employ a modified sound bridge in which the switch to source-disconnected sound occurs before the cut rather than after it. In other words, the sound cut precedes the visual transition. In Mike Nichols's *The Graduate* (1967), a striking sequence expresses the social and emotional alienation of the young hero, Benjamin (played by Dustin Hoffman), when he dons a scuba suit

GLORY (COLUMBIA TRI-STAR, 1989)

The voice of Col. Robert Shaw (Matthew Broderick) provides the sound bridge unifying these reaction shots of African-American soldiers. The sound bridge connects the space and time of these shots, which contain almost no visual elements in common. Frame enlargements.

and seeks refuge at the bottom of his parents' swimming pool. The camera films him alone and isolated in the depths of the pool. As the camera tracks slowly away from him, viewers hear sound from the next scene (which occurs in a phone booth) for 13 seconds before the image cuts to that scene. It is Benjamin talking on the telephone to invite Mrs. Robinson, the family friend, to meet him at a local hotel.

The sound of Benjamin on the phone, asynchronous with the shot of him in the pool, technically violates the time and space of the pool scene, but viewers accept the sound editing as a novel, interesting, and offbeat way of signaling the transition to the

THE GRADUATE (AVCO-EMBASSY, 1967)

A creative noncorrespondence between image and sound in *The Graduate*. The sound bridge to the next scene begins well before the end of the final shot in this, the previous scene. As the camera pulls away from Benjamin (Dustin Hoffman) in the swimming pool, viewers hear him talking on the telephone in the next scene. Frame enlargement.

next scene. When *The Graduate* was released in 1967, this was an innovative way of making the transition, but it has become a fairly standard technique today.

OFF-SCREEN SOUND   Just as the distinction between source-connected and source-disconnected sound is relevant for understanding principles of sound continuity, it also helps to explain how sound can extend the viewer's perception of visual space. **Off-screen sound** is part of the dramatic action of a scene, but its source is off-camera. This kind of sound enlarges the coordinates of the world represented on screen. That world is not coextensive with the images on screen. Instead, through sound information, it extends into an indefinite, acoustically defined area of off-screen space.

Filmmakers quickly grasped the creative possibilities. Produced only a few years into the sound era, Fritz Lang's classic *M* (1931) brilliantly uses off-screen sound to signal the lurking, unseen presence of a serial killer. The murderer compulsively whistles the theme from the *Peer Gynt* suite, and his rapid, repetitive whistling occurs off-camera in many scenes throughout the film as a means of building suspense, anxiety, and mystery. As a little girl looks in a store window and then runs down the street, the off-screen whistling conveys his stalking presence and desperate hunger for a new victim. Lang had quickly grasped the power of sound to fire the audience's imagination. The unseen, conveyed through sound, is far more frightening than how the killer proves to look when the camera finally shows him. This sonic extension of the frame into off-screen space would become an essential technique in horror films in which monsters lurk just out of sight.

The famous ending of *All Quiet on the Western Front* (1931) shows the hero—a German soldier in the trenches of World War I—killed by a sniper as he reaches tenderly for a butterfly that has alighted on the fields of carnage. In close-up, the viewer sees the hero's hands reaching for the butterfly and then hears an off-screen gunshot and sees the hands drop lifelessly to the ground. At this moment, the ambient (and off-screen) sounds of battle cease, as the soundtrack deadens to convey the hero's passing.

The distinction between **diegetic sound** and **non-diegetic sound** can provide a useful way of thinking about relationships between sound-producing sources and the story world represented on screen. Diegetic sound originates within the story world,

M (1931)

Director Fritz Lang's classic film vividly demonstrated the power of off-screen sound space. The whistled leitmotif of the serial killer (Peter Lorre) suggests his lurking presence as he stalks his victims from off-screen. Here, frustrated in his hunt, he pauses by a store window. Rows of knives reflected in the glass encircle his body, suggesting that he is a prisoner of his lethal desires. Frame enlargement.

and can include sources, like character dialogue or sound effects, that are on-screen as well as off-screen. Diegetic sound can be heard by characters in the story. Non-diegetic sound originates outside of the story world, and a good example is movie music. If a character plays music within a scene from a radio or a phonograph, that's diegetic sound. When the music is provided by the score composed for the film, that's non-diegetic sound. The terms are helpful in describing situations where the distinctions to be drawn about the use of sound involve being inside or outside of the story world rather than on-screen or off-screen.

SOUND MONTAGE   Contemporary multitrack sound design is based on montage, the editing of sounds into highly intricate and complex patterns that create meaning and

ALL QUIET ON THE WESTERN FRONT (UNIVERSAL, 1931)

As the hero (Lew Ayres) reaches tenderly for a butterfly, a sniper's bullet, fired off-screen, abruptly ends his life. To simulate his passing, the soundtrack goes dead, all ambient noise ceasing. Frame enlargement.

APOCALYPSE NOW (UNITED ARTISTS, 1979)

The beginning of *Apocalypse Now* shows Captain Willard (Martin Sheen) in a Saigon hotel room. A complex sound montage replaces Saigon's city sounds with jungle sounds to suggest Willard's desire to return to the jungle. Frame enlargement.

emotion. *Apocalypse Now* (1979) features an exceptionally creative sound montage during the opening scene as Captain Willard (Martin Sheen) lies on his bed in a Saigon hotel. Willard longs to be back in the jungle where he can safely satisfy his violent appetites in combat and by working as a paid assassin. As he lies in the hotel, Willard imagines himself in the jungle. The soundtrack carries an audio representation of this inner fantasy. Sound designer Walter Murch systematically replaced city sounds with a series of jungle sounds. Urban noises—a policeman's whistle, the engines of cars and motorcycles—give way on the soundtrack to the squawk of jungle birds, the buzzing of insects, and the cries of monkeys. Murch pointed out that these sound manipulations convey the idea that, although Willard's body is in Saigon, his mind is in the jungle.

Visual montages arrange shots to express meanings not contained in any single shot taken in isolation. This scene from *Apocalypse Now* uses the same principle, transposed to sound. The total arrangement of sounds expresses the reality of Willard's fantasy in a way that the individual sounds, taken in isolation, cannot.

The multi-channel systems used for playback in theater auditoriums and consumer home video have accentuated the montage structure of contemporary sound design. By spatializing sound—sending discrete elements to different speakers positioned about the viewer—multi-channel playback emphasizes the richness and density of sound montages. The expanded dynamic range provided by digital sound has enabled filmmakers to construct ever more complex audio montages and has helped make this an essential feature of contemporary sound aesthetics.

SUMMARY

Though moviegoers may not be explicitly aware of sound design, its contribution to film cannot be overstated. The next time you watch a favorite movie, turn off the sound and see how impoverished the pictures become. Without sound, a movie loses much of its emotional impact.

Sound design works with the three types of sound—dialogue, music, and effects. Dialogue in film tends to be either voice-over narration or character speech. Sound effects are created using Foley techniques or more elaborate electronic manipulations as part of a comprehensive sound design. Music in film tends to be composed within a late romantic style, whose musical conventions and range of coloring are familiar to most moviegoers. Movie music helps set the locale and atmosphere of time and place in the story, adds psychological and emotional meaning to a scene, provides background filler, establishes continuity, and calls attention to climaxes and conclusions of scenes.

Sound design creates a complex audio environment to accompany film images, establishing dynamic audiovisual relationships and shaping in subtle and almost subliminal ways the viewer's interpretation of those images. Sound design is orderly and rule-based, following a set of basic codes, some of which establish perceptual correspondences with the viewer's real-world audio experience.

Dialogue, music, and effects are controlled to establish a hierarchy of sound relationships with dialogue being given primary importance. Direct, reflected, and ambient sound levels are carefully related to camera position to create sound perspective. Editors alternate between establishing on-screen and off-screen sound–image relations to keep camera perspective flexible and to maintain continuity. Sound editing establishes continuity across cuts, primarily by allowing sound to flow over the cut, as in the use of sound bridges. Sound is also used to prepare viewers for visual transitions, as when a sound cut precedes a visual cut, and to establish off-screen space that extends the viewer's physical sense of the image. Finally, sound montages may establish intellectual and emotional associations that go beyond the content of the images.

KEY TERMS AND CONCEPTS

ADR   183
ambient sound   184
cue sheet   187
dialogue   179
diegetic sound   209
direct sound   203
effects   179
Foley technique   184
leitmotif   192
music   179

non-diegetic sound   209
off-screen sound   209
postdub   206
production
   track   183
realistic sound   197
reflected sound   203
room tone   204
soundstage   177
sound bridge   207

sound design
   (designer)   196
sound field   175
sound perspective   201
speech   179
spotting   187
synthetic sound   197
temp track   187
voice-over
   narration   179

SUGGESTED READINGS

Rick Altman, ed., *Sound Theory/Sound Practice* (New York: Routledge, 1992).
Michel Chion, *Audio-Vision*, ed. and trans. Claudia Gorbman (New York: Columbia University Press, 1994).
Kathryn Kalinak, *Settling the Score: Music and the Classical Hollywood Film* (Madison: University of Wisconsin Press, 1992).
Fred Karlin, *Listening to Movies: The Film Lover's Guide to Film Music* (New York: Schirner Books, 1994).
Sarah Kozloff, *Overhearing Film Dialogue* (Berkeley: University of California Press, 2000).
Vincent LoBrutto, *Sound-on-Film: Interviews with Creators of Film Sound* (Westport, CT: Praeger, 1994).
Michael Schelle, *The Score: Interviews with Film Composers* (Los Angeles: Silman-James Press, 1999).
Elizabeth Weis and John Belton, eds., *Film Sound: Theory and Practice* (New York: Columbia University Press, 1985).

7

The Nature of Narrative in Film

OBJECTIVES

After reading this chapter, you should be able to:

- explain why a script serves as the foundation for a film

- explain why the storytelling function came to film early in its history

- explain the relationship between narrative and the mass production of film

- explain the three basic elements of narrative

- differentiate between story and plot and explain how filmmakers may creatively manipulate this distinction

- explain the concept of authorship in cinema and why it is a problematic concept

- distinguish between real and implied authors

- explain how point of view operates in film narratives

- describe the classical Hollywood narrative

- distinguish explicit causality from implicit causality and explain their different narrative effects

- explain the counter-narrative tradition in cinema
- describe the viewer's contribution to narrative

- define the nature of film genre
- describe the types of stories found in the major film genres

Stories are found in all cultures. Narrative is a universal human activity used for entertainment, instruction, and socialization. It is also an essential way that people think about themselves and their world. To explain how things change or how they got to be, people tell stories. Given the universality of narrative, it is not surprising that cinema, in its popular forms, has been a narrative medium.

Commercial filmmakers use the camera, light, color, actors, sound, and editing to tell stories. Fiction films are distributed internationally, and fans of Westerns, science fiction films, and other genres turn to them for pleasure and enrichment. Narrative is also central to the tradition of documentary filmmaking. Many documentary filmmakers will say that they cannot define the structure of their film until they find the story that they are going to tell.

The importance of narrative for popular movies cannot be overestimated. What, then, is narrative, and what are its structural elements in film? This chapter explains when and why narrative came to the movies, examines some of the basic elements of narrative structure, and concludes by examining what the viewer contributes to the experience of narrative.

STORY AND SCRIPT

Though cinema is an audiovisual medium, it begins with the written word. The initial step in the production of a film is completion of a script. Much like a play, the script tells the story in a scene-by-scene fashion, with dialogue and character interactions written out in detail. The script furnishes the basic structure of story and dramatic action that filmmakers will transform into picture and sound. There is no substitute for these attributes at the scripting stage; filmmakers find it difficult to develop them once a production has commenced and is before the cameras. Shekhar Kapur, the director of *Elizabeth* (1998), joined that project when the script was in its third revision, and nothing went before the cameras until the script was in its thirteenth draft. The resulting film is uncommonly rich and well designed, in large part because of its solid, scripted foundation.

The elegance of structure found in such exquisitely told narrative films as Hitchcock's *Rear Window* and *Vertigo* originated in outstanding scripts. (For *Vertigo*, Hitchcock went through three screenwriters before he got what he wanted.) Because of the structural complexity of filmmaking, a great deal about the medium must be preplanned and predetermined. As a result, filmmakers cannot simply improvise shots and action and expect their finished film to have a sophisticated and intricate visual and narrative design. This design must be planned in advance. As we saw in other chapters, filmmakers use the camera, sound, and editing to shape stories and bring them to life as cinema. But all this begins with a script, even though the screenwriter, in practice, will specify few details of camerawork. (That is an area left to the director.) The audiovisual design of a film falls outside the domain of the screenwriter. The script, however, furnishes the narrative, dramatic action, and dialogue that a director then has the job of visualizing, using all the tools that the craft of filmmaking offers.

TIME CODE (SCREEN GEMS, 2000)

In this unusual film, a split-screen technique divides the frame into four grids, with each conveying a separate storyline, but all centering on the same events and characters. The plots even move from grid to grid, and the narrative becomes a kaleidoscopic mosaic. Changes in the sound mix "tell" viewers which grid to concentrate on. Director Mike Figgis shot on digital video in extended takes running almost 90 minutes. The only "editing" is that which occurs when the viewer compares the picture information across the four grids. Frame enlargement.

THE TURN TO NARRATIVE IN EARLY FILM HISTORY

The storytelling function in cinema arrived quickly. Public exhibition of projected motion pictures dates from 1895, when the photographic equipment manufacturers Auguste and Louis Lumière held a public screening of their short films. Called "actualities," they focused on everyday life and did *not* assume a narrative format. Subjects included parents feeding a baby, workers knocking over a wall, a train pulling into a station, and workers leaving a factory.

One film on the early program, however, *The Gardener Gets Watered* (1895), anticipated the use of film as a storytelling medium. A gardener watering his lawn is tormented by a mischievous boy who kinks the hose and then straightens it, spraying the gardener's face. He retaliates by chasing and spanking the boy. The film thus shows a series of events that were clearly staged for the camera and which present an episode of narrative action ordered in time, with a beginning and an end.

In the United States, movies were an early attraction on the vaudeville stage, where motion picture presentations coexisted with slapstick comedians, singing

THE GARDENER GETS WATERED (1895)

The use of film to tell stories followed soon after the invention
of cinema. This early Lumière
film, *The Gardener Gets Watered*,
staged events for the camera and
sequenced them as narrative.
Frame enlargement.

performances, dramatic recitations, and animal shows. By 1902, however, narrative films, particularly comedies, began to appear and were greeted enthusiastically by the public.

They coexisted, however, with a vast amount of nonfiction film material, including travelogues (films showing beautiful, exotic, or faraway places) and films focused on topical events such as a yacht race or political parade. Narrative film, though, quickly became the predominant form, displacing these nonfiction formats. The public was enthusiastic about story films, including comedies, dramas, chases, or trick films (films favoring such special optical effects as characters appearing and disappearing or moving in fast or slow motion). Nickelodeons—storefront theaters where the public could see an entire program of films for 5 or 10 cents—sprang up in great numbers, by 1910 attracting about 26 million Americans per week (a little less than 20 percent of the national population).

The nickelodeon boom demonstrated the explosion of popular interest in the movies, and it challenged producers to optimize film production so that it could meet the growing popular demand for motion picture entertainment. In this regard, story films offered decisive advantages over nonfiction production. Stories could be written as fast as films were needed, and they could capitalize on the scenic features of a given production company's locale. By contrast the documentary filmmaker was a hostage to events. Production had to wait for the interesting yacht race or parade to occur. The only limit on the production of story films was the imagination of the writers and the physical resources of the production companies.

Historian Robert Allen has argued that the shift to narrative films can be explained in part by these advantages and points out that by 1909, fiction films represented 97 percent of the industry's total output. Public interest and the needs of the expanding industry decisively shifted film production into the narrative mold. The narrative sophistication of early film rapidly matured. The work of director D. W. Griffith, beginning in 1908, displayed a special narrative brilliance and an unprecedented sophistication of visual design. Since the first decade of the medium's history, then, narrative has been an essential ingredient in the popular appeal of cinema, and it furnished the key basis on which the industry could flourish.

D. W. Griffith

In early film history, D. W. Griffith perfected (though he did not invent) the essential techniques of motion picture narrative. Griffith's understanding of the principles of film structure and the methods of cinematic storytelling was uncommonly sophisticated. Viewed today, the camerawork and editing in his films seem thoroughly modern, even though the melodramatic stories appear somewhat dated.

Griffith was born in Kentucky in 1875, into a family ruined and impoverished by the Civil War and Reconstruction. Determined to become an actor and playwright, Griffith loved the theater and considered it to be a legitimate art. By contrast, he thought the movies were a bastard offspring, and he came to them reluctantly after failing to launch a successful theatrical career. In 1908, Griffith made his first film at the Biograph Studio in New York, where he continued to work until 1913. In his Biograph films, Griffith developed an increasingly complex and expressive visual style that he used to punch his stories across with maximum emotional impact. He perfected this style by directing a huge number of films. He directed 86 films in 1910, for example, and 70 films in 1911. Their subjects fell into categories that would define the basic Hollywood genres: gangster films, Westerns, biblical films, and war films.

At Biograph, Griffith strained against the narrative restrictions imposed by the one-reel format (one reel was approximately 10 minutes). In 1911, he made *Enoch Arden* in two reels, and in 1913 he made the biblical epic, *Judith of Bethulia*, his final Biograph film, in four reels. By moving to longer forms, Griffith was able to tell increasingly complex stories. After leaving Biograph, Griffith made two epics, *The Birth of a Nation* (1915) and *Intolerance* (1916), which masterfully wove together multiple plotlines and featured huge casts of characters. At silent speeds, each film ran approximately three hours.

Griffith's films are a virtual catalogue of modern motion picture technique. By using multiple camera positions and fluid editing, he fractured a scene into its constituent shots, intercutting freely to create smooth continuity. Each shot was dramatically incomplete, recording just a fragment of the action

and acquiring meaning in relation to the other shots that made up the scene. He drastically varied camera position and angle, freely incorporating low- and high-angle shots, as well as long shots, medium shots, and close-ups. In *Enoch Arden*, Griffith used a psychological image to show what a character is thinking. The camera draws close to the character's face, then Griffith cuts to another scene that represents the character's mental image.

Griffith skillfully placed his cameras to frame shots in highly expressive ways. In *The Birth of a Nation*, when the Little Colonel returns home from the Civil War, he is greeted by his mother. Rather than showing the mother's face, Griffith discreetly shows only her arms reaching out from inside the house to embrace him. This discreet framing, with its use of off-screen space, intensifies the emotions of the reunion by emphasizing their private nature.

By 1915 and 1916, when Griffith completed his epics, *The Birth of a Nation* and *Intolerance*, he had perfected the essential building blocks of modern motion picture narrative: rapid changes of camera position and angle, close-ups used to intensify the drama and reveal emotion, complex editing used to fracture a scene into a series of dramatically incomplete shots, camera movement used to extend the frame and follow action, and cross-cutting of multiple story lines.

Unfortunately, Griffith's brilliant grasp of film structure accompanied racist and reactionary attitudes. Most notoriously, *The Birth of a Nation* portrayed the Civil War and Reconstruction as catastrophes that destroyed the happy plantation life of the South and, by freeing southern slaves, unleashed a tide of black villainy against virtuous white aristocrats. In the film's climax, the Ku Klux Klan saves southern honor and white virtue by restoring order throughout the South. Because of its virulent racism, *The Birth of a Nation* remains as inflammatory today as when it was first screened. Its explosive nature is evidence of Griffith's filmmaking skill. Its visual power and emotional manipulation of audiences make its racism all the more vicious and repugnant.

Griffith tried to rebut charges that he was a racist and calls for censoring the movies with

(continued)

THE BIRTH OF A NATION (1915)

Griffith was a director of remarkable visual brilliance. In this moment of quiet intimacy from *The Birth of a Nation*, a soldier returning from the Civil War is greeted by his mother and sister. Their arms encircle and draw him into the house. The image is eloquent in its restraint and simplicity. Frame enlargement.

Intolerance, a complex film weaving together a modern story of crime and gangsters with stories about the fall of Babylon, the massacre of the Huguenots in medieval France, and the crucifixion of Christ. Griffith drew an epic portrait of social intolerance by telling these stories simultaneously, cutting back and forth among them to create dramatic and emotional connections. Its elaborate narrative structure made *Intolerance* a film far ahead of its time. Even today, it remains a challenging film.

Griffith continued to make several more outstanding films (*Broken Blossoms*, 1919; *True Heart Susie*, 1919; *Way Down East*, 1920; *Orphans of the Storm*, 1922), but during the 1920s his melodramatic stories seemed increasingly old-fashioned, and except for two productions, the coming of sound put an end to his career. His last picture was the undistinguished *The Struggle* (1931). On his death in 1948, at age 73, he was a lonely, forgotten man who spent his last years living on the fringes of a Hollywood that had passed him by. ■

THE BIRTH OF A NATION (1915)

By 1915, cinema had reached artistic maturity and attained great narrative sophistication. *The Birth of a Nation* presented an epic (and intensely racist) narrative of unprecedented structural complexity. The circular masking on this shot is an iris—commonly used in silent cinema—which director D. W. Griffith employs to focus the viewer's attention on the Little Colonel (Henry B. Walthall) as he defiantly rams a flag into the barrel of an enemy cannon. Frame enlargement.

ELEMENTS OF NARRATIVE

Narratives have three fundamental characteristics: (1) an understanding between viewers and the filmmaker about how the story should be judged, (2) a story and plot sequencing events into a particular order that forms the narrative, and (3) a narrator and narrative point of view.

The Fictive Stance

Audiences evaluate fictional stories differently from nonfictional ones, and they generally want to know to what degree a story is fiction or nonfiction. With fiction, the audience willingly suspends its disbelief in order to experience the pleasures of an imaginary world. The audience agrees to accept the contents of the story as real at one level of make-believe while knowing, at another level, that it is only a story. Critic Peter Lamarque has termed this agreement the "fictive stance."

If a story is clearly fiction, the audience does not hold the filmmaker accountable for its truth or veracity. Instead, the audience applies a different set of criteria dealing with the artistic structure and organization of the story. Is it compelling, convincing, thrilling, entertaining, or amusing? By contrast, with nonfiction, audiences measure the tale according to notions of factual truth and honesty.

This seems like a clean and clear distinction, yet many stories and movies occupy gray areas. Are they fiction or nonfiction? How does one decide? In a movie such as *Star Wars* (1977), viewers clearly have a fictional story. The events in George Lucas's film do not exist in this world or in any easily imaginable world of the near future. By contrast, Oliver Stone's *JFK* (1991) seemed to want to play both ways with its audience, mixing fact and fiction in ways that were often hard to detect. On the one hand, the film presents an exhaustive summary of the facts surrounding the assassination of President Kennedy, supported by real, archival news footage. The film uses this fact-based history to critique and debunk the Warren Commission's finding that Lee Harvey Oswald acted as a lone

SPIDER-MAN 3 (COLUMBIA PICTURES, 2007)

Spider-Man is a clearly fictional story, based on the adventures of a comic book character. The setting is an alternative world to our own, the characters have no real-life counterparts, and the story events are entirely imaginary. Viewers of this film have no difficulty deciding whether to evaluate it and experience it as fiction. Frame enlargement.

JFK (WARNER BROS., 1991)

Kevin Costner as District Attorney Jim Garrison in *JFK*. Oliver Stone's film created controversy because of its fluid mixture of real archival footage of the Kennedy years, faked footage made to look archival, and fictional characters who had no counterpart in the historical record. Director Stone meticulously sifted through the factual record surrounding the assassination, questioned the official findings that a lone assassin killed Kennedy, but often described his film as a myth. As a result, viewers could not tell where the film's factual ambitions turned into the fictions of myth; nor could they be sure the filmmaker knew where the differences lay. In comparison with a film such as *Spider-Man*, the fictional status of this film is more ambiguous and harder to evaluate. Frame enlargement.

assassin. On the other hand, Stone intermixes the archival footage with re-enactments filmed so that they would look like part of the documentary record, and he concocts an entirely speculative explanation for the assassination based on the unproved premise that Kennedy intended to withdraw U.S. forces from Vietnam and was killed by those committed to escalating the war. There is virtually no evidence to support this contention, and Stone said that he was offering a countermyth to oppose what he regarded as the dominant mythology of a lone assassin. Where did that leave the film: fiction, nonfiction, myth, history? *JFK* is an uncomfortable mixture of these modes that leaves the audience unable to tell where the filmmaker believes their differences lie.

Audiences want very much to know the truth value of the tales they are told. When filmmakers like Stone fudge the distinctions between fiction and nonfiction, they often stir up controversy. When Robert Zemeckis used real footage of President Clinton speaking about the Oklahoma City bombing victims in a fictional context in *Contact* (1997)—the film makes it seem as if Clinton is addressing a space shuttle explosion—many people criticized what they regarded as the unethical use of the news footage. Filmmakers, though, can work in the other direction quite successfully, presenting a clearly fictional story as if it were the record of real events. *The Blair Witch Project* (1999), for example, is a horror movie about the disappearance of a film crew that left footage of its terrifying last moments, and the film is constructed as a documentary that examines this footage and tries to reconstruct the story it tells.

Narrative Structure: Story and Plot

How the story is told is every bit as important as its content. **Story** and **plot** are fundamental characteristics of every narrative, and their relationship determines its

structure. Plot refers to the sequencing of events as shown in a given film. It designates the way narrative events are arranged in the film. Story designates the larger set of events of which the plot is a subset. Any given narrative points beyond itself to imply a set of events that are not directly portrayed, as well as those that are shown. Story refers to the comprehensive set of all events, shown or implied, that make up the narrative.

Unlike the events of one's daily life, which often appear to be somewhat unstructured, random, and in flux, events in a narrative have a clear shape and sequence. Not all story events need to be included in the plot, and this is where the distinction between story and plot arises. Many events can be implied or do not need reference at all. In the case of mystery or suspense films, events are withheld from the audience to be revealed at a later time. Viewers enjoy mysteries, for example, because they try to figure things out before the detective does.

In many films there is little structural distinction between a film's plot and a film's story. Often, a plot is linear, presenting a story from start to finish. The vast majority of commercially produced movies are told in a linear, chronological fashion. However, many films make use of flashbacks, a narrative structure that was especially common in Hollywood films of the 1940s (*Casablanca*, 1942; *Double Indemnity*, 1944; *Sunset Boulevard*, 1950). *Passage to Marseilles* (1944), starring Humphrey Bogart, boasted an uncommonly intricate flashback structure, with flashbacks inside of flashbacks. The plot of *Citizen Kane* (1941) is structured as a series of flashbacks, which portray overlapping events narrated by different characters. In all these cases, the flashbacks change the sequencing of story events in the films' plots.

Many contemporary films cleverly exploit the story–plot distinction. Quentin Tarantino's *Pulp Fiction* (1994) constructs a narrative composed of three relatively separate plots, each peopled by the same gallery of characters (primarily two professional killers, played by John Travolta and Samuel L. Jackson, and a washed-up boxer, played by Bruce Willis). These characters and their separate plots cross paths at several strategic points in the film, most significantly when the boxer murders one of the hired guns (Travolta). Writer–director Tarantino stages this killing midway through the film,

PULP FICTION (MIRAMAX, 1994)

John Travolta's hit man in *Pulp Fiction* is killed off midway through the film only to reappear in the concluding plot segment. Quentin Tarantino's film playfully exploits the story–plot distinction by re-arranging its narrative events in a nonchronological way. Frame enlargement.

during the second plot segment, and then brings Travolta's character back in the third, concluding plot. The viewer realizes, with a jolt, that this last episode is occurring earlier in story time than the second and watches Travolta with some sadness, already knowing how that character will die.

Sliding Doors (1998) shows how differently the life of Helen (Gwyneth Paltrow) would turn out, depending on whether she took a subway train home early one day

MULHOLLAND DR. (UNIVERSAL, 2001)

The narrative in David Lynch's mysterious film is like a dream that becomes a nightmare. Betty (Naomi Watts) is a chirpy, aspiring actress, and Rita (Laura Elena Harring) is a mystery woman tormented by amnesia. They may or may not be the same person, and the entire story may represent Betty/Rita's last moment of consciousness before death. Lynch demolishes the classical Hollywood narrative in order to achieve a surreal poetry. Frame enlargement.

or missed it. The film intercuts these two scenarios and shows how this seemingly minor difference sets in motion chains of events that produce alternate fates for the character. Intercutting the alternate storylines suggests the existence of parallel worlds.

In a similar fashion, *Run Lola Run* (1998) shows a desperate 20-minute sprint by Lola to retrieve a stolen bag of cash to save her boyfriend. If she can't retrieve it, gangsters will kill him. The plot shows the episode of her run three separate times, with seemingly chance events each time altering the outcome and changing the fates of the characters. The plot of *Irreversible* (2002) moves backward from a vengeance killing to the rape that motivated it and then to the romantic couple (she the future

Case Study MEMENTO

Director Christopher Nolan is fond of clever, complex narratives. *Inception* (2010) has a multi-layered narrative, constructed of characters who are dreaming inside of other people's dreams. The plot structure works like a puzzle in which viewers must figure out what is real and what is dream. Nolan's earlier film, *Memento* (2001), presents a story that is told backward, beginning with the end and working in reverse to the beginning. Leonard Shelby (Guy Pearce) suffers from a brain disorder that robs him of short-term memory. He knows who he is (or once was—he was married and worked as an insurance investigator), but he can't remember any details of his present life or recent past.

Leonard is obsessed with finding his wife's killer, but to do so he must struggle with his memory disorder. When he finds a clue, he tattoos it onto his body, photographs it, or writes it on the back of the photo so that it will not be forgotten. The movie becomes a mystery in reverse, opening with Leonard's execution of a man he believes is the killer and then moving backward to explain how he found his victim.

This main story line is woven together with three other narrative frames: scenes of Leonard alone in his hotel room, flashbacks of his married life, and flashbacks of an insurance case he investigated involving a man named Sammy Jenkis, who lost all short-term memory following a traffic accident. The case foreshadows Leonard's fate. Intercutting these narrative frames throughout the film produces a plot structure that is rich and kaleidoscopic, but the film's main line of action—Leonard's efforts to find his wife's killer—is a linear one (though in reverse order). No scenes could be removed from it, or placed in a different order,

without damaging its clarity. Each scene is a crucial link in the narrative chain of events.

The film's story is further enriched by the ambiguities that accumulate as the plot moves backward and in and out of Leonard's memories. He is, it turns out, an unreliable narrator because he cannot remember the things he has already done or said. He has killed other men, believing them to have been his wife's killer, but he doesn't recall doing so. Natalie (Carrie-Anne Moss), the girlfriend of a drug dealer, and Teddy (Joe Pantoliano), a cop, offer him help but may, in fact, be manipulating him for their own purposes. Memories can deceive and distort. Where does the truth lie?

Director Nolan gives the ingenious narrative structure a careful visual design. The opening credits appear overtop a Polaroid photo that begins to undevelop and fade to white, and the first scene—Leonard's killing of Teddy—plays in reverse action. These strategies tell the viewer about the way the film will be organized.

Furthermore, the visual design of the different narrative frames always makes it clear which one the viewer is in. The main story line is in color, and the scenes of Leonard in his hotel room (these form the present tense of the story) are in high-contrast black-and-white and are filmed with a handheld camera. The Sammy Jenkis flashbacks are also in black and white, but these are more brightly lit and less grainy and do not feature a hand-held camera.

The narrative design is clever, highly organized, and visually marked to assist the viewer in making sense of it. The pleasures of *Memento* lie in *how* the story is told, revealing the mysteries and ambiguities of the worlds that we believe our memories contain.

(continued)

MEMENTO (NEWMARKET, 2001)

This ingenious film mixes a linear narrative running in reverse with flashbacks and with a present-tense time frame that shows Leonard Shelby (Guy Pearce) in his hotel room. Tracking his wife's killer and with no short-term memory, he relies on photographs to recall important details. The story develops great mystery as it progresses. Natalie (Carrie-Ann Moss) may be manipulating Leonard for her own ends; without a working memory, he is an easy victim and an unreliable narrator. To accentuate Leonard's isolation from people and places, the filmmakers shot in anamorphic widescreen 2.35:1, taking advantage of that format's shallow depth of field to focus on Leonard and make the backgrounds soft. Frame enlargements.

rape victim, he the future murderer) in happier times. The plots of *Annie Hall* (1977) and *Memento* (2001) jump around in many different time frames, leaving it to the viewer to assemble events in proper chronology.

Authorship and Point of View

One of the peculiar characteristics of cinema is that it is often difficult to determine the author of a film. In literature, the author of a novel is generally understood to be a single individual, the writer. Films, by contrast, are made by groups of people, and it is often difficult to say with any certainty which member of the production team—director, cinematographer, editor, sound designer—is responsible for a particular effect on screen. In this sense, films have multiple authors. Films do have writers, but the author of a screenplay typically furnishes dialogue, narrative, and dramatic action but not a film's visual or audio design. Cinematography, editing, sound—these vital areas of filmic design fall outside the domain of a screenplay.

Some years ago, the critic Pauline Kael attempted to argue that the real "author" of *Citizen Kane* (1941) was Herman J. Mankiewicz, the author of its screenplay. While Mankiewicz's script was undeniably brilliant, he had nothing to do with the film's extraordinary audiovisual design. The cinematography (by Gregg Toland), the art direction (by Van Nest Polglase), the music score (by Bernard Herrmann), and the editing (by Robert Wise) are all world-class accomplishments, and director Orson Welles was the key person organizing and integrating the contributions of these individuals. Kael's intentions to honor the film's writer were noble, but her case for Mankiewicz's authorship of the film failed to account for many of the features that have made *Citizen Kane* an outstanding and classic work of cinema.

Because the director typically has the controlling creative authority on a given production, the convention has evolved of treating the director as the author of a film. This should be done, however, in a cautious and conservative manner, with the understanding that no director is ever a film's sole author, as the writer of a novel is.

REAL AND IMPLIED AUTHORS   The collaborative nature of filmmaking gives the distinction that has existed in literary theory between the **real** and the **implied author** a special intensity. Literary critic Wayne Booth developed the notion of a real versus an implied author as a means of avoiding the biographic trap that sometimes ensnares a critic. In discussing the novels of Ernest Hemingway, for example, one cannot reduce their stylistic and literary structure to the facts of biography.

In other words, for Booth, "Hemingway," the literary persona (and the implied author) seemingly present in the writings, is relatively distinct from Ernest Hemingway, the man, who was born in Illinois in 1899, served as a reporter on the *Kansas City Star*, fought in World War I, settled in Paris after the war, and died in Idaho in 1961. The novels have their own emotional logic and power, and one can speak of "Hemingway," the literary persona that hovers in the shadows of the writings, as being relatively distinct from Hemingway, the man.

A film critic might study the work of such filmmakers as "Hitchcock," "Ford," "Spielberg," "Godard," "Bertolucci," or "Kurosawa" and treat these as implied rather than real authors, the names as labels given to bodies of film and used to describe the characteristics of those films rather than the characteristics of those individual people. In this way, "Hitchcock" designates a narrative world characterized by a certain Catholic conception of sin, guilt, transgression, and punishment and a visual design marked by such recurring features of style as high-angle shots used in moments of dramatic crisis.

The difficulty with maintaining a hard and complete distinction between the implied and the real author is that many directors do draw on personal experience in crafting their films so that a correlation does exist between who they are as people and the content of the films. Directors such as Ingmar Bergman, Steven Spielberg, and Alfred Hitchcock undeniably have based aspects of their films on personal experiences. Knowing something about their personal history can help to

TO CATCH A THIEF (PARAMOUNT, 1956)

Character meets author. On the run from the police, jewel thief John Robe (Cary Grant) hops aboard a bus and, glancing toward the window, discovers the film's director (Alfred Hitchcock) seated next to him. As a director, Hitchcock transformed his personal experiences, interests, and anxieties into brilliant film images and narratives, but the richness of these films transcends any biographic basis they might have. Moreover, Hitchcock depended on collaboration with his regular cinematographer (Robert Burks), editor (George Tomasini), and composer (Bernard Herrmann), as well as screenwriters like John Michael Hayes. As an implied author, "Hitchcock" designates the creative result of these partnerships—an unparalleled series of elegant, witty, and suspenseful films. Frame enlargement.

clarify structural features of their films. But biographic correlations can be misleading and are easily overemphasized. Because of this, the distinction between real and implied authors is useful to maintain, not in any fixed or absolute sense, but as a way of keeping clear the many ways in which film structure, produced as a collaborative enterprise by teams of filmmakers in a medium that has multiple authors, may transcend the facts of an individual filmmaker's biography.

POINT OF VIEW IN CINEMATIC NARRATIVES   As with authorship, narrative **point of view** has special conditions in cinema that differentiate it from its literary context. Literary narratives customarily use the first-person or third-person point of view. If point of view is in first-person, then the narrator employs the first-person pronoun: "I went there." "I did that." Third-person pronouns help to produce a third-person narrative: "He went there." "She did that." While novels may use either, movies almost always use third-person narration. In most films, the camera assumes a point of view that is detached and separate from the literal viewpoint as seen by each of the characters.

However, there are times when filmmakers wish to suggest a character's literal point of view. To do so, the filmmaker would use a **subjective shot** or point-of-view shot, in which the camera literally views through the eyes of the character. This kind of shot creates a brief interlude of first-person perspective. Generally, the shift from third to first person in film is signaled by showing the character reacting to something off-screen, then cutting to a view of what the character sees, the subjective view, and then closing the subjective moment with a cut back to the character from a third-person perspective.

In cinema, first-person point of view is more commonly present in an *implicit* way. In *Memento* (2001), although we see Leonard Shelby on camera, the story is told from his point of view. We share his confusion and difficulty piecing events together, and our knowledge of the story is restricted to what he knows. We learn new information only when he does.

(a)

(b)

(c)

(d)

STRANGERS ON A TRAIN (WARNER BROS., 1951)

First-person perspective typically occurs in cinema for brief intervals through the use of a subjective shot, representing what a character sees. Hitchcock often used subjective shots in remarkable ways. Guy (Farley Granger) and Bruno (Robert Walker) quarrel, in a camera setup (third-person perspective) that represents neither character's viewpoint (**a**). When Guy punches Bruno, however, Hitchcock abruptly inserts a subjective shot (**b, c**), showing this action from Bruno's perspective. Thereafter, he returns to a more normative, third-person framing (**d**). Frame enlargements.

Through performance, production design, lighting, color, editing, and the use of sound and camera, directors can suggest the emotional or psychological perspective of a character in a scene. George Stevens's *Shane* (1953) deals with the arrival of a mysterious gunfighter in a farming community in Wyoming. He stays at the home of farmer Joe Starrett and is revered by Starrett's young son, an impressionable little boy whose father is somewhat distant and who yearns for an attractive male authority figure to worship. He finds this in Shane, and it is implied very strongly that the story of the film is filtered through the point of view of young Joey Starrett.

There are, however, few subjective shots from Joey's perspective. Instead, the systematic visual presentation of Shane as an extremely romantic and idealized figure, clad in golden buckskins, establishes an implicit first-person narration, one that correlates with Joey's point of view. Shane's idealized visual and emotional presentation makes him precisely the sort of hero a young boy, starved for attention, might desire.

Extended First-Person Narration   Although *extended and explicit* first-person point of view is rare in film, there are a few spectacular examples. *Lady in the Lake*, a detective film made in 1946 from a Raymond Chandler novel, is distinguished by the novelty of having the camera take the detective's first-person point of view throughout. Viewers see the detective when he pauses in front of a mirror or examines his reflection in a store window. At other times his hand or an item of his clothing might intrude into the frame.

More recently, *84 Charlie MoPic* (1989) presented its narrative entirely through a subjective camera as MoPic, a combat cameraman, follows and films a dangerous seven-man reconnaissance mission to the central highlands during the Vietnam War. The action is presented as he sees it through the lens of his camera, and the gimmick works well in making the viewer a participant on the mission.

Filmmakers rarely employ subjective point of view so extensively, and the reason is clear. It becomes awkward and interferes with a flexible presentation of narrative information. First-person perspective ties the camera to a character's physical position,

SHANE (PARAMOUNT PICTURES, 1953)

Shane's (Alan Ladd) smooth, handsome face, golden buckskins, and refined manner establish an implicitly first-person perspective in *Shane*. It is a boy's view of a romantic and idealized Western hero. Frame enlargement.

and filmmakers customarily want to film scenes from a variety of camera positions. Filmmakers therefore find it more effective to employ third-person camera positions but to use light, color, sound, performance, and composition to imply the emotional and psychological points of view of characters in a scene. Taken together, these elements of structure help create the cinema's distinctive narrative point of view: explicit third-person narration with implied first-person components.

THE CLASSICAL HOLLYWOOD NARRATIVE

A plot is not a random collection of events. It places events in a time sequence that usually imparts a clear sense of purpose. The story seems to be moving in a certain direction, and in most cases, the viewer understands that it will come to a deliberate end, and reach a purposeful and satisfying conclusion. Causality is the glue that holds the various events and episodes in the story together. One event in the story causes another event. Some plots are tightly constructed with events chained in a strong causal sequence. By contrast, other plots are loose, open-ended, or almost shapeless, with causality present in a minimal or implicit way.

The **classical Hollywood narrative**, named after the films produced by the Hollywood studios in the 1930s to 1950s, is still prevalent in popular cinema. *Titanic* (1997), *The Lord of the Rings* trilogy (2001–2003) and *Avatar* (2009) are classical Hollywood narratives, as are almost all popular film entertainments.

Such films feature a main line of action and one or more subordinate lines of action (subplots) tied to it. The plot is directional—activated by a main character pursuing a goal—and one event follows another in tight causal relationships, as links in a chain. The goals of the action are announced early in the film, and the plot follows a line of rising interest and tension as the characters confront impediments to their goals. The conclusion of the film sees the characters either achieving or failing to achieve their goals in a way that brings the narrative to a satisfying conclusion that resolves all outstanding story issues. It is this sense of completeness, resulting from the resolution of all lines of action, that gives the classical narrative its satisfying quality. In the cases of *The Lord of the Rings* trilogy, the story lines arc across several films before achieving complete resolution.

Alternatives to the Classical Narrative

While classical Hollywood narratives have proven to be very popular with audiences, and a great many films each year are produced in this format, alternative narrative forms have been an important and vital part of cinema. The example cited earlier in the chapter of narrative structure in *Memento* shows a case of nonclassical narrative.

Films made outside of mainstream Hollywood production often use alternative narrative structures. In these cases, causality may be minimized in favor of ambiguity. No clearly dominant line of action may emerge. The sequence of events may be loosely organized, giving the viewer a weaker sense of the direction in which the story is moving.

Many European films, for example, prize ambiguity over causality in structuring their narratives. Bernardo Bertolucci's *Last Tango in Paris* (1972) is a French-Italian co-production that portrays the emotional devastation of an American named Paul (Marlon Brando), living in Paris, whose wife has just committed suicide. Her suicide is the fundamental motivating event for all the film's action, but the film does not reveal what has happened until well into the narrative. As a result, considerable ambiguity surrounds Paul's behavior.

Unlike *Memento*, where the plot rearranges the chronology of story events, Bertolucci does not alter the chronology of events in *Last Tango*. But he omits key scenes and delays giving the viewer important information needed to understand the story. Thus the viewer cannot at first comprehend the reasons for Paul's extreme emotional distress. The reasons for his distress (namely, his wife's suicide) are not made

Case Study   THE SEARCHERS

John Ford's *The Searchers* (1956), a renowned and prestigious Western, illustrates the goal-directed, highly motivated action of the classical Hollywood narrative. At the beginning of the film, Ethan Edwards (John Wayne) returns from the Civil War to his brother's cabin in Texas. Ethan has been away for a number of years, engaged in activities that remain mysterious. He arrives at Aaron's and Martha's homestead, where relations between the brothers are tense, and where it is hinted that Ethan and Martha share an unspoken love. Shortly after Ethan's arrival, Indians attack the homestead, burn the cabin, and wipe out the family, except for Aaron's and Martha's two daughters, whom they abduct. Driven by a powerful hatred of Indians, Ethan becomes obsessed with returning his nieces to the white community.

This is the goal-directed activity that generates the remainder of the film's narrative and takes the character on a five-year search. The opening act of the film served to define the essential conditions—Ethan's love for Martha, his rootless and stubborn nature, and his pathologic hatred for Indians—that motivate the ensuing action. As the plot progresses, however, Ethan encounters impediments to his goal, chief among them being his own savagery. Ethan's hatred for Indians poisons his feelings for Debbie (the one abducted niece who survives) once he realizes that she is living among the Comanche as a member of their culture. His original goal of rescuing Debbie is replaced by another and darker quest: to destroy her.

In its last act, *The Searchers* generates considerable excitement as Ethan finds Debbie and chases her down a ravine to the mouth of a cave. He lifts her in his arms and the viewer is afraid that he is going to bash her brains out, but in a last-minute turn of events, he forgives her, forgives himself, and honors his original quest, returning her to the white community of Texas settlers.

Ethan's quest for Debbie is the main line of action in the film, but it is conjoined with a subplot showing the relationship of Marty, a relative accompanying Ethan, with a family of settlers, whose domestic lives hold more attraction for him than they do for Ethan. The subplot is interrelated with the main line of action—Marty decides that his real task will be to prevent Ethan from killing Debbie when he finds her—and both lines of action are resolved at the end. Debbie is rescued. Marty joins the family of settlers and will (it is implied) marry their daughter. In the last scene, he enters the family's home, whereas Ethan chooses not to do so, walking away from the cabin into the desert and back to the rootless existence from which he appeared at the film's beginning.

The classical Hollywood narrative makes use of **explicit causality.** One event clearly causes another in the chain that forms the narrative. The Comanche attack on the cabin prompts Ethan's quest. Ethan swears to return Debbie to her rightful community. He undertakes a five-year search. During the course of the search, he comes to hate Debbie. What will he do when he finds her? The tension surrounding this latter question generates the climax of the film and its surprising last-minute turn of events in which the character redeems himself in a way that allows him to honor the original goal, the one that had driven the narrative from its beginning.

Because of its explicit causality, classical Hollywood cinema features a clear hierarchy of narrative events. Certain episodes stand out as the most important links in the narrative chain, whereas others are less decisive and less important. If viewers are asked to summarize this kind of highly motivated film narrative, they can easily identify the most important narrative events. Asked to summarize *The Searchers*, a viewer might say that a band of Commanche attacks a Texas homestead, and one of the survivors vows revenge, searches for many years for a young girl, and finally locates and rescues her. These events could not be subtracted from the film without radically altering or damaging the story. ◼

(a)

(b)

(c)

(d)

(e)

(f)

THE SEARCHERS (Warner Bros., 1956)

The highly motivated and goal-oriented classical Hollywood narrative. Ethan (John Wayne) returns from years of wandering to visit his brother's family and Martha, whom he loves (**a–c**). Comanches massacre the family and abduct the children. Ethan views the carnage with horror (**d**) and resolves to find and rescue the children. After years of searching, he returns with one child (**e**). In the last image (**f**), he stands alone, now without purpose in his life, turns and walks away, into the desert. Frame enlargements.

clear until 30 minutes into the film. This gives many scenes during the intervening period an unclear and ambiguous status. In one, Paul stands in a bathroom as a maid cleans a tub full of blood. He waits silently as the maid describes how she was questioned by the police. At this point in the narrative, though, the viewer doesn't know what happened here, why the police are involved, or what relationship this has to Paul.

The important questions in the narrative—who Paul is, where the blood in the bathroom has come from, why he is in such distress—are answered slowly and incompletely. As a result, the narrative in *Last Tango* presents the viewer with serious interpretational challenges. Bertolucci's viewer must sort out the particulars of Paul's distress and his wife's suicide and their marital relationship by working through a plot structure that is not organized to facilitate the answering of these questions.

Independent filmmaking is another mode of production in which classical Hollywood narrative is often conspicuously absent. The narrative in many independent films is often very episodic, with events joined in a loose fashion, with minimal or **implicit causality**. John Sayles is one of the most successful independent filmmakers, with

LAST TANGO IN PARIS (UNITED ARTISTS, 1972)

The narrative structure of *Last Tango in Paris* withholds key pieces of story information. As a result, first-time viewers have great difficulty piecing the story together. Paul's anguish is, at first, unexplained. When he visits the scene of a suicide, viewers struggle to grasp its significance for him. The film's narrative design deliberately poses interpretive challenges for its viewers. Frame enlargements.

a long and respected filmography (*Return of the Secaucus Seven*, 1980; *Lone Star*, 1996; *Men With Guns*, 1998). Although he has used linear classical narrative in *Matewan* (1987), in other films he has moved far from it. *City of Hope* (1991) contains one of his more radical narrative structures. The film portrays a decaying urban economy and community in the 1990s. The narrative is not driven by the personal goals of a protagonist or a main line of action. Sayles instead follows an ensemble—a group—of characters as the narrative winds through the city to reveal a cross section of its inhabitants: a corrupt city contractor, his disillusioned son, an idealistic city councilman, a group of cynical policemen, and citizen groups of various racial and ethnic backgrounds. Summarizing the story of this film is much more difficult than with *The Searchers* because narrative events are not tightly chained together, and no single line of action predominates. The narrative focus is diffuse, unified by the common theme of showing a multitude of responses to urban decay. Alejandro Inarritu's *Amores Perros* (2000) and Paul Haggis' *Crash* (2004) offer similarly episodic narratives focusing on an ensemble of characters.

THE COUNTER-NARRATIVE TRADITION   The most extreme alternatives to classical Hollywood narrative can be found in the **counter-narrative** tradition. Radical attempts at narrative deconstruction—at making films that decompose and take apart their own narratives—have been popular among more philosophically inclined directors. In their work, narrative is treated as a problem, as something to be refused or attacked.

CLOSE-UP

Three Acts or Four?

One way to understand the structure of a classical Hollywood narrative is to break it down into major structural units. Syd Field is an influential author of numerous books aimed at aspiring screenwriters. His books provide advice on how to write screenplays, and Field has argued that a Hollywood narrative is composed of three acts. Act One, which he calls the *set-up,* introduces the story, characters, and setting. Act Two, the *confrontation,* focuses on the conflicts that come between the main characters and their goals. Act Three, *resolution,* settles these conflicts and ties up the various plot lines. Field argues that a "plot point" occurs at the transitions between these acts, and this plot point introduces something that hooks into the action "and spins it around in another direction," creating a transition to the next act.

In contrast to Field, film scholar Kristin Thompson has suggested that there are four acts in Hollywood movies. The *set-up* establishes the action and character goals. The *complicating action* introduces a new situation that the characters must respond to. The *development* shows the characters attempting to reach their goals. The *climax* resolves the various conflicts. Thompson suggests that these acts are roughly equal in length, around 20–30 minutes each, and that the film overall has a mid-point, a plot development that occurs about midway through the running time. This is a turning point in the plot that marks the onset of the development section. She suggests, for example, that the scene in *Alien,* during which the baby monster bursts through the stomach of one of the astronauts and then runs off to hide on board the ship, is the central turning point of the film. It marks the onset of the development section, which is all about the efforts of the surviving crew members to hunt down the monster and kill it. This scene occurs almost exactly midway through the film.

One way, then, to understand the organization of narrative in Hollywood movies is to perform a structural analysis, which aims to break the films into their basic segments. You can easily do this by thinking about where the turning points in the narrative occur, and whether they work to break the film into three or four acts. ■

(continued)

ALIEN (20TH CENTURY FOX, 1979)
The narrative mid-point introduces a new, complicating line of action that preoccupies characters in the development section, according to scholar Kristin Thompson. The alien monster bursts through the chest of an unfortunate astronaut and goes on a rampage in the spaceship, compelling the remaining characters to confront it in a life-and-death struggle. This mid-point action occurs almost exactly in the middle of the film, measured by its running time. Frame enlargement.

Case Study   LAST YEAR AT MARIENBAD

French director Alain Resnais, in the classic modernist film *Last Year at Marienbad* (1961), presents a narrative that deliberately refuses to organize itself. *Last Year at Marienbad* deals with a murky, cloudy, unclear set of events taking place at a luxurious hotel. During the film, an unnamed man attempts to persuade an unnamed woman that they have met the year before at a fancy spa. Whether they actually did or not is never resolved.

Resnais's editing prevents the emergence of clear space and time relationships between scenes. For example, a number of shots are joined with matched cuts and continuous dialogue, which imply that no time has elapsed, but the characters' costumes change, as do the locales. These are contradictory cues that indicate time is both passing and not passing.

Last Year at Marienbad self-consciously studies the creation of narrative. In the film, a story tries to organize itself but never quite does. The movie opens in a kind of prenarrative state without characters and without a clear setting. The camera tracks through empty hotel hallways, past doors, friezes, columns, paintings,

and tapestries. Voice-over narration, of unidentified origin, poetically states that this is an environment of soundless rooms where voices sink into rugs so deep that no step can be heard, where halls and galleries are from another age, where hallways cross other hallways that endlessly open onto deserted rooms.

During the course of the camera's movements through this poetically and mysteriously defined environment, a group of people appears in frozen, still-life postures, characters existing as sculptures in this strange hotel. Gradually the characters unfreeze, begin to move, and start delivering dialogue during which the mysterious man attempts to convince the unnamed woman that they have met the year before. The narrative comes to life.

Last Year at Marienbad is a film that deliberately sets out to provoke, puzzle, challenge, and undermine assumptions about what narrative is and how it operates in film. There is no sense of direction to the plot, and no real conclusion is reached either. Instead, endless repetition—of images, camera movement, dialogue—is the defining structural characteristic. In this respect,

Last Year at Marienbad stands as an extreme departure from the terms of narrative in popular, mass-market movies, and it can be classified as a modernist film in that it does not wish to tell a story so much as to talk about what stories are and how they may be structured on film.

Jean-Luc Godard's *Le Gai Savoir* (1969) is another example of counter-narrative filmmaking. Here, two characters gather in an empty French television studio to inquire into the nature of images and to understand better how television and other visual media communicate. They meet for seven nights, and their comings

LAST YEAR AT MARIENBAD (1961)

Antinarrative in *Last Year at Marienbad*. Characters move through richly detailed settings, but the narrative fails to emerge. The film's use of narrative to play with and tease the viewer was a major influence on such later films as *Inception* and *Memento*. Frame enlargement.

LE GAI SAVOIR (1969)

Godard's *Le Gai Savoir* offers poetry and philosophy in place of a narrative. Many modern, stylistically radical directors believe that all the stories have already been told in cinema, and they reject or deform the medium's storytelling function. Frame enlargement.

(continued)

and goings, and their philosophical reflections about the nature of pictures, constitute what plot there is. The soundtrack is punctuated by the noise of static and by Godard's own voice in a kind of running, anxious commentary about the nature of images and his own film. *Le Gai Savoir* reduces narrative to a minimum in order to construct a film that functions more on the lines of an essay than a story. In this respect, like *Last Year at Marienbad*, *Le Gai Savoir* illustrates the impatience with stories felt by many modern, stylistically radical directors.

Such filmmakers regard narrative as an obstacle to their creative interests. Telling a story gets in the way. It obligates them to create, delineate, and motivate characters and to emphasize the story, treating other,

nonnarrative elements as background components. Filmmakers whose interests are essayistic, poetic, or didactic often take the medium in a nonnarrative direction when they consider narrative to be incompatible with their artistic goals. Viewers of popular movies may find this antinarrative orientation difficult to understand or seemingly perverse because the basic pleasure offered by popular cinema is precisely the storytelling function. Such viewers may find the antinarrative films to be a strange experience or to offer little of the familiar pleasures they are accustomed to finding in movies. But the antinarrative tradition in cinema is very real, and it has influenced many important filmmakers whose work has enlarged the creative boundaries of cinema. ■

CLOSE-UP

The French New Wave

Jean-Luc Godard and Alain Resnais were filmmakers who were part of the French New Wave—a new generation of directors who established careers in the 1960s and rebelled against the traditional formulas of studio filmmaking by experimenting boldly with narrative and film style. Existing visual designs and story templates were twisted, stretched, and re-imagined, transforming the heritage of French cinema and redefining its future. Francois Truffaut's *The 400 Blows* (1959), for example, takes a naturalistic approach to its story of a young delinquent but ends with a freeze-frame that abruptly halts the story and leaves the fate of the main character unresolved and ambiguous. The freeze-frame creates an open ending that avoids the tidy resolutions commonly found in movie narratives. The freeze frame boldly announced to viewers that the film's narrative was refusing traditional forms of closure.

Alain Resnais' *Hiroshima, mon amour* (1959) uses flash cuts to blend the war-time memories of an actress (Emmanuelle Riva) with her present life, making the narrative a subjective one with images that capture the free flow of thought itself as the character (identified as SHE in the script) reflects on earlier traumas and on her present love affair with a Japanese architect (Eiji Okada). The narrative concludes in an enigmatic and poetic way, with the two lovers addressing each other not by personal name

but with the names of cities associated with losses in World War II. "Hiroshima. Hiroshima. That's your name," she tells him.

The New Wave directors loved film, and they filled their movies with self-conscious references to cinema and with riffs on Hollywood. Such extensive winks and homages were unprecedented in the period, although they are more common today largely because of the New Wave's influence. Frankie (Jean-Paul Belmondo) in Godard's *Breathless* (1959) gazes adoringly at a poster of Hollywood star Humphrey Bogart and models himself on Bogart. Godard's *Contempt* (1967) casts famed director Fritz Lang (*Metropolis*, 1927) as a filmmaker struggling with a crass American producer. Prominent Hollywood director Sam Fuller has a cameo at a party in Godard's *Pierrot le Fou* (1965). Asked what is cinema, he replies famously, "A film is like a battleground. It's love, hate, action, violence, death. In one word, emotions." Maoist guerillas in Godard's *Weekend* (1967) communicate by radio using movie titles as call signs: "Johnny Guitar calling The Searchers;" "Battleship Potemkin calling Gosta Berling." A cut-out of director Alfred Hitchcock appears in the background of a shot in Resnais' *Last Year at Marienbad* (1961).

Truffaut made *The Bride Wore Black* (1968) in the style of an Alfred Hitchcock film, and director

Claude Chabrol embarked on an entire career's worth of Hitchcock-style thrillers. Truffaut's *Day for Night* (1973) portrayed a film crew at work on a production, a movie within the movie, with Truffaut appearing as the film's director. The title—*Day for Night*—refers to movie magic, the filming during broad daylight of scenes scripted as taking place at night.

Jacques Demy's *The Umbrellas of Cherbourg* (1964) is a stylized musical modeled on Hollywood movies, with flamboyant color design and characters who sing all of their dialogue instead of speaking. Agnes Varda's *Cleo from 5 to 7* (1962) opens with a color sequence and then switches to black-and-white for the remainder of the film, reminding viewers of style and structure. At the beginning of

THE 400 BLOWS (Les Films du Carosse, 1959)

The film's concluding freeze frame shows Antoine Doinel (Jean-Pierre Leaud) staring back at the camera, facing an uncertain future in his life. The concluding image is both defiant and ambiguous. The shot looks very grainy because the close-up was enlarged on an optical printer, causing generational loss of image quality. Frame enlargement.

PIERROT LE FOU (Janus Films, 1965)

Maverick Hollywood director Sam Fuller, with sunglasses and an ever-present cigar, drops in to Godard's film to explain the nature of cinema. Frame enlargement.

(continued)

Godard's *Tout va bien* (1972), he offers a montage showing all of the checks that need to be written to pay for the film and its crew, emphasizing the film's status as a manufactured object and not a window on reality. And Godard himself appears in *Cleo from Five to Seven* in a short, silent film within the movie, along with the actress Anna Karina who frequently starred in Godard's own films.

The New Wave directors were passionate devotees of cinema (some had begun their careers as film critics) and in their playful approach to narrative and their self-conscious cinematic designs, they invited viewers to share in this passion for movies. Their influence has been huge, re-shaping the nature of cinema and what viewers have come to expect from it. Contemporary filmmakers have winked in return to acknowledge their debt to this tradition. Quentin Tarantino, for example, named his production company A Band Apart, in honor of Godard's early film about bumbling gangsters, *Band a part* (1964). ∎

THE UMBRELLAS OF CHERBOURG (Madeleine Films, 1964)
Hollywood musicals inspired Jacques Demy to make this stylized variation in which all dialogue is sung, not spoken. Intense color design evokes a world of heightened emotion while the story stays close to psychological realism, unusual for musicals. Frame enlargement.

THE VIEWER'S CONTRIBUTION TO NARRATIVE

Viewers participate in the storytelling process, and filmmakers design narratives in ways that encourage this participation. In his choice of narrative technique, Hitchcock preferred suspense over surprise because the former condition drew viewers into the story as participants, whereas surprise tended to exclude them. **Suspense** as a narrative technique depends on giving viewers information, whereas **surprise** depends on withholding it. If Hitchcock began a scene by showing viewers a ticking bomb under a table around which a group of friends were playing cards, he could then film the card game for five or ten minutes of excruciating suspense, during which the audience is saying to the cardplayers, "Stop playing cards, there's a bomb under your table!" Conversely, if he did not show the bomb and it then exploded, it would produce a brief moment of shock and surprise.

Filmmakers use the elements of narrative structure to encourage the viewer's active contribution. The action of the popular thriller *The French Connection* (1972) deals with a New York cop's obsessive hunt for a powerful French drug smuggler. At the end of the film, the cop corners the smuggler in a warehouse. The cop chases him into a back room, but the camera stays outside the room, leaving both characters off-screen. After a pause, a gunshot is heard off-screen, and the image fades out. The film is over, and the viewer is left wondering who fired the shot and whether the cop got his man. As the end credits roll, that final gunshot reverberates in the viewer's mind. What did it mean, and why was it presented in such a mysterious way? How does the story *end?* Its structure challenges the viewer to make sense of the film's puzzling conclusion, its final withholding of information, and its lack of explicit narrative closure.

As the ending of *The French Connection* illustrates, storytellers can hook the audience by deliberately omitting important pieces of story information. The audience infers and fills in this information as its contribution to the story, binding storyteller and audience in a close creative relationship. In a mystery film, viewers will try to guess the identity of the murderer before the detective or the narrative reveals it. The final shot of the ice pick under the bed in *Basic Instinct* (1992) teases the audience

THE SIXTH SENSE (HOLLYWOOD PICTURES, 1999)
This uncommonly clever ghost story sprung an unforgettable twist ending on its viewers, many of whom felt compelled to return to the film for a second viewing to see how it was done. The story is psychologically rich and has a slow, meditative pacing. These are not the typical characteristics of a box-office blockbuster, and they demonstrate that the pleasures offered by a well-told story do not go out of fashion. Compositions showing Malcolm (Bruce Willis) and Cole (Haley Joel Osment) together in the frame are quite rare in the film. Most often they are framed in separate shots, a strategy director M. Night Shyamalan uses to subliminally suggest that the characters inhabit different realms—the living and the dead. Frame enlargement.

with the possibility that the real killer in the narrative is still at large and may strike again.

The Sixth Sense (1999) vividly illustrates this storytelling partnership between filmmaker and audience. Its narrative is uncommonly clever, and in its closing moments, it springs a last-minute surprise on the viewer that completely changes everything the viewer has assumed about the characters and story. The film's phenomenal box-office success was due to the pleasure that its remarkable twist gave viewers and to repeat business. Viewers came back to see the movie again, intrigued by its clever design, curious to see how the twist was accomplished and whether there were any clues to the ending that they had missed. *The Others* (2001), a ghost story starring Nicole Kidman, works in a similar fashion.

The viewer's participation in a narrative activates a basic operational principle of the human mind—the search for pattern. Perception and interpretation are not mechanical responses to information but are active, goal-directed processes. Narrative activates these processes by inviting the audience to search for the overall pattern within a given narrative structure, the story to which the plot points. The desire to see the completed pattern is experienced by viewers as the need to find out "what happens next" in a story. The clear causality and motivation in a classical Hollywood narrative such as *The Lord of the Rings* stimulates this desire by organizing the story in a linear fashion that moves forward, with increasing momentum, toward its conclusion. The more fragmented structure of *Memento* or *Last Tango in Paris* stimulates this desire by burying the master pattern—the story—inside a narrative structure—a plot—that hides it. In each case, the act of storytelling binds the audience to the narrative as participant and co-creator, strengthening the bond between audience and storyteller as they both help create the story.

These considerations point to an important conclusion: Meaning is not *in* the film but is formed by the interaction of the film's audiovisual and narrative design with the

INCEPTION (WARNER BROS., 2010)
Meaning is not *in* a film but arises through the interaction of viewers with movies. *Inception* capitalizes on this interaction by creating an ambiguous narrative that invites viewers to provide a resolution. The ending, for example, teases viewers by holding out two possibilities that are mutually exclusive. Dom Cobb (Leonardo DiCaprio) believes he has returned to reality from the dream-world that he has inhabited. But has he? The film's ambiguous ending provokes viewers to interpret, and thereby to create, its meaning. Frame enlargement.

viewer's own horizon of perceptual and social experience—the viewer's interpretive contribution. The implication of this is enormous. It means that filmmakers cannot control the meaning of their films because the experiences, values, and assumptions that viewers bring to those films and that establish their frameworks of interpretation are incredibly diverse and variable.

Obviously, viewers use a variety of criteria to evaluate the aesthetic qualities of a narrative. Is it coherent? Is it pleasurable? Is it convincing? Does it make sense? These are evaluations of narrative structure—how the story is aesthetically organized and told.

In a story where events are linked in a tight causal chain, with few digressions, viewers tend to expect an ending that ties up the loose ends by resolving all outstanding story issues. If they are given, instead, an ambiguous ending, as occurs in *The French Connection* (1972), some viewers may feel frustrated, whereas others find the ambiguity exciting and are stimulated to fill in the missing information. Viewers routinely evaluate how the story is told and whether, given the type of film it is, the story is told in a satisfying way.

Because so many movies establish screen worlds that are recognizably similar to their own, viewers also evaluate narratives using standards borrowed from personal and social experience. Here, it is not so much the narrative design that is evaluated as the way the narrative portrays people or situations. Arab-Americans protested the Arnold Schwarzenegger thriller *True Lies* (1994) because of its portrayal of Arabic groups as terrorists. Some African-Americans felt that the hyenas in Disney's *The Lion King* (1994) were unpleasantly close to a caricature of black people. The mannerisms and Caribbean accent of Jar-Jar Binks in *The Phantom Menace* (1999) aroused similar complaints. Viewers assess the narrative portrayals against their own understanding of the issues, situations, or groups. Does the narrative square with their own sense of things, or does it seem unreasonably biased or distorted in a way that style cannot justify?

The standards viewers apply when evaluating narratives, then, are quite diverse, and they range from judgments about the artistic design of the story to judgments about its success in representing familiar things or people. Filmmakers can influence but they cannot control these evaluations. Filmmakers *can* control the audiovisual design of their films, but viewers are the essential co-creators of the meanings that arise from those designs.

FILM GENRES

Many popular films fall into **genres**, which are sets of interrelated stories and their associated images. The most popular and historically significant American film genres include the Western, the gangster film, the horror film, the musical, film noir, the war film, and the science fiction film. One of the most important characteristics of genres is that the stories are repeated again and again, with rules, or **conventions**, about what can happen within the genre. Moreover, many conventions are unique to a given genre. What viewers accept in a musical film might appear ridiculous in a gangster film.

The repetition of story situations throughout a genre produces two effects: It enables viewers familiar with the genre to anticipate likely narrative developments and outcomes, and it enables filmmakers to achieve highly concentrated meanings within the genre. Consider these simple terms common to Westerns: *gunfighter, Indian, cowboy*. Each word conjures up a host of associated images and potential story situations for viewers who are familiar with the genre.

A viewer critical of genres, who objects that all Westerns or all horror films are the same, is missing the point. Film scholar Robert Warshow has pointed out that "one does not want too much novelty" from a genre film. Fans of a genre derive pleasure from the small variations that are worked out within the pre-established order of story and setting. Repetition of familiar material is very important, and too much novelty or originality can place a film outside a genre's framework.

The Western

The Western is one of the oldest screen genres. Indeed, the Western as a cultural category predates the cinema. It emerged near the end of the nineteenth century and was established in a variety of pre-cinematic forms: the dime novel, the Puritan captivity narratives, the Leatherstocking tales (1823–1841) of James Fenimore Cooper, theatrical plays and shows (e.g., Buffalo Bill's Wild West Show), and painting (ethnographic studies of Indian cultures, as well as Frederic Remington's action scenes).

The Western, then, already existed when the cinema was invented at the turn of the century. The cinema supplied movement and exciting visual images to flesh out existing cultural stories about westward expansion and conflict between settlers and Native Americans. The Western rapidly established its popularity in cinema. By 1910, 21 percent of all U.S. pictures were Westerns. During the next decades, Hollywood produced Westerns in great quantities, and many of the industry's most popular stars were closely identified with the genre: Gary Cooper (*The Virginian, The Westerner, High Noon*), John Wayne (*Stagecoach, She Wore a Yellow Ribbon, Hondo*), Clint Eastwood (*High Plains Drifter, The Outlaw Josey Wales, Unforgiven*). John Ford, perhaps the

THE TOLL GATE (1920)

The Western is one of the oldest screen genres and quickly achieved enormous popularity. William S. Hart was one of the most popular Western stars in the silent period. Hart aimed to portray the West with realism and with a serious, adult outlook that contrasted with the adolescent appeal of stars such as Tom Mix. Frame enlargement.

finest director of the Hollywood period, made many of the genre's enduring classics: *Stagecoach, My Darling Clementine, Fort Apache, The Searchers, The Man Who Shot Liberty Valance.*

Beginning in the 1970s, however, the genre's popularity notably diminished, and since then, it has never recovered the close relationship with a mass audience that it once enjoyed. Important and fine Westerns continue to be made—*Tombstone* (1993), *Unforgiven* (1992), *Open Range* (2003)—but the genre's high period of creativity and appeal to a wide audience seems to have ended. It remains, though, the quintessential American genre, the one most closely tied to the theme and mythology of the nation's experience and identity.

The Western is defined by period, setting, and theme. The period is that interval of time between the Civil War and World War I, and the setting is west of the Mississippi River, on the plains or in the desert or the mountains. Films that fall outside these specifications may lie on the periphery of the genre, but they are not Westerns. This period and setting contain the great historical stories that have furnished the genre with its material: waves of migration via the overland trails, the Indian wars, the building of the railroads, the cattle drives, the gold rushes, the frontier marshals and town tamers, the gunfighters.

While the genre has many themes, the one at its heart is the conflict between cultural ideas about civilization and the wilderness in stories that explain why violence is necessary for the preservation of community. The theme is linked to an enduring pattern of imagery. In the highly conventionalized opening typical of many Westerns, the central character, a man of violence, rides in to a town or settlement from the wilderness. A narrative situation—the approach of a violent individual to a community—is linked to a particular setting and image, the wilderness of desert or mountain. The long shots integrate the character with the surrounding wilderness, and by showing how large and expansive the wilderness is, they stress the fragility and vulnerability of the settlement or community. The struggle between violence and law

UNFORGIVEN (WARNER BROS., 1992)

Clint Eastwood is the Western's last big star, and his work as director–producer demonstrates genuine mastery and feeling for the genre. In *Unforgiven*, he probes the destructive consequences of violence and offers a revisionist treatment of his star image. Frame enlargement.

is embodied in this visual contrast. As a figure of violence, the gunman comes from the wilderness to the community, and frequently at the end of the films, he must leave the settlement to return to the mountains or plains.

The Western is among the most rule-bound of film genres. It links specific story situations to particular settings. In many Westerns, the violent skills of the protagonist are tested in a public arena. This arena often is a saloon, where armed and violent confrontations occur in close proximity to the bar. The genre has coded this location for violence. By contrast, schoolrooms and churches are impermissible locations for violent confrontations. Gunfights or brawls almost never occur there.

The regularity of story in the Western is most apparent in the necessity for a gunfight at the conclusion of the film. The gunfight resolves the narrative conflicts by granting that at this moment of primitive social development, violence is needed on

3:10 TO YUMA (LIONSGATE, 2007) and THE ASSASSINATION OF JESSE JAMES BY THE COWARD ROBERT FORD (WARNER BROS., 2007)

Contemporary filmmakers continue to make Westerns, although production in the genre remains small. In his remake of *3:10 to Yuma,* James Mangold used fast-paced action to give the genre a more contemporary feel. In contrast, *The Assassination of Jesse James* was slowly paced and more poetic, with Roger Deakins' cinematography lending the film a very stylized and pictorial design, evident in the sepia tone and selective blurring of the frame found in this shot. Ford (Casey Affleck, center) gazes adoringly at Jesse (Brad Pitt, left), whom he is destined to kill. Frame enlargements.

behalf of the community. Because genres *are* so rule-bound, too much variation from the formulas can produce **deviant plot structures** that viewers may deem unsatisfying. Howard Hawks's 1948 production of *Red River* is a case in point. It deals with the first cattle drive over the Chisholm Trail. Tom Dunson (John Wayne) leads his cattle on this perilous trek, assisted by his adopted son, Matthew Garth (Montgomery Clift). During the drive, Dunson grows tyrannical and becomes a borderline psychopath obsessed with preventing cowboys from quitting the drive and threatening to hang those who do. Eventually, he becomes unbearable, and the men revolt. Matthew Garth takes the herd and leaves Dunson behind. Dunson swears revenge and tells Matt that he will kill him when they next meet.

The plot moves in traditional Western fashion toward the promise of a climactic gunfight. But it never occurs. Instead, a comical fistfight between Matt and Dunson leads to their reconciliation. Many viewers have felt somewhat cheated by this ending, which is at odds with the genre. (From the standpoint of the director's other films, however, this ending seems less deviant because in most of his work Hawks tended to prefer comedy and comradeship over tragedy.)

The Western makes an excellent tool of study for students who wish to understand how genre works. It has a long history, is extremely rule-bound and precise in the application of those rules, and yet it shows an impressive diversity of style and subject matter. This is the essential and fascinating aspect about a genre: It shows diversity within constraint, variations within an abiding master pattern.

The Gangster Film

The gangster film is nearly as old as the cinema, having clear precursors in the early silent era. The genre emerged as a powerful force in U.S. film, however, at the time of the Great Depression. In the years 1930–1932, three films—*Little Caesar, The Public*

LITTLE CAESAR (WARNER BROS., 1931)

One of the biggest in a long line of movie gangsters, the snarling Rico Bandello (Edward G. Robinson) in *Little Caesar*. Pictured here, he is at the height of his power and wealth, but in a classic rise-and-fall story, the gangster eventually must lose. Rico is so smug and self-centered that when death finally comes, he can scarcely believe it. Riddled by a police machine gun, he asks in disbelief if his life has reached its end. Frame enlargement.

Enemy, and *Scarface*—defined the essential narrative patterns, settings, images, and types of social conflicts that would characterize the genre during the next decades.

In the classical gangster structure, the narrative focuses on the rise and fall of a career criminal, from his early, humble, frequently immigrant origins to the zenith of his success, and then to his decline from power and violent death. This narrative pattern characterizes *Little Caesar, The Public Enemy*, and *Scarface*, as well as many later gangster films, including the *Godfather* films, the 1983 remake of *Scarface* by Brian De Palma, and Mario Van Peebles's *New Jack City* (1991). Other gangster films, of course, deviate from the classical narrative. Mike Newell's *Donnie Brasco* (1997) forgoes the epic style of a rise-and-fall story in its low-key account of the last days of a small-time New York hood (Al Pacino). Martin Scorsese's *Goodfellas* (1990) has elements of the rise-and-fall story in its tale of a young Brooklyn man's aspirations to join the local mob, but its main focus is a kind of ethnography of mob behavior and ritual.

In the classical structure, the gangster hero represents a perverse version of the American myth of success. He is an inverted and dark embodiment of the Horatio Alger myth, which stipulated that opportunities to advance were open to everyone, no matter how humble their origins. His determination and persistence enable him to achieve great economic success, but he must use harsh and violent tactics to do so, and his appetite for power, wealth, and violence is boundless. The gangster Tony Montana (*Scarface*, 1983) dreams of possessing the world and all in it.

The roots of the gangster film in U.S. culture include this Horatio Alger myth of success, as well as the example of the nineteenth-century robber barons, who, like the film gangster, amassed great fortunes through frequently ruthless methods. The genre's cultural roots also include the impact of the Great Depression and its demonstration of economic injustice and the influence of Prohibition, which eroded respect for law-and-order and generated popular sympathy for the rum-running gangster.

Each of these cultural factors helped to make the movie gangster what he was and ensured that the genre offered a sustained critique of society. If society, after all, created gangsters like Little Caesar or Scarface, how healthy could it be? Francis Ford Coppola's *The Godfather* (1972) opens with a dark screen, as a voice intones, "I believe in America." As the lights come up, Don Corleone confers with an Italian man who has come to him because the courts have not provided justice. His daughter has been raped and assaulted, and the legal system failed to convict her assailants. He seeks from Don Corleone a more primitive kind of justice, one that involves violent retribution.

With his ability to exercise this kind of justice and his rejection and repudiation of established society, with his attainment of wealth and power, the gangster character appeals to an implicit dissatisfaction on the part of movie audiences with their social and economic status. By succeeding and becoming wealthy, the gangster fulfills the culture's deepest ideals, but he does so by violating its norms. This appeal is nowhere more apparent than in the conventions that surround the death of the movie gangster. As dictated by the rules of the genre, the gangster's death must be spectacular, and it often contains a powerful social critique. In *High Sierra* (1941), Roy Earle (Humphrey Bogart) is a romantic and sympathetic gangster with great compassion and empathy for the poor and downtrodden. The film presents his death as a cowardly act by the legal authorities.

Earle is not simply killed; he is shot off a mountaintop and falls from a great height, a hero of legendary stature brought down by callous authority. Shot in the

DONNIE BRASCO (COLUMBIA TRISTAR, 1997)

Much distinguished work in the genre lies outside its classic narrative structure. Small-time hood and hanger-on Lefty Ruggerio (Al Pacino) is not the stuff of a rise-and-fall story. Rather than an epic hero like Little Caesar or the Godfather, he's a nobody, a foot soldier in the neighborhood mob. But he is a compelling character who illuminates the low end of gangsterdom, and the film invests the story of his last days with compassion. Frame enlargement.

back, he is felled by a police sniper. His death is witnessed by Marie, the woman he loved, and in the closing moments of the film she murmurs, "Freedom," equating Earle's death with a final escape from unjust social authority. The end credits are presented on a scroll that moves toward the top of the frame in a visual design that echoes the distant High Sierra mountains and symbolizes the idea of transcendence and escape that Earle's death embodies in the narrative.

At the conclusion of *White Heat* (1948), the psychopathic gangster Cody Jarrett immolates himself atop a huge chemical storage tank. In one of the most famous moments in all U.S. cinema, he screams, "Made it, Ma, top of the world!" just before he and the tank explode. The erupting mushroom cloud, which is the film's final image, situates Jarrett's crazed violence within the postwar atomic age and its nuclear anxieties. Jarrett is a violent psychopath, yet the energies of violence embodied in modern society and represented by the atomic weapon and the mushroom cloud are infinitely greater. The ending of the film suggests a nuclear apocalypse. Jarrett has made it to the top of the world, and now the world ends.

The famous montage that concludes *The Godfather* (1972), in which editor Peter Zinner cuts back and forth between the baptism ceremony for Michael Corleone's infant nephew and the execution of Corleone's enemies, suggests Michael's own violent and corrupt nature and also the violence and corruption at the heart of established society. Michael has attained a position of eminence, wealth, and political power and commands sufficient social prestige to ensure a proper baptism for his nephew in one of the city's largest and most prominent churches, even as he wipes out his enemies.

At the conclusion of Brian De Palma's *Scarface*, Tony Montana (Al Pacino) is gunned down by a small army of South American narco mercenaries, but not before he engages them in a prolonged, hyper-violent gun battle. Although Tony has the appetites and moral sensibility of a shark, the ferocity with which he fights lends his death, when it comes, a stature befitting the genre, even though as a character he lacks the romantic appeal of Roy Earle or the sentimental rendering given Cody Jarrett or the Godfather.

HIGH SIERRA (WARNER BROS., 1941)

Cornered in the Sierra Nevada Mountains, Roy Earle (Humphrey Bogart) dies a noble death, and the film's credit design, with titles rolling toward the heavens, suggests that in death Earle has at last found freedom and transcendence. Frame enlargements.

WHITE HEAT (WARNER BROS., 1948)

Cody Jarrett (James Cagney) seconds before his explosive death in *White Heat*. Jarrett's fiery end is a cautionary note for the nuclear age. Jarrett's spectacular death is a moment of such visual brilliance that it has become part of cinema's folklore, comparable with King Kong's last stand atop the Empire State Building. Both monsters, Kong and Jarrett, find an unforgettably poetic death. Frame enlargement.

The film ends by invoking the social critique inherent to the genre: The camera moves past Tony's body to a statue bearing the inscription, "The World is Yours."

Each of these films presents the gangster's death in a spectacular manner that contains an implicit social critique. The genre stipulates that the gangster must have a great deal of charisma. The gangster's appeal invites the viewer to ask about the kind of society that produces such seductive forms of corruption and violence. Like the cowboy, the movie gangster is a highly charged cultural symbol. (In other ways, though, he is the opposite of a Western hero. The gangster works hard, dreams big, and talks nonstop; the Western hero rarely holds a job,

SCARFACE (UNIVERSAL, 1983)

Defiant to the end, Tony Montana (Al Pacino) finds a flamboyant death in a hyper-violent gun battle with South American narco bandits. One of the most unredeemable of movie gangsters, he nevertheless gains a savage stature in the manner of his death. Frame enlargement.

THE DEPARTED (WARNER BROS., 2006)

Gangsters remain enduringly popular figures in American cinema, and in this Martin Scorsese film Jack Nicholson joined the ranks of screen actors with memorable gangster characters to their credit. His Irish mob boss is corrupt, sinister, and violent, yet also vividly human. Frame enlargement.

cares only about his horse and what possessions he can carry with him, and is silent and stoic.) The gangster embodies the danger of chaotic lawlessness as well as popular resentment of legal authority. The movie gangster represents a highly complex social fantasy about the prize and price of success. As such, in its uniquely American rendering, the gangster is a figure tied closely to a capitalist economy and is an expression of social ambivalence toward such an economy. In this respect, unlike the Western, the gangster genre remains timely and contemporary, its appeal never fading or going out-of-date.

The Musical

Unlike the Western and gangster films, which appear in cinema during the silent era, musicals owe their origin to sound filmmaking. Indeed, the film that is popularly credited as being the first "talkie," *The Jazz Singer* (1927), is a musical built around the singing of star Al Jolson. Sound made the cinema a receptive medium for the talents of the singers and dancers who would proliferate in musicals, and the genre flourished from the 1930s to the 1960s.

In the 1930s, Busby Berkeley choreographed and/or directed a string of hit musicals—*Footlight Parade* (1933), *42nd Street* (1933), and *Gold Diggers of 1935* (1935)—that were enlivened with extravagant sets and his trademark manner of filming a chorus line as if it were a visual kaleidoscope. Dance partners Fred Astaire and Ginger Rogers epitomized grace and elegance in a long film series including *Flying Down to Rio* (1933), *The Gay Divorcée* (1934), *Top Hat* (1935), and *Swing Time* (1936). In the 1940s and 1950s at MGM, producer Arthur Freed established a production unit that turned out a steady stream of the genre's classics, many of which starred Astaire, Gene Kelly, and Judy Garland: *The Wizard of Oz* (1939), *Meet Me in St. Louis* (1944), *An American in Paris* (1951), *Singin' in the Rain* (1952), and *The Band Wagon* (1953). These decades, and Freed's work in particular, may be regarded as the genre's golden age.

During this period, the genre's essential stories centered on the courtship rituals of a romantic couple who sang and danced to express their desire for each other. Viewers knew that the characters played by Astaire and Rogers were right for one another because they moved so uniquely well together. At the same time, the genre broke its visual style into two domains. Dialogue scenes were shot in a realist style, whereas the musical sequences take filmmaker and viewer far from realism. These scenes include the wild geometric forms of Busby Berkeley, popular in the 1930s, and the aggressive color design of the ballet sequences from *The Band Wagon* (1953) and *An American in Paris* (1951). In the latter film, the compositions and color schemes evoke the style of French Impressionist painters. For filmmakers who wanted to experiment with radical color and image styles, the musical was an ideal genre, offering them possibilities unmatched by any other film format.

Contemporary audiences frequently have trouble accepting the genre's bifurcated style. The transitions from everyday reality to the musical scenes with their extravagant song, dance, color, lighting, and camerawork often seem jarring to modern viewers, who may react nervously when a character in a classic musical suddenly breaks into song and dance.

Once again, though, it is important to understand the connection between these visual and narrative conventions and the underlying social values they express. The classical musicals—*Singin' in the Rain* (1952), *Meet Me in St. Louis* (1944), *The Band Wagon* (1953), and *An American in Paris* (1951)—belong to a less cynical age, and they express a cultural optimism and innocence that contemporary viewers find quite foreign. The musical is a joyous celebration of life, romance, and desire, whereas modern audiences may be more accustomed to cynical representations of life on movie screens.

Furthermore, the musical is an antirealist, relatively **antinarrative** format. A semblance of realism only prevails during the dialogue scenes. By contrast, the musical

SINGIN' IN THE RAIN (MGM, 1952)

The relatively naturalistic presentation of dialogue scenes in the musical gives way to elaborately stylized musical sequences, which gave filmmakers opportunities to explore color, light, and movement with complete imagination. The musical's antirealism is the most extreme of any film genre, and narrative is relatively unimportant. Frame enlargement.

interludes are about the possibilities for stylizing color, sound, and movement in cinema, freed from the necessity to ground those styles in anything that smacks of realism. The story line in a musical is often the least important of its elements. The stories are typically very slight, without much elaboration, and serve mainly as a way of connecting the musical sequences, which is where the heart of the genre really lies. The musical genre is about the pure poetry of image and sound, freed from all literal consideration. As a narrative art, it celebrates the rituals of courtship, in which music

MOULIN ROUGE (20TH CENTURY FOX, 2001)

Director Baz Luhrmann added tremendous style to the movie musical with this fanciful, energetic tale of Satine (Nicole Kidman), a popular singer at the famous nineteenth-century French club. The movie's frantic pace and self-conscious use of wildly different musical sources, including Madonna, Elton John, and *The Sound of Music*, make this a very untraditional musical and show how flexible genre can be. Frame enlargement.

serves to herald love and heartbreak. Like the Western, this genre has notably diminished in recent years. The cinema is a poorer medium for its loss.

The Horror Film

Like Westerns and gangster films, horror has roots in the early silent period and existed as a literary and theatrical genre long before the invention of cinema. In the silent era, Lon Chaney (known as "The Man of a Thousand Faces") used horrific makeup to create memorably grotesque characters in *The Phantom of the Opera* (1925) and *The Hunchback of Notre Dame* (1923). Actor John Barrymore played a strikingly repellent Mr. Hyde in *Dr. Jekyll and Mr. Hyde* (1920). Using distorted sets and compositions, the German expressionists created hauntingly bizarre worlds, such as that in F. W. Murnau's vampire classic *Nosferatu* (1922).

Beginning in the 1930s, Universal Pictures gave the cinema its classic monsters: *Frankenstein* (1931), *Dracula* (1931), *The Mummy* (1932), and *The Wolf Man* (1941). The brilliant makeup and set design and the classic visual conceptions given to the monsters have made these Universal productions the golden age of movie horror, and they have exerted an enduring influence on popular conceptions of Dracula, the Frankenstein monster, and werewolves. During this period, producer Val Lewton at RKO made a series of poetic and atmospheric horror films—*Cat People* (1942), *Isle of the Dead* (1945), and *I Walked with a Zombie* (1943)—in which horrible or uncanny things were suggested rather than shown. Since then, horror has been big box office, an enduring genre that has never been long out of favor with audiences.

Critic Robin Wood defines the basic narrative situation in horror films as one whereby "normality" is threatened by the monster. Monster films from *Frankenstein* (1931) and *Dracula* (1931) to *Halloween* (1978) and *The Fly* (1988) often define normality in terms of the romantic, heterosexual couple or the family, particularly parent–child relationships (*The Exorcist*, 1973; *The Omen*, 1976). This is

THE MUMMY
(UNIVERSAL, 1932)

THE MUMMY (UNIVERSAL, 1999)

In its golden age, the horror genre created its enduring monsters using brilliant makeup designs applied to the face and body of actors Boris Karloff, Bela Lugosi, and Lon Chaney. Lacking a comparable generation of monster movie actors, today's films use high-tech effects and digital animation. Karloff's classic mummy used makeup and lighting to give the actor a sinister look; by contrast, the remake featured a monster created and animated in the computer. Frame enlargements.

not, though, an invariable pattern. John Carpenter's remake of *The Thing* (1982), for example, is set amid an all-male community of scientific researchers based in Antarctica. But in virtually all cases, normal life, however it is portrayed in a given film, is under threat from something unspeakable, horrific and/or supernatural.

SAW (LIONSGATE, 2004)

Graphic violence returned to the horror film with the onset of the *Saw* and *Hostel* series of films. In the gruesome but clever *Saw*, a psychopath subjects his victims to outlandish tortures and deaths, and continued to do so in the film's many sequels. Frame enlargement.

Aside from the obvious physical danger it typically poses to ordinary, normal characters in the films, the monster poses a larger and more profound threat to the classification systems that define reality and on which culture and society rest. Whether a vampire, a mummy, a werewolf, or a vengeful psychopath, the monster represents a confusion—a violation—of social categories that specify boundaries between normal and abnormal, human and animal, living and dead. The monster typically occupies an uncertain middle ground between these distinctions, neither living nor dead, neither fully human nor fully an animal, abnormal but bearing disturbing traces of the human. Stories in the horror genre address the fragility of human identity by showing, through the monster, the loss, destruction, or violation of humanity.

The screen's most famous monsters—Bela Lugosi's Dracula, Boris Karloff's Frankenstein's monster, Lon Chaney Jr.'s wolfman, Freddie Kreuger, Jason Voorhees—demonstrate that the monstrousness of the monster lies in its display of both human and inhuman characteristics. As such, the horror film questions the viewer's most deeply cherished notions about what it means to be a human being. By centering on imaginary creatures who dwell in the margins of human life and consciousness, the horror film terrifies viewers by undermining their secure sense of where human identity lies in relation to the world of the dead, of animals, or of things.

DRACULA (UNIVERSAL, 1931); FRANKENSTEIN (UNIVERSAL, 1931); THE WOLF MAN (UNIVERSAL, 1941)

The greatest and most enduring monsters are those that remain recognizably human while being undeniably monstrous. This recognition that human identity and monstrosity are one is the genre's deepest secret and most profound source of terror. Frame enlargements.

The monsters in the *Alien* series, for example, are genre classics, genuinely creepy creatures, from which audiences recoil with primordial fear and disgust. The "face huggers," blending arachnid and crustacean anatomy, seed their human hosts, and the baby aliens gestate inside the human victim, destroying their host as the human gives birth to the monster. The narrative arc of the first three films brings the creatures ever closer to Ripley, the series heroine, until it transpires that she, too, has been seeded and is no longer fully human. The third film ends with her destruction.

The appeal of such films shows that in cinema negative emotions—fear, anxiety, dread, experiences that in life are often quite unpleasant—can become sources of pleasure. The safety of the movie theatre or viewing room enables spectators vicariously to experience negative emotions without the real consequences that follow from such things in actual life. Staying within the imaginative domain of a fictional story enables viewers to experience these states as symbolic emotions rather than as real responses to actual, life-threatening situations. Many viewers, though, do not enjoy the experience of negative emotions in cinema, and for them the horror genre is one they avoid.

EVOLUTION OF THE HORROR FILM   The evolution of the horror film demonstrates how genre conventions change. Old conventions become exhausted, and filmmakers search for new ones in their never-ending challenge to retain the interest of the audience. Horror films of the 1930s and 1940s depicted the monster using an actor in (often brilliant) makeup, whereas contemporary films often use computer-based visual effects to visualize the creatures. Moreover, horror films during their golden age tended to end on a very comforting note. The monster was destroyed, and the romantic couple reached safety unharmed. Horror often was left to the viewer's imagination in contrast with the graphic gore of modern films, which use contemporary effects technology to visualize the elaborate violence that is now basic in the genre. (In this respect, *The Blair Witch Project* [1999], *The Sixth Sense* [1999], and *The Others* [2001], all of which work through suggestion rather than graphic violence, are a return to the golden age of horror.)

ALIEN 3 (20TH CENTURY FOX, 1992)
One of the monsters inspects Ripley (Sigourney Weaver) and then gives her a tender caress because she is no longer fully human. Gestating inside her is a baby alien. The horror genre terrifies by violating the conditions that define human identity. Frame enlargement.

By the 1970s and 1980s, in such films as *Halloween* and the never-ending *Nightmare on Elm Street* and *Friday the 13th* series, the monster became indestructible and undefeatable. These monsters—Freddy, Jason, Michael Myers of the *Halloween* films, and the aliens in the *Alien* series—remain alive at the end of each episode, and viewers know they will come back again to haunt and terrify. Contemporary horror films, therefore, can be more disturbing and unsettling than horror was in previous decades, when narrative conventions insisted that normality be restored and secure at film's end. Perhaps because the modern viewer's sense of what is normal is more precarious and more easily undermined, the destruction of order and security may strike contemporary audiences as a more authentic vision of life. The monsters today are everywhere, and they cannot be defeated, a perception that the narrative design of contemporary horror emphasizes.

Science Fiction

This genre and its close ally, the fantasy film, are the most popular of contemporary film genres, and arguably, they have made the strongest impact on popular culture by way of such series as the *Star Wars, Lord of the Rings*, and *Matrix* films.

The genre has its cinematic roots in the "trick" films that appeared with the birth of cinema. *A Trip to the Moon* (1902), *The Whole Dam Family and the Dam Dog* (1903), and many others used double exposures, miniature models, stop-action jump cuts, and in-camera mattes to simulate fantastic worlds, unexpected optical effects, and alterations of time and space. *The Lost World* (1925) used rear projection of animated dinosaur models blended with live actors matted in as foreground elements. Such early classics as *Metropolis* (1927) and *Things to Come* (1936) created visions of fantastic, often futuristic cities, establishing a tradition that continues today in *Blade Runner* (1982), *Dark City* (1998), *The Fifth Element* (1997), *Sin City* (2005), and the *Star Wars* and *Lord of the Rings* films, where fabulously inventive cities are a key part of fantasy décor.

METROPOLIS (UFA, 1927)

Science fiction movies had been made before *Metropolis* but never in such grand, epic, and imaginative terms. This film, with its futuristic city, has exerted a huge influence on over a century of science fiction and fantasy films. In terms of this influence, one could say that the science fiction genre in cinema begins with *Metropolis*. This scene shows the master creation of the evil inventor Rotwang, a humanoid robot. Frame enlargement.

THE TIME MACHINE (MGM, 1960)

Director–producer George Pal was a master of science fiction and fantasy in the 1950s. His films were imaginative and literate and did not go overboard on special effects, using them instead to advance the story. *The Time Machine* is one of the best adaptations from sci-fi literature ever made. Pal's other work includes *When Worlds Collide* (1951) and *War of the Worlds* (1953). Frame enlargement.

Low-budget Buck Rogers and Flash Gordon sci-fi serials were plentiful in the 1930s, but other genres, such as the Western and gangster film, were hugely popular. Science fiction did not emerge as a major genre until the 1950s, when the Cold War emphasis on space exploration, coupled with anxieties about nuclear weapons, stimulated a tremendous amount of film production. *Rocketship X-M* (1950), *Destination Moon* (1950), and *Forbidden Planet* (1956) offered early depictions of space travel, whereas nuclear anxieties were displaced onto a gallery of mutant creatures spawned by radiation in *The Beast from 20,000 Fathoms* (1953), *Them!* (1954), *Tarantula* (1955), and others.

Twenty Million Miles to Earth (1957), *Invaders from Mars* (1953), and *Invasion of the Body Snatchers* (1957) expressed the Cold War paranoia of the period, with alien invaders standing in for the fear of communist attack. In *Earth vs. the Flying Saucers* (1956), alien invaders destroy monuments and government buildings in Washington, D.C., in a manner that anticipates the action of *Independence Day* (1996).

The formative literature of Jules Verne and H. G. Wells influenced a number of distinguished adaptations in this period: *20,000 Leagues Under the Sea* (1954), *Journey to the Center of the Earth* (1959), *The Time Machine* (1960), and *Mysterious Island* (1961).

20,000 Leagues Under the Sea and *The Time Machine* are especially distinguished, with the former a lavish Technicolor Disney extravaganza and the latter a thoughtful, careful adaptation of Wells' novel with outstanding special effects by George Pal. Compare it with the sorry remake (2002), which turned Wells' speculative novel into action adventure. (Wells' *The Time Machine* has inspired many time-travel films over the years, some of which are more fantasy than science fiction—*Time After Time* (1979), *The Final Countdown* (1980), *Somewhere in Time* (1980), *Time Bandits* (1981), and *12 Monkeys* (1995).

For the most part, science fiction diminished in the 1960s as a popular genre, although that decade saw one of its masterworks, Stanley Kubrick's *2001: A Space Odyssey* (1968), as well as *Planet of the Apes* (1968), the first and best of a series. Kubrick's film is a deliberately mysterious, perplexing meditation on humankind's encounter with alien intelligence, and it departs from film conventions by showing space as a silent void (no space ships here sounding like souped-up race cars). With its mystical visions of the cosmos, *2001* connects with the intellectual focus of much science fiction literature, which the *Star Wars* series discarded when it seized on the Buck Rogers–Flash Gordon serials as its model. But it was *Star Wars* in 1977 that revived the genre's vitality. The *Star Wars* saga (1977–2005) reawakened popular interest in science fiction, and the genre has remained extraordinarily popular ever since.

During the era spawned by *Star Wars*, the long-running *Star Trek* series (1979, 1982, 1984, 1986, 1989, 1991, 1994, 1996, 1998, 2009) helped to keep alive the intellectual elements of the science fiction enterprise. But unlike the low-tech television series on which the movies were based, the films offered state-of-the-art visual effects, as did other high-profile productions, such as the *Jurassic Park* series (1993, 1997, 2001). In addition to *Star Trek*, other distinguished films that have used the genre to explore ideas, in contrast to action adventure, include *Brazil* (1985), *Gattaca* (1997), and *A.I.: Artificial Intelligence* (2001).

Although science fiction lends itself to utopian visions of the future, in practice, very few films fall into this category. Many take a darker outlook; in the process, they reflect back to us our anxieties and fears about the present. Even though the *Star Wars* saga ends (in *Return of the Jedi*, 1983) in a utopian world, the series climaxes (in terms of the production sequence of the films) with *Revenge of the Sith* (2005), in which Anakin Skywalker joins the dark side and becomes Darth Vader.

In this respect, science fiction gives filmmakers a powerful means for exploring anxieties about where our world is heading, and many films take a grim and pessimistic view, seeing a decaying environment, antidemocratic governments, and ruthless corporations controlling the world—*Escape from New York* (1981), *Robocop* (1987), *Blade Runner* (1982), the *Alien* series (1979, 1986, 1992, 1997, 2004), the *Terminator* series (1984, 1991, 2003), *Starship Troopers* (1997), and *Minority Report* (2001). *I, Robot* (2004) offers reflections on the erosion of civil liberties and threats to democracy in the United States following 9/11. Even a comic film such as *Men in Black* (1997) finds the earth continuously poised on the edge of annihilation.

Epic struggles with titanic evil inform the *Star Wars* films, and their success influenced similar depictions in the *Matrix* and *Lord of the Rings* series. The latter series, though, belongs to fantasy and locates its battles between good and evil in an ancient mythic world. As such, it draws from a somewhat different set of influences. These include the battle epics of directors Akira Kurosawa (*Seven Samurai*, 1954) and Sergei Eisenstein (*Alexander Nevsky*, 1936), as well as earlier epics of ancient world mythology (Fritz Lang's *Siegfried*, 1924, and *Kriemhild's Revenge*, 1924).

The *Lord of the Rings* films are also deeply influenced by the fantasy creatures designed by effects wizard Ray Harryhausen in ancient-world pictures such as *The Seventh Voyage of Sinbad* (1958), *The Three Worlds of Gulliver* (1959), *Jason and the Argonauts* (1963), and *One Million Years B.C.* (1967).

2001: A SPACE ODYSSEY (MGM, 1968)

Whereas *Metropolis* is the towering classic of the silent period, *2001* is the genre's greatest masterpiece of the sound era. Stanley Kubrick's mystical and spectacular epic of human discovery follows the intellectual tradition established in sci-fi literature. Frame enlargement.

DISTRICT 9 (TRISTAR, 2009)

Contemporary science fiction often projects visions of the future or of alternative worlds based on speculations about contemporary problems and fears. *District 9* uses the era of racial segregation and oppression in South Africa, known as "apartheid," to depict a world in which a race of aliens trapped on Earth is confined to slums and detention camps and kept under military surveillance. The story situation also resonates with a post-9/11 world. Dramatizing contemporary problems in disguise enables science fiction to remain relevant to the lives of its viewers. Frame enlargement.

As *The Lord of the Rings* series premiered over a span of three years, many people remarked that the creative torch in science fiction/fantasy seemed to have been passed from George Lucas (and *Star Wars*) to Peter Jackson (and *Lord of the Rings*). Like so much of science fiction, though, the Jackson films envision a world in crisis while enabling the filmmakers to use cinema effects with imaginative delight. Here lies the essential appeal of the science fiction genre—giving form to contemporary doubt while conjuring magic tricks unlike any seen before.

THE WAR FILM

With classics such as *The Big Parade* (1925) and *All Quiet on the Western Front* (1930), the war film extends back to the silent and early sound eras. *The Birth of a Nation* (1915) has a Civil War sequence of startling realism. But it was the World War II era and its immediate aftermath that saw the Hollywood studios produce this genre in its greatest numbers. Hollywood joined the war effort, and in such pictures as *Objective, Burma!* (1945), *Flying Tigers* (1942), *They Were Expendable* (1945), and *Sands of Iwo Jima* (1949), American film showed the home audience why the war had been fought and celebrated the patriotism and sacrifice of its soldiers.

But World War II was the last war about which America held a clear consensus of opinion, and the films about subsequent wars have been much more ambivalent and critical. Korea in *The Bridges at Toko-Ri* (1954) and *Pork Chop Hill* (1959), Vietnam in *Apocalypse Now* (1979) and *Platoon* (1986), the Persian Gulf War in *Three Kings* (1999), and the Iraq War in *The Hurt Locker* (2008) are depicted as conflicts without a clear rationale or moral foundation.

As these examples suggest, narrative in the war film is often reflective of the political and social context that surrounds a given war. When that context is generally free of controversy, as in World War II, the celebration of heroism in a picture such as *Saving Private Ryan* (1998) is much easier to achieve.

SANDS OF IWO JIMA (REPUBLIC, 1949)

Hollywood's films about World War II were part of the war effort and were meant to instill patriotic feelings in their viewers. John Wayne appeared in many of these films as a hero engaged in a good fight about which neither he, nor the viewers, had doubts. No war since has been shown by American film in so untroubled a fashion. Frame enlargement.

THE HURT LOCKER (VOLTAGE PICTURES, 2008)

Recent wars have lacked the moral and political clarity that surrounded World War II, and the genre has reflected this with more ambiguous or critical portraits of modern war. The Iraq War that followed 9/11, for example, has been depicted in many films as an ill-considered campaign lacking clear objectives. *The Hurt Locker* takes a close-in view, portraying the experiences of a bomb demolition expert (Jeremy Renner, right) whose addiction to the adrenaline rush of combat alienates him from the other soliders in his squad. Frame enlargement.

By contrast, it has proven much harder to portray Korea or Vietnam or the Iraq War on film with the moral clarity and heroism of Hollywood's World War II films. In fact, Hollywood avoided making films about Vietnam until the late 1970s and 1980s, and contemporary depictions of the Iraq War often are bleak and without heroic affirmation.

War films tend to come in three formats. *Battle epics* provide a large-scale overview of the strategies and objectives that are involved in major military confrontations. The story in these films moves from high-level military decision-making to front-line action, providing a bird's-eye view of the unfolding battle. *The Longest Day* (1962), *In Harm's Way* (1965), *Tora! Tora! Tora!* (1968), and *Pearl Harbor* (2001) exemplify this format, which is closely associated with World War II. But it is also a format that lends itself very well to depictions of the ancient world, as in *Alexander* (2004), *Troy* (2004), and *Spartacus* (1960).

Combat films take a close-in view of the fighting and often concentrate on a small unit of soldiers engaged in ferocious and sustained battle. Unlike the battle epics, combat films tend not to show the high-level decision-making that has resulted in the fighting. This close-up focus often makes the politics of a given war more distant and less relevant to the immediate tasks faced by the characters of staying alive and prevailing against forbidding odds. Thus combat films tend to be about heroism under fire, regardless of what controversies may surround the war itself. This format has proven to be enduringly popular, and examples can be found from a wide variety of conflicts—World War II (*Bataan*, 1943), Korea (*Pork Chop Hill*), Vietnam (*Platoon; Hamburger Hill*, 1987; *We Were Soldiers*, 2001), and Somalia (*Black Hawk Down*, 2001).

PLATOON (ORION, 1986)

Combat films focus up-close on the experience of battle, often portraying small units engaged in ferocious fighting. *Platoon* redefined the treatment of the Vietnam War on film with its close attention to jungle combat. No film about Vietnam had shown jungle warfare so intensively before. Frame enlargement.

Home-front dramas concentrate on the difficulties faced by families at home while loved ones fight overseas or on the problems faced by veterans who return home after combat. The home-front drama generally avoids much depiction of combat, preferring to concentrate on domestic sacrifice. This format was especially effective during World War II, as such powerful films as *Since You Went Away* (1944) and *Mrs. Miniver* (1942) demonstrate. *Coming Home* (1978) is a Vietnam era home-front drama. *Grace Is Gone* (2007) examines the impact of the Iraq War on the husband and children of a soldier killed in combat.

An interesting subgenre of the war film is the submarine picture, which deals with the stress of manning a submarine in dangerous waters. Sometimes these films portray war, as in *U-571* (2000), *Destination Tokyo* (1943), *The Enemy Below* (1957), *Up Periscope* (1959), and *Das Boot* (1981), the greatest film about submarine warfare ever made. Other films, however, put more stress on the hazardous nature of submarine duty and may incorporate a crisis in the chain of command with a threatened mutiny, with war or global conflict as a background element—*K-19: The Widowmaker* (2002), *Crimson Tide* (1995), *The Hunt for Red October* (1990), *Gray Lady Down* (1978), *Ice Station Zebra* (1968), and *The Bedford Incident* (1965).

As these films illustrate, a genre does not have a fixed and firm boundary, and many films may exist on the edge of a genre, blending genre and nongenre elements.

While many war films have celebrated glory and patriotism, the horror and savagery of war have produced a much darker tone in many others. In fact, many war films can be described as antiwar because they concentrate on the brutalizing effects of combat or on the oppressiveness of the military itself. *The Big Parade* (1925) is a powerful indictment of the slaughter in World War I, as is *All Quiet on the Western Front* (1930), a classic antiwar picture. Stanley Kubrick's *Paths of Glory* (1957) and *Full Metal Jacket* (1987) are powerful critiques of the mechanism of war, the military

Many war films have focused on conflict involving submarines, giving rise to a popular and enduring subcategory of the genre. These films emphasize the hazards and stress of serving on board a submarine in a theater of war. Many, but not all, are set during World War II, as is *U-571*. Frame enlargement.

system, and the sacrifice of young lives. So too is Sam Peckinpah's *Cross of Iron* (1977). Robert Aldrich's *Attack* (1956) and Terrence Malick's *The Thin Red Line* (1998) indict the brutality of command and the dehumanizing effects of combat.

The critical tone of these films is counterbalanced by the stirring portraits of heroism offered in pictures such as *Glory* (1989) and *Saving Private Ryan* (1998). The war film, therefore, encompasses affirmation and critique, as well as liberal and conservative points of view. One of the most powerful and complex of human behaviors, war has fascinated filmmakers and drawn them to it, and they have responded from a variety of moral and political perspectives. The great war films are about the specifics of a particular conflict, as well as the timeless issues that war raises.

PATHS OF GLORY (UNITED ARTISTS, 1957)

Numerous films in the genre have an antiwar point of view or are highly critical of a particular conflict or of the military. One of the genre's antiwar classics, *Paths of Glory* shows three soldiers in World War I framed for cowardice by a corrupt officer intent on covering his mistakes, put on trial, and then executed. Stanley Kubrick's film shows the machinery of war as a vast, powerful institution against which the individual is relatively powerless. Frame enlargement.

FILM NOIR

Film noir emerged much later than many of the other genres, which have roots in the silent era. Noir began in 1941 with *Citizen Kane* and *The Maltese Falcon*. *Citizen Kane*'s visual design featured shadows and low-key lighting, which created a dark, ominous-looking world on screen, and this look became an enduring part of film noir. *The Maltese Falcon*'s story of crime, betrayal, and corruption helped establish the themes and type of story that would be central to noir.

Noirs are dark, pessimistic films, telling stories about crime, often with an urban setting emphasizing shadows and darkness. The classic period of noir lasted until 1958, but the genre has influenced so many contemporary directors that the term *neo-noir* is used to describe the films they make in the genre today.

A huge number of noir films were made in the classical period. Their titles very often express the defining noir mood of anxiety, paranoia, corruption, and violence—*Raw Deal* (1948), *Brute Force* (1947), *The Dark Corner* (1946), *Criss Cross* (1949), *In a Lonely Place* (1950), *Night and the City* (1950), *They Live by Night* (1949), and *Kiss Me Deadly* (1955).

The hero is often a victim in these stories, caught in a web of crime and betrayal, and the mood of fatalism is strong, the sense that his acts and choices are foredoomed. The films often tell the story using flashbacks and voice-over narration, which add to the sense that all will go wrong for the characters. Walking the streets at night in *Double Indemnity* (1944), the hero, Walter Neff (Fred MacMurray), realizes that he cannot hear his own footsteps, that his is the walk of a dead man.

The hero is often menaced by a seductive but dangerous woman, known as a *femme fatale*, or "deadly woman." This character type is one of noir's most famous and can be found in *Double Indemnity, Sunset Blvd.* (1950), *Kiss Me Deadly*, and many others.

The classical period of noir is tied to World War II and the Cold War, and these eras certainly helped to influence the sense of anxiety in the genre. But noir also has roots in crime fiction, particularly the hard-boiled crime and detective novels of

DOUBLE INDEMNITY (PARAMOUNT, 1944)

Even in daylight, the world of noir was dark. The slanting shadows of Venetian blinds fall on Walter Neff (Fred MacMurray) in a room barely illuminated by the afternoon sun. The Venetian blind imagery was used widely in the genre. Frame enlargement.

MURDER, MY SWEET (RKO, 1944)

The world of film noir is one of anxiety, paranoia, darkness, and crime, given memorable visual expression in moody black-and-white cinematography. The crime novels of Raymond Chandler and others furnished many of the genre's stories. Here, Chandler's hero, private investigator Philip Marlowe (Dick Powell), is startled by the sudden appearance of a thug, reflected in his office window. Frame enlargement.

Raymond Chandler, James M. Cain, and Dashiell Hammett, many of which were made into film noirs—Cain's *Double Indemnity* and *The Postman Always Rings Twice* (1946) and Hammett's *The Maltese Falcon* and *The Glass Key* (1942).

Chandler created noir's most enduring private investigator, the character of Philip Marlowe, who has appeared in numerous movies adapted from Chandler novels— *Farewell My Lovely* (1944 and 1975 remake), *The Big Sleep* (1946 and 1978 remake), *Murder My Sweet* (1944), *The Lady in the Lake* (1946), *Marlowe* (1969), and *The Long Goodbye* (1973).

Noir also was influenced by paintings and photographs of the city stressing loneliness and alienation (the paintings of Edward Hopper and the photographs of Arthur Fellig, known as "Weegee"). But whereas the gangster film defines the city as a place of excitement, glamour, and power, film noir used these influences from painting and photography to portray it as a place of danger and fear.

The genre also found a key influence in the visual style of German expressionist cinema, particularly its low-key lighting and exaggerated camera angles portraying a world that is off-kilter. Many of the German directors and cinematographers who had created these films immigrated to Hollywood and began making film noirs.

Numerous influences, then, combined to create film noir, and the genre's striking visual design attracted some of the best cinematographers of the period. John Alton, for example, created some of the deepest and blackest shadows to be found anywhere in American film in such pictures as *T-Men* (1947), *Raw Deal*, and *The Big Combo* (1955). He also shot with wide-angle lenses to exaggerate his shadowy lighting. The last shot of *Big Combo* is one of the definitive and most famous images of noir, showing the film's two principal characters, backlit as silhouettes, walking away from the camera and into a mysterious, undefined region of fog and mist.

The shadows and low-key lighting of noir achieved their power in the black-and-white cinematography of that period. For the most part, noir in its classical phase is a black-and-white genre, and this is as it should be. The contrast of light and dark achieved in low-key lighting is far more powerful and expressive in black-and-white.

THE BIG COMBO (ALLIED ARTISTS, 1955)

John Alton was the genre's most radical cinematographer, with the deepest shadows and most extreme compositions. Here, a table lamp dominates most of the frame, with the three characters placed in shadows in the background. In the film's last shot, Alton uses fog and silhouette lighting to create a poetically undefined environment. Frame enlargements.

Color cinematography tends to soften shadows, to weaken the contrast of light and dark, by supplying the additional information about coloration that is lacking in black and white. Color cinematography can use low-key lighting, but the result lacks the sharp contrasts that black-and-white achieves.

NEO-NOIR   For this reason, perhaps, the classical phase of noir ends about the time that color cinematography replaced black-and-white as the norm of film production. The last classical film noir is generally considered to be Orson Welles' *Touch of Evil* (1958), with brilliant black-and-white cinematography by Russell Metty.

But the genre proved to be an enduring one, revived by contemporary filmmakers drawn to its visual style and its moral pessimism. **Neo-noir** films are shot in color but

CHINATOWN (PARAMOUNT, 1974)

Noir has endured long past its classical phase. Neo-noir films revive the genre in color. In *Chinatown*, set in the 1940s, Jack Nicholson plays a Philip Marlowe–like private investigator who uncovers a scheme to control Los Angeles' water supply. Neo-noirs also may be set in the present day, such as *Palmetto* or *Femme Fatale*. Frame enlargement.

use a low-key lighting style to evoke some of the visual qualities of noir in its classical period. The noir revival began in the 1970s and is still ongoing. *Chinatown* (1974), more than any other film, revived the genre for the contemporary era, and modern filmmakers were immediately attracted to noir's stylish stories of greed, temptation, and defeat. *Taxi Driver* (1975), *Body Heat* (1981), *Blood Simple* (1984), *At Close Range* (1986), *The Grifters* (1990), *After Dark, My Sweet* (1990), *Gun Crazy* (1992), *Red Rock West* (1993), *L.A. Confidential* (1997), *Palmetto* (1999), *Femme Fatale* (2002), and *Sin City* (2005) are just a few of the recent neo-noirs.

Sin City includes many of the elements of classic noir—a detective hero, a gritty and dangerous urban locale, a visual look defined by shadows and darkness. And yet it owes as much to the Frank Miller comics from which the film's three stories have been drawn. Moreover, the urban settings are entirely digital; they were never actually photographed the way that cities were in classic noir.

In this respect, *Sin City* illustrates one of the enduring questions about noir—Is it a genre or is it really a visual style that can be attached to different kinds of film? Scholars of film have debated this question for years because many films, which are not noirs, have used the style. *Blade Runner* (1980), for example, is a science fiction film whose central character is a detective straight out of film noir. The Christmas classic *It's a Wonderful Life* (1946) has a nightmare sequence that becomes a film noir. And *Batman Begins* (2005) visualizes the comic book character in terms of a noir visual design. All these films include noir elements, but none would be considered film noir.

Ultimately, noir is both a style and a genre. Stylistically, it defines a look that many films can emulate of whatever genre. But as a genre, it has clear origins in the hard-boiled school of crime fiction that flourished in the 1920s–1940s, and filmmakers in that period knew that they were making film noirs, even though the name itself wasn't coined until later. A dead-on parody of film noir appears in 1947. *My Favorite Brunette*, starring Bob Hope as a nebbish who wants to be a hard-boiled detective like he's seen in the movies, satirizes noir slang, flashback plotting, and voice-over

BLADE RUNNER (LADD CO., 1982)
Scholars and critics have debated whether noir is a genre or simply a visual style. Whatever the answer, it is certainly true that the style of noir has been tremendously influential, appearing in numerous films outside the genre. *Blade Runner*, for example, a science fiction film, uses noir's low-key lighting and 1940s-style fashions to evoke its world of crime and anxiety. Frame enlargement.

narration and includes an uncredited cameo appearance by a big noir star of the period, Alan Ladd. Such a thorough parody suggests strongly that noir was a clearly recognized genre of film.

Film noir is one of American cinema's most famous, distinctive, and enduring creations. Today's directors will continue to make neo-noirs because they love the look and the stories and because doing so connects them to a great heritage of Hollywood film.

SUMMARY

In their most popular form, movies tell stories, yet the film medium also can inform and instruct by observing real events (these movies are called documentaries), or it can represent pure shape, line, color, and form rather than real things (these are experimental, "underground," or avant-garde films). Yet it is narrative films that have captured the popular audience. The turn toward narrative emerged very early in film history and has been present ever since.

Present in all cultures, narrative thinking is an essential human ability. Fictional narratives, the kind movies typically employ, grow out of a particular context in which the storyteller and the audience agree to play make-believe in a way that grants the fictional story a special status: Its truthfulness is not counted to be as important as its artistic organization and its power to delight and to compel belief.

Filmmakers create narrative structure by establishing discrepancies between plot and story. Using flashbacks, the omission of detail, or other devices, filmmakers can re-arrange the proper order of story events and/or create obstacles to the viewer's assimilation of story information. If skillfully done, this will arouse the viewers' interest and make them keenly interested in seeing the full outcome of events. Among the most popular of plot structures is the classical Hollywood narrative, which offers a clearly dominant line of main action and one or more interrelated secondary lines of action. This narrative type is clearly motivated, forward moving, and establishes explicit causal relationships among its story events. Alternatives to the classical Hollywood narrative may feature implicit or minimal causality or, in extreme cases, an antinarrative orientation.

All stories are told by someone, although the collaborative nature of cinema makes it difficult to identify a single or sole author. In film, narration is produced by the complex of structural elements—the camera, lights, sound, color, set design, costumes, and other elements of structure. While these can be used to imply a character's subjective perspective, point of view in the cinema is usually third person, with implicit first-person components.

KEY TERMS AND CONCEPTS

antinarrative   251
classical Hollywood
   narrative   229
convention   241
counter-narrative   223
deviant plot
   structures   245

explicit causality   230
genre   241
implicit causality   232
implied author   225
neo-noir   267
plot   220
point of view   226

real author   225
story   220
subjective shot   226
surprise   238
suspense   238

SUGGESTED READINGS

Rick Altman, *Film/Genre* (London: BFI, 1999).

David Bordwell, *Narration in the Fiction Film* (Madison: University of Wisconsin Press, 1985).

Seymour Chatman, *Coming to Terms: The Rhetoric of Narrative in Fiction and Film* (Ithaca, NY: Cornell University Press, 1990).

Seymour Chatman, *Story and Discourse: Narrative Structure in Fiction and Film* (Ithaca, NY: Cornell University Press, 1978).

John L. Fell, *Film and the Narrative Tradition* (Norman, OK: University of Oklahoma Press, 1974).

Syd Field, *The Screenwriter's Workbook* (New York: Delta, 2006).

Avrom Fleishman, *Narrated Films: Storytelling Situations in Cinema History* (Baltimore: Johns Hopkins University Press, 1992).

Jane Gaines, ed., *Classical Hollywood Narrative: The Paradigm Wars* (Durham, NC: Duke University Press, 1992).

Barry K. Grant, *Film Genre Reader II* (Austin: University of Texas Press, 1995).

Andrew Horton, *Writing the Character-Centered Screenplay* (Berkeley: University of California Press, 2000).

Kristin Thompson, *Storytelling in the New Hollywood: Understanding Classical Narrative Technique* (Cambridge, MA: Harvard University Press, 1999).

George M. White, *Narration in Light: Studies in Cinematic Point of View* (Baltimore: Johns Hopkins University Press, 1986).

Visual Effects

OBJECTIVES

After reading this chapter, you should be able to:

- describe the roles that visual effects play in cinema

- explain what a composited image is and its relation to visual effects

- describe a travelling matte

- describe the Schufftan process

- distinguish between rear and front projection

- explain what a Z-depth map is used for

- distinguish between male and female mattes

- describe the role of forced perspective

- explain what an optical printer does

- explain rendering and multi-pass compositing

- describe how stereoscopic cinema works

- explain the role of a stereographer

Many of cinema's most artistically significant and many of its most popular films feature an intensive use of visual effects—*Citizen Kane* (1941), *Metropolis* (1927), *The Wizard of Oz* (1939), *Gone With the Wind* (1939), *North by Northwest* (1959), *Titanic* (1997), *The Lord of the Rings* trilogy. Visual effects are an essential structural component of cinema, enabling filmmakers to create worlds of the imagination and to overcome the limitations of time, budget, and place. A filmmaker must visualize the world described in a story and place it upon the screen. Very often, the places and characters of that story cannot be directly filmed because they never existed or they no longer exist or they are inaccessible. The majesty of the ocean liner *Titanic* belongs to a bygone world, but it can be visualized using models, mattes, and digital animation. An imaginary planet, Pandora, can be created for *Avatar* (2009). San Francisco no longer looks as it did in the 1960s, but it can be digitally built for a historical drama like *Zodiac* (2007). The actor Andy Serkis can be transformed into the wizened Gollum or the giant ape King Kong.

To a popular audience, these are examples of "special effects," and, indeed, for several decades this was the industry's term for the special photographic effects that were added to a film. The first Academy Award for Achievement in Special Effects was bestowed in 1937. In 1964, the wording was changed to Achievement in Special Visual Effects; in 1972 it became Special Achievement in Visual Effects; and in 1981 it became Achievement in Visual Effects.

The industry still uses the term "special effects," but it now carries a very narrow and restricted meaning—it designates mechanical effects, such as explosions or physical stunts such as cars flipping over. Everything else that a popular audience would call a "special effect" is today referred to in the film industry as a **visual effect**, and, accordingly, that is the terminology that will be used here.

This chapter explains fundamental visual effects techniques, surveys their use throughout the history of cinema, and explains the artistic designs they help to accomplish.

TITANIC (20TH CENTURY FOX, PARAMOUNT, 1997)

Visual effects enable filmmakers to overcome the limitations of time, budget, and place that otherwise would restrict the stories they could film. Matte paintings, miniature models, animation, and other tools allow moviemakers to film imaginary worlds and bygone eras from the past. Without visual effects, there often is no cinema. Frame enlargement.

A COMPOSITED MEDIUM

Cinema is a composited medium, assembled from many pieces of picture and sound. A **composite** image or sequence is one that is composed of elements created separately and then combined together. Visual effects are composites; the final image is a layered blend, conjoining different elements—for example, live action, miniature models, matte paintings or animation. Understood in these terms, editing is a visual effect. An edited sequence creates a composite reality by joining together shots that were filmed separately from one another. The *Rear Window* example examined in Chapter 5 establishes that Jeffries (James Stewart) watches his neighbors across the apartment courtyard when, in fact, actor Stewart saw none of the things that the editing suggests his character can see. In a historical context, editing was one of the first tools filmmakers used to create visual effects.

The first known example occurs in *The Execution of Mary, Queen of Scots* (1895). Just before the executioner's axe falls, the cameraman, Alfred Clark, stopped filming. All of the actors on set froze and held their positions while a dummy was substituted for the actress playing the queen. Filming was resumed, the axe fell, and the head rolled off; when projected on screen, the action flowed in an unbroken and, for the time, shocking fashion.

Stopping the camera to create a hidden cut in the action fast became a popular visual effects technique. Georges Melies used it frequently in his films, such as *A Trip to the Moon* (1902), enabling lizard-like moon people to appear and disappear in puffs of smoke. R.W. Paul's *An Extraordinary Cab Accident* (1903) uses stop-action substitution to visualize a man run over by a horse-drawn carriage, and Edwin S. Porter in *The Great Train Robbery* (1903) uses it to switch out an actor with a dummy that is then thrown from a moving train.

Filmmakers quickly devised a repertoire of techniques that enabled a new genre of "trick films" to emerge. These were movies that offered viewers astounding images that contradicted physical reality. In *Upside Down, or The Human Flies* (1899), a set

A TRIP TO THE MOON (1902)

Georges Melies was a magician who turned to cinema for its ability to create magical effects. He built his own studio and made more than 500 films full of trick effects, perfecting stop-motion substitution, painted backgrounds, mirror distortions, perspective cheats, deceptive camera positions, and matted images. Melies today is the most famous visual effects filmmaker who worked during cinema's infancy. Here, brave French astronomers gaze at the city—a painted backing with live smoke effects—before embarking on their trip to the moon. Frame enlargement.

THE ? MOTORIST (1906)

Producer Robert W. Paul made documentaries and historical re-creations as well as trick films. This delightful fantasy is among his best work. In the climax, the motorists circle the rings of Saturn, courtesy of an animated miniature and a painted backdrop. This fast, witty, and charming film shows how visual effects stimulated filmmakers to reach for new heights of creative expression. Frame enlaragement.

constructed upside-down and filmed with an inverted filmstrip inside the camera made a group of houseguests seem to cavort and party on the ceiling. In *The Cheese Mites, or Lilliputians in a London Restaurant* (1901), previously filmed footage inserted into a scene makes doll-sized people appear on top of a restaurant table before the incredulous eyes of the diner. In *The Clown Barber* (1899), a man gets a novel shave when the

A RAILWAY COLLISION (1900)

This R. W. Paul production shows how visual effects served filmmakers in creating portraits of a real rather than imaginary world. Paul visualizes a train wreck using miniature models of locomotives and the mountainous landscape. Frame enlargement.

barber removes his head, cuts the whiskers, and then re-attaches the head. R.W. Paul's *The ? Motorist* (1906), one of the greatest of the trick films, uses miniature models, animation, painted backdrops, and stop-action substitution in a delightful story of two motorists who drive their car so fast that it flies off into space, circles the sun, and lands on the rings of Saturn.

But it wasn't only the trick films that used visual effects. Dramatizations and recreations of newsworthy events were very popular with early audiences. Filmmakers used miniature models of buildings, landscapes, and ships to recreate *The Battle of Santiago Bay* (1898), *Windsor Hotel Fire* (1899), and *Eruption of Vesuvius* (1906) and to visualize *A Railway Collision* (1900).

MATTES

Mattes enabled filmmakers to selectively expose a portion of the frame and furnished one of the most important methods for creating composite images. A **matte** is a type of mask, a dark or opaque area that blocks light from a film negative and prevents an image from being formed or exposed there. Matting selected areas in the frame enabled filmmakers to combine separately created images to form a composite visual effect. Using mattes for composites helps prevent double-exposures, super-imposed images where both are visible on top of and through each other.

The earliest mattes were performed in-camera. In *The Great Train Robbery*, Edwin Porter used mattes to show moving landscapes visible through the windows of indoor sets. In one instance, a passing locomotive can be seen through the window of a telegraph operator's office. A matte and counter-matte created the composite of the office set with the train in the window. The **counter-matte** masks the frame in an inverse manner to the matte. The matte/counter-matte system quickly became an established means of creating composite images.

Porter shot the scene's action—outlaws burst into the office and hold the telegraph operator hostage—with a matte blocking the window area and preventing this part of the film from being exposed. The film was rewound in the camera, and a passing train was filmed using the counter-matte, which blocked the entire frame except for that portion corresponding to the window opening. The composite image that resulted from these two exposures placed the train inside the window of the set without allowing the separate exposures to overlap and create ghosting or a double-image.

Although in-camera matting became less common as filmmakers developed more elaborate methods of producing composites, some spectacular examples can be found in modern cinema. The second section of Stanley Kubrick's *2001: A Space Odyssey* (1968) portrays a landing on the moon by astronauts and their discovery of a mysterious, giant black monolith that suggests the presence of an intelligent, alien life form. Shots of the lunar excavation area around the monolith combine live action (the astronauts) with a miniature model of the moon's surface. The live action was shot first, and the 65mm negative was left unprocessed for more than a year as Kubrick and his crew worked on other sections of the film. When it came time to film the miniature, it was filmed using the undeveloped live action footage bi-packed in the camera with a counter-matte blocking the previously exposed area (the live action component). A bi-pack camera is capable of running two strips of film, so in this case one strip contained the live action and another the counter-matte. The result was an extremely sharp, clear, in-camera composite image combining the miniature model with the live actors on a set.

THE GREAT TRAIN ROBBERY (1903)

Edwin S. Porter used an in-camera matte to place footage of a passing locomotive in the window of the set depicting the telegraph operator's office. Filmmakers rapidly seized on the matte/counter-matte system for creating composited images. Frame enlargement.

2001: A SPACE ODYSSEY (MGM, 1968)

Astronauts investigate a lunar excavation site where a mysterious giant monolith has been found. The actors and the excavated site were shot on a studio stage in England and matted in-camera with a miniature model of the rocky, mountainous lunar surface. Frame enlargement.

TRAVELLING MATTES

Cinema is a medium of *motion* pictures, and matting techniques need to be capable of accommodating moving action. **Travelling mattes** enable filmmakers to insert moving foreground figures into a landscape or other type of background that has been filmed separately. Accordingly, travelling mattes are an extremely valuable and widely used tool of visual effects. They involve the application of a matte and counter-matte in order to prevent double-exposures. In our example of Superman flying to the rescue, the composite image could be produced using rear screen projection (a technique explained later in the chapter), but we will treat the scene as if produced using a travelling matte. Christopher Reeve as Superman is the foreground element and has been filmed separately in a controlled studio environment. If we simply printed the foreground and background elements together, they would be double-exposed; Superman would look transparent because the desert landscape could be seen through him. Using mattes to selectively expose portions of the composite image, we can prevent this kind of double-exposure.

A **male matte** is created from the foreground element (Superman, in this case). A male matte, also known as a holdout matte, is a black silhouette of the foreground element with all other areas of the film frame being transparent. The opaque silhouette will block light from being transmitted through the film in this area during printing (or, if working digitally, during compositing). A **female matte** (also known as a cover matte) must also be created as the inverse of the male. The female matte is an opaque frame in which the foreground figure is transparent. The opaque area of the female matte will block light during printing.

Several steps are needed to produce the final composite image. The background element (the desert landscape) is printed together with the male matte. The new strip of film that results shows the landscape now with a "black hole," an area without an image that corresponds with the foreground figure. Using the female matte, we can now print our foreground figure of Superman onto the landscape footage that was printed with the male matte. The foreground figure fits into the black hole, and the female matte prevents additional light from hitting the previously exposed area of background. The resulting composite image shows Superman flying across a desert landscape.

Filmmakers developed numerous methods for generating male and female mattes. The earliest was the Williams Process, patented in 1918, which involved filming the foreground element against a black background and then copying the resulting image onto high contrast black-and-white film to generate a male matte. The process did not at first employ a female matte, but Williams refined it to include one, at which point it was known as the Williams Double-Matting process. It was used extensively in *King Kong* (1933) to combine the miniature model of Kong, animated using stop-motion, with live action footage. An example is Kong's dramatic appearance inside the enormous gates of the compound on Skull Island. Kong is the moving foreground element (though in the shot's composition he appears in the background) matted into the live action set and crowd of extras.

Most travelling matte processes used colored light to generate the male and female mattes because color can act as a filter, useful for blocking or transmitting light. The first of these, developed in the late 1920s, was the Dunning-Pomeroy Self-Matting Process. It used orange and blue light to create an in-camera matte for compositing foreground and background and was employed on *Tarzan the Ape Man* (1932) as well as *King Kong* (1933). Subsequent processes using blue-screens to

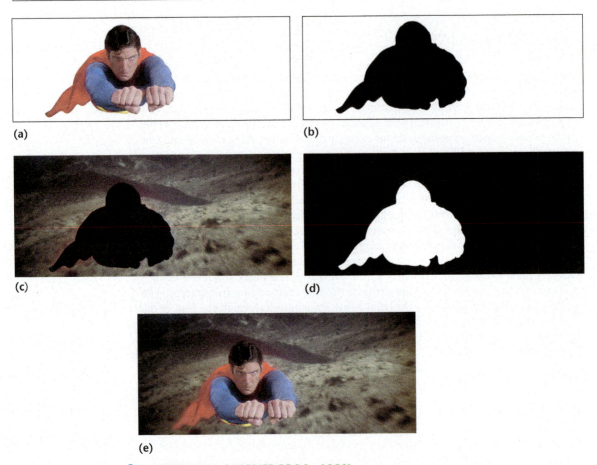

(a)

(b)

(c)

(d)

(e)

SUPERMAN II (WARNER BROS., 1980).

Principles of travelling mattes. A. Foreground element is shot in a studio against a colored backing and is then extracted from that backing. B. Male matte is produced from the foreground element. C. The male matte is composited with the background image to produce a "black hole" (an area with no picture information) into which the foreground element will be inserted. D. The male matte is inverted to produce a female matte. E. Using the female matte, the foreground element (A) is composited into the background footage (C) to produce the final composite (E). Frame enlargement.

separate the foreground element or, alternatively, a yellow screen, developed from the 1930s onward.

All of these travelling matte systems tended to leave artifacts in the composited image. Visible matte lines, such as a black or colored line around the foreground figure, pointed to the join between composited elements. Registration was sometimes imperfect, visible as a noticeable jiggling or wiggle between the elements. Color fringing might occur around fine areas of detail such as hair, produced by colored light from the background screen bleeding through porous or sheer areas of the foreground object.

Digital tools today enable much cleaner matte extraction and virtually perfect registration among the composited elements. In a digital image, each pixel is allocated

KING KONG (RKO, 1933)

King Kong forces open the compound gates to attack the villagers of Skull Island. Kong is a miniature puppet animated with stop-motion photography. He was then matted into the shot using the Williams Process. Frame enlargement.

THE AFRICAN QUEEN (UNITED ARTISTS, 1951)

Optically printed travelling mattes sometimes exhibit artifacts where image elements have been extracted or joined together. Matte lines are visible here around actors Katharine Hepburn and Humphrey Bogart, and her hair shows some color fringing. Frame enlargement.

four channels, three of which are the red, green and blue components that together comprise its color. The fourth channel—the **alpha channel**—specifies the pixel's degree of transparency, and this channel can be used for generating male and female mattes. A visual-effects artist working with the alpha channel can easily and automatically extract or "pull" a matte from any element in a digital image. Once a male matte is pulled, its alpha values can be inverted to produce a female matte. Moreover, the interaction of matted moving elements can be more complex in a digital composite because Z-depth mapping enables precise calculations about the distances of all objects in the frame from the camera. The **Z-axis** refers to the depth in the image along which objects are arranged or through which they move. A **Z-depth map** uses gray-scale values to visualize these distances, ranging from white (objects nearest the camera) to shades of gray to black (objects farthest from the camera). The optical composites used in earlier generations of Hollywood films did not allow for the complex, three-dimensional interactions among moving matted elements that digital tools facilitate.

GLASS PAINTINGS, FOREGROUND MINIATURES, AND MIRRORS

Paintings produced on sheets of glass were an early and extremely effective visual effects technique. Norman Dawn, Edward Rogers and Ferdinand Pinney Earle were creating glass shots in the teens, and by the 1920s glass shots were being combined with the matte-and-counter-matte system to create high-quality, complex visual effects shots. A glass painting could be produced on location. Using a sheet of glass set up between the camera and the set or location, a painter would supply vistas, buildings, trees, or other elements as needed for a scripted scene. Glass shots are early instances of matte paintings in cinema. Areas to be filmed as live action would be left unpainted on the glass and filmed through this opening. Alternatively, live action could be matted into the painting.

The silent version of *Ben-Hur* (1926) includes numerous extraordinary glass shots created by Earle, whose epic paintings add a sense of grandeur to many scenes. *Ben-Hur* also brilliantly incorporated hanging **foreground miniatures** used as set extensions. The Coliseum where an elaborate chariot race occurs was built only as a one story structure; the upper stories were a foreground miniature outfitted with small wooden figurines that could be moved to suggest the responses of a crowd of spectators.

Foreground miniatures are suspended in the air at the top of the frame and between the camera and a distant set that has been partially built. The hanging miniature is much closer to the camera than is the set, and it supplies the missing sections of set. If it is positioned properly and is built to the correct scale, from the camera's viewpoint it will appear on film to be an actual part of the set.

Because hanging miniatures create illusions of scale and depth, camera movement must be restricted in such shots, lest the disconnection between set and miniature become apparent. Limited pans and tilts are possible using a **nodal tripod**, one that pivots or tilts around the optical center of the lens and therefore produces no motion perspective. Normal tripods pivot and tilt a camera on an axis well behind the lens, and the distance between this area and the lens (which captures the image) produces motion perspective. This, in turn, will reveal the presence of a miniature, which will appear to move more quickly past the camera than will the more distant set. The

BEN-HUR (MGM, 1926)
This visual effects masterpiece features a brilliant blend of glass shots, foreground miniatures, and color tinting. Top: A matte painting on glass composited with actors visible in the lower right of frame. Bottom: Foreground miniatures complete the stadium as set extensions. Frame enlargements.

chariot race in *Ben Hur* includes a pan across the miniature, and the absence of motion perspective preserves the illusion.

Hanging foreground miniatures are among the most magical of visual effects, and they have been used throughout film history. In *Gone With the Wind* (1939), when Scarlet (Vivian Leigh) returns to Twelve Oakes Plantation, now devastated by the

THE AVIATOR (MIRAMAX, 2004)

Elaborate foreground miniatures—the airplane and wing, the rocky sea-break and concrete seawall, the tent, garbage cans and automobiles, the oil derricks—were positioned in front of the camera, and the actors performed the scene some sixty yards away. The illusion is perfect. Everything looks real, and the differences of scale and distance remain invisible. Frame enlargement.

war, she stands in the ruined mansion at the foot of the grand staircase. The lower part of the set was constructed in scale, and the upper portion, showing the staircase and second floor of the mansion, was created as a hanging miniature. The studio, Selznick International, had a nodal tripod for their Technicolor cameras which enabled them to do modest pans and tilts in shots with miniatures. As Scarlett looks at the ruined mansion, a pan and tilt follow the implied line of her gaze and reveal more of the set and the hanging miniature and establish a visual bridge connecting the two.

The final sequence in Martin Scorsese's *The Aviator* takes place after Howard Hughes lands his Hercules H-4 transport airplane and is celebrated by fans in a large tent next to the pier where the plane is docked. In the shot reproduced here, nearly everything in the foreground is a hanging miniature—the airplane, the rocky seawall, the concrete seawall, the tent, the oil derricks, and the automobiles in front of the tent and the aircraft's pontoon. The actors performed the scene sixty yards away from the miniatures, and as the frame enlargement demonstrates, the illusion is perfect. Scorsese remained fond of hanging miniatures, and in the final shot of *Shutter Island*, the lighthouse is a foreground miniature.

Foreground miniatures create illusions of perspective, making something close by seem much farther away. Many visual effects tools work by creating perspective illusions, and miniatures generally are built in ways that create deceptive perspectives. **Forced perspective,** for example, takes informational cues about depth and distance—such as the way parallel lines seem to converge in the distance or the way objects seem to grow smaller as they get farther away—and exaggerates these to convey on the small scale of a miniature model an impression of great size or distance. Many of the miniatures in *The Lord of the Rings* movie work this way, and many sets and props

THE LORD OF THE RINGS: THE FELLOWSHIP OF THE RING (NEW LINE, 2001)
Visual effects often create perspective illusions. Sets built with forced perspective create the illusion that actors Ian McKellen and Ian Holm are different sizes. Frame enlargement.

in those movies were built to different scales to convey illusions about the size of the hobbits relative to other characters. When Gandalf (Ian McKellen) sits at a table with Bilbo Baggins (Ian Holm), Bilbo's small size is conveyed by placing the actor, Ian Holm, farther away from the camera than McKellen and making Bilbo's section of the table larger so that, being farther away, the camera would see it as being the on the same scale as McKellen's section of table.

Alfred Hitchcock loved visual effects and made sure that his movies included plenty of them. *Saboteur* (1942) was especially ingenious. Hitchcock's art director, Robert Boyle, used a small indoor studio set to create the illusion of a lengthy circus caravan traveling along a dusty desert road. The film's hero, Barry (Robert Cummings), is running from police and takes refuge in the caravan. Several point-of-view shots show the line of trucks halted as police with flashlights search them. The caravan and the cops seem to stretch from the foreground way into the distance, but this was an illusion created with forced perspective. The road was painted on the concrete studio floor and outlined with dirt and was raised up in the rear of the set to simulate distant space. Real trucks in the foreground were succeeded by painted toy trucks in the background, and cops played by actors in the foreground became tiny cut-out figures with lights in the distance. Speaking about the methods of forced perspective used in the shots, Boyle said, "You're achieving a large space in a limited space. You bring the background up, and you force everything smaller."

Miniature models can be combined with live action using mirrors, and the **Schufftan process** is a famous example of this technique. Eugene Schufftan was a cinematographer who invented a method of filming live action with the reflected image of a miniature model or a matte painting. By placing a mirror, that reflects the image of the miniature or painting, at a 45-degree angle to the camera, live action elements can be filmed through portions of the mirror that have been scraped away to leave transparent glass. The camera sees the live action through the glass and sees the miniature

SABOTEUR (UNIVERSAL, 1942)

This highway and circus caravan stretching into the distance were built on a small, indoor studio stage. Normal-sized vehicles in the foreground give way to miniatures in the background and a raised floor to suggest increasing distance. The forced perspective is ingeniously designed. Frame enlargement.

reflected in the glass. The actors and the miniature or painting are thereby filmed simultaneously. The Shufftan process famously was used throughout the science fiction epic *Metropolis* (1927) to place live action inside miniature sets of the futuristic city. Alfred Hitchcock used the process in *Blackmail* (1929) to combine actors with miniatures of the London Museum. The Schufftan process facilitated a shot in *Aliens* (1986) that required a larger set than what could be constructed on budget. The filmmakers needed a shot of two characters entering a bar in the off-world boom town but didn't have a full set. So they built a full-size door the actors could enter, and the rest of the building and surrounding area was a miniature reflected to the camera by a mirror.

THE HOLLYWOOD STUDIO ERA

From the late 1920s until the 1960s, it was very rare for American films to be shot on real locations. Instead, films were shot on indoor studio sets and outdoor studio properties, a practice that has become known as "backlot filmmaking." Rather than traveling to Paris to film *An American in Paris*, for example, MGM, the studio producing the movie, built the city with sets, miniatures, and matte paintings. Environments built in this fashion on studio backlots relied on visual effects to simulate story settings.

Warner Bros.' great adventure film, *The Sea Hawk* (1940), provides an example. Errol Flynn stars as Captain Geoffrey Thorpe, a 16th-century English raider targeting Spanish ships. Thorpe leads his men on a guerrilla raid into Panama to seize Spanish treasure. The Panamanian jungle, of course, is no such thing, having been created with fog machines and tropical plants dressed on a studio soundstage. When Thorpe and his men escape from the jungle to the shore and row out to their ship to head for England, they walk from the jungle backlot into beach shots filmed on the Pacific coast in Ventura County, and from there to a partial model of a rowboat placed in a studio rear projection set, and then to shots in which they climb aboard a full scale model of a 135-foot ship placed in a specially constructed studio maritime soundstage and surrounded by a muslin cyclorama painted with a skyscape. Their brief trip from jungle to ship takes place in these

Printer head / process projector   **Process camera**

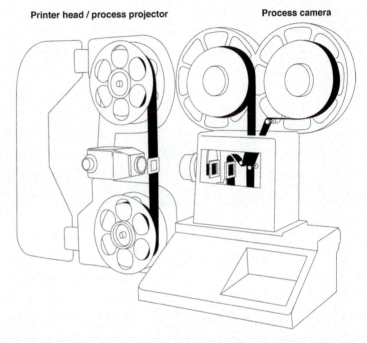

Optical printers were the visual effects workhorses of the Hollywood studio era. Featuring an interlocked camera and projector, they enabled visual effects artists to build composited shots by separately photographing each of their elements. Optical printers were also used to create credit sequences in films and basic editing transitions, such as fades, dissolves, and wipes. They facilitated the use of split-screen effects, as in this sequence from *An American in Paris*, introducing the character of Lise (Leslie Caron) by playfully contrasting her many moods and personalities. Frame enlargement.

composited environments, in which the sea and sky are, alternatively, real, a photographic projection and a painted backdrop.

Two important effects tools used extensively in this period were the optical printer and rear-screen projection. **Optical printers** were used to photograph and physically combine the elements of a composited effects shot. Optical printers were made of a synchronized process camera and a process projector that was called the printer head. Master positive footage of effects elements—models, travelling mattes, animation—was loaded into the printer head and run through and photographed frame by frame in the process camera. (A process camera is one used in the laboratory for effects work, in distinction to a production camera used to film live action.) The final composite (the finished effects shot) was created gradually by this process of re-photographing each of its components. The composite negative in the process camera had to be re-wound each time so that each component of the shot could be photographed. Here lay one of the drawbacks of optical printing—it works with dupe footage (dupe footage is several generations away from the camera negative) and ultimately creates a dupe negative, a copy of a copy. It's very common to see generational losses of image quality in optically printed shots. The more elements an effects shot contained, the more elaborate the printing process became. Two- and four-head optical printers enabled the photographing of multiple image elements in one pass, speeding the work of compositing.

Linwood Dunn, who became head of RKO's photographic effects department, designed the Acme-Dunn Special Effects Optical Printer which was widely used throughout the studio era. Editing transitions in generations of Hollywood films, such as wipes, fades and dissolves, were created on optical printers, as were split screen effects and the opening and closing credits for a film. Many photographic effects could be achieved in optical printers by moving the printer head to simulate a move by the production camera or by enlarging a shot to simulate a zoom or camera move. Dunn estimated that 50 percent or more of the shots in *Citizen Kane* had been composited on an optical printer. These included some of the film's famous deep focus shots, with the optical printer being used to exaggerate the depth of field captured on set by Gregg Toland, the cinematographer, and camera moves, such as the famous tracking shot through the glass skylight of the El Rancho nightclub.

Rear-screen projection was used so extensively that it became perhaps the most common visual effects tool of the Hollywood period. Rear-screen projection, or back projection, combines live action in the foreground with a background projected as a moving image upon a screen positioned behind the actors and set. The background images are projected *behind* the screen, which is, therefore, translucent. Many outdoor locations were simulated as rear projections, filmed with actors on indoor studio sets. Driving scenes, for example, where characters are shown riding in automobiles, were invariably done as back projections.

An ingenious variation of back projection is **miniature rear projection**, which enables filmmakers to place live actors in a miniature model or set. The method was used extensively throughout *King Kong* (1933) because all of the shots in which Kong interacts with human characters necessitated the use of miniature models and sets. Another variation was developed by visual effects artist Ray Harryhausen for his creature movies combining stop-motion animation and live action. In such films as *20 Million Miles to Earth* (1957) and *The 7th Voyage of Sinbad* (1958), the live action components of scenes were back projected behind Harryhausen's creatures.

CITIZEN KANE (RKO, 1941)

Many shots in *Citizen Kane* are optically printed composites. These often create extended depth-of-field effects, complementing the deep-focus cinematography of Gregg Toland. In this regard, the film's famous deep-focus style is a joint product of cinematography and visual effects. In this shot, Raymond the butler (Paul Stewart) opens a door and sees Kane (Orson Welles) standing in another doorway at the end of a long corridor. Actor Stewart and the doorway next to him are the live action elements. Welles, backlit and silhouetted, is matted into the shot, and the intervening hallway with Kane's reflection on the tiled floor is a matte painting. Frame enlargement.

Less frequently used, **front projection** systems projected the background image in front of and *on top of* the actors and set. 3M's invention in 1949 of Scotchlite, a highly reflective surface used in road signs, helped make front projection viable for motion pictures. Projection screens made of Scotchlite reflect light in a straight path directly back to its source and with almost no loss in brightness. In a front projection system, the camera faces the actors and set, and a Scotchlite screen is behind them. Set at a ninety degree angle to the camera's line of sight is a projector which throws its image onto a two-way, beam-splitting mirror positioned at a 45, degree angle in front of the camera. The mirror reflects the projector's footage onto the Scotchlite screen and, from there, back to the camera. Because the mirror is two-way, the camera can see through it to film the scene. The bright set lighting on the actors washes out the projector footage covering them, and the camera photographs them normally.

2001: A Space Odyssey was the first major film to use front projection. The opening sequence, showing the dawn of the apes in Africa, was shot on an indoor set in London. The background landscapes were front projections of high-resolution photographs taken in Africa, and the illusion is perfect. A viewer watching the film cannot tell that the shots are in-camera composites. Other films to use front projection include *Where Eagles Dare*, *Superman*, *The Fugitive*, *Moonraker*, *Outland*, and *Cliffhanger*.

TO CATCH A THIEF (PARAMOUNT, 1955)

Back projection in the Hollywood era was a standard method of depicting driving scenes. Actors Cary Grant and Grace Kelly play characters driving along the French Riviera. In reality, they are in a partial model of an automobile shot in a studio in front of rear projected imagery. Frame enlargement.

Composite shots achieved with rear or front projection offered an alternative to optical printing because the effects were achieved in-camera, but rear projection, too, left visual artifacts in a scene. Because the rear projections used dupe footage, generational differences in image quality were often visible between the live action components and the back projections. Differences in lighting and color and the grain structure of the film stocks often prevailed as well. But in general back projection provided a very serviceable illusion of being on location and was widely used until, in the 1960s, shooting on location became a predominant practice.

Already well-established in the teens and 1920s as a vital effects tool, matte painting flourished during the studio era. Each of the major studios had a matte painting department and used optical printers to composite painted and live action images. A common misperception about visual effects is that they are found mainly in

KING KONG (RKO, 1933); THE 7TH VOYAGE OF SINBAD (COLUMBIA, 1958)

Variations on basic rear projection include miniature back projection, used in *King Kong* to insert live actors into miniature sets. Actor Bruce Cabot, as a projected image lower frame left, plays a character hiding in a cave, where he is menaced by Kong. Visual effects artist Ray Harryhausen specialized in stop-motion animation and devised a system combining the live action element as a rear projection, composited with animated puppets. Here, Kerwin Matthews as Sinbad, back projected, battles a skeleton brought to life by an evil wizard. Frame enlargement.

genres like science fiction and fantasy to provide spectacle. In fact, however, the great majority of feature films, irrespective of genre, make use of visual effects. Thus in Hollywood movies during the studio era, matte paintings and other effects might be found in Westerns, musicals, horror films, war films, dramas, and comedies.

Gone With the Wind, for example, is a visual effects-intensive film. Producer David O. Selznick said, "I could not even hope to put the picture on the screen properly without an even more extensive use of special effects than had ever before been attempted in the business." The film's epic historical landscapes were composites, formed from split-screen effects used to double the size of crowds, front and rear projection, miniature projection, and especially matte painting. Clarence Slifer, who worked with

2001: A SPACE ODYSSSEY (MGM, 1968)

Front projection throws a background image overtop of performers and set. Set lights prevent the camera from seeing the projection on the actors, and a highly reflective screen behind them returns the projected image to the camera. The African landscapes in the first sequence of Kubrick's film are high-resolution photographs front projected onto actors in ape suits and a minimal set. Frame enlargement.

Jack Cosgrove, the head of Selznick's special effects department, estimated that approximately 100 matte paintings were used in the film. The paintings are blended subliminally with live action and miniatures and were used to create set extensions, fill out landscapes, add skies above sets and actors, and provide dramatic vistas.

Slifer had designed an aerial optical printer that enabled him to achieve new effects with matte painting. With **aerial image printing**, an image (such as a matte painting) is projected to a focal plane in space (rather than onto a surface) where it can be photographed by the process camera in the optical printer. That footage can be combined with live action footage and other optical elements. Cosgrove and Slifer used aerial printing throughout the film to add smoke or fire effects to matte paintings. In a shot showing the Atlanta train station, smoke pours from a locomotive parked in front of the station. Footage of smoke against a clear background was placed in the projector head of the optical printer. Another projector threw an aerial image of the painting behind the smoke footage. The printer then photographed both. By photographing the painting in this manner, the smoke seemed to naturally cover the painted train station roof as it would in a real 3D world.

Aerial imaging was also used in the famous pull-back of Scarlet and Gerald O'Hara against a dramatic sunset in the scene where he tells her that he will leave Tara to her after his death and that land is the only thing that endures. The pull-back by the camera shows the characters as silhouettes standing next to a tree with Tara visible in the distance. The shot composites live action footage of the characters (stand-ins doubling for stars Vivien Leigh and Thomas Mitchell) with two matte paintings, depicting the sky and a distant view of Tara (projected into the composite as an aerial image). The tree in the foreground is a miniature model. The complexity of the shot is apparent in the less than perfect registration—the pull-back (which appears to be a crane shot but was, instead, created in the optical printer as a visual effects move on the paintings) occasions some jiggle among the image elements.

GONE WITH THE WIND (SELZNICK INTERNATIONAL, 1939)

Wounded Civil War soldiers pour into the Atlanta train station. The station is a studio set. The station roof is a matte painting projected as an aerial image behind footage of smoke against a clear background. Composited in this way on the optical printer, the smoke looks quite real, covering the painting as actual smoke would do a real roof. Frame enlargement.

TORN CURTAIN (UNIVERSAL, 1966)

Actor Paul Newman walks into a matte painting and then a series of them in a bravura sequence lasting two minutes on screen. In the sequence, director Alfred Hitchcock and Albert Whitlock create a series of virtual environments for the actor, and they dare the audience to notice. Few viewers do. Frame enlargement.

Alfred Hitchcock was very fond of matte paintings and worked often with the great matte artist Albert Whitlock, who produced extraordinary painted environments for numerous Hitchcock films including some very famous shots in *The Birds* (1963). One of Whitlock's greatest achievements is a bravura, two-minute sequence in Hitchcock's *Torn Curtain* (1966), where the main character, Michael Armstrong (Paul Newman), walks through an East German art museum. Because it was the Cold War, Hitchcock couldn't shoot on location, so he had Whitlock create the museum's exterior and interior as a series of six matte paintings into which the character is composited. Although the term "virtual environment" is identified today mainly with digitally created images, virtual environments have always been a part of cinema, achieved with visual effects. The art museum sequence in *Torn Curtain* gives viewers an entirely convincing series of virtual environments.

MOTION CONTROL

Camera movement provides filmmakers with a very important tool for blending and joining the optical elements in an effects shot. Nodal tripods were used to create limited camera moves when matte paintings were filmed on glass in front of a live action set or location. But for much of the studio era, when matte paintings were created in the studio and composited on an optical printer with live action, the traditional practice was to lock the camera down and composite the shot without camera movement on any of its elements.

The pull-back from Scarlett and her father in *Gone With the Wind* was a simulated camera move. To introduce camera movement into effects shots, filmmakers needed a mechanical system of motion control, enabling them to exactly reproduce a camera movement on all of a composited shot's optical elements. Motion control systems became available in the late 1940s and changed the look of visual effects. The Dupy Duplicator, developed at MGM by Olin Dupy, provided a means of recording camera movement in a live-action shot and then match-moving in the same way as a process camera shooting a matte painting. When both elements were optically composited, the film's viewer seemed to see on-screen a single, unbroken camera move. The system debuted with a shot in *Easter Parade* (1948) that tilts up from a studio set depicting Fifth Avenue to a matte painting of Manhattan buildings. The opening and closing of *An American in Paris* (1951) used the Dupy Duplicator to join partial sets with matte paintings depicting set extensions. In a shot introducing Jerry (Gene Kelly), the camera pans from a sidewalk café (the real set) up the three-story building where he lives, revealing him looking out of a top story window. Above the second-floor level, the image is a painting, including roof and sky, and the motion-control blend of the image elements is perfect. Even if a viewer knows where the join is, it cannot be seen. Paramount Pictures had a proprietary motion repeater system, which it used in *Samson and Delilah* (1949) to replicate camera moves on live action and miniature model elements in a composite.

The famous Slitcan sequence in *2001: A Space Odyssey* used motion control to create an abstract play of light and color. With its shutter held open, the camera moved along a fourteen-foot track toward a slit behind which were various pieces of backlit colored art. It took up to a full minute for the camera to finish its move, and each frame of film was exposed twice while the camera's focus was continually changing, creating an impression of infinite depth of field, a sensation

EASTER PARADE (MGM, 1948)

The Dupy Duplicator enabled motion control cinematography at MGM, allowing filmmakers to match-move a laboratory camera over a matte painting or miniature and composite that footage with a camera move on set. The Fifth Avenue Easter parade that concludes the film was staged on an MGM backlot. A camera tilt begun on the set finishes with another move in the laboratory over the matte painting depicting Manhattan buildings. The two elements were composited on an optical printer. Frame enlargement.

that the astronaut David Bowman (Keir Dullea) was plunging into an infinity of space and consciousness.

Computerized motion control systems arrived with *Star Wars* (1977). The spaceships were miniature models made to fly by slowly, moving the camera past them while filming. The moves had to be repeated numerous times to build up the layers of an effects shot, and computer control of the camera enabled extremely precise matchmoving. Digital motion control systems are now the norm for producing match-moves in effects sequences.

STAR WARS (20TH CENTURY FOX, 1977)

Computerized motion control enabled new levels of precision in building composited shots featuring camera movement. This X-wing fighter comes to life as a miniature model thanks to multiple-passes of a motion-controlled camera. Frame enlargement.

THE IMPACT OF *STAR WARS*

Star Wars revived and reinvigorated visual effects in cinema, and its impact on effects and the popular culture surrounding them cannot be overstated. In the late 1960s, the studio system had broken apart, and no studios retained the extensive technical crews of matte painters and model builders that they once had. Most studios, in fact, apart from Disney, had shut down their matte painting departments because filmmaking had moved beyond the backlot practices of earlier decades. In the 1960s, movies were shot on location, and screen environments were not as extensively fabricated with effects tools as they were in the backlot era.

George Lucas loved matte paintings and miniature models and the magic these create on screen, and in *Star Wars* he embraced these traditions of film production. Moreover, until *Star Wars*, the Hollywood studios had remained tight-lipped about visual effects, keeping them relatively secret and unpublicized. Norman O. Dawn, who pioneered the use of glass paintings and matte shots, worked at Universal for five years beginning in 1916, and recalled that studio heads "didn't believe in telling anybody about effects...They considered anything that was a drawing or a glass shot a fake. So they didn't want to let the exhibitors know that this was a cheap picture full of fakes. They kept all that quiet...no matter if it was nothing more than an ordinary double exposure." More than any other single event, the release of *Star Wars* in 1977 changed these attitudes. George Lucas had enthusiastically embraced visual effects, and the huge popular response to the film opened a new era in which visual effects were extensively publicized. Cinema effects today have a huge fan following, as well as serious journals devoted to them, like *Cinefex* which chronicles the history, technology, and aesthetics of visual effects.

FILMMAKER SPOTLIGHT

George Lucas

Though he has directed few films, George Lucas's influence on contemporary cinema is enormous. He has been one of the industry's technological visionaries, fixed on the digital future of cinema and helping transition the industry toward all-digital production methods. A graduate of the University of Southern California Film School, Lucas took one of his student projects and expanded it into his first feature as director. *THX-1138* (1971) is a grim, science fiction vision of a totalitarian future. Its somber tone is galaxies removed from the spirited hijinks of his subsequent *Star Wars* series.

Lucas followed *THX-1138* with the hugely popular *American Graffiti* (1973), portraying the bittersweet antics of high-school graduates at summer's end on the threshold of the sixties. Its complex sound design resulted from Lucas's collaboration with sound designer Walter Murch, who also worked on *THX-1138*. Committed to optimizing cinema sound, Lucas teamed with another top sound designer, Ben Burtt, on the *Star Wars* trilogy and built a state-of-the-art postproduction sound facility at Skywalker Ranch, his corporate headquarters.

Lucas wanted to streamline film production using digital methods, and he began funding systematic research into digital applications in film production. In 1978, he recruited Edwin Catmull from the New York Institute of Technology to start a computer graphics program at Lucasfilm.

(continued)

STAR WARS (20TH CENTURY FOX, 1977)

Obi-Wan Kenobi (Alec Guinness) battles Darth Vader (David Prowse) as Imperial storm-troopers gather in the background. Like Fritz Lang's *Metropolis* and Kubrick's *2001: A Space Odyssey*, Lucas's film is a definitive visual effects classic. In its embrace of matte paintings and miniatures, *Star Wars* embraced cinema's enduring traditions of movie magic. Frame enlargement.

Lucas had three objectives. He wanted a nonlinear editing system that could speed up the work of editing, a complementary system for digitally processing and mixing sound, and a digital film printer to replace existing optical printers. There was no point in developing computer graphics unless the results could be scanned to film for exhibition.

Although digital effects were not part of Lucas' original vision, the effects created by the artists at his company, Industrial Light and Magic (ILM), became widely identified with the filmmaker as his primary influence on cinema. In light of this, ironically, Lucas was relatively slow to incorporate digital effects into his own films. *Star Wars* (1977) included a brief 3D computer graphic visualizing the planned attack on the Death Star. The other computer screens shown in the film display hand-animated graphics. The innovative computer work on *Star Wars* lay not in digital effects but in motion control cinematography. A computer-controlled camera made multiple, exactly repeatable passes, photographing miniature models numerous times to create the image layers needed for a composite. On *The Empire Strikes Back* (1980), ILM considered using CGI to animate an X-wing fighter, but in the end the film contained no computer graphics. The

sequel, *Return of the Jedi*, used only a small amount of digital animation to simulate graphics displays.

Lucas shot the next set of *Star Wars* movies on high definition video. *The Phantom Menace* (1999) originated partly on film because high speed HD video needed for effects work wasn't yet viable. Lucas persuaded Sony to build a customized hi-def camera for his needs, and using the Sony HDW-F900, Lucas shot all of Episode II in the second trilogy, *Attack of the Clones* (2002), on HD video. He used an improved version of Sony's camera on the next installment, *Revenge of the Sith* (2005). In doing so, he demonstrated for the industry the viability of digital capture. Capturing images digitally facilitated effects work because there was no need to scan from film to digital video.

In the meantime, ILM became an industry powerhouse in the area of visual effects, producing work for Lucas' films and for many other filmmakers. Steven Spielberg had planned to make *Jurassic Park* as he did *Jaws*, with animatronic models. But the artists at ILM convinced him that it was possible to do the dinosaurs digitally, and although Spielberg retained some animatronics in the film, it was the digital dinosaurs that made the movie a must-see event for audiences. ILM's work on *Jurassic Park* persuaded Hollywood that digital visual effects would henceforth be a vital part of contemporary film.

Following *Star Wars*, Lucas stepped out of the director's chair and turned his attention to getting ILM and his production company, Lucasfilm, into good financial condition and to producing films for other directors. In this capacity, he oversaw completion, and co-wrote, the other two films in the trilogy (*The Empire Strikes Back*, 1980; *Return of the Jedi*, 1983) and each of the three Indiana Jones films directed by his pal Steven Spielberg (*Raiders of the Lost Ark*, 1981; *Indiana Jones and the Temple of Doom*, 1984; and *Indiana Jones and the Last Crusade*, 1989).

Lucas returned to directing, and to his *Star Wars* project, with *The Phantom, Menace* (1999), *Attack of the Clones* (2002) and *Revenge of the Sith* (2005). He believes that celluloid film is now a relic of history and that the medium will be moving in an all-digital direction. Through ILM, Lucas has exerted a profound influence over visual effects in contemporary film. And in the mix of adventure, fantasy and visual effects he perfected in *Star Wars*, he helped shape the very definition of a Hollywood blockbuster.

There is no denying the enormous popular acceptance of his work or its trend-setting importance for mainstream filmmaking. Lucas's digital paradigm is, in all probability, the future of cinema. ∎

THE DIGITAL ERA

In the 1960s and 1970s, a tremendous amount of research conducted at universities and corporate and government laboratories focused on computer graphics (CG), the creation and display of pictures in computers. Research scientists and visual artists had to learn how to simulate the properties of light and how to model solids, liquids and gases and spatial relationships among them in ways that would be convincing and would look naturalistic. These were extremely difficult tasks, and as they were solved computer graphics became increasingly photorealistic.

Computer graphics began appearing in feature films in small ways in *Westworld* (1973) and *Future World* (1976) and then more significantly in *Tron* (1982), *Star Trek II: The Wrath of Khan* (1982), *The Last Starfighter* (1984), *Young Sherlock Holmes* (1985), *The Abyss* (1989), *Terminator 2* (1991), and *Death Becomes Her* (1992). But the jury was still out, as far as the film industry was concerned. Many of these movies performed poorly at the box office, and it was not yet clear that digital effects could make a real difference for a film's box-office success.

With its $1 billion global box-office gross, Steven Spielberg's *Jurassic Park* (1993) became the film that showed the industry the financial and creative potentials of digital effects. *Jurassic Park's* digital dinosaurs were more vivid than any prehistoric beasts seen on screen before, and Spielberg brilliantly blended old and new effects techniques. There are only about 50 digital effects shots in the film, and most scenes with dinosaurs blend the digital beasts with **animatronic models** (a model that is motorized and moves) and old-fashioned man-in-a-monster-suit performers. In many shots, Spielberg subliminally shifts among the suited performers, the models and the digital creatures, and unless a viewer knows exactly what to look for, the changes remain invisible.

Jurassic Park ushered in a new generation of digital effects that gave filmmakers an expanded toolbox for designing images. Digital tools did not alter the role of visual effects in cinema; instead, filmmakers used digital tools to build on and further develop existing stylistic traditions.

JURASSIC PARK (UNIVERSAL, 1993)

ILM's dinosaurs re-defined the nature of visual effects by taking them into the digital domain in ways that electrified audiences and made the Hollywood industry take note. It wasn't the first digital effects film, but it was the most important. The digital dinosaurs co-exist on screen with animatronic models and performers in dinosaur costumes. Steven Speilberg brilliantly combined digital and non-digital effects tools in ways that were largely seamless and invisible. Frame enlargement.

Digital composites replaced optical printers. Rather than photographing image elements on an optical printer to create a blend, digital composites worked directly on pixels and blended image layers by transforming pixels. A matted object could be produced, for example, by adding or subtracting pixels in an image. Digital **rendering** replaced optical printing. Rendering is the process during which a synthetic digital image is created from the files and data that an artist has assembled. **Multi-pass compositing** creates a final, rendered image from separate operations carried out upon different image layers. Multi-pass compositing had been carried out on optical printers. Some of the optical printer effects shots in *Return of the Jedi* were so complex that they required more than a hundred passes.

But doing multiple passes digitally allows for much greater precision and control of image elements. A depth pass can be carried out on the Z-depth channel to manipulate focus and depth of field. A specular pass controls the size and positioning of specular highlights (shiny surfaces). An ambient pass builds general, directionless levels of light in the environment. An ambient occlusion pass generates soft shadows. A beauty pass builds the shot with its greatest levels of color and detail. Unlike optical printing, digital passes introduce no image degradation. Everything remains first generation in visual quality.

Moreover, importing images to an electronic realm makes them infinitely variable. Digital tools can simulate many features of camera perspective and lighting, and all-CG films, such as *WALL-E*, can be given a specific photographic look. Andrew Stanton, *WALL-E*'s director, wanted the movie to look as if it had been shot as a 1970s-era sci-fi movie in anamorphic widescreen. The images were digitally rendered,

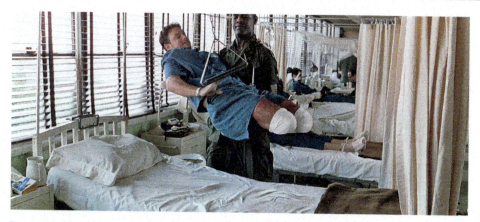

FORREST GUMP (PARAMOUNT, 1994)

In the wake of *Jurassic Park*, digital effects assumed a new importance for feature film-making. The digital erasure of actor Gary Sinise's lower legs, so that he could play a paraplegic Vietnam veteran, became a famous and much talked-about effect when the film was released. Many viewers knew this was a digital effect, but this knowledge did not undermine the credibility of the images. The filmmakers believed strongly that the effect brought them closer to a realistic style than had been the case in past films where an actor playing a paraplegic would hide a limb in costume. Frame enlargement.

therefore, to emulate many of the characteristic flaws and idiosyncrasies of anamorphic cinematography, such as horizontally spiked lens flares.

When digital tools started being adopted in films, many filmmakers and critics feared that digital applications would replace traditional effects tools. To date, that has not happened. Digital tools co-exist with the traditional techniques of models, stop motion, animatronics and location filming, as movies like *The Lord of the Rings* trilogy (in which miniature models and matte paintings were used extensively) and *Inception* demonstrate. *Inception*'s director, Christopher Nolan, blended location filming, practical effects created in-camera, and physical sets and props with digital images. The real locations included Paris streets where stars Leonardo DiCaprio and Ellen Page were filmed. The real location was then treated digitally for a spectacular scene in which the urban environment folds up into a cube containing the actors. Nolan felt these blends would enhance the perceived realism of the film's more fantastic moments.

Although digital methods have changed matte paintings, painting remains an essential effects tool. Many contemporary films—*The Lord of the Rings* trilogy, *The Curious Case of Benjamin Button, The Day After Tomorrow*—rely intensively upon matte painted images. Today matte paintings are created using programs like Autodesk Maya and Adobe Photoshop, and painters work with mouse and keyboard rather than paint and brush. In the analog era, a matte painting was a flat, 2D image element placed at the rear of a shot, and apart from the pans or tilts facilitated by a motion control system like the Dupy Duplicator, the painting could not be integrated dynamically into shot movement on screen. A digital matte painting, by contrast, can be **camera-mapped** onto the 3D geometry of a CG scene or set. This involves wrapping the painting around the wireframe objects that form the underlying geometry of the scene and specifying perspective as established by the camera's position and lens focal length. The wireframe objects can be rotated in computer space to simulate the changing perspective of a

WALL-E (PIXAR, 2008)

Digital animation does not require a camera to film live action. Almost nothing was filmed in this animated sci-fi movie, but its director Andrew Stanton wanted the movie to look as if it might have been filmed in anamorphic widescreen during the 1970s. Accordingly, Hollywood cinematographer Roger Deakins consulted with Pixar's animators on issues of lighting, showing them how a cinematographer would work. The Pixar artists emulated the characteristic features of anamorphic lenses, building these artifacts into the film. The artifacts include lens flares that spike in a horizontal direction, as in the shot pictured above. Anamorphic lens perspective organizes the aesthetic design of *WALL-E*, and this was achieved not with a camera but as a digital graphic design. Frame enlargement.

moving camera. When this is done, the camera-mapped painting exhibits the motion perspective produced by the moving camera. Digital matte paintings, therefore, are 2 ½-D elements—not fully 3D because they are texture wrappings on 3D wireframe objects—and as such can undergo dynamic spatial changes within a shot. This is a major difference compared with the way paintings functioned in the analog era.

THE DAY AFTER TOMORROW (20TH CENTURY FOX, 2004)

Digital matte paintings are extremely common in contemporary film and can be spatially dynamic in ways that earlier generations of paintings could not. The Statue of Liberty freezes over due to global warming, and the matte painting supplies an appropriately apocalyptic composition. Frame enlargement.

ALICE IN WONDERLAND (DISNEY, 2010)
Digital methods can offer new performance opportunities for actors. Helena Bonham Carter played the wicked Red Queen in costume on a greenscreen soundstage. Effects artists then enlarged the size of her head and gave her a tucked, narrow waistline. The character was then composited into environments dressed with digital props and objects. Frame enlargement.

Digital tools have not replaced actors but have helped to create dynamic extensions of performance. Obviously, many creatures in film today can be digitally created; when they are, they typically begin life as a **maquette,** a small, 3D sculpture that forms the basis for subsequent digital animation and demonstrates the continuing role that miniatures play in the digital era. Using motion capture (explained in Chapter 4), a live actor's performance can furnish the basis for a character that is digitally animated (as with the blue-skinned Na'vi in *Avatar*) or digitally transformed in ways that go beyond what traditional makeup can supply. An example is the digital head replacements in *The Curious Case of Benjamin Button* that enabled Brad Pitt to play a character who ages in a backwards fashion. Costumes as well can be created digitally. In *Iron Man 2*, actor Robert Downey wore an incomplete costume as Iron Man. The full costume was motion tracked onto Downey as a digital element in postproduction.

THE CURIOUS CASE OF BENJAMIN BUTTON (WARNER BROS., 2008)
Digital environment creation returns contemporary film to the backlot traditions of the studio era. The digital backlot offers an alternative to location shooting. All of the scenes in which Benjamin (Brad Pitt) sails aboard the tug *Chelsea* along the eastern seaboard are virtual environments, created from a blend of digital matte paintings, miniatures, and CGI. Nothing was filmed at sea. Frame enlargements.

Digital tools have built on existing effects traditions. A clear example is today's counterpart of studio backlot filmmaking—the **digital backlot**. Locations that cannot be filmed can be built or augmented digitally. Numerous films today—*Changeling* (2008), *Zodiac* (2007), *Master and Commander* (2003), *The Curious Case of Benjamin Button* (2008)—simulate locations on digital sets, using painting, animation, and miniatures in combination with live action.

STEREOSCOPIC (3D) MOVIES

The widespread adoption by Hollywood of digital imaging has produced a resurgence of 3D movies. 3D today is a digital visual effect and is typically used in movies that are intensively oriented toward effects—*Avatar, Alice in Wonderland, Thor*.

The term "3D" is actually a poor one because conventional cinema is already 3D. Watching a movie in a theater activates most of the same informational cues about depth and distance that operate in real life. These are **monocular depth cues**, that is, they do not depend on seeing with two eyes but can be perceived with one eye only. Examples of these cues are overlap (near objects hide more distant objects along a single line of sight), relative size (objects appear smaller with increasing distance), height in the picture plane (farther off looks higher up), and motion perspective (differences in the apparent rate of an object's motion depending on its distance from the camera or observer). These cues provide information about a three-dimensional world, and conventional cinema has always used them because they work perfectly well on a flat picture surface like a movie screen.

CORALINE (FOCUS FEATURES, 2009)
Stereoscopic cinema uses two images to produce a left-eye and a right-eye view of scene action. The two views are displaced from one another in ways that position objects in stereoscopic space, in front of and behind the screen. Unlike conventional cinema, stereoscopic cinema uses binocular disparity and convergence to provide viewers with an enhanced experience of depth and distance. Frame enlargement.

A better term for a 3D movie, therefore, is **stereoscopic cinema**. Stereoscopy is perception with two eyes, and it includes all of the monocular depth cues as well as several that require two-eyed viewing. The two relevant to stereoscopic cinema are **binocular disparity** (each eye has a different angle of view on the world) and **convergence** (movement of the eyes toward each other to sight a near object). Where stereoscopic cinema differs from conventional cinema is in using information about binocular disparity and convergence to create for the viewer an enhanced impression of spatial depth, one that extends behind the screen as well as in front of it. Stereoscopic cinema works by creating simultaneous left-eye and right-eye (binocular) views, whereas conventional cinema offers a monocular (single-eyed) perspective.

Stereoscopic movies today are digitally shot and digitally projected, and they are often visual effects-intensive, making them a purely digital medium. Scientific knowledge about stereoscopy and stereoscopic devices preceded the invention of photography, and continuing attempts throughout cinema history were made to create and project stereoscopic motion pictures. Celluloid film, though, was a flawed medium for this purpose and proved unable to create perfectly aligned and matching right-eye and left-eye views. Digital capture and digital projection largely solved these problems, which is why stereoscopy today has returned to feature filmmaking.

How is the stereoscopic illusion created? Binocular images can be created either at the point of filming or in postproduction. If produced during filming, then two cameras are used to shoot the film in order to get separate right-eye and left-eye views. But two cameras are not necessary; a second view can be created digitally in post-production. The separation between our eyes—**interocular distance (IO)**—averages 65mm and, as a result, each eye receives a differently angled view of solid objects. This difference increases as we converge our eyes to view very close objects. Stereoscopic space in cinema is created by manipulating these variables—interocular distance corresponds with the distance between two camera lenses, and convergence corresponds with the size of the angles at which the cameras are pointed. IO settings determine how large or small an object appears to be in stereoscopic space. Convergence settings determine how near or far it seems relative to the viewer.

Ideally, IO will replicate the average 65mm separation of the viewer's eyes, but in practice filmmakers vary this setting depending on the screen action or the focal length of the lens used in a shot. IO settings on *Avatar*, for example, ranged from one-third-inch to slightly more than two inches. Wide-angle lenses may require a smaller IO setting because of the manner in which they scale perspective information. Objects close to the camera in a wide angle view will appear much larger, requiring less stereoscopic volume for effect and therefore a smaller IO setting.

A camera move from an object in close-up to a wider view will be orchestrated with continuous changes in IO so that the viewer perceives a physically continuous space on screen and does not feel like s/he is growing larger or smaller in relation to that space. This is one of the paradoxes of interocular settings—their variation can induce a sensation in the viewer of growing larger or smaller in relation to the screen world. A camera move in *Coraline* (2009), an animated film with puppets as the characters, began with a puppet's face in extreme close-up and pulled back to show a house and yard. The move was orchestrated with an IO change from 0.5mm to 18mm because spatial volume could be minimized in the extreme close-up and maximized for the wider view. The IO settings were smaller than 65mm, the distance between people's eyes, because of the need to scale space according to the size of the puppets and the sets and models they inhabit. Coraline's puppet eyes were 19mm apart. Using a human IO setting

Negative Parallax : Left-eye and Right-eye images are crossed

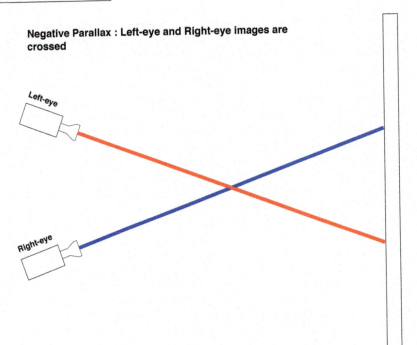

Left-eye

Right-eye

Positive Parallax : Left-eye and Right-eye images are displaced but uncrossed

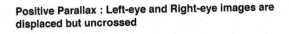

Left-eye

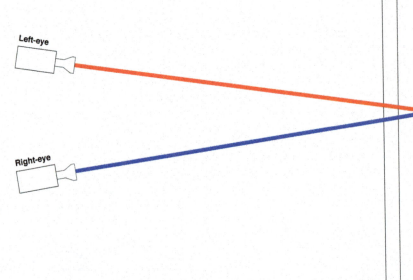

Right-eye

Filmmakers position objects in front of or behind the screen by adjusting negative and positive parallax. Crossed-eye images (negative parallax) require the viewer to converge her/his eyes in order to fuse the images into one, with the result that objects appear to be in front of the screen. Uncrossed viewing places objects behind the screen. Objects at the screen surface exhibit no binocular disparity.

would produce the phenomenon of dwarfism in relation to the 1/6 scale puppets and sets. Dwarfism results in stereoscopic displays from excessive IO distances. It can make the observer feel hundreds of feet tall and make distant environments look abnormally small. The visual reality of *Coraline*'s puppet world depended on making the viewer feel like an inhabitant there rather than like a giant looking at a miniature world. The smaller IO settings created an appropriately scaled space for this illusion.

Convergence settings determine how close objects in stereoscopic space seem to be in relation to the viewer. They vary according to how much the left-eye and right-eye views are displaced from one another. A filmmaker can place an object or character in front of the screen (between screen and viewer) by adjusting convergence settings so that they have **negative parallax**—the left-eye image is on the right, and the right is on the left, requiring that viewers converge their eyes to fuse the images. Objects or characters behind the screen surface have **positive parallax**; the right and left eye images are not crossed. The screen itself is a zero parallax area; no displacement of right- and left-eye images exists there. The two images are aligned. Filmmakers, therefore, can position objects in front of the screen or behind it by setting negative or positive parallax values. One of the biggest differences between the gimmicky use of 3D in earlier eras and today is the conservative use of parallax. Unlike the garish fly-out effects of the 1950s, excessive parallax is minimized or avoided today so that viewers will not be presented with discomforting image fusion tasks.

In stereoscopic cinema, the screen itself can move around. Filmmakers can reposition its apparent location by using what is called a "floating window" to make

TOY STORY 3 (PIXAR, 2010)

Stereoscopic cinema is naturally biased toward deep focus compositions, maximizing positive and negative parallax. Stereoscopic cinema also emphasizes longer shot lengths, rather than fast cutting, so that viewers have time to visually explore the extended depths and spaces that the format supplies. In these ways, stereoscopic filmmaking reconfigures some of the stylistic features (principally, shallow focus and fast cutting) of contemporary film. Frame enlargement.

the screen surface seem nearer or farther from the viewer. This is often done in order to choreograph framing and depth of field to minimize the image fusion tasks that a viewer is presented with.

Stereoscopic movies tend to require different compositional and editing styles from conventional cinema. Stereoscopy privileges depth of field, deep space framings, wide-angle lenses, and a slower cutting rate so that viewers have time to visually explore the stereoscopic frame and are not presented with fast changes of perspective that can be jarring in 3D. To design all of this, a new member of the production crew—the **stereographer**—consults with the director about the orchestration of binocular space. The stereographer creates a **depth score**, a kind of thematic pattern in the way that stereoscopic space is configured throughout the film in relation to the characters and their conflicts. For *Bolt 3D* (2008), stereographer Robert Neuman used negative parallax (placing characters in front of the screen) in order to heighten the viewer's emotional connection and involvement with them. In *Tron: Legacy* (2011), the depth score distinguished between the film's two narrative worlds—the everyday world of ordinary reality was shot in a monocular fashion, whereas the computer world of Tron was stereoscopic.

Stereoscopy is sometimes dismissed as a fad or a gimmick, an intrusion onto cinema for purely commercial ends. And some viewers don't like 3D movies. But the long history of stereoscopic devices and the continuing use of binocular display systems in cinema suggest that there is a natural connection between cinema and stereoscopy. In the hands of gifted filmmakers, such as James Cameron (*Avatar*), Steven Spielberg (*The Adventures of Tintin,* 2011), and Werner Herzog (*Cave of Forgotten Dreams,* 2010), stereoscopy reconfigures the nature of the medium and extends and enhances cinema's artistic potential.

NARRATIVE AND SPECTACLE

Surveying early film history, scholar Tom Gunning suggested that one of cinema's primary appeals for viewers was its ability to provide startling, eye-popping imagery. He emphasized that cinema's ability to provide startling and pleasurable illusions often was more important than storytelling, that spectacle offered its own pleasures and that these could be greater than those of narrative. He identified trick films and visual effects as examples of what he called "the cinema of attractions." By this term, he meant entertainments that were based around spectacle.

Visual effects often are identified with spectacle, and many films, such as *Transformers* (2007), appeal to viewers based on eye-popping imagery. But visual effects perform many functions in cinema; while these include spectacle, often the functions are narrative ones. Visual effects may create settings and locations in a story, describe characters and visualize dramatic conflicts, and in general enable filmmakers to tell stories about places and situations that they cannot directly film but can create using effects tools.

Most visual effects artists agree that story is critically important for the quality of a film and that good effects cannot save a badly told story. As effects artist Stan Winston said, "*Jurassic Park* wasn't successful because of the effects. *Terminator* wasn't successful because of its effects. *Lord of the Rings* wasn't successful because of its effects. They were all great stories."

Cinema has never existed without visual effects. They are a core component of the medium, an essential part of cinema structure. And like so many other elements of cinema, what counts, finally, in determining the quality of a visual effect is the intelligence and skill of the filmmaker.

KEY TERMS AND CONCEPTS

aerial image printing   291

alpha channel   280

animatronic model   297

binocular disparity   303

camera-mapping   299

composite   273

convergence   303

counter-matte   275

depth score   306

digital backlot   302

digital composite   298

female matte   277

forced perspective   283

foreground miniature   280

front projection   288

interocular distance
   (IO)   303

male matte   277

maquette   301

matte   275

miniature rear
   projection   287

monocular depth cues   302

multi-pass
   compositing   298

negative parallax   305

nodal tripod   280

optical printer   287

positive parallax   305

rear-screen projection   287

rendering   298

Schufftan process   284

stereographer   306

stereoscopic
   cinema   303

travelling matte   277

visual effect   272

Z-axis   280

Z-depth map   280

SUGGESTED READINGS

Ron Brinkman, *The Art and Science of Digital Compositing*, second edition (New York: Morgan Kaufmann, 2008).

Linwood G. Dunn and George Turner, eds., *The ASC Treasury of Visual Effects* (Hollywood, CA: ASC Holding Company, 1983).

Lenny Lipton, *Foundations of the Stereoscopic Cinema: A Study in Depth* (New York: Van Nostrand Reinhold Co.. 1982).

Shilo T. McClean, *Digital Storytelling: The Narrative Power of Visual Effects in Film* (Cambridge: MIT Press, 2007).

Dan North, *Performing Illusions: Cinema, Special Effects and the Virtual Actor* (New York: Wallflower Press, 2008).

Stephen Prince, *Digital Visual Effects in Cinema: The Seduction of Reality* (Rutgers University Press, 2011).

Richard Rickitt, *Special Effects: The History and Technique* (New York: Billboard Books, 2007).

Michael Rubin, *Droidmaker: George Lucas and the Digital Revolution* (Gainesville, FL: Triad Publishing, 2006).

Mark Cotta Vaz and Craig Barron, *The Invisible Art: The Legends of Movie Matte Painting* (San Francisco: Chronicle Books, 2002).

Mark Cotta Vaz, *Industrial Light and Magic: Into the Digital Realm* (New York: Ballantine Books, 1996).

Ray Zone, *Stereoscopic Cinema and the Origins of 3-D Film, 1838-1952* (Lexington: University of Kentucky Press, 2007).

Modes of Screen Reality

OBJECTIVES

After reading this chapter, you should be able to:

- explain the basic modes of screen reality

- describe the principles of narrative, character behavior, and audiovisual design that operate in each mode of screen reality

- differentiate ordinary fictional realism, historical realism, documentary realism, and fictional documentary realism

- describe how the cinema functions as a medium that can record properties of the visual world before the camera as well as transform the appearance of that world

- explain how this double capacity for recording and transforming relates to the basic modes of screen reality

- explain the importance of production design for the mode of fantasy and the fantastic and how fantasy settings achieve credibility

- distinguish two modes of cinematic self-reflexivity

- explain why multiple modes of screen reality are possible in cinema

This chapter examines how filmmakers use the elements of structure (lighting, editing, camera position, etc.) to create versions of representational reality on screen. Audiences routinely view a wide variety of films, ranging from comedies and Westerns to serious dramas, science fiction, and gangster films. The worlds represented on screen vary considerably among such films. Each possible screen world establishes its own validity, and a filmmaker must convince the audience that what they are seeing is plausible and is, taken on its own terms, real.

The concept of **screen reality** pertains to the principles of time, space, character behavior, and audiovisual design that filmmakers systematically organize in a given film to create an ordered world on screen in which characters may act and in which a narrative may unfold. Obviously, different kinds of films create different representational realities on screen and relate in different ways to the actual social worlds inhabited by their flesh-and-blood spectators. A film's screen world is a systematic, artistic transformation of the viewer's personal and social frames of reference. This process of transformation is complex and multileveled. This chapter explains the basic modes or types of screen reality and why there are several different but equally acceptable modes.

The cinema can configure physical, social, or psychological reality in many different ways or modes. Cinema persuades film viewers to believe in the validity of various uniquely constituted on-screen worlds. There are five fundamental modes of representational reality on screen: **realism, expressionism, fantasy and the fantastic, cinematic self-reflexivity,** and **animation.** (For the purposes of the discussion, each mode will be treated as an ideal type. In practice, however, a given film may draw on elements from several modes.) How do these modes operate and how are films constructed from within them?

REALISM

This is one of the most commonly encountered modes of screen reality, but one must be careful in discussing it. The term *realism* is probably the most overused and overworked item in critical discussion and daily conversation about film. *Realism* is a slippery term, with meanings that can be difficult to pin down or with connotations that ill-fit the medium of cinema. Nevertheless, it is an essential term for describing some of the attributes and functions of cinema, provided one is clear and cautious in using it.

The difficulty that the cinema poses for the term *realism* is that the medium involves so much artifice. What these chapters have termed the *transformational function* of cinema is its ability to go well beyond the viewer's visual and social experience, to create novel images that have no counterpart in life, and to do so using structural elements—wide-angle lenses, for example—that transform normal vision. On the other hand, though, the camera is a recording mechanism that produces images of the things that once were in front of its lens, and these images can correspond very closely to the viewer's experience and sense of the world. Recording the things and events that were before the camera connects the cinema in a powerful way to the real world. The camera can take pictures of that world. Thus the realistic components of cinema are generally those that accord with the medium's abilities to record and correspond with experience. Since these are very important attributes, one or more concepts of realism become essential to understanding the medium. Three broad types or categories of realism clearly exist in film: **ordinary fictional realism, historical realism,** and **documentary realism.**

Ordinary Fictional Realism

In this mode, the world on screen closely resembles the one that the viewer inhabits. Time and space operate much as they do in viewers' ordinary lives. Characters belong to readily recognizable social worlds and communities (though these may differ from the viewer's), and they do not have magical powers or behave in ways that are exotic, strange, or incomprehensible. In other words, films in this category seem to have an ordinary, everyday kind of realism. This mode characterizes a large number of films. Among them is *A Beautiful Mind*, the 2001 Academy Award winner for Best Picture. Russell Crowe portrays John Nash, a brilliant mathematician whose mind was clouded by schizophrenia. Three fundamental components of ordinary fictional realism operate in *A Beautiful Mind*, as in other films belonging to this mode.

Naturalistic Visual Style

The first of these components is the lack of overly pictorial, expressive interventions in the visual style of ordinary fictional realist films. Explicit, readily recognized stylistic manipulations are generally absent. These might include extreme lighting effects, elaborate camera movements, editing for discontinuity, or elaborate production design. Such elements will call the viewer's attention to a film's formal design, emphasizing surface and texture. By contrast, the visual style of ordinary fictional realism is relatively unobtrusive. As a film's formal design becomes more elaborate and insistent, the film begins to move out of this mode.

The camerawork in *A Beautiful Mind* serves the characters, the dialogue, and the story, providing viewers with compositions that focus attention on the emotional meaning of scenes and on important events and turns in the narrative. Doing so, the camerawork does not announce its presence with stylistic flourishes. Instead, it observes the characters and their doings, and most viewers would find it difficult to recall details of the cinematography, though not details of the story that the cinematography has illuminated.

Like most films in this mode, *A Beautiful Mind* employs continuity editing to replicate, on screen, basic perceptual cues that viewers use to infer relations of time and space in their daily lives. The film uses the eyeline match, shot-reverse-shot cutting, inserts matching the master shot, the 180-degree rule, and transitional material to prepare for changes of screen direction. As a result, the editing creates very strong visual and narrative continuity. The action flows over the cuts, and the screen world built from shot to shot links up in a physically coherent way.

The editing creates a realistic impression of time and space in which the physical constancies in the world on screen do not depart in fundamental ways from those that viewers observe in their own lives. The physical positioning of characters does not change arbitrarily from shot to shot. In a similar fashion, the lighting, set, and costume design all aim for an unobtrusive naturalism. Visual design and shot construction in *A Beautiful Mind* achieve an impression of ordinary realism by avoiding cinematic designs that look excessively artificial or elaborately arranged.

Linear Narrative Structure

Films in this mode often employ a linear narrative in which the sequence of events has a clear logic, that is, in which events are chained together as a series of causes and effects. The action at the beginning of the film sets in motion events that lead to the final outcome. The narrative thus moves forward in one predominant direction. The story traces Nash's life from the onset of his schizophrenia, when he is a student at Princeton in 1947, to his winning of the Nobel prize in 1994. The story has a linear and chronological structure, and

A BEAUTIFUL MIND (UNIVERSAL/ DREAMWORKS, 2001)

Balanced compositions and camera positions that facilitate continuity editing—note how the close-ups match the master shot and use the eyeline match—help give *A Beautiful Mind* its naturalistic visual style. The visual design serves the characters and dialogue and calls little overt attention to itself. In this scene, Nash's wife (Jennifer Connelly) visits him when he is confined to a psychiatric hospital. Frame enlargements.

it shows the viewer how Nash battled his psychological disorder and ultimately triumphed over it. His victory, and his winning of the Nobel prize, gives the story a satisfying and up-beat resolution.

NONLINEAR DESIGNS Narratives that are nonlinear tend to move films out of the mode of ordinary realism. Nonlinear designs emphasize a film's style and structure, and in cases where the designs are especially elaborate, they may require the viewer to work actively to make sense of the story. The kaleidoscopic structure of Woody Allen's *Annie Hall* (1977), for example, presents the story of Alvy Singer's relationship with Annie in a nonchronological fashion, leaping in and out of different time periods in the lives of the characters. This doesn't prevent the audience from enjoying the movie, laughing at the gags, or feeling sad when Annie and Alvy finally break up. But the film's complex design sets some challenges for the audience. Because it is so fragmented, the story is not as easy to follow as it is in *A Beautiful Mind*. Furthermore, viewers notice the fragmented narrative as a *design*; the film's structure announces itself in an assertive manner.

Multiple flashbacks are a common way of breaking up what would otherwise be a linear narrative. One of the most famous films to employ multiple flashbacks is Akira Kurosawa's *Rashomon* (1950). The film's story is set in Japan's twelfth century and centers on the details surrounding the rape of a noblewoman and the death of her samurai warrior husband. The events of the crime are recalled differently by four separate narrators: the bandit accused of the rape, the noblewoman herself, the spirit of the dead samurai accessed through a medium, and a woodcutter who was an unseen witness to the tragedy. As each narrator presents a different version of the events under question, the film flashes back to the crime, but each time the story told in the flashback changes. In the case of *Rashomon*, the multiple flashbacks signal a didactic intent on the part of the filmmaker and encourage the viewer to extract the following lesson: that truth is relative and that people will perceive those versions of reality that best suit their own self-images.

Plausible Character Behavior

Characters should behave in believable ways. This is one of the most important constituents of the viewer's sense that films in this mode are realistic. When characters act in ways that are unmotivated or improbable, the viewer's level of belief in the fiction suffers, and such a viewer is likely to say that the film was not very realistic. Viewers are scrupulous judges of character behavior. If that behavior is not dictated by the demands of genre or story formula, viewers expect that it will conform with their own sense of what is right and appropriate under the circumstances.

Nash's schizophrenia becomes worse—he becomes delusional and sees people who aren't there—when he stops taking his medication. Although it has very destructive consequences, his decision not to take his pills seems entirely plausible because the pills dull his mind, which he cannot accept when it becomes difficult to work out scientific problems. Even worse, the pills have made him physically unresponsive to his wife.

Because images and stories in this mode seem so accessible, critics and viewers sometimes regard ordinary fictional realism as an easy accomplishment or as synonymous with no style at all. On the contrary, the elements of linear narrative, unobtrusive visual design, and plausible character behavior do not denote the absence of cinematic style. They should not be misunderstood as indicating a zero-degree level of style, nor should one assume that a filmmaker can readily achieve these attributes. Like the others, this mode is a highly constructed one, involving the deliberate design and manipulation of elements of structure. The appearance of ordinary realism is one that is *constructed* and *created*. That this is a paradox in no way diminishes the achievement.

Historical Realism

Ordinary fictional realism generally represents a time or place not too far removed from the social world of the film's audiences. Many films in the realist mode, however, aim at the recreation of a more distant past. Such films include Martin Scorsese's *The Age of Innocence* (1993), set in late nineteenth-century, aristocratic New York society;

CLOSE-UP

Italian Neo-realism

Filmmakers who value realism often try to achieve it by shooting on real locations and by minimizing stylistic flourishes, such as elaborate lighting designs or camera movements. By minimizing stylistic manipulation, filmmakers may feel that they get closer to a realistic portrait by getting farther from cinematic artifice and embellishment. Using real locations and non-professional actors can help to strip away common forms of stylistic adornment.

One of cinema's most important traditions of realism, in this regard, was practiced by Italian filmmakers in the 1940s and 1950s and became known as **neo-realism** (the new realism). The neo-realists produced many film classics (*Open City, Bicycle Thieves, Umberto D*), and their work has been tremendously influential.

Neo-realism developed as a reaction against the style of studio-made films that typified Italian cinema before and during World War II. In 1942, critic and screenwriter Cesare Zavattini called for a new kind of filmmaking and argued that studio-made entertainment films (like those produced by Italy's Cinecitta studio and by Hollywood) produced a false consciousness in their viewers because, by emphasizing glamour, wealth and romance, they offered distorted views of society. Zavattini urged filmmakers to use the cinema as a medium for documenting and recording authentic social reality, rather than for creating glossy, if entertaining, fantasies. He wanted filmmakers to show the everyday rather than the exceptional, to show things as they are rather than as they seem, to show the relation of the people to their society rather than to their dreams, and to show the common people, workers and peasants, rather than idealized heroes and wealthy, upper-class aristocrats.

In 1943, critic Umberto Barbara coined the term "neo-realism" to describe this approach to cinema. Luchino Visconti's *Ossessione* (1943), a dramatization of a U.S. crime novel, signaled a decisive break with Cinecitta style by capturing the bleakness and poverty of the contemporary Italian countryside, and it is often regarded as the first neo-realist film. Roberto Rossellini's *Open City* (1945) received international acclaim for its shot-on-location portrait of resistance fighters in the Nazi-occupied city of Rome. Equally powerful is Vittorio de Sica's *Bicycle Thieves* (1948),

BICYCLE THIEVES (PRODUZIONI DE SICA, 1948)

Ricci (Lamberto Maggiorani) and his wife, Maria (Lianella Carell), struggle to keep their family together when Ricci loses his job. Their struggle takes place amid widespread unemployment, and De Sica's use of locations visualizes their economic desperation. As Ricci searches for his bicycle, De Sica's camera takes the viewer on a visual journey through post-war Rome. Frame enlargement.

(continued)

about the desperate search by an unemployed laborer and his son for the stolen bicycle that the laborer needs in order to work.

Neo-realist Techniques

Neo-realists like Rossellini and de Sica preferred to shoot on location rather than using artificial sets and to employ non-actors or semi-professional actors. Lamberto Maggiorani, for example, who plays Ricci, the owner of the stolen bicycle, had been a factory worker before De Sica cast him in the film. He gives an affecting, honest performance, fresh and powerful because it does not rely on a trained actor's carefully developed techniques.

The neo-realists aimed to avoid intricate plots and fancy narratives. They believed that elaborate plotting and intricate storytelling (as in, for example, *Citizen Kane)* tended to create movies with artificial designs. Neo-realists also employed a casual, open style of composition instead of deliberate and complex framings. Camera set-ups tended to be functional and basic. The neo-realists avoided elaborate equipment like booms and dollies and the extravagant camera movement these make possible.

Lighting set-ups tended to be very spare and unadorned. The neo-realists avoided the elaborate high-contrast and low-key lighting popular in Hollywood cinema in the 1940s because it required expensive studio resources and because it communicated the glossy production values that neo-realism aimed to avoid. As with lighting, composition, and camera movement, the neo-realists used editing with restraint. They avoided montage as a way of achieving effects, believing it to be an inherently unrealistic structural device and overly manipulative of the viewer's response.

Using these simple approaches, neo-realist directors concentrated on what was in the frame rather than on the properties of the image itself. Neo-realist directors did not wish to create images so complex and self-conscious that they called attention to themselves as artificial creations. Instead, they wanted to portray authentic subjects rooted in the conditions of postwar Italian society. The results were often uncompromising and powerful. *Bicycle Thieves* ends with Ricci, driven by desperation and the inability to find his bike, attempting to steal one. The attempt fails; he is detained by a crowd and humiliated before his son, who has witnessed his father's crime. The crowd allows Ricci to go, and as the film ends, father and son disappear into the city, jobless, penniless, without prospects. In a Hollywood movie, Ricci would be a hero, and he'd find his bike. De Sica

THE 400 BLOWS (LES FILMS DU CARROSSE, 1959)

A new generation of portable, lightweight cameras and sound recording equipment enabled director Francois Truffaut to shoot this autobiographical film about his childhood on location in Paris. The city's presence in the film is so extensive that is becomes a kind of character and enhances the authenticity of the childhood world that Truffaut dramatizes. Frame enlargement.

THE BATTLE OF ALGIERS (RIALTO PICTURES, 1966)

Italian neo-realism exerted a powerful influence on this landmark film about the Algerian war for independence, waged against French forces occupying the country. Director Gillo Pontecorvo shot the film in Algeria using nonprofessional performers, some of whom were guerillas who had fought the French. In the film's many crowd scenes, Algerians played themselves, enacting emotions—nationalist pride, anger at French colonialism—that were still deeply felt. The results were extraordinary. Although the film recreates events, it feels completely authentic, as if Pontecorvo's cameras were witnessing history, catching events as they occurred. Frame enlargement.

concludes the movie in a way that is true to the situation and avoids a melodramatic triumph.

Neo-realism disappeared as a distinct film movement in the 1950s, but its methods have been highly influential. Many of the French New Wave films broke with studio traditions by shooting on location, and the city of Paris appears so extensively throughout Francois Truffaut's *The 400 Blows* (1959), Jean-Luc Godard's *Breathless* (1959), and Agnes Varda's *Cleo from 5 to 7* (1962) as to become a character in these movies. Steven Spielberg worked mainly on location for *Schindler's List* (1993) and avoided expensive equipment, using mostly hand-held cameras to achieve a more observational, less calculated style. Much of the power of Elia Kazan's *On the Waterfront* (1954) was created by shooting on the streets and dockyards of New York City. These are not neo-realist films, but they are influenced by the tradition and what it demonstrated. Stripping away the medium's customary tools and visual embellishments and emphasizing real locations—these have become essential methods used by filmmakers for creating what they feel are honest and truthful depictions of the world. ∎

James Ivory's *The Remains of the Day* (1993), set among the British aristocracy circa World War II; and Steven Spielberg's Oscar-winning *Schindler's List* (1993), which aims at a visual and cultural re-creation of Poland and Germany during the Nazi era. The most prolific filmmakers to work consistently in this mode have been director James Ivory and producer Ismail Merchant, a team whose literate and nuanced films include *The Bostonians* (1984), *A Room with a View* (1985), *Howard's End* (1992), *The Remains of the Day* (1993), and *Jefferson in Paris* (1995).

The historical realist mode works by accumulating authentic period detail. Meticulously decorated sets and costumes evoke now-vanished eras. Production

BARRY LYNDON (WARNER BROS., 1975)

Production design is a key element of style that helps establish the period setting of films in the mode of historical realism. Director Stanley Kubrick conducted extensive research into 18th-century European society, and the production design by Ken Adam and Roy Walker brings this period to life with exacting detail. Frame enlargement.

design, therefore, is extremely important in this mode. Nominees for Academy Awards in the categories of art direction and costume design are often dominated by historical realist films. In 1994, for example, these included *The Age of Innocence*, *The Remains of the Day*, and *Schindler's List*.

To achieve this detail, filmmakers often conduct extensive historical research. Janusz Kaminski, the cinematographer for *Schindler's List*, based the visual design of his images on the photography of Roman Vishniac, who photographed European Jewish communities in the 1920s and 1930s and published these photographs in a book called *A Vanished World*. Seeking to recreate these communities for the film, Kaminski emulated Vishniac's photographs. To do so, Kaminski tried to work as if he were photographing the film using the technology of 50 years ago, with no fancy lights, dollies, or tripods.

Robert Altman's *Gosford Park* (2001) portrays the codes of social etiquette that bind a house full of English aristocrats in the 1930s with the service staff that waits on them and tends to their every need. An American filmmaker, Altman knew little about this historical period and the behaviors appropriate to it, but he wanted to get it right. He therefore hired a former butler, a housemaid, and a cook, all of whom, now in their eighties, had entered domestic service in the 1930s. They became technical advisors on the film, instructing the actors and filmmakers on the precise ways to prepare meals, clean shoes, set a dinner table, and for the actors to carry themselves properly as service staff in this period. Arthur Inch, the butler advisor, for example, corrected errors of costuming. He pointed out that a livery footman always wore a white bow tie, not a black one. This and other advice helped the filmmakers capture the small, accurate details of dress and behavior that helped the film achieve its vivid historical realism.

The weight of such detail, in conjunction with characters whose behavior must conform to different social norms than those that prevail today, works to persuade viewers of the authenticity of the screen world. Many such films—*Sense and Sensibility* (1995), *Howard's End, Titanic* (1997)—depict the confining nature of social class by showing the conflict between what a person desires to do and what his or her station in life demands. Construed according to the dictates of a historical period, character behavior furnishes an important index of historical realism, provided the norms of the era are clearly understood and the behavior is plausible within those norms.

An especially powerful depiction of such a conflict, *Elizabeth* (1998), portrays the accession to the throne of Queen Elizabeth I in sixteenth-century England, from which she commenced a 40-year rule known as England's golden age. The film was shot on location in a variety of historical settings throughout the United Kingdom, including Durham Cathedral, Haddon Hall, and Bamburgh Castle, providing the film with regional authenticity. Director Shekhar Kapur envisioned the core of the film as Elizabeth's journey from youth and love to ruthlessness, power, and the renunciation of her personal needs and feelings, and he stylized the film so as to bring out this core meaning. He used white light—as in several fades to white—to suggest the transcendent religious meanings on which she would model her image as queen. To embody the ruthlessness and cruelty of the political world she inherits, Kapur chose sets made of stone. English castles at the time included wood in their design, but Kapur felt that stone would better convey the coldness and harshness of power and would imply that these structures—castles and halls—would outlast the people living in them. To emphasize the forces of history and destiny, he also shot from extremely high angles, with the camera looking sharply down on the figures below. The climactic sequence late in the film, in which Elizabeth consolidates her throne by assassinating her political enemies, is modeled on a comparable, famous sequence in *The Godfather* (1972), wherein Michael Corleone (Al Pacino) violently rids himself of his enemies. These choices of light, set, camera position, and narrative structure demonstrate that filmmakers who aim for historical realism need not be shackled by an overly literal

GOSFORD PARK (USA FILMS, 2001)

To recreate the social world of English high society in the 1930s, the filmmakers hired special consultants to advise on details of setting, dress, and behavior. The consultants, then in their eighties, had been domestic servants in the period that the film portrays. Their advice helped bring to life a now-vanished period in English history. Frame enlargement.

ALI (COLUMBIA, 2001)

This film biography of the world champion boxer includes very stylized camerawork but weaves elements of historical realism into its account of Ali's life. For the scene depicting the assassination of the Reverend Martin Luther King, the filmmakers modeled their composition on a well-known news photograph showing King's associates clustering around his body and gesturing to a rooftop where the gunfire that killed King originated. The movie image (shown here) acquires its impression of realism through its close visual relationship with the news photograph. The filmmakers intend for viewers to make this comparison. Frame enlargement.

depiction of the past. They are free to invent and to stylize their materials in ways that clarify the core meanings that are inherent in the past being depicted. Historical realism, therefore, is compatible with inventive methods of visual stylization.

Documentary Realism

Concepts of realism in the cinema are closely tied to traditions in which the camera is used as an instrument of reportage and documentation. Films that fall into this tradition are frequently termed **documentaries**, although such films may employ a wide range of styles. While the topic of documentary filmmaking is an extremely broad one, and generally falls outside the confines of this textbook, a word on the subject is in order in relation to concepts of realism.

While the camera can be used as a recording instrument to capture events, situations, and realities that may be transpiring independently of the filmmaker, the camera is also an instrument of style. A filmmaker's choices about lenses, film stocks, and camera positions and angles alter the raw material of the event unfolding before the camera so that it becomes a cinematic event that has a stylistic organization and design. It is naive, then, to believe that documentary filmmaking is the equivalent of raw reportage. A filmmaker's structural choices transform the raw material before the camera into an organized cinematic design.

BASIS OF DOCUMENTARY REALISM   Documentary films exist in a state of tension, caught between the camera's recording and transformative functions. The documentary filmmaker aims to report on an event that has occurred, yet, to do so, he or she must transform that event into cinema. How, then, does the concept of realism operate within the documentary tradition? How can realism be squared with a filmmaker's need to shape structure? Are documentary films essentially like fiction films in that they speak a language of structure and style that is unique to the cinema?

To some extent, documentaries *are* like fiction films. In each, a filmmaker confronts the same array of choices: where to put the camera, where to cut the shot, how to join several images together, whether and how to impose a narrative logic on the events to be depicted. Despite these similarities, however, two unique characteristics distinguish documentary realism from ordinary fiction films. First, audiences and most documentary filmmakers assume the existence of a noncinematic referent, some person, event, or situation that exists prior to, and independently of, the film that is being made. This assumption does not hold for fiction films in which the characters are clearly made up for the purposes of the story.

CLOSE-UP

9/11 and Documentary Film

Cinema often attains great power when it is placed in an observational mode, recording and documenting events. The attacks of September 11, 2001, elicited an outpouring of documentaries, made within a wide range of styles and points of view. There were partisan films that argued and advocated for particular ways of interpreting the meaning of the disaster. These included Michael Moore's *Fahrenheit 9/11* (2004) and a film made in response to Moore's, *Fahrenhype 9/11* (2004). There were also paranoid conspiracy films, like *Loose Change* (2007) and *The Great Conspiracy: The 9/11 News Special You Never Saw* (2005), that claimed 9/11 was an inside job, an attack by the U.S. government on its own citizens.

But the best and most significant documentaries were those that avoided partisan argumentation and aimed to observe and by doing so to provide an archival record of what happened, how the events looked and sounded, and how people responded. *WTC: The First 24 Hours* (2001), for example, breaks with documentary tradition by avoiding narrative entirely and also by not using a narrator or any interviews with subjects and witnesses. The film is an eloquent and poetic compilation of video footage taken in the rubble of the smashed Trade Center during the evening, night, and morning following the collapse. The ruined architecture is poetic and powerful, especially as captured on digital video with only ambient sound and without commentary.

The images furnish a rare glimpse inside the remains of the ruined buildings.

102 minutes elapsed between the instant that the first plane hit the North Tower of the World Trade Center and when the tower fell (the South Tower, hit later, fell first). During that interval, onlookers in Manhattan and New Jersey trained hundreds of cameras on the burning buildings and the surrounding streets, filming the unfolding catastrophe.

These professional and amateur photographers and videographers produced a massive amount of footage that filmmakers have used to create documentaries composed of candid views of the events caught on film as they were happening. *9/11* (2002) was improvised on the spot by two French filmmakers, Jules and Gedeon Naudet, who were in Manhattan making a documentary about New York's Fire Department. Jules was on the street filming a routine incident when he looked up and caught American Airlines Flight 11 striking the North Tower. He accompanied firemen into the lobby and filmed the destruction that had occurred there from burning jet fuel. And when the South Tower came down, he kept the camera running as he ran for safety.

In Memorium: New York City (2002) portrays the interval during which the buildings were burning by cutting among viewpoints provided by amateur cameras stationed throughout the city and into New

(continued)

102 MINUTES THAT CHANGED AMERICA (A&E, 2008)

The North Tower of the World Trade Center burns during the interval before the second plane hits the South Tower. The attacks of September 11 were among the most photographed events in history. Many documentaries have used the candid footage captured by witnesses to create a visual history of events as they unfolded that morning. The filmic style is observational and attains great power. Frame enlargement.

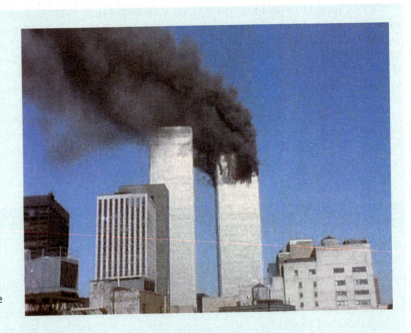

Jersey, creating a kaleidoscopic portrait composed of multiple, simultaneous views. *7 Days in September* (2004) examines the debates, vigils, and memorial services that proliferated in Manhattan following the collapse of the towers, and *102 Minutes That Changed America* (2008) uses the candid footage to provide a linear narrative of events, anchored by a digital time clock that displays when things were occurring.

Because the events were so terrible, many people taking pictures found themselves reflecting on ethical issues posed by filming atrocity. Jules Naudet, for example, turned his camera away from burn victims in the North Tower lobby, feeling strongly that no viewer of his film should see those victims. Some onlookers with cameras spontaneously filmed jumpers falling from the towers and then felt that doing so was wrong. Taking the pictures made these photographers feel that they were complicit in the deaths. In *7 Days in September*, an amateur videographer impulsively films one of the bodies falling and zooms in on the detail. But then he turned off his camera, remarking in a subsequent interview "I didn't want to have anybody else's death on my hands." In *In Memoriam: New York City* as a camera operator films a falling body, the camera's sound card captures someone standing nearby

saying, "Come on. Don't take pictures of that. What's the matter with you?"

Taking such pictures was not necessarily wrong. Such details were part of the truth of what was happening. But photographing events can be an ethical and moral act, with positive as well as negative value. By taking a picture, a photographer or filmmaker enters into a relationship with the people or events being recorded. It is important for documentary filmmakers—and for candid witnesses with cameras—to reflect on those values. These reflections, too, became part of the meaning of what happened that day.

Many viewers resented it when filmmakers created fictional or docudrama recreations of 9/11, believing that nothing was to be gained by re-enacting those events for a movie. In this sense, fiction and docudrama struggled under a burden of proof—such movies needed to justify their existence, according to many Americans. But documentary escaped this burden of proof. Documentary is an assertive mode, unlike fiction. About historic events, documentary asserts *this is*—these things occurred, and they looked and sounded and felt like such. And that assertion is commonly recognized by viewers as being important. ■

The second basis on which documentary realism rests is the perceived absence of fictionalizing elements. These might include the presence of actors performing a role or a narrative structure that alters the time chronology of the event. Audiences and most documentary filmmakers assume that fictionalizing tendencies begin with the presence of actors and an invented narrative structure. Critics charged that the documentary about the collapse of the auto industry in Flint, Michigan, *Roger and Me* (1989), violated documentary ethics because it re-arranged and re-ordered the chronology of events leading to the demise of the General Motors auto plant. The film condensed events that occurred over a long period of time so that they seemed to happen virtually overnight. Assumptions of a noncinematic referent and the absence of key fictional elements are central to the mode of documentary realism, but in practice, there is considerable flexibility for individual films to negotiate their own unique approaches with reference to these issues, particularly when a filmmaker wants to offer a stylistic commentary on the events or people the film depicts. Documentary filmmaker Errol Morris, for example, in such films as *The Thin Blue Line* (1988) and *Standard Operating Procedure* (2008), routinely uses actors to re-enact key events, but he employs music or visual cues to mark these episodes for the viewer.

DOCUMENTARY FILMMAKING—FAIR AND BALANCED?

Many viewers believe that there is a clear line dividing documentary films from fiction films, that the categories are quite distinct from one another. In fact, there is much similarity and overlap.

Robert Flaherty's *Nanook of the North* (1922) is one of the earliest documentary features and a classic of the form. Flaherty spent ten years studying and filming the Eskimo communities of Canada's Hudson Bay area, and he built his film around the charismatic hunter, Nanook. He filmed Nanook with his family, on hunting and

NANOOK OF THE NORTH (PATHE, 1922)

Robert Flaherty spent a decade filming in Canada's Hudson Bay region and eventually found Nanook, a renowned hunter of the Itivimuit Eskimo, to be the central character of his film. Backed by a French distributor after Hollywood turned it down, Flaherty's film was a critical and box office hit. With this success, the documentary feature film was born. Frame enlargement.

fishing trips, and while building igloos and repairing boots. The footage provides a vivid record of Eskimo life.

Flaherty, however, altered and embellished many of the things that he filmed. For a sequence where Nanook and others hunt a walrus, Flaherty insisted they use a harpoon, a traditional weapon but one that the men had discarded long ago in favor of rifles. The harpoon would be more dangerous for the men—the enraged and wounded walrus could drag them into the sea—but it would make a more dramatic and visually exciting film sequence, and this was Flaherty's chief objective.

In this scene and others, Flaherty changed the conditions of the lives he was film-ing so as to produce a more vivid portrait. While a documentary filmmaker today might feel more restraint than Flaherty did at the time, the essential truth is this—documentary filmmakers must satisfy the requirements of cinema, and sometimes this leads them to manipulate the situation or their footage.

Many viewers may believe that documentary films must be fair, objective, unbiased, and completely factual. Journalism, television documentaries, and Hollywood's old "March of Time" newsreels probably influenced this ideal, but it does not begin to account for the wide variety of film styles and approaches that we call *documentary*.

Let's examine three fundamental types of documentaries that differ from this ideal—films of advocacy, visual poetry, and direct cinema.

Case Study   ADVOCACY: FAHRENHEIT 9/11

The best-known documentary of recent years probably is Michael Moore's *Fahrenheit 9/11* (2004), a passion-ate attack on the Bush administration's stated reasons for going to war in Iraq. Moore uses all the filmmaker's tools—montage, music, humor, even switching to ani-mated cartoon footage—to make the film a lively one, and he injects his own persona into the film. Moore's specialty is using humor to be obnoxious and rude to politicians and institutions of power, such as when he interviews a congressman on the street and tries to per-suade him to send his own children to fight in Iraq. This was a situation that he set up and provoked rather than one that he found and filmed, but he believed that the responses he caught on film would reveal a truth that was otherwise hidden from view.

Moore also included in the film a great deal of footage and news information that had been suppressed or mini-mally covered by mainstream media. This included the infamous seven minutes of video showing President Bush continuing to read with a group of school children after learning of the World Trade Center attack, the protests that surrounded President Bush's first inauguration, the U.S. government's efforts to fly prominent Saudi Arabian executives and politicians out of the United States

following the World Trade Center attack, and graphic footage of persons wounded or killed in the Iraq War.

In all of this, Moore's point of view was crystal clear. He was advocating the ideas that the Iraq War was a criminal enterprise, that the government had lied about its reasons for going to war, and that the war was a diversion from the hunt for Osama bin Laden and the actual people who had attacked the United States.

Many viewers who disagreed with these ideas felt that Moore's film lacked the objectivity that they believed documentary requires. Others, filmmakers among them, responded in kind. *Fahrenhype 9/11* (2004), for example, critiqued Moore and his film by using his own style against him.

However, whether one finds Moore's film credible or not, there is little in it that is inconsistent with the documentary tradition because that tradition includes a clear line of advocacy filmmaking. In the 1930s, British filmmaker John Grierson supervised a series of classic films that championed the cause of working-class life. In pictures such as *Drifters* (1929), *Housing Problems* (1935), *Coal Face* (1936), and *Night Mail* (1936), Grierson used film, as he said, like a hammer and not a mirror. "I look on cinema as a pulpit," he said.

FAHRENHEIT 9/11 (MIRAMAX, 2004)
Political and social advocacy is a historical part of the documentary film tradition. Michael Moore's film—a criticism of the Bush administration's response to 9/11—is a recent example of this enduring tradition. In this scene, Moore badgers members of Congress with questions about whether they will send their own children to serve in the Iraq War. Frame enlargement.

In that same period, Pare Lorentz made two classics about the Dust Bowl and the farming crisis in Depression-era America, *The Plow That Broke the Plains* (1936) and *The River* (1937), that criticized the government policies which, in his view, had helped create these problems.

The Iraqi War was a direct stimulus for *Fahrenheit 9/11*, and wars have motivated many of the advocacy classics of documentary. Frank Capra's *Why We Fight* (1943–1945) series used footage of the German, Japanese, and Italian enemy to advocate the cause of U.S. participation in World War II. John Huston's *The Battle of San Pietro* (1944) vividly showed the violence of the Italian campaign in World War II from the standpoint of the infantrymen caught in it. Because the film was so candid in its portrait of battlefield death, it was criticized

by the Pentagon as being "against war." Huston replied, "Well, sir, whenever I make a picture that's *for* war— why, I hope you take me out and shoot me."

More recently, *Hearts and Minds* (1973) offered a strong indictment of the Vietnam War, and from the other side of the political spectrum, the "Swift Boat Veterans" critiqued the war record of presidential candidate John Kerry in a series of short films that helped cost him the election.

Political advocacy, then, is a vital and enduring part of the documentary film tradition. Objectivity does not play a role in this tradition of filmmaking. Instead, the filmmaker tries to persuade and to arouse viewers; many classic documentaries have aimed, in Grierson's words, to use film as a hammer. ▪

Visual Poetry

The documentary tradition includes another line of filmmaking in which the emphasis is on the poetic properties of cinema, on the expressive possibilities that color, light, texture, movement, editing, and the elements of sound hold for the filmmaker.

One of the most popular documentaries of recent years is *Winged Migration* (2001), a study of the flight paths of migratory birds in different areas of the world.

**WINGED MIGRATION
(BAC FILMS, 2001)**
The documentary tradition includes numerous works that aim for visual poetry, that seek rich, artistically appealing manipulations of image and sound. The extraordinary cinematography of this film celebrates majestic images of birds in flight. Frame enlargement.

Although the film features voice-over narration informing the viewer about the different birds on display, the real heart of the film is the flying sequences, composed of amazing shots that track the birds on their flight paths. Gliding through the air with the birds, the camera seems to come so close that a viewer could touch their feathers. The visual poetry in these shots is astonishingly beautiful, and they convey the sensation of flight more strongly and sensually than anything put on film before. In fact, the poetry of flight here is so powerful and pleasurable to experience that the film could have done without the voice-over narration.

Comparable films that use nature photography or outdoor action to modify one's perception of reality include deep-sea documentaries like *Aliens of the Deep* (2005), which display novel and exotic colors and shapes in the form of rarely glimpsed ocean creatures. A recent series of surfing documentaries—*Step into Liquid* (2003) and *Riding Giants* (2004)—uses special camera rigs and slow motion to take the viewer inside the experience of surfing a giant wave, slowing down time and magnifying space in ways that enhance the visual spectacle. These films are less about providing information on what surfers do than about picturing the physical thrills of riding a huge wave.

On a more abstract level, one that does not visualize a specific location or activity, are the "life out of balance" films that Godfrey Reggio has been making since the 1980s—*Koyaanisqatsi* (Life Out of Balance, 1983), *Powaqqatsi* (Life in Transformation, 1988), and *Naqoyqatsi* (Life as War, 2002). Reggio's films are a dizzying montage of footage showing landscapes, cities, people, and cultural practices across the world. Connecting the shots is a poetic logic that explores oppositions between rural and urban life, premodern communities and industrial ones, pristine nature and the ravages of pollution. The imagery expresses an underlying theme that the modern world is out of balance and is exploiting, consuming, and despoiling the environment on which all life depends. These ideas are explored in purely visual and musical terms (with music by composer Phillip Glass), without narration, spoken dialogue, or interview footage.

The visual poetry of these films is part of a long tradition in documentary, which includes the "city films" of the silent and early sound era. Dziga Vertov's *The Man With a Movie Camera* (1929) is a montage of life in the Soviet Union, showing people working,

THE MAN WITH A MOVIE CAMERA (1929)
Dziga Vertov's documentary about Russian life in city and country is a dazzling montage of shots that show ordinary people as well as the cameraman traveling around to get his shots and the film's editor assembling the footage. The poetics of Vertov's montage include these references to the machinery of cinema. The film begins with this image of the cinematographer atop a huge camera. For Vertov, documentary realism is a matter of what the camera sees and how it sees it. Frame enlargement.

playing, and sleeping and the city environment itself, traffic, monuments, and bridges. The film documents its era with poetry and self-consciousness. An impressionistic logic connects the shots, there is no narration, and through it all we see the film's cameraman, moving through traffic and climbing buildings to get the shots. We see the film's editor at work, and in a stop-motion animated sequence, we even see the camera assembling itself and walking off on its tripod.

Walter Ruttman's *Berlin: Symphony of the City* (1927) provides a dawn-to-dusk montage of the city awakening, coming to life in its daily bustle, and then slowing down again as the day ends. There is no plot, narration, or characters; instead, the visual rhythm formed by the editing of often abstract shots (e.g., a stroboscopic series showing railroad tracks and telephone lines) provides the film's organizing design. Alberto Cavalcanti's *Only the Hours* (1926) explored Paris in an identical fashion.

Filmmakers take tremendous delight in using the tools of their medium, and the documentary tradition enables them to do this. Documentary is not incompatible with poetic expression, and many of its classics aim to provide viewers with an intensely stimulating audiovisual experience.

Direct Cinema

The ideal of documentary as an "objective" medium may seem, at first, to be consistent with **direct cinema,** a style of documentary that minimizes the filmmaker's overt manipulations of the material. The style emerged in the 1960s, characterized by films that seemed to be merely observations, without advocating a set of politics or point of view, and in which the filmmaker's editorial role seemed relatively neutral.

The most famous direct cinema filmmaker is Frederick Wiseman, whose films have focused mostly on social institutions, which are identified in the title—*High School* (1968), *Law and Order* (1969), *Hospital* (1970), and *Juvenile Court* (1975). Much of Wiseman's work has been funded by and shown on public television.

Case Study   CAPTURING THE FRIEDMANS

Andrew Jarecki's *Capturing the Friedmans* (2003) is an extraordinarily powerful recent example of direct cinema. Jarecki's film portrays the destruction of a family when the father and one of the sons are arrested on charges of child molestation. Incredibly, the family made its own home movies of the terrible, raging arguments that followed the arrests, as the husband, wife, and children exchanged bitter recriminations. Jarecki used much of this footage in the film, providing a disturbingly candid portrait of family breakdown.

By seeming merely to observe what had happened, Jarecki allowed the situation to remain very ambiguous. On the one hand, the father did have child pornography stashed in the house. On the other hand, the children who made the accusations were counseled by therapists whose specialty was uncovering repressed and unconscious memories using techniques that, since then, have been discredited. Some of the children later recanted their charges.

The film is explosive in its emotional power—and much of this power is due to Jarecki's reluctance to make any overt commentary on the events. This policy sustains ambiguity and uncertainty about whether the abuse as charged actually occurred. It is very common for two people who see the film to come to very different conclusions about the father's guilt.

At the same time, Jarecki skillfully manipulates his material. The father was a gay man living a closeted, heterosexual life. Jarecki reveals this point slowly over the course of the film, and he withholds knowledge that the father's brother is gay, until a very calculated camera move late in the film reveals that the brother, interviewed throughout in a tight close-up, is in fact sitting next to his lover. The addition of this context late in the film forces the viewer to reassess the emotional dynamics of the family's life as they've been shown until now.

These aspects of the film's design point toward a basic truth about direct cinema, namely, that it does *not* provide an unfiltered, objective portrait of reality. No film can accomplish such a task, nor would one wish it to do so. A filmmaker inevitably exercises editorial control over the material. Direct cinema is a style in which this seems minimized, but it is always, in fact, a part of filmmaking. ◼

CAPTURING THE FRIEDMANS (MAGNOLIA PICTURES, 2003)

The mysteries and ambiguities of reality are explored in disturbing fashion by filmmaker Andrew Jarecki. The film examines a family's disintegration when the father and son are arrested and charged with terrible crimes. Frame enlargement.

Wiseman's films dispense with a "story" or plot, and by shooting many hours of material and carefully editing it down, he manages to show the complexity of these institutions and the ways that they wield power over people.

Wiseman's work, and direct cinema in general, was made possible by new developments in the late 1950s that led to highly mobile cameras and synchronized sound recorders. These enabled documentary film for the first time to make extensive use of interviews and recorded dialogue in natural, relatively uncontrolled settings. Thus Wiseman could capture and show the remarks of people, naturally and in action, in the institutions he studied.

Documentary Today

Documentary is more alive and vital today than perhaps at any point in its long history. Moreover, in the last few years, a significant number of films have "crossed over" into mainstream distribution, attracting audiences that are much broader than is typical for the form. *March of the Penguins* (2005) is an impressive example, grossing $117 million worldwide after eight months in release. Warner Independent Pictures and National Geographic Feature Films acquired a French film entitled *The Emperor's Journey,* directed by Luc Jacquet. Warner and National Geographic retitled the film, added a new music score, and eliminated the talking penguins of the original, replacing their voices with spoken narration by Morgan Freeman. The resulting film's popularity and Academy Award recognition showed how powerful documentaries have become in today's film culture. In addition to such pictures as *Capturing the Friedmans, Fahrenheit 9/11,* and *Step into Liquid,* others include *Spellbound* (2002), a highly dramatic portrait of children's spelling bee competitions; *The Fog of War* (2003), an evocative series of interviews with Robert McNamara, the architect of the Vietnam War; *Enron: The Smartest Guys in the Room* (2005), about the crash of the Enron Corporation and its fraudulent practices; and *Murderball* (2005), about a bone-crunching sport played by quadriplegics.

The Internet provides documentary filmmakers with a new means of sales and distribution. Producer–director Robert Greenwald's *Outfoxed: Rupert Murdoch's War on Journalism* (2004) and *Uncovered: The War on Iraq* (2004) were principally sold and distributed via the Internet, bypassing the traditional distribution routes of theaters and television.

Many have remarked that the best stories on film in the last few years have been found in documentaries. Certainly, it is the documentary that most connects film with the conditions of our lives, and the form is quite flexible, enabling filmmakers to use cinema at the height of their artistic powers.

SUPER SIZE ME (HART SHARP, 2004)

Filmmaker Morgan Spurlock used himself as the guinea pig in this documentary about the health effects of eating fast food. Spurlock spent a month eating three meals a day at McDonald's and turned the camera on himself, filming the physical and psychological changes that resulted. Made for $65,000, the film grossed nearly $30 million, and its popular impact led to McDonald's discontinuing its Super Size portions. Frame enlargement.

Distribution and sales of DVD via the Internet enable film-makers to take their work directly to an audience, bypassing traditional the-atrical distribution. Robert Greenwald used the Internet and political lobbying group MoveOn.org as primary delivery systems for this cri-tique of news reporting on the Fox television network. Nontraditional approaches to production and distribution hold great promise for docu-mentary filmmakers today. Frame enlargement.

MOCKUMENTARIES   Suppose that a filmmaker deliberately uses a style of documen-tary filmmaking but in a wholly fictitious context. To the extent that documentary is a film *practice*—specifying a method of working as well as stylistic designs that are permissible and those that are not—there is nothing to prevent a filmmaker from imitating this practice, that is, from making a fake documentary, or **mocku-mentary**, such as *The Blair Witch Project*. Rob Reiner's *This Is Spinal Tap* (1984) is a well-known example of a fake documentary. In the film, director Reiner plays fic-titious director Marty DiBergi who is making a documentary film about British rock group Spinal Tap. No such group exists, of course, except in the pretend world of this film parody, which accurately skewers many of the conventions of rock docu-mentaries.

The film opens with Reiner, as DiBergi, seated by a camera and lighting equip-ment as he tells viewers about his first meeting with Spinal Tap in 1966 and explains the genesis of what he calls a rockumentary, that is, a documentary about rock. DiBergi talks directly into the camera with cinema equipment prominently displayed behind him. Because viewers think documentaries are more real than fiction films, shrewd filmmakers can emphasize this impression by displaying the cinema equipment used to create the images on screen. Such an on-screen display of camera equipment is unthinkable in the mode of ordinary fictional realism, but within documentary real-ism, it serves to authenticate the special nonfiction status of the film by communicat-ing to the audience that the filmmaker is not trying to "fool" viewers into mistaking the film's images for reality itself.

Other codes of rock documentaries that the film employs include people-on-the-street interviews with fans talking about what Tap means to them. These interviews are intercut with faked concert footage and faked behind-the-scenes glimpses of backstage preparation for concerts. Other faked documentary codes include a series of interviews with the band members (all of whom, of course, are actors) and even faked black-and-white kinescope

THIS IS SPINAL TAP (EMBASSY PICTURES, 1984)

This Is Spinal Tap applies documentary techniques to completely fictitious events and characters. The film looks like a documentary but is really an elaborate hoax. Representational reality may be unreliable or ironic. In the case of *This Is Spinal Tap*, the filmmaker expects the audience to recognize the irony. Frame enlargement.

footage, supposedly from 1965, dramatizing an early television appearance by Tap (like the Beatles on Ed Sullivan).

The popularity of *This Is Spinal Tap* has led to other films in the fake documentary mode. Among the best are three by Christopher Guest—*Waiting for Guffman* (1997), about a small-town theater troupe putting on a show; *Best in Show* (2000), about the nutty contestants in a prestigious dog show; and *A Mighty Wind* (2003), about competing styles of folk music. Like *Spinal Tap*, these films imitate many of the rules of documentary filmmaking, but much of their humor depends on the viewer getting the ironies and appreciating the elaborate fakery.

BEST IN SHOW (WARNER BROS., 2000)

Filmmaker Christopher Guest has specialized in fake documentaries. This one is a hilarious comedy about a group of oddballs who've entered their dogs in a prestigious show. Fake interviews and apparently impromptu situations abound. Frame enlargement.

EXPRESSIONISM

Expressionism is an extremely stylized mode of screen reality in which filmmakers use visual distortion to suggest emotional, social, or psychological disturbances or abnormalities. The distortions may be subtle, but most often they are manifest and explicit. In this regard, expressionism is an antirealist mode that aims to move far from naturalism, emphasizing instead strange or bizarrely poetic designs using lighting, color, lenses, camera position, and set design. Expressionism in its pure form, as it characterized German cinema in the 1920s, is distinct from expressionism as it survives in contemporary cinema.

Classic German Expressionism

The expressionist mode in its purest form is found in 1920s German cinema. Expressionism began in German painting and theater in 1908 and, by the 1920s, had spread to the cinema, where it characterized a series of classic films including *The Cabinet of Dr. Caligari* (1920), *Nosferatu* (1922), an early version of Dracula, and the science fiction classic *Metropolis* (1926).

In these and other films of the early German cinema, the expressionist style was overtly opposed to realism; it emphasized elaborate distortions in the mise-en-scène. Lighting designs employed a prevalence of shadows and violent visual contrast. Decor and set design used aberrant architectural forms to create dwellings whose off-kilter, skewed designs embodied decentered, anxiety-ridden screen worlds. Normal, rectilinear architectural forms (dwellings where walls, floor, and ceiling are at right angles to each other and in parallel planes) were replaced with skewed structures built with diagonals and nonparallel planes.

These filmmakers integrated the actors' physical appearance and movements with the architectural forms. In the accompanying illustration from F. W. Murnau's *Nosferatu*, the vampire's thin, elongated body is linked at a visual level

NOSFERATU (1922)

Expressionistic integration of character and decor in *Nosferatu*. Expressionist distortions included architectural design as well as the human figure. Note how the vampire's elongated body fits within the arched doorway. The expressionist style linked people and settings to form a uniquely stylized screen reality. Frame enlargement.

with the arched door frame in which he lingers before pouncing on his victim. Expressionist acting frequently employed a distorted physical appearance, and as the image from *Nosferatu* illustrates, these strange body types functioned as expressive forms and were integrated seamlessly with the shapes and textures of the set design.

Expressionist filmmakers often used odd camera angles to enhance the decentering of the screen world. The camera's positioning, the lighting design, and the decor all work together to achieve maximum distortion in expressionist mise-en-scène. These distortions often were correlated with a particular kind of subject matter. Characters might be grotesques, as in the vampires of *Nosferatu* or the mad doctor in *Metropolis*. They inhabited fantasy realms of myth, as in Fritz Lang's *Seigfried*, or futuristic worlds, as in Lang's *Metropolis*. Correlated with these extrahuman or subhuman characters were their extreme and sometimes deranged emotional states. The terror of the victim of the sleepwalking killer in *The Cabinet of Dr. Caligari* and the killer's own anxiety-laden flight across the rooftops are expressively conveyed in the wild decor pictured in the on page 332 illustration.

German expressionism entered the United States via a wave of émigré German filmmakers working in Hollywood, and the style was popularized in the series of horror films produced in the 1930s at Universal Studios. James Whale's 1931 production of *Frankenstein* features the grotesque characters and diagonal visual forms that link it closely with the German horror and fantasy films that flourished in the 1920s. In the opening scene, Dr. Frankenstein and his evil assistant Fritz hide in a graveyard, waiting until the gravediggers have finished burying a body. They plan to dig it up and steal the corpse for use in their gruesome medical experiments. Visual designs emphasizing extreme antirealism and distortion effectively convey the film's horror content.

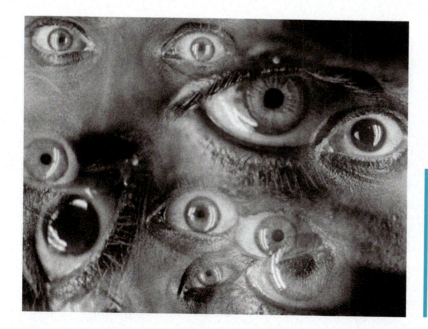

METROPOLIS (1926) (UFA, 1926)

Multiple in-camera exposures helped to produce this startling image of a crowd of excited spectators at a futuristic nightclub. Expressionism favors optical distortions, dream-like imagery, and visual poetry instead of realist designs. Frame enlargement.

THE CABINET OF DR. CALIGARI (1919)

Expressionist set design created a bizarre, strange, off-kilter world in the classic *The Cabinet of Dr. Caligari*, the first expressionist film. Note the disturbing diagonal lines suggesting disorder and instability throughout the set in place of normal rectilinear architecture. Frame enlargement.

Contemporary Expressionism

While the pure expressionism characterizing German cinema of the 1920s is rarely found in contemporary filmmaking, modern directors often employ the visual distortions of expressionist style.

OTHER RECENT CASES   More recent productions have drawn on the expressionist heritage. Spike Lee's *Crooklyn* (1994) features a 20-minute sequence shot with uncorrected anamorphic perspective—making the characters and settings look thin and elongated—to visualize a city girl's disorientation at living in the suburbs. One of the chief villains in Tim Burton's *Batman Returns* (1992) is the industrialist

FRANKENSTEIN (UNIVERSAL STUDIOS, 1931)

Expressionist set design—note the sloping diagonals—in the Universal horror genre. Dr. Frankenstein (Colin Clive) digs up a fresh corpse for his experiments. Subsequently, his monster rages against confinement in a castle cell. Frame enlargements.

Case Study ALFRED HITCHCOCK

Alfred Hitchcock was probably the best-known filmmaker to use expressionism as an ongoing feature of his work. In *Psycho* (1960), a striking low-angle shot of Norman Bates, the psychopathic killer, dehumanizes his face. By emphasizing the working of his gullet as he chews on some candy, it transforms him visually into a birdlike creature. This is appropriate because Norman is a taxidermist by hobby and keeps his office stuffed with birds of prey, which he has mounted on the walls. Hitchcock said that these birds are perfect symbols of Norman himself. They are birds of the night—predators—and he sees his own guilt mirrored in their eyes.

In *Strangers on a Train* (1951), a demented fan of a famous tennis player kills the athlete's greedy and selfish wife, believing that he is doing the celebrity a favor. Hitchcock films the killing from a memorably distorted perspective, in an image refracted by the wife's eyeglasses, which have fallen to the ground in her struggles with the killer. After she is dead, the killer reaches for the glasses, and the refracted image gives him giant lobster hands, dehumanizing him in a poetic manner (in the film's first scene, he wears a vulgar, lobster-print necktie).

In *Notorious* (1946), about a woman who is coerced into spying for the U.S. government, an early scene shows her waking up with a hangover. She looks up and sees a government agent hovering in the doorway of her bedroom. Hitchcock employs a subjective expressionistic shot to represent her point of view and to make the agent seem very threatening and sinister. The agent appears as a silhouette. As he walks toward her and she turns her head to look up at him, tracking his movements, his figure pirouettes upside down across her field of vision.

In *Vertigo* (1958), to suggest the approaching despair and madness of the detective hero (James Stewart), Hitchcock included a completely artificial sequence. The detective's nightmare hallucination is represented, in part, through animation. A bouquet of flowers, held by a ghostly character in the film,

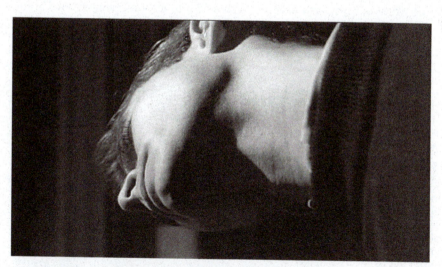

PSYCHO (PARAMOUNT PICTURES, 1960)

This strange, low-angle shot of Norman Bates (Anthony Perkins) in *Psycho* turns him into a bird. This adds a symbolic dimension to the narrative because Norman is a taxidermist specializing in stuffing predatory birds. The bizarre image suggests that Norman, too, is a predator, a creature of the night, like his birds. Hitchcock appreciated the special power of expressionistically distorted images to transform normal visual reality. Frame enlargement.

(continued)

STRANGERS ON A TRAIN (WARNER BROS.,1951)

Hitchcock shows a murder as the distorted reflection in the lens of a pair of discarded eyeglasses. Having finished with his victim, the killer then reaches for the glasses, and the optical distortion turns his hand into a giant lobster claw. Frame enlargements.

suddenly splits apart and the petals fly menacingly toward the viewer. Hitchcock departs from realism here so thoroughly that it sometimes confuses modern viewers, uncertain whether they are seeing an example of inferior visual effects or a genuinely radical visual design.

As these examples from Hitchcock's cinema illustrate, the director learned from the expressionists about the power of a distorted visual image and employed such designs systematically throughout his career when he needed to suggest intensified states of emotional disturbance. ◼

NOTORIOUS (RKO, 1946)

In *Notorious*, Cary Grant, as an American government agent, appears in this bizarre, upside-down perspective. The angular distortion represents the anxious point of view of a character reclining on a bed. In this respect, the visually unstable point of view replicates the original aims of German expressionism, which were to visually represent subjective states of mind. Frame enlargement.

NOTORIOUS (RKO, 1946)
With a subtle expressionistic touch, Hitchcock designs this shot from *Notorious* so that the cup of poison (foreground) looms gigantically beside the woman who is being poisoned (Ingrid Bergman, background). To get the shot, Hitchcock instructed his prop crew to construct an enormous cup and then placed the camera in this low-angle position to emphasize its size. Frame enlargement.

Max Schreck (Christopher Walken). In name and appearance, he evokes the 1920s German classics. "Max Schreck" was the name of the actor who played the vampire in *Nosferatu,* and as the character appears in Burton's film, he sports a flamboyant shock of white hair that makes him look like the mad scientist Rotwang in Fritz Lang's *Metropolis.* In other respects as well, Burton's film evokes classic expressionist mise-en-scène. The huge fireplace in Bruce Wayne's mansion strongly resembles the giant fireplace used in *Bride of Frankenstein* (1935). These details of design and character are explicit homages to the German cinema, used to explicitly evoke some of its best-known stylistic features.

Martin Scorsese's *Cape Fear* (1992) employs a number of striking expressionistic motifs in the opening title design. The film deals with a vengeful psychopath, newly released from prison, who wreaks a terrible plan of destruction on the family of the lawyer he blames for his conviction. The film's title is derived from the river in North Carolina where the climax occurs. The title also evokes, in a poetic and symbolic manner, the climate of terror and anxiety that is established in the story when the psychopath begins stalking and tormenting the lawyer's family.

During the opening credits, the waters of the Cape Fear River reflect several distorted expressionistic forms. A predatory bird swoops down near the surface of the water, its shadow extended and disturbed by the river's rippling surface. Superimposed over the water is a terror-stricken eye, glancing about with extreme agitation. Later in the sequence, a screaming mouth appears, the teeth fearsomely exposed. Next looms a dark, ominous figure of a man, skewed on a diagonal. Finally, a drop of blood drips from the top to the bottom of the screen, bringing with it a wave of red color.

A dissolve links the end of the credit sequence to a close-up of the eyes of the lawyer's young daughter, viewed as a negative image. Here, Scorsese revived an expressionist technique from Murnau's vampire classic *Nosferatu.* To suggest the phantom world, Murnau showed Dracula's coach and horses as film negatives. Scorsese pulls viewers out of the expressionist title sequence and inserts them into the world of the

NIGHT OF THE HUNTER (UNITED ARTISTS, 1955)

For this story about a psychotic preacher (played by Robert Mitchum, right), director Charles Laughton used many visual elements drawn from silent cinema. These included the expressionist tradition of set design and chiaroscuro lighting. Note how Mitchum's pose and raised arm harmonize with the sloping walls of the set, integrating character and architecture in the visual manner that expressionists preferred. In this scene, set design and lighting make the bedroom look like a chapel. The slashing blades of light mimic the knife that Preacher Harry will use to murder Willa Harper (Shelly Winters, on bed, right). Frame enlargement.

LEMONY SNICKET'S A SERIES OF UNFORTUNATE EVENTS (PARAMOUNT, 2004)

The set design of Count Olaf's house recalls classic German expressionism in its use of diagonals and sloping graphic elements. The appearance is unsettling and disorderly, an effective visual portrait of this villain's lair. Frame enlargement.

SWEENEY TODD: THE DEMON BARBER OF FLEET STREET (DREAMWORKS, 2007)

Director Tim Burton often incorporates the expressionist mode into his films, such as *Batman Returns* (1992) and *Sleepy Hollow* (1999). For this set representing the room that Sweeney (Johnny Depp) rents from Mrs. Lovett (Helena Bonham Carter), Burton asked his production designer to incorporate the large slanting window because it would be reminiscent of classic German expressionism. Frame enlargement.

narrative proper by using negative imagery, suggesting, at a visual level what the narrative will establish, a world in which human behavior and values are dangerously inverted.

Used by filmmakers as diverse as Hitchcock, Burton, and Scorsese, expressionism constitutes a powerful mode of screen reality permitting a filmmaker to break with realism and skew images and characters in ways expressive of social or psychological abnormality. In this regard, the style has transcended the context (silent German cinema) in which it first flourished to become an essential and ongoing mode of screen reality.

FANTASY AND THE FANTASTIC

This mode of screen reality sometimes overlaps with expressionism (as, for example, in the case of *Batman Returns*, 1992). There are, however, important distinctions between them. Expressionism can be employed within a relatively naturalistic framework, as in the films of Alfred Hitchcock, where the expressionistic elements are of relatively brief duration and occur within scenes whose overall style is more naturalistic. By contrast, in films employing a fantasy or fantastic mode, settings and subjects, characters, and narrative time are often displaced from the viewer's own realm into other realms, sometimes futuristic ones, where normal laws of time and space may not apply. Characters might have superpowers, like Superman, or advanced technology that lends them superpowers,

A TRIP TO THE MOON (1902)

One of the cinema's fundamental roots lies in fantasy. Since the inception of the medium, filmmakers have used it to picture the imagination. Early filmmaker Georges Melies filmed a band of intrepid astronomers traveling to the moon and dreamed up this memorable image, picturing their spaceship landing in the eye of the man in the moon. Frame enlargement.

like Robocop. Adventurers can pilot starships to new galaxies as in *Star Wars*, and artificial beings, created by mad inventors, can become suburban hairdressers, like Edward Scissorhands. Angels can assume material form and fall in love with humans, as in *City of Angels*.

This mode is as old as cinema. One of the earliest films was Georges Melies's *A Trip to the Moon* (1902), which took viewers on the titular journey and depicted the moon as inhabited by a species of lizard people who chase their visitors from Earth merrily about. *A Trip to the Moon* is a science fiction fantasy, but the mode of fantasy in cinema transcends genre. Fantasy is essential to science fiction but it also can characterize romance (*Always, The Ghost and Mrs. Muir, City of Angels, Ghost*), drama (*Stairway to Heaven*), the war film (*A Guy Named Joe*), and Arthurian legend (*Excalibur, First Knight*).

The success of the *Lord of the Rings* film trilogy has made fantasy into one of the currently most popular modes of filmmaking. *Rings*-style films about magical lands, sorcery, mythical creatures, and children embarking on epic adventures have proliferated in recent years. They include *The Chronicles of Narnia: The Lion, the Witch and the Wardrobe* (2005), *The Chronicles of Narnia: Prince Caspian* (2008), *Nim's Island* (2008), *The Bridge to Terabithia* (2007), *The Golden Compass* (2007), *Beowulf* (2007), and *Eragon* (2006).

Ways of Making Fantasy Credible

Viewers are willing, even eager, to suspend disbelief in order to enter an enchanting, amusing, or thrilling fantasy world. Filmmakers, though, have to work to sustain this willingness and make the unreal seem credible for the duration of the film. One way of doing this is to set the fantasy within recognizably real surroundings, as in *City of Angels* (1998), where well-known Los Angeles settings (and some in San Francisco) provide a convincing locale for the action. So intent were the *City of Angels* filmmakers on evoking the realities of an urban setting that they placed the actors (Nicolas

THE CHRONICLES OF NARNIA: THE LION, THE WITCH AND THE WARDROBE (DISNEY, 2005)

The success of *The Lord of the Rings* films has led to many more productions in the mode of fantasy. Among the most successful have been adaptations of C.S. Lewis's *Chronicles of Narnia* novels, about the adventures of four children in the magical, mythical kingdom of Narnia. Frame enlargement.

Cage and Dennis Franz) high atop a real skyscraper construction site for a dialogue scene that has the characters sitting on a girder overlooking the city. Having evoked place in this detailed manner, the film shifts easily into its moments of explicit fantasy—angels defying time and space to move with lightning speed, angels guiding the dying into a transcendent realm of light, an angel's hand unharmed by a knife that has sliced through his finger.

Another effective way to establish the credibility of a fantasy world is through the sheer accumulation of narrative detail. The more thoroughly a filmmaker can render the fantasy world, the richer its tapestry of detail—characters, places, events—the more convincing it will come to seem to viewers. George Lucas is a master at working in this manner. The hugeness of his *Star Wars* project—encompassing to date six films produced over more than two decades—and the expanse and wealth of story information that he gave to his mythopoetic world are quite unprecedented in modern cinema. By beginning his saga in the middle of the story (*Star Wars* is "Episode IV"), Lucas abruptly plunged his viewers into a well-defined fantasy universe, and each subsequent film elaborated on the intricate network of characters and locations that the films were constructing, installment by installment. By the end of *Return of the Jedi*, this imaginative universe contained a galaxy of uniquely differentiated and vividly rendered planets where critical episodes of the story line occur. *The Empire Strikes Back* opens on the ice world of Hoth and a deadly clash between the Empire and the rebel forces, which have gone into hiding after launching (from the planet of Yavin 4) their assault on the first Death Star in *Star Wars*. The heroes, Luke, Han, and Princess Leia, escape the battle, with Luke journeying to the jungle world of Dagobah, where he encounters the Zen-like but diminutive Yoda. Han and Leia seek refuge on Bespin in the Cloud City run by Lando Calrissian. Darth Vader, though, sets a trap, freeze-dries Han, and sends him to Tatooine, the desert world where Luke grew up and where the toad-like gangster Jabba the Hut has his headquarters. The climax of the Empire–rebel struggle occurs in *Return of the Jedi* on Endor, a forest planet that is home to the Ewok, a race of furry, cute, but fierce rebel allies. Filling out this remarkably detailed gallery of places and characters are bounty hunters (Boba Fett, Greedo), monsters (the sand-dwelling Sarlacc), and Wild West cantinas (Mos Eisley). The elaborate effects that Lucas and his artists created for the films are certainly a major part of their appeal. But the intricately layered narrative details extending across six films arguably have done more to establish the fantasy and make it convincing.

A third way of establishing credibility in this mode is by using production design to make unreal settings seem tangible and convincing. Consider the work of Tim Burton, one of the most popular filmmakers currently working in fantasy. His films include *Beetlejuice* (1988), *Batman* (1989), *Edward Scissorhands* (1990), *Batman Returns* (1992), *Mars Attacks! (1996),* and *The Legend of Sleepy Hollow* (1999) and, as producer, *The Nightmare Before Christmas* (1993). *Batman* features a brilliant production design by Anton Furst that evokes Gotham City as a dark, congested metropolis rife with crime. As in other films about dark cities of the future—*Blade Runner* (1982), *Dark City* (1998), and *The Matrix* (1999)—the metropolis of *Batman* is one of the stars of the film, taking a commanding visual presence alongside the major characters. Rendered with sets, mattes, and miniature models, Gotham is a wholly imaginary creation, but its visual design is so powerful that it comes convincingly to life.

In *Edward Scissorhands*, production designer Bo Welch daringly drops Edward's medieval castle into the middle of suburbia, even showing it perched ominously at the end of a street of trim houses with manicured lawns. It's an ostentatious design concept, almost daring the audience to react with disbelief. Yet, when a saleswoman (Dianne Wiest) calls on its occupant, the castle proves to be adorned with so much Gothic detail that it becomes unquestionably *real*.

In fantasy, the real is limited only by a filmmaker's imagination, and whatever an audience can be persuaded to believe in becomes real for this mode. In this regard, fantasy offers filmmakers tremendous flexibility of style and freedom of invention

EDWARD SCISSORHANDS (20TH CENTURY FOX, 1990)
All things are possible in fantasy, even a gothic castle perched in the middle of suburbia. Frame enlargement.

because audiences do not require plausibility in the way that they ask it from a film-maker working in the realist mode. An enduring cliché of science fiction films demonstrates the freedom to invent that fantasy offers its filmmakers. Except mainly for Stanley Kubrick's *2001: A Space Odyssey* (1968), which showed spacecraft gliding silently through space, most science fiction spacecraft emit loud, powerful rumblings from their engines. In *Star Wars'* first scene, for example, a series of spaceships approaches the camera, and then, in a reverse angle cut, the group flies away. The roar of the engines gives these visual-effects creations an impressive physicality. Multichannel sound, with the dedicated bass channel, has accentuated this cliché because now spacecraft can emit wall-shaking low-frequency sound as they pass by. Doppler effects are routinely employed to create the changes in pitch (higher pitch for approaching objects, lower for receding ones) correlated with movement.

While the Doppler effects are accurate for Earth-bound experience, in the outer-space context they are impossible. In space there is no sound because there is no medium, such as the air or atmosphere on earth, to transport sound waves. Consequently, spaceships should make no perceivable noise at all. But this would be dramatically flat and uninteresting. Thus the cliché has developed—which viewers happily endorse—that spaceships traveling through a void make noise.

Fantasy and Cinema Technology

The fantasy mode is tremendously popular throughout the world. The *Harry Potter, Lord of the Rings, Spider-Man,* and *Star Wars* series have generated billions of dollars in global markets. To take advantage of this popularity, fantasy films now showcase the industry's most important technological advances. Digital multichannel sound debuted in three high-profile fantasy films. Dolby Digital premiered its system in *Batman Returns* (1992). Digital Theater Systems (DTS) unveiled its CD-playback system with *Jurassic Park* (1993). Sony Dynamic Digital Sound (SDDS) came online in *The Last Action Hero* (1993).

George Lucas is a major figure in modern movie fantasy and in pushing the industry to develop the next generation of effects technology. These two attributes are interconnected. In 1975, he created Industrial Light and Magic (ILM), which became the industry's premiere effects house, creating effects for dozens of major productions—the *Star Trek* series, the *Indiana Jones* series, *Who Framed Roger Rabbit* (1988), and *Jurassic Park* (1993)—and doing research on the next generation of effects tools, those that would be supplied by digital imaging and digital methods of production. By the mid-eighties, Lucasfilm had a computer-assisted electronic editor (EditDroid) online and an all-digital sound editor (SoundDroid) used to mix and create effects for *Indiana Jones and the Temple of Doom*. To achieve cutting-edge sound in the films that he produced, Lucas constructed the industry's state-of-the-art postproduction sound facility, the Technical Building at Skywalker Ranch, Lucas's corporate headquarters in Marin, California.

As with sound, the revolution in digital imaging developed in cinema for films in the fantasy mode. Computer-animated sequences first appeared in *Future World* (1976), *Tron* (1982), *The Last Starfighter* (1984), and *Star Trek II: The Wrath of Khan* (1982), but the box-office failure of the first three pictures delayed the widespread application of digital imaging for several years. But, by the late eighties and early nineties, digital imaging had attained new levels of sophistication, and the next generation of digital effects films created tremendous interest in the technology

WHO FRAMED ROGER RABBIT (DISNEY, 1988); THE MASK (NEW LINE, 1994)

Fantasy has been on the cutting edge for new developments in cinema technology. Traditional (nondigital) methods of compositing visual effects images reached their zenith in *Who Framed Roger Rabbit*, an expert blend of live action with animated characters. The widespread application of digital imaging in the years following *Roger Rabbit* took the visual potential of cinema into new dimensions. Fantasy films showcased these breakthroughs. Frame enlargements.

throughout the industry and excited audiences with fantasy creatures that seemed impossibly real: the slithery water alien in *The Abyss* (1989), the gleaming, shape-shifting *Terminator 2* (1991), and the dinosaurs of the *Jurassic Park* series (1993, 1997, 2001).

The vividness of Spielberg's dinosaurs—created by ILM—convinced George Lucas to return to his *Star Wars* series since digital effects offered a new arsenal of powerful tools for envisioning anything a filmmaker could imagine. Lucas had long wanted to shift the industry toward all-digital methods of filmmaking, and he pursued this ambition with the new *Star Wars* films. *Attack of the Clones* (2002) was shot on digital cameras that were custom-built for Lucas by Sony, and the film was exhibited theatrically in digital format at selected locations around the country. Lucas's ambitions are big ones, and the industry is transforming itself to meet them. The long-term result will be comparable with the coming of sound in the late 1920s; that is, it will change everything. It will cut the industry off from the photomechanical technology to which it has been wedded since its inception and take it into an all-electronic realm.

The fantasy mode has been a key player in this drama. It is now synonymous with state-of-the-art cinema technology. In this regard, fantasy is tremendously important for contemporary cinema. It generates huge box office success and is propelling the industry into its all-digital future.

CLOSE-UP

Pan's Labyrinth (2006)

Fantasy constructs alternative worlds to our own. What is the relationship between the two? What role or purpose does fantasy fulfill? Pan's Labyrinth, an international award-winning film written and directed by Guillermo del Toro, examines these questions by creating a parable about a young girl's encounters with a mysterious faun that lives inside an old maze or labyrinth.

The story takes place in Spain during the fascist era of World War II, and Ofelia (Ivana Baquero) travels with her mother, Carmen, to a military post where Captain Vidal (Sergi Lopez I Ayats), her stepfather and her mother's husband, is hunting guerillas that are fighting against the country's military dictatorship.

Vidal is a cruel man who delights in murder and torture, and he values Ofelia's mother only for the son she will bear him. At the post, Ofelia encounters the faun who tells her she is the reincarnation of a princess who lived with her parents in the Underground Realm. Princess Moanna grew curious about the human world, left her parents, and went above, where she grew old, forgot her past, and died, and all traces of her vanished from the

PAN'S LABYRINTH (WARNER BROS., 2006)
The faun comforts Ofelia after the death of her mother and promises her she can enter the safety of the Underground Realm if she performs a final task. Del Toro's extraordinary film explores the role fantasy plays in a world of darkness and cruelty. Frame enlargement.

(continued)

world, a fate that befalls all people. But her parents believed always that her spirit would return and live forever in the Underground Realm.

The faun tells Ofelia she is the princess and that she must perform three tasks to prove herself worthy of returning. Del Toro intercuts this plot line with Vidal's harsh treatment of Carmen and his brutal interrogations of captured guerillas. Carmen's pregnancy goes bad, and she dies while giving birth.

Fearing for the life of her infant brother, and on the faun's instructions, Ofelia abducts him from Vidal's quarters and rushes into the maze, pursued by Vidal. He seizes the child and callously shoots Ofelia with his pistol before the anti-fascist guerillas capture and execute him. Mercedes, Vidal's housekeeper who became friends with Ofelia, finds her body and weeps beside it.

As she dies, and in a colorful sequence with glowing imagery, Ofelia appears in the Underground Realm where she is joyously welcomed home by her parents and by the faun. Del Toro has counterpointed the film's two narrative lines. Ofelia's adventures with the faun and her visit to the underworld kingdom have been entwined with the brutal political drama of Captain Vidal's efforts to torture and kill the anti-fascist resistance fighters. They've been entwined as well with Ofelia's experiences of violence, cruelty, and loss.

Furthermore, the film begins with imagery of Ofelia bleeding and dying from the gunshot wound, with the visit to Vidal's post, her mother's death, and the experiences with the faun presented as a flashback at the moment of her death. As a narrator explains the legend of Princess Moanna, a close-up of Ofelia's lifeless face shows time moving backward, her blood flowing back into her body rather than out of it.

Del Toro thus poses a question about the Underground Realm—is it real? Does Ofelia find an immortality with her lost parents that is denied ordinary people, each of whom is fated to die and vanish from the earth? Are the faun and the mythical kingdom true? Or are they a psychological fantasy that provides Ofelia with some comfort in the final moments of her life but has no authenticity beyond this function?

Del Toro shows that Ofelia's fantasy is a response to unbearable cruelty in a world of pain and violence that overwhelms her. The Underground Realm provides her with a safe and protected space. Is this the role that fantasy plays in human life—by creating imaginary worlds as alternatives to the real one, does it make life less unbearable?

The film's power lies in its ambiguity. Del Toro leaves open both possibilities—that the Underground Realm is real and, alternatively, that it represents the final flicker of consciousness in a dying mind. The ambiguity gives the film its poetic force and its haunting power. In *Pan's Labyrinth*, Del Toro constructs a beautiful but scary parable about fantasy and the human longing for an escape from pain and mortality. ■

CINEMATIC SELF-REFLEXIVITY

However unusual or fantastic their settings and design, the other modes of screen reality aim to persuade the viewer that the world depicted on screen is real, that it is, for the purposes of the narrative, a valid world whose premises are not questioned within the body of the film. The fantasy world that George Lucas creates in the *Star Wars* films is, taken on its own terms, a self-enclosed and internally valid one.

By contrast, the self-reflexive mode makes no pretense that the world represented on screen is anything other than a filmic construction. Films in this mode remind viewers that what they are watching is, after all, a movie. Self-reflexive films tell the viewer that the reality on screen is a movie reality. These acknowledgments take a variety of forms. Typically, they fall into two categories. They tend to be either comic or made with didactic intent.

ANNIE HALL (UNITED ARTISTS, 1977)

Woody Allen, as Alvy Singer, turns toward the camera and speaks to the film's viewers in this scene from *Annie Hall*. Allen breaks the illusion of make-believe in a moment of comic self-reflexivity. In popular films, self-reflexivity is quite common in comedy but rare in drama. Frame enlargement.

Case Study AUSTIN POWERS *AND* KILL BILL

Contemporary screen comedy often makes use of a self-reflexive style. *Scary Movie* and *Scary Movie 2*, for example, play with the viewer's familiarity with the horror movie conventions that are being satirized. Like Woody Allen, Mike Myers has made playing to the camera an integral part of his ironic comic persona. His *Austin Powers* films (1997, 1999, 2002) include numerous moments of self-conscious comedy, in which Myers jokes with the camera, making humor by acknowledging its presence. He winks at it, grins broadly to it, and uses it to make a formal introduction of key scenes, such as when he leans forward, smiles, and says into the camera, "Ladies and gentlemen, Mr. Burt Bacharach," introducing cameo appearances by the composer, who then performs selections from his songs. Bacharach's songs were very popular in the 1960s and 1970s, and their catchy melodies are major emblems of the popular culture of those periods. Myers's introductions of Bacharach, then, are moments of nostalgia and affection, and his use of a self-reflexive camera emphasizes them.

A secret agent from the 1960s, Austin Powers is based on the many screen spies who had popular film series in that era. These include James Bond, Derek Flint, and Matt Helm. Myers weaves numerous references to those movies into his own. *Austin Powers in Goldmember* (2002), for example, costars Michael Caine as Powers's father. Caine is an actor closely identified with the sixties spy craze, having played secret agent Harry Palmer in several pictures (including *The Ipcress File*, 1966). His presence in *Goldmember* evokes this history. Furthermore, *Goldmember* plays with the title and character of one of the most famous James Bond films, *Goldfinger* (1964).

While not a laugh-out-loud comedy like the *Austin Powers* films, Quentin Tarantino's *Kill Bill*, released in two parts (2003, 2004), contains a lot of dark humor and outrageous wit. Veering from one mode of screen reality to another, the films have a flashy, in-your-face style that makes reference to many of Tarantino's favorite films.

(continued)

AUSTIN POWERS (NEW LINE, 1997)

Austin Powers (Mike Myers), the international man of mystery, jokes and confides with the camera and viewers, thereby acknowledging the presence of each. Here, he offers an affectionate introduction to a cameo appearance by composer Burt Bacharach. Frame enlargement.

He audaciously switches from color to black-and-white for a climactic sword fight (this also helped the film keep its R rating) and, without warning, goes from live action to an extended animé sequence for a flashback showing a character's childhood.

With swordfights and graphic blood spurts, the story focuses on a female assassin seeking revenge on those who betrayed her. It is derived from (and it makes reference to) *Lady Snowblood* (1973), a Japanese film that is one of Tarantino's favorites. Along the way, he also makes many visual and musical references to Sergio Leone's spaghetti Westerns, especially *The Good, the Bad and the Ugly* (1966), to the Shaw Brothers martial arts movies of the 1970s, and to Japan's *Streetfighter* film series. The star of those films, Sonny Chiba, has a major role in *Kill Bill*, as the master swordsman who makes the heroine's sword.

The pleasures of *Kill Bill*, then, lie in its self-reflexive style, as Tarantino calls the viewer's attention to his playful movie in-jokes and to his audacious manipulations of picture and sound.

KILL BILL (MIRAMAX, 2003, 2004)

Like all of Quentin Tarantino's films, *Kill Bill* is very self-conscious about its relationship to other movies. Tarantino references his favorite films and filmmakers, and he playfully manipulates picture and sound in striking, attention-grabbing ways. Frame enlargement.

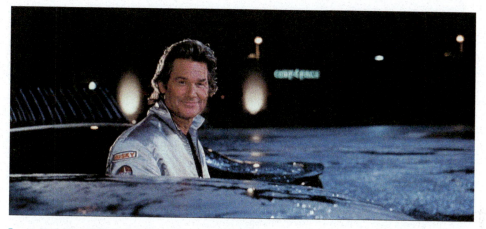

GRINDHOUSE (DIMENSION FILMS, 2007)

Directors Quentin Tarantino and Robert Rodriguez teamed up to evoke the style of 1970s exploitation pictures. Their film is a double feature composed of *Deathproof* (Tarantino directed) and *Planet Terror* (Rodriguez directed) and includes fake trailers directed by other filmmakers including Eli Roth and Rob Zombie. Throughout, the footage is scratched and torn and has frames missing to evoke the experience of watching an old print that has been run many times through a projector. The entire project is an extended wink at the audience. Here, villain Kurt Russell pauses to grin at the camera just before he does something really nasty. Frame enlargement.

The self-reflexive mode works extremely well for comedy because it promotes the intimate relationship with an audience that is integral to effective humor. *Austin Powers* and *Kill Bill* invite the audience to play along and be as hip as they are by enjoying the jokes.

The comic possibilities of the self-reflexive mode assume that the viewer will understand the social norms, movies, and movie characters that are being referenced. Only viewers who "get" the references will enjoy the humor these films offer.

Comic Self-Reflexivity

The tradition of self-reflexivity most commonly found in popular mass-market movies employs a comic design. Throughout *Annie Hall* (1977), director and star Woody Allen continually interrupts the narrative with a series of humorous asides and confessions made to the camera. By speaking to the camera, of course, he speaks directly to the film's audience. Looking at the camera lens, he looks directly at the eyes of the viewer. During one scene, when Alvy Singer (Woody Allen) and Annie Hall (Diane Keaton) quarrel over whether she said going to psychoanalysis will change her life or change her wife, Alvy breaks off the argument, turns to the camera, and reminds the film's viewers that they know what was said because they have been there all along, listening to the quarrel. Likewise, in a subtle way, the tradition established by director Alfred Hitchcock of making guest appearances inside his films reminds viewers of his controlling presence as director and, therefore, of the film's status *as* a film.

Didactic Self-Reflexivity

The second category of self-reflexive film style is used for didactic purposes and falls within the aesthetic tradition identified with the theater of playwright Bertolt Brecht. Brecht was an active playwright and poet from the 1920s until his death in 1956, and his plays include such classics as *The Threepenny Opera, Galileo*, and *The Caucasian Chalk Circle*. As a Marxist, Brecht sought in his art to have a direct impact on his social world and historical period, and to do so, he developed a unique and very influential approach to drama.

Impatient with the conventions of the theater of his day, Brecht created his own theatrical forms that he termed *epic* and that tried to break down the barriers that separated spectators from the play they were watching. Brecht considered the illusion of naturalism or realism, as created in theater or film, to be an obstacle preventing playgoers or film viewers from reflecting on the connections between their own lives and the events depicted on stage or screen.

Case Study   *THE BRECHTIAN LEGACY IN FILM:* WEEKEND

Brecht's work in the theater continues to exert an enormously powerful influence on filmmakers. French director Jean-Luc Godard is probably the most famous Brechtian filmmaker currently working. Godard's films offer a virtual catalogue of Brechtian cinematic techniques, that is, techniques that break the illusion that the spectator is watching a real, authentic world on screen rather than a movie. These techniques enable Godard to speak directly to his audience as author rather than indirectly through the characters and action of a film. *Weekend* (1967), Godard's savage satire of modern consumer society, employs three kinds of didactic, self-reflexive techniques. These are the use of printed titles, nontraditional camera techniques, and the incorporation of imaginary characters and moments of performance self-disclosure.

Titles

Title cards break up the narrative action of *Weekend*, which follows the comic and violent misadventures of a middle-class couple journeying across France on holiday. The printed titles offer ironic and poetic commentaries on the narrative. During the opening credits of the film, two title cards proclaim, with some irony, that this is "a film adrift in the cosmos" and "a film found on a dump." A long musical sequence in the middle of the film, during which a pianist performs a Mozart sonata as the camera tracks three times around the perimeter of a farmyard, is introduced by flash-cut inserts of the title "Musical Action."

Throughout the film, title cards serve to (1) introduce and set off a given scene from the surrounding context of the narrative, (2) tell viewers what it is they are about to see, (3) remind viewers of the filmmaker's intrusion on the narrative, and (4) emphasize the way the filmmaker has chosen to shape and organize the structure of the film. By calling attention to the film's methods of constructing its images and narrative, each of these functions is consistent with the Brechtian goal of breaking the illusion of reality exerted by the screen world.

The title card "Totem and Taboo" prefaces the film's most horrific sequence, dealing with the cannibalism and mutilation of English tourists at the hands of a guerrilla army based in the countryside. This title derives from a famous book by Sigmund Freud dealing with primitive social organization and behavioral taboos in human ancestry. Here, the self-reflexive qualities are multiple. In addition to the four functions described above, the title card tells the viewer that the scenes that follow will contain shocking and taboo imagery, as indeed they do, and for viewers who know the reference, this acknowledgment positions the scenes in relation to Freud's famous work.

Nontraditional Camera Techniques

These are a second method used by Godard to create self-reflexive style in *Weekend*. Two sequences stand out for their use of radical camerawork. The tracking shot along the row of stalled cars (described and discussed in Chapter 1) and the circular tracking movements around the farmyard during the musical interlude extend the length of these shots and scenes to a point many viewers find unbearable, especially because no new narrative information is being disclosed. However, the tracking shots go on for so long that the visual device—camera movement—becomes the subject of the shots. By elaborating camera movement at such length, the style becomes self-reflexive by making the viewer acutely aware of the visual design. As in comic uses, however, self-reflexiveness depends on the viewer's knowledge of the norm that is being violated. In this case the norm is that camerawork is subordinated to the action of a scene rather than vice versa.

Imaginary Characters and Performance Self-Disclosure

Weekend is filled with imaginary storybook characters. These establish a third area of self-reflexive technique. During one episode in the middle of the film, the vacationing couple, Corinne and Roland, encounter poet Emily Brontë and a companion dressed in storybook costumes.

Corinne and Roland ask for directions to their destination, Oinville, but Brontë and her companion reply with metaphysical riddles. When Roland asks for the directions, Brontë inquires if he is interested in poetical or physical information. When Roland tells her that they only want to know how to get to Oinville, Brontë tells him that physics doesn't really exist, only individual

sciences, prompting Roland to mutter that the film they are in (and the viewer is watching) must be rotten—it's full of crazy people. His remark is a moment of performance self-disclosure in which the actor steps out of character to evaluate the quality of the film in which he appears. Of course, Godard does not believe he's making a rotten film and so the evaluation is ironic.

For the Brechtian tradition, this is precisely the attitude to be combated, and it is what motivates the use of self-reflexive techniques. By breaking the spell of reality cast by film or play, these techniques point to the enormous differences between life and the constructed spectacles on stage or screen.

The scene culminates in a moment of horror. Roland drives away Brontë's companion and then sets her on fire. As the poet burns and cries, a shaken Corinne says that this is bad, that they shouldn't have torched her, prompting Roland to remark that is doesn't matter because they are imaginary characters.

Brontë's fiery destruction by Roland illuminates the emotional paradox of cinema. Though the film presents Brontë as a storybook character dressed in a fairy-tale costume, her violent death strikes the viewer as a terrible crime. Despite her obviously fictional status, her death is disturbing. This paradox—a film's ability to compel emotion and belief from the viewer despite the fictional artifice of its characters—is the phenomenon that the Brechtian tradition seeks to control, understand, and influence.

WEEKEND (NEW YORKER FILMS, 1967)

Storybook characters dressed in fairy-tale costumes help shatter realism in Godard's *Weekend*. Dressed in these outlandish costumes, Emily Brontë and Le Gros Poucet step into the film from some alternate poetic reality. They quarrel with Corinne and Roland, who promptly burn them for violating the standard of realism. Frame enlargement.

(continued)

The Legacy of Godard

Godard's self-conscious, radical cinematic techniques have exerted an enormous influence on other filmmakers, as has the Brechtian tradition that nourished his work. Spike Lee is a contemporary director who freely mixes modes of screen reality in his films, incorporating ordinary fictional realism, fantasy sequences, and modes of self-reflexivity. The black-and-white narrative of *She's Gotta Have It* (1986), for example, is punctuated by one striking color sequence, a musical fantasy, that departs greatly in tone and style from the surrounding narrative.

In *Do the Right Thing* (1989), Lee displays a precise understanding of how Brechtian techniques can be used to contain and control the emotions generated by the story on screen. During the famous racial slur sequence, a gallery of characters hurls obscenities and insults at targeted social groups. A young Italian man (John Turturro) insults African-Americans, Mookie (Spike Lee) insults Italian-Americans, a Hispanic gang member insults Koreans, a cop insults Hispanics, and a Korean merchant condemns Jews. Each character is filmed in an identical fashion: The camera quickly tracks from long shot to medium close-up to add visual emphasis to the verbal invective.

The sequence is emotionally powerful and inflammatory because it gives full-throated voice to various racisms. Spike Lee realized that he needed to break down and contain the emotions unleashed in the scene and that were likely to be aroused in the film's audiences. Accordingly, he breaks the hypnotizing power of the racist rhetoric with an explicitly didactic, Brechtian conclusion. A black radio deejay breaks into the montage, telling the characters to cool down, shut up, and break that nonsense off. The deejay heartily condemns the racial antagonisms of the characters, restoring calm and sanity.

Filmmakers such as Lee or Godard use self-reflexive techniques in a didactic manner to maintain a measure of control over the social impact of their films and the messages inside those films. These techniques enable the filmmakers to insert editorial remarks into the film, offering the viewer explicit guidance about how a scene should be interpreted or understood. The Brechtian tradition is a major aesthetic influence on filmmakers who want to speak directly to their audience and who wish to assert maximum control over the impact of their social messages.

He wanted his plays to become a stimulus to social action and reform, to have direct real-world consequences, and so he deliberately broke with realist and naturalist traditions by incorporating explicitly didactic techniques into his theater. Actors on stage might speak directly to the audience, or the social contradictions dramatized by the action of a play might be announced directly via titles projected on a screen above the stage. These methods were anti-illusionist in that they sought to dispel the illusion of a self-contained fictional world created by conventional drama and stagecraft.

Impact on Viewers of Self-Reflexive Techniques

The comic and didactic modes of cinematic self-reflexivity tend to pull viewers out of the reality represented on screen by reminding them that it is a cinematic construction. The illusion created by a screen world, however, is very powerful. It can sustain the digressions and intrusions of self-reflexive techniques. Such techniques typically dispel, *momentarily*, the emotional pull the viewer experiences from the screen world, but it is difficult to disrupt this emotional pull for very long. It tends quickly to reassert itself.

In *Weekend*, for example, despite all the title cards, the radical camera movements, and the moments of performance self-disclosure, the basic spectacle of Corinne and Roland's comic and increasingly violent car journey across France is exceptionally compelling. While one appreciates the social responsibility that Lee demonstrates as director when he brings on the calm deejay to conclude the racism scene in *Do the*

DO THE RIGHT THING (UNIVERSAL, 1989)

Mookie (Spike Lee) in the famous racial slur sequence from *Do the Right Thing*. Director Lee uses a self-reflexive technique to maintain artistic control over the sequence's inflammatory stream of racist insults. By alternating between different modes of screen reality, Lee evokes the poisonous intensity of racial hatred and then contextualizes it with a clear and direct condemnation. Frame enlargement.

Right Thing, one nevertheless remembers the scene for its extraordinarily hypnotic stream of racial insults.

The represented world on screen can be manipulated by filmmakers using self-reflexive techniques, but for spectators, the screen world tends to retain its emotional integrity and validity. Viewers know that Austin Powers and Bill are just movie characters. They admit this themselves, but viewers still want to spend time with them. The cinema compels emotional belief in its modes of screen reality even when filmmakers admit to viewers that it's all just a movie.

ANIMATION

Because it is susceptible to the optical illusions on which cinema depends—beta movement and persistence of vision—the human eye can be fooled into seeing movement in a series of hand-drawn images just as with a series of still photographic images. The creative possibilities of animation—of making a still image or model appear to move—have long fascinated filmmakers.

The illusion of movement in cinema is not dependent on seeing live action images—it can work for any type of image. Filmmakers have animated line drawings created by hand as well as stationary objects, built either as three-dimensional models or as virtual objects inside computer space. Animation forms a distinct mode of screen reality in which the constraints imposed by live action drop away.

Most significantly, as a mode of screen reality, animation takes cinema away from the photographic tradition that informs virtually all feature films. The camera in

an animated film is not focused on live actors and real sets or locations that get photographed to make the movie. (Performance capture, to be discussed shortly, is the exception to this rule in animation.)

A line drawing with minimal detail like Gertie the Dinosaur can come to life, and the fish of *Finding Nemo* (2003) or Remy the rat in *Ratatouille* (2007) can speak and act with personalities that would be unconvincing in live action. Because this mode of screen reality departs from photographic origins, audiences readily accept things in an animated world that they would not in a live action world. In an animated world, if a cartoon character accidentally drives a car off the edge of a cliff, the car will hang suspended in space, just long enough for the character, now wise to the danger, to grimace at the camera. Then gravity grabs the car and down it goes.

This mode of screen reality has been with cinema since the beginning, and the techniques for creating an animated screen world have changed over the decades.

The earliest film cartoons appeared shortly after the invention of cinema. J. Stuart Blackton's *Humorous Phases of Funny Faces* (1906) used chalk and a blackboard to animate a series of amusing facial expressions. The French cartoonist Emile Cohl created over 75 film cartoons between 1908 and 1910 and then came to the United States to continue his work with *The Newlyweds and Their Baby* (1912), a movie cartoon based on a comic strip. One of the earliest and most popular cartoon characters with a distinct personality was Windsor McCay's lovable *Gertie the Dinosaur* (1914). McCay made 10,000 separate drawings to bring this one reel film to life.

2D Animation

2D animation is the process of photographing flat artwork, typically a combination of characters and background. Until the development of computer animation in the 1990s, cartooning in cinema traditionally was a two-dimensional (2D) process. Characters such as Bugs Bunny and Mickey Mouse were drawn on **cells** (transparent sheets of celluloid, the same material that a strip of film is made of). These are placed overtop a painted background. In order to create a movement, such as Bugs popping up from his rabbit hole, many cells are drawn, each containing a fragment of Bugs's movement, and these are then photographed separately against the background. Thus, in 2D animation, the background art remains relatively unchanging; most movement occurs in the foreground characters.

This method of animating cells against a painted background was developed in 1914. While it became an industry standard, it was limited in the amount of three-dimensional (3D) depth information that it could convey. If a character moved away from the camera into the distance, the camera could not follow into the depth of the scene. Furthermore, early cartoons such as *Gertie* or the popular Felix the Cat (a major character in the 1920s) involved very few light and shadow effects, which are a key means of creating the impression of depth.

Walt Disney achieved the key breakthroughs in these and other technical areas, and his work dominated cartooning in the 1930s. (Max Fleischer's popular Betty Boop and Popeye the Sailor cartoons were key competitors with Disney.) Disney made the first sound cartoon in 1928 with *Steamboat Willie,* starring his new character Mickey Mouse, and then a Technicolor animation in 1932 with *Flowers and Trees.* He introduced Donald Duck in 1934, whose popularity (along with Goofy and Pluto) displaced Mickey Mouse.

The short films that Disney was making with Mickey, Donald, Goofy, and Pluto were wildly popular, but determined to push the creative boundaries of animation, Disney resolved to produce a full-length animated feature.

To do this, he had to solve the problem of limited depth perspective. The feature needed to be completely cinematic. It would have to do many of the same things as a live-action feature film—create lighting effects, depth perspective, and camera movement—in order for the audience to accept it.

To achieve this, the Disney team created a **multiplane camera,** which thereafter became a standard tool of 2D animation. A multiplane camera is mounted above a series of cells, each containing separate elements of the scene. Because the cells are mounted at varying distances from the camera, if it pans or moves toward them, an effect of motion perspective is created (near objects moving more rapidly than distant objects), which is a powerful source of depth perception.

Moreover, the multiplane camera enabled animators to create depth-of-field effects. They could shift focus from a tree on a foreground cell to Mickey Mouse on a cell mounted farther from the camera, again creating an animated equivalent of depth perspective. And moving-camera shots could be simulated by moving a series of cells past the camera and at different rates to simulate motion perspective. The camera, the background art, and the cells could be adjusted in 64 different ways for every frame of film, a huge increase in the amount and variety of visual information.

Snow White and the Seven Dwarfs (1937), Disney's first animated feature, capitalized on these innovations, as well as fine attention to lighting effects, in particular a new ability to create transparent shadows attached to solid characters, achieved by underexposing the cells containing the shadows. Disney and his team also perfected the difficult art of personality animation. As a result, Snow White and her seven dwarves were as emotionally involving as live-action characters. The film was a stupendous hit.

The success of *Snow White* opened the door to the golden age of 2D animation, during which Hollywood's major studios started their own animation departments. Disney dominated features in this period, with *Snow White*, *Pinocchio* (1940), *Fantasia* (1940), *Dumbo* (1941), *Bambi* (1942), and *Cinderella* (1950). But the other studios excelled at shorts. 20th Century Fox had Terrytoons, with animated stars Heckle and Jeckle, Mighty Mouse, and Deputy Dawg. Universal had a series produced by Walter Lantz, starring Woody Woodpecker. Columbia had cartoon stars Krazy Kat and Mr. Magoo, MGM had Tom and Jerry, and Paramount had Popeye and Casper the Friendly Ghost.

But it was Warner Bros. that produced more cartoon stars and classic cartoon shorts than anybody else. Warners was home to Bugs Bunny, Daffy Duck, Elmer Fudd, Porky Pig, the Road Runner, Wile E. Coyote, Yosemite Sam, Tweety, Pepe LePew, and many others. Animators and directors Chuck Jones, Tex Avery, Bob Clampett, Frank Tashlin, and Fritz Freleng and vocal artist Mel Blanc were among the key people responsible for this amazing run of cartoons that lasted until the end of the 1950s.

Rising production costs and television killed the golden age. Former MGM animators Bill Hanna and Joe Barbera developed a "limited movement" approach for television that quickly became the standard in *The Yogi Bear Show*, *Quick Draw McGraw*, *The Flintstones*, *Top Cat*, *The Jetsons*, and *Magilla Gorilla*.

2D animation survives in today's world of digital film. *The Iron Giant* (1999) combined traditional 2D animation with digital animation in a well-written tale about a friendly space traveler who lands in the United States during the paranoid Cold War era of the 1950s.

Japan's pre-eminent animator, Hayao Miyazaki, helped to pioneer the revival of animated features with *Princess Mononoke* (1997), *Spirited Away* (2001), and *Howl's Moving Castle* (2005). He has remained committed to hand-drawn animation with minimal use of digital effects. Working on *Spirited Away*, Miyazaki told his staff, "This is a two-dimensional film. This is our strength," and he believes that hand-drawn work gives the creator more freedoms than digital.

RABBIT SEASONING (WARNER BROS., 1952)

Beginning in the 1930s, Warner Bros. launched a cartoon series released under the banners Looney Tunes and Merrie Melodies featuring a gallery of now-classic characters: Bugs Bunny, Daffy Duck, Porky Pig, Elmer Fudd, Road Runner, and others. This was the golden age of 2D animation. Frame enlargement.

COMBINING LIVE ACTION WITH 2D ANIMATION   The combination of live action (real people and places as traditionally photographed in cinema) with cartoon footage was an irresistible creative temptation for filmmakers. The **rotoscope** is a combination camera–projector that makes this possible. It projects previously filmed footage onto a series of cells that animators then use to create the cartoon elements. Because they can see the film footage on their cells, they can precisely align the animation with the live-action elements. The cells are then filmed and composited with the live action.

The MGM musical *Anchors Aweigh* (1945) featured an impressive and funny rotoscoped scene in which star Gene Kelly danced with Jerry the mouse, a cartoon character. The dance choreography was carefully worked out, and the result was a highly convincing illusion.

But the most elaborate blend of live action and animation, achieved with non-digital means, is unquestionably Disney's *Who Framed Roger Rabbit* (1988). The film features more than 1000 shots in which live action and animation are joined, and the story premise is remarkably clever. Taking place in the 1940s and modeled on Hollywood's own films noir of that period, the story features private eye Eddie Valiant (Bob Hoskins) investigating the murder of a cartoon character. His quest eventually takes him to Toontown, where all the film industry's cartoon characters live and which is a kind of alternate universe where cartoon laws apply (a character, for example, who falls out of a window will hang in the air for a moment before dropping).

Director Robert Zemeckis, cinematographer Dean Cundey, and effects artists from Industrial Light and Magic took elaborate steps to maximize the illusion that Eddie really co-exists with Roger Rabbit and the other 'toons. To blend the two domains, they used elaborate camera moves and atmospheric texture such as filming

WALTZ WITH BASHIR (SONY PICTURES CLASSICS, 2008)

Animation is a very flexible mode of screen reality because it departs from the tradition of photographic realism that has been so powerful and pervasive throughout cinema. But this does not mean that an animator cannot investigate the real world. *Waltz With Bashir*, for example, is an animated documentary, conjoining two modes of screen reality that are almost never combined with one another. Filmmaker Ari Folman uses animation to explore the events surrounding the massacre of Palestinians gathered in a refugee camp during the 1980 Israeli invasion of Lebanon. Frame enlargement.

the 'toon characters through smoke or fog. Full-figure cutouts stood in for Roger and Jessica Rabbit and other 'toons, and lighting, camera moves, and the live actors' performances were rehearsed in relation to these cutouts, which were then removed for filming. Finally, everything was shot on wide-gauge VistaVision film to maximize clarity and resolution, important because all the effects shots were done with traditional optical compositing, which involves multiple-rephotographing of the blended elements.

It's not just the amazing blend of live action and animation that makes *Who Framed Roger Rabbit* a great film. It is also extremely well-written and well-performed and is filled with a love for cinema and its great cartoon characters, many of whom make guest appearances—Bugs Bunny, Tweety Bird, Dumbo, Porky Pig, Pinocchio, Donald Duck, Yosemite Sam, Mickey Mouse, and Betty Boop. And it's a picture that has given us one of the great movie lines—"I'm not bad. I'm just drawn that way."

3D Animation

3D animation involves the use of puppets or other real models or animation within three-dimensional (3D) computer space. The animation of puppets or models is a traditional tool of cinema and has been used widely in various methods of **stop-motion animation**. This involves posing a model, exposing one frame of film, then re-posing

WHO FRAMED ROGER RABBIT (DISNEY, 1988)

Rotoscoping enables filmmakers to combine live action and animation. It has a long history in cinema, and it reached its pinnacle of accomplishment in *Roger Rabbit*, where real actors and cartoon characters combine to create an animated film noir. Frame enlargement.

the model, exposing another frame of film, and so on, with a matte or mask used to block that portion of the frame in which live actors will be inserted.

Many classic special-effects films used this technique. Willis O'Brien's *The Lost World* (1925) brought its dinosaurs to life as animated miniature models, with live actors matted into the shots. *King Kong* (1933), about the giant ape who lives on Skull Island, is probably the most famous example of this type of animation. In this film, O'Brien inserted the live actors into the effects shots as film footage projected behind the puppets and miniature models.

Ray Harryhausen was another genius at stop-motion animation, perfecting his own system called "Dynamation" in a series of films based on Jules Verne novels, on Greek myths, and on tales of the Arabian Nights (*The Seventh Voyage of Sinbad*, 1958; *Mysterious Island*, 1961; *Jason and the Argonauts*, 1963; and *Clash of the Titans*, 1981).

One of Harryhausen's most famous and brilliant sequences is Jason's battle with a group of skeleton warriors. Because Harryhausen had to move all their arms and legs, animating the seven skeletons required him to make 35 separate movements for every frame of film, or 840 movements every second (35 × 24 frames per second), all of which had to be choreographed with the live actor in order to simulate a convincing sword fight.

More recently, Tim Burton's *The Nightmare Before Christmas* (1993) used stop-motion techniques to animate its puppet figures, as did Matt Stone and Trey Parker's *Team America: World Police* (2004).

Since the 1990s, visual effects have moved inside the computer, and animation has benefited from this revolution. Popular cartoon features today—*Toy Story,*

THE LOST WORLD (FIRST NATIONAL, 1925)

3D animation has deep roots in cinema, going back to the silent era. The dinosaurs in this special-effects film were animated as miniature models (18 inches high) by moving and photographing them a frame at a time, with a portion of each frame blocked (matted) from exposure. The film was then rewound, with the exposed area matted this time. Live actors were then photographed in the area of the frame that had been originally matted and unexposed. The finished image combined live action (the actor in the lower-right frame) and animation (the brontosaurus). Frame enlargement.

Shrek, Finding Nemo—tend to employ **digital animation**, with characters created as models inside three-dimensional computer space. This gives animators all the impressive visual-effects tools that live-action features have been using to impress audiences. Digitally created lighting effects can be very elaborate and, when used with texture mapping of skin and other surfaces, can create remarkable illusions of depth.

Unlike traditional 2D animation, which employs a real camera, the all-digital films are shot with a **virtual camera,** which is a program that simulates the many ways in which a camera might view the scene, mimicking the optical effects of different lenses, depth of field, rack focusing, and panning-and-tracking movements. As a result, the illusion of depth and motion perspective is much more powerful in digital animation, and these films capture far more of the visual qualities of live-action features than 2D animation could accomplish.

Furthermore, digital animation can be more efficient because the animator only needs to create **key frames,** those points at which the characters' positions change substantially. Once the key frames are specified, the computer will then fill in all the intervening frames of motion.

The efficiency and creative power of digital have led to a significant increase in the production of animated features. Until the 1990s, animated features were relatively rare and hardly existed outside of Disney. Now, however, they are plentiful and are among the biggest box office films of any given year.

Two studios—Pixar and DreamWorks—have specialized in digital animation features. Pixar formed in 1986 and signed a coproduction deal with Disney in 1991, and its first feature was *Toy Story* (1995). Other Pixar hits include *Monsters, Inc.* (2001), *Finding Nemo* (2003), and *The Incredibles* (2004). Pixar combined high-quality digital animation with an innovative blend of humor aimed at adults as well as children. This blend has proven extremely popular—parents enjoy these films along with their children.

UP (PIXAR, 2009)

The virtual camera—computer simulation of camera movement, angle, and lens perspective—has revolutionized animation, and the increasing sophistication of digital software enables animators to create detailed renderings of three-dimensional fantasy worlds. The animated feature film has returned in digital form as a contemporary blockbuster. Pixar's films look back to the Disney tradition in that photorealism is *not* the goal. Instead, like Disney's animators, Pixar's artists embrace caricature as a means of creating believable characters and getting to emotional truth. Frame enlargement.

DreamWorks' features—*Antz* (1998), *Prince of Egypt* (1998), *Shrek* (2001), *Shrek 2* (2004), *Shark Tale* (2004), and *Madagascar* (2005)—offer a similar blend of state-of-the-art computer animation with adult wit and children's gags.

A key factor in the success of these films is the use of star voices. This dates from Robin Williams's turn as the wizard in Disney's *Aladdin* (1992). Tom Hanks and Tim Allen voiced *Toy Story*, and Renee Zellweger and Will Smith voiced *Shark Tale* (2004). More recently, stars have been paid enormous revenues to do these films. DreamWorks paid $10 million apiece to Mike Myers, Cameron Diaz, and Eddie Murphy for *Shrek 2*. Ancillary rights bring in even more money, with a 5 percent royalty on all merchandise using an actor's voice. On this scale, Eddie Murphy would get 50 cents from the sale of every $10 talking toy based on his donkey character.

In this regard, digital animation has brought cartoon features into the world of movie blockbusters, requiring high-power stars and aggressive marketing in order to generate tremendous revenue streams.

PERFORMANCE CAPTURE   In the world of 2D animation, the rotoscope was invented in 1917 and was used occasionally to project live-action footage onto a cell, and an animator then drew over the top of the photographic image. In this case, rather than being combined with animation, the live action furnished a visual template for the animation.

A CHRISTMAS CAROL (DISNEY, 2009)
Jim Carrey (right) plays Scrooge in this animated version of Dickens' Christmas tale. Carrey's performance was transformed into digital animation for director Robert Zemeckis, who has made a series of performance capture-based films. In them, Zemeckis aims to give animation a strikingly photo-realist appearance. Frame enlargement.

In the digital world, **performance capture** works in a similar way, using a live actor's performance as the model for an animated figure. The actor wears a special suit with reflective markers at the joints and is filmed by multiple cameras, each of which sends a beam of light to the markers. The light is reflected back into the camera lens and recorded onto film as a series of white dots against a black background. The dots correspond to the location of the reflectors and provide a 2D portrait of the filmed movement. By comparing in a computer the views taken by the multiple cameras, a 3D model of the movement is created.

Robert Zemeckis made *The Polar Express* (2004) in this fashion. Actor Tom Hanks, in a skin-tight body suit and with 152 reflective pellets on his face (to capture facial expressions), was filmed by more than 100 cameras. Digitizing his performance and rendering it as animation enabled him to play five different characters, including a child, inhabiting an all-digital world. The results were somewhat less than satisfactory—the faces of the animated characters looked flat and unexpressive. Zemeckis used the technique again on *Beowulf* (2007), with approximately the same results.

Zemeckis brought 2D animation to one of its greatest achievements in *Who Framed Roger Rabbit*. He believes that performance capture and digital animation will be tremendously liberating to the filmmaker, with nothing that cannot be visualized, the only limits being those of the imagination. At the same time, this method represents a digital extension of an old and traditional technique, namely, rotoscoped images.

The Future of Animation

Animation is an enduring mode of cinema, and it has co-existed with live-action movies since the beginning of the medium. The pleasures offered by animation lie in its ability to depart from photographic realism in order to create a visual world that is more imaginative and magical than what live action can accomplish. A photographic image is more constrained by time and space than an animated image. The talking fish of *Finding Nemo* seem quite real as animated beings; they wouldn't seem real if the filmmaker tried to make the film by photographing actual fish. Whether 2D or 3D, animation will always be present as an essential mode of cinema, enabling filmmakers to create works of imagination that they could not achieve with live action.

SUMMARY

Because the camera has a double capacity, functioning as a medium that can both record properties of the visual world set before it and manipulate and transform the appearance of that world, filmmakers can create differing styles or modes of screen reality. The mode of ordinary fictional realism employs an audiovisual and narrative design that aims to replicate on screen, with a fair degree of resemblance, the spectator's understanding of space, time, causality, and the dynamics of human behavior.

The expressionistic mode makes available to filmmakers a range of extremely explicit stylistic distortions and manipulations that are used to express heightened, extreme, or abnormal states of feeling, thought, or behavior. The mode of fantasy and the fantastic establishes a realm of time and space far removed from ordinary reality in which character behavior can retain recognizably human dimensions or possess magical and extraordinary powers and abilities. The mode of animation frees filmmakers from the constraints of live action, enabling them to populate a screen world with talking non-human characters and bend the laws of time, space, and behavior even more radically than in the mode of fantasy.

The mode of cinematic self-reflexivity is available to filmmakers who wish to reveal and display the constructed and artificial basis of the cinema. Typically, filmmakers employ this mode for either a comic effect or for communicating an urgent social message directly to their audience. In the latter case, filmmakers will use this mode if they feel that the necessity of having to speak indirectly through characters and a story will prevent them from getting their message across or may leave the message itself muddied and muddled.

While the cinema has several distinct stylistic modes available to it, the divisions and boundaries between these modes are not hard and fast. In fact, many films incorporate one or more distinct modes. Musicals such as *Singin' in the Rain* and *An American in Paris*, for example, typically draw on ordinary fictional realism as well as fantasy and the fantastic. These stylistic modes are extremely flexible, and filmmakers can move in and out of several different modes.

Screen reality is constructed partly by the manipulations of film design discussed in this chapter, and it can vary widely across films. It is, however, also constructed by viewers. Representational reality seems real only when a viewer decides that it does. Representational conventions change over time, as does the viewer's response to them. Contemporary audiences react with disbelief when gunshot victims in 1940s movies clutch their stomachs, double over, and slowly sink out of frame. Screen reality exists in relation to viewers who judge its perceived levels of credibility and validity. By manipulating film structure, filmmakers hope to influence viewers' judgments, but their ability to control viewer response is limited. Like so much else about film, the creation of screen reality is a collaborative production.

KEY TERMS AND CONCEPTS

SUGGESTED READINGS

Jonathan Bresman, *The Art of Star Wars: Episode I: The Phantom Menace* (New York: Del Rey, 1999).

Lotte Eisner, *The Haunted Screen: Expressionism in the German Cinema* (Berkeley: University of California Press, 1989).

Bill Nichols, *Representing Reality: Issues and Concepts in Documentary* (Bloomington: Indiana University Press, 1992).

Irving Singer, *Reality Transformed: Film as Meaning and Technique* (Cambridge, MA: MIT Press, 1998).

Robert Stam, *Reflexivity in Film and Literature: From Don Quixote to Jean-Luc Godard* (New York: Columbia University Press, 1992).

Mark Cotta Vaz, *Industrial Light and Magic: Into the Digital Realm* (New York: Del Rey, 1996).

10

At the Crossroads of Business and Art

OBJECTIVES

After reading this chapter, you should be able to:

- identify the Hollywood majors

- describe how a film's box office success is measured

- explain why box office gross is a misleading indicator of a film's economic performance

- identify the ancillary markets and explain their significance

- describe the box office performance of U.S. films in world markets

- explain how the U.S. film industry facilitates the marketing of its product

- describe three key forms of Hollywood's stylistic influence on world cinema

- explain how contemporary filmmaking operates within an integrated market

- define blockbuster production

- define product tie-ins and product placement

- describe the international marketing of *Jurassic Park*

- explain how Hollywood absorbs and transforms foreign film style

363

Previous chapters have examined the aesthetics of cinema in terms of the medium's expressive, structural elements. These include light, color, sound, editing, and so forth. It would be naïve, though, to claim that cinema's expressive components exist in a pure state or that filmmakers can work with complete freedom to pursue their visions. The aesthetics of cinema are bound up with technological, social and economic factors, and an introductory understanding of movies and meaning would be incomplete if it focused only on cinema aesthetics in isolation from these other factors.

The art of cinema resides at a crossroads, where technology, industry, and society intersect. Movies are a business as well as an art, and cinema is a global phenomenon.

This chapter examines the business of film art, the economic context in which filmmakers work and that shapes the medium's artistic possibilities. The inscription on the famous MGM studio logo was "ars gratia artis" or "Art for art's sake." But few studios or funding agencies underwrite a production solely for the sake of art. Cinema aesthetics resides at the crossroads, where technology meets industry in a social context.

FROM LARGE SCREENS TO SMALL

A convenient way to illustrate the relationship of technology, business, and aesthetics is to consider changes in the size of cinema's image and in how and where viewers encounter the medium. For more than a century, the experience of cinema was a theatrical experience. Moviegoers left their homes and viewed large-screen images projected on celluloid film in theaters dedicated to that purpose.

The Hollywood studio system from the 1920s into the1950s was star-driven, and the special iconic power of a film star lay substantially in the pleasure viewers derived from seeing stars projected to giant proportions on a large theater screen. It was their on-screen charisma that distinguished movie stars, charisma that the large screen magnified rather than diminished. Not all screen performers were successful in this regard—a star had to command the large screen and not get lost or be overwhelmed by its size.

Theaters, too, were big, especially during the 1920s which became the era of "movie palaces." Expensively furnished, ornate, flamboyantly decorated, and above all huge, movie palaces transported viewers to another domain, a heightened, intensified screen world distinct from that of a viewer's everyday life. It was distinct because it was glamorous, exciting, and because story conflicts on film reached emotionally satisfying conclusions, unlike life. But it was distinct also because viewers had to leave their homes to experience it, to physically take leave of their everyday surroundings and enter a theatrical world of big-screen projection.

Moviegoing became a cultural ritual with massive appeal. Eighty million Americans went to the movies weekly in 1930, representing 65 percent of the national population. In 1946, 90 million people attended movies weekly. By comparison, in 2000, 27 million attended weekly. By 2010, moviegoers went out to theaters on average six times per year.

Theatrical screenings—the established venue for seeing movies—profoundly shaped cinema aesthetics. Because viewers saw big images, filmmakers generally kept their cameras at a comfortable distance from the actors on set or on location, covering much of a scene's action in full shot or medium shot framings and reserving close-ups for dramatic moments. Shots ran longer than they do today; cuts between shots did

For most of its history, cinema has been a big-screen medium. Audiences left their homes to view films in large theatres, and in the 1920s and 1930s these were luxurious and elaborately decorated. Virginia's Lyric Theater, pictured here, opened in 1930, during the Great Depression, and was one of the first theatres to show sound pictures. Listed in the National Register of Historic Places, the theater operates today as a nonprofit, offering screenings of foreign and independent films.

For most of its history, cinema was a film-based medium, with images captured on strips of celluloid. Theaters required large projectors with high-intensity lamps to throw a bright, huge image upon the screen. The Lyric's projector, pictured here, is a Simplex X-L, a model first marketed in 1949 and based on the original Simplex designed in 1908. Co-designed by Edwin S. Porter (director of *The Great Train Robbery*, 1903), the Simplex was widely adopted by theaters and became one of the industry's great workhorses. Today most viewers do not experience cinema primarily as a celluloid image projected upon a large screen. (The silver reel visible above the project on the right belongs to a smaller, 16mm projector that stands next to the Simplex.)

Celluloid film is a bulky medium, and theaters traditionally operated two 35mm projectors (known as a two-reel system), switching between them at the start and end of a reel of film to maintain continuous projection. A platter system, shown here, requires only one projector. The entire film is assembled on a single reel and then placed on a set of horizontal tables, providing a continuous feed to the projector and automatic take-up of the film as it exits the projector, eliminating the need for rewinding.

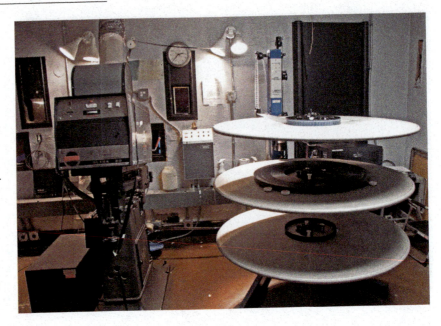

not occur as frequently or quickly. Thus for contemporary viewers, older movies seem to have a slower pace, but viewed on a large screen, the compositions and editing are powerful.

This way of framing a scene's action enabled actors to perform with their whole bodies, whereas today it is mainly their faces. Blocking of scene action was complex and required actors to move on set with their bodies in ways that the camera would see. The frame became a unit of design—scene action was choreographed within the frame to be meaningful and centered, and a considerable amount of story material might unfold within a single, extended shot. Films made before 1960 have an average shot length of 8–11 seconds, whereas contemporary movies average 4–6 seconds or less.

Whereas rapid cutting today serves to hold a viewer's attention, in the earlier period screen size commanded audience attention, along with the special luminous power of film itself. Celluloid film contains bits of silver halide, visible as image grain, suspended in a gelatin covering adhering to a strip of plastic that runs through camera and projector. Silver halide in an unexposed film negative reacts to light, and the film image is captured by this reaction and in these grains. But the grain structure of every frame on a strip of film is relatively unique; the distribution of silver halides includes a degree of randomness that gives life to cinema's film image. Every frame is different from every other, and when projected, the luminous film image pulses with life; each image is both similar and randomly different from every other. Twenty-four times a second—the projection rate of celluloid film—the screen image is renewed, but it also offers viewers a unique visual experience 24 times a second, making film live in a glowing, pulsating way that video does not duplicate. The hypnotic power that film commanded during this ritual period of high, sustained consumption by audiences largely derived from its special, luminous qualities and from its unchallenged place in popular entertainment. No other moving image media with the popular appeal of cinema competed with it.

CASABLANCA (WARNER BROS., 1942)

The special luminous power of film, projected onto a large theater screen, gave cinema the extraordinary appeal that the medium enjoyed in earlier decades. The grain structure of celluloid film helped create glowing images of cinema stars, such as Ingrid Bergman (pictured here). Film grain—bits of silver suspended in the emulsion on celluloid—made the screen image glitter. And because the distribution of silver halides changed from frame to frame, film came alive in a way that was unique to the medium. Frame enlargement.

With the marketing of television in the late 1940s, however, cinema began to lose its unique and unchallenged hold on the popular audience. This process accelerated with the advent of home video in the 1980s. The appeal of watching movies at home on VHS videotapes began to shift the medium away from its theatrical mode and toward alternative modes of consumption. DVD, brought to market in 1997, and Blu-ray in 2006, drove the low-resolution VHS medium into extinction. The availability of movies on tape and disk inaugurated an era of personal ownership that was quite unique in film history. Before this, movies were screened in theaters and then disappeared; in the television era, they might be broadcast for the small screen after a theatrical run, but in each case, viewers randomly encountered a given film and never owned it outright (except illegally by 35mm or 16mm collectors). Home video gave birth to the cultural notion that film ownership by consumers was not only a prerogative but a right.

Beginning in the mid-1980s, people saw movies more often on home video than they did in theaters, and cinema began a kind of reverse journey into various miniaturized forms. It was a reverse journey because the move toward smaller-screen viewing challenged the iconic and ritual power the medium had assumed to this point and challenged, too, its aesthetic design.

The move to small screens, over time, led filmmakers to rely more on close-ups and fast cutting to hold viewer attention. Cutting rates increased, as did overall pacing, and as close-in framings became increasingly privileged, actors more often were called on to "stand and deliver," to stand still and deliver dialogue filmed at close range, rather than move in full-figure framings and in complexly choreographed camera set-ups as in earlier decades. Shallow focus compositions explicitly directed a viewer's attention and worked well on small-screen viewing devices. Depth of field did not, nor did long shots or lengthy shots.

The great cinema directors of earlier periods—Ingmar Bergman, Akira Kurosawa, Jean Renoir, Chaplin, Keaton, John Ford—made films for the large screen and for a medium that was unique and unlike any other. A filmmaker today makes a movie for a theatrical screening as well as for home video and for streaming video to a variety of small viewing devices. The great large-scale epics from the theatrical era—Abel Gance's *Napoleon* (1927), Akira Kurosawa's *Seven Samurai* (1954), David Lean's *Lawrence of Arabia* (1962), Stanley Kubrick's *2001: A Space Odyssey* (1968)—are incompatible with cinema viewed on an iPhone or YouTube. They are not shot or edited for these viewing venues, and in this regard they challenge the emerging, contemporary idea that cinema is wherever one finds it, on large screens or small. They are designed for large-image venues, and their long running times require the special kind of immersion that large-screen imagery provides. Thus it is essential that students developing a specialized, introductory understanding of the medium see that *how* a film is viewed influences and often determines *what* a filmmaker has designed (because filmmakers work with an ideal end-viewer in mind) and how that movie is experienced.

For more than a century, the theatrical venue defined cinema, its aesthetics, and its special appeal for viewers. In contrast, video streaming to small viewing devices is a proliferating form of cinema today. The extraordinary profitability of such devices for their manufacturers is helping to drive the new markets for small-screen viewing. Apple, for

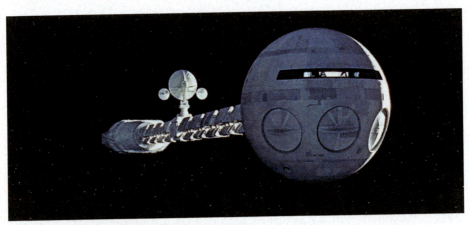

2001: A SPACE ODYSSEY (MGM, 1968)

Stanley Kubrick intended for his epic science fiction film to provide viewers with a grand, spectacular visual experience. Large-screen viewing was essential for this experience to work. The content and composition of his shots, and the pacing and rhythm of the editing, are calibrated for the big screen. Cinema aesthetics developed, historically, in close relationship with the medium's traditional theatrical venue. Frame enlargement.

Today *2001: A Space Odyssey* can be viewed as streaming video on an iPhone or on a comparable portable consumer electronic device. The iPhone provides a miniaturized cinema experience. It fits easily on a bookshelf as pictured here. Because the device is portable, and the streaming images are instantly accessible wherever one goes, cinema becomes a placeless experience as well as a miniature one.

example, drew more than $330 million in profit from the first three days of iPhone sales, and half of its $25 billion revenue in 2011 derived from iPhones and related products.

Streaming video can be viewed on YouTube or other Internet sites or can be sent directly from companies such as Netflix to one's laptop computer, Ipad, or cell phone. The move to streaming video and video-on-demand is changing the era of movie ownership that has flourished since the 1980s. If many films are available for instant viewing, why buy them? Moreover, video streaming enables studios to retain control over their films in a way that the sale of physical media, such as a DVD, does not. Ownership and physical media are interrelated; moving from physical media can mean moving away from ownership and from the special connoisureship that building a permanent collection of movies tends to inspire. It also involves a shift toward lower resolution image and sound. As cinema becomes more portable and instantly accessible, overall image and sound quality declines.

For young cinema viewers today, the medium is not distinct or unique, and it is not rooted in a history of celluloid film or theaters. Cinema now is wherever a moving image narrative happens to be encountered. It has lost its medium-distinctiveness as electronic media have proliferated. Cinema today is everywhere and nowhere.

Viewing cinema often is not a ritual experience as in decades past. To many readers of this textbook, it does not matter how or where a movie is encountered or experienced. A YouTube viewing seems as legitimate to many young consumers as a big-screen experience. But small-screen viewing tends to accompany multitasking. The darkened theater auditorium is a jealous lover that tolerates no distractions or interruptions. It invites sustained interaction with a film. Movie viewing at home or on small electronic screens typically occurs in environments where others things are going on and laying claim to one's attention.

As cinema proliferates across these formats, it risks losing a defining aesthetic profile and becoming immersed in a vast sea of moving-image media. Movies developed especially for iPhones or iPads need not display the subtleties of composition or lighting or performing found on the large screen since miniaturized viewing devices tend to neutralize such things; they don't play as well on a small screen. Abel Gance's *Napoleon,* Kurosawa's *Seven Samurai,* and David Leans's *Lawrence of Arabia* lose their allure in shrunken formats. But as cinema becomes miniaturized, it is also moving toward high-resolution home media, along contrary paths of development. Blu-ray offers viewers the opportunity to view great-looking cinema images at home and only works meaningfully on relatively large-screen devices. Cinema thus moves in two directions—toward high-resolution home viewing and large-screen formats and toward miniaturized devices that can be carried wherever one goes and which make cinema a placeless experience in that it is not tied to a particular viewing environment.

THE ART FILM ERA

The emergence of widespread public recognition that cinema is an art form occurred during the period when theatrical exhibition was the dominant form of movie watching, when cinema was a singular medium displayed on large screens, a time when moving image media were not as extensive and common as they are today.

The Venice Film Festival, the world's oldest, was established in Italy in 1932 to provide "an international exhibition of cinematographic art," and the Cannes Film Festival began in France in 1946. International distribution of foreign film enabled the

THE GRAND ILLUSION (RAC, 1937)

Jean Renoir's enduring classic portrays French officers and enlisted men in a German prisoner of war camp during World War I. Distributed internationally to great acclaim, the film won numerous prizes. The conjunction of film festivals with theatrical distribution of foreign film helped to inaugurate the art film era. Frame enlargement.

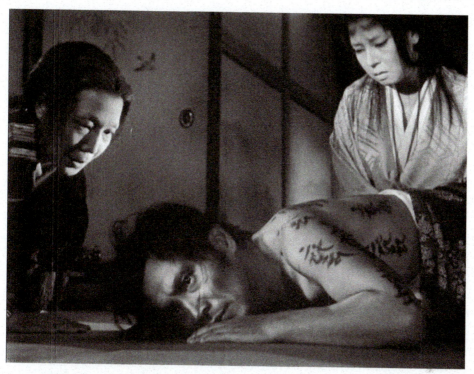

UGETSU MONOGATARI (DAIEI, 1953)

The discovery by overseas audiences of national cinemas was an exciting part of the art film era. Works by Japanese filmmakers were screened widely for international audiences following the success of Kurosawa's *Rashomon* (1950) at the Venice Film Festival. *Ugetsu Monogatari*, a ghost story set amid the turmoil of Japan's medieval samurai wars, has a poetic visual beauty sustained by Mizoguchi's ability to compose action for the moving camera and in lengthy, unbroken shots. Frame enlargement.

"art film" to proliferate. These were films made by directors who aimed to express ambitious themes by way of strikingly original and creative cinematic styles.

Numerous, enduring film classics emerged during this period of international film distribution. Jean Renoir's *Grand Illusion* (1937) became the first foreign language film nominated for an Academy Award for Best Picture, and it won a prize at Venice in 1938. Renoir followed it with *The Rules of the Game* (1939), confirming his reputation as one of cinema's greatest directors and this pair of films as among the finest works produced in French cinema. Roberto Rossellini's *Open City* (1945) won the Grand Prize at Cannes in 1946 and premiered that year in the U.S. Numerous classics of Italian neo-realism followed in its wake.

When Akira Kurosawa's *Rashomon* won the Golden Lion for best film at Venice, it launched Japanese cinema into world distribution. Kurosawa went on to make such landmark films as *Ikiru, Seven Samurai*, and *Throne of Blood*, and other directors found acclaim overseas. Kenji Mizoguchi's *Ugetsu Monogatari* (1953), for example, won a Silver Lion at Venice for Best Direction in 1953 and is today regarded as an enduring classic.

L'AVVENTURA (PCE, 1960)

International film distribution enhanced the cultural prestige of directors whose films were embraced by domestic and overseas audiences. These included Michelangelo Antonioni, whose films about anxiety and alienation were honored as bold statements about the modern condition. In *L'Avventura,* Sandro (Gabriele Ferzetti) and Claudia (Monica Vitti) are unable to console one another as they search for a missing friend. Frame enlargement.

Ingmar Bergman's severe psychological portraits of religious and emotional anguish were essential viewing for anyone who claimed to know cinema. These included *The Seventh Seal* (1957), *Wild Strawberries* (1957), and *Persona* (1966), and Bergman was a frequent prize winner at international festivals. Michelangelo Antonioni's *L'Avventura* (1960) won a special jury award at Cannes for the beauty of its images and for its novel stylistic design. Antonioni's great theme was psychological alienation in the modern world, and his drifting, de-centered compositions offered precise visual statements of this condition. He followed *L'Avventura* with two similar films, *La Notte* (1960) and *L'eclisse* (1962).

Luis Bunuel (*Belle de Jour,* 1967; *The Discrete Charm of the Bourgeoisie,* 1972) and Federico Fellini (*La Dolce Vita,* 1960; *8½,* 1963) were other major figures in this period and were joined by the filmmakers of the French New Wave (Francois Truffaut, Jean-Luc Godard, Agnes Varda) and the New German Cinema (Rainer Werner Fassbinder, Werner Herzog).

International cinema culture continues to thrive today, but the era of theatrical distribution for films from overseas has largely ended and been replaced by distribution in nontheatrical venues such as home video. Films from throughout the world are more accessible today on video than they were during the art film era, but cinema today exists on a crowded media landscape where it competes for a viewer's attention with other media devices and software delivery systems. Moreover, international film confronts an elephant in the room, and that is the global dominance of Hollywood cinema.

THE GLOBAL DOMINANCE OF HOLLYWOOD

The Majors

The Hollywood industry is composed of the **majors** (large studio–distributors that fund film production and distribute films internationally) and a number of small, independent production companies and distributors. The Hollywood majors are Sony Pictures Entertainment/Columbia Pictures (*Spider-Man 3* (2007), *The Da Vinci Code* (2005)), *Bewitched* (2005)); Warner Bros. (*Inception* (2010), *Batman Begins* (2005), *The Polar Express* (2004), *Ocean's Twelve* (2004)); Disney (*Toy Story 3* (2010), *Pirates of the Caribbean: On Stranger Tides* (2011)); 20th Century Fox (*Avatar* (2009), *Die Hard 4* (2007), *X-Men 3* (2006)); Universal (*The Bourne Ultimatum* (2007), *King Kong* (2005)); and Paramount (*True Grit* (2010), *Iron Man* (2008)). MGM (*The Pink Panther* (2005)), *Legally Blonde 2* (2003)) at one time was a major but is no longer. Each year the majors fund 10 to 15 productions and distribute an additional 10 to 12 films produced by other companies, usually the independents.

The soaring costs of film production prevent the majors from expanding their production activities beyond this relatively modest number of films. At the same time, however, some low-budget independent films (*The American* (2010), *The Waitress* (2007), *Memento* (2001), *The Blair Witch Project* (1999)) have performed well at the box office, and this makes the independent market attractive to the majors. Accordingly, they look for promising independent films to put into distribution.

The two markets are quite different in size and scale. Production costs are much lower for independent films, as are publicity costs, because the films are not distributed as widely or promoted as aggressively. A *Lord of the Rings* will saturate theaters nationwide; a *Memento* will be released only in selected regions of the country. Thus the industry refers to independent film distribution as the **limited-release market**.

MAJOR STUDIOS Motion Picture Producer/Distributors	OWNED BY
Sony Pictures Entertainment/ Columbia Pictures—Tri-Star	Sony (Japan)
Disney (Buena Vista)	Walt Disney Co.
Paramount	Viacom
20th Century Fox	News Corp. (Australia)
Warner Bros.	Time Warner
Universal	General Electric

FIGURE 10.1
The Hollywood majors.

THE LORD OF THE RINGS: THE RETURN OF THE KING (NEW LINE, 2004)

The size of the global film market is staggering, especially so if one adds the revenue from related product merchandising. The *Lord of the Rings* trilogy has grossed more than $4 billion from global box office, home video and television sales, and merchandising. Frame enlargement.

CLERKS (MIRAMAX, 1994)

Because of their low production costs, independent films don't have to be blockbusters to perform well at the box office. Shot in grainy black and white, *Clerks* found a sizable audience. The relative popularity of pictures like *Clerks* has attracted the majors to the independent market, most of whom now distribute such pictures through their own subsidiaries. Miramax, the distributor of *Clerks*, had been unaffiliated with the majors for most of its operating history. Disney now owns it. Frame enlargement.

Partly because of limited publicity and distribution, independent films typically earn far less at the box office than the majors' productions. *Memento*'s total box office earnings were $25 million, which is extremely high for the limited-release market. More typical are pictures like *Winter's Bone* (2010) with $8 million worldwide. Many independent films do not gross over $1 million. By contrast, *Spider-Man 3*

SHREK FOREVER AFTER (DREAMWORKS, 2010)
Computer-animated characters, voiced by Hollywood stars such as Cameron Diaz, Eddie Murphy, and Mike Myers, can be a key ingredient in the success of a blockbuster. Most blockbusters are showcases for visual effects, and the blend of CGI and warm, witty characters made the *Shrek* films into huge hits in the global film market, where they grossed over $900 million. Frame enlargement.

earned $151 million in its first *three days* of national release. Independent films do occasionally become box office hits. *My Big Fat Greek Wedding* (2002) grossed over $200 million, and *The Blair Witch Project* (1999) over $100 million, but most have modest earnings that match their modest budgets.

JUNO (FOX SEARCHLIGHT, 2007)
This appealing film about a young woman's unplanned pregnancy was produced on a small budget of $7 million and grossed nearly $230 million in worldwide markets. This level of success is extremely unusual for independent films, most of which struggle to find distribution and an audience. Frame enlargement.

For the majors, the **domestic theatrical market** (United States and Canada) is but a small part of their total box office earnings. The world cinema market is huge, and overseas revenue can be enormous. Hollywood films produced by the majors dominate this market. In 2010, *Harry Potter and the Deathly Hallows: Part I* earned twice as much overseas as it did in the United States and Canada. Of the top 125 films worldwide in 2001, only four were foreign pictures unreleased in the United States. In other words, American film production/distribution accounted for 99.9 percent of the world's top-earning films that year. *Harry Potter and the Deathly Hallows* is not unique. Many films earn more overseas than domestically. With its release spanning 2003–2004, *The Lord of the Rings: The Return of the King* grossed $742 million overseas compared with $377 million domestically. The world market for these pictures is more important in terms of box-office revenue than the domestic U.S. market. The highest-earning picture in world markets is *Avatar* (2009), with a global **gross** of $2.8 billion. The U.S. market generated only 27 percent of this total.

The overseas market is a vital source of revenue for Hollywood because the cost of producing and marketing a film has exploded in the last two decades. Costs hover upwards of $100 million. In 2007, for example, the average production cost was $71 million, plus $36 million for advertising. The industry no longer publicizes the average cost, perhaps because it has gotten so high.

THE FALLING BOX OFFICE   In reality, only a handful of films earn the fantastic revenues just cited. And all films today, even these blockbusters, have to earn their box office in a very short span of time. Box office revenue falls off almost instantly, with most films earning a substantial chunk on their opening weekend. *Spider-Man 3* had the biggest opening weekend box office of 2007—$151 million—and its

THE BLAIR WITCH PROJECT (ARTISAN, 1999)

Because of its extremely low production cost and huge box-office earnings, this independent film has been called the most profitable film in history. Frame enlargement.

box-office earnings fell 62 percent on the following weekend. *Harry Potter and the Deathly Hallows* fell 61 percent in its second week, and from there fell another 65 percent its third week. Virtually all films today show these steep declines after their opening weekend. This creates tremendous pressure on the industry to create high-profile films that can scoop up money quickly and get out of town fast if they need to.

Avatar bucked this trend because people felt very strongly that they needed to see it on the big screen. Its earnings declined a mere two percent in the second week. In week five they *rose* eight percent,, and in weeks 9–10 *rose another* 29 percent, behavior that is virtually unheard of.

Box-office revenues have remained flat for many years. In 2010, the industry announced U.S. market revenues of $10.6 billion, exactly what it had been the previous year. This helps to explain one reason the industry is so excited about 3D movies. They generated 21 percent of US/Canada box office. Annual ticket sales, rather than box-office gross, provide a better measure of the industry's performance. Annual ticket sales have remained relatively flat for many years, hovering around 1.3 billion. This suggests that the motion picture audience is not a growth market.

These patterns cause great uncertainty in the executive offices of the studios, as the industry finds it harder to connect with a public.

Movies at the theater now must compete with video games, online activities, and home video viewing, and the industry's greatest fear is that theatrical film may be declining relative to these other outlets. A 2005 nationwide poll by the Associated Press and AOL News was unsettling. It found that three-quarters of adults preferred watching movies at home.

A weakening box office makes the overseas markets ever more important. In 2010, 67 percent of industry revenue came from overseas markets. The larger problem that the industry faces is that it is very hard to make money from film production. How can this be, the reader justifiably wonders, given the millions earned by top-grossing films? Nevertheless, profits are hard to find, and this essential fact explains much about how the industry presently operates and is organized.

Splitting the Box-Office Dollar

Where does the money go? The popular media report box-office grosses, but these are distinct from the **rentals**, which are the revenues returned to the studio distributor and from which profit arises after expenses. Information about gross earnings, taken out of context, is nearly meaningless. In its first month of release, *Iron Man* (2008) grossed $353 million in world markets, but it cost $186 million to make. By contrast *300* (2007) cost $60 million to make and grossed $456 million worldwide, a better cost-to-earnings ratio. *The Blair Witch Project* (1999), which only cost $35,000 to produce, grossed over $120 million, leading many to describe it as the most profitable film in history.

Gross earnings must be evaluated in relation to a film's production cost, which, in the industry's vocabulary, is known as its **negative cost**. This is the expense the production has incurred, which includes the salaries for everyone from stars to the production crew, the costs of printing the film in the lab, and all the resources involved in the production (set design, costuming, special effects, etc.). Expensive star salaries will drive up negative costs. For *The Matrix* (1999), which had a negative cost of $60 million and grossed $350 million worldwide, Keanu Reeves earned 10 percent

FIGURE 10.2

Where the box office dollar goes.

Source: Adapted from Harold L. Vogel, *Entertainment Industry Economics,* 6th ed. (New York: Cambridge University Press, 2004).

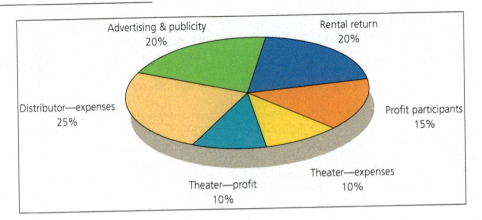

of the film's gross, which likely earned him in excess of $30 million. That is money the studio distributor will never see.

Box office earnings are diverted at multiple points by individuals and groups that have a claim on those moneys. To illustrate this, let's consider where your money goes when you buy a ticket. Of every dollar, the theater keeps 10 percent (10 cents) for its operating expenses and an additional 10 percent for its profit. The distributor keeps 25 percent to cover its operating expenses (studio distributors operate worldwide organizations). Advertising and publicity for a film will consume 20 percent of the box office-dollar. Profit participants who receive a cut of the gross may take anywhere from 10 to 30 percent. Subtracting all these deductions from the gross revenue leaves around 20 percent as the rental revenue for the studio, which must cover the negative cost and then (if possible) begin to generate profit. However, with negative costs now at an average of $64 million, 20 cents on the dollar hardly begins to cover these expenses.

Powerful stars, directors, and producers will take a percentage of a film's gross. This practice, known as taking *points*, greatly reduces the revenue available to the production company and distributor. The amount of money that can be involved is breathtaking. On *Meet the Fockers* (2004), 28 percent of its $514 million worldwide gross went to director Jay Roach and stars Ben Stiller and Robert De Niro. On *Catch Me If You Can* (2002), 35 percent of the gross ($351 million worldwide) went to director Steven Spielberg and actors Tom Hanks and Leonardo DiCaprio. Director Peter Jackson saw 20 percent of the gross on *King Kong* (2005).

Stars and directors who take points are **profit participants** because they share in a film's revenue along with the studio. Another category of profit participants consists of the outside investors who help to finance the cost of a production. These profit participants will be paid before a studio sees its profit. Fifty percent of the gross was promised to participants on *Terminator 3* (2003)! That fact, plus the film's huge production cost—$200 million—virtually guarantee that this film will never earn a profit.

The paradox, therefore, is resolved—despite the industry's seemingly impressive yearly earnings, the high cost of producing and promoting films leaves little profit from theatrical revenues. For this reason, Hollywood relies heavily on earnings from ancillary markets.

HARRY POTTER AND THE DEATHLY HALLOWS PART I (WARNER BROS., 2010)
One of the biggest box office films of 2010, it earned nearly $1 billion in global revenue by the end of its theatrical release. And that's just box office revenue. The movie also drove a global wave of merchandizing based around the popular characters. Author J. K. Rowling created those characters, but Time Warner now owns the copyright, enabling it to generate profits in multiple media markets. For the film industry, this is the key element of a blockbuster—its ability to drive consumer spending on a wave of related products in the ancillary markets. Frame enlargement.

Ancillary Markets

These are all the nontheatrical markets in which viewers watch movies or from which studios derive revenues. Warner Bros.' *Batman* (1989) earned money as a motion picture, a comic book character, a soundtrack album, a book about the making of the film, a Saturday morning cartoon series, and a wide range of toys, games, clothing, and other associated products carrying the Batman logo. Revenue earned by the Batman character from these products, both domestically and overseas, returns to Time Warner, the parent corporation that owns the rights to the character and that controls the media in which the Caped Crusader is marketed.

Ancillary markets include broadcast and pay cable television (both domestically and worldwide), home video royalties realized through rental and sale of DVDs and Blu-ray, digital distribution (video on demand), and the licensing of film characters and logos to merchandisers and retailers.

Beginning in the mid-1980s, revenue from home video surpassed box-office earnings. Since that time, the majors earned more from sales of films to video and cable markets than from ticket sales in the nation's theaters. *Shrek* (2001), for example, grossed $268 million at the domestic box office but earned $470 million in VHS/DVD sales and rentals. The DVD market in particular had generated huge revenues. *Spider-Man* sold $145 million of DVDs in its first week of home video release.

DVD had been a fabulously successful source of revenue for the studios. DVD sales and rentals in 2004, for example, totaled $21 billion, compared with a $7 billion box office. But now that golden goose has stopped laying its eggs. DVD sales and rentals reached a high of $20 billion in 2006 and have fallen steadily since then, reaching a low of $14 billion in 2010. Revenue from Blu-ray and video-on-demand is rising, but these markets presently are very small in comparison to DVD.

It seems likely that the boom years for the DVD market are over, and many people in the industry regard Blu-ray as the last form of packaged media that movies will assume. Digital distribution—movies available as downloads-to-own or as video viewing on demand—is seen as the future of home entertainment.

While big screen theaters once were the traditional venue for movies, the growth of home entertainment and the push to digital distribution demonstrates that the markets for motion picture entertainment are integrated—the theatrical market exists in conjunction with the ancillaries—and corporate survival depends on the control of these markets. This environment creates a distinct rationale for **blockbuster** production. The blockbuster film, especially **franchise** series featuring *Spider-Man, Harry Potter, Lord of the Rings*, and *Star Wars*, has enormous audience appeal that spreads across a variety of media categories. These films do a huge business in the theatrical market, which, in turn, generates big revenues in ancillary markets. But to create blockbusters and to market them across the ancillaries requires that a film studio be **diversified**, with its business activities spread across a range of products, media, and associated markets. Diversification positions a film studio to compete within the integrated entertainment market, enables it to perform in overseas markets, and facilitates the marketing of blockbuster films.

Film and Product Merchandising

Film-based product merchandising is a direct function of diversification into multiple media markets. Blockbuster films—*Harry Potter, Lord of the Rings, Spider-Man*— often feature mechanical or fantasy characters that lend themselves to manufacture and merchandising as diverse products. There is a direct correlation between these mechanical characters and the imperatives of product merchandising. As the licensing director of Amblin Entertainment (the production company responsible for *Gremlins*) remarked, "Whenever you have a nonhuman type of character, it lends itself to

THE LORD OF THE RINGS: THE RETURN OF THE KING (NEW LINE, 2004)
Parent company Time Warner had a very good year with its subsidiary New Line Cinema. *Lord of the Rings: The Return of the King* grossed $1.1 billion worldwide. Although the film was funded and distributed by New Line, its revenue stayed in-house at Time Warner. The global media market is ruled by a relative handful of giant companies like Time Warner. Frame enlargement.

merchandising." Film-based merchandising takes two forms: the product tie-in and product placement.

PRODUCT TIE-INS   With their skyrocketing box office gross, Steven Spielberg's *Jaws* and George Lucas's *Star Wars* in the mid-seventies announced the onset of the blockbuster era. The phenomenal impact of *Jaws* in the summer of 1975 was intensified by the enormous range of **product tie-ins** marketed around the release of the film. These products included T-shirts, plastic tumblers, the soundtrack album, a paperback about the making of the movie, beach towels, bike bags, blankets, costume jewelry, shark costumes, hosiery, hobby kits, inflatable sharks, iron-on transfers, games,

CLOSE-UP

High-Definition DVD

For movie lovers, the most exciting ancillary market is now unquestionably high-definition DVD. It offers unprecedented clarity, sharpness, and color reproduction, as well as audio formats that are superior to what conventional film theaters can offer (see High-Definition Audio in Chapter 6). When displayed on a high-definition widescreen set of even modest size, a hi-def DVD is markedly superior to standard DVD. When projected onto a large screen, the differences are even more striking. Detail and texture pop off the screen in images that look far more like film than like video.

Standard DVD offers 480 lines of picture information that are interlaced in the fashion of conventional television as alternating fields, each containing only 50 percent of the picture information. High-definition DVD, by contrast, offers 1080 lines that are progressively displayed, producing a much smoother and sharper picture without the artifacts, such as jagged lines, associated with an interlaced signal.

Blu-ray emerged as the standard format for high-definition DVD after a short war with the competing HD-DVD format. This struggle dated back to 2002 and the rivalry between Sony (promoting Blu-ray) and Toshiba (pushing HD-DVD). Both formats offered equivalent picture quality, but Blu-ray proved better at handling the numerous different audio formats carried on high-definition DVD.

The format war ended in 2008 when Warner Bros., which controlled nearly a quarter of the home video market, announced it would back Blu-ray exclusively, and similar announcements followed from the mail-order video rental firm Netflix and the big-box discounter Best Buy. Along with Sony, Warner has placed the most titles onto Blu-ray.

Presently, hundreds of films are available on Blu-ray, with most, predictably, being recent box-office successes. But an increasing number of older films have found their way to high definition, such as *The Longest Day* (1962), *Butch Cassidy and the Sundance Kid* (1969), *Dirty Harry* (1971), *Bullitt* (1968), and several films by Stanley Kubrick. *2001: A Space Odyssey* (1968), for example, looks fabulous in this format. Classic silent films have also been released on Blu-ray, offering home viewers an unprecedented opportunity to see them in their cinematic glory. Buster Keaton's *The General* (1926), F. W. Murnau's *Nosferatu* (1922) and *City Girl* (1930), and Douglas Fairbank's *The Black Pirate* (1926) are among the best.

While many viewers would probably say that standard DVD is "good enough," high-definition DVD is a tremendous step forward toward a high-quality, in-home cinema experience. As more titles appear on high definition and more viewers invest in the necessary playback equipment, it is conceivable that high definition will replace standard DVD as the preferred medium of viewing choice. And high-quality home theaters will begin to cut into the business of conventional movie theaters, becoming, in effect, the first-run cinemas of the future. Alternatively, if low-resolution streaming formats kill packaged media, as many in the industry hope, Blu-ray may be the last hard media format to showcase the special beauty of cinema. ■

(continued)

THERE WILL BE BLOOD (Paramount, 2007)
High definition creates a film-like viewing experience because of its ability to capture small details and render them in crisp resolution. In *There Will Be Blood*, Daniel Day-Lewis plays an obsessive, driven oil baron, and the high-definition image presents the detailing on his face with exceptional clarity. Frame enlargement.

Case Study   TIME WARNER

Warner Bros. belongs to parent company Time Warner, which is the largest media and entertainment company in the world, a vast media empire with holdings in film, book publishing, and music recording. Time Warner's revenue in 2010 was $27 billion, a huge figure that provides some idea of the size of this corporation. Hollywood film is only one of many entertainment media controlled by Time Warner, which are grouped in three segments: cable television networks, filmed entertainment, and publishing.

Filmed Entertainment provided 40 percent of Time Warner's earnings in 2010. Several companies operate here, providing film and television revenue. Warner Bros. Pictures is the film studio, producing hits like *Inception* (2010), *Clash of the Titans* (2010), and the *Harry Potter* films. New Line Cinema Corp. also produces films, often specializing in independent films, and had a giant hit with the *Lord of the Rings* series. New Lines revenues dropped in subsequent years, however, and Time Warner dissolved the company as a separate subsidiary and absorbed its operation.

Warner Home Video controls 20 percent of the video sales and rental market in the United States. For ten years, it has been the market leader in home video sales and rentals. It offers titles drawn from Warner's library of 6,000 theatrical films and 54,000 television titles. The *Lord of the Rings* and *Harry Potter* series have been huge sellers on home video, as have boxed sets of television shows, including *Sex and the City* and *The Sopranos*. In the early days of DVD, Warner Home Video was the most aggressive champion of the format among all the Hollywood majors. By 2002, it had released nearly 900 titles on DVD.

Warner Bros. Television Group produces programming for network and cable and had more programming on the air during the 2004–2005 season than any other studio. Its shows include *Smallville*, *The West Wing*, and *Cold Case*.

Networks also include companies that deliver cable television programming—Turner Broadcasting System (TBS, TNT, CNN, the Cartoon Network), Home Box Office (HBO and Cinemax). TNT reaches 100 million households, and HBO is the number one pay cable network. HBO also produces a large amount of film and television programming, including *Deadwood*, *The Sopranos*, and *Empire Falls*.

SPIDER-MAN 3 (Sony Pictures, 2007); PIRATES OF THE CARIBBEAN: AT WORLD'S END (Buena Vista, 2007)

Because of high negative costs, studios look for properties that can generate revenue across several installments. Such films are called "franchises" because the property or brand is appealing enough to audiences to motivate several productions. *Spider-Man 3's* negative cost was $258 million, but it was the year's highest-grossing movie. As long as a franchise's earnings potential lasts, studios are reluctant to abandon the format. *Pirates of the Caribbean: At World's End,* for example, concludes with action that sets up the sequel, *On Stranger Tides* (2010). Frame enlargement.

The core area of publishing consists of magazines and books. Time, Inc., publishes 90 magazines globally, including *Time, People, Entertainment Weekly*, and *Sports Illustrated.* But with the decline of print media, this area contributes only 14 percent of company revenues.

Time Warner used to operate a huge cable hardware business and had also partnered with AOL to offer Internet access and services. It got out of these businesses and now looks to the future with Warner Bros. Digital Distribution, a division of Warner Home Video. It licenses films and television programs for distribution via cable, satellite, the Internet, and PCs, laptops, and cell phones. Nokia, Samsung, and Dell cell phones and PCs come pre-loaded with Warner films to be marketed to consumers.

(continued)

As this brief profile indicates, Time Warner creates media programming *and* seeks to influence or control the distribution systems (the Internet, theaters, video, cable and broadcast TV) needed to get that programming to its audience. What are the advantages of such diversification? One advantage is that Time Warner can offset the loss accruing to any one area of business operations from profits associated with others. The major advantage, however, is that Time Warner keeps in-house all revenues from the performance of its products across a wide range of media markets.

Creative artists, however, may construe this as a disadvantage, arguing that a vertically integrated company's incentive to keep revenue streams in-house may cause it to pass up higher bids from outside companies for DVD or publishing rights. This is exactly what director Peter Jackson argued in a suit he filed in 2005 against New Line, whose divisions handled home video, merchandising, and television rights for *The Lord of the Rings.* Jackson claimed that outside companies would have made higher bids for these rights and that New Line's "self-dealing" harmed the resulting revenues.

The financial health of the industry, however, depends on these kinds of self-dealings. The *Harry Potter* films have been among the biggest box-office films in the world, and Time Warner owns the trademarks and copyrights to the characters. Thus it can market Harry as a movie, a soundtrack album, a DVD, and videocassette and receive revenue from the tidal wave of Harry Potter merchandise.

Similarly, Batman has been a hugely successful comic book, movie, video, record, and line of toys. The Batman character originated in D.C. Comics, which Time Warner owns and publishes. The *Batman* films are produced by Warner Bros., books about the making of the *Batman* movies are published by Warner Books, the soundtrack albums have appeared on Warner Bros. Records, and revenue from the release of the films to the home video market is generated through Warner Home Video.

Thus, regardless of how the Harry Potter or Batman characters appear—as a movie, record album, book, video viewed in the home, comic strip, or toy model or board game—Time Warner is assured a steady stream of money. Revenues from the theatrical market are insufficient to cover today's high cost of film production. As a result, the Hollywood majors are held by larger firms that operate in multiple media markets. This is the only way that expensive film production can be a winning game for the industry.

---

posters, sharks' teeth necklaces, sleepwear, children's sweaters, swimsuits, ties, and water pistols.

The majors derive huge revenues from licensing movie characters and props to merchandisers. Hollywood's product licensing revenues totaled $70 billion in 2001, and the contemporary blockbuster is designed to maximize this revenue.

This kind of marketing is now a standard feature of film distribution. The *Star Wars* movies have grossed more than $1 billion at the U.S. box office, but merchandising related to the films has generated more than four times as much money! The James Bond adventure *Die Another Day* (2002) carried $120 million worth of advertising by 20 brands, a promotional windfall for the film's distributor, MGM, which spent $30 million to promote the film. All the extra advertising was a virtual freebie for MGM.

PRODUCT PLACEMENT   A second category of film merchandising illustrates the deep connection between modern film and the consumer economy. **Product placement** is a form of product advertising that appears inside a motion picture. Today, if Will Smith or Cameron Diaz drinks a can of beer in a movie, it is not going to be a generic fictitious label such as Ajax beer. It will be a popular, commercially available beer such as Budweiser or Michelob. Famous brand labels don't appear accidentally on screen. They are there because manufacturers paid a placement fee to studios to guarantee their labels a visible spot on screen. The size of the fee depends on how prominently

JAWS (UNIVERSAL, 1975)

While *Jaws* terrified summer audiences, it was accompanied by a marketing blitzkrieg pushing shark products. Blockbuster films are huge engines driving the leisure-time economy. They stimulate massive cycles of consumer purchasing. Their economic impact sometimes is more significant than the artistic merits they may possess. *Jaws,* however, is a superbly made film by a brilliant director (Steven Spielberg). Frame enlargement.

the product is displayed. Studios count on income from product placements to offset expensive production costs, which accounts for the growing frequency of product placements.

In 1990, the Center for the Study of Commercialism, based in Washington, D.C., conducted a study to determine the pervasiveness of product placement. It found that

CAST AWAY (20TH CENTURY FOX, 2000)

This scene from *Cast Away* shows especially blatant product placement. In terms of the composition, the Wilson volley ball is visually more important than the film's main character, played by Tom Hanks. "Wilson," the ball, even becomes a character in the film. Note how the product's positioning ensures high visibility for the brand label. Frame enlargement.

the year's top-grossing film, Paramount Pictures's *Ghost*, contained 23 references to 16 different brand-name products. The second highest-grossing film that year, Disney's *Pretty Woman*, contained 20 references to 18 brand names. *Total Recall*, the sixth highest-grossing film that year, was the champion. It contained 55 references to 28 brand-named products including Heinz ketchup, *U.S.A. Today*, Ocean Spray juices, the Hilton Hotel, Pepsi, Fuji Film, Hostess snacks, Panasonic TV, Nike shoes, Coca-Cola, Kodak film, Sony television, Beck's Beer, Campbell's soup, Northwest Airlines, Killian Red Beer, Miller Light Beer, Miller Genuine Draft Beer, Gordon's Liquor, Jack-in-the-Box restaurants, ESPN, and Evian water.

Given the emphasis on product placement in today's Hollywood, obvious issues of creative control arise. Do paid advertisements within the context of a film narrative subtly alter the shape and focus of that narrative? At least with certain films, the answer is an unqualified "yes." *Total Recall* is a science fiction thriller in which the villains are ruthless futuristic corporations in league with gangsters running a brutal mining operation on Mars. The film's satire and criticism of corporate control are compromised by its massive reliance on product placements. These render the film's anticorporate satire less than coherent. At a minimum, product placements will tend to bias the social perspective of a film toward an unquestioning or unexamined acceptance of the contemporary consumer economy with its engineered leisure-time markets and products. This subverts the effort by a film such as *Total Recall* to satirize a future world overtaken by for-profit leisure-time industries. Its massive reliance on product placement makes *Total Recall* into the very thing it would satirize.

WAYNE'S WORLD (PARAMOUNT, 1992)

Product placement became so prominent and enduring a feature of contemporary film that Wayne and Garth could not resist making fun of it. In this scene, while pretending to complain about big stars who "sell out," they happily push products by Coke, Pizza Hut, and others. Frame enlargement.

TOTAL RECALL (TRI-STAR PICTURES, 1990)

Total Recall, starring Arnold Schwarzenegger, featured more product placements than any other film of 1990. The film's satirical content suffered from the constant on-screen product advertising. Frame enlargement.

Economic Significance of the Blockbuster Film

Besides being superprofitable, blockbuster films have two additional characteristics. Their stories frequently depend on fantasy or visual effects (this is the magic that Spielberg referred to), and their characters are often superhuman or mechanical and nonhuman (the shark in *Jaws*, the robots in *Star Wars*, the alien in *E.T.*, the robots in *Terminator 2* or *Transformers*, and the dinosaurs in *Jurassic Park*). Visual effects promise to provide audiences with visions of things never before photographed, and this is a big part of the allure of blockbusters. Furthermore, as we have seen, mechanical characters lend themselves quite well to reproduction across diverse product lines. (Not all blockbusters have each of these elements. *Forrest Gump* (1994), *Home Alone* (1990), and *Beverly Hills Cop* (1984), for example, are not dependent on mechanical or nonhuman characters. *Gump*, though, is a visual-effects showcase, whereas *Home Alone* and *Beverly Hills Cop* boast cartoonlike plots with ultra-powerful heroes (played by Macaulay Culkin and Eddie Murphy) at their center.) Blockbuster filmmaking crosses a wide range of media sources and merchandise lines. As such, the shark frenzy generated by *Jaws* in 1975, the dinosaur craze created by *Jurassic Park*, and the wave of *Phantom Menace* toys that swept retailers in 1999 represented cultural phenomena far greater than the films themselves. The shark and dinosaur and *Star Wars* markets extended well beyond the revenues created by motion picture ticket sales.

Here lies the most important principle represented by blockbuster production. The blockbuster motion picture is merely the hub of a giant wheel of interconnected services and products. The film provides the stimulus for a huge array of merchandising and marketing in the nation's and the world's restaurants, toy stores, and other retail outlets, and it creates audience interest that sustains revenues in the cable and home video markets.

Sometimes, an aggressive product-licensing campaign can have an unintended effect. Even with a big box-office hit, efforts to license products can fail if the merchandise and the film provide a poor fit. *Star Wars Episode I: The Phantom Menace* (1999) sold more than $2 billion of merchandise worldwide, but many millions of unsold toys and products remained on retailers' shelves, leaving retailers feeling burned and believing that the film had been oversold and overhyped. Accordingly, Lucasfilm acknowledged its mistake and reduced the number of product tie-ins for *Episode II: Attack of the Clones*, concentrating on core items such as action figures, video games, and books and eliminating fringe items such as the Anakin Skywalker inflatable chair and the Obi-Wan Kenobi clip-on hair braids.

The performance of *Jurassic Park*, the number one film in world markets in 1993, offers a more successful example of product licensing. Products associated with *Jurassic Park* included ice cream, frozen pizza, cakes, juices, cookies, key rings, chairs, sneakers, and, of course, toy dinosaurs. Video and computer games were a huge chunk of the product merchandising conducted with the film. Ocean Software paid $2 million

as an advance royalty in exchange for worldwide rights to all *Jurassic Park* video games. It was a good deal. In France, the film opened on October 20, and by the end of December, Ocean Software had already sold 250,000 video games there. So stunning was the early performance of *Jurassic Park*–themed computer games, food, clothing, books, and toys that the vice president of international merchandising for MCA/Universal, the studio conglomerate that produced the film, predicted that international sales of *Jurassic Park*–licensed products would outperform domestic U.S. sales.

Long-term planning before the film's release helped to ensure the successful marketing of the film and its associated products. The previous international box office champion was another Spielberg film, 1982's *E.T.: The Extra-Terrestrial*. Studio marketing executives believed they had fumbled the ball with *E.T.* more than a decade ago. Because the main character in *E.T.* is an ungainly little alien, the executives underestimated the market potential for product tie-ins, and they actually had difficulty finding manufacturers who were interested in bringing out *E.T.*-themed lines of merchandise.

THE PHANTOM MENACE (20TH CENTURY FOX, 1999)
Although this film was a major hit worldwide, many of its product tie-ins failed to move off of store shelves. *Phantom Menace* merchandise oversaturated the market, and many of the items for sale—clip-on hair braids, for example—were poor fits with the film. Lucasfilm scaled down its merchandising efforts with the next installment in the series. Frame enlargement.

E.T. (Universal Studios, 1982)
Despite its long-time position as box office champ before being dethroned by *Jurassic Park* and then *Titanic, E.T.* never realized its full potential as a catalyst for product marketing. In comparison with the early 1980s, the film industry today heavily depends on product placement and marketing for additional revenue streams. Throughout the 1980s, the industry carefully reorganized itself to capitalize as much as possible on the profit potential of diverse leisure-time markets. Frame enlargement.

Marketing executives were determined not to repeat this mistake with *Jurassic Park*. Accordingly, two years before the film's premiere, the studio put teams of licensing, promotional, and manufacturing personnel to work preparing for the film's global launch. A major component of the marketing strategy was the *limited* disclosure of information about the film. Spielberg did not want to reveal too much about the film in early trailers and publicity. The secrecy was designed to keep the audience in suspense about the mysterious film prior to its release. Marketing programs were drawn up in countries throughout the world using only one graphic illustration from the film, an image showing the head of a dinosaur tipping over a park vehicle.

As the film's premiere drew closer, minimal, teasing information gave way to full media blitzes. For example, the film premiered September 3 in Sweden, Finland, and Norway and two weeks later in Denmark. Television was the major media form promoting the picture in these Scandinavian countries. Massive advertising campaigns saturated television viewers with promos for the film. In Norway, 97 commercials were presented in the nine days before the film's premiere. Heavy television advertising also whet viewers' appetites in Sweden, Denmark, and Finland. As a result, from the less than 24 million people inhabiting these countries, the film grossed $15 million.

Spielberg's Assessment

Surveying the extraordinary performance of his film in global markets, Spielberg likened its appeal to the magic of a compelling story told around a campfire. In earlier times, communities would sit by the campfire and listen attentively as a storyteller cast a spell with tales of magic and fantasy. Today, Spielberg pointed out, the gathering around the campfire is the entire world. From Europe to Asia to Central and South America, people gather in multiplex theaters. He stated that the success of the film was due to good storytelling and not to the economic dominance in global markets of American cinema.

Spielberg's feeling of satisfaction was deserved. He has made some of the most popular pictures of all time, and even his serious, adult-themed films (*Schindler's List, Saving Private Ryan*) have reached wide audiences. But more than the magic of good storytelling was at work in the global performance of *Jurassic Park*. Without American corporate control of a global media industry and control of revenue from interlocking media formats (movies, books, records, home video, and retail merchandising), the *Jurassic Park* phenomenon could not have existed. The global reach of U.S. media industries is fundamental to the success of blockbuster films. Despite what Spielberg has said, this economic framework cannot be easily dismissed. ◼

MEN IN BLACK (COLUMBIA TRISTAR, 1997)

Blockbuster films typically showcase state-of-the-art visual effects and fantasy narratives populated by eccentric or mechanical characters. *Men in Black* portrayed an Earth overrun by aliens, including the giant, and mean-spirited, Edgar bug. Frame enlargement.

Blockbuster filmmaking, therefore, is about more than just the making of a single film. Successful blockbuster production stimulates the creation of a huge network of associated products and productions. This is why the integrated market is so important. Because the appeal of blockbuster film characters crosses media classes and product lines, parent corporations who own the film studios that produce those characters must also control all of the other markets in which the film and its characters will appear.

This is accomplished by controlling the multiple ways that consumers will encounter the film and/or its characters. Whether consumers view it as a theatrical motion picture, as a video on home television, or by way of pay cable, whether they listen to the film's music on a soundtrack album, or read a paperback book about the making of the movie, or buy dolls, games, or clothing tied into the film's characters, the revenue streams generated by these media markets stay in-house. By licensing the use of the blockbuster characters to other manufacturers, the potentially huge revenue stream generated by product tie-ins throughout the world helps enlarge corporate earnings.

In its truest sense, then, blockbuster filmmaking is about the production and manufacture of commodities on a national and global scale. Film is only a means toward this pattern of global production. Blockbuster films are the engines that drive the global entertainment markets. Understood in economic terms, the blockbuster film's importance is measured only in its ability to stimulate a huge wave of consumption of film-themed leisure-time products and services. With their blockbuster productions and aggressive promotional campaigns, U.S. film studios have made the world their marketplace. The danger in this is that global film production becomes increasingly homogenized, increasingly the same from country to country, given over to special-effects-driven fantasy narratives or violent action spectacles featuring superhuman heroes.

Steven Spielberg

Judged by box-office receipts, Steven Spielberg has been the most popular filmmaker in the world. *Jurassic Park* (1993) broke world box office records, and the top-grossing film it displaced was *E.T.* (1982), another Spielberg creation. His other hits—*Jaws* (1975), *Raiders of the Lost Ark* (1981), and *Indiana Jones and the Last Crusade* (1989)—are among the highest-grossing films of all time. But unlike Spielberg's public, until recently critics have remained divided over the merits of his work.

During the 1970s and early 1980s, critics dismissed him as a maker of popcorn movies, built around visual effects and strong emotions. The mechanical shark, the spacecraft and aliens of *Close Encounters of the Third Kind* (1977), and *E.T*—critics disparaged these as movies that evoked a range of uncomplicated feelings, mainly awe and wonder, issuing from unexpected encounters with fantasy creatures. But popular audiences responded enthusiastically to the energy of Spielberg's storytelling and the power of his images.

As a filmmaker, Spielberg was a genuine boy wonder. Unlike his contemporaries, he did not attend film school but went straight into the industry. Born in Cincinnati in 1947, he was just 21 when hired as a television director by Universal Studios, where he was in charge of episodes of *Night Gallery*, *Marcus Welby*, and *Columbo*. His first feature film, *Duel* (1971), made for television, was a gripping thriller of a traveling salesman menaced on the road by a mysterious, anonymous truck driver.

At the age of 26, Spielberg began filming a similar story about a confrontation between ordinary people and the unknown, but this time with an aquatic setting. *Jaws* (1975), the work of a hungry young filmmaker eager to prove himself, caused a sensation the summer of its release. People were afraid to go in the water, just as they had been afraid to take showers when Hitchcock had finished with them in *Psycho* (1960) a decade and a half earlier. A ferocious thrill machine, *Jaws* evoked a primitive terror in its audience that Spielberg never again

attempted to duplicate. He quickly turned to spirited evocations of childlike wonder and adolescent adventure: *Close Encounters of the Third Kind* (1977), *Raiders of the Lost Ark* (1981), *E.T.* (1982), and *Indiana Jones and the Temple of Doom* (1984). Their spectacular success obliterated his only early career misfire, *1941* (1979), an overblown and unfunny attempt at a World War II slapstick comedy.

But Spielberg was more ambitious than critics at the time recognized. He began to expand his range with more mature subjects. With *The Color Purple* (1985), he adapted Alice Walker's novel about an African-American woman's experiences with an abusive husband. *Empire of the Sun* (1987), another World War II film, and *Always* (1989), a remake of a classic 1943 Hollywood film, were critical and commercial disappointments, but in both cases Spielberg conspicuously stepped away from popcorn moviemaking. Moreover, they demonstrated something that was hard to see at the time, that World War II had special resonance for Spielberg and that he would become one of its most important cinematic chroniclers.

He next broke through the digital threshold with *Jurassic Park* (1993), providing not the first but the most spectacular demonstration of next-generation computer-based effects. It was *Schindler's List*, though, released the same year, that earned Spielberg the critical respect that had, until then, eluded him. This grim black-and-white film portrays the horrors of the Nazi extermination camps in Poland with a depth of emotional feeling and an adult sensibility that Spielberg had never before demonstrated in his work. Moreover, he extended his historical and moral sense of obligation by helping launch a vast project documenting and recording the oral histories of Holocaust survivors, accounts that will be digitized and become part of the world's historical record. He felt a special urgency in carrying out this project because many of the survivors were quite elderly.

Beginning with *Schindler's List*, Spielberg came into his own as a filmmaker of considerable artistic and moral ambition. Fashioning brilliant images,

(continued)

RAIDERS OF THE LOST ARK (PARAMOUNT PICTURES, 1981); MINORITY REPORT (DREAMWORKS, 2002)

During the 1980s, Speilberg was box-office gold, crafting popular hits like *Raiders of the Lost Ark*, an **homage** to old Hollywood serial adventures. In the 1990s and after, he often turned to dark-themed material, such as *Minority Report*, a frightening portrait of an authoritarian future where the state has access to people's thoughts and the power to arrest them for thought crimes. On these later films, Spielberg collaborated with cinematographer Janusz Kaminski to design cold and grainy images that rejected the glossy surfaces of more audience-friendly films. Frame enlargements.

he now used film to examine issues of human evil and moral redemption. *Amistad* (1997) graphically showed the horrors of slavery in its portrait of a historic rebellion of African slaves in Colonial America. *Saving Private Ryan* (1998) showed the D-Day invasion of the Normandy beaches in a way that caught the savagery of the combat with a ferocity unprecedented in commercial cinema. Intended to dramatize the heroism of that generation of U.S. soldiers, the film aroused tremendous interest in their example and public respect for their sacrifice.

Spielberg's somber historical dramas are his most artistically ambitious films; most encouraging in this respect, they have performed solidly at the box office. The greatest strength of U.S. film has always been its conjunction of popular appeal with work of artistic distinction. More than many other directors now working, Spielberg exemplifies this principle.

After *Saving Private Ryan*, Spielberg took an unusual (for him) break from filmmaking. His next two features, *A.I.: Artificial Intelligence* (2001) and *Minority Report* (2002), were an ambitious and challenging return to the genre of science fiction, but without the children's orientation of *E.T.* and *Close Encounters*.

Both are grim and disturbing films, aimed for adults, and suggested that Spielberg, who had always been a visionary director, was pursuing his artistic ambitions as vigorously as he once courted the box office. Following the destruction of the World Trade Center, Spielberg made three films that reflected on 9/11: *The Terminal* (2004), *War of the Worlds* (2005), and *Munich* (2005), one of his finest films. He then returned to the Indiana Jones franchise with *Indiana Jones and the Kingdom of the Crystal Skull* (2008). ■

INDEPENDENT FILM

Many viewers probably think of independent films as being wholly distinct and different from blockbusters and from mainstream studio movies. In fact, though, the category of independent film includes many different types of movies, some of which may have rather high budgets, big stars, and a major studio distributor. *Cold Mountain* (2003), for example, a drama about the Civil War, starring Nicole Kidman and Jude Law, cost $83 million to make and was distributed by a subsidiary of Disney, one of the major studios. *Star Wars Episode III: Revenge of the Sith* (2005) was made by George Lucas' production company, Lucasfilm, without studio control or interference.

At the other end of the spectrum of independent film, *Open Water* (2003) cost only $130,000 to make. This drama about two divers who are stranded in the ocean when their dive boat returns to shore and who are preyed on by sharks had a very low production cost because it was shot on digital video and was a two-character film, with the ocean as the main set. Most famously, *The Blair Witch Project* (1999) required only $35,000 to complete. *My Big Fat Greek Wedding* (2002) also was a very inexpensive film.

"Independent," then, does not always mean that a film was low budget or was made completely outside the studio system. It is better to think of this category as containing a range of films, at different budget levels, that were either financed or produced or distributed by sources outside the major Hollywood studios, although the studios may have some level of involvement. A film such as *Outfoxed: Rupert Murdoch's War on Journalism* (2004) was made completely outside the system, with no participation at any level by a Hollywood major. On the other hand, Clint Eastwood's *Million Dollar Baby* (2004) was financed independently but was distributed by Warner Bros., one of the majors.

The film industry, therefore, is not divided into two camps, one mainstream and one independent. The industry is decentralized and fragmented into many separate production companies and distributors, and the relationships among these can be complex and fluid.

While financing and distribution arrangements provide a very good measure of a film's degree of independence, another characteristic that many viewers may hold in mind when thinking about independent film is artistic experimentation.

THE KING'S SPEECH (THE WEINSTEIN COMPANY, 2010); WINTER'S BONE (WINTER'S BONE PRODUCTIONS, 2010)

Independent film is diverse, occupying a range of budgets and styles. Some pictures, such as *The King's Speech*, may have relatively large budgets and prominent stars, such as, in this case, Helena Bonham Carter, Colin Firth, and Geoffrey Rush. During its widest distribution, it played in 2500 theaters. In contrast, *Winter's Bone*, nominated for an Academy Award as Best Picture, screened in only 141 theaters. Frame enlargement.

Independent film is often thought to be more daring, off-beat, or radical in its artistic design, with filmmakers taking more risks than they would be able to in a studio project.

This is sometimes true, sometimes not, again because independent film is a big category that contains a large range of movies. *Sin City* (2005) clearly takes an experimental approach in placing live actors against digitally rendered sets and props.

Memento (2001) famously tells its story backward, and *The Machinist* (2004) offers a thriller with numerous ambiguities and a grainy black-and-white look.

As noted, though, *Cold Mountain* and *Million Dollar Baby* are also independent films because of their financing arrangements, and these pictures feature strong stories, told in a straightforward way, with characters whose fates are emotionally moving and who are played by charismatic stars. These are characteristics of mainstream Hollywood films as well.

Independent film, then, is a very flexible category and a very big one. Most of the films that are in release in any given year are independents. While films by the Hollywood majors tend to generate most of the media coverage (because these include the blockbusters), the independent distributors actually put more films into circulation than the majors. In 2010, for example, the majors released 141 films, whereas independent distributors released 419, and this ratio has held constant for several decades.

The downside to independent distribution is that these films go into fewer theaters and will be seen by smaller audiences. On the other hand, with so much product in circulation, an independent filmmaker has many opportunities for getting a film produced and distributed.

A convenient way to understand independent film is to examine it in terms of its production companies, film festivals, and filmmakers.

Production Companies

Miramax was the most prominent producer and distributor of independent films. Run by Bob and Harvey Weinstein, Miramax began as a stand-alone company and

SEX, LIES & VIDEOTAPE (MIRAMAX, 1989)

Winning numerous awards from film festivals and critics' associations and distributed to great success by Miramax, this film launched the modern era of independent filmmaking. It helped put Miramax on the map as the pre-eminent distributor of independent film. With its focus on the sexual hang-ups of three characters and its atypical style, it also solidified the reputation of independent film as being an outsider to mainstream Hollywood product. Frame enlargement.

became famous when it acquired Steven Soderbergh's *sex, lies & videotape* (1989) at the Sundance Film Festival. The Soderbergh film went on to become one of the most prominent and popular "indies" of its era, and its release by Miramax is often regarded as the opening chapter of the modern independent film era.

The Weinstein brothers moved aggressively to put a large number of films into distribution. They proved to be very shrewd judges of the marketplace, and many of the films they acquired performed extremely well and have become classics of the indie movement—*The Crying Game* (1992), *In the Bedroom* (2001), *Kill Bill* (2003, 2004), *House of Sand and Fog* (2004), and *Sin City* (2005).

The Weinsteins also championed the careers of emerging directors by funding and distributing their work and aggressively publicizing it for Academy Award nominations. The most famous of the Miramax directors are Quentin Tarantino and Michael Moore. Miramax's backing of *Reservoir Dogs* (1992), *Pulp Fiction* (1994), *Jackie Brown* (1997), and *Kill Bill* (2003) demonstrated that independent film could have considerable box-office earning power, as did *Roger & Me* (1989), *Bowling for Columbine* (2002), and *Fahrenheit 9/11* (2004).

Tarantino's films have been massively influential on a generation of young filmmakers, as has Michael Moore's approach to the documentary format. In this respect, Miramax left a lasting legacy to American cinema.

Disney acquired Miramax in 1993, and the Weinsteins used their connection to a Hollywood major to expand the budgets and production resources of their films. The Miramax productions that followed blurred the line between independent film and the larger scale and scope of Hollywood productions. These big-budget indies included *The English Patient* (1996), *Cold Mountain, Gangs of New York* (2002), and *The Aviator* (2004).

The relationship with Disney, though, had a downside—corporate control from above running counter to the spirit of independent filmmaking. This issue was very apparent in the fight that erupted over *Fahrenheit 9/11*. Disney, which had contracted to release the film, decided not to distribute it once the picture had been completed. Many suspected that the film's anti-Bush politics had prompted Disney's decision, although Disney denied that this was the case.

The Weinsteins lobbied Disney to negotiate new terms that would allow them to find another distributor, and after much back-and-forth, they were successful. But the episode showed how corporate control of the media can threaten to restrict the flow of ideas and expression, and it helped to sour the relationship of Miramax and Disney.

The era from 1989 to 2005 may be seen in retrospect as the classical era of independent filmmaking, personified most visibly by Miramax. In 2005, the Weinsteins broke with Disney but were not allowed to keep the name of their company or its library of films. They formed The Weinstein Company and distributed such notable indies as *Blue Valentine* (2010), *Miral* (2010), and *The King's Speech* (2010), which won an Academy Award for Best Picture.

OTHER INDIE COMPANIES   *sex, lies & videotape* eventually earned more than $100 million on a production cost of $1.2 million, and this record drew the attention of the Hollywood majors, all of whom created their own subsidiaries to finance or distribute independent films. These included Fox Searchlight (*One Hour Photo*, 2002), Sony Pictures Classics (*Baadasssss*, 2004), and Universal's Focus Features (*Billy Elliot*, 2000; *Crouching Tiger, Hidden Dragon*, 2001). Many have now ceased operating.

BLACK SWAN (FOX SEARCHLIGHT, 2010)

The relative popularity of independent films led the Hollywood majors to get in on the action. The majors formed subsidiary companies to finance or distribute independent pictures. Fox Searchlight distributed this thriller by director Darren Aronofsky about a ballerina (Natalie Portman) suffering a psychotic breakdown. Frame enlargement.

Stand-alone companies, unaffiliated with the majors, include Lion's Gate (*Monster's Ball*, 2001; and *Beyond the Sea*, 2004), Summit Entertainment (the *Twilight* movies), and Focus Features (*Brokeback Mountain*, 2005; *Lost in Translation*, 2003). Film stars and directors also have formed their own production companies. Mel Gibson's Icon Productions financed and distributed *The Passion of the Christ* (2004) when none of the Hollywood majors was willing to take the project on. Gibson made the film exactly the way he wanted it, including elements the majors considered unmarketable, such as extremely graphic violence and dialogue spoken in Aramaic and accompanied by subtitles. Impressed with the film's box-office performance, 20th Century Fox agreed to distribute it on DVD.

The Independent Film Channel (IFC) on cable television also has provided financing and distribution through several of its divisions. IFC Productions has provided financing for films that include *Boys Don't Cry* (1999), with distribution by Fox Searchlight and an Oscar-winning role for actress Hillary Swank. Independent Digital Entertainment produces digital films (*Tape*, 2001). IFC Originals produces films for the IFC cable channel, and IFC Films concentrates on production for theatrical markets (*My Big Fat Greek Wedding*, 2002).

The network of companies involved in independent production and distribution illustrates an interesting contradiction about the film industry. It is both highly centralized, with significant control exerted by the majors, and also quite decentralized, with many arenas where production can occur and many avenues to distribution and the marketplace. And the sheer output of the independent sector means that a great many of the films that viewers see are, in fact, indies.

Festivals

Film festivals provide an important mechanism for sustaining the independent film scene. Fledgling directors compete for slots at a festival, where they hope the screening of their work will attract a deal with the distribution companies whose reps attend looking for product. Festivals also provide a public expression for the enthusiasm and passion of filmmakers and viewers who are looking for artistry and vision beyond what mainstream film can provide.

The Sundance Festival, founded by Robert Redford in 1986 and held yearly in Park City, Utah, is perhaps the best-known indie festival. Over the course of 10 days, Sundance screens more than 100 films and gives a series of awards, including a Grand Prize. Winners at Sundance are picked up by distributors and often go on to make a strong mark at the box office. The list of winning films at Sundance shows how effective this festival is as a launching pad for a film's performance in the marketplace. Sundance festival winners include *You Can Count on Me* (2000), *American Splendor* (2003), and *Forty Shades of Blue* (2005).

Acceptance rates at Sundance demonstrate the festival's prestige as well as the over-populated nature of the independent film sector. For the 2010 festival, Sundance received 1,058 films competing for sixteen prizes in dramatic feature categories, producing an acceptance rate of 1.5 percent.

The cultural visibility and economic importance that Sundance has achieved led to criticism that it's become too glitzy and status-conscious for the health of independent film, and the criticism spawned break-away competitor festivals, such as Slamdance. Sundance, though, has remained the key festival for independent cinema.

Other notable festivals include the Toronto International Film Festival and Telluride Film Festival, held Labor Day weekend in Telluride, Colorado.

CHE (IFC FILMS, 2008)

Steven Soderbergh directed this epic, four-and-a-half-hour portrait of revolutionary Che Guevara (Benecio del Toro), chronicling his role alongside Fidel Castro in the Cuban Revolution and his ill-fated campaign to create a revolution in Bolivia, where he was captured and killed. Soderberg shot the film on digital video. It had an abbreviated release to a handful of theaters, but the ancillary aftermarkets—chiefly, home video and cable television—brought the film most of its viewers. These markets serve an important function for indie filmmakers because the costs of distributing a picture to the theatrical market are often too high. Frame enlargement.

Filmmakers

Many of today's most notable and prominent directors started out in or have remained part of independent film. Quentin Tarantino has become such a superstar that it is easy to forget that he's an independent filmmaker. Steven Soderbergh achieved remarkable success alternating between independent films (*sex, lies & videotape; The Limey,* 1999; *Che,* 2009) and studio product (*Ocean's Twelve,* 2004; *Erin Brockovich,* 2001).

Joel and Ethan Coen have written and directed a steady supply of films for two decades, including *Blood Simple* (1984), *Raising Arizona* (1989), *Fargo* (1996), *The Big Lebowski* (1998), and *O Brother, Where Art Thou?* (2000). They scored a major commercial and critical success in 2010 with *True Grit.*

John Sayles, who is today's pre-eminent independent filmmaker, has written, produced, and financed his own films since 1980s *The Return of the Secaucus Seven,* and his output includes *The Brother From Another Planet* (1984), *Matewan* (1987), *Lone Star* (1996), and *Casa de los babys* (2003).

Independent film has gained a considerable artistic reputation in today's film world, and this has led the major studios to recruit notable independent filmmakers for mainstream projects. As noted, Steven Soderbergh regularly alternates between the two categories of film. Similarly, Robert Rodriguez followed the success of *El Mariachi* (1992) and *From Dusk Till Dawn* (1996) with the digital studio blockbusters *Spy Kids* (2001) and *The Adventures of Shark Boy and Lava Girl in 3-D* (2005). Rodriguez makes his movies using his own equipment and studio located in Austin, Texas.

SIDEWAYS (FOX SEARCHLIGHT, 2004)

Director Alexander Payne also has forged a career path outside the Hollywood majors. Payne's films—*Citizen Ruth* (1996), *Election* (1999), *About Schmidt* (2002), *Sideways* (2004), and *The Descendants* (2011)—are more quirky and character-driven than Hollywood allows its big-budget films to be. Thus far Payne has been very successful at finding commercial distribution for films made with the artistic freedom of an independent filmmaker. Frame enlargement.

Christopher Nolan's indie films *Memento* (2000) and *Insomnia* (2001) led Warner Bros. to recruit him to make *Batman Begins* (2005), a blockbuster intended to revive the Batman film series. The risk for a filmmaker who transitions from the scarce resources of indie films to expensive studio productions is that the new level of resources can become seductive, even as a filmmaker's creative control of the project may diminish in inverse proportion to the size of the budget. A filmmaker enmeshed in blockbusters may never find his or her way back to the innovative and creative vision of his or her independent work. Nolan, however, has bent blockbusters to his own creative interests in such unusual and idiosyncratic films as *Inception* (2010) and *The Dark Knight* (2008).

INTERNATIONAL INFLUENCE OF HOLLYWOOD STYLE

With its global economic power, the U.S. cinema influences foreign directors in three key ways: (1) by colonizing foreign cinemas, it provokes overseas filmmakers to position their work in relation to it, (2) it employs émigré directors, and (3) it remakes foreign films and then distributes these overseas.

Influence on Foreign Filmmakers

The visibility of Hollywood cinema can make it hard to ignore for overseas filmmakers who may point to it in their own work, even when that work is politically or

ANTONIO DAS MORTES (1968)

Glauber Rocha was the most prominent member of Brazil's Cinema Novo movement, dedicated to forging a new, nationalist cinema for Brazil that would be reflective of its indigenous cultural and artistic traditions rather than imitating film styles from abroad. This epic about a gunman turning on the landowners who hired him is infused with Brazilian history, folklore, and song, even as it nods defiantly at the Hollywood Western. Frame enlargement.

stylistically opposed to the Hollywood model. One reason for this is Hollywood's voracious appetite for colonizing foreign markets. A visitor to Tokyo, for example, sees numerous film posters advertising American movies, whose market saturation can drive out indigenous films.

Director Glauber Rocha belonged to Brazil's *cinema novo* (new cinema) movement, a turn by Brazilian directors away from Hollywood-style entertainment movies and toward a more radical style of filmmaking that embraced the idea of revolution and the needs of the country's vast, impoverished peasantry.

His most famous film, *Antonio Das Mortes* (1968) is an epic fusion of folklore, politics, music, and dance, portraying a *cangaceiro* (a bandit and bounty hunter) who fights corrupt landowners on behalf of the poor. The film is steeped in Brazilian history and culture, but its imagery of the dusty, arid sertao region, and its gunfighter

FILMMAKER SPOTLIGHT

Akira Kurosawa

Kurosawa is one of the giants of world cinema. His artistic tastes were very diverse, and his work conjoins Japanese cultural traditions with international styles of painting, literature and theatre. Unlike the filmmakers of Brazil's *cinema novo*, he did not reject Hollywood style but assimilated some of its influences and turned them to his own purposes. In *The Bad Sleep Well* (1960), a thriller about corrupt corporations, Kurosawa borrows from Warner Bros. crime films of the 1930s in using montages of newspaper headlines to announce major plot developments. *Yojimbo* (1961), a samurai film about a warrior who manipulates two criminal gangs into annihilating each other, uses for its main set a dusty, wide street in a T-design that recalls the main street of many a Hollywood Western. The climatic showdown in *Yojimbo* occurs here just as it has in countless Westerns. *Yojimbo* also includes a reference to the well-known Western *High Noon* (1952) and a scene lifted directly from the 1942 crime drama, *The Glass Key*.

At the conclusion of *Sanjuro* (1962), two samurai confront each other. They draw their swords like guns from holsters, and the faster draw wins. Quicker to get his sword out of its scabbard, the hero kills his opponent. Kurosawa has clearly modeled this showdown on Western gunfights. In *Kagemusha* (1980), another samurai drama, the film's horizon shots of samurai on the march were

modeled on the Monument Valley compositions of John Ford's classic Hollywood Westerns (these included *Fort Apache* [1948], *She Wore a Yellow Ribbon* [1949], and *The Searchers* [1956]).

Kurosawa borrowed from Ford, but he also played against Hollywood tradition. The climax of *Kagemusha* features a charge by samurai mounted on horseback against an opposing clan armed with rifles. The scene visualizes an important Japanese battle that has historic significance because it was the first demonstration of the effects of organized firepower on an army carrying only swords and lances. As the riders charge, they are mowed down and wiped out by their enemy.

Kurosawa had the riflemen shoot the horses out from under the riders, deliberately reversing a well-known Hollywood convention in which one invariably fired to hit the rider and not the horse.

But while Kurosawa nodded at the American cinema in these ways, his gigantic stature in world cinema rests upon his brilliant command of film technique and his storytelling abilities. *Seven Samurai* has been remade by filmmakers around the world probably more often than any other film, and filmmakers everywhere have learned from Kurosawa's mastery of editing and method of filming with multiple cameras running simultaneously. His influence on others far outweighed the things that he borrowed.

(continued)

SEVEN SAMURAI (TOHO, 1954); KAGEMUSHA (TOHO, 1980)

One of the most influential films ever made, Kurosawa's portrait of Japan's 16th-century samurai wars is a brilliant example of epic storytelling and historical portraiture. *Seven Samurai* is culturally specific even as it addresses universal themes and emotions. Kurosawa often returned to the period film and the samurai heritage because it furnished a powerful way of symbolizing contemporary conflicts. *Kagemusha* portrays the destruction of the powerful Takeda army by an enemy clan using rifles, an episode Kurosawa understood as representing the destruction of tradition and the dawn of a modern world of automated violence. Frame enlargements.

Kurosawa's films were deeply responsive to his own cultural heritage and to Japanese viewers. He made movies about Japan's devastation from World War II (*Drunken Angel, Stray Dog*), about the country's economic boom, the growth of large corporations and the threats to democracy these posed (*The Bad Sleep Well, High and Low*), and, most famously, about Japan's samurai heritage (*Seven Samurai, Yojimbo, Ran*).

He drew from Japanese literature, painting and theatre and transposed these forms into his movies, and he made movies based on foreign literary traditions. The most famous are the Shakespeare adaptations, *Throne of Blood* and *Ran*, which Kurosawa brilliantly transposed into Japan's medieval period of samurai warfare, sensing there a historical parallel with Shakespeare's themes.

Kurosawa's artistic sensibility, then, was extremely powerful. He assimilated artistic and cultural traditions in original and striking ways, blending foreign influences with Japan's cultural heritage. The filmmaking that resulted was uncommonly rich, ambitious and cinematically brilliant. And, in the long run, Kurosawa's influence on world cinema was far more powerful than were the influences that he selectively drew from it. ∎

characters, also gesture defiantly toward the Hollywood Western. Rocha transformed the film's politics into allegory and myth as a way of escaping censorship by the country's military dictatorship and of rejecting Hollywood norms.

Absorption of Foreign Filmmakers

Hollywood cinema continually attracts and absorbs talented filmmakers from abroad, who, in turn, help to modify and change U.S. film style. Beginning in the late 1920s, a major wave of émigré filmmakers arrived in Hollywood from Germany. These included cinematographer Karl Freund; directors Fritz Lang, F. W. Murnau, and Ernst Lubitsch; scriptwriter Carl Mayer; and actors Emil Jannings and Conrad Veidt. Lang had directed such classic German films as *Metropolis* (1926) and *M* (1931), and he went on to have a long career in Hollywood, frequently specializing in dark crime films before he returned to Germany near the end of his career to direct his final films.

Many of Hollywood's enduring classics were created by filmmakers who began their careers in other countries. The jaunty adventure classic *The Adventures of Robin Hood* (1938), the popular romantic drama *Casablanca* (1942), and the superpatriotic portrait of composer George M. Cohan, *Yankee Doodle Dandy* (1944), were all directed by Michael Curtiz, who was born in Hungary and worked in Germany during the early part of his film career. Hollywood's superstar director Alfred Hitchcock arrived in the United States in 1939 after a lengthy and distinguished career as a director in the British cinema. While apprenticing in the British system as an assistant director, Hitchcock worked and studied in Germany for two years, absorbing the style of expressionism then prevalent in German cinema. Hitchcock's subsequent U.S. movies are strongly marked by the elements of German expressionism that he found so impressive while studying in Germany in 1924 and 1925.

RECENT ÉMIGRÉ FILMMAKERS   In recent years, émigré directors have created some of the U.S. cinema's most distinguished or popular films. Based on a series of stylish, frenzied action films—*A Better Tomorrow* (1986), *The Killer* (1989), *Bullet in the*

ROBOCOP (ORION PICTURES, 1987)

The critical and popular success of *Robocop*, a savage social satire of 1980s America, launched the Hollywood career of Dutch director Paul Verhoeven. Like many foreign filmmakers before him, Verhoeven found the huge resources and popular impact of Hollywood filmmaking to be powerful lures. Unlike some of his less successful predecessors, though, Verhoeven enjoyed great popular success with his American productions. Frame enlargement.

Head (1990), and *Hard Boiled* (1992)—Hong Kong director John Woo emigrated to Hollywood but found the U.S. system unable to accommodate his audacious style. Thus his initial U.S. films—*Hard Target* (1993) and *Broken Arrow* (1996)—were disappointments, but Woo eventually prevailed with a critical and popular success in *Face/Off* (1997).

Peter Weir established his career in Australia with such memorable films as *Picnic at Hanging Rock* (1975), *The Last Wave* (1978), and *Gallipoli* (1981), the latter film starring Australian actor Mel Gibson, who subsequently became a major Hollywood star. Weir then went on to direct the well-regarded U.S. films *Witness* (1985) and *Dead Poets' Society* (1989) with such established U.S. celebrities as Harrison Ford and Robin Williams. Weir's colleague in the Australian cinema, George Miller, established his international reputation with the hits *Mad Max* (1979) and *The Road Warrior* (1981), both starring Mel Gibson. In the U.S. cinema, Miller directed one segment of *Twilight Zone—The Movie* (1983), *The Witches of Eastwick* (1987), and *Lorenzo's Oil* (1992).

Remakes of Foreign Films

In its constant search for story material, Hollywood often turns to films from overseas. The Danish film, *The Girl With the Dragon Tattoo* (2009), became an international hit, as did two follow-up films (*The Girl Who Played with Fire*, *The Girl Who Kicked the Hornet's Nest*), all based on novels by Stieg Larsson. Hollywood can't resist an international success, and a remake starring Daniel Craig and directed by David Fincher was released in 2011, a mere two years after the original film.

For his follow-up to *Memento*, director Christopher Nolan selected a 1997 Norwegian film, *Insomnia*, and "Americanized" it by switching the setting from Norway to Alaska and casting actors Al Pacino, Hilary Swank, and Robin Williams.

The success of the horror market in Japan and the United States led Hollywood to recruit Japanese filmmakers to remake their hits here. Takashi Shimizu remade his *Juon* (2003) as *The Grudge* (2004), starring Sarah Michelle Gellar. Hideo Nakata directed *Ringu* (1998) and *Ringu 2* (1999) in Japan and then their Hollywood remakes, *The Ring* (2002) and *The Ring 2* (2005), with star Naomi Watts. Another Nakata film, *Dark Water* (2002), was remade in 2005 by Brazilian director Walter Salles for Disney's Touchstone Pictures.

Many star vehicles have been remakes of foreign films. *Vanilla Sky* (2002), starring Tom Cruise, was based on a 1997 Spanish film called *Open Your Eyes*. *K-Pax* (2002), with Kevin Spacey, was an unofficial remake of another Spanish film, *Man Facing Southeast* (1986). *Twelve Monkeys* (1995), with Bruce Willis, was a feature-length remake of the classic French short, *La Jetée* (1962). The Richard Gere–Jodie Foster vehicle *Sommersby* (1993) was a remake of a popular French film, *The Return of Martin Guerre* (1982). The comedies *Three Men and a Baby* (1987) and *The Man with One Red Shoe* (1985) also were remakes of popular French hits. The Nicolas Cage–Meg Ryan romance *City of Angels* (1998) was an Americanized remake of Wim Wenders's German production, *Wings of Desire* (1986). *Last Man Standing* (1996), starring Bruce Willis, was a remake of Kurosawa's *Yojimbo*. While remakes of foreign hits have been especially common in recent years, it is not a new trend. The classic Western *The Magnificent Seven* (1960) Americanized Akira Kurosawa's magnificently filmed Japanese epic, *Seven Samurai* (1954).

THE GIRL WHO PLAYED WITH FIRE (NORDISK FILM, 2009)

Noomi Rapace plays Lisbeth Salander, a hacker who teams up with an investigative journalist to expose high-level crimes in a film trilogy based on Stieg Larsson novels. The novels and films were popular in Denmark and abroad, and Hollywood director David Fincher released an American remake in 2011. Frame enlargement.

The challenge Hollywood faces in remaking foreign films is to translate story material from one cultural context to another. In some cases, the translations are fairly successful, as with *Three Men and a Baby*, mainly because the original was a piece of comic fluff not bound closely to a particular cultural context. By contrast, the Americanized Western *The Magnificent Seven* simplifies and eliminates much of the historical and philosophical complexity of the Japanese original. This is because no parallel cultural relationship exists in the American West with that between the samurai warrior and the peasant farmer in medieval Japan. Unable to translate the class conflicts and historical framework of Kurosawa's feudal drama to the American West, the screenwriters working on the remake simply eliminated large chunks of the original film. As a result, while the U.S. remake is somewhat entertaining, it has never achieved the international stature of Kurosawa's film.

Case Study LET ME IN

The American horror film *Let Me In* (2010) was in theaters a mere two years after release of the Swedish film *Let the Right One In* (2008), on which it was based. Both films derive from a best-selling novel by John Ajvide Lindqvist, originally published in Swedish and then translated into several languages. *Let Me In* joins many contemporary Hollywood horror movies that are remakes of foreign films.

In this case, the remake machinery got underway very quickly. Rights for an English-language remake were sold as soon as *Let the Right One In* premiered in the U.S. at the Tribeca Film Festival. The Swedish film was an unusual and suspenseful vampire story, and producers for the American market saw how easily it could be transposed. The remake was in production the following year, with Matt Reeves as director. Reeves had made the stylish horror film, *Cloverfield* (2008), about a giant monster attacking New York City.

Unlike many horror films today, *Let Me In* emphasizes atmosphere and tone rather than gruesome violence. It follows very closely the first film's storyline, duplicating its tone, rhythm, and pacing, and where the original film minimizes the novel's explicit violence, so, too, does the remake. Several long, horrific scenes that are in the novel are omitted in both films.

Lindqvist's story is about the friendship between a boy, Oscar, and a mysterious young girl who lives in the apartment next door. The girl, Eli, turns out to be a vampire, and Oscar develops such strong feelings for her that he eventually becomes her protector and procurer, finding human victims for Eli to feast upon.

The novel and first film feature cold, snowy Swedish landscapes and a principle location in suburban Stockholm. The remake shifts the locale to New Mexico and changes the names of Oscar and Eli to Owen and Abbey in order to Americanize the story.

While both films follow the novel's storyline closely, they omit some of the book's most provocative and disturbing content. In the movies, Eli/Abbey tells Oscar/Owen that she's not a girl, by which she means to say that she is a vampire and not a human being.

In the novel, however, Eli is really a boy named Elias, and scenes in the novel where Eli cuddles with Oscar and kisses him are homoerotic, an element that neither film presents. The novel's Eli was castrated and vampirized by a decadent aristocrat centuries ago, a ritual that neither film portrays or alludes to.

When Oscar meets "her," Eli is living with an adult named Hakan, whom Oscar assumes is her father but who, in fact, procures human victims for her. Neither movie portrays this character in any detail, perhaps because the novel's presentation is so perverse. There, Hakan is a pedophile who likes young boys, and Eli plays on his desires in order to keep him with her, on occasion allowing Hakan to touch her if he'll agree to bring back blood from a new victim. Hakan becomes obsessively devoted to Eli, thinking of her as his beloved.

Even though both movies are horror films with some gruesome scenes (in one, a man burns his face off with acid), production decisions were made to exclude the novel's more perverse elements and avoid placing them on the screen. Producers on both films evidently felt that doing so was necessary if the films were to succeed commercially and in the international markets.

And succeed they did, critically and commercially. Eli's story exemplifies the interconnected markets in the modern media economy. Originating from a novel, the character spawned two movies and a comic book miniseries. Produced by Dark Horse Comics, the series was offered as a prequel and a tie-in to *Let Me In*. It supplements the film by inventing a back story for Abbey as she and Hakan (now renamed Thomas and evidently rehabilitated from his proclivities in the novel) travel around and try to survive. Careful adaptations by Swedish and then by American filmmakers transformed the novel's premise of a child vampire traveling with a pedophile into a less perverse narrative scenario, one that became a successful product in theatrical and ancillary movie markets. ◼

LET THE RIGHT ONE IN (EFTI, 2008); LET ME IN (HAMMER FILM PRODUCTIONS, 2010)

The *Twilight* movies and books led to a renewed interest in vampires as a profitable source of screen entertainment. *Let the Right One In* was an unusual and atmospheric vampire story and attracted remake interest almost immediately. *Let Me In* Americanizes the original film's Swedish setting and characters but follows the storyline and visual design of that film almost exactly. Both films, however, omit some of the novel's darker elements. Frame enlargements.

SUMMARY

In his autobiography, published in 1974, the great French director Jean Renoir wrote that cinema history is characterized by warfare between filmmakers and the industry. Renoir's view reflected his concern that the filmmaker-artist should be free to buck convention, break rules, and create original, interesting work rather than copy the patterns of yesterday's box-office successes.

Renoir's view neglects the many filmmakers, such as Akira Kurosawa and Alfred Hitchcock, who flourished in the industry even while creating movies that were recognized as great works of art.

But it remains true that for most of its history, cinema has been an expensive medium in which to work, and so filmmakers have been subject to commercial constraints and calculations. Cinema exists at the crossroads of art and business, and as it became an industry with global reach and potentially huge revenue returns, those constraints and calculations have become more influential than in Renoir's days.

U.S. filmmaking exerts a global influence throughout world markets. This influence has a clear economic basis. U.S. film studios are owned by diversified parent corporations whose holdings equip them to compete in an integrated world entertainment market. Blockbuster filmmaking, driven by special effects and mechanical or superhuman characters, is an ideal means of dominating domestic and overseas markets. The blockbuster film is enormously popular, generates huge audience interest, and lends itself to extensive lines of product merchandising. With its multinational corporations, the U.S. cinema is able to perform very aggressively in global markets.

Hollywood exerts strong international influence not just economically, but stylistically as well. The style and content of U.S. films have a major impact on world cinemas in three ways: (1) foreign filmmakers confront, reject or borrow images, characters, and story situations from the U.S. cinema; (2) filmmakers who have established their careers in other countries come to Hollywood to make U.S. films; and (3) Hollywood remakes foreign films according to the norms and standards of U.S. film and popular culture.

But filmmakers who celebrate indigenous national and cultural styles and traditions create works that offer alternatives to the blockbuster model. So, too, does the "indie" film sector. The tensions in cinema between art and business can be productive as well as destructive, a source of great filmmaking and a source that prevents it. The aesthetics of cinema, which this book has spent many pages exploring, rarely escape the shaping influence of a filmmaker's need for funding and the industry that provides it.

KEY TERMS AND CONCEPTS

ancillary markets 379
blockbuster 380
diversification 380
domestic theatrical
   market 376
franchise 380

gross 376
homage 392
limited-release
   market 373
majors 373
negative cost 377

product tie-ins 381
product placement 384
profit participants 378
rentals 377
streaming video 369

SUGGESTED READINGS

Tino Balio, ed., *The American Film Industry*, rev. ed. (Madison: University of Wisconsin Press, 1985).

John W. Cones, *Film Finance and Distribution: A Dictionary of Terms* (Los Angeles: Silman-James Press, 1992).

Peter Cowie, *Variety International: Film Guide 2000* (Los Angeles: Silman-James Press, 2000).

Peter Lev, *The Euro-American Film* (Austin: University of Texas Press, 1993).

Barry R. Litman, *The Motion Picture Mega Industry* (Boston: Allyn and Bacon, 1998).

Stephen Prince, *A New Pot of Gold: Hollywood Under the Electronic Rainbow, 1980–1989* (New York: Scribner's, 2000).

Jason E. Savire, ed., *The Movie Business Book* (New York: Fireside, 1992).

Justin Wyatt, *High Concept: Movies and Marketing in Hollywood* (Austin: University of Texas Press, 1995).

Film Theory and Criticism

OBJECTIVES

After reading this chapter, you should be able to:

- explain the nature of film theory and the types of questions it investigates

- describe the characteristics, strengths, and limitations of realist models

- describe the characteristics, strengths, and limitations of auteurist models

- describe the characteristics, strengths, and limitations of psychoanalytic models

- describe the characteristics, strengths, and limitations of ideological models

- describe the characteristics, strengths, and limitations of feminist models

- describe the characteristics, strengths, and limitations of cognitive models

- select the most appropriate theoretical model for the particular type of questions that need answers

- understand that multiple theoretical perspectives are required because the cinema is multidimensional

Film theory and criticism are closely related to one another. Criticism aims to evaluate the merits of a film or set of films and explore thematic content. A critic evaluates the quality of a filmmaker's work. How are the shots designed and composed? How effective is the direction of actors, and what contribution does performance make to the whole? How is the story told? Is the film's thematic content supported by the movie's structural design? The critic might incorporate one or more elements of theory into the evaluation and thereby produce an auteurist interpretation or an ideological interpretation.

Criticism seeks to arrive at an aesthetic understanding of the expressive designs and achievements of one or more films and to produce novel and interesting interpretations of them. Criticism describes relevant features of a film and interprets these and seeks to persuade the reader that the interpretation is sound.

Theory is not as concerned with evaluating aesthetic achievements. Theory deals with broader questions. Theory is a systematic attempt to think about the nature of cinema: What it is as a medium, how it works, how it embodies meaning for viewers, and what kind of meanings it embodies.

Six models of **film theory** have been especially important to critics and scholars. These are the realist, auteurist, psychoanalytic, ideological, feminist, and cognitive models of film theory. Each model is especially good at dealing with some aspects of film style and the viewer's experience while being limited in its ability to deal with other aspects. As a result, each model constructs a somewhat different portrait of the medium from the others.

REALIST MODELS

This textbook has emphasized that the cinema has a double capacity. It both records and transforms the people, objects, and situations before the camera lens. Filmmakers use cinema as a recording medium to make pictures of the events, people, and situations in front of the camera, but they can also use the complex tools of their craft to manipulate the visual and acoustical design of their films. This tension within cinema between its recording functions and the power it gives filmmakers to stylize and transform reality poses a challenge for film theory when it attempts to locate a basis for realism and for realistic film styles. On which attributes of cinema should a theory of realism depend?

Theories of realism in the cinema look for points of correspondence between film images and the social, psychological, and physical realities before the camera. Typically, **realist film theory** restricts a filmmaker's manipulations of audiovisual design in order to honor and respect the integrity of the events and situations before the camera. Realist theory often implies that there is a threshold beyond which stylistic manipulation begins to falsify or distort the truths that the realist filmmaker pursues. Italian neorealists, for example, aimed to define such a threshold by holding a filmmaker to the creation of relatively simple stories and the use of nonprofessional actors and real locations, the better to honestly record the social realities of postwar Italy.

Elements of Realist Theory: Bazin

Questions about the nature of social or psychological reality, where it properly lies, and how the cinema relates to it are extremely difficult problems. French theorist Andre Bazin offered an ingenious and famous solution. Composed in the 1940s and 1950s, his essays on cinema exerted an enormous influence on the French film critics writing for the journal *Cahiers du Cinema*, who would themselves later become film

Case Study   OPEN WATER

Theories and concepts of realism often will dictate specific filmmaking practices. A theorist or filmmaker aiming for realism will wish to minimize the artificiality of the situations being filmed. Filmmaker Chris Kentis felt that everything he saw in films today seemed computer-generated and looked correspondingly fake. He wanted to go as far in the direction of realism as he could in filming this story about two divers stranded in shark-infested waters when their tour boat returns to shore without them.

The film was shot like a documentary to maximize the sense of realism. Kentis used a cast of relatively unknown actors, avoiding stars because their presence would diminish the sense of authenticity he wished to create. He then put the actors playing the two divers into the ocean and surrounded them with real sharks, throwing chum (bloody fish parts) into the water to attract the predators. As his cameras filmed them, the real sharks swam around the actors, evoking very real fear responses from the performers.

Kentis was a skilled diver, had worked with sharks before, and felt secure that he could film this action safely. Nevertheless, he hired a professional shark wrangler to handle the creatures, and the actors wore chain mail on their bodies below the water line and out of sight to the camera. But still, the actors had to be willing to get into the water with gray reef sharks—which have attacked people before—and swim with them while the sharks fed on chum.

Kentis kept his camera above the water because he knew this perspective—not seeing the predators below—would be more frightening. The viewer sees what the characters nervously see—the shark fins circling around them. The movements were real, not like the smoothly gliding fins that movies have shown traditionally and which are not typical of sharks. Actual fins look, in Kentis' words, like "rat tails flopping all over."

The realism of *Open Water* (2003), then, was a matter of making the filming conditions as much like the story situation as possible. Kentis' approach was based on a belief in photographic realism—that making the situation in front of the camera real would enhance the perceived danger in the story and would feel very different to the viewer than what computer-generated effects might accomplish. ◼

OPEN WATER (Lions Gate, 2003)

Real actors in a real ocean surrounded by real predatory sharks—filmmaker Chris Kentis wanted to get as far from the fakery of computer-generated images as possible. Not surprisingly, the fear responses called for in the story came naturally to the actors. Frame enlargement.

directors (see the section on the French New Wave in Chapter 7). Bazin based his theory on an ethical assumption about the nature of reality, and he suggested specific elements of film structure as the ones best suited for a realist style.

COMPONENTS OF BAZIN'S REALISM   Realistic film styles for Bazin were those that respected and reproduced the viewer's experience of reality. As people move about in the world, they experience visual and physical space as being whole and continuous, rather than chopped up in the manner established by editing in cinema. Bazin believed that reproducing the experience of spatial wholeness should be a key objective for a realist design.

He felt that each person's perspective on the world was, to a significant degree, uniquely his or her own and differed from the perspective of others. In this regard, reality possessed an ambiguous quality. Different people viewing the same scene or situation would tend to extract differing interpretations of it. Bazin believed that filmmakers should develop a style that respected these ambiguities and that did not unfairly coerce or manipulate viewers into sharing a single, mass emotional response to the scene or film. He believed that filmmakers should employ techniques that honor and enhance the ambiguities of reality and give viewers room to develop their own interpretations and responses. These conditions would form the basis of a realist style.

Bazin also argued that the special photographic nature of cinema pointed the medium in a realist direction. Photographs are **indexical signs,** that is, they are physically connected to what they represent; they bear the trace of the object or things they depict. A photograph of one's mother, for example, is imprinted by the reflected light that the camera captured from her presence in front of it. The photographic image testifies to her presence before the camera. It provides evidence of her reality.

Many theorists of photography and of cinema have stressed this aspect of the photographic image. As an indexical sign, it points to, is physically connected with, the existence of that for which it furnishes an image. According to this view, as a photographic medium, cinema is naturally biased toward realism.

STRUCTURAL BASIS FOR BAZIN'S REALISM   Bazin suggested that particular elements of film structure were more or less suited to representing the experience of spatial wholeness and the ambiguities of reality and giving spectators freedom of response. Bazin felt that the techniques best suited for realism were **deep-focus cinematography** (where a great distance separates sharply focused foreground and background objects) and the **long take** (shots of long duration) in a style that minimizes the importance of editing.

Shots employing deep focus can create multiple areas of interest and activity within the frame, ranging in crisp focus from foreground to background. As a result, viewers have more to study in a deep-focus shot than in a more conventional shot that is organized around one main area of interest. For Bazin, such shots are more ambiguous than shots composed using a narrow plane of focus because they afford viewers multiple ways of viewing and responding to the material in the frame. Used in conjunction with deep focus, long takes enhance this visual ambiguity by extending the deep-focus compositions in time. For Bazin, deep focus "brings the spectator into a relation with the image closer to that which he enjoys with reality. Therefore, it is correct to say that independently of the contents of the

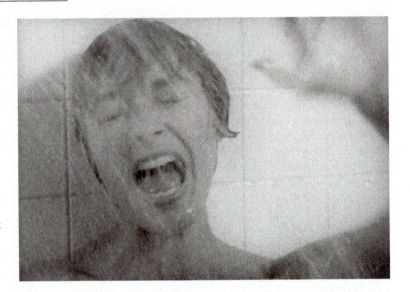

PSYCHO (PARAMOUNT PICTURES, 1960)

Mass-emotion films, such as *Psycho*, fail Bazin's test of a realist film by provoking all spectators to share a uniform emotional response (fright, in the case of *Psycho*). Frame enlargement.

image, its structure is more realistic." By contrast, for Bazin "montage by its very nature rules out ambiguity of expression."

By minimizing editing, deep focus and the long take respect the wholeness and richness of space and reality. By contrast, montage fractures and divides this whole-ness. For Bazin, therefore, it was incompatible with a realist style. Bazin criticized filmmakers who used montage to control the audience, manipulate their responses, and elicit mass emotional reactions. Montage-oriented directors who would fail Bazin's ethical basis for a realist aesthetic include such masters as Alfred Hitchcock and Sergei Eisenstein.

Using very brief shots edited at a frenzied pace, the shower sequence from *Psycho* achieved Hitchcock's goal of making the audience share a single, uniform response—scream with fright. Hitchcock said about *Psycho* that he wasn't interested in the actors or their performances or even the story, but only in using the elements of pure cinema, primarily editing, to make the audience experience a mass emotion. A similar strategy operates in Steven Spielberg's *Jaws* (1975), where editing, specifi-cally cross-cutting, creates considerable suspense and terror about the shark's attacks. Like *Psycho*, *Jaws* is a mass-emotion film in which the filmmaker uses technique with brilliance and sophistication to ensure that all members of the viewing audience experience the same intense reactions.

This uniformity of response is precisely what Bazin wished to avoid. Montage editing has an inherit tendency to manipulate the viewer's response, and this placed it outside the ethical basis of his film realism.

BAZINIAN FILMMAKERS   Bazin praised the work of directors who employed deep-focus compositions and the long take. He greatly esteemed French director Jean Renoir (*The Grand Illusion*, 1937; *The Rules of the Game*, 1939) for his use of deep-focus cinematography and for his tendency to employ camera movement rather than mon-tage. *The Grand Illusion* and *The Rules of the Game* contain a series of remarkably fluid camera moves and mobile framings. Rather than cutting to a new camera setup,

THE RULES OF THE GAME (NEF, 1939)

Several areas of action ongoing simultaneously in a deep focus shot. Director Jean Renoir relied on the moving camera to choreograph a scene's action and to keep the shots running, enabling actors to perform for longer intervals on screen. His compositions often used extended depth of field, emphasizing the spatial wholeness of a scene as well as the psychological and emotional dynamics among the characters. Bazin praised his work as realistic. Renoir, interestingly, said about this film that he wanted to leave naturalism far behind and to work in the classical style of Moliere and the Commedia del Arte. He described the film as the portrait of a society that is rotten to the core. Condemned by French society upon its release, *The Rules of the Game* is today recognized as one of cinema's greatest films. Frame enlargement.

Renoir kept his camera and the actors in nearly constant motion, extending the length of his shots past the point at which other directors would cut and using deep focus to create multiple areas of activity within the frame. The resulting richness of his compositions was the essence of Bazinian realism.

Renoir, too, believed that his technique was realistic because it captured what he felt was an essential truth of human life, namely, that people are interconnected rather than being solitary individuals. Renoir believed that close-ups tend to convey the idea that individuals are isolated from one another.

Bazin also admired U.S. director Orson Welles. In *Citizen Kane* (1941), Welles filmed entire scenes in one or two lengthy shots. In the scene where Kane's parents make arrangements with a banker to raise him and to act as young Charlie Kane's guardian, Welles composed the scene in two shots. The action begins with a long shot showing young Charlie playing in the snow, and the camera pulls inside the

CITIZEN KANE (RKO, 1941)

Deep focus in *Citizen Kane*. Young Charles Kane plays outside while his parents sign away control of his future to a banker. Note the crisp focus in foreground, midground, and background. Frame enlargement.

window of young Charlie's home to reveal his parents and the banker. The camera tracks in front of his mother as she crosses from the window to a table to sign the papers, and Welles records this scene in an extraordinary deep-focus shot. In the second shot of the scene, the camera is outdoors and tracks across the porch of the cabin to young Charlie in the snow, where the adults join him and announce his fate.

The two extended takes that compose this scene, running nearly four minutes, represent a clear stylistic alternative to the standard rules of continuity editing, which would mandate using first a master shot and then inserts matching action to the master. But instead of editing from shot to shot, Welles uses camera and character movement to change the compositions, effectively editing *within* the shot. As Bazin pointed out with respect to Welles's films, "dramatic effects for which we had formerly relied on montage were created out of the movements of the actors within a fixed framework."

The supreme example of a filmmaker who employs deep focus, rather than montage, to create rich compositions with multiple areas of interest is the French director Jacques Tati. In films like *Playtime* (1967), editing plays virtually no creative role at all. This comic film about the encounters of a bumbling Frenchman with a bewildering modern world of steel skyscrapers and plastic commodities is played out entirely in lengthy shots composed in deep focus where an amazing number of things are happening simultaneously within the frame.

Summary

Bazin's theory of realism has important strengths. It connects film style with a viewer's physical and perceptual experience of the world and locates a realist style on the basis of that connection. It also stresses the ethical contract that exists between a filmmaker and an audience, and it challenges filmmakers and viewers to think about the cinema's potential for unfairly manipulating its audiences. Bazin cited ample evidence throughout film history to support his argument that the ethically motivated film-maker, seeking to respect the viewer's experience of reality, should avoid a style that is overtly manipulative and based in montage.

If Bazin was right that individuals' subjective experiences of reality are varied and that a basis for realist style lies in employing cinematic tools that respect this variety, then it follows that filmmakers who use cinema to manipulate audiences into holding socially objectionable reactions are engaging in an unfair or unethical exploitation of their viewers. Although Bazin wrote about film beginning in the 1940s until his death in 1958, his work has important implications in this respect for contemporary film, which tends to use fast cutting to manipulate viewer responses and to elicit uniform reactions from viewers. For a Bazinian realist, such films fail to respect the integrity and uniqueness of each viewer's perception of the world. Bazin's theory of realism has much to say about the ethical contract that obtains between filmmakers and viewers and about the extraordinary potential for coercing emotions that filmmakers have at their command.

At the same time, Bazin's realist aesthetic tends to exist as a potential, as an ideal that is never fully realized in any given film. Some of the filmmakers Bazin cites as practitioners of deep focus or the long take also employ montage. *Citizen Kane* in-cludes a number of celebrated sequence shots composed in deep focus, but it also em-ploys some striking montages.

Very few films do without the expressive power of editing. In *Rope* (1948), Alfred Hitchcock tried to dispense with editing. Most of the shots in *Rope* run a full ten minutes. Hitchcock only cut when the camera ran out of film, and even then he went to great pains to disguise the cut by having it occur at moments when a character or some other obstruction blocks the camera's view. Hitchcock, however, found the practice unsatisfying, and he discontinued the experiment after *Rope*, rec-ognizing that without editing, he had very little ability to create dramatic and psy-chological rhythm and tempo. Few films representing a pure application of Bazinian principles exist.

Another limitation in the theory is its tendency to minimize the degree to which even deep-focus–long-take cinematography can shape the viewer's perceptions. In Jacques Tati's *Playtime*, when Tati needs viewers to look at a particular area of the frame, he uses a sudden loud noise, a rapid movement, or a bright color to draw at-tention there. Even within the long-take–deep-focus approach, filmmakers can still guide and influence viewer perceptions.

Although it has been extremely influential, Bazin's approach is not the only basis for a theory of film realism. In Chapter 8 we examined documentary realism, which offers filmmakers a method for documenting social conditions and events by minimiz-ing the use of fictionalizing techniques.

Another approach to realism emphasizes the nature of the perceptual information found in cinema and its correspondence with the perceptual information people use in everyday life. This approach may be called **perceptual realism** because it locates a source of realism in cinema at the perceptual level. Film technique builds on a view-er's ordinary perceptual habits and ways of processing the visual and auditory world. Through lighting, sound design, and camera placement, filmmakers build sources of three-dimensional information into their images and can selectively emphasize these sources. As a result, film images look three-dimensional rather than as they truly are, a two-dimensional projection on a flat surface.

Wide-angle lenses, for example, emphasize depth cues. Near objects will appear larger in size than distant objects; this is an everyday perceptual cue that the eye and brain use to infer information about depth and distance. Wide-angle lenses exaggerate these size disparities, making near objects somewhat larger than they are and distant objects somewhat smaller. Thus wide-angle lenses convey this kind of depth information with special vividness (and, as a result, are the basis for the deep-focus realism of Bazinian theory), in contrast to telephoto lenses, which tend to reduce these differences by magnifying the size of everything in the frame. The appearance of depth and distance in the film image is thus a realistic perception because it uses the same information that is found in the three-dimensional world. (Though Bazin did not write in terms of perceptual science, its findings furnish a strong foundation to his theory.)

Realist theory is a little different from the other models examined in this chapter because a critic might do an auteurist, feminist, ideological, psychoanalytic, or cognitive interpretation of a film but would be less likely to do a "realist" interpretation of a film. If, then, realist theory does not provide a roadmap or procedural guide to interpreting films in the ways that the other models do, it nevertheless deals with essential issues that a theoretical understanding of cinema must confront. These include the nature of cinema's connection with the world and how recording technologies like cameras and microphones "capture" that world.

Because cinema largely has been a photographic medium for most of its history, concepts of realism have been tied to its photographic nature. As cinema shifts into digital modes, theorists have asked whether these undermine the indexical nature of photographically-derived images. Because a digital image can be endlessly transformed, and often in imperceptible ways, does that make digital images less real, and does it mean that realism is a term that cannot be applied to digital images?

While some theorists have answered "yes" to these questions, digital cameras are recording instruments just as analog cameras have been. The 9/11 documentaries examined in Chapter 9 are composed largely of digital images. Questions about realism do not lose their relevance in the digital era—they become more important. People care deeply to know the truth value of the images they encounter. In this respect, the problems of realism in cinema that theory investigates are always with us.

AUTEURIST MODELS

Auteurist film theory studies film authors. Approaching cinema as an art presupposes the existence of one or more authors. Movies are created by groups—the team of production personnel whose coordinated efforts bring a film to completion—but one or more people have creative control over the team of artists assembled for a production. Auteurist theory looks for these authors and studies film as a medium of personal expression in which artists leave a recognizable stylistic signature on their work. The prime artist in cinema is generally taken to be the director. The term *auteur* derives from the French word meaning "author," and this model of theory and criticism has become the most commonly employed and most deeply ingrained method of thinking about film. When approaching film as a creative medium, the director emerges as the central figure of creative authority.

The French origins of auteur theory occurred in the 1950s when the critics for *Cahiers du Cinema* began to write director-centered film criticism and suggested that even in the Hollywood system a handful of auteurs produced great films. This was a controversial assertion because in the 1930s and 1940s, during the high period of the Hollywood system, directors often were hired functionaries who filmed the script as economically and quickly as possible and who answered to the film's producer. Nevertheless, the auteur critics suggested that John Ford, Alfred Hitchcock, and others were true auteurs by virtue of having a recognizable and consistent artistic style from film to film. By contrast film directors today enjoy more prestige and public recognition as artists. In fact, many directors today achieve superstar status, and even directors who have made only one or two films are allowed to place their name above the film title and claim possessive credit, as in "A Film By..."

Auteurist criticism developed among the French New Wave critics and then was imported to the United States in the 1960s. Today, director studies are among the most common forms of film criticism. They trace the style of key directors regarded as important artists and as the major creative influence shaping the materials and design of their films. Such directors include Akira Kurosawa in Japan, Ingmar Bergman in Sweden, Federico Fellini in Italy, and in the United States, Alfred Hitchcock, John Ford, Francis Ford Coppola, Martin Scorsese, and many others.

Elements of Auteurism

An auteurist critic looks for consistency of theme and design throughout a director's films. In practice, this means that the critic looks at three correlated elements: cinematic techniques, stories, and themes.

Case Study   ALFRED HITCHCOCK

In the case of Alfred Hitchcock, a director frequently studied from an auteur perspective, these consistent and recurring elements include stories about characters falsely accused of crimes (the "wrong man" theme, found in such films as *The 39 Steps*, *The Wrong Man*, *Strangers on a Train*, and *North by Northwest*) and visual elements such as cross-tracking shots, the subjective camera, high-angle shots, mirror imagery, and long stretches of film without dialogue but with an intensively visual design that Hitchcock called "pure cinema."

In addition, the critic developing an auteur study of Hitchcock might seek correlations between Hitchcock's upbringing and private life and the subjects and techniques of his films. An auteur critic might draw a connection between Hitchcock's intense relationship with his mother and the frequently recurring mother figures in the films or between Hitchcock's Catholic upbringing and attendance at a Jesuit school and the narratives of

guilt, sin, transgression, and crime so common in his films. Hitchcock's fascination with crime, his attendance of murder trials at England's Old Bailey Court, his visits to the Black Museum of Scotland Yard, his attraction to the suspense writer Edgar Allen Poe, and his fascination with celebrity killers such as England's famed John Christie, who buried the bodies of his victims under the floorboards of his house, would seem to have an obvious bearing on the films.

The auteur critic also could draw on anecdotes told by Hitchcock as a standard part of interviews, such as the imprisonment story about the time his father allegedly took him to a police station where Hitchcock was locked in a cell and then subsequently released with a warning by the police that "this is what we do to naughty boys." By telling such anecdotes, Hitchcock encouraged the search for connections between his personal life and his films. He said, "I was terrified of the police, of the Jesuit fathers, of

(continued)

STRANGERS ON A TRAIN (WARNER BROS., 1951)

In Hitchcock's moral universe, everyone is guilty of something, if not by deed then by thought. Accordingly, many of his films focus on a "wrong man" theme, with a character falsely implicated in a crime he did not commit. Guy (Farley Granger) is unwillingly drawn into a bizarre plot to murder his wife, and though he does not commit the deed and even protests against it, he has harbored murderous thoughts about her. To suggest this moral guilt, Hitchcock frames him behind bars, with his face half in shadow. Frame enlargement.

PSYCHO (PARAMOUNT PICTURES, 1960)

Hitchcock's lifelong fascination with crime certainly influenced his screen work. He studied the careers of England's famous murderers and helped create some of the screen's most famous villains. Norman Bates (Tony Perkins) in *Psycho* remains one of cinema's most chilling monsters. Frame enlargement.

physical punishment, of a lot of things. This is the root of my work."

To the extent that the auteur critic can find consistent themes, stories, and audio-visual designs running through the body of a director's films, and can even tie these elements to the filmmaker's private life, the critic can argue that such a director is a true auteur whose films embody a personal and artistic vision. ■

Summary

Auteur criticism has helped elevate cinema to the level of art in the eyes of critics, film-makers, and the general public. By stressing the uniformity and integrity of a director's artistic vision, the auteur critic argues in favor of a unified body of work. By doing so, the critic implies that film is more than just a business, a product manufactured for profit, or an ephemeral and diverting entertainment. By stressing film as an art, auteur criticism undeniably bolsters the power of directors relative to producers and other members of the production crew and has helped to legitimize the film medium.

Moreover, in many cases, the director *is* the catalyst of a production, the key crew member who synthesizes, directs, and helps guide the contributions of other personnel. Production designers and cinematographers emphasize the need to subordinate their artistic vision and interests to the desires of the director in an effort to help the director get the results he or she wants. With many directors, therefore, it is legitimate to argue in favor of some degree of auteurism.

If one looks at enough films of any director, however, visual and narrative patterns probably will begin to emerge, but not all of these are meaningful, nor should they necessarily be attributed to the director. Filmmakers sometimes execute an effect simply because they like the way it looks or even, more mundanely, because they had to shoot or edit a scene a certain way owing to uncooperative weather, the scheduling of in-demand actors, or simply running out of money. Many factors that influence the look of a finished film are things over which filmmakers have little or no control. Japanese director Akira Kurosawa was asked about his framing of a scene in *Ran* (1985), a film about samurai warfare in sixteenth-century Japan. Kurosawa's response says much about the realities of filmmaking. He replied that he had to shoot from the angle he used: Any other angle would reveal the Sony factory and airport nearby, incompatible with the film's period setting.

One problem with a strict auteur approach is that film production is collaborative. It is often impossible to assign responsibility for an effect to a particular individual such as the director, even when the filmmaker in question is one with a readily recognizable style, such as Alfred Hitchcock. Hitchcock collaborated with the screenwriters on most of his films but mainly to guide the design of the narrative and ensure that it afforded him opportunities to create interesting visual effects. Constructing a narrative from scratch and building it into an elegant finished structure was something Hitchcock did not do on his own, in the manner of a filmmaker such as Woody Allen. He needed the services of accomplished screenwriters. The elegant charm and light spirit of *Rear Window* (1954), *To Catch a Thief* (1955), and *The Trouble With Harry* (1956) have an important point of origin in the scripts John Michael Hayes furnished for these films. Much of Hitchcock's other work lacks the unique spirit of his collaborations with Hayes, and this suggests that Hayes played a considerable role in shaping the style of these pictures.

Some of Hitchcock's finest films, such as *Notorious* (1946), about U.S. agents infiltrating a nest of Nazi spies in Brazil, were shaped by decisive creative intervention from the producer. In the case of *Notorious*, producer David O. Selznick insisted again and again that the scripts from Hitchcock and his writers were not good enough and needed merciless revision. As was his custom, Selznick even offered specific suggestions for changing the characters and story situations. Only when the revisions satisfied Selznick was Hitchcock allowed to begin filming.

The auteur critic detects consistent patterns across the body of a director's films and hopes that those things attributed to the director are, indeed, justified. In most cases, though, the critic attributes things on faith, without documentation in the form of interviews or written records about who on the crew did what. Many auteur critics respond to this problem by claiming that, by "Hitchcock," they mean not the private individual but rather the body of films with their unified themes and visual designs. Accordingly, "Hitchcock" becomes a construction required by theory, referring to the films and not to the man. This stratagem is a way of dealing with the objection that a critic can never really know who is responsible for what in a film, and it corrects some, but not all, of the reasons for making the objection.

It is also important to note that many fine directors do *not* impose a consistent stylistic signature across a body of films. Their talent lies in being able to film scripts in consistently intelligent, interesting, and *diverse* ways. Hollywood director Michael Curtiz, for example, has never been regarded as an auteur. And yet, if one looks at the films he directed, an astonishing body of great filmmaking is there. These include classic swashbuckling adventures starring Errol Flynn (*Captain Blood,* 1935; *The Charge of the Light Brigade,* 1936; *The Sea Hawk,* 1940) and major films showcasing Hollywood's biggest stars, such as James Cagney (*Angels With Dirty Faces,* 1938; *Yankee Doodle Dandy,* 1942), Humphrey Bogart (*Passage to Marseille,* 1944; *Casablanca,* 1942), Joan Crawford (*Mildred Pierce,* 1945), and John Garfield (*Four Daughters,* 1938; *The Breaking Point,* 1950). Curtiz was comfortable working in genres from the Western (*Virginia City,* 1940) to the musical (*White Christmas,* 1954).

Norman Jewison (*In the Heat of the Night,* 1967; *Moonstruck,* 1987) and Sidney Pollack (*Tootsie,* 1982; *Out of Africa,* 1985) also were fine filmmakers who fall outside of the auteur framework. They directed many films that are diverse

BROKEN EMBRACES (UPI, 2009)

Distinctive filmmakers may establish careers as international auteurs, recognized in global film culture as important artists. Pedro Almodovar is a prominent, contemporary Spanish director whose films are noted for their sexually flamboyant content, highly saturated colors, intensive melodrama, and focus on strong women. He established a long-term, collaborative relationship with actress Penelope Cruz. In *Broken Embraces,* her fourth film with Almodovar, she plays an aspiring actress involved with a manipulative, jealous patron. The collaborative partnership between Almodovar and Cruz recalls other great director–actor pairings, including Michael Curtiz and Bette Davis and Ingmar Bergman and Liv Ullmann. An auteur director often rises to distinction based on close relationships with key collaborators, including cinematographers and scriptwriters as well as actors. Frame enlargement.

and stylistically varied, unified only by the fact that the work is intelligent, well-designed and sharply focused. The auteur perspective has had difficulty coming to terms with such filmmakers, who by any definition are great directors but who subordinated their own self-branding to the needs of the script and varied their signatures accordingly.

While, then, an auteur approach is essential to understanding cinematic artistry, it highlights directors who have a recognizable signature across a body of films and tends to overlook other fine directors who don't meet this criterion.

PSYCHOANALYTIC MODELS

Drawing primarily from the writings of Freud and French psychoanalyst Jacques Lacan, **psychoanalytic film theory** emphasizes film's elicitation of unconscious sources of pleasure and desire. For psychoanalytic critics, the film medium activates deep-rooted psychological and nonrational desires and drives.

Elements of Psychoanalytic Models

In his landmark book *The Interpretation of Dreams* (1899), Freud wrote that dreams provided access to the workings of the unconscious mind. He argued that our conscious thoughts and feelings represented only a small portion of our mental life and that the most significant and strongest motivations underlying our behavior are unconscious. For Freud, the mind was not a unified whole but was, instead, fractured into relatively separate components. Thoughts, feelings, and ideas we are aware of belong to the ego; those that were unconscious belonged to the id, and many of these were formed by repression, the blocking from consciousness of impulses and desires that are socially prohibited but which nonetheless remain active.

A famous example that he wrote about was castration anxiety, suffered by a male child when he realizes that his mother lacks a penis. The resulting fear of sexual difference—rooted in the realization that women are physiologically different beings from men—in Freud's view causes the male child tremendous anxiety, which is repressed and may resurface in the form of fetishes and other obsessive behaviors.

Psychoanalysis was Freud's method for uncovering the impulses of the unconscious mind, and the interpretation of dreams was a key component of psychoanalytic technique. Dream imagery when properly interpreted, Freud believed, reveals the repressed contents of an individual's unconscious. What a person remembers of a dream when awake is its manifest, or surface level, content. Its true content is latent and accessible only to psychoanalysis.

Dreams work according to mechanisms of **condensation** and **displacement**. Psychic energy and impulses become condensed into one or more resonant dream images. Often these images are displacements, substitute objects that take the place of the more fundamental and forbidden desire. Dreaming is an act of secondary revision; it imposes a narrative coherence upon the raw stream of imagery generated by the unconscious. The object of psychoanalytic dream interpretation is to connect the narrative in the dream to its underlying latent content.

Freud's model of the mind and of dream analysis has exerted a strong influence upon filmmakers as well as film critics and scholars. Movies have been likened to dreams, and the act of watching a movie has been compared with a state of dreaming-while-awake.

Numerous films throughout cinema history have tried to reproduce the weird logic and imagery of dreams or have incorporated dream sequences into the narratives. Luis Bunuel and Salvador Dali's *Un Chien Andalou* (1929) is a surrealist attack on polite society that works by evoking the irrationality of dreams—a man bicycles dressed as a nun, two priests drag a pair of pianos into an apartment on top of which is a bleeding animal carcass, narrative events are contradictory and fail to cohere or to observe unities of time and place.

Buster Keaton's *Sherlock, Jr.* (1924) uses the connection of movies to dreams as a source of comedy. Keaton plays a projectionist at a movie theater who wants to become a famous detective and win the respect of his girlfriend. He achieves these things when he falls asleep at the theater and steps into the movie on screen which functions according to the logic of dreams. The seashore abruptly changes to a wintry landscape, so that Keaton's dive into the water lands him in a snowbank. The dreamworld of cinema fulfills the character's deepest desires and fantasies.

The ambiguity of dreams, seeming more real than reality to the sleeper, has enabled filmmakers to play with the logical status of dreaming and wakefulness. In Luis Bunuel's *The Discrete Charm of the Bourgeoisie* (1973), characters throughout the film suddenly awaken in bed and remark that everything a viewer has just seen was a dream. Dreams within dreams become so numerous that the viewer can no longer tell what is a dream and what events belong to the waking life.

SHERLOCK, JR. (BUSTER KEATON PRODUCTIONS, 1924)

Longing to be a famous detective, but in reality working as a janitor and projectionist at a movie theater, Buster falls asleep and enters the dream world of a film where his fantasies come true. The connection of movies and dreams has been recognized by filmmakers the world over. Frame enlargement.

Christopher Nolan's *Inception* (2010) works in a similar way, placing characters inside dreams within dreams, taking them down into deep layers of the unconscious mind such that a viewer, watching the film's final moments, cannot tell whether the main character, Cobb (Leonardo DiCaprio), has returned to consciousness or remains within a dream. The logical status of all the narrative events in David Lynch's *Mulholland Dr.* (2001) is suspect, with the story becoming increasingly weird as it

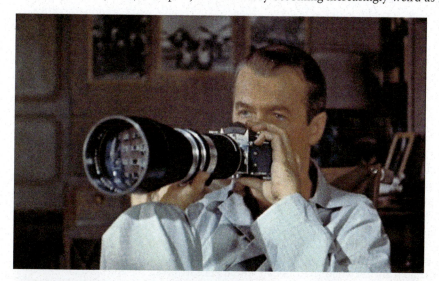

REAR WINDOW (PARAMOUNT, 1954); VERTIGO (PARAMOUNT, 1958)

Greatly influenced by Freud, Hitchcock used film to explore the repressed, unconscious desires of characters. From a psychoanalytic standpoint, *Rear Window* is a drama about castration anxiety and sublimated potency. In *Vertigo*, Scotty Ferguson (James Stewart) has a phobia of falling from high places. This fear is a displacement of his desire for death. Hired to trail a mysterious woman (Kim Novak), he falls in love while voyeuristically watching her. In the shot pictured here, he conceals himself in a back room and gazes at her while she visits a flower shop. Watching her in secret arouses his desire for her. To Freud, scopophilia was the erotic pleasure of **voyeurism**, and Hitchcock considered it to be one of the fundamental appeals offered by cinema. Frame enlargements.

progresses until it seems probable that everything in it is the dream of a character (Naomi Watts) undergoing a psychotic breakdown.

A psychoanalytic interpretation of cinema examines the dream-like qualities of film narrative and film technique, with particular attention to repressed, unconscious desires and motives on the part of characters in a film and to the ways that cinema may elicit such desires from viewers.

As a director, Hitchcock was very influenced by Freud's work, and many of his films are quite rewarding for Freudian analysis. In *Rear Window*, Jeffries (James Stewart) is a photographer confined to his apartment with a broken leg. Bored, he takes to spying on his neighbors, watching them through their windows using his camera's long-focus lens. He constructs fantasies and imaginary stories about the lives he sees from a distance in ways that make his situation as a voyeur comparable to the cinema viewer, who also derives pleasure from watching people on screen from the safety of a darkened auditorium.

Jeffries fears Lisa (Grace Kelly), the woman who loves and wants to marry him. He fears her differences as a woman from his preferred ways of living. If he marries her, she'll change his life, and he isn't sure he wants that to happen. *Rear Window*, then, can be seen in part as a movie about castration (fear of Lisa and her sexual difference, a fear symbolized by Jeffries' broken leg) and displacement. Jeffries displaces his anxieties onto the pleasures he derives from fantasizing about the substitute worlds of his neighbors' lives. Using his long-focus lens, Jeffries sublimates his lost potency by connecting it to the fantasy world that gives him pleasure. And he accepts Lisa only when she steps into that fantasy world, going across the courtyard to enter one of the apartments where Jeffries can watch her retrieving the clue to a crime.

For Freud, "scopophilia" was the erotic pleasure that a person derived from looking at people or things, and psychoanalytic models of cinema take it as a medium that provides scopophilic pleasures to its viewers, offering them voyeuristic opportunities. In a classic essay called "Visual Pleasure and Narrative Cinema," Laura Mulvey argued that cinema mobilizes a scopophilic drive and that women are presented as objects for the male gaze. Cinema techniques, such as close-ups, can draw the viewer's attention to aspects of the screen spectacle that arouse scopic pleasures. Male directors, for example, may use long, lingering close-ups to examine the glamorous, sexy appearance and costuming of female stars such as Marlene Dietrich or Marilyn Monroe, who embody male erotic desires.

FETISHIZING THE BODY   Psychoanalytic critics describe Dietrich's elaborate costuming and ritualistic visual presentation in a series of films she made for director Josef von Sternberg (*Morocco*, 1930; *Shanghai Express*, 1932; *Blonde Venus*, 1932; *The Scarlet Empress*, 1934; *The Devil Is a Woman*, 1935) as a kind of visual fetish. With lingering attention, the camera studies the precise outline, design, and appearance of Dietrich as an erotic object. While the Sternberg films enjoy a high critical reputation owing to their exquisite artistic design, many less reputable films display the bodies of their performers in a fetishized fashion, a practice that includes male stars as well as female ones.

Mulvey argued that male characters are not subject to the controlling gaze of the camera or a viewer in ways that are scopophilic, but many films made after the 1970s, when she wrote her essay, seem to do precisely this. The glistening, well-defined muscles of Sylvester Stallone or Arnold Schwarzenegger command a great deal of attention in their action films. This attention emphasizes their bodies as idealized sexual objects conforming to an exaggerated cultural ideal of male potency and power.

GENTLEMEN PREFER BLONDES (20TH CENTURY FOX, 1953)

Psychoanalytic theory examines the gaze in cinema as a gendered construction. Female stars, such as Jane Russell and Marilyn Monroe (pictured here), were constructed by color design, composition, and camera set-ups as objects appealing to the gaze of male viewers. Male stars in earlier decades were rarely presented in such overtly erotic terms to female viewers. Frame enlargement.

But, significantly, such attention is disavowed and its erotic component is repressed, absorbed by violent action and physical combat that the narratives view as appropriately male behavior. The engorged muscles of Stallone and other action heroes are examples of condensation, a site of erotic energy and attention, energy that is repressed in the films through displacement onto spectacles of violent action.

Films offer spectacles of sex and violence that excite viewers in ways they would deny in polite society. Viewers of *The Silence of the Lambs* (1991) eagerly spend time in the company of serial killer Hannibal Lecter, whereas in real life they would shun such a person. Unlike real-life violence, bloodshed and killing on screen give many viewers intense aesthetic pleasure. For psychoanalytic critics, the cinema's ability to excite viewers with spectacles of sex and violence illustrates its powerful appeal to an audience's primitive, nonrational desires. Polite society restricts outward expressions of sexual or aggressive behavior, yet the cinema displays these in extremely arousing ways.

Summary

Psychoanalytic criticism emphasizes the complex ways that film arouses an audience's repressed emotions and desires. These desires may not be conscious or fully understood by viewers, yet films can reach deep inside viewers' minds to influence the ways they understand their world, themselves, and their feelings. Sometimes the emotional response of an audience is so extraordinarily intense and concentrated, at such an unbearable pitch, that a psychoanalytic explanation seems warranted.

RAMBO: FIRST BLOOD PART II (TRI-STAR, 1985)

Rambo is tortured by his Vietnamese captors, but first he must be undressed in order to display his body. Sylvester Stallone's engorged, glistening muscles exemplify the Freudian ideas of condensation and displacement. As a symbolic image, they concentrate ideas about the erotic appeal of male bodies coded in terms of physical action and suffering. Action displaces the erotic energy that is otherwise on such obvious display. Frame enlargement.

THE SILENCE OF THE LAMBS (ORION PICTURES, 1991)

Hannibal Lecter (Anthony Hopkins) in *The Silence of the Lambs* exerts a powerful fascination for viewers who are repulsed by his monstrousness yet attracted by his wit and intelligence. The special power such a character has over viewers may require a psychoanalytic explanation because it seems to contradict a viewer's rational judgment that such a person is evil and to be avoided. Frame enlargement.

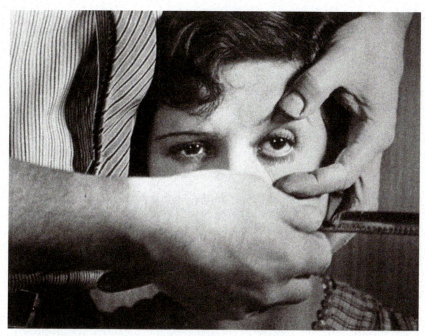

UN CHIEN ANDALOU (1929)

Luis Bunuel and Salvador Dali aimed to assault the viewer's eye and mind with a catalog of irrational, disturbing, and offensive imagery and to explode narrative with a collection of illogical and disconnected episodes. They intended *Un Chien Andalou* to be an act of violence committed against the medium of cinema and for its images to appeal to the primitive, unconscious mind of its viewers. To symbolize this assault on mind and vision, in the film's opening moments, director Bunuel pulls out a straight razor, opens a woman's eye, and slices. The camera does not look away. Frame enlargement.

As an example, consider the opening of Luis Buñuel's and Salvador Dali's *Un Chien Andalou* (1928), which features one of the most shocking images in screen history. In the scene, a man (played by Buñuel) stands behind a seated woman. He pulls out a straight razor and opens her left eye. The film then cuts to a long shot of clouds slicing across a moon, as the audience breathes a sigh of relief, thinking that, as usual, the camera has turned away from something that promises to be too horrifying.

In the next moment, though, the filmmakers show what viewers most dread. The razor slices into an eye that pops and disgorges a blob of gelatinous fluid. This is an old movie, and violent images have a way of becoming less intense and horrifying over time. This, though, is not one of those cases. The image has a special, sustained power to disturb and nauseate viewers. Contemporary audiences recoil with the same intensity and disgust that viewers felt in 1929.

A psychoanalytic explanation can help here. As Freud suggested, among all the parts of the body that might potentially be wounded, people seem most sensitive about their eyes. Freud connected this anxiety to fears of castration. Whatever one might think of such a connection, Freud seemed correct in noting the special intensity of the instinctual anxiety over the threat of wounds to the eyes. When an object or situation is so charged with emotional energy, psychoanalysis looks toward the unconscious for an explanation. The anxieties seem, in some way, to be fundamental and primitive components of human identity, and, for psychoanalytic theory, the unconscious is the most primitive part of the mind. Psychoanalytic theory, then, enables critics to ask about why certain film images seem so charged with emotional energy and about how, in such moments, the cinema provokes and intensifies the reactions of its audience.

A psychoanalytic approach must be careful not to overextend itself, to be used as a means of explaining all dimensions of an audience's emotional response to movies. Psychoanalysis emphasizes mainly repressed and irrational desires and perceptions. On the contrary, though, many aspects of the viewer's response to movies are entirely rational and do not require special explanation with reference to the unconscious mind. Among these are the demands for reference and correspondence with experience that viewers expect from a photographically-based medium like cinema.

IDEOLOGICAL MODELS

Critics use **ideological film theory** to examine the relationship between movies and society and, specifically, how film represents social and political realities. An **ideology** is a set of beliefs about society and the nature of the world, involving assumptions and judgments about the nature of right and wrong, good and evil, justice and injustice, law and social order, and human nature and behavior.

Societies contain multiple ideologies, and these are not always coherent or harmonious. Because of this, all societies are subject to ideological tensions and conflicts. Among conflicting ideologies in U.S. culture are the commitments to individual freedoms, on the one hand, and, on the other, the power of state and local governments to enforce law and maintain public order.

The ongoing controversies over gun control illustrate these conflicting ideologies. Proponents of gun control emphasize the need for government to ensure public safety by getting guns off the street. Opponents emphasize the individual right to own and bear arms. Such conflicts are very difficult to resolve and tend to arouse a great deal of emotion on each side, as the ongoing battles about gun control illustrate. Ideological conflict is a typical social phenomenon arising from the simple fact that not all of the belief systems that circulate through a society are compatible or consistent with one another.

Elements of Ideological Models

Ideological film critics study the ways film portrays society and gives voice to one or more social ideologies. The ideological critic often starts by describing certain social trends or habits of thought and then demonstrates how these are represented in given bodies of film. Ideological critics, for example, emphasize the way that many Hollywood Westerns, which portray Native Americans as villains and as obstacles to be removed, support traditional cultural beliefs about manifest destiny, the inalienable right of European settlers to claim the wilderness and divest Native Americans of their land.

LEVELS OF IDEOLOGY   Social ideologies exist in films on either first- or second-order levels, that is, they are either explicit or implicit. *Rambo: First Blood Part II* (1985), about a super U.S. warrior who returns to Vietnam many years after the war and defeats the Vietnamese in battle, offers U.S. culture a kind of substitute and vicarious symbolic victory in a war the nation lost. By virtue of its explicit treatment of social, political, and historical topics, it is an overtly ideological film. Its story deals with anxieties about the role of the United States as a world super-power and with lingering questions about its defeat in Southeast Asia. As such, the images and narrative of *Rambo* are ideological in an immediate, explicit, first-order way.

Films that are ideological on a second-order level present social messages and portraits of society that are implicit, indirect, and subtle. Examples of second-order ideological films are *Back to the Future* (1985) and *Field of Dreams* (1989), both of which are intimately connected to the mood of the era in which they were produced, especially the nostalgic myth of a return to the past represented by 1980s political culture.

In *Back to the Future*, the hero, Marty McFly (Michael J. Fox), travels back in time, and Ray Kinsella (Kevin Costner) from *Field of Dreams* mysteriously recreates the past in an Iowa cornfield of dreams. Both characters meet their parents from the past, and by doing so, they reclaim their boyhood. An ideological critic would show how these narratives correlate with the political culture of the 1980s, particularly its nostalgic embrace of an ideal past and the folklore of small towns and close-knit communities that underlay the appeal and vision of the Reagan presidency.

Unlike *Rambo*, where the political ideologies are up-front and out in the open, *Back to the Future* and *Field of Dreams* do not strike one immediately as political films. An ideological critic, however, could argue, correctly, that these films are closely entwined with the political culture of their period. As a result and despite their overt appeal as entertainment vehicles, they are ideological in a second-order, implicit, and indirect way.

IDEOLOGICAL POINT OF VIEW   Just as films may be directly or indirectly ideological, they also may take up a variety of positions with respect to the ideologies they portray and the views of society developed in their narratives. Although a wide range of such positions exists, three main categories are the most important. Films can support established social values, criticize established values, or offer an incoherent, ambiguous, and unresolved presentation of social values. To describe the ideological position of a film, a critic must specify two things: the constellation of social values within the film and its attitude toward them, and, second, the social groups to whom those values belong.

Position One: Ideological Support   The first position—support for established social values—is illustrated by many contemporary war films, which take a very positive and patriotic stance with respect to America's military forces. *Black Hawk Down* (2001), for example, recounts the horrendous fighting in Somalia between a local warlord's army and U.S. Marines. Consistent with war films since *Saving Private Ryan*, the depiction of battlefield violence is graphic and intense. This violence, though, serves to emphasize the heroism, bravery, and determination of U.S. forces, qualities that the film stresses.

CLOSE UP

9/11 and Hollywood Film

Imagery of the terrorist attacks on September 11, 2001, captured in photographs and videos by onlookers, seared the national consciousness. The imagery included throngs of panicked New Yorkers fleeing the collapsing towers of the World Trade Center, the cloud of ash and dust that followed the collapse, and, before this, the gaping holes in the buildings, the fires and black smoke, and the blizzard of paper that blew out of the towers' offices. And in the days to come, crowds gathered around numerous pictures of missing loved ones that had been posted throughout the city.

In general, Hollywood films stayed away from direct portraits of 9/11 because the event was so tragic and emotional that few moviegoers wished to see a dramatization of it on the screen. But many films that were not about 9/11 used the iconic imagery of that day to give their stories an extra resonance. *Cloverfield* (2008), for example, depicts a monster destroying Manhattan and uses jittery, hand-held video cameras to create images of fleeing crowds that resemble the footage produced by witnesses on 9/11. The monster-movie spectacle of Manhattan's destruction is keyed to the disaster on 9/11.

From an ideological standpoint, Hollywood feared making films about 9/11, believing that they would be box-office disasters and in bad

THE DARK KNIGHT (Warner Bros., 2008)

Batman's nemesis, the Joker, is depicted in this film as a terrorist seeking to create chaos and destruction. The Joker and his men bomb numerous buildings in Gotham City, and Gotham's politicians and police debate whether to use harsh interrogation tactics—torture—on the terrorists in order to stop them. In its focus on terrorism, the film becomes an ideological account of post-9/11 America and the dilemmas it has faced. The scene pictured here, showing Gotham firefighters coping with the aftermath of a bombing, recreates iconic 9/11 imagery of firefighters at work in the devastated remains of the World Trade Center. Frame enlargement.

taste as well if they were made as entertainments. But many Hollywood filmmakers felt compelled to use film to acknowledge 9/11, and most did so in an indirect way, giving their films ideological content in a second-order and implicit manner.

Steven Spielberg, for example, made three films that were indirectly about 9/11. *The Terminal* (2004) is a comedy about the closing of America's borders by Homeland Security. *War of the Worlds* (2005) uses the iconic 9/11 images of destruction and fleeing crowds in telling a story about alien invasion (based on H.G. Wells' novel). *Munich* (2005) depicts Israel's response to the killings of its Olympic athletes in 1972 by the Black September terrorist group and treats this event as a precursor to 9/11. The film's closing image shows the 1970s-era New York skyline with the twin towers of the World Trade Center in prominent view. These are a digital effect because when the film was made the towers could no longer be photographed. But Spielberg intends for the image to make an ideological point, connecting the events in *Munich* with our contemporary experience.

WAR OF THE WORLDS (PARAMOUNT PICTURES, 2005)

In the aftermath of 9/11, many Hollywood films incorporated iconic images of that day of destruction. Steven Spielberg's film depicts terror-stricken crowds fleeing alien invaders and shows an airplane that has crashed into a building. But the film's ideological perspective on 9/11 gets some important things wrong. Speilberg shows people turning on another with anger and hatred, screaming, and fighting among themselves. It is a very negative portrait of how people might behave in situations of danger. It fails to square with what all reports about 9/11 have shown, namely, that those in the stricken World Trade Center calmly made their way to the exits and helped others who were hurt. People were at their best because they were in the worst of circumstances, a fact of human behavior that eludes the film's ideological portrait. Frame enlargement.

(*continued*)

WORLD TRADE CENTER (PARAMOUNT PICTURES, 2006)

In one of the few Hollywood films to directly portray the events of 9/11, Nicolas Cage plays New Jersey Port Authority Officer John McLoughlin, who, with three other Port Authority Officers, was trapped in an underground concourse beneath the rubble of the Trade Center's south tower when it collapsed. McLoughlin and one other officer were rescued. The characters and events are real, presented by the film in an emotional and inspiring way. The story is one of lives saved whereas one of 9/11's most important meanings lies in the number of lives that were lost. Ideological meaning in film often arises from the way that events are selected, portrayed, omitted, or emphasized. *World Trade Center* searches for a positive experience to offer moviegoers, and while it is a fine film, the events that it selects to portray do not include a recognition of the scale of death that occurred on 9/11. Frame enlargement.

Like many contemporary war films, *Black Hawk Down* does not offer a political perspective on the fighting. In fact, it avoids political analysis and, instead, offers a straightforward tribute to America's military by concentrating on the close-in details of hand-to-hand fighting.

More recently, *We Were Soldiers* (2002) portrays the courage and determination that enabled a battalion of 400 U.S. Army soldiers to prevail over 2000 enemy soldiers during the Vietnam War in 1965. The movie stresses the strong family and religious background of the main character, Lt. Col. Hal Moore (Mel Gibson). Many scenes show Moore at home and his devotion to family. He frolics with his kids, has heart-to-heart talks with them, and prays with them before bedtime. By giving family and religion such emphasis, the film scores ideological points. The character is defined in terms of a very positive vision of a good, moral life, and this moral framework is then transferred to the battle scenes in Vietnam, helping them to become a statement about American patriotism and bravery.

(a)

(b)

BLACK HAWK DOWN (COLUMBIA, 2001); WE WERE SOLDIERS (PARAMOUNT, 2002)

Many contemporary war films avoid dealing with the politics of war and questions surrounding the projection of U.S. power overseas. Instead, they take a close-up view of battlefield violence and stress the bravery and patriotism of American soldiers. In *Black Hawk Down* (a), Americans find themselves outgunned in Somalia but manage to prevail. In *We Were Soldiers* (b), Lt. Col. Hal Moore (Mel Gibson) prays with his children at bedtime while his wife looks on approvingly. The film uses family and religion for ideological purposes, stressing that virtue and patriotism are the essential meanings of the Vietnam War. Frame enlargements.

The major ideological effect of *We Were Soldiers* lies in the way that it erases the war's controversy, substituting for that a redemptive and heroic vision of American sacrifice. Toward this end, the filmmakers deleted a key scene placed at the end of the film in which, after the battle, Moore warns Pentagon officials that the Vietnamese will be a tough enemy, suggesting that a decision to pursue the war would be foolish. The scene added a very different point of view, one that was more critical of the war. It was, therefore, cut out. Consistent with many contemporary Vietnam War movies,

We Were Soldiers portrays a controversial war by ignoring the controversy and emphasizing instead traditional elements of patriotism.

Because societies contain multiple communities and multiple ideologies, films might support social values that have currency within one community or subgroup but that are disdained or rejected by other groups. *Longtime Companion* (1990) examines the spread of AIDs in the 1980s by focusing on a small, closely knit community of gay men in New York City. When released, the film was controversial because its affectionate, supportive portrait of gay life clashed with the values of groups convinced that gay sexuality is wrong or who blamed the gay community for the spread of AIDs.

Position Two: Ideological Critique Films offering a genuinely critical view of established social values are less common in the U.S. industry than those that offer clear support for such values. Nevertheless, in the late 1960s, films such as *Easy Rider* (1969) and *The Wild Bunch* (1969) presented heroes who were outlaws or rebels dissatisfied with and struggling against what was then termed "the establishment." In *Easy Rider* and *The Wild Bunch*, audiences sympathized with the outlaws and not with mainstream society; the heroes' rebellion exposed the pettiness and intolerance of society. More recently, *Robocop* (1987) offered a savage critique of the social Darwinism that underlay 1980s economic policies, especially those cutting the social safety net from under the poor while revising the tax laws to benefit the very wealthy.

Outside relatively rare social satires such as *Robocop*, critiques from a left-wing perspective are uncommon within the U.S. industry. By contrast, European

PHILADELPHIA (TRISTAR PICTURES, 1993)

Commentators and critics argued over the ideological content of *Philadelphia*, which focused on the film's portrayal of a homosexual man (played by Tom Hanks) with AIDS. Some critics suggested that the film minimized the character's gay identity and sexuality in the interest of appealing to heterosexual audiences that traditionally have avoided gay-themed films. Frame enlargement.

THE WILD BUNCH (WARNER BROS., 1969)

The savage violence of *The Wild Bunch* contained a powerful indictment of society. The film viewed society as being hopelessly corrupt, and its outlaw heroes were only slightly less bad than everyone else. Frame enlargement.

filmmakers are much sharper in their political critiques. Italian director Gillo Pontecorvo, in *The Battle of Algiers* (1965) and *Burn!* (1969), critiqued the imperialism of France and England at the time of their empires; these films portrayed heroic guerrilla struggles for revolution and independence. Furthermore, by implication, *Burn!* offered a critique of U.S. intervention in Vietnam. This kind of left-wing, socially critical filmmaking is virtually nonexistent in the U.S. industry.

The reasons are not hard to understand. Many millions of dollars are at stake in a film production today, and Hollywood is not eager to risk losing big chunks of its market with hard-edged social criticism. It is easier, and potentially more profitable, to reinforce existing ideologies than to challenge them in fundamental ways. *Starship Troopers* (1997) offers an instructive lesson in this regard. Director Paul Verhoeven and screenwriter Ed Neumeier tried to use the format of World War II propaganda films in order to equate war with fascism, but this critique was overwhelmed by the film's intense violence and bravura special effects. These made the film very marketable and more conventional and conservative by blunting the sharpness of its political critique of imperialism and militarism.

Position Three: Ideological Conglomeration Radical ideological criticism is rarely found in the U.S. industry. Hollywood films more commonly assume a position of ideological conglomeration; that is, they contain a mixed set of appeals and social outlooks. This is an understandable result from the conditions of mass-market production. Major studio films are designed for consumption by large, heterogeneous audiences composed of diverse groups, communities, and subcultures. To appeal to these diverse groupings, Hollywood often puts, ideologically, a little of this and a little of that into a film. The resulting mix creates a sufficiently ambiguous product calculated to attract as many members of the target audiences as possible while offending few. Ideological conglomeration enables Hollywood to appeal to a multitude of different viewers.

The futuristic social satire *Total Recall* (1990) portrayed ruthless corporations exploiting workers on a Martian mining colony and using the media back on earth to camouflage and disguise political reality. Excessive product placements in the film undermined its social satire. *Total Recall* was 1990's product-placement champion; the film that featured more placements than any produced that year. The anticorporate satire of *Total Recall* did not sit well with the continual corporate advertising carried by the product placements. By helping to tame the film's anticorporate satire, the product placements provided a greater degree of social familiarity and ideological comfort to viewers watching the movie's disturbing futuristic world.

African-American Film

Ideology in film is determined in part by the social perspectives that given films express. These, in turn, are related to the distribution of power, privilege and opportunity within the larger society. Throughout film history, this distribution of power and privilege has operated to deny or to marginalize the voices of social groups, based on gender, race, ethnicity or class. In older Hollywood films, nonwhite ethnic groups are almost always stereotyped and caricatured. A brief examination of how African-Americans have fared in the Hollywood industry can help to illustrate how films have reflected social inequalities and then began to change as these, too, have changed.

Before the 1990s, it is nearly correct to say that no African-American directors worked in Hollywood. Sidney Poitier, a prominent actor, directed occasional films in the 1970s and 1980s, which included *Uptown Saturday Night* (1974) and *Stir Crazy* (1980). Michael Schultz directed *Cooley High* (1975) and *Car Wash* (1976), but these are relatively rare examples.

THE 1990s GENERATION   Of the filmmakers who emerged during and after the 1990s, their African-American identity is sometimes highly visible and relevant to their work. But not always—sometimes the result is simply an entertaining popcorn movie. The industry has made room for this new generation of filmmakers in a variety of ways, which include blockbusters at the highest levels of industry financing.

Tim Story, for example, followed his breakthrough comedy *Barbershop* (2002) and *Taxi* (2004) with the summer blockbuster *Fantastic Four* (2005). Director Antoine Fuqua has moved easily from cop films such as *Training Day* (2001) and *Brooklyn's Finest* (2010), with their sharp sense of the streets and contemporary racial issues, to the medieval world of *King Arthur* (2004), where the focus is on legend and myth.

Carl Franklin has moved from a brilliant adaptation of *Devil in a Blue Dress* (1995), based on the Walter Mosley novel that re-imagines the detective genre from the standpoint of a black detective, to *One True Thing* (1998), an accomplished melodrama about a white family in which the mother is dying of cancer.

This is a healthy situation in which black filmmakers can work on a variety of projects aimed at differing audiences. Compared with the rigid racial policies that prevailed in Hollywood 50 years ago, the creative situation today is far more fluid and flexible, and this is largely due to the influence of a new generation of filmmakers, keen to work on a variety of projects rather than be confined to making one kind of film for one kind of audience.

Spike Lee was the first of this group to emerge. After *She's Gotta Have It* (1986), which was one of the most prominent independent films of its period, Lee's *Do the*

Right Thing (1989) achieved a high degree of visibility by stimulating dialogue and discussion around the country about the state of race relations in America. Lee's portrait of a neighborhood in Brooklyn, New York, showed numerous racial and ethnic tensions among the black, white, Latino, and Asian characters. The tensions climax with a protest that elicits police violence, and Lee ends the film with an ambiguous contrast between the pacifist philosophy of Dr. Martin Luther King, Jr., and the more aggressive and radical teachings of Malcolm X.

Lee then embarked on a series of stylized, imaginative productions, many of which took race among their primary themes. These included *Mo' Better Blues* (1990), *Jungle Fever* (1991), *Malcolm X* (1993), *Get on the Bus* (1996), *Four Little Girls* (1997), *Clockers* (1995), and *Bamboozled* (2000). *25th Hour* (2002) is one of the best of that era's 9/11-themed films. Lee has also been very active as a documentary filmmaker, work that includes the acclaimed HBO production, *When the Levees Broke: A Requiem in Four Acts* (2006), about Hurricane Katrina and the flooding of New Orleans.

John Singleton was the next major director to appear after Spike Lee. His *Boyz N the Hood* (1991) was a highly acclaimed directorial debut, and its appearance following Lee's films confirmed that a major change was taking place in American cinema. The film was a melancholy portrait of the crime, violence, and lack of opportunity that was decimating a generation of black men in the cities. He then made three very original pictures—*Poetic Justice* (1993), *Higher Learning* (1995), and *Rosewood* (1987)—before joining the Hollywood remake game with *Shaft* (2000), a slick updating of the "blaxploitation" classic. His more recent efforts have been action films—*2 Fast 2 Furious* (2003) and *Four Brothers* (2005).

Like Singleton, Albert and Allen Hughes made a highly acclaimed debut with *Menace II Society* (1993), also about the gun violence claiming young black men. This was the most profitable film of its year owing due to its low production cost and good box office return. Julie Dash directed the acclaimed independent film, *Daughters of the Dust* (1991), a period drama about a family migrating from the Sea Islands off the

DO THE RIGHT THING (UNIVERSAL, 1989)

Spike Lee was the first to emerge of a new generation of black filmmakers in Hollywood in the 1990s. *Do the Right Thing*, his breakthrough film, stimulated wide-ranging national discussions about race in America. Frame enlargement.

Carolina coast to the U.S. mainland. This was the first African-American film directed by a woman to go into general theatrical release.

At a much higher level of box-office success are the comedies of Keenan Ivory Wayans. These include *Scary Movie* (2000), *Scary Movie II* (2001), and a fond parody of 1970s-era "blaxploitation," *I'm Gonna Git You Sucka* (1988).

ACTORS   Among the present generation of African-American actors, the most prominent is Denzel Washington, who became one of the few actors to make a successful transition from television (the 1980s series *St. Elsewhere*) to the big screen. Washington has specialized in playing relatively noble characters in pictures such as *Devil in a Blue Dress* and *Philadelphia* (1993). He made a dramatic switch in *Training Day* (2001), where he played a ferociously bad cop, and the industry took notice. He won the Academy Award for Best Actor with that role.

Washington has often teamed with director Tony Scott (*Man on Fire*, 2004; *The Taking of Pelham 1 2 3*, 2009; *Unstoppable*, 2010), and he has directed two films, *Antwone Fisher* (2002) and *The Great Debaters* (2007).

In 2005, he returned to the New York stage, playing Brutus in *Julius Ceasar*, and his star charisma drew huge audiences and helped to make the play one of its season's hits.

The same year Washington won his Oscar for *Training Day*, Halle Berry won as Best Actress for *Monster's Ball*. The twin victories were highly symbolic. No black actor had won the award since Sidney Poitier in 1963, and few had even been nominated. The symbolism of the dual wins enabled the industry to announce the importance of African-American films and audiences and to acknowledge that it had been slow to reach this point. Unfortunately, Berry followed her victory with some bad career moves, roles in the James Bond film, *Die Another Day* (2002), and *Catwoman* (2004), which audiences avoided.

Thus there are currently no African-American female stars of the magnitude of Denzel Washington or Will Smith. Angela Basset seemed poised for a major career after the hit *How Stella Got Her Groove Back* (1998), but she then suffered the same kind of career halt that afflicts many women working in film today (discussed in the subsequent section of this chapter).

Like Washington, Will Smith successfully transitioned from television series to big-screen films while carrying with him his trademark wisecracking humor. Smith has made action thrillers (*Enemy of the State*, 1998) and straight drama (*Malcolm*, 2001; *Hitch,* 2005) but has found some of his biggest hits in science fiction. He battled aliens in *Men in Black* (1997) and *Independence Day* (1996) and an army of robots in *I, Robot* (2004). The latter film is especially interesting in the way that it uses Smith's persona to lend a racial subtheme to the film. Smith plays a black cop who is a bigot—he is prejudiced against the robots who help people with their chores and who are second-class citizens.

He eventually overcomes his prejudice by learning to appreciate the humanity in one of the robots who assists him in his case. While the racial subtheme is not a major part of the film, it adds an interesting resonance to the movie, and it could not have been achieved in the same way with a white actor.

Numerous supporting players bring their distinctive personalities to contemporary film. Morgan Freeman is one of the most dignified and regal actors ever to appear in Hollywood movies. He carries a natural authority and bearing that have distinguished his appearances in a huge number of films, including *Glory* (1989),

Unforgiven (1992), *Se7en* (1995), *Deep Impact* (1998), and *An Unfinished Life* (2005). Clint Eastwood cast him as Nelson Mandela in *Invictus* (2009).

Samuel L. Jackson's street-smart persona, his cockiness, and his extraordinarily expressive voice are essential to *Pulp Fiction* (1994), *Jackie Brown* (1997), *Shaft* (2000), and other films that denote "cool." He has supplied the cartoon voice of Frozone in *The Incredibles* (2004), and providing one measure of his star quality, he was given one of the most startling and breathtaking death scenes in recent film in *Deep Blue Sea* (1999).

Queen Latifa moved from recorded music to an ongoing film career, which only occasionally makes use of her exceptional singing talent—*Living Out Loud* (1998), *Chicago* (2002), and *Beauty Shop* (2005).

Don Cheadle has built a thriving career on memorable character roles in *Devil in a Blue Dress* (1995), *Boogie Nights* (1997), *Ocean's Eleven* (2001), and *Ocean's Twelve* (2004), and he was nominated for a Best Actor Oscar for his lead performance in *Hotel Rwanda* (2004). Other memorable supporting players include Ving Rhames, Ice Cube, and Ice T. To understand why the changes in contemporary film that have brought these players and directors forward are significant, one needs to look at how things were during the first eight decades of Hollywood film.

A SEGREGATED INDUSTRY   During the silent and sound film eras, Hollywood movies reflected the racial inequalities that prevailed in America. African-American screen characters were stereotyped and marginalized and were background elements of the plot.

In fact, in silent and many early sound films, black actors did not appear at all. Black characters were played by white actors in blackface makeup. D. W. Griffith's *The Birth of a Nation* (1915) told an epic story of the Civil War and Reconstruction,

HOTEL RWANDA (LIONS GATE, 2004)

Don Cheadle plays Paul Rusesabagina, a hotel manager who sheltered Tutsi victims of a Hutu-led massacre in Rwanda. Cheadle has an extraordinary range and has played characters as diverse as stone killer Mouse Alexander (*Devil in a Blue Dress*), singer Sammy Davis, Jr. (*The Rat Pack*), and straight-laced District Attorney John Littleton (TV's *Picket Fences*). Frame enlargement.

and its many black characters had notably Caucasian features because of the white actors who impersonated them.

Griffith's film was brilliantly made, and it was extremely racist, offering the terror group the Ku Klux Klan as the film's hero, saving the South from the chaos of black rule. Griffith's filmmaking skill made the film's racist politics explosive. Its hateful view of race relations—basically saying that African-Americans should have remained slaves—triggered rioting and protests when it premiered.

In its long-term impact, *The Birth of a Nation* proved to have two kinds of influence. The first, a very negative influence, is that it established the basic gallery of black stereotypes that Hollywood film would perpetuate for the next 40 years. The stereotyped black characters in *Gone With the Wind* (1939), for example, owe much to Griffith's film.

The second influence, a very positive one, is that it led to the emergence of a black film industry. Black civic leaders and entrepreneurs realized that film was far too important a medium to be left in the hands of bigots like Griffith or other white filmmakers who would create demeaning or stereotyped portraits of black communities.

In the wake of *The Birth of a Nation*, a number of black production companies sprang forth, making black-themed films for African-American audiences. Since Hollywood had no interest in doing this, these companies operated outside the orbit of the major Hollywood studios, producing and distributing films on their own circuits for audiences in major urban centers.

The Lincoln Motion Picture Company (1916–1922), for example, offered audiences messages of racial integration and black middle-class life in such films as *The Realization of a Negro's Ambition* (1916). The Ebony Motion Picture Company of Chicago made black-themed adaptations of famous literary works such as *Black Sherlock Holmes* (1918).

But the most important and energetic black producer, director, and financier in this period of film history was Oscar Micheaux, who wrote, produced, and/or directed 24 films from 1919 to the early 1940s. This was an extraordinary accomplishment, given that he did not have the support and infrastructure of a major studio behind him. Micheaux's films aimed to counter the stereotypes of black people found in Hollywood film, and his work includes *Symbol of the Unconquered* (1921) and *Body and Soul* (1924).

The black film industry was an indigenous response to the problems of Hollywood studio films. Although the Ebony, Lincoln, and Micheaux films were made on relatively low budgets and lacked the technical resources that Hollywood made available to its filmmakers, they gave their audiences much-needed imagery and stories of African-American life. Hollywood film remained uninterested in providing this for many decades.

THE HOLLYWOOD ERA   During the studio era, from the 1930s to the 1950s, black actors did appear on screen but always in small, supporting roles and often in a demeaning manner. Stepin Fetchit played slow, dim-witted characters who were lazy and always looking to avoid work. The Mills brothers were incredibly talented dancers, but they had no chance of playing the lead role in a musical. Their career consisted of guest appearances in a genre dominated by white dancers such as Fred Astaire and Gene Kelly.

WITHIN OUR GATES (MICHEAUX BOOK & FILM CO., 1919)

Producer-director-writer-entrepreneur Oscar Micheaux was the most important and prolific black filmmaker to emerge in the wake of *The Birth of a Nation*. Micheaux wanted to counter the hateful images of Griffith's films but also to dramatize the realities of racial oppression in his time. Thus, in this picture, made just four years after *The Birth of a Nation*, he showed a subject that was absolutely taboo in Hollywood film—the rape of a black woman by a white man. Frame enlargement.

Hattie McDaniel, who played Mammy in *Gone With the Wind* (1939), felt very conflicted about playing this character, whose sole purpose in the story is to look after her white master, Scarlett (Vivien Leigh). McDaniel reconciled herself to the task by deciding that it was better to play a maid than to have to work as one.

Dooley Wilson was her male counterpart in *Casablanca* (1942), playing Sam, a pianist and sidekick of the film's hero, Rick (Humphrey Bogart). Sam spends the film in the background of the scenes, worrying about Rick and fussing over his welfare.

Although there were exceptions to these trends—King Vidor's *Hallelujah* (1929) featured an all-black cast, and Vincente Minnelli's *Cabin in the Sky* (1943) featured black singers Ethel Waters and Lena Horne in rare starring roles—for the most part Hollywood film centered on white characters living in a white world.

Sidney Poitier   The first major African-American Hollywood star did not appear until the 1950s, at a time when the studio system was breaking apart under the influence of television and the rise of independently produced and distributed films. These influences helped to change the character and content of American film.

Sidney Poitier came to the United States from Cat Island in the Bahamas. He made his film debut in *No Way Out* (1950) and quickly established a powerful screen persona. He played dignified characters who frequently worked professional occupations (doctor, detective) but whose tolerance and humanity were tested by racism and segregation. Facing these trials, Poitier would do a slow burn on screen but never lose his cool. His characters would prevail but in ways that demonstrated the ideals of racial tolerance and accommodation. His high-profile work in the period contains many screen classics—*The Defiant Ones* (1958), *Lilies of the Field* (1963), *A Raisin in the Sun* (1961), and *In the Heat of the Night* (1967).

While continuing as an actor, he went on to produce and direct films, a very rare accomplishment in that period, and some of these pictures became huge hits,

IN THE HEAT OF THE NIGHT (UNITED ARTISTS, 1967)
Sidney Poitier was the first African-American male star in Hollywood cinema. He typically played characters of grace and noble bearing who confronted discrimination in a racially prejudiced America. Here, he plays a detective from Philadelphia who reluctantly helps the chief of police in a backwater southern town solve a murder. Frame enlargement.

especially when they starred Bill Cosby or Richard Pryor (*Uptown Saturday Night*, 1974; *Stir Crazy*, 1980).

"BLAXPLOITATION"   As the civil rights struggle heated up in the late 1960s, Sidney Poitier's film characters came under attack by segments of the black community for being too polite and accommodating in the face of racism. An angrier, more aggressive set of black characters appeared in a genre of crime films aimed at African-American audiences. The genre began with the huge box-office success of two films in 1971 by black directors, *Sweet Sweetback's Baad Asssss Song* and *Shaft.*

Hollywood took notice, and the studios began producing scores of black-themed crime films that were hugely popular until the production cycle ended at mid-decade. Because their focus was on crime, drugs, and violence instead of the moral uplift of Poitier's films, national civil rights groups condemned the movies and began referring to them as **"blaxploitation."** At the time, the term was a negative one. Today, however, the term is used more affectionately because these movies were important. They offered the first triumphant black heroes and heroines in Hollywood cinema and gave charismatic actors—Ron O'Neal, Richard Roundtree, Jim Brown, Pam Grier, Fred Williamson, and Gloria Hendry—starring roles.

Melvin van Peebles' *Sweet Sweetback's Baad Asssss Song* (1971) kickstarted the era of "blaxploitation." This scruffy, low-budget independent picture about a black hustler, Sweetback (van Peebles), on the run after killing a pair of racist cops was enormously popular with urban audiences, who had seen plenty of movies about a black man chased by police but never one in which he got away. *Sweetback* was made expressly for the black community, and its success showed Hollywood that there was

Case Study NOTHING BUT A MAN

One of the most outstanding black films of this period was made by two white, Jewish filmmakers, whose Jewish sensitivity to segregation and racial bigotry led them to identify with the plight of African-Americans in mid-1960s America. *Nothing But a Man* (1964) was shot in six weeks for $160,000 during a period of heightened civil rights activity and racist backlash. During production, the Rev. Martin Luther King, Jr., delivered his "I Have a Dream" speech, NAACP field secretary Medgar Evers was murdered, and the 16th Street Church in Birmingham was bombed, killing four young girls.

Nothing But a Man portrays the efforts of Duff (Ivan Dixon), a black railroad worker in the South, to marry and start a family with Josie (played by jazz singer Abbey Lincoln in a luminous performance) while reconciling with his own embittered father (Julius Harris) and the son that Duff abandoned years ago. Ivan Dixon strongly identified with the character of Duff, and his scenes with Lincoln and Harris are extraordinarily powerful and well-acted.

The film was unique in its time for showing African-American actors in close-up, for showing a black couple courting and kissing, and for its quiet, naturalistic depiction of ordinary life. But the movie offers no easy answers. It powerfully shows the economic factors that preyed on black families, targeting men by making it difficult for them to find work and thereby eroding the family structure. As the film's director Michael Roemer put it, "You take away a man's ability to make a living, and you take away his manhood." This is the dilemma that Duff must struggle with.

Although the film was made by two white men, actors Ivan Dixon, Abbey Lincoln, and Julius Harris all felt that its portrait of southern black life in the sixties was true and very accurate. The film showed African-American characters in their communities and played by black actors in leading roles at a time when this was extremely rare to see on American screens. Sidney Poitier's films, for example, tended to feature a mostly white cast of characters. *Nothing But a Man* showed that independent film could get closer to the truth in this period than the well-intentioned studio films that Hollywood was producing. No less an authority than Malcolm X loved this film.

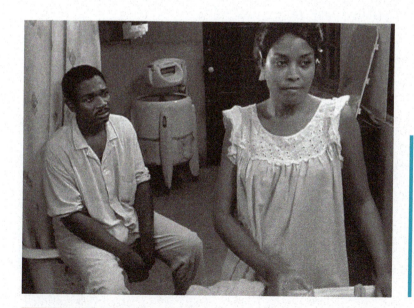

NOTHING BUT A MAN (Cinema V, 1964)

A film unique in its time for depicting ordinary African-American life in the South, and made in cooperation with the NAACP, it portrays a black man coming to terms with fatherhood, with his own father, and with the meaning of manhood in an economically unjust society. Frame enlargement.

an untapped market here, hungry for a new and different kind of film. (Van Peebles' son, Mario, made *Baadassss* [2004], a tribute to his father and the film, with son Mario playing his dad attempting to get the legendary film made.)

That same year, Gordon Parks' *Shaft* (1971) offered a new and popular hero, private investigator John Shaft (Richard Roundtree), who, unlike the more wary and cautious characters played by Poitier, was comfortable, confident, and in control of his dangerous urban environment. During the opening credits (set to Isaac Hayes' sensational music), Shaft gives the finger to a motorist who almost runs him down, and this was one of the first times audiences had seen an angry black man on screen. *Shaft* was so popular that Roundtree returned in two sequels, *Shaft's Big Score* (1972) and *Shaft in Africa* (1973). He also had a cameo in the 2000 remake by John Singleton.

Another hero of "blaxploitation" was *Superfly* (1972), a heroin dealer, played by Ron O'Neal, who is looking to get out of the drug business and has to pull off a scam against a group of crooked white cops to do so. A huge outpouring of films followed—*Slaughter* (1972), *Hell Up in Harlem* (1973), *Black Caesar* (1973), *Coffy* (1973), *Cleopatra Jones* (1973), *Foxy Brown* (1974), and numerous other flashy gangster, cop, and action pictures. In *Foxy Brown* and other films, Pam Grier emerged as one of the stars of the movement, and Quentin Tarantino paid tribute to the "blaxploitation" era by casting Grier as the lead in *Jackie Brown* (1997).

By the mid-1970s, the "blaxploitation" era was ending. Although many of these films were financed by Hollywood studios and were made by white directors, the films were supported by African-American audiences. Although they were controversial in their day for offering what some said were negative and stereotyped portraits, today there is a great deal of affection and nostalgia for these pictures. They were funky, flashy, in-your-face entertainments and were unapologetic about it—a rare combination of qualities in any era.

Moreover, until the generation of African-American filmmakers who emerged in the 1990s, "blaxploitation" represented the only flourishing of black-themed films since the era of Oscar Micheaux. They were aimed exclusively at black

BAADASSSSS (SONY PICTURES CLASSICS, 2004)

Writer–director Mario van Peebles plays his father, Melvin, making his epochal film, *Sweet Sweetback's Baad Asssss Song* (1971). Mario intended this as a tribute to his father and to the picture that started the era of "blaxploitation." Frame enlargement.

SHAFT (MGM, 1971)

Black detective John Shaft (Richard Roundtree) was a new kind of movie hero—tough, street wise, defiant of "the man," and most important, African-American. Hollywood had a long tradition of tough-guy heroes, but they had always been white. Roundtree made Shaft into a charismatic figure for the times, and he returned in two sequels and a remake in 2000. Frame enlargement.

audiences because Hollywood did not believe that black-themed films or films with African-American actors in the lead roles would draw white viewers.

All that has changed today. African-American films are now among the industry's most successful mainstream pictures. *Are We There Yet?* (2005), starring Ice Cube and Nia Long, grossed $83 million in the United States and Canada, and studio market research found the audience to be 43 percent white, 26 percent black, and 18 percent Hispanic. *Barbershop* (2002), a comedy about black neighborhood life, also with Ice Cube, grossed $76 million and drew an audience that was 60 percent black and 40 percent white. *Hitch* (2005), a romantic comedy starring Will Smith, grossed $177 million domestically. Nothing succeeds in Hollywood like success. The mainstreaming of African-American film has replaced the segregated market in which "blaxploitation" was introduced and should be considered one of contemporary film's great success stories.

Narrative and Ideology

A final component of ideological film criticism should be noted. This is the close relationship that exists between narrative and ideology. Ideological film critics regard narrative as an especially good vehicle for ideology. A film's narrative shows a series of changes in a situation or a state of affairs and concludes by explaining how some condition has come about. By so doing, it can embody an ideological *argument*.

Fatal Attraction (1987), for example, tells a story about a happily married lawyer whose casual adultery produces a nightmare for his family when the woman he is seeing turns out to be a violent psychopath. In telling a story that moves from the allure of casual sex and the excitement of adultery to terror and anxiety and concluding with the death of the female villain and reunification of the family, *Fatal Attraction* constructs an argument about the importance of family and fidelity and about the violation of trust and love that can result from casual adultery.

Note, though, that this is an ideological argument and that all these categories—family, love, fidelity, adultery—are ones that the film constructs in the course of developing its argument. As such, one can quarrel with some of the definitions. Was it really necessary, for example, to turn the lawyer's lover into such a monster? In the real world, adultery does not inevitably have such horrific and monstrous consequences. It is essential for the film's ideological argument, though, that these consequences ensue. They enable the film to invoke the importance of family and to conclude its ideological argument with a vision of family triumphant.

Summary

Because many films are ideological in an implicit and second-order way, such criticism usefully uncovers otherwise unnoticed aspects of social meaning. Good ideological criticism prevents viewers from becoming too complacent, too naive about the way film can display and distort important social and political realities. Ideological criticism keeps viewers vigilant against the egregious screen distortions of important social issues.

FATAL ATTRACTION (PARAMOUNT PICTURES, 1987)

Fatal Attraction builds its ideological argument about the sanctity of marriage and family through a narrative about a psychopath, Alex (Glenn Close), terrorizing her former lover, Dan Gallagher (Michael Douglas), and his family. In this scene, a knife-wielding Alex invades the Gallagher home and attacks Dan's wife, Beth (Ann Archer). The film's ideology is conveyed by its narrative. Frame enlargement.

Oliver Stone

With much thunder and rage, Oliver Stone revitalized a left-wing and overtly ideological vision in mainstream U.S. cinema, although to call his political vision left-wing is to give it perhaps more unity than it actually possessed. After serving in the infantry in Vietnam and subsequently studying filmmaking at New York University, Stone scripted several violent, pulp films (*Midnight Express*, 1978; *Conan the Barbarian*, 1982; *Scarface*, 1983; *Year of the Dragon*, 1985) and directed a routine horror film (*The Hand*, 1981).

In his second film as director, the remarkable *Salvador* (1986), he began to define his niche as a powerful, sometimes strident critic of U.S. society and foreign policy. Completed during the Reagan era of the early- and mid-1980s as a criticism of the administration's support for a brutal military regime in El Salvador, Stone's film is an act of political courage and commitment. Like most of his work, however, it is not without ambiguity and ambivalence. It skillfully dissects the duplicity of U.S. policy in El Salvador and the violence of the regime the United States supported but backs away from acknowledging the peasant revolutionaries as a viable alternative. As a result, Stone cannot find any solution to the horrors he portrays, and his political engagement turns into despair.

Stone's next film, *Platoon* (1988), put him in the big leagues as a filmmaker. As an antidote to the comic book fantasies embodied by Sylvester Stallone's Rambo character, Stone's film was hailed by veterans and critics as the most realistic portrait of the Vietnam War yet made. *Platoon* does have a surface realism, yet it also employs explicit religious symbolism and generic narrative formulas. Its political view of the war is murky, but it portrays with great intensity the suffering and loss of U.S. soldiers.

Stone next applied his *Platoon* narrative formula—a young man torn between good and bad father figures—to U.S. capitalism in *Wall Street* (1987) and then made one of his least popular but best films, *Talk Radio* (1988), which powerfully portrays the free-floating popular rage and anxiety that threatens U.S. society and democracy.

A grandiose style and an increasingly strident tone mar some of his subsequent films. *Born on the Fourth of July* (1989) contains an extraordinary Tom Cruise performance as Vietnam vet Ron Kovic, but Stone's audiovisual style is unrelentingly bombastic. The viewer is pummeled by its grandiloquence and by a one-dimensional view of how young Kovic was brainwashed by macho, jingoistic U.S. culture, personified by John F. Kennedy in the period the film portrays.

Stone apparently revised his view of Kennedy for *JFK* (1991), which portrays a dovish president eager to withdraw from Vietnam and killed by Washington

PLATOON (ORION PICTURES, 1986)

Platoon was one of the most influential films of its decade. Avoiding Rambo-style heroics, it shows the war as a horrifically destructive event. The film mixes realism with religious symbolism, as in the Christian imagery employed in this shot showing an American soldier's death. Stone returned to the war in several subsequent films, but *Platoon* remains his best work on that subject. Frame enlargement.

(continued)

powers intent on prosecuting the war. While the film is structurally brilliant in its complex montage editing and clear summary of a mountain of assassination data, Stone weakens his case by building his argument on a speculative and unproven thesis that Kennedy was going to withdraw from Vietnam. As a result, the film occupies a muddy middle ground, neither a clear fiction nor a responsible historical document.

Attacked by many media commentators for the conspiracy theories of *JFK*, Stone lashed back with *Natural Born Killers* (1994), an ugly account of two mass murderers whose crime spree is glamorized by the news media and who are portrayed as celebrities by reporters eager to promote the latest scrap of tabloid sensationalism. The film is a mishmash of disjointed MTV-style technique—flash cuts, off-kilter camera angles, jerky handheld camerawork, random pans, and other visual manipulations that exist for their own sake. The film glorifies and embodies what it pretends to attack: the violence and ugliness in modern U.S. society and its promotion via film and television.

Nixon (1995) is a surprisingly compassionate portrait of Richard Nixon's life and presidency, with a masterful performance by Anthony Hopkins in the role. *U Turn* (1997) is an unpleasantly violent film noir that returned to the disjointed and off-kilter style of *Natural Born Killers*.

Stone's films had been vociferous, cinematically powerful attacks on the power structure in U.S. society. In carrying out this project, he was virtually unique among contemporary U.S. directors, who generally prefer box office returns to social messages. But Stone grew weary of the controversy his films were provoking and felt that he had taken a terrific beating over remarks that he made following 9/11 that suggested the attacks were the result of U.S. policies overseas. He lowered his public profile, and as a result, his recent filmmaking has lost the sharp edge it once possessed. *World Trade Center* (2006) is an inspirational tale of lives rescued on 9/11, a film that takes no political perspective on the day's events. *W* (2008) is a compassionate portrait of the young George W. Bush, and *Wall Street: Money Never Sleeps* (2010) is a sequel to *Wall Street* that lacks the earlier film's anger about high financial crimes.

Whether Stone will return to the aggressively ideological quality of his earlier work remains to be seen. ■

A weakness of ideological criticism occurs when a critic too quickly collapses different levels of meaning, moving too rapidly from the specificity of the film, the particulars of the characters and their situations, to the extraction of a more abstract and generalized ideological message. *Back to the Future* (1985) may be a key film of the 1980s, connected with the era's zeitgeist, but it should not be reduced to that. It is also a clever, multileveled comedy that speaks to its viewers in a variety of ways.

When an ideological critic or theorist pays scant attention to the particular and concrete details of a film's characters and story situations, in favor of a more abstract social message, it weakens the force and logic of the analysis. It may be that the ideological argument of *Fatal Attraction* is that sex is bad if it takes place outside of marriage, but the enormously complex concrete details of the film, and the intricacies of its narrative, should not be reduced to such an abstract and blanket statement. Sophisticated ideological analysis maintains a clear separation between these levels.

FEMINIST MODELS

Critics use **feminist film theory** to analyze representations of gender on screen and the forms of pleasure associated with them, as depicted for characters in a film and also for spectators, whose gender identities are constructions of biology as well as of society and its values. Feminist models seek to open up traditional definitions of gender as portrayed in film and to make these problematic by revealing hidden assumptions and repressed meanings. Feminist models of criticism often blend elements of psychoanalytic and ideological analysis. The psychoanalytic component is found in attempts to understand the ways that cinema arouses pleasure and desire in audiences and how this might differ on a gender basis. The ideological component is found in the efforts of feminist criticism to relate the depiction of gender in film to prevailing social attitudes, assumptions, and practices found in the general society of which film is part.

Elements of Feminist Models

IMAGES OF GENDER IN FILM   Feminist film criticism tends to assume two forms. The first is an analysis and description of the ways that films portray gender. Feminist critics may examine the way that visual spectacle and the use of the close-up function in film to present women as visual and erotic objects for the contemplation of a male audience. For feminist critics, the extraordinary visual attention given to the bodies of stars such as Marilyn Monroe or Marlene Dietrich turns these performers into erotic objects for a male audience.

Feminist analyses focus on narrative strategies as well as specifically visual ones. A feminist analysis of *Fatal Attraction* might concentrate on the fate of the film's nominal villain, Alex (portrayed by Glenn Close). A feminist critic could emphasize the way that the film ideologically constructs the character of Alex as a monster whose outrageous behavior toward the hero's family requires that she undergo an extraordinary amount of suffering and physical punishment to atone for her crimes.

Because the film presents Alex as such a monster, the feminist critic might reasonably suggest that *Fatal Attraction* regards female sexuality that is unconstrained by the institutions of marriage and family with a great deal of fear, suspicion, and loathing. Alex is an independent, single, aggressive, and very sexual woman. In the film, she is ideologically suspect because of these very qualities, and the gender confusion represented by her masculine name points toward this villainy. By creating and then destroying this monster, the film offers a very traditional message about the ideal role of women as wives and mothers rather than as single professionals.

Feminist theory also focuses on prevailing gender roles assigned to men in commercial cinema. These investigations have included the phenomenon of the "hard-bodied" male action hero (Sylvester Stallone, Arnold Schwarzenegger, Jean-Claude Van Damme), a figure of great violence, exaggerated physical prowess, few words, and little introspection. Feminist theory asks about the ideal of "maleness" that such a figure embodies and its implications for ordinary men and women.

In recent films, women have assumed this character type. In *Lara Croft: Tomb Raider* (2001), Angelina Jolie plays the kind of muscle-bound action hero, blazing away with automatic weapons, that male action stars have long played. At the same time, a regressive, and perhaps even sexist, view of women comes through. Lara Croft can kick butt, but the camerawork and costuming play up her Barbie-doll figure, with outlandishly large breasts. Is this progress, a feminist critic might ask?

DISRUPTIVE READINGS Feminist analyses often practice a strategy of disruption, aiming to offer formulations that counter prevailing stereotypes and assumptions about gender and sexual identity or to focus on films that disrupt existing assumptions about what is "natural" and appropriate. Countering or disrupting dominant myths is a way of shedding new light onto old problems.

In the 1920s, for example, Rudolph Valentino was a huge star of romantic melodramas in which he played exotic characters—a matador, an Arab warrior, numerous European aristocrats—whose allure for the films' heroines was irresistible. The movies were extended rituals of seduction, in which Valentino's sexual aura overcame the heroine's resistance and the Victorian morality which insisted that she must resist.

Valentino and his movies held great appeal for female viewers. He was a surrogate lover for millions of women in the moviegoing audience, and the nature of his appeal, therefore, offers inviting questions for theory to investigate. Accordingly, feminist critics have examined the special qualities of his films, which were unusual for presenting Valentino as an erotic object for the camera's gaze, precisely the terms by which women are more typically presented in films for male viewers. Valentino's films—*The Sheik* (1921), *Blood and Sand* (1922), *A Sainted Devil* (1924), *Son of the Shiek* (1926), and others—concentrated on his qualities as an erotic object, chiefly his physical beauty but also his androgynous mixture of masculine and feminine traits.

The pleasures offered by these movies to Valentino's female fans (and gay male following as well) exceeded the boundaries of what society officially permitted for women in the period. Women were expected to be wives and mothers, and, for the sake of domestic morality, to subordinate their desires to these domains and responsibilities. Scholar Miriam Hanson points out that the Valentino films, by contrast, offered audiences the vision and the possibility of female desire outside

LARA CROFT, TOMB RAIDER (PARAMOUNT, 2001)

Muscle-bound action heroes are now played by women, not just men. Lara Croft is comfortable with a variety of weapons and never met a man she couldn't outpunch and outshoot. And yet the film gives great emphasis to her exaggerated Barbie-doll figure. Is this progress or merely the same old formula of a woman's body put on display in cinema? Frame enlargement.

BEYOND THE ROCKS (FAMOUS PLAYERS-LASKY, 1922)
Gloria Swanson plays a woman unhappily married to an older man. On vacation, she meets a dashing nobleman played by Rudolph Valentino, with whom she falls in love. She swoons when Valentino kisses her hand. A major star in the period, Valentino's films showcased him as an object of erotic beauty and desire for female and gay male viewers. Frame enlargement.

of motherhood and family. From this viewpoint, Valentino's movies appealed to impulses in the popular audience that the society of the time was suppressing and denying expression. The films offered "an ideal of erotic reciprocity," a beautiful male lover who desired the woman as much she desired him, an erotic attraction that had nothing to do with social duties and responsibilities and, instead, offered a glorious liberation from them. Offering these transgressive pleasures to Valentino's fans, the movies explicitly sexualized an ideal of male beauty, represented in Valentino, presenting him as an object of erotic adoration.

Disruptive readings—interpretations that aim to deconstruct prevailing social myths and assumptions—have focused productively upon the work of director Douglas Sirk, a Hollywood director who, in the 1950s, made numerous romantic melodramas that used lighting, color, set design and the staging of emotional conflicts among the characters to probe the dark areas of American society—intolerance, prejudice, sexual repression.

The concept of "excess" is often applied by scholars and critics to Sirk's work, designating moments where emotional displays, color saturation, music scoring, or other elements of style become overwrought or intensively expressive in ways that seem unmotivated by the storyline. Such excessive moments are taken as signs of displacement, marking the presence of feelings and desires that polite society does not accept.

ALL THAT HEAVEN ALLOWS (UNIVERSAL, 1955)

Douglas Sirk found melodrama to be an excellent vehicle for exploring social repressions and taboos. Cary Scott (Jane Wyman) is an aging widow with grown children who falls in love with a much younger man (Rock Hudson) and incurs the wrath of her children, her friends, and her social community for selecting a lover everyone feels is too young for her. Sexual desire in a woman of her age is socially unacceptable. Pressured by her children to cut off the affair, she agrees and gazes sadly at the wintry landscape outside her window. Sirk films the scene so that the window panes become the bars of Cary's prison. Frame enlargement.

FEMINIST FILMMAKING   A second focus of feminist criticism is closely related to the first. It is the exploration of alternative, feminist forms of filmmaking and images of characters. In this respect, feminist filmmaking has sometimes been described as creating a counter-cinema, though in practice it needn't result in that.

One of the great—and most audacious—works of modern cinema is Chantal Akerman's *Jeanne Dielman, 23, quai du Commerce, 1080 Bruxelles* (1975). As its title, which is the main character's name and address, suggests, this is a film focused on the mundane, banal, and trivial details of daily life, but its brilliance lies in Akerman's ability to invest these with great mystery and a compelling sense of the strange.

Akerman was influenced by experimental filmmakers, such as Andy Warhol and Michael Snow who expanded the viewer's sense of duration, of time's slow crawl, by filming nonmoving subjects or by doing slow camera moves or zooms through empty rooms. Akerman, too, emphasizes the fullness of time and the emptiness of space. She refuses the standard grammar of narrative cinema, composing the film instead in a series of long takes that are precisely framed according to a principle of frontality, so that the camera, most often, is at a 90-degree angle to the back wall of a room or set and regards the characters in a frontal fashion.

In place of the condensed time that operates in most movies, whose plots omit banal and uninteresting details in order to concentrate on dramatic highlights, Akerman insists upon duration, upon the experience of time passing slowly. The film is very long—201 minutes—and very little happens. Over a three-day span of narrative, the camera watches Jeanne Dielman, a widow living with her son and who also works as a

JEANNE DIELMAN, 23 QUAI DU COMMERCE, 1080 BRUXELLES (OLYMPIC FILMS, 1975)

Jeanne (Delphine Seyrig) performs her daily chores, framed by Chantal Akerman's static camera in long takes and frontal compositions. In silence and quiet spaces, Jeanne slowly comes apart. Her obsessive-compulsive behaviors grow erratic, and she remains unable to express the loneliness and despair that overtake her. Akerman's landmark film is an audacious work of radical cinema that disrupts the medium's conventional forms in order to move toward a non-narrative experience of time, its flow, and its duration. Frame enlargement.

prostitute, as she performs her daily routines—peeling potatoes for dinner, making coffee, cleaning the bathroom, going into town to shop for food, receiving male clients.

Jeanne spends most of her days alone, and the filming style gradually becomes alienating, capturing an essential loneliness that engulfs Jeanne and that is perhaps partly responsible for the psychological breakdown that the film's second half shows. Jeanne's ordered, obsessive-compulsive routines start to come apart—she forgets to turn off a light when leaving a room; she overcooks dinner; she wanders from room to room carrying a pot of food, uncertain where to place it. The film ends with an abrupt and unexplained act of violence.

Jeanne exemplifies two of the archetypal categories to which women have been assigned by men: mother and whore. By meticulously filming Jeanne's daily rituals and the emotionless way in which she conducts them, Akerman's poetic, haunting and disturbing film subverts the categories, making them as problematic as the surfaces of Jeanne's domestic life come to seem, arenas and spaces laden with anxiety and an alienation that Jeanne cannot articulate.

Agnes Varda's *Cleo from 5 to 7* (1962) is a classic of French New Wave cinema, and Molly Haskell has called Varda "the premiere female director of her generation." The film studies the emotional turmoil in a pop singer, Cleo (Corinne Marchand), as she spends ninety minutes awaiting the results of a medical test that she fears will bring a cancer death-sentence. Cleo takes an inner journey during the length of this nearly real-time film (the film's running time corresponds very

CLEO FROM 5 TO 7 (CINE TAMARIS, 1962)

Mirrors and reflective surfaces point toward Cleo's false consciousness, happy to bask in the adoring gazes of others and preoccupied with her own beauty. The slivered images suggest a fracturing of self, a lack of personal integration. Cleo grows as she learns to be the author of her own gaze, to look out at the world-and to take an interest in other people. Frame enlargement.

closely to the time depicted in the story), moving from a self-centered and shallow outlook, wherein Cleo cannot listen or relate to others, to becoming a more open, curious, and empathetic person. This change correlates with a shift in Cleo from drawing pleasure in being seen by others to finding pleasure in seeing the world around her.

Varda shows this change in cinematic terms. As the film begins, Cleo is content to be looked at by men and by fans for her beauty. Cleo believes that being alive means being beautiful. Varda emphasizes mirrors, glass windows and other reflecting surfaces, and composes shots that show Cleo's reflections, creating prismatic, split-image views of the character that comment on her narcissism, selfishness, and lack of emotional integration.

As Cleo becomes more responsive to the people and world around her, she becomes the author of her own gaze, and the self-reflective, split-image compositions change to ones that show Paris and its people from Cleo's point of view as she regards them with a new level of unselfish curiosity. At film's end, the shadow of illness still pursues Cleo, but she greets the future with a new sense of hope.

Shot on location in Paris, full of charm and energy, *Cleo from 5 to 7* is a cinematically brilliant depiction of a woman's spiritual journey, realized in a clear, eloquent visual design that correlates the connections between self and others with acts of seeing and, for Varda, of filming.

Varda's background lies in art history and photography, and she has been keenly interested in images, as they bear traces of self and world, as they serve as props for memory, and as they show time's cruel effects on people and places. Her work has alternated between narrative films and documentaries. The latter include *Daguerreotypes* (1976), portraits of the people and shops on the rue Daguerre, the Paris neighborhood where she has lived for decades. The title references the neighborhood as well as the early form of photography—daguerreotypes—that involved imprinting an image in-camera on the silver surface of a copper or brass plate.

Her narrative films include two additional classics. *One Sings, the Other Doesn't* (1977), about the friendship between two women amid the militant women's movement of the 1970s, focused particularly upon the struggle over abortion. This widely-known film was a landmark of feminist cinema, in France and abroad, although its straightforward nature makes it a lesser work than *Cleo* or *Vagabond* (1985), which has been called Varda's masterpiece.

Vagabond portrays the reactions of farmers, shopkeepers, itinerant laborers, and bourgeoisie who briefly come in contact with Mona (Sandrine Bonnaire), a vagabond wandering the bleak landscapes of southern France in winter. When the film begins, Mona's lifeless, frozen body is found in a ditch, and Varda offers the film as an inquiry into who Mona was and what she represented to those who briefly knew her.

Mona is a paradox to those whom she comes in contact with. She smells, she's filthy, she lives outside of society and is uninterested in friendship, work, sex, any sort of relationship, all the sources of personal identity that an individual typically uses to create a sense of self. She's smart, lively, with a sense of humor, an ability to enjoy life, and she refuses all efforts to help her. She thus eludes the social categories that people try to put on her or use to explain her behavior. Mona is a riddle, and the film gains its power from Varda's refusal to explain this character.

The movie shows how she is worn down from exposure to rain and cold, from hunger, and from aimlessness to a point where she stumbles into a ditch and, lacking the strength to climb out, freezes to death. *Vagabond* is attentive to the labels and perceptions that people attach to women—all of the witnesses interviewed in the

VAGABOND (CINE TAMARIS, 1985)

Agnes Varda's masterpiece portrays an enigmatic character, Mona (Sandrine Bonnaire), a drifter whose refusal to conform to social expectations challenges the belief systems of all who encounter her. Mona's aimless existence leads to her death, but Varda offers no easy answers or conclusions. The film is precisely conceived and designed. All of its tracking shots, for example, following Mona as she wanders a wintry landscape, move from right to left, opposite the direction in which Western cultures read printed text. The camera movements materialize Mona's rejection of society. Frame enlargement.

film have hypotheses about Mona that explain her peculiar behavior—but the movie gathers considerable and haunting power from its refusal to validate any and from its acceptance that Mona is fundamentally unknowable. Varda's film looks onto the ambiguities of human personality and behavior, and while it explores gender in social terms, its poetic force resides in its acceptance of mystery and in the sobering notion that people can remain unknowable.

The Piano, written and directed by Jane Campion, stars Holly Hunter (Best Actress Oscar winner for the role) as a mute Victorian unwed mother who travels to New Zealand to fulfill an arranged marriage to an English farmer living there. Ada arrives in New Zealand accompanied by her child and her piano. The film explores her torturous reception as both a woman and an artist. She confronts a culture that is alien to her and places her into the most restrictive of sex roles, expecting her to be a dutiful wife to a well-meaning but insensitive and ultimately brutal husband (played by Sam Neill).

The most telling measure of his insensitivity is his refusal to transport her piano from the beach to their plantation home. Unable to speak or unwilling to do so for reasons that in the film remain mysterious, Ada's only form of communication with the world is her music. Denied this by her husband, who abandons the piano and who later mutilates one of her hands, Ada becomes progressively more alienated from her surroundings, sexually, emotionally, aesthetically. A feminist critic might point to the improbability of a male screenwriter or director demonstrating this degree of sensitivity to a woman's psychological and physical plight and such a complex metaphorical understanding of the close relationship between the social oppression of women and control over the rights to speech, art, and communication.

Whereas Varda and Akerman have used cinema in highly personal ways that rework its narrative modes and stylistic traditions, Kathryn Bigelow works within

THE PIANO (MIRAMAX, 1993)

In *The Piano*, Holly Hunter portrays Ada, an unmarried mother coping with life in a rustic, remote New Zealand community. Written and directed by Jane Campion, the film emphasizes Ada's viewpoint and treats the narrative's male characters as supporting, rather than lead, players. Frame enlargement.

traditional forms, specifically the action genres traditionally associated with male directors. Her films include *Blue Steel* (1990), an urban police thriller, *Point Break* (1991), about a string of perfect bank robberies and the FBI agent sent to investigate, *Strange Days* (1995), a futurist thriller about virtual reality, *K-19: The Widowmaker* (2002), a thriller about sailors trapped aboard a crippled Soviet nuclear submarine, and *The Hurt Locker* (2009), about a bomb disposal expert in the Iraq War. Because these are

FILMMAKER SPOTLIGHT

Dorothy Arzner

In the Hollywood studio era, film directing was regarded as man's work, and few women established careers as directors. Dorothy Arzner, however, directed eleven films at Paramount Pictures, one of the major studios, from 1927–1932. After that, she left Paramount and worked as an independent director-for-hire in Hollywood, making another six films before she ceased directing features. In the 1960s and 1970s, she became a professor, teaching directing and screenwriting at UCLA.

Arzner began working in the industry as a writer and an editor. She edited the popular Rudolph Valentino movie about bullfighting, *Blood and Sand* (1922), and James Cruze's epic Western, *The Covered Wagon* (1923). Now an editor of note in Hollywood, she convinced Paramount to give her a vehicle to direct. The box-office success of *Fashions for Women* (1927) launched her directing career, and she made three more silent films before Paramount entered the sound era and put Arzner in charge of its first talkie, *The Wild Party* (1929), featuring Clara Bow, a major star in the period.

In the early sound era, Arzner flourished as a distinct artist in Hollywood. When the Production Code Administration began operating in 1934, American film grew more conservative and restrictive in its depictions of morality, sexuality, crime and religion, and the years of sound filmmaking from 1930–1934 showcase movies that are much freer and more explicit in their depictions of these topics.

Arzner's feminist sensibilities synchronized with this open and tolerant period in American cinema to produce remarkable films, such as *Working Girls* (1931), a portrait of two sisters struggling with issues of identity and self-determination during

the Great Depression. As she did in many of her films, Arzner explores the ways that society defines women in terms of marriage and motherhood and, in so doing, undermines a woman's ability to chart a course of independence and self-determination as men are allowed to do.

Arzner's movies are keenly focused on women's issues, and *Christopher Strong* (1933) depicts a world-famous aviatrix, Lady Cynthia Darrington (Katharine Hepburn), who is so devoted to flying that she has no time for men or for sex. She rises early to train and stay in peak physical shape for difficult flights, such as a round-the-world race that she wins. Darrington's life, however, becomes messy and complicated when she falls in love with a married man, Christopher Strong, and he asks her to give up flying. She refuses to do so, and, upon learning that she is pregnant, returns to the air, sets an altitude record, and then removes her oxygen mask, losing consciousness as she crashes to her death.

The film does not moralize about its topics of adultery and out-of-wedlock pregnancies, and, in fact, suggests that many marriages are stale and unhappy and that this is why adultery is so common. In these respects, it shows how the openness of "pre-Code" Hollywood enabled Arzner to produce startlingly original work.

But more importantly, watching *Christopher Strong* is like glimpsing an alternative path that Hollywood film might have gone down, had there been more women working as directors to make movies, as Arzner did, about strong women seeking independent and self-fulfilling lives. Hepburn's Lady Darrington is a dazzling character of a sort not to be

(continued)

CHRISTOPHER STRONG (RKO, 1933)
Katharine Hepburn is a tough, self-reliant, independent aviatrix who has no time for romance, until she falls for a married man. Dorothy Arzner's remarkable film illuminates a pathway that American cinema might have taken in the Hollywood era but didn't. Frame enlargement.

glimpsed again in American film for many decades. Instead, women depicted in movies directed by men in this period too often are either unconvincing as female characters or are defined primarily by their relations to men, principally those of wife and mother.

Arzner's films, however, such as *Christopher Strong* or *Craig's Wife* (1936) often turn the conventional focus of Hollywood films inside-out because they do not reaffirm the clichés that were so standard in the period, such as the idea that a woman should find happiness not through holding a career but by making a home for a man. *Craig's Wife* is a particularly scathing treatment of this idea.

Feminist film scholars have found Arzner's films to be fascinating instances of a kind of counter-cinema to the Hollywood model, and the movies do offer striking material to this effect. *Dance, Girl, Dance* (1940), for example, has a startling scene where

Judy (Maureen O'Hara), an aspiring ballerina who is working temporarily in a burlesque show, steps out of character on stage to lecture the men in the audience about how pathetic they are in their desire to watch her undress. It's an instance of the male gaze being turned back upon itself.

Arzner, however, considered herself to be a Hollywood professional, not a radical, which is to say that her films are remarkable in many ways but don't reduce to thesis-filmmaking or sloganeering. Like the best Hollywood filmmakers, her movies are tight and crisp. The dialogue is snappy, and the camera is always in the right place to frame the action and to comment on it. These are attributes of strong filmmaking. Arzner was an important Hollywood auteur, and her work is still relatively neglected today. Most of her films, for example, remain unavailable on DVD. ■

genre pictures, a feminist critic might be interested to uncover minor variations that a director such as Bigelow might create within these standard and traditional formats. Bigelow is an articulate filmmaker and a proponent of the view that women directors must not be ghettoized as makers of soft, sensitive films. Her work is indistinguishable, stylistically, from male-directed action pictures, and they demonstrate that women can excel as filmmakers in precisely the kinds of material long claimed by men.

Women in Film

Under the old Hollywood studio system, few women worked as directors, but many had very successful careers as performers in front of the camera. Many also worked behind the camera as editors or costume designers. One might think that all this has changed in today's film world, but in fact, the changes have not been so extensive. And in one respect—working in front of the camera as an actor—things today are not as good as they were 50 years ago. This history provides one of the contexts that feminist film theory seeks to address and make an intervention into. A brief examination of how women have fared in the Hollywood industry can help to illustrate why issues of feminist filmmaking and of the images of women on film have been important ones for theory to explore.

Actors

Women working as actors tend to have relatively short careers today. Because the prime audience for movies is composed of teenagers and young adults, studios court this segment of viewers very aggressively, and actors who fit this age range or who can play it on screen tend to get the most work most easily.

Reese Witherspoon has exemplified the young-adult category where women actors today tend to find the most roles. In pictures such as *Vanity Fair* (2004), *Legally Blonde 2* (2003), *Sweet Home Alabama* (2003), and others, she brings zest, charm, and great good humor to her roles. Her characters set out on the road of life with spirit and self-confidence.

Will she sustain her career over the next decade or longer as she ages beyond the young-adult demographic that she currently plays? She clearly has the range of talent to do so. The question is whether the industry will accommodate the change.

Unfortunately, many women today who age beyond this demographic find that the character roles available to them grow fewer and fewer. The industry makes few films built around mature adult female characters, so the roles start to dry up for actors once they move out of the young-adult age range.

Charlotte Rampling kept her career alive as she aged into her fifties and sixties by doing most of her later work in European film. In the 1980s, she appeared prominently in Woody Allen's *Stardust Memories* (1980) and Sidney Lumet's *The Verdict* (1982), but thereafter she worked mostly in France. She worked steadily, with major roles, including the leads in *Under the Sand* (2000) and *Swimming Pool* (2003), where she played the kind of mature woman who is rarely seen as the major character in Hollywood film.

Another problem is sustaining a career following a breakthrough role. Many fine actors who enjoyed success in high-profile or well-received films experience difficulties getting the next role. Mary Elizabeth Mastrantonio (*The Color of Money*, 1986; *The Abyss*, 1989), Elizabeth Shue (*Leaving Las Vegas*, 1995), and Linda Fiorentino (*The Last Seduction*, 1994; *Men in Black*, 1997) all gave very strong performances in successful films but have not thereafter enjoyed a sustained series of leading roles.

Virginia Madsen (*Candyman*, 1992) would have been a big star in the old Hollywood studio era. She projects a mature, smoldering sensuality and power that would have brought her great success in the 1940s, but today there are very few pictures for this kind of persona. After appearing in a long string of horror pictures, she got rave reviews for her performance in *Sideways* (2004) but did little film work the following year.

Stars today that are sustaining careers through a series of adult roles with an impressive level of accomplishment include Julia Roberts, who carries the high-power wattage and maturity of the great female stars of old Hollywood. She's played an impressive range of roles, and she's one of the few adult actresses whom the industry allows to carry a film in the lead role (*Erin Brockovich*, 2000). One reason that Steven Soderbergh cast her in *Ocean's Eleven* (2001) is because her character does not make an appearance until midway through the film. He wanted an actor with the charisma to make an instant and strong impression on viewers, and Roberts gave him that.

Nicole Kidman also has sustained an impressive career, making consistently good choices about projects and seeking out challenges by working with great directors or great material (*Eyes Wide Shut*, 1999; *The Hours*, 2002; *Dogville*, 2003; and *Cold Mountain*, 2003). These have included the master Stanley Kubrick, the Danish filmmaker Lars von Trier, and characters as differentiated as the civil war widow in *Cold Mountain*, the writer Virginia Woolf in *The Hours*, and Samantha the witch in *Bewitched* (2005). She's also one of the rare film actors today who is extremely skilled at delivering long monologues (in, for example, *Eyes Wide Shut* and *Birth* [2004]).

RABBIT HOLE (OLYMPUS PICTURES, 2010)

Nicole Kidman maintains a careful and shrewd balance in her work between entertainment films (*Moulin Rouge, Australia*) and challenging, character-centered dramas with limited box-office appeal. In *Rabbit Hole*, she plays a woman distraught with grief over the death of her child and whose inability to recover from this loss threatens her marriage. Frame enlargement.

Compared with today, old Hollywood had many such front-rank stars who sustained long careers. Bette Davis made more than 100 films from 1931 to 1989, with roles ranging from Queen Elizabeth to romantic leads in two of the great movie melodramas, *Dark Victory* (1939) and *Now, Voyager* (1942). During the 1930s, she appeared in from three to six films per year.

Katharine Hepburn specialized in strong career women. Although she made fewer films than Davis, she still appeared in more than 50 movies, a great many of which are classics—*Alice Adams* (1935), *Holiday* (1938), *Bringing Up Baby* (1938), *The Philadelphia Story* (1940), and *The African Queen* (1951).

Other major stars included Jean Arthur (more than 90 films, including *Mr. Smith Goes to Washington*, 1939), Joan Fontaine (nearly 50 films, including *Rebecca*, 1940), Ingrid Bergman (more than 50 films, including *Casablanca*, 1941), Myrna Loy (more than 130 films, including *Libeled Lady*, 1936), Joan Crawford (nearly 100 films, including *Mildred Pierce*, 1945), and Carole Lombard (more than 70 films, including *Nothing Sacred* 1932, in a career cut short by early death).

What has changed today is that the industry does not make enough films with the kind of content that would sustain a large gallery of lead female actors. Therefore, while we have a Julia Roberts or a Nicole Kidman, the type of films the industry funds leaves little room for others to join them.

"Indie" opportunities

While the industry rarely gives a blockbuster film project to a female director, women are more likely to find work as directors in independent film or on smaller-budget pictures picked up by the majors.

After graduating from film school at New York University, for example, Nicole Kassell made *The Woodsman* (2004), about a child molester (played by Kevin Bacon in a critically praised performance) coping with life in the world after being released

NOW, VOYAGER (WARNER BROS., 1942)

Leading roles for women were much more plentiful during the classic Hollywood era of the 1930s and 1940s. Bette Davis, for example, specialized in playing tough, strong, independent women and made more than 100 films in her career. In *Now, Voyager,* her character undergoes a transformation from shrinking wallflower to a poised, powerful figure of high society. Frame enlargement.

from prison. Independent film enabled her to transition from film school to professional directing.

After working as a production designer, Catherine Hardwicke transitioned to directing independent films. Her first feature, *Thirteen* (2004), is a powerful portrait of Tracy (Evan Rachel Wood in an outstanding performance), a seventh-grader on the skids, involved with drugs and petty crime. She continued her focus on teen characters in a follow-up feature, *The Lords of Dogtown* (2005). She then had a huge box-office success with the vampire story, *Twilight* (2008), made for indie production company Summit Entertainment.

Sofia Coppola attained a remarkable level of success (for an indie feature) with *Lost in Translation* (2003), about the friendship between a melancholy movie star (Bill Murray) and a neglected newlywed (Scarlett Johansson). The film was nominated for several Academy Awards, and she followed it with a period film, *Marie Antoinette* (2006).

Working on smaller budgets outside the orbit of the major studios can provide more creative freedom and an opportunity to work regularly, although, even here, getting the next project can be a problem. After directing several episodes of the TV series, *Homicide: Life on the Street*, Lisa Cholodenko wrote and directed the highly acclaimed feature film *High Art* (1998), a character piece about two women sharing an apartment who become lovers. It was a comeback film for Ally Sheedy, who had been one of the popular "brat pack" actors in the 1980s. Critics praised her blazing performance, but Cholodenko did not have another feature film in release until *Laurel Canyon* (2002).

LOST IN TRANSLATION (FOCUS FEATURES, 2003)

After winning critical praise for *The Virgin Suicides* (1999), director Sofia Coppola found critical and popular success with *Lost in Translation*. This quirky low-budget independent film grossed an amazing $119 million worldwide, a level of success that gave Coppola a new degree of bargaining power in the industry. She followed *Lost in Translation* with a period film, *Marie Antoinette* (2006). Frame enlargement.

THE KIDS ARE ALL RIGHT (FOCUS FEATURES, 2010)

Nic (Annette Benning) and Jules (Julianne Moore) share an awkward meeting with the birth father (Mark Ruffalo) of their children. Lisa Cholodenko's film exemplifies the character-centered dramas that are more commonly found on today's indie circuit than in big studio pictures. Frame enlargement.

In that picture, which Cholodenko also wrote, she gave Frances McDormand one of the best roles of her career as a free-spirited music producer living in the famed bohemian neighborhood long favored by folk and rock musicians. The film explores issues of aging, parenting, and sexuality with real sensitivity and insight. She returned to these issues in *The Kids Are All Right* (2010), in which Annette Bening and Julianne Moore play a gay couple whose children search out their birth father. Made for indie Focus Features, the film was nominated for a Best Picture Oscar.

Case Study REAL WOMEN HAVE CURVES

Home Box Office (HBO) has been very receptive to the work of women directors and grants its filmmakers a great deal of artistic freedom. Lisa Gay Hamilton's *Beah: A Black Woman Speaks* (2005), Liz Goldwyn's *Pretty Things* (2005), Ivy Meeropolis' *Heir to an Execution* (2004), and numerous other films produced and directed by women have found a home on HBO.

The HBO production *Real Women Have Curves* (2002) is one of the best films of recent years to portray what it means to grow as a woman, and a Latina, in the United States today, where oppressive beauty standards stigmatize women who are not thin and health-club toned. The film is a coming-of-age story about Ana (played by first-time actress America Ferrera), a Mexican-American woman from a working-class family who has an opportunity to go to college on scholarship. Her mother opposes this because she does not want Ana to leave the neighborhood or her class background, and Ana must decide what she will do.

The film gracefully integrates its many observations about class, ethnicity, gender, and sexuality and adds a great deal of humor to the mix. Ana is heavy (her mother calls her "fatty"), but she feels good about her weight and about herself, and she attracts the romantic attentions of a boy in her class.

Ana works with a group of overweight women at the sewing factory run by her sister Estella, where, for low wages, they make inexpensive dresses that are then sold by others at high prices in swanky department stores. One of the themes of the film is to be comfortable with the type of body that you have, and in one of the film's best scenes, the women, sweating in the hot factory, remove their outer clothes and work in their underwear, comparing their cellulite and rolls of flesh while joking and dancing with a new sense of energy. Ana's mother is appalled, but Ana admonishes her, saying that real women look like this.

(continued)

REAL WOMEN HAVE CURVES (HBO, 2002)

America Ferrera is Ana Garcia, struggling with issues of beauty, class, and success in a sensitive coming-of-age story that avoids cliches. Screenwriter Josefina Lopez based the story on her own experiences. Frame enlargement.

The film's writer and director are Latinas who were determined to show a different image of Hispanic characters, who are often portrayed in mainstream films in a context of crime, guns, or drugs. Director Patricia Cardoso is a graduate of film school at the University of California Los Angeles, and she came to the United States from Columbia in 1987. Screenwriter Josefina Lopez was born in Mexico and came to the United States with her family as undocumented residents. She became a legal resident in 1987 through the Simpson–Rodino Amnesty Law, passed in 1985, that provides amnesty for undocumented aliens. While living as an "illegal," she worked in the sewing factories of Los Angeles,

and from that experience, she wrote the play from which the film was adapted.

The play focused on the women in the sewing factory, working and joking but always fearful of an INS raid. Her screenplay moved the focus to Ana and made the film into a coming-of-age story, a portrait of class in America, and a critique of contemporary beauty standards. The movie masterfully balances and integrates all this material and does so with heart and humor.

Well directed as the film was, though, Patricia Cardoso did not have another film in production until *Nappily Ever After* (2005). This is the enduring challenge that independent filmmakers confront. Finishing one film does not make getting the next one necessarily any easier. ▪

Production Executives and Personnel

Achieving an active and successful career actually can be easier outside directing. In the executive offices of Hollywood's major studios, some of the most powerful people in the industry have been women. These have included producers and studio executives.

Kathleen Kennedy has produced many of the industry's most successful and highest-profile pictures—*War of the Worlds* (2005), *Seabiscuit* (2003), and *Signs* (2002). Gale Ann Hurd's track record as producer includes *Terminator 3: Rise of the Machines* (2003), *Hulk* (2003), and *Armageddon* (1998). Until her recent death, Debra Hill maintained an active producing career—*Crazy in Alabama* (1999), *Escape from L.A.* (1996), and the *Halloween* series. As their credits demonstrate, the industry's most powerful female producers are not ghettoized into making "women's pictures" or "chick flicks." Their work includes some of the most prominent contemporary action films.

Working at the highest level of industry influence, Sherry Lansing was a studio chief. She was chair of Paramount Pictures, one of the Hollywood majors, from the early 1990s until 2005. She was responsible for such films as *Braveheart* (1995), *Titanic* (1997), and *Saving Private Ryan* (1998). In its 2003 Women in Entertainment Report, *The Hollywood Reporter* named her Number 4 on its list of the 100 most powerful people in Hollywood.

After two years as entertainment president of Fox Broadcasting, Gail Berman was appointed president of Paramount Pictures. Amy Pascal became chairman of Columbia Pictures in 1999 and was promoted to chairman of its parent company, Sony Pictures Entertainment, in 2003, where she oversees all the company's production in movies, television, DVD and video, games, and mobile phone technologies.

And in terms of production personnel, two of the most brilliant and steadily working film editors have been Ann V. Coates (*Lawrence of Arabia*, 1962; and *Unfaithful*, 2002) and Thelma Schoonmaker (*Raging Bull*, 1980; *Taxi Driver*, 1976; *The Aviator*, 2004). Women, however, traditionally have found work as editors, even during Hollywood's classic period, because editing, like costume design, was regarded by men in the industry as "women's work."

Thus, while women have long worked as editors, their employment as powerful studio executives and chiefs is a significant development. Despite this, however, the industry remains relatively lopsided in the opportunities that it grants to women, with clear boundaries existing in the roles that are available in front of the camera and the slots that are available behind it. For women actors and filmmakers, Hollywood remains a difficult environment in which to work.

Summary

Feminist criticism has made a major contribution to the understanding of how gender perspectives and gender biases influence film images about the world and the way narratives are organized to privilege male characters and experiences at the expense of strong female characters. To a large extent, this bias in favor of male experience results from the extraordinary power male filmmakers have long enjoyed relative to the much smaller number of women directors in charge of major productions. Because of this power, men have constructed images of women in films, and, for a feminist, these images necessarily say more about men than women. Accordingly, feminist criticism emphasizes the importance of women directors having an artistic voice in the world of cinema as a means of balancing the voices that male directors have long commanded.

Feminist theory has also called attention to the work of repression in cinema, that what a film does *not* show or say may reveal key assumptions about gender and about the way the social world is structured. Resistant and disruptive interpretations by a critic can reveal these hidden and repressed areas of meaning and the prohibited or taboo areas of content they point to.

Gender is one of the many screens through which human experience is filtered, and, while it has a profound impact on the terms by which people live their lives, it is not the only means for ordering one's experience of the world or organizing the design of films. Sophisticated feminist criticism understands when best to apply accounts emphasizing gender differences and to what degree. The feminist sensibility behind *Cleo From 5 to 7* or *The Piano* is more profound and enters more deeply into the design of those films than does the fact that *Blue Steel* or *Point Break* are directed by a woman. In the latter case, the weight of genre and traditional commercial formulas tends to minimize the distinctive voice that a female director might use. As with all models of criticism, the feminist critic must develop a sensitive understanding of which material will most benefit from her or his distinctive tools of analysis.

COGNITIVE MODELS

Cognitive film theory studies the ways viewers understand and interpret visual and auditory information in film and how specific structural features, such as editing or lighting, may cue responses or invite particular kinds of interpretations. Cognitive film theory focuses on (1) the viewer's perception and emotional experience of visual and sound information, and (2) the ways that viewers organize and categorize these perceptions in order to derive meaning from a film. With its emphasis on perceptually based interpretation and understanding, cognitive film theory derives many of its principles and assumptions from research in perceptual psychology, computer science, and communications. The cognitive film theorist is less concerned with developing an interpretation of the content of a specific film than with understanding how viewers in general process audiovisual information in order to extract meaning from films.

Elements of Cognitive Models

For cognitive film theorists, viewers understand visual and auditory information by using **perceptual** and **interpretive processing**. Perceptual processing refers to sensory perception by viewers. Interpretive processing refers to the higher-level interpretations that are placed on sense information. Let's consider how cross-cutting—a convention of continuity editing used to suggest that two or more events are occurring simultaneously—elicits both levels of response from viewers.

Understood in terms of perceptual processing, a viewer watching a cross-cut sequence sees a succession of shots flashing by on the screen as an alternating series. One series, for example, may show a swimmer desperately racing for shore while the other series shows a shark cutting through the water. Understood in terms of interpretive processing—the cognitive or active interpretational response to sensory information—the viewer draws an inference from the alternating series of recurring images. That inference is a presumption of simultaneous action, the assumption that the narrative lines presented in the cross-cut sequence are occurring at the same moment of time.

These two levels of processing emphasize the basic perceptual skills that the medium of cinema builds on as well as the viewer's contribution to the creation of meaning in cinema. The distinction between the terms highlights the difference between the actual on-screen audiovisual information and what a viewer attributes to that information. Cognitive film theory, therefore, studies the ways that specific audiovisual designs in cinema communicate information to the viewer who responds with an active interpretation. Another example can help to clarify this. A basic rule of continuity editing is the **eyeline match**. In terms of perceptual processing, a viewer watching a sequence cut using the eyeline match sees a series of close-ups or medium shots of actors oriented so that the directions of their gazes are in complimentary directions—one looks screen left, the other looks screen right. From the interpretive perspective, viewers respond to this editing code by inferring a relation of proximity and communication between the characters. The

MOONSTRUCK (MGM/ UNITED ARTISTS, 1987)
Cognitive theory stresses how viewers perceive and interpret audiovisual information. Viewers give that information a higher-order level of meaning and structure than the images and sounds themselves convey. These two shots from *Moonstruck* illustrate the eyeline match. In terms of perceptual information, all a viewer sees are separate images of Cher and Nicolas Cage looking in different directions. But viewers organize the shots by inferring, across the cut, that the performers are looking at each other. This level of information is not in the images themselves; the viewer supplies it. Frame enlargements.

viewer infers that characters presented using the eyeline match are communicating with one another and/or are near each other.

SCHEMAS   Attention to interpretive processing enables cognitive film theorists to examine the ways that a viewer's responses to film are guided by a series of **schemas**, or frameworks of interpretation. A fundamental assumption of cognitive film theory is that viewers' responses to film are not strictly sensory driven, that is, are not entirely explainable as immediate responses to the visual and auditory information contained in the film. Viewers bring to this information a large set of schemas, or frameworks of interpretation, that they have developed through personal experience in the world, as members of given cultures and societies, and as experienced film viewers.

Using schemas, a viewer can understand and interpret visual and narrative information in an extremely efficient and rapid fashion. To viewers familiar with science fiction movies—viewers whose experience in this genre has enabled them to develop an extensive set of interpretational schemas—a bright light on a character's face coupled with an awestruck expression instantly evokes the idea of an alien presence. Viewers familiar with Westerns will have schemas attuned to that genre. They know that a cowboy

The cross-dressing
villain in *The Silence
of the Lambs* breaks
cultural rules regarding
proper gender behavior.
The filmmakers count
on this violation of
a viewer's culturally
influenced schemas to
generate strong disgust
and condemnation of
the character. Frame
enlargement.

walking into a saloon will order whiskey, but seated around a campfire will prefer coffee. The more audience knowledge a filmmaker can assume, the more efficient is story
presentation. Less needs to be explained.

Filmmakers often count on the existence of specific interpretational schemas in
their target audience and design their films to exploit these schemas. The gender-
bending villain in *The Silence of the Lambs*, who cross-dresses and makes himself up
to look like a woman, triggers an audience's cultural schemas regarding the acceptable range of gender displays and sexual behavior. The villain's flagrant violation of
conventional schemas regarding proper gender display provokes, as the filmmakers
intended, anxiety and disapproval from most audience members.

WHY FILM IS COMPREHENSIBLE   In addition to studying the ways that audiences apply
schemas to process visual and narrative information, cognitive film theory investigates
the more general question of what makes film so comprehensible, accessible, and enjoy-
able to audiences worldwide. The answers provided by cognitive theory emphasize the
correspondences that exist between film and a viewer's real-world perceptual and social
experience. For the cognitive theorist, film is comprehensible, accessible, and enjoy-
able because it builds many similarities between the means used to represent a world
on-screen and the spectator's familiar habits of perception and social understanding.
Cognitive theory takes the viewer as a rational agent, whereas the psychoanalytic approach emphasizes irrational elements in the viewer's responses. The two approaches
differ considerably from one another in this respect.

Perceptual Correspondences   The viewer sees a three-dimensional world on the flat
surface of the screen because the photographic images reproduce important real-
world sources of information about spatial depth, about the location and distribution
of objects in space, about volume, texture, and movement. Just as this information
tells viewers where objects are located in the real, three-dimensional world, it provides the same information in the represented reality of a screen world. Today, many
film images are created not with a camera but in the computer. Software programs
routinely create this information to make the computer-created image look convincingly three-dimensional. Second, the codes of continuity editing used to build scenes

create a consistent projective geometry within the represented three-dimensional world on screen that is analogous to the viewer's own visual and physical experience. Throughout a scene edited using continuity principles, the screen coordinates of up, down, front, back, right, and left remain consistent, regardless of changes in camera position and angle.

Third, point-of-view editing establishes, for the viewer, easy narrative comprehension because the judicious use of long shot and close-up clarifies important narrative information and emphasizes characters' emotions. Viewers see everything they need to know and are given all the information they need in order to understand the narrative. Fourth, in the film image the viewer reads and understands the significance of characters' facial and gestural expressions, just as the viewer does with real people in daily life. Viewers are extremely good at decoding the meaning expressed on people's faces and through gestures, and they use these skills when watching a movie. Actors are professionals trained to mimic the range of gestural and facial cues significant within their culture so as to evoke the emotions typically associated with those expressions and gestures.

Pointing to these complex correspondences between the information contained in film images and the viewer's real-world perceptual habits and skills, cognitive film theorists persuasively explain why films are so easily understood by large numbers of people.

Social Correspondences   A second set of correspondences connects the screen world to viewers' experiential skills and knowledge. Viewers apply to the screen world many assumptions and judgments about people and proper role-based behavior that are derived from social experience. These assumptions co-exist with, and are modified by, others that the viewer derives from narrative formula and genre. Characters in a horror film, for example, behave like viewers expect characters in a horror film to behave—they always go down into that dark basement where a monster is lurking!—but these behaviors also must correlate with dimensions of human experience that the viewer finds credible or valid.

NOTORIOUS (RKO, 1946)
The three-dimensional information contained in this shot from Hitchcock's *Notorious* includes the relative sizes of the men, the converging parallel lines on the floor, and the diminishing size and spacing of the floor tiles. These cues—which derive from everyday visual experience—establish the illusion of depth and distance in the image. Frame enlargement.

Research involving preschool children and adolescents indicates that a close relationship prevails between a child's developing stock of moral and ethical concepts and his or her abilities to use these concepts to interpret character behavior in movies. Very young children are likely to judge a character as good or bad depending on whether the character looks attractive or ugly. Older children override such appearance stereotyping with more complex evaluations based on the moral or ethical content of the character's behavior.

Person perception, then, is a process that commonly underlies nonfilmic interpersonal and social experience and the inferences and evaluations viewers make about characters in movie narratives. Filmmakers draw from this important source of correspondence in creative ways. The presentation of Hannibal Lecter in *The Silence of the Lambs*, the film's stress on his wit, intelligence, and compassion for the heroine Clarice Starling, as well as his sadistic cruelty, complicates the viewer's desire to establish a stable moral and ethical evaluation of that character. Viewers are attracted by his positive qualities and charisma yet repulsed by his violation of normative human behavior.

Summary

The strengths of cognitive film theory are twofold. First, this model, unlike many of the others, is research-based. The assumptions and principles of the theory are supported by empirical data, which make the theory directly testable, and, accordingly, give it a great deal of explanatory power.

Because of its empirical dimension, cognitive theory provides a strong foundation for understanding how viewers make sense of film images and narratives. Rather than relying on critical speculations that may or may not be applicable to real viewers, the cognitive theorist studies the perceptions and interpretations of actual viewers and is able to help clarify the factors that make film an intelligible medium for its audience.

Second, by providing explanations for the intelligibility of motion pictures, cognitive film theory provides an understanding of why the cinema has become so popular across cultures. Cinema provides viewers with an easily understood spectacle, and this helps ensure its enormous popularity throughout the world. If the motion picture medium was difficult to understand, it would never have become so popular.

Because the cognitive model stresses perception and cognition, one might think that it has had little to say about the emotional components of the viewer's experience. In fact, cognitive scholars have devoted great attention to this area and have published numerous studies about the ways in which film elicits emotional responses from viewers. At the same time, cognitive film theory has had relatively little to say about the transformative functions of cinema, the way films go beyond and imaginatively transform the boundaries of the viewer's experience. Films are not mere copies or mirrors of that experience; they re-organize and reconfigure it in complex ways. Moreover, the determinants of meaning in film are manifold. How a filmmaker manipulates structure, what a viewer brings to a film, and the visual and narrative traditions and genres in which a given film is located, all these are part of the elaborate mixture that produces meaning in film.

WRITING A CRITICAL PAPER

Film criticism does not mean that one criticizes a movie in the sense of pointing up its flaws or its failed ambitions. Neither does it involve reaching a decision about whether a film is "good" or "bad." Few films are such unconditional achievements

THERE'S SOMETHING ABOUT MARY (20TH CENTURY FOX, 1998)
Cognitive theory helps explain why and how viewers readily understand cinema, and a great deal of research from a cognitive perspective has been conducted on emotional responses and appeals. *There's Something About Mary* was a huge popular hit with audiences who delighted in its humor. Cognitive theory explores the manner in which films elicit emotion and the ways that filmic technique, such as facial close-ups, work to identify character emotions and solicit a viewer responses including empathy, laughter, and disgust. Frame enlargement.

that they can be described as good or bad. Most movies are a mixture of things that work and some that don't, ambitions attained and those that eluded the filmmaker, and nearly all films contain levels and layers of meaning that skillful criticism can uncover and clarify.

Criticism is not a negative act. A critic's interpretations add meaning to a film, enrich its context, and enrich a viewer's appreciation for context and for aesthetic design and accomplishment.

As a student writing a critical paper, you explore the multidimensional meanings of a given film and/or its stylistic, structural design. Often, this means clarifying implicit or subtle meanings, identifying and exploring seemingly contradictory messages or values in a given film, describing and illuminating significant elements of design, and, ultimately, creating a new and interesting way of interpreting or understanding a film. This last function is the central act of criticism: the creation of a new interpretation that extends or deepens a viewer's appreciation of a film.

The approach you take will depend on the kind of analysis that you have been asked to undertake. Analyzing a genre involves searching for and clarifying patterns—the narratives, themes, and images that typify the genre. Genre patterns can be explained by comparing various films that are part of the genre. Analysis that aims to explore how an individual film connects with a genre would specify how such patterns are present within the film and what variations on them may be present as well. Too much variation takes a film outside of a genre it might otherwise belong to, but insufficient variation is often the mark of lesser genre films. Interesting variations often are introduced by individual filmmakers. In such cases, genre and director studies may intersect. John Ford's Westerns are very different from those of Budd Boetticher and Anthony Mann, and some of these differences can be attributed to the ways that directorial style and sensibility rework generic material.

Moreover, certain theoretical models lend themselves to particular genres. Psychoanalysis has been especially useful in clarifying the workings of horror films and of avant-garde cinema, many of whose filmmakers were quite influenced by Freud's writings.

Analyses that aim to explore issues of film and society often seek to explicate the ideological material found in given films and to connect this with social forces and dynamics, or the critic might be interested to investigate the representations of gender or race found in particular films. The critic should be attentive to how a film defines what is "natural" or "true" and how these representations necessarily omit, deny or repress alternative constructions. By reading against the grain, by doing a deconstructive reading, the critic often can uncover repressed meanings surrounding gender and race that structure the discourse presented by a film.

A formal film analysis typically is concerned with examining the details of a film's audiovisual design, with identifying and interpreting how lighting, color, editing, and other elements of structure convey meaning. This type of analysis can be an end in itself, providing students with training in looking at and analyzing the audiovisual features of film. Alternatively, formal analysis may be a component of ideological or auteur criticism and, in fact, should play some role in those approaches. Analyzing Hitchcock's work from a purely thematic point of view, omitting the remarkable structural designs in his work, may produce less convincing interpretations than ones that use formal analysis to advance thematic ideas by showing connections between the two, the ways that Hitchcock's themes are grounded in particular cinematic designs.

An auteur analysis investigates questions of authorship, which usually are posed in terms of the director, although cinematographers and screenwriters might also be studied as auteurs. Like genre analysis, auteur study involves a search for patterns, for signature narratives, themes and image designs that seem to identify a cohesive artistic profile in a director's work.

Begin your paper with a clear understanding of the kind of analysis you have been asked to produce. The objectives of a genre paper will differ, for example, from those of a purely formal analysis.

Once you have a clear understanding of the objectives of the assignment, you should view the film or films you will analyze at least two or three times. Search for material in the film—key scenes, character interactions, aspects of narrative structure, and elements of audiovisual design—that you find striking and interesting and can identify as a potential fit with the objectives of your task. Having found such material, be sure to carefully describe it. You needn't describe everything in a shot or scene, only what is relevant to the interpretation you are developing. If a detail doesn't fit, don't force it. The people reading the criticism will know if your interpretations are well-supported by the evidence you cite.

Precisely label all aspects of visual design, quote dialogue accurately, and spell character names correctly.

Learning to identify what you see on screen is a very important task. The camera doesn't "swoop"—it moves on a crane or boom, on tracks, on a dolly, or as a Steadicam mounted to the operator's body. A fade and a dissolve are distinctly different transitions. A critic who loses track of these distinctions will lose credibility.

Be careful about imposing personal prejudices and value judgments on films that are old and/or are produced from other cultures and societies. Old films may reflect social worlds that no longer exist and differ from the contemporary one that you inhabit, and other cultures and societies may have different rules governing behavior and emotional displays. But being careful does not mean avoiding a contemporary filter—the racism and sexism that was taken for granted in earlier generations of filmmaking can only be clarified from a point of view that is outside the cultural prisms that operated in earlier periods.

It often is essential to further research the subjects or issues addressed by the film that you are analyzing so that you can develop a basis for evaluating how the film treats them. It also may be helpful to view other films produced by the same director or movies by other filmmakers that deal with the same topic or genre. This will enable you to become familiar with a body of work that you can use to contextualize the film that you are critiquing.

You might also read what scholars and critics have said about the film because this will stimulate your own thinking and help you generate ideas. It will also allow you to see how other writers have constructed their critical arguments. Remember, though, that the goal of criticism is to produce a novel or original interpretation, not to recycle someone else's ideas. *Any* material that you borrow or use from a published source needs to be identified as such and attributed to that source. Failing to do so is plagiarism.

Pursue your ideas and their implications as far as you reasonably can. A flaw in the work produced by beginning writers, or by beginning film critics, is the failure to explore the implications of one's ideas or of the issues one raises in building a critical argument. Experienced writers are sensitive to the productive implications of a good idea and skilled at exploring them, at going down the intellectual pathways they open up. Beginning writers often fail to see and consider the implications raised by their ideas and arguments. Taking an idea as far as it can reasonably go is the hallmark of good writing, good analysis, and good film criticism. A novice critic often will have an interesting insight and then fail to consider where it can take the writer. As you examine your paper—and all serious writers do this, no one ever turns in a first draft because nobody is so good or brilliant as to produce polished and crafted work in a first draft—reflect upon the issues raised by your ideas. Have you fully explored them? During the time spent away from your early draft, new ideas often present themselves. Follow them where they take you, and integrate them into your argument.

There is no single formula or method for constructing a critical argument. However, all the rules normally associated with good writing also apply to film criticism. You want to persuade the reader that your interpretation of the film reveals important patterns and layers of meaning that are not immediately apparent or explicitly conveyed during a casual viewing.

Be careful, therefore, to build your argument by clearly guiding the reader through all of the steps and stages in your critical thought, from describing your initial premises to the citation of evidence and the statement of conclusions. Good writing is clear, connected, and forceful. Because criticism is a rhetorical act, the quality of the writing is as important as the quality of the ideas in swaying the reader to your positions. Finally, remember that good criticism is provocative. If your ideas are challenging, if the connections that you draw across the images and narrative episodes are novel and insightful, you will enrich the readers' understanding of the film and may send them back for another and wiser viewing.

SUMMARY

Because cinema is such a rich and powerful medium of communication, because it affects viewers' lives and their thinking about the world in so many ways, it is important to reach an understanding of what the medium *is,* independently of its existence in any given film. Film theories are systematic attempts to think about, and explain, the nature of cinema, how it works as a medium, and embodies meaning for viewers.

Because the cinema is multidimensional, no one theory has all the answers. Each theory is best suited to answering certain kinds of questions. Realist theory emphasizes the cinema's recording and documenting functions and the ability of filmmakers to use photographic images and naturalistic sounds to capture social realities existing before the camera. Theories of realism tend to define a threshold beyond which the cinema's transformation of social realities is regarded as fictitious, duplicitous, stylized, or distorted. To this extent, realist theories stress the ethical contract that exists between filmmaker and audience.

Realist models aim to establish difficult distinctions between the cinema's recording and documenting functions and its transformative abilities. It is often very hard, though, to know where these distinctions lie. Every camera position implies a viewpoint, and some degree of stylistic transformation of the raw material before the camera is inevitable. It is the job of realist theories to say how much transformation is too much.

Auteur theory stresses the human qualities of cinema and emphasizes that mechanically produced sights and sounds can be organized by artists into an aesthetically satisfying design. Auteurism insists that this mechanical, twentieth-century medium is capable, in the right hands, of producing art.

Psychoanalytic theory emphasizes the enormous potential of cinema to provoke emotional responses in its viewers that may be unconscious, primitive, nonrational, and even contrary to the behaviors polite society demands. Psychoanalytic theory is drawn to explain the highly charged poetic and emotional power of certain images and why they seem to exert such a hold over viewers.

As a medium seen by millions, cinema inevitably has a social impact, and its images and stories construct politically and socially charged views of the world. Ideological film theory uncovers the often subtle terms by which cinema codes its views of reality and, by revealing them, can give viewers control over them.

Feminist film theory reveals the gender biases at work inside the views of social reality offered by films made by men within an industry where power is still largely wielded by men. Images of women in film frequently have been defined by male filmmakers, and feminist theory looks for the alternative artistic and social voices of female filmmakers. Feminist theory reminds viewers that gender is one of the most powerful screens through which film images and stories pass and that male filmmakers may tend to organize those images and stories differently than female filmmakers.

Cognitive theories aim to provide answers to some of the most basic questions about cinema. Why is it intelligible to viewers? Why are many films so easily understood? How can a filmmaker facilitate an audience's understanding of shots, scenes, and stories? How do viewers base their interpretations of films on analogies with their own perceptual and social experience? Cognitive theory points to the ways in which cinema works as a medium of communication.

All of these theoretical models are important because motion pictures are never just one thing. Films offer portraits of the world that can seem realistic but that code and transform sociopolitical content into an emotionally powerful experience. Each theory provides a different point of entry for analyzing a film's design and its effects on viewers.

Film viewers should always keep in mind the extraordinary richness of the motion picture medium. It is what makes cinema such a challenging medium to study and one that is so powerful to experience. Hopefully, these chapters have indicated something of that richness. Equipped with this knowledge, you can embark on an exciting journey. A world of cinema—composed of films from different decades, countries, and genres—awaits exploration. Let intelligence and curiosity be your guides, and enjoy an incredible diversity of film experiences. It is easy to love the cinema. It gives so much back in return.

KEY TERMS AND CONCEPTS

auteurist film theory   418
blaxploitation   446
condensation   423
cognitive film theory   468
deep-focus
   cinematography   413
displacement   423
eyeline match   468

feminist film theory   451
film theory   411
ideological film theory   430
ideology   430
indexical signs   413
interpretive processing   468
long take   413
perceptual processing   468

perceptual realism   417
psychoanalytic film
   theory   423
realist film theory   411
schema   469
taboo images   000
voyeurism   425

SUGGESTED READINGS

Dudley Andrew, *The Major Film Theories* (New York: Oxford University Press, 1976).

Andre Bazin, *What is Cinema?*, 2 vols., ed. and trans. Hugh Gray (Berkeley and Los Angeles: University of California Press, 1971).

David Bordwell and Noel Carroll, eds., *Post-Theory: Reconstructing Film Studies* (Madison, WI: University of Wisconsin Press, 1995).

Diane Carson, Linda Dittmar, and Janice Welsch, eds., *Multiple Voices in Feminist Film Criticism* (Minneapolis, MN: University of Minnesota Press, 1994).

Molly Haskell, *From Reverence to Rape: The Treatment of Women in the Movies* (New York: Holt, Rinehart, and Winston, 1974).

E. Ann Kaplan, ed., *Psychoanalysis and Cinema* (New York: Routledge, 1990).

Annette Kuhn, *Women's Pictures: Feminism and Cinema* (London: Routledge and Kegan Paul, 1982).

Gerald Mast, Marshall Cohen, and Leo Braudy, eds., *Film Theory and Criticism: Introductory Readings*, 4th ed. (New York: Oxford University Press, 1998).

Stephen Prince, *Visions of Empire: Political Imagery in Contemporary American Film* (New York: Praeger, 1992).

GLOSSARY

3D digital matte   A matte painting that has been camera mapped onto a 3D geometrical model in computer space. The digital matte can then be moved or rotated to simulate the perspective of a moving camera. See also **camera mapping**.

Additive Color Mixing   A system used for creating color on television where red, blue, and green lights are mixed together to create all other hues.

ADR   *Automated dialogue replacement* (ADR) is a post-production practice in which actors re-record lines of dialogue or add new ones not present at the point of filming. Computer software enables proper synching of these lines with the performer's lip movements as recorded on film.

Aerial Image Printing   Method of producing dimensional effects using matte paintings in an optical printer. An image (such as a matte painting) is projected to a focal plane in space (rather than onto a surface) where it can be photographed by the process camera in the optical printer. That footage can be combined with live action footage and other optical elements.

Aerial Perspective   A visual depth cue in which the effects of the atmosphere make very distant objects appear bluish and hazy.

Alpha Channel   In a digital image, this channel of information specifies a pixel's degree of transparency. The alpha channel is often used for generating male and female mattes.

Ambient Sound   The background sound characteristic of an environment or location. For a film such as *The Last of the Mohicans*, set in a forest, ambient sounds include the rustle of branches and the cries of distant birds.

Anamorphic   Method of producing a widescreen (2.35:1) image by squeezing the picture information horizontally and stretching it vertically. This method is used for both theatrical films and for DVD home video formatted for 16 × 9 (widescreen) monitors or projection systems. Unsqueezing the picture information during projection or viewing produces the widescreen image.

Ancillary Market   All of the nontheatrical markets from which a film distributor derives revenue. These include home video, cable television, and foreign markets.

Angle of View   The amount of area recorded by a given lens. Telephoto lenses have a much smaller angle of view than wide-angle lenses.

Animation 2D   Traditional form of animation in cinema which involves photographing flat artwork, typically a combination of characters and background. Camera movement and three dimensional depth perspective is fairly limited.

Animatronic Model   A motorized, moveable miniature model, often used for creature effects.

Animation 3D   Animation of miniature models or puppets or animation inside three-dimensional computer space.

Antinarrative   A narrative style that tends, paradoxically, toward eliminating narrative by employing lots of digression, avoiding a clear hierarchy of narrative events, and by suppressing the causal connections among events.

Art Director   Working under the production designer, the art director supervises the translation and sketches into sets.

Art Film   Films made by overseas directors in the 1950s and 1960s that explored weighty and timeless themes and took film style in new, unexplored directions.

Aspect Ratio   The dimensions of the film frame or screen image. Aspect ratio is typically expressed in units of width to height.

Attributional Errors   Mistakes of interpretation that arise when a critic erroneously decides that some effect in a film has a meaning expressly intended by its creators or incorrectly assigns the creative responsibility for an effect to the wrong member of the production crew. Uncovering these errors typically requires documentation of a film's production history.

Auteur   A director whose work is characterized by a distinctive audiovisual design and recurring set of thematic issues. Auteurism is a model of film theory and criticism that searches for film authors or auteurs.

Auteurist Film Theory (Auteur Theory)   A model of film theory that studies the work of a film auteur (or author). Directors are generally considered to be the prime auteurs in cinema. Auteurist theory studies the films of a cinema auteur as works of personal expression.

Back Light   The light source illuminating the space between performers and the rear wall of a set. Along with key and fill lights, back light is one of the three principal sources of illumination in a scene.

Beta Movement   A perceptual illusion in which the human eye responds to apparent movement as if it were real. Because of this illusion, viewers think they see moving figures on a film or television screen when, in fact, there is no true movement.

Binocular Disparity   Each eye has a different angle of view on the world, and this difference or disparity provides a source of information about depth, distance and spatial layout. Stereoscopic cinema incorporates binocular disparity to create an impression of 3D.

"Blaxploitation"   The cycle of films that emerged in the early 1970s aimed at African-American audiences. Most of the "blaxploitation" films were crime and action thrillers.

Blockbuster   A hugely profitable film usually featuring a fantasy theme and a narrative heavily dependent on special effects.

Boom Shot   A type of moving camera shot in which the camera moves up or down through space. Also known as a *crane shot*, it takes its name from the apparatus—a boom or crane—on which the camera is mounted.

Camera Mapping   Method of projecting a 2D matte painting onto a 3D geometrical model in computer space. Once the image is projected onto the model, it can be treated as a 3D object and moved or rotated to simulate the perspective of a moving camera.

"Camera Pen"   The term used by Alexandre Astruc to designate the use of cinema as a medium of personal expression. The concept was a major influence on French New Wave directors and their conviction that cinema was a director's medium (see Auteur).

Camera Position   The distance between the camera and the subject it is photographing. Camera positions are usually classified as variations of three basic setups: the long shot, the medium shot, and the close-up.

Canted Angle   A camera angle in which the camera leans toward screen right or screen left, producing an imbalanced, off-center look to the image. Filmmakers often use canted angles to capture a character's subjective feelings of stress or disorientation.

Cells   Transparent sheets of cellulose on which an animator draws and paints. A completed scene may be composed of numerous cells photographed one behind the other.

Cinematic Self-Reflexivity   A basic mode of screen reality in which the filmmaker establishes a self-referential audiovisual design. A self-reflexive film calls attention to its own artificially constructed nature.

Cinematography   The planning and execution of light and color design, camera position, and angle by the cinematographer in collaboration with the director.

Cinephilia   Love for cinema. This designates a deep passion for the medium of cinema, not merely a fondness for this or that individual film.

Classic Hollywood Narrative   Type of narrative prevalent in Hollywood films of the 1930s to 1950s and still popular today. The plot features a clear, main line of action (with subordinate subplots), marked by a main character's pursuit of a goal, in which the story events are chained in tight causal relationships. The conclusion cleanly resolves all major story issues.

Close-Up   One of the basic camera positions. The camera is set up in close proximity to an actor's face or other significant dramatic object that fills the frame. Close-ups tend to isolate objects or faces from their immediate surroundings.

Cognitive Film Theory   A model of film theory that examines how the viewer perceptually processes audiovisual information in cinema and cognitively interprets this information.

Composite   in a visual effects shot, combining the image layers to create the finished shot.

Composition   The arrangement of characters and objects within the frame. Through composition filmmakers arrange the visual space on-screen into an artistic design.

Computer-Generated Images (CGIs)   Images that are created and designed using computer software rather than originating as a scene before the camera that is photographed. Sophisticated software enables digital artists to render textures, lighting effects, movement, and other three-dimensional pictorial information in highly plausible and convincing ways. Bearing this information, CGI can be married (composited) with live action photography to stunning effect, as the exciting interaction of real actors and CGI dinosaurs in *The Lost World* demonstrates.

Condensation   A concept in psychoanalytic film theory that denotes the concentration of meaning found in images that are highly charged with emotional or dramatic significance. This concentration is symptomatic of repressed content that find expression in a condensed, indirect manner.

Continuity Editing   As its name implies, continuity editing maximizes principles of continuity from shot to shot so that the action seems to flow smoothly across shot and scene transitions. Continuity editing facilitates narrative comprehension by the viewer.

Contrast   The differences of light intensity across a scene. A high-contrast scene features brightly illuminated and deeply shadowed areas.

Convention   A familiar, customary way of representing characters, story situations, or images. Conventions result from agreements between filmmakers and viewers to accept certain representations as valid.

Convergence   Movement of the eyes toward each other that occurs when viewing near objects. Stereoscopic cinema uses convergence information to elicit 3D effects.

Costume Designer   Individual who designs costuming worn by actors.

Costumes   The clothing worn by performers in a film. Costumes help establish locale and period as well as a given film's color design.

Counter-Matte   A **counter-matte** masks the frame in an inverse manner to a matte. Used in combination with a matte, the matte/counter-matte system provides a means of creating composite images. See also **Traveling Matte.**

Coverage   The shots an editor uses to bridge continuity problems in the editing of a scene. By cutting to coverage, rather than relying on the master shot, an editor can finesse many problems of scene construction and can improve an actor's performance.

Crane Shot See **Boom Shot.**

Criticism The activity of searching for meaning in an artwork. The critic seeks to develop an original interpretation by uncovering novel meanings inside a film.

Cross-Cutting A method of editing used to establish simultaneous, ongoing lines of action in a film narrative. By rapidly cutting back and forth between two or more lines of action, the editor establishes that they are happening simultaneously. By decreasing the length of the shots, editors can accelerate the pace of the editing and imply an approaching climax.

Cue Sheet A breakdown of a scene's action, listing and timing all sections requiring musical cues.

Cut A type of visual transition created in editing in which one shot is instantaneously replaced on screen by another. Because the change is instantaneous, the cut itself is invisible. The viewer sees only the change from one shot to the next.

Deduction The method by which the critic works, using the general goals of the critical model to guide the search for supporting evidence.

Deep-Focus Cinematography A style of cinematography that establishes great depth of field within shots. Gregg Toland's cinematography for Orson Welles's *Citizen Kane* is a classic example of deep-focus composition.

Depth of Field The area of distance or separation between sharply focused foreground and background objects. Depth of field is determined by the focal length of a lens. Wide-angle lenses produce deep focus or great depth of field, whereas telephoto lenses have a shallow depth of field.

Depth Score The way that stereoscopic (3D) space is choreographed on screen in order to express a film's underlying themes and story issues.

Description A stage in creating criticism wherein the critic fully describes those relevant features of narrative or audiovisual design on which the critical interpretation will be based.

Design Concept The underlying creative concept that organizes the way in which sets and costumes are built, dressed, and photographed on a given production.

Deviant Plot Structure A narrative whose design and organization fails to conform with viewers' expectations regarding what is proper or permissible.

Dialogue One of the three basic types of film sound, it includes speech delivered by characters in a scene and voice-over narration accompanying a scene or film.

Diegetic Sound Sound that can be heard by characters in a scene and by film viewer. See also **nondiegetic sound.**

Digital Animation Animation inside three-dimensional computer space, aided by software to produce many photographic-like effects. Digitally created lighting effects, for example, can be very elaborate, and when used with texture mapping of skin and other surfaces, these can create remarkable illusions of depth.

Digital Backlot Practice of simulating locations using digital tools as an alternative to location shooting.

Digital Composite A composited shot produced digitally, rather than using an optical printer, by adding, substracting or otherwise transforming pixels.

Digital Effects The computer-designed components of a shot that may be composited with live action elements.

Digital Grading Method of digitally altering image elements, such as color balance and saturation, contrast, gamma, and filtration. *O Brother, Where Art Thou?* was the first feature, shot on film, to be entirely digitized and then color-corrected in this fashion. Also called *digital timing*.

Digital Intermediate The version of a film on digital video that is subjected to digital grading or the computer correction of color, contrast, and other image qualities. After these corrections are made, the footage on digital video is then scanned back onto film.

Digital Rendering The process during which a synthetic digital image is created from the files and data that an artist has assembled.

Digital Video An increasingly accepted alternative to celluloid film, this format captures picture information as an electronic signal in binary code. Images captured on digital video look different than those captured on film, but, once in binary format, images can be stored and manipulated by computer programs for editing and special effects work.

Direct Cinema A documentary style that emerged in the 1960s and sought to minimize all appearances that the filmmaker was shaping or manipulating the materials of the film.

Direct Sound Sound that is captured and recorded directly on location. Direct sound also designates an absence of reflected components in the final recording.

Director The member of the production crew who works closely with the cinematographer, editor, production designer, and sound designer to determine a film's organizing, creative structure. The director is generally the key member of the production team controlling and synthesizing the contributions of other team members. On budgetary issues, however, the director is answerable to the producer who has the highest administrative authority on a production.

Displacement A concept in psychoanalytic film theory whereby repressed ideas, emotions or impulses find a substitute outlet in disguised form as they are projected onto nonthreatening aspects of a scene or situation.

Dissolve A type of visual transition between shots or scenes, created by the editor. Unlike the cut, the dissolve is a gradual screen transition with distinct optical characteristics. The editor overlaps the end of one shot with the beginning of the next shot to produce a brief superimposition.

Diversification A corporate structure in which a company conducts business operations across a range of associated markets and product categories.

Documentary   A type of film dealing with a person, situation, or state of affairs that exists independently of the film. Documentaries can include a poetic, stylized audiovisual design, but they typically exclude the use of overt fictional elements.

Documentary Realism   A subcategory of the realist mode of screen reality. The documentary realist filmmaker employs the camera as a recording instrument to capture events or situations that are transpiring independently of the filmmaker. Documentary realism is also a stylistic construction in that the filmmaker's audiovisual design imposes an artistic organization on the event that has unfolded before the camera.

Dolly   A type of movable platform on which the camera is placed to execute a tracking shot. Tracking shots are sometimes called *dollies* or *dolly shots*.

Editing   The work of joining together shots to assemble the finished film. Editors select the best shots from the large amount of footage the director and cinematographer have provided and assemble these in the proper narrative order.

Editor   The member of the production crew who, in consultation with the director, designs the order and arrangement of shots as they will appear in the finished film and splices them together to create the final cut.

Effects (Sound)   One of the three basic types of film sound. Effects are all of the nonspoken, nonmusical sounds in a film (e.g., footsteps, breaking glass, etc.).

Emulsion   The light-sensitive surface of the film. Light sensitivity varies among film stocks. Fast films feature emulsions that are very light sensitive, requiring minimal light for a good exposure. Slow films feature emulsions that are less light sensitive, requiring more light on the scene or set for proper exposure.

ENR   Named for Ernesto N. Rico, this method of film processing retains a portion of the silver in film emulsion, which is normally removed during developing. This has the effect of making shadows blacker, de-saturating color, and highlighting the texture and edges of surfaces.

Errors of Continuity   Disruptions in the appropriate flow of action or in the proper relation of camera perspectives from shot to shot. These errors may include the failure to match action across shots or to maintain consistent screen direction.

Establishing Shot   A type of long shot used to establish the setting or location of a scene. In classical continuity editing, establishing shots occur at the beginning of a scene and help contextualize subsequent close-ups and other partial views of the action.

Explicit Causality   The tight chaining of narrative events into a strong causal sequence in which prior events directly and clearly cause subsequent events. Characteristic of Hollywood filmmaking.

Expressionism   A basic mode of screen reality in which filmmakers use explicit audiovisual distortions to express extreme or aberrant emotions or perceptions.

Extras   Incidental characters in a film, often part of the background of a shot or scene.

Eyeline Match   The matching of eyelines between two or more characters who are engaged in conversation or are looking at each other in a scene, in order to establish relations of proximity and continuity. The directions in which the performers look from shot to shot are complementary. That is, if performer A looks screen right in the first shot, performer B will look screen left in the next shot.

Fade   A visual transition between shots or scenes created by the editor. Unlike the cut, the fade creates a gradual transition with distinct visual characteristics. A fade is visible on screen as a brief interval with no picture. The editor fades one shot to black and then, after a pause, fades in the next shot. Editors often use fades to indicate a substantial change of time or place in the narrative.

Fall-Off   The area in a shot where light falls off into shadow. Fast fall-off occurs in a high-contrast image where the rate of change between the illuminated and shadowed areas is very quick.

Fantasy   A basic mode of screen reality in which settings and subjects, characters, and narrative time are far removed from the conditions of the viewer's ordinary life. Fantasy characters may have super powers or advanced technology that lends them extraordinary abilities.

Feature Film   A film typically running between 90 and 120 minutes.

Female Matte   In a matte/counter-matte system, the female matte (also known as a cover matte) is an opaque frame in which the foreground figure is transparent. The opaque area of the female matte blocks light during printing.

Feminist Film Theory   A model of film theory that examines the images of women in film and issues of gender representation.

Fetishizing Techniques   As emphasized in psychoanalytic film theory, these are elements of style that concentrate the viewer's attention for extended periods upon erotic imagery or material in a way that displaces other components of a scene or shot.

Fill Light   A light placed opposite the key light and used to soften the shadows it casts. Along with key and back lights, fill light is one of the three principal sources of illumination in a scene.

Film Noir   A cycle of crime and detective films popular in the U.S. cinema of the 1940s. Low-key lighting was a major stylistic attribute of this cycle.

Film Stock   Camera negative identified by manufacturer and number. Stocks vary in terms of their sensitivity to light, color reproduction, amount of grain, contrast, and resolution.

Film Theory   A philosophical or aesthetic model that seeks to explain the fundamental characteristics of the medium of cinema and how it expresses meaning.

Final Cut   The finished edit of a film. The form in which a film is released to and seen by audiences.

Flashing   A technique used to de-saturate color and contrast from a shot and to create a misty, slightly hazy effect. Film stock is flashed by exposing it to a small amount of light prior to developing.

Flicker Fusion   Along with persistence of vision and beta movement, this is one of the perceptual foundations on which the illusion of cinema rests. The human eye cannot distinguish the individual still frames of a motion picture because of the speed at which they are projected. Flicker fusion designates the viewer's inability to perceive the pulsing flashes of light emitted by the projector. These flashes and the still pictures they illuminate blend together to produce an illusion of movement.

Focal length   The distance between the optical center of the lens and the film inside the camera. Lenses of different focal lengths will "see" the action in front of the camera very differently. See **Wide-Angle, Telephoto, Normal,** and **Zoom Lenses.**

Foley   The creation of sound effects by live performance in a sound recording studio. Foley artists perform sound effects in sync with a scene's action.

ForcedPerspective   Perspective distortion that takes informational cues about depth and distance—such as the way parallel lines seem to converge in the distance or the way objects seem to grow smaller as they get farther away—and exaggerates these to convey on the small scale of a miniature model or a matte painting an impression of great size or distance.

Foreground Miniature   A miniature model suspended between the camera and the set or location and photographed as part of the dramatic action.

Frame   The borders of a projected image or the individual still photograph on a strip of film. Frame dimensions are measured by aspect ratio.

Framework of Interpretation   The intellectual, social, or cultural frames of reference that a critic applies to a film in order to create a novel interpretation. It is the general intellectual framework within which an interpretation is produced.

French New Wave   The group of filmmakers that emerged in France beginning in 1959 and whose films broke with existing studio style. They were very fond of American films, and in time their work influenced such Hollywood films as *Bonnie and Clyde* and *Easy Rider.*

Front Projection   Method for simulating locations by projecting location footage from a position in front of the actors and set.

Genre   A type or category of film such as a Western, musical, gangster film, or horror film that follows a set of visual and narrative patterns that are unique within the genre.

Glass Shot   Often used in early cinema, this was a method for producing a composited image in-camera by filming a scene with a matte painting on glass used to represent part of the set or location.

Gray Scale   A scale used for black-and-white cinematography that measures color intensity or brightness. Black-and-white film and the black-and-white video camera can differentiate colors only if they vary in degrees of brightness. The gray scale tells filmmakers which colors will separate naturally in black and white.

Greenscreening   Filming of live actors against a blank and colored (green) screen for subsequent compositing with digital elements.

Gross   The total box office revenue generated by a film before expenses are deducted.

Hand-Held Camera   A camera that is physically held by the operator rather than being mounted on a tripod, dolly, or other platform. It permits more freedom of movement and is especially suited for scenes where the action is spontaneous and unpredictable.

Hard Light   Light that is not scattered or diffused by filters or reflecting screens. Hard light can establish high contrast.

Hard-Matted   Method of producing letterboxed video transfers of widescreen films. The widescreen ratio is preserved for viewing on a 4:3 monitor by masking that part of the video signal that displays on the top and bottom of the monitor's screen and displaying the widescreen image in the unmatted area.

High-Angle   A camera angle usually above the eye level of performers in a scene.

High-Definition Video   Compared with standard video, which has 480 scan lines of picture information, hi-def video has up to 1080 scan lines. The Sony/CineAlta HD24P format, which George Lucas used to shoot the latest installments of his *Star Wars* series, runs at 24 frames per second, like film, and carries a resolution of 1920 × 1080 pixels.

High-Key Lighting   A lighting design that minimizes contrast and fall-off by creating a bright, even level of illumination throughout a scene.

Historical Realism   A subcategory of the realist mode of screen reality. Historical realist films aim to recreate in close detail the manners, mores, settings, and costumes of a distant historical period.

Homage   A reference in a film to another film or filmmaker. The climatic gun battle on the train station steps in Brian De Palma's *The Untouchables* (1987) is an homage to Sergei Eisenstein's *The Battleship Potemkin* (1925), which features the famous massacre on the Odessa steps.

Hue   One of the basic attributes of color. Hue designates the color itself. Red, blue, and green are primary hues. They are not mixtures of any other color.

Identification   A stage in creating criticism wherein the critic selectively identifies those aspects of the film that are relevant for the critical argument being developed. The identification of selective film elements enables the critic to simplify and reduce the wealth of material in the film.

Ideological Film Theory   A model of film theory that examines the representation of social and political issues in film.

Ideology   A system of beliefs characteristic of a society or social community. Ideological film theory examines the ways in which films represent and express various ideologies.

Implicit Causality   The loose sequencing of narrative events. Narrative causality is minimized, and the viewer's sense of the direction in which the story is moving is weaker than it is in films that feature explicit causality.

Implied Author   The artistic perspective implied and embodied by a film's overall audiovisual design.

Intensity   A basic attribute of color. Intensity measures the brightness of a hue.

Internal Structural Time   The dynamic tempo of a film, established by its internal structure (camera positions, editing, color and lighting design, soundtrack). Perceiving this internal tempo, viewers label films as fast or slow moving, yet internal structural time never unfolds at a constant rate. It is a dynamic rhythm. Filmmakers vary the tempo of internal structural time to maintain viewer interest.

Interocular Distance   The amount of distance or separation between human eyes. Stereoscopic cinema scales interocular distance in terms of dual camera position to elicit 3D effects.

Interpretation   The goal of criticism. By examining a film's structure, a critic assigns meaning to a scene or film that it does not immediately denote.

Interpretive Processing   The viewer's attribution of meaning to audiovisual information, as distinct from perceptual processing, which is the purely perceptual response to this information. Film viewing involves both components. Understood in terms of perceptual processing, a viewer watching a cross-cut sequence sees a succession of shots flashing by on screen as an alternating series. Via interpretive processing, the viewer attributes a representation of simultaneous action to the alternating series. This attribution is not a meaning contained within the images themselves. It is the viewer's contribution.

Iris   An editing transition prevalent in silent cinema. A circular mask closed down over the image (an iris out) to mark the end of a scene or, alternatively, opened up (an iris in) to introduce a new scene.

Jump Cut   A method of editing that produces discontinuity by leaving out portions of the action.

Key Frames   In digital animation, the points at which a character's position changes substantially. The animator specifies and creates these key frames, and a software program then creates the intervening frames.

Key Light   The main source of illumination in a scene usually directed on the face of the performer. Along with fill and back lights, it is one of the three principal sources of illumination in a scene.

Latent Meaning   Meanings that are indirect or implied by a film's narrative and audiovisual design. They are not direct, immediately obvious, or explicit.

Leitmotif   A recurring musical passage used to characterize a scene, character, or situation in a film narrative.

Letterbox   A method of formatting wide-screen motion pictures for video release. Black bars mask the top and bottom of the frame, producing a wider ratio picture area in the center of the frame. While the aspect ratio of a letterboxed video image closely matches the original theatrical aspect ratio, the trade-off is a small and narrow image as displayed on a television monitor.

Limited-Release Market   The theatrical distribution of independent film, typically on a smaller scale than the release market for major studio productions.

Linear Editing System   Until the late-1990s, editors worked on celluloid film, with the footage in their workprints derived from camera negative. Using a linear system, the editor searched for material by running footage from beginning to end and joined shots sequentially, one after another. Such editors were in physical contact with actual film, unlike those using nonlinear systems who access an electronic signal via a keyboard.

Live Action   Those components of a special effects shot or scene that were filmed live before the camera. These elements may then be composited with digital effects.

Long Shot   One of the basic camera positions in which a camera is set up at some distance from the subject of the shot. Filmmakers usually use long shots to stress environment or setting.

Long Take   A shot of long duration, as distinct from a long shot, which designates a camera position.

Low-Angle   A camera angle usually below the eye level of performers in a scene.

Low-Key Lighting   A lighting design that maximizes contrast and fall-off by lighting selected areas of the scene for proper exposure and leaving all other areas underexposed.

Majors   The large studio-distributors that fund film production and distribute films internationally. Collectively, these companies constitute the Hollywood industry. They are Columbia Pictures, Warner Bros., Disney, MGM/UA, Paramount, 20th Century Fox, and Universal.

Male Matte   In a matte/counter-matte system, the male matte, also known as a holdout matte, is a black silhouette of the foreground element with all other areas of the film frame being transparent. The opaque silhouette blocks light from being transmitted through the film in this area during printing (or, if working digitally, during compositing).

Master Shot   A camera position used by filmmakers to record the entire action of a scene from beginning to end. Filmmakers reshoot portions of the scene in close-up and medium shot framings. Editors cut these into the master shot to create the changing optical viewpoints of an edited scene. When used to establish the overall layout of a scene or location, the master shot can also double as an establishing shot.

Matched Cut   A cut joining two shots whose compositional elements strongly match. Matched cutting establishes continuity of action.

Matte A painted landscape or location that is composited with the live action components of a shot. Mattes were traditionally done as paintings on glass, but many contemporary films use digital mattes created on a computer. Matte can also refer to a mask that is used to block or hide a portion of the frame, as when producing a widescreen image in theatrical projection. See **Soft-Matted, Hard-Matted, Counter-Matte, Traveling Matte**.

Maquette A small, 3D sculpture that forms the basis for subsequent digital animation. Often used in creature effects.

Medium Shot One of the basic camera positions in which a camera is set up to record from full- to half-figure shots of a performer.

Melodrama The predominant dramatic style of popular cinema, emphasizing clear moral distinctions between hero and villain, exaggerated emotions, and a narrative style in which the twists and turns of the plot determine character behavior.

Method Acting An approach to screen performance in which the actor seeks to portray a character by using personal experience and emotion as a foundation for the portrayal.

Miniature A small-scale model representing a portion of a much larger location or building.

Mise-en-scène A film's overall visual design, created by all of the elements that are placed before the camera. These include light, color, costumes, sets, and actors.

Mockumentary A fiction film that uses the style of documentary to create the illusion, typically for comic effect, that it is a documentary.

Monocular Depth Cues Informational sources about depth, distance and spatial layout that can be perceived with one eye.

Montage Used loosely, *montage* simply means "editing." In a strict sense, however, *montage* designates scenes whose emotional impact and visual design are achieved primarily through the editing of many brief shots. The shower scene from Hitchcock's *Psycho* is a classic example of montage editing.

Motion Control Cinematography in which the camera's movements are plotted by computer so that they can be replicated when designing the digital components of the shot.

Motion Parallax Also known as *motion perspective*, the term designates the changing positions of near and far objects as the viewer or the camera moves through space.

Motion Perspective The change in visual perspective produced by the camera's movement through space. The visual positions of objects undergo systematic changes as the camera moves in relation to them. Camera movement will produce motion perspective but a zoom shot will not.

Multiplane Camera A standard tool of 2D animation used to produce effects of camera movement and motion and depth perspective. Cells are arranged at varying distances from a multiplane camera. It can move toward or away from them, and they can be moved across its field of view.

Multipass Compositing Method for creating a final, rendered image from separate operations carried out upon different image layers. Prior to the digital era, multi-pass compositing had been carried out on optical printers. Some of the optical printer effects shots in *Return of the Jedi* were so complex that they required more than a hundred passes.

Music One of the three basic types of film sound. Film music may include the score that accompanies the dramatic action of scenes as well as music originating on screen from within a scene.

Negative Cost Accounting term for the expenses incurred by a film production, excluding the cost of advertising and publicity.

Negative Parallax In stereoscopic cinema, placement of the left-eye image on the right, and the right-eye image on the left, requiring that viewers converge their eyes to fuse the images. This results in positioning objects in front of the screen.

Neonoir Film noir made in the contemporary period and shot in color.

Neorealism A filmmaking style that developed in postwar Italian cinema. The neorealist director aimed to truthfully portray Italian society by avoiding the gloss and glitter of expensive studio productions, emphasizing instead location filmmaking, a mixture of non- and semiprofessional actors, and simple, straightforward visual technique.

Newspaper/Television Reviewing A mode of film criticism aimed at a general audience that performs an explicit consumer function, telling readers whether or not they should see the film being reviewed. Film reviews presented as part of television news or review programs also belong to this mode.

New Wave A new stylistic direction or design appearing within a national cinema in the films of a group of (usually young) directors who are impatient with existing styles and seek to create alternatives.

Nodal Tripod Camera mount that enables a camera to pivot around the optical center of the lens, producing no motion perspective. Often used in shots employing hanging miniatures to disguise the presence of the miniature.

Nondiegetic sound Sound that cannot be heard by characters in a film but can be heard by the film's viewer. See also **diegetic sound.**

Nonlinear Editing Systems Computerized editing on digital video. This system gives editors instantaneous access to any shot or scene in a film and enables them to rapidly explore different edits of the same footage. Once a final cut has been reached on the digital video footage, the camera negative is then conformed (edited to match) this cut. Unlike an editor using a linear system who would actually handle film, the nonlinear editor uses a computer keyboard to find shots and join them together.

Nonsynchronous Sound   Sound that is not in synch with a source visible on screen.

Normal Lens   A lens of moderate focal length that does not distort object size and depth of field. The normal lens records perspective much as the human eye does.

Off-Screen Sound   A type of sound in which the sound-producing source remains off-screen. Off-screen sound extends the viewer's perception of a represented screen location into an indefinite area of off-screen space.

180-Degree Rule   The foundation for establishing continuity of screen direction. The left and right coordinates of screen action remain consistent as long as all camera positions remain on the same side of the line of action. Crossing the line entails a change of screen direction.

Open Matte   Formatting of 1.85:1 aspect ratio films for the television/home video ratio of 4:3 by transferring the film full frame without the matting that was used during projection in theaters.

Optical Printer   Device used to composite effects shots during the Hollywood studio era. Optical printers were made of a synchronized process camera and a process projector that was called the printer head. Master positive footage of effects elements—models, travelling mattes, animation—was loaded into the printer head and run through and photographed frame by frame in the process camera. (A process camera is one used in the laboratory for effects work, in distinction to a production camera used to film live action.) The final composite (the finished effects shot) was created gradually by this process of re-photographing each of its components.

Ordinary Fictional Realism   A subcategory of the realist mode of screen reality. Such films feature a naturalistic visual design, a linear narrative, and plausible character behavior as the basis for establishing a realist style.

Pan   A type of camera movement in which the camera pivots from side to side on a fixed tripod or base. Pans produce lateral optical movement on-screen and are often used to follow the action of a scene or to anticipate the movements of performers.

Pan-and-Scan   A method of formatting wide-screen motion pictures for video release. Only a portion of the original wide-screen image is transferred to video. A full screen image appears on the video monitor, but it represents only a portion of the original wide-screen frame.

Parallel Action   An editing technique that establishes multiple, ongoing plot lines and simultaneous lines of action. Editors generally use the technique of cross-cutting to establish parallel action.

Perceptual Correspondence   Those properties of cinema that duplicate the visual information that viewers encounter in the everyday world. These include information about object size, light and shadow, movement, and facial expression and behavior as signs of emotion and intention.

Perceptual Processing   The film viewer's perceptual response to audiovisual information, as distinct from interpretive processing, which is the active interpretation of that information. Film viewing involves both components. The viewer sees color, depth, and movement (perceptual processing) in cinema and may attribute particular meanings to those perceptions (interpretive processing). Understood in terms of perceptual processing, a viewer watching a cross-cut sequence sees a succession of shots flashing by on-screen as an alternating series. Via interpretive processing, the viewer attributes a representation of simultaneous action to the alternating series. This attribution is not a meaning contained within the images themselves. It is the viewer's contribution.

Perceptual Realism   The correspondence of picture and sound in cinema with the ways viewers perceive space and sound in the real, three-dimensional world.

Perceptual Transformation   Those properties of cinema (e.g., a telephoto lens or a simultaneous zoom and track in opposite directions) that distort or alter the visual information that viewers encounter in the everyday world or that create completely novel visual experiences that have no basis in real-world experience. An example of the latter would be the high-speed bullet effects used in *The Matrix*.

Performance Capture   Digital means for extracting the movements of a live actor and compositing these into a cartoon or special effects character. The live actor's performance is thereby mapped onto the digital character.

Performance Style   The actor's contribution to the audiovisual and narrative design of a film.

Persistence of Vision   A characteristic of the human eye in which the retina briefly retains the impression of an image after its source has been removed. Because of persistence of vision, viewers do not see the alternating periods of light and dark through which they sit in a theater.

Phi Phenomena   The many different conditions under which the human eye can be fooled into seeing the illusion of movement. Beta movement is one of the phi phenomena.

Photogrammetry   Method of building a 3D environment in the computer by using photographs. By tracing the camera's lines of sight in multiple photographs of the same area, and plotting their intersection, a 3D model of the depicted area can be assembled.

Pictorial Lighting Design   A lighting design that does not aim to simulate the effects of an on-screen light source. Instead, the design moves in a purely pictorial direction to create mood and atmosphere.

Pixel   With reference to computer-based images, a pixel is the smallest unit of a picture capable of being digitally manipulated. The sharpness or resolution of an image is a function of the number of pixels it contains. High-end computer monitors, used in sophisticated film effects work, may have 2000 pixels per screen line.

Plot   The order and arrangement of story events as they appear in a given film.

Point of View   The perspective from which narrative events are related. Point of view in cinema is typically third-person perspective, although filmmakers routinely manipulate audiovisual design to suggest what individual characters are thinking or feeling. Point of view in cinema can assume a first-person perspective through the use of voice-over narration or subjective shots in which the camera views a scene as if through the eyes of a character.

Point-of-View Shot   See **Subjective Shot**.

Positive Parallax   In stereoscopic cinema, placement of the left-eye image on the left, and the right-eye image on the right, enabling viewers to fuse the images without converging their eyes. This results in positioning objects behind the screen.

Polyvalence   The attribute of having more than one meaning. Motion pictures are polyvalent because they possess multiple layers of meaning.

Postdubbing   The practice of recording sound effects and dialogue after principal filming has been completed. *ADR* is the contemporary term for postdubbing. In the case of postdubbing dialogue, the technical challenge is to closely match the rerecorded dialogue with the performer's lip movements in the shot.

Postproduction   The last stage of filmmaking, following the shooting and sound recording of scenes, that includes the editing of image and sound and finalizing of digital effects.

Practical (Light)   A light source visible on a set used for exposure.

Preproduction   The stage of filmmaking that precedes the shooting and sound recording of scenes. It is the planning and preparation stage.

Previsualization   Any of a number of methods by which filmmakers try to visualize a shot before actually exposing film in the camera. Storyboards are a form of previsualization, as are various software programs that will model a set as seen by different camera positions and lenses.

Producer   A production administrator who hires a director and supervises a film's production to ensure that it comes in under budget and on schedule. While directors work under a producer, in practice producers generally allow directors considerable creative freedom.

Production   The stage of filmmaking that includes the shooting and sound recording of scenes.

Production Design   The planning and creation of sets, costumes, mattes, and miniatures according to an overall concept articulated by the production designer in collaboration with the director.

Production Track   The soundtrack as recorded at the point of filming. The final soundtrack mix included on release prints to theaters includes portions of the production track along with a great deal of sound created in postproduction.

Production Values   Those elements of the film that show the money invested in its production. These typically include set designs, costumes, locations, and special effects.

Product Placement   The appearance of products on screen as part of a film scene. These appearances are advertisements for which the merchandiser pays a fee to a product placement agency. Film production companies derive revenue from these fees.

Product Tie-Ins   Products marketed in conjunction with the release of a blockbuster film. For example, a *Jurassic Park* video game. These products often bear the logo or likeness of characters in the movie.

Profit Participant   An individual who is contractually entitled to receive a portion of a film's profits. This is often a star or director who receives a percentage of gross revenue, a practice known as *taking points*.

Prop Master   Individual who supervises the design and construction of props used in the film.

Psychoanalytic Film Theory   A model of film theory that examines the unconscious, sometimes irrational, emotional, and psychological relationship between viewers and films or between characters within films.

Real Author   The actual flesh-and-blood author of a film, as distinct from the implied author, the artistic perspective embodied by a film's overall audiovisual design.

Realism   A basic mode of screen reality. Ordinary fictional realism, historical realism, and documentary realism are subcategories of the realist mode.

Realist Film Theory   A model of film theory that seeks to explain how filmmakers may capture, with minimal distortion, the essential features of real situations and events, or, in the case of fictionalized events, how filmmakers may give them an apparent real-world status.

Realistic Lighting Design   A lighting design that simulates the effects of a light source visible on screen.

Realistic Sound   Sound that seems to fit the properties of a real source. In practice this is an elastic concept because many sounds that seem to be realistic are, in fact, artificial and derive from sources other than the one that is designated on screen.

Rear Screen Projection   A technique for simulating location cinematography by projecting photographic images of a landscape onto a screen. Actors are photographed standing in front of the screen as if they were part of the represented location.

Recces   Scouting trips to find locations by the production designer and crew.

Reflected Sound   Sound that is reflected off surfaces in a physical environment before being captured by the microphone. By manipulating characteristics of sound reflection, sound designers can capture the physical attributes of an environment.

Rental   Accounting term for the revenues returned to a film distributor.

Rhetoric   The use of language to persuade and influence others. Film criticism is a rhetorical activity.

Room Tone A type of ambient sound characterizing the acoustical properties of a room. Even an empty room will emit room tone.

Rotoscope A combination camera–projector used to combine live action with animation. Live-action footage is projected frame by frame onto a series of cells, enabling the animator to produce drawings that exactly fit the live action.

Rough Cut The film editor's initial assembly of shots in a scene or film before the editing is tightened and perfected in the fine cut.

Running Time The amount of real time it takes a viewer to watch a film from beginning to end. Most commercial films run between 90 and 120 minutes.

Saturation A basic characteristic of color. Saturation measures color strength and is a function of how much white light is mixed into the color. The more white light that is present, the less saturated the color will seem to be.

Scenic Artist Individual who supervises design and matte paintings.

Schema This term derives from the psychology of perception and designates a mental category or framework used to organize information. Applied to cinema, it helps explain the function of devices like the master shot, which provides viewers with a schema or map of a location and the characters' positions within it. Viewers use the visual schema provided by master shots to orient themselves to changing camera positions and to integrate partial views of a scene provided by close-ups.

Scholarly Criticism A mode of criticism aimed at a specialized audience of scholars, employing a technical, demanding vocabulary, and exploring the significance of given films in relation to issues of theory or film history.

Schufftan Process Method for combining live action and miniature models or matte paintings. By placing a mirror that reflects the image of the miniature or painting at a 45 degree angle to the camera, live action elements can be filmed through portions of the mirror that have been scraped away to leave transparent glass. The camera sees the live action through the glass and sees the miniature reflected in the glass. The actors and the miniature or painting are thereby filmed simultaneously.

Screen Reality The represented reality depicted by a fictional film. Screen reality is established by the principles of time, space, character behavior, and audiovisual design as these are organized in a given film.

Sequence Shot A long take whose duration extends for an entire scene or sequence. Such a scene or sequence is accordingly composed of only one shot and features no editing.

Set Decorator Individual who dresses a set with furnishings and props.

Sets The controlled physical environment in which filming occurs. Sets may be created by blocking and lighting an area of ground outdoors or by building and designing a physical environment indoors.

Shading A visual depth cue in which gradations and patterns of light and shadow reveal texture and volume in a three-dimensional world and can be used to create a three-dimensional impression on a flat theater or television screen.

Shot The basic unit of film structure, corresponding to the amount of footage exposed in the camera from the time it is turned on until it is turned off. Shots are visible on-screen as the intervals between cuts, fades, or dissolves.

Shot-Reverse-Shot Cutting A type of continuity editing generally used for conversation scenes. The cutting alternates between opposing over-the-shoulder camera set-ups showing each character speaking in turn.

Shutter Device inside the camera that regulates the light reaching the film. In a film projector, the shutter functions like an on/off switch, regulating the light reaching the screen to produce beta movement and critical fusion frequency.

Sign In communication theory, that which embodies or expresses meaning.

Snorkel Lens A lens that is mounted to the end of an elongated arm, which itself is attached to the camera body. The lens can be rotated, tilted, and maneuvered separately from the camera body to produce the illusion of camera movement through a miniature model.

Soft Light Light that is diffused or scattered by filters or reflecting screens. Soft light creates a low-contrast image.

Soft-Matted The use of mattes during projection to mask the top and bottom of the film frame and produce a widescreen (1.85:1) image.

Sound Bridge Sound used to connect, or bridge, two or more shots. Sound bridges establish continuity of place, action, or time.

Sound Design (Designer) The expressive use of sound throughout a film in relation to its images and the contents of its narrative. Working in conjunction with the director, the sound designer supervises the work of other sound personnel.

Sound Field The acoustical space created by all the speakers in a multichannel, surround-sound system.

Sound Hierarchy The relative priority given to dialogue, effects, and music in a given scene. In most cases, dialogue is considered the most important of these sounds and rests atop the sound hierarchy.

Sound Montage A type of sound editing that conjoins many discrete sound effects and sources.

Sound Perspective The use of sound to augment visual perspective. Sound perspective often correlates with camera position. In a long shot reflected sound may prevail, whereas in a close-up direct sound may prevail.

Soundstage The acoustical space created by the front speakers in a multichannel, surround-sound system.

Speech Dialogue spoken by performers playing characters in a narrative.

Spotting A collaborative process between the director and composer during which they spot or identify passages in the film that require musical scoring.

Star The highest profile performer in a film narrative. Stars draw audiences to theaters and establish intense personal relationships with their publics.

Star Persona The relatively fixed screen personality of a star.

Stereoscopic Cinema Films and filmmaking that employ binocular disparity and convergence to depict three-dimensional depth in the frame.

Stereographer Member of a production crew who consults with the director and choreographs stereoscopic (3D) space on screen.

Steadicam A camera-stabilizing system that enables the camera operator to work with a hand-held camera and produce steady, jitter-free images. It is especially suited for producing lengthy, extended moving camera shots.

Stop-Motion Animation Method used for animating three-dimensional models, such as King Kong. The model is moved and photographed a frame at a time.

Story The entire sequence of events that a film's plot draws on and references. The plot arranges story events into a given order, which may differ from the story's proper chronology.

Story Time The amount of time covered by the narrative. This may vary considerably from film to film. The narrative of *2001: A Space Odyssey* begins during a period of primitive prehuman ancestry and extends into the era of space travel, while the narrative of *High Noon* spans, roughly, 90 minutes, closely approximating that film's running time.

Structure The audiovisual design of a film. The elements of structure include the camera, lights and color, production design, performance style, editing, sound, and narrative.

Subjective Shot Also known as a *point-of-view shot*. The camera's position and angle represent the exact viewpoint of a character in the narrative.

Subtractive Color Mixing The method for creating color in film. Magenta, cyan, and yellow dyes combined in color film produce all other hues.

Super 35 Widescreen format that captures a 2:1 aspect ratio image on the camera negative. This image is then typically cropped to 2.35:1 for theatrical release and to 1.33:1 for full-frame home video release.

Supervising Art Director During the classical Hollywood era, this was the head of the art department who supervised art design in all the films under production at a studio.

Supporting Player A performer in a secondary role who does not receive either the billing or the pay of a major star. Many performers first establish themselves as supporting players before they become stars.

Surprise A narrative technique used to jolt or startle the viewer. Creating surprise depends on withholding crucial narrative information from viewers, whereas creating suspense depends on providing viewers with necessary information. Showing the audience the bomb under the table before it goes off will create suspense. Not showing the bomb before it goes off will create surprise.

Surrealism Influenced by Freudian psychoanalysis, this art style aims to appeal to the viewer's subconscious and irrational mind by creating fantastic and dream-like images. David Lynch's *Blue Velvet* is a surrealist film.

Suspense A narrative technique used to create tension and anxiety in the film viewer. Creating suspense depends on revealing rather than withholding narrative information. Showing the audience the bomb under the table before it goes off will create suspense. Not showing the bomb before it goes off will create surprise. Unlike suspense, surprise depends on withholding information from the audience.

Synthetic Sound Artificially designed sound that does not match any existing source. The sounds of the light sabers in the *Star Wars* films are examples of synthetic sound.

Taboo Images Imagery depicting forbidden or disturbing subjects, often of a sexual or violent nature.

Technical Acting An approach to acting in which the performer thinks through the requisite gestures and emotions and then exhibits them. In contrast to method acting, the technical actor does not look to personal experience as a basis for understanding the character.

Telephoto Lens A lens of long focal length that distorts object size and depth of field. Telephoto lenses magnify the size of distant objects and by doing so compress depth of field and make them appear closer than they are.

Temp Track A temporary musical track usually derived from an existing film that a director uses early in production to show the composer the type of musical composition he or she wants.

Thematic Montage A style of editing that draws an explicit comparison between two or more images, as when Charles Chaplin compares workers and sheep in a pair of shots at the beginning of *Modern Times*.

Tilt A type of camera movement in which the camera pivots up and down on a fixed tripod or base. Tilts produce vertical movement on screen and are often used to follow action and reveal detail.

Tracking Shot A camera movement in which the camera physically moves along the ground to follow action or to reveal significant narrative information. Tracking shots can be executed by pushing the camera along tracks, by attaching the camera to a moving vehicle such as a car, or by using a handheld Steadicam mount, in which case the camera operator runs or walks alongside the action. Tracking shots are sometimes called *dolly shots*, after the "dolly" or movable platform on which the camera is sometimes mounted.

Translite A photographic image, enlarged and backlit, this is one of the basic tools of production design, used to simulate a large, scenic view in the background of a set.

Traveling Matte Travelling mattes enable filmmakers to insert moving foreground figures into a landscape or other type of background that has been filmed separately. Accordingly, travelling mattes are an extremely valuable and widely-used tool of visual effects. They involve the application of a matte and counter-matte in order to prevent double-exposures. These are composed of male and female mattes. A male matte, also known as a holdout matte, is a black silhouette of the foreground element with all other areas of the film frame being transparent. The opaque silhouette will block light from being transmitted through the film in this area during printing (or, if working digitally, during compositing). A female matte (also known as a cover matte) is the inverse of the male. The female matte is an opaque frame in which the foreground figure is transparent. **Tromp l'Oeil** Optical illusions created by painting or other visual media. Matte paintings in cinema routinely employ tromp l'oeil techniques to achieve the effects of perspective, scale, depth and distance.

Typage The manipulation of a screen character's visual or physical characteristics to suggest psychological or social themes or ideas.

Unit Art Director In the classic Hollywood studio system in the 1930s and 1940s, the unit art director oversaw the creation of sets and costumes for a given production. The unit art director worked under a studio's supervising art director who supervised set and costume design on all of the studio's productions.

Virtual Camera Simulation via computer of the many ways in which a camera might view a scene. 2D animated films are shot with a real camera. 3D computer animation uses a virtual camera, mimicking the optical effects of different lenses, depth of field, rack focusing, and panning-and-tracking movements. These are far more vivid in digital animation than in 2D animation.

Visual Effects Supervisor Member of the production crew who oversees the design of a film's special effects.

Voice-Over Narration Dialogue spoken by an off-screen narrator. This narrator may be a character reflecting in voice-over on story events from some later point in the narrative or, as sometimes occurs in documentary films, the narrator may exist independently of characters in the story.

Voyeurism A basic pleasure offered by cinema, derived from looking at the characters and situations on screen.

Wavelength The characteristic of light that corresponds to color. Colors are visible when white light is broken down into component wavelengths.

White Telephone Films Derogatory term for the glossy studio films produced by Cinecitta, Italy's national studio, during the Mussolini period.

Wide-Angle Lens A short focal length lens that exaggerates depth of field by increasing the size of near objects and minimizing the size of distant objects. Because they can focus on near and far objects, wide-angle lenses can capture great depth of field.

Widescreen Ratios Any of a large number of aspect ratios that exceed the nearly square, 1.37:1 ratio of classical Hollywood film and 1.33:1 ratio of conventional television. Wide-screen films must be reformatted for video release using methods of letterboxing or panning-and-scanning.

Wipe An editing transition prevalent in earlier decades of sound film. A hard- or soft-edged line (generally vertical) traveling across the frame marked the border of the outgoing and incoming shots. Although wipes are rare in contemporary film, George Lucas used them extensively in *Star Wars Episode I: The Phantom Menace* to evoke the style of old movie serials.

Z-Axis Specifies the amount of depth in a digital image along which objects are arranged or through which they move.

Z-Depth Map An image that supplies a graphic rendering of depth values in a shot. It uses gray-scale values to visualize distances, ranging from white (objects nearest the camera) to shades of gray to black (objects farthest from the camera).

Zoom Lens A lens capable of shifting from short (wide-angle) to long (telephoto) focal lengths. Using a zoom to change focal lengths within a shot produces the impression of camera movement, making it seem as if the camera is moving closer to or farther from its subject.

INDEX